Everyman, I will go with thee,
and be thy guide

Edmund Spenser

THE FAIRY QUEEN

A modernised selection edited by
DOUGLAS BROOKS-DAVIES
University of Manchester

EVERYMAN
J. M. DENT · LONDON
CHARLES E. TUTTLE
VERMONT

Modernised selection, introduction, notes and other critical apparatus
© J. M. Dent 1996

The Faerie Queene Books I to III
first published as an Everyman Classic in 1987
This edition first published in Everyman Paperbacks in 1996

J.M. Dent
Orion Publishing Group
Orion House, 5 Upper St Martin's Lane,
London WC2H 9EA
and
Charles E. Tuttle Co., Inc.
28 South Main Street,
Rutland, Vermont 05701, USA

Typeset in Sabon by CentraCet Ltd, Cambridge
Printed in Great Britain by
The Guensey Press Co. Ltd, Guernsey, C. I.

British Library Cataloguing-in-Publication Data
is available upon request.

ISBN 0 460 87572 8

CONTENTS

NOTE ON THE AUTHOR AND EDITOR

EDMUND SPENSER was born in London, probably in 1552. He was educated at Merchant Taylors' School, and Pembroke Hall, Cambridge. By 1579 he was employed in the Earl of Leicester's household and had become acquainted with Sir Philip Sidney; in the same year he married Machabyas Chylde. The year 1580 saw him in Ireland as secretary to Lord Grey, the Lord Deputy, and from this time Ireland was his home, though he retained a strong attachment to Elizabeth and her court. The success of *The Fairy Queen* (1590) can be measured in part from the grant by the queen of an annual pension of £50 in 1591. The mid 1590s saw Spenser in a remarkable frenzy of creativity: *Amoretti and Epithalamion* – the formalised narrative of his courtship and marriage to his second wife, Elizabeth Boyle – appeared in 1595; *Colin Clout's Come Home Again* was published the same year; and three more books of *The Fairy Queen*, together with *Prothalamion* and the *Four Hymns*, appeared in 1596. In 1598 Spenser's estate at Kilcolman, near Cork, was attacked by the Earl of Tyrone's forces, and a few months later he was sent to London with dispatches for the Privy Council. He arrived on Christmas Eve, but died in Westminster on 13 January 1599. He is buried in Westminster Abbey.

DOUGLAS BROOKS-DAVIES was born in London and educated at Merchant Taylors' School, Crosby, and Brasenose College, Oxford. Until 1993 he was Senior Lecturer in English Literature at the University of Manchester and is currently Honorary Research Fellow there, as well as being a stained-glass artist. His publications include: *Spenser's 'Faerie Queene': A Critical Commentary on Books 1 and 2* (1977); *The Mercurian Monarch* (1983); *Pope's 'Dunciad' and the Queen of Night* (1985); *Spenser: 'The Faerie Queene', Books 1–3* (Everyman, 1987; rev. 1993); *Oedipal Hamlet* (1989); *Silver Poets of the Sixteenth Century* (Everyman, 1992, rev. 1994); *Edmund Spenser: Selected Shorter Poems* (1995); he was also a major contributor to the *Spenser Encyclopedia* (1990). More recently, he has prepared a critical edition of L. P. Hartley's *The Go-Between*.

CHRONOLOGY OF SPENSER'S LIFE

Year   *Age*   *Life*

1552(?)   Born, probably in London; nothing known with
certainty of his family origins

Year	Literary Context (Britain)	Historical Events
1551-2		Council of Trent (second session)
1552	Sir Walter Ralegh born	Second Edwardian Prayer Book; Calvin's *Concerning Predestination*
1553	Gavin Douglas, *Aeneid* trans.; Thomas Wilson, *Art of Rhetoric*	Death of Edward VI; Lady Jane Grey proclaimed queen; accession of Mary Tudor (Catholic); arrest of Protestant bishops
1554	Philip Sidney born; *Book* 4 of Surrey's *Aeneid* trans.	Lady Jane Grey executed; full restoration of Roman Catholicism in England; Mary marries Philip of Spain
1555		John Knox unites Scots Protestants
1556		Philip II succeeds to Spanish throne
1557	Surrey's *Aeneid* trans., Books 2 and 4; *Tottel's Miscellany* of poems by Surrey, Wyatt, etc.	Incorporation of Stationers' Company
1558		Death of Mary I; accession of Elizabeth I; John Knox: *First Blast of the Trumpet against the Monstrous Regiment of Women*
1559	*Mirror for Magistrates*	Elizabeth I crowned; English Church re-established with Act of Supremacy and Elizabethan Prayer Book
1560	Barker's trans. of Xenophon's *Cyropaedia*	Geneva Bible
1561	Mary Sidney born; Stow's edn of Chaucer; Castiglione's *The Courtier*, trans. Hoby	Knox establishes constitution of Scottish Church Norton's trans. of Calvin's *Institutes of the Christian Religion*

Year   *Age*   *Life*

15(?)–1569 17   Merchant Taylors' School, London, under the headship
                 of the celebrated humanist and scholar, Richard
                 Mulcaster

1569   17   English translation of Jan van der Noot's Dutch
                 Protestant *A Theatre for Worldlings* published,
                 including epigrams translated by Spenser from Petrarch;
                 sonnets translated by him from Du Bellay; and four
                 sonnet paraphrases from the Book of Revelation
                 20 May matriculates at Cambridge; sizar (i.e., poor
                 scholar) at Pembroke Hall, Cambridge; becomes friend
                 of Gabriel Harvey (college fellow, 1570)

Year	Literary Context (Britain)	Historical Events
1562	Sackville and Norton, *Gorboduc* (first English blank verse tragedy); Heywood, *Works*	John Hawkins starts Africa–America slave trade; Europe: Council of Trent resits; Sternhold and Hopkins, *Whole Book of Psalms*; Jewel, *Apologia pro ecclesia Anglicana*
1563	John Foxe: *Book of Martyrs* (Protestant martyrology); Samuel Daniel born	Council of Trent finishes
1564	Shakespeare, Marlowe born; Anne Bacon's trans. of Jewel's *Apology*; John Dee, *Monas Hieroglyphica*	Calvin, Michelangelo die
1565	Arthur Golding's trans. of Ovid's *Metamorphoses* Books 1–4 published; Stow, *Summary of English Chronicles*	Hawkins's second South America voyage (1564–5)
1566	Nicholas Udall, *Ralph Roister Doister* (first English comedy) published	James VI of Scotland (future James I, England) born; Nostradamus, astrologer, dies
1567	Full text of Golding's Ovid published; Parker's edn of an Aelfric homily; Drant's trans. of Horace, *Art of Poetry*; Turberville's poems	Mary Queen of Scots abdicates; Hawkins's third voyage (to West Indies and Guinea)
1568	John Heywood's interlude, *The Four P's*; Skelton's *Works*	Douai College (seminary for training English Catholic priests) founded; Mary Queen of Scots flees to England; Bishops' Bible
1569	Sir John Davies (poet), born	
1570	Roger Ascham, *The Schoolmaster*	Papal Bull *Regnans in Excelsis* excommunicates Elizabeth I

Year	Age	Life
1573	21	Graduates BA
1576	24	Graduates MA
1578	26	Employed as secretary to John Young, Bishop of Rochester, formerly Master of Pembroke
1579	27	Early October: Spenser employed by Earl of Leicester; acquainted with Philip Sidney, John Dyer and Daniel Rogers 27 October: an 'Edmounde Spenser' (presumably the poet) marries Machabyas Chylde at Westminster (they will have two children, Sylvanus and Katherine) 5 December: *The Shepherds' Calendar* entered in the Stationers' Register
1580	28	June: the Gabriel Harvey–Spenser *Familiar Letters* published; contain first reference to *The Fairy Queen* Appointed private secretary to Arthur, Lord Grey of Wilton, Lord Deputy of Ireland 12 August: probably arrives in Ireland with Grey; works as Clerk of the Privy Council at Dublin Castle; will remain in Ireland, with occasional trips to England
1581	29	March: succeeds the poet Lodowick Bryskett as Clerk of the Chancery for Faculties while remaining under Grey December: leases castle and manor at Enniscorthy, County Wexford, for brief period; subsequently leases dissolved monastery at New Ross, County Wexford; a house in Dublin; and New Abbey, County Kildare (lease for the latter forfeited 1590 after failure to pay rent)

Year	Literary Context (Britain)	Historical Events
1571		Cecil becomes Lord Burghley; London Royal Exchange opened; Turks capture Cyprus from Venetians
1572	Ben Jonson (dramatist) born	Drake attacks Spaniards in South America; August 23/4, French Protestants murdered in Paris (St Bartholomew Massacre); John Knox dies
1573	George Gascoigne, *A Hundred Sundry Flowers*	Drake views Pacific from Panama; Tasso, *Aminta*
1575	Comedy *Gammer Gurton's Needle* (acted 1566) published; Gascoigne, *Poesies*; John Marston (dramatist) born	Elizabeth I offered (and declines) sovereignty of Netherlands; Tasso, *Gerusalemme liberata*
1577	Peacham, *Garden of Eloquence*; Gascoigne dies; Robert Burton born	Drake begins voyage round world
1578	Holinshed, *Chronicles*; Lyly, *Euphues, or the Anatomy of Wit*	English College moved from Douai to Rheims
1579	North's trans. *Plutarch's Lives*; John Fletcher, dramatist, born	The Duc d'Alençon courts Elizabeth
1580	Philip Sidney, *Apology for Poetry* (publ. 1595); Lyly, *Euphues and his England*	Francis Drake returns from circumnavigation of globe
1581	Sidney completes *Arcadia*	Act against English Catholics; Tasso, *Gerusalemme Liberata* (revised)

Year	Age	Life
1582	30	Grey recalled to England
1583	31	Spenser appointed Commissioner of Musters for County Kildare
1585	33	Prebendary of Effin (non-resident living attached to Limerick cathedral)
1586	34	Assigned Kilcolman Castle, with 3,000 acres (confiscated along with another 245,000 acres from the Irish Earl Desmond); undertakes to assist in colonisation of Munster by populating it with English immigrants; takes possession 1588(?); granted full perpetual lease to the property 1590
1589	37	Succeeds Bryskett as Clerk of the Council in Munster October: Spenser to England with Sir Walter Ralegh ready to present *Fairy Queen*, Books 1–3 (the 1590 *Fairy Queen*) to Queen Elizabeth 1 December: *Fairy Queen*, Books 1–3 entered in Stationers' Register
1590	38	January: *Fairy Queen*, Books 1–3 published by William Ponsonby in London 29 December: *Complaints: containing sundry small poems of the World's Vanity* entered in Stationers' Register

Year	Literary Context (Britain)	Historical Events
1582		Jesuit mission to China; Gregorian calendar introduced into Catholic Europe
1583	Stanyhurst's trans. *Aeneid*, Books 1–4; Massinger (dramatist) born	Discovery of Throckmorton plot against Elizabeth in favour of Mary Queen of Scots; Sir Thomas Smith, *De republica Anglorum* published
1584	Peele, *The Arraignment of Paris*; Bruno, *Lo Spaccio della bestia trionfante* published in London (followed by *De gli heroici furori*, 1585); Scott, *Discovery of Witchcraft*; James VI, *Essays . . . in the Divine Art of Poesy*	Ralegh discovers Virginia; English acts against Jesuits and seminary priests
1586	Camden, *Britannia*; Warner, *Albion's England*	Sidney dies; trial of Mary Queen of Scots
1587	Marlowe's *Dr Faustus*, *Tamburlaine* acted; Day's trans. of Longus, *Daphnis and Chloe*	Mary Queen of Scots executed; English expedition against Cadiz; Knox, *History of the Reformation in Scotland* published
1588	Anti-episcopal *Marpelate Tracts* published (–1590); Lyly, *Endimion*	Spanish Armada; William Morgan's Welsh trans. of the Bible
1589	Puttenham, *Art of English Poesie*	
1590	Marlowe, *Tamburlaine*, *Jew of Malta*, Sidney, *Arcadia* printed	

Year	Age	Life
1591	39	Returns to Ireland having been granted considerable annual pension of £50 by queen (February); *Complaints* published by William Ponsonby; *Daphnaida* published by William Ponsonby 27 December: date of Dedicatory Epistle to Sir Walter Ralegh of *Colin Clout's Come Home Again* (not published until 1595)
1594	42	Queen's Justice for Cork 11 June: marries Elizabeth Boyle (they have one child, Peregrine, who will die in 1642) 19 November: *Amoretti and Epithalamion* entered in Stationers' Register
1595	43	Publication of: *Colin Clout's Come Home Again* (published with *Astrophel: a pastoral elegy upon the death of the most noble and valorous knight, Sir Philip Sidney*); *Amoretti and Epithalamion*. Ponsonby published both sets of works
1596	44	Publication of: *Fairy Queen*, Books 4–6 (published with Books 1–3); *Four Hymns*; *Prothalamion*, all by Ponsonby *A View of the Present State of Ireland* written (unpublished) King James VI of Scotland claims Spenser slandered his mother, Mary Queen of Scots, in figure of Duessa in *Fairy Queen*, Book 5

Year	Literary Context (Britain)	Historical Events
1591	Harington's trans. of Ariosto, *Orlando Furioso*; Sidney, *Astrophil and Stella*; Shakespeare, 2 and 3 *Henry VI*; George Ripley, *Compound of Alchemy*	Death of Spanish mystic, St John of the Cross
1592	Shakespeare, 1 *Henry VI*; Marlowe, *Edward II*; *Dr Faustus* printed; Kyd, *Spanish Tragedy*; Constable, *Diana*; Daniel, *Delia*	Presbyterianism established in Scotland; remains of Pompeii discovered; Montaigne dies
1593	Marlow, *Massacre at Paris*; Shakespeare, *Venus and Adonis*, *Richard III*, *Comedy of Errors*; Barnaby Barnes, *Parthenophil and Parthenophe*; Marlowe dies; George Herbert born	
1594	Hooker, *Ecclesiastical Polity*, 1–4 (completed 1597); Shakespeare, *Titus Andronicus*, *The Taming of the Shrew*, *Two Gentlemen of Verona*; Nashe, *Unfortunate Traveller*	Palestrina dies
1595	Shakespeare, *Love's Labour's Lost*, *A Midsummer Night's Dream*, *Richard II*; Chapman, *Ovid's Banquet of Sense*; Daniel, *Civil Wars*, 1–4; Robert Southwell (poet and priest) martyred	
1596	Shakespeare, *The Merchant of Venice*, *King John*	English attack Cadiz
1597	Shakespeare, *Romeo and Juliet*; Joseph Hall, *Virgidemiae* (*Harvest of Rods*)	

Year	Age	Life
1598	46	Named Sheriff-designate for County Cork October: Kilcolman attacked and burned by forces led by Earl of Tyrone 24 December: Spenser brings dispatches from Governor of Munster to Privy Council in London
1599	47	13 January: Spenser dies at Westminster; funeral in Westminster Abbey, paid for by Earl of Essex
1609		Publication of *The Fairy Queen*, including *Two Cantos of Mutability*
1611		Publication of folio works: *The Fairy Queen; The Shepherds' Calendar: together with the Other Works of England's Arch-Poet, Edm. Spenser*

Year	Literary Context (Britain)	Historical Events
1598	Part of Chapman's trans. *Iliad* printed; Jonson, *Every Man in his Humour*; Marlowe/Chapman, *Hero and Leander*; Shakespeare, *1 Henry IV*, *Much Ado About Nothing*; John Stow, *Survey of London*; Francis Meres, *Palladis Tamia, Wit's Reflections*	Philip II of Spain dies
1599	Jonson, *Every Man out of his Humour*; Shakespeare, *Henry V*, *Julius Caesar*; James VI, *Basilikon Doron* (defending kingly Divine Right)	Oliver Cromwell born; Juan de Mariana, *De Rege et Regis institutione* (defends tyrannicide); Essex appointed Deputy in Ireland
1600	Shakespeare, *As You Like It*, *The Merry Wives of Windsor*, *Twelfth Night*; Fairfax's trans. of Tasso, *Jerusalem Delivered*; Dekker, *Shoemaker's Holiday*; Jonson, *Cynthia's Revels*	East India Company founded; James VI appoints bishops in Scotland; Giordano Bruno burnt by Inquisition for heresy
1601	Shakespeare, *Hamlet, Troilus and Cressida*; Jonson, *The Poetaster*	Essex executed for attempted rebellion
1602	Marston, *Antonio's Revenge*	Tommaso Campanella, *City of the Sun*; Bodleian Library opened
1603	Shakespeare, *All's Well That Ends Well*; Jonson, *Sejanus*	Elizabeth dies, James VI succeeds as James I, grants tolerance to Catholics

INTRODUCTION

The Fairy Queen was published in two instalments. Books 1–3 appeared in 1590, by which time Spenser had already, in October 1589, travelled from his home in Ireland to London (in company with his neighbour Sir Walter Ralegh), to present the poem to its dedicatee, Queen Elizabeth I. Books 4–6, together with a slightly revised Books 1–3 and a more splendidly monumental dedication to the queen, were published in 1596 (for further details, see Note on the Text).

If the queen is the poem's dedicatee, she is also its subject in the form of the Fairy Queen, known as Gloriana, from whose court (the *Letter of the Author's*, reprinted in the Appendix, tells us) each knight in turn travels on his – or, in one case, her – particular adventure. She is also the goal of the poem's super-hero's quest, for Prince Arthur, embodiment of the all-inclusive virtue of Magnificence (*Letter of the Author's*), and the knight whose function it is to rescue victims who are beyond mere mortal aid, is perpetually seeking her after she visited him in a dream (1. 9. 13–15). Born of the attempts under Elizabeth I, after her excommunication in 1570, to stifle and oppose both native and European Catholicism, the poem is thus a Protestant icon: a shimmering multi-faceted reflection of the queen to whom it is dedicated. This queen is head of the English Church (by the Settlement of 1559) and of the militant Protestant Order of the Garter (Una and the Redcross knight, St George, in Book 1); the embodiment of temperance – that ability to control opposites through the exercise of reason which was regarded as the essential preliminary virtue in a monarch and which also carried with it the power of self-transcendence – the power mystically to transform opposites into a new whole (Belphoebe and Alma in Book 2); and the Virgin warrior man–woman whose function it is to redeem female history from the erasures it has been placed under by successive generations of males (Britomart in Book 3).

The Fairy Queen is not a simple poem. In the first place its length guarantees this (by 1596 it comprised six books each of twelve cantos, with each canto containing between forty and fifty nine-line stanzas); secondly its gestation period also contributes to its complexity. Begun, apparently, by 1579 (Gabriel Harvey mentions 'your *Faerie Queene*' in a letter to Spenser published in *Three Proper, Witty, Familiar Letters*, 1580), it eventually appeared in two instalments with the announced intention of extending it to a twelve-book epic on the model of the *Aeneid*, and even twenty-four books, on the Homeric model (*Letter of the Author's*). It even insisted on posthumous birth, the *Two Cantos of Mutability* – presumably part of a putative Book 7 – being published in the 1609 edition, a decade after Spenser's death.

It is perhaps symbolic that the *Two Cantos* (printed in full in this edition) tell of Mutability's claim to supremacy and of her defeat by the logic of divine order that controls time and can bestow eternal rest at the end of time. For, in a sense, most of Spenser's poetry is impelled by the beliefs (Spenser would have recognised them as Platonic and Christian) that temporal process operates in the service of God and that we shall eventually see him 'face to face' (1 Corinthians 13:12). In other words, it enacts the metaphor that one's life is a journey towards light, the divine One, characterised by the givens of decay, a corrupted will and partial understanding (our inheritance from the Fall: Genesis, 3); that it is a pilgrimage through a wasteland of temptation, shadow and darkness in which the devil often masquerades as his opposite. Hence *The Fairy Queen* is in essence a quest poem obsessed with the gap between desire and attainment, governed by the oppositions of good and evil, light and dark. It is predicated upon the Tudor belief that the court is the centre of virtue, patronage, taste, and religion, and that the centre of the court is the sovereign who reigns on earth as a manifestation of God's blazing light. Thus, as the *Letter of the Author's* explains, each titular knight of *The Fairy Queen's* books sets out from court on his/her adventure to avenge a particular wrong.

In Book 1 Holiness and Protestant national identity, in the figure of St George, the knight of the Red Cross, prevail over the Catholic Antichrist; in Book 2 Temperance vanquishes its opposite; in Book 3 Chastity succeeds in banishing the forces of sexual torment. The excerpt from Book 4 in this edition shows us Scudamour winning Amoret, his beloved, from the Temple of Venus, and Florimell's release from imprisonment under the ocean by Proteus (thus returning us to, and completing, fragments of stories begun in Book 3); while the excerpt from Book 6 – Calidore's interruption of the dance of Venus's Graces and attendant maidens about an unidentified 'fourth maid' – presents us with one of the most important moments in the whole poem. For in this canto Spenser shows us his own poetic *persona* – the one he had used in his first published poem, *The Shepherds' Calendar*, and which, borrowed from John Skelton's *Colin Clout* (1521–2?), he returned to again and again – charming the dancing women into existence as products of his art. This means that to some extent he owns them. But one escapes his possessiveness – the mysterious fourth Grace, the country lass who is and is not Venus, Gloriana, or the supreme embodiment of virginity, Diana. The episode demonstrates how the poet constructs but also how even he, in the end, must acknowledge his powerlessness to name the ineffable, and to recall it once gone. While lesser men – Calidore in this instance – are positively lumpen: a moment's thoughtlessness and they destroy it, retaining only the idea and the memory, as Trojan Paris was left with a phantom Helen while imagining all the time he was making love to the real one (see 3. 8. 5–9 note). The theme is picked up again when Faunus in the *Cantos of Mutability* presumes to encroach on the ideal and is punished as Actaeon was by Diana (see *Mutability*, 6. 42 note); and it has already been a topic in Book 3, where the female knight Britomart releases Amoret from the enchanter Busirane's attempt to impose his own perception of womanly identity on her. Time and again, then, throughout *The Fairy Queen* we see women's identity scrutinised and male limitations of understanding of the feminine exposed.

Spenser wrote his poem in the blend of current courtly English, archaism, dialect and neologism that he had made his own as early as his first published poem, *The Shepherds' Calendar*. But this time he invented a topography as well, placing his tale in the half-mediaeval, half-dream, land of fairy; and wrote the whole as a chivalric romantic epic on the model of Virgil and his Italian successors. Spenser had to imitate Virgil's *Aeneid* in praise of Augustus not only to prove that, as a native Englishman, he could assert English as a poetic medium in accordance with Renaissance theories of imitation and arguments over the literary efficacy of the vernacular tongue, but also because Elizabeth, via the well-known story of Aeneas's great-grandson, Brutus (legendary founder of Britain: see Book 3, canto 9), claimed ancestry from Aeneas and his Trojan forefathers and hence equality with Augustus. Of the Italian successors Ariosto is perhaps the most important because his *Orlando Furioso* offered for imitation a post-Virgilian vernacular epic set in the time of Charlemagne which thus shadowed the achievements of the Holy Roman Emperor Charles V whom, even more than his secular predecessor as first presider over the Roman empire, Augustus, Elizabeth sought to rival in her claim to be supreme Protestant emperor in Europe and just inheritor of Christendom. And *The Fairy Queen* had to be chivalric because the 1570s saw the revival of the mediaeval courtly code in the form of tilts held annually to celebrate Elizabeth's accession day, 17 November (hence the 'annual feast' at Gloriana's court, during which, the *Letter of the Author's* tells us, the knights leave on their adventures).

But though so apparently full of certainties, sixteenth-century England was in as big a state of crisis as her late-twentieth-century counterpart, with religion explicitly at the forefront of things. Catholic, then with allegiance to the Pope forbidden under Henry VIII; devoutly Protestant under Edward VI; zealously Catholic under Mary Tudor; ineluctably Protestant under Elizabeth: how did those who lived from one of these reigns into the other (and, as we are ignorant of his exact year of birth, Spenser may, for all we know, have been baptised a Catholic), know where Truth was supposed to lie? Assuming that they had the leisure to care, this state control and manipulation of faith must have led to private revolt or cynicism. And what about the fundamental matter of transubstantiation – the Catholic doctrine that in the Mass Christ is corporeally present, wine changed to blood, bread to flesh, versus the new, Protestant, insistence that at communion the bread and wine, while acting as vehicles of Christ's grace, remain themselves, and so are more in the nature of being symbols? Did not that reflect on the position of the monarch, insisting on a shift away from divine right theory to the Machiavellian view that leaders prevail through brute strength, opportunism, cunning and the mere symbolism of their office? For the fact is that you cannot revise faith without fracturing every other certainty. If wine can no longer be blood – if it is now symbol not transubstantiated mystery – it is mere liquid fermented from grapes to be played around with by furtive choristers. If the queen succeeds to the throne amid adulation but is forced (or decides she is forced) to execute her relative and rival, Mary Queen of Scots (just as much a crowned and anointed queen as she herself), then how can the court believe in her authority as deriving from anything other than Machiavellian pragmatism?

Some of these tensions at least found their way into *The Fairy Queen* as, from the considerable distance of Ireland, and beleaguered by what he regarded as the Irish rebels, Spenser paused from secretarial and other duties, over a period of many years, to write his epic. He dedicated it to an empress. But in his daily life he saw (and if he is a poet worth reading he sympathised profoundly with) the wretched state of those over whom she ruled. He thought of the Irish faith and of the queen's (and his) opposite, Protestant, one. He thought of things as they ought to be, and of things as they were: the Virgin Queen who had succeeded in usurping the place of the Virgin Mary in her people's affections, yet who grew embarrassingly and vulgarly jealous whenever one of her favourites fell in love and married (Leicester; Ralegh). He thought of secularisation: of what happens when faith dies in a welter of bickering and schism. And as a result he wrote a poem that contained dreams of things as they might be and embodied the nightmare of things as they were. Some modern critics would call it self-deconstructing, but terminology doesn't matter. What does matter is that we recognise how it constantly charts the gap between desire and the goal of desire.

Spenser wrote and published *The Fairy Queen* in fragments – to announce himself publicly (and to gain attention from the queen, which he received in the not inconsiderable form of a pension of £50 a year) but also to register that its vision was provisional, even anti-holistic: to affirm that parts are separate testaments to the fragmentariness of experience. And although he seems to have had time to continue it beyond Book 6 and the two surviving *Mutability Cantos*, he didn't. He was tired; preoccupied; disenchanted (all readers of Book 6 have noticed how in it courtly forms and displays disappear as epic converts

to its generic opposite, pastoral, culminating in Spenser's evoca-
tion of himself as his own discarded radical shepherd *persona*,
Colin Clout, in canto 10). Yet simultaneously he bound – or
attempted to bind – the whole poem together with an astonish-
ing numerological virtuosity which insists that its books march
solidly to the scale of the planetary week (Book of the Sun, Book
of the Moon, Book of Mars and Minerva, etc.), and that its
narrative harmonies are those of the God-ordained universe: see
A. Fowler, *Spenser and the Numbers of Time* (1964).

Spenser conceived of *The Fairy Queen* as an Arthurian epic,
with his Arthur the embodiment of the ultimate virtue, Magnificence (*Letter of the Author's*), and his role the redemptive one
of Providence and/or grace (his appearance in the eighth canto
of each book – except the third – alludes to the redemptive
symbolism of the number in Christian mythography from 1
Peter 3: 20–1). Arthur, the great Cambro-British world conqueror, was another of Elizabeth's supposed ancestors, so the
poem's Arthurianism functions to consolidate the Elizabethan
imperial myth of the 1590s. Or does it? Spenser's Arthur is
prince, not king, and although the *Letter* explains this away as
necessary to the portrayal of his private virtues, assuring us that
this Arthur may well be succeeded by King Arthur demonstrat-
ing 'the politic virtues', this young knight recalls the queen's
uncle, Prince Arthur, elder brother to her father Henry VIII,
who died in 1502 at the age of sixteen amid considerable
mourning. And Arthur's ghostly evocativeness is supported by
the uncanniness of his narrative role. Redemptive he may be,
but his is the absent presence lamented by sonneteers like Sidney
and Spenser himself: there and not-there, by Book 3 he has
diminished into a lovesick melancholic chasing the wrong girl.
While even his tale to Book 1's heroine, Una, of his vision of the
fairy queen who visited him one night and has left him pursuing
her ever since, is too similar to the Red Cross knight's dream of
a false Una sent by Archimago in canto 1 for us not to feel that
he, too, is contaminated by the darkness of the world's riddles,
the distance between signifier and signified. Moreover, while the
deferral of his arrival in the poem (to canto 7 of Book 1) is
reminiscent of ceremonial delay (after false images the true solar
prince emerges out of darkness in triumph), it is also suggestive
of comic travesty: the deflation of heroic pretension in Rabelais
as it was to be followed by Cervantes.

And as with Arthur, so with Gloriana, by whom 'I mean glory in my general intention, but in my particular I conceive the most excellent and glorious person of our sovereign the queen' (*Letter of the Author's*): Elizabeth as manifestation of divine light and hence (according to the neo-Platonist Marsilio Ficino's *Commentary* on Plato's *Symposium*) essential Beauty itself, the goal of eros or desire. But although we hear of her in the *Letter*, we never see her. Maybe we would have done at the poem's end, in Book 12 or 24, but, as we have seen, Spenser seems to have done his best to ensure that it didn't, in any formal sense, end.

Then, within the books themselves there are strange, questioning riddles. Why at the threshold of Book 1, after our introduction to Una/Oneness/Truth/the queen as the sole head and governor of the Church (the multiplicity of her signifieds may reflect the Apuleian adage that the goddess has many names, but it sits rather strangely on the shoulders of a woman called One), do we meet Error as a snake-woman eaten by her offspring in imitation of the story that the mother pelican, if she can obtain no other food for her young, pierces her breast with her beak and feeds them with her blood? The pelican was associated with Elizabeth as nursing mother of her realm (to quote the Isaian text – 49: 23 – used in the coronation liturgy), so is Error here Una's opposite, the queen perceived as terrible mother? The identification would not have surprised Jung. It doesn't surprise us once we begin to recognise the other clues to the poem's double vision, its secret other text. For example, Una's appearance dressed in black and white, the personal colours of Elizabeth which were also the colours favoured by Mary Queen of Scots (compare Elizabeth's 'Sieve' portrait with the 1583 portrait of Mary and the young James): the reading of Una by a Stuart loyalist would have been very different from that of an ideal Protestant supporter of Elizabeth. Or consider the usurping sun queen Lucifera (1. 4), whose name seems to signify that she is a proud Lucifer (Satan) and thus a Mary Queen of Scots figure opposite to all that good queen Gloriana/Elizabeth stands for. Yet she, like Una and like the Virgin Queen herself, is called 'a maiden queen' (1. 4. 8); and *Lucifera* is a name of Diana, the Virgin Queen's main mythological *persona* (Cicero, *On the Nature of the Gods*, 2. 27). What, too, of the rigorous condemnation of Catholicism (through the figures of Duessa and

Orgoglio particularly), while Redcross, at the moment of his purgation in the House of Holiness, undergoes a ritual penance that could have come straight out of any treatise written by a believer in the old faith?

Similar riddles are posed by Books 2 and 3. Acrasia, for example, labelled 'Intemperance' by her name, is the destructive venerean witch who, at the centre of her bower in 2. 12, nevertheless recalls the bride of the Song of Solomon as 'a garden enclosed' and hence one imagistic strand associated with the Virgin Queen via the iconography of the Virgin Mary. Why? To say that she is a 'parody' of the queenly ideal, another 'terrible mother', is too simple. Spenser seems much more interested in exploring the dynamics of the process by which an ideal collapses into its opposite through the limitations of human perception (in this case, that of the peeping Sir Guyon whose creation she is as he gazes, lusts, and then destroys). As with Guyon so with all of us, says Spenser: we produce the queen as the image of our desires in all their forms, while her production of herself into hieratic image is inevitably subject to contamination by the viewer/consumer. While in Book 3, Britomart marches through the text in armour that, although it reputedly belonged to the Saxon queen Angela, who supposedly named the Angles and hence England (3. 3. 58–9), is sufficiently similar to the armour of male knights to make her so convincing a transvestite that Malecasta (the unchaste queen of canto 1) creeps into her bed and starts to think about plundering her body in the time-honoured masculine way. The comedy is considerable – if the predictable stuff of Greek romance and picaresque novel – and, like the mad King Lear, raises all sorts of handy-dandy questions about woman's 'real' role. If, for instance, she overrides natural law to become queen – the begetter of John Knox's *First Blast ... against the Monstrous Regiment of Women* – does she have to assume masculine traits? Does she, in Spenser's *reductio ad absurdum* here, have to mimic all the swaggering male postures? Then again, the fact that this transvestite knight, *persona* of Virgin Queen Elizabeth, is passionately in love with the image of Artegall poses several questions. After all, the queen was long past marriage, yet Spenser brings the three-book *Fairy Queen* of 1590 to a climax with a legend of chastity, not virginity; with an image of love's triumph, not, for example, of the victory of Diana over Actaeon or an equivalent icon of virginal femininity's triumph over the male. Finally, given the primacy of the Trojan–British myth, it is at least a matter of curiosity that, after the solemn mythologising of British history in 2. 10 and 3. 3 (omitted from this edition for reasons of space), its Trojan roots should be mocked in 3. 9, when Sir Paridell, descendant of the Paris who abducted Trojan Helen and thus started the Trojan war (the subject of the *Iliad* and the *Aeneid* and the legendary origin of Britain and of Queen Elizabeth, the Virgin Queen), champions the memory of his lustful ancestor, then proceeds to seduce and abduct the wife of his host Malbecco, whose name is Hellenore: Helen yet once more. So the Spenser who laments male appropriation of heroic deeds and asks why the ancient glory of women has been erased from modern records (3. 2, 3. 4) and who even dares reverse the Genesis-given fiat that women should give birth in pain as a punishment for Eve's part in the Fall (Chrysogone in 3. 6), doubles back to remind us that Tudor history, originating with Troy, is bound up with that of a whore, the same whore who generated the major epic texts of western civilisation, including Spenser's own. Britomart may counter Paridell by voicing the conventional history, but Paridell has been heard.

Thematic analysis

BOOK I

(1) *Subject*: Holiness: i.e., devotion to God that ideally culminates in spiritual perfection. On earth it marks you out as one of the saints (God's elect); posthumously, you will be one of the elect in heaven, maybe even a canonical saint. Hence the titular knight of Book 1 is revealed, in a Protestant revision of a Catholic legend, to be St George (see 1. 10. 66).

(2) *Allegorical method*: more than any other book in *The Fairy Queen*, Book 1 depends on the three-fold (four-fold if you count the literal level) scheme followed for biblical interpretation by the Church Fathers and used, for example, by Dante in the *Divine Comedy*. *Allegory* in this convention signifies historical allegory (narrative events corresponding to events in national history); *tropology* signifies moral allegory; *anagogy* signifies the allegorical level that is concerned with spiritual mysteries, God's

providential plan for humanity. The levels do not operate continuously or, necessarily, simultaneously.

(3) *Sources*: best understood in relation to (2) above. They are, mainly, (a) the St George legend (in which the knight kills the dragon that has been terrorising a city and demanding human sacrifice; the knight arrives when it is the turn of the king's daughter to be devoured and he encounters her waiting with her lamb); (b) the Bible in the Protestant Geneva translation of 1560 (many times reprinted), especially the Song of Songs and Revelation. The Geneva version contained marginal glosses offering various allegorical readings of its texts. The Song, a series of love songs between bride and bridegroom embodying their passion and desperate quest for each other, was anagogised in Geneva (and other versions) as signifying Christ's love for his Church 'which he hath sanctioned and appointed to be his spouse, holy, chaste'. In Song 3:2 the bride rises to 'go about . . . by the open places, [to] seek him that my soul loveth'. Compare Una, abandoned by Red Cross, searching for him between cantos 2 and 7. *Anagogically* she thus represents the Church, appearing as the bride of her knight/Christ in canto 12. *Allegorically* she is the English Church (and Elizabeth I as the head of that Church). Slightly more complicatedly, she represents Truth embodied in the English Church (as subscribing Elizabethans understood it). Redcross separates from her having been deceived into believing her to be false, and succumbs to Duessa (twoness, duplicity: canto 2): he is *allegorically* England (figured in her national saint) tied to a corrupt Catholicism, moving toward, and awaiting the revelation of, the true faith. This movement is paralleled by Redcross's *tropological* development, his journey as embodiment of fallen man through error (canto 1), pride (worldly and spiritual: cantos 4, 7–8), lust (his attraction to Duessa throughout, but especially at the beginning of canto 7 when he strips off his armour – the armour of the Christian man, as the *Letter of the Author's* tells us – to make love to her), despair (canto 9), repentance (canto 10), and consequential fitness to battle with the dragon of the sins (canto 11).

The Book of Revelation – a vision of the end of the world culminating in the marriage between Christ (the Lamb) and the New Jerusalem, the heavenly city of the elect (the Church

transferred to heaven) – supports the allegorical levels suggested
by the Song of Songs. Una is again the bride, Redcross her
espoused Christ; but Revelation's insistence on the defeat of the
dragon Satan (chapters 12, 20, etc.) focuses Book 1's various
dragons more precisely, while its Whore of Babylon (chapter
17) is a prototype for Duessa (one of the Geneva glosses
announces allegorically that she is 'the spiritual Babylon, which
is Rome'), and the woman clothed with the sun of chapter 12
('a type of the true and holy Church': Geneva gloss) adds
another layer to Una's significance (note the connection between
Una and the sun at 1. 3. 4; 1. 6. 4; 1. 12. 23).

(4) *Structure*: this operates through Spenser's characteristic
method of analogical (or parallel) patterning. Just as characters
correspond (Una: Duessa; Redcross: Archimago; etc.), so canto
1 is answered by 11 and 12 (forest displaced by the restored
Eden when Una's parents are released; dragon of error defeated
again in the dragon of 11); cantos 6 and 7 form a parallel core
pair (Una in the forest encounters the wood folk in their pagan
ignorance; Duessa and Redcross embrace in a shady grove and
engender the Catholic (specifically papal) ignorance of the giant
Orgoglio); and canto 4, with Lucifera's palace of pride, is
answered by canto 10, Dame Celia's humble house of holiness.

BOOK 2

(1) *Subject*: Temperance: i.e., control of the passions by reason;
or (see 2. 1. 58 note), it is the mid point between extremes of
excess and defect. The book's concerns are the passions traditionally allocated to the extreme parts of the tripartite soul:
concupiscence (which can be subdivided into lust and avarice)
on the one side, irascibility on the other. The main episodes and
characters of the book fall into place around this scheme.

   However, important as it is as a basis of moral behaviour
(and thus the foundation from which the moral and spiritual
edifice of *The Fairy Queen* can arise: Book 2, as it were, begins
at the beginning, whereas Book 1 has given us an overview of
the difficulties besetting the Christian's – and Christianity's –
life on earth and its *telos*), Aristotelian (classical) temperance
has, of necessity, been redefined by Christianity. This being so,
the passions are not, now, subject simply to the willed assertion

of reason's controlling power, for Christianity states that they were corrupted by the fall of man with original sin (this is what the bloody-handed babe Ruddimane signifies in cantos 1 and 2). Our willingness to battle with sin is signalled first by baptism (note the frequency with which water flows through the book), then by faith and by God's willingness to impart grace to us (the angel who appears at the beginning of canto 8). The *Palmer* is the symbol of faith as also of Christian experience, wisdom and suffering in the book. When he advises, Guyon is (just about) safe; when he is absent, Guyon is endangered. In other words, Christian truth supplements and transcends the moral knowledge available to the ancients. The titular knight, Guyon, recalls chivalric romance heroes (e.g., Guy of Warwick) and the river of paradise, Gihon, identified with temperance (see Book 2 proem 5 note).

(2) *Allegorical method*: essentially tropological (moral), with the characters representing the various passions.

(3) *Structure*: even more symmetrical than Book 1 in order to enact the mediating principle of rational control. The origin and goal of the book's journey is Acrasia (the witch of intemperance who is based on the Circe of *Odyssey*, 10): she killed Mortdant (an Adamic figure who has succumbed to lust as Adam succumbed to Eve: canto 1); she has Verdant (a recycled Mortdant, renewed as lust renews with every generation) entrapped in her bower in canto 12 (the bower parallels the Eden of Book 1's end). Guyon has to avenge the one by freeing the other. On his way, he has to learn the virtue he practises by encountering various excesses: anger in the form of Furor and Pyrochles; lust and sloth in the form of Cymochles and Phaedria. More seriously, he encounters avarice, the other side of lust, in Mammon (more seriously, because worship of gold can be understood as idolatry: Mammon is the god of this world, and his hellish cave is in effect a reminder that Judas set pieces of silver above Christ).

In contrast to the negatives, the narrative erects three female positives: Medina (the middle way; Aristotle's reason); Belphoebe (who reconciles opposites within herself to become an embodiment of self-transcendence: she is the queen in her private capacity as 'a most virtuous and beautiful lady', according to the *Letter of the Author's*, icon of virtue to the realm; that realm's history – seen in terms of a constant battle of reason over passions, kings over unruliness – is the subject of canto 10); and Alma (the rational soul herself, mistress of the temperate castle of the body which is, as all bodies are, subject to the attacks of the senses and original sin; Maleger, canto 11).

BOOK 3

(1) *Subject*: Chastity: i.e., that aspect of temperance relating to sexual behaviour and attitudes which in Elizabethan thought comprised both virginity and marital fidelity. The book's titular knight, Britomart, embodies the virginal ideal in her name (3. 1. 7–8 note); matrimonial chastity is her destiny (marriage with Artegall). Book 3 (1590 edition) ends with an epithalamic vision to answer the betrothal of Una and Redcross at the end of Book 1: Amoret (in a sense a sexual double for Britomart) embraces her husband Scudamour (double, momentarily, for Artegall), and they melt into a hermaphroditic union that sums up all the attempts at reconciliation and self-transcendence that have occurred, or been hinted at, in the previous books.

(2) *Method*: The most Ariostan of the books in its episodic structure and characterisation (Britomart is, in addition to her other precursor selves, Ariosto's Bradamante; Florimell his fleeing Angelica: *Orlando Furioso*, canto 1, etc.), it is also the most mythic of the three, the least obviously allegorically reductive. It is concerned with sexuality, but on a less didactic, more shadowy – even psychological and anthropological – level than Books 1 or 2, its main symbols in this respect being Venus and Adonis (subject of the tapestry in canto 1, mysterious centre of the book in the Garden of Adonis in canto 6); Narcissus (embodied in Marinell, beloved of Florimell who refuses to marry her but who, wounded by Britomart, lies in a stupor of self-involvement; the symbolism is implied at 3. 4. 29); Proteus, god of Marinell's element, the sea [Latin *mare*), symbol of passion, moral fluidity, and the depths of the imagination, as well as Venus's life-source (she was born from the waves, and her emblem is the fish: thus Florimell, having fled the forester, finds herself, in canto 8, in a boat (cf. Venus in her traditional scallop shell); and when her sleeping companion attempts to

rape her and, in doing so, covers her with fish scales, the moment is at once sexually suggestive and also mythologically apt); and the three maidens Amoret, Belphoebe and Florimell, who represent the three Graces who were the traditional hand-maids of Venus.

(3) *Structure*: episodic but also symmetrical. The tapestry of Venus and Adonis (anong others) in Malecasta's palace (1) is answered by the tapestries and triumph of Cupid in Busirane's castle (11, 12), and both reflect into canto 6 (the Garden of Adonis, which is itself the opposite of Acrasia's Bower of Bliss in 2. 12). Less symmetrically, Britomart's love quest, as a result of which she discovers from Merlin her destiny as mother of a progeny which will culminate in the birth of an imperial, virginal, Queen Elizabeth (canto 3), is answered in the second half by cantos 9 and 10, which tell of the seduction of Malbec-co's wife by Paridell, the firing of Malbecco's castle (so that it goes up in flames like ancient Troy), and the abandoning of Hellenore to a life among the satyrs where, marginalised and bestialised, she can fulfil her sexual appetite and be happier than she ever was married to a husband whose avarice was the visible sign of his constant and ubiquitous jealousy.

This revision of the tale of Helen of Troy is orthodox in being anti-Helen, heterodox in suggesting sympathy for her plight. As such it belongs to Spenser's avowed defence of women's function in history, confirming that the best way to begin to understand Book 3 is as a defence of chastity illuminating Elizabeth I's special role as Virgin Queen married to her realm which expands to become a consideration of women's role in social history and myth.

DOUGLAS BROOKS-DAVIES

NOTE ON THE TEXT

General

There is no surviving manuscript of any part of *The Fairy Queen* (or, indeed, of any other of Spenser's poems). Books 1–3 were first published in 1590 by Spenser's printer–publisher, William Ponsonby; three issues of the text have been identified. In 1596 Ponsonby published a second edition, containing six books: it reprinted Books 1–3 from 1590, with a few substantive changes and some changes in accidentals; revised the dedication to the queen; and altered the ending to Book 3 by removing the closure of Amoret's and Scudamour's embrace (Scudamour now leaves Busirane's castle before being reunited with Amoret in order that their tale can continue into Book 4). In addition, the 1596 edition contained the first printing of Books 4–6. (The *Two Cantos of Mutability* were first published in the 1609 edition, some ten years after Spenser's death.) The *Letter of the Author's* was appended to the 1590 edition but omitted from the 1596 text, as were all but three of the commendatory verses and all of the dedicatory sonnets that appeared with the 1590 text.

Modernisation

Spenser scholars seem generally agreed that the original spelling should be retained in editions of his poetry. I have, however, argued the case for a modernised edition of the shorter poems elsewhere (see under Editions in Further Reading). Reluctance to modernise *The Fairy Queen* seems even greater (if that were possible) than critical unwillingness to countenance modernised texts of Spenser's other works – in part, perhaps, because of an over-zealous deference to the particular fairyland he devised as the location for his great epic. For, the conservative argument goes, this land, at once England and not-England, the late sixteenth century and some chivalric time that never quite was, demanded its own language – a blend of archaism, dialect, standard courtly English, recent imports and neologisms. In other words, the language, like the poem's setting and topography, hovers on the brink of the familiar while being distinctly alien.

But the language Spenser uses in *The Fairy Queen* differs very little from that in his other poems, and is nowhere near as dialectally and archaically difficult as that employed in his *Shepherds' Calendar*. Far from being specially developed for *The Fairy Queen*'s other England, in fact, the language of that poem merely possesses all the hallmarks of Spenser's general poetic idiolect. Once this special case argument collapses, and when we recall that, in the absence of holograph texts, it is impossible to rescue authorial spelling and punctuation in this period since they are almost invariably compositorial, then the case for a modernised text seems incontrovertible. At the very least, a modernised *Fairy Queen* will enable the present-day reader to encounter the poem without artificial obstacles of quaintness interfering with his or her responses. It is an appropriate way to mark the quatercentenary of the six-book *Fairy Queen*'s publication.

The present edition

For reasons of space, the present edition is a selection only. But it is a generous one, ensuring narrative and thematic continuities by offering Book 1 complete; Books 2 and 3 with considerable fullness; cantos 10 and 12, with a fragment of canto 11, from Book 4; the 'core' canto, 10, from Book 6; and the *Cantos of Mutability*. The *Letter of the Author's* is printed in the Appendix. Copy text is the 1596 edition with substantive corrections where necessary; accidentals have been modernised, as has spelling, except where this would affect metre or rhyme or where a word is so archaic or otherwise alien that to modernise would be to destroy Spenser's intention to shock with strangeness.

The uniqueness of a modernised text has been complemented in this edition by marginal lexical glosses which, as well as explaining meanings, also signal, within the limits of present knowledge, the chronological status of significant words. This is effected by the use of signs, thus: * indicates a word that was, according to the *Oxford English Dictionary*, out of general literary use by Spenser's time; ‡ indicates a word that appears to have gained literary currency after the mid 1530s; † indicates a word that appears to have been first used by Spenser (either in *The Fairy Queen* or elsewhere). Occasionally, the signs are used in conjunction: thus *† signifies an archaism reinvented and given a different meaning by Spenser; ‡* signifies a word of recent origin which Spenser (or a near contemporary) appears to have been the last to use.

For textual information on *The Fairy Queen*, see: *The Fairy Queen* ed. Smith; *Variorum*; *The Fairy Queen* ed. Roche (under Editions in Further Reading). Also W. P. Williams in *Spenser Encyclopedia*, pp. 90–3, 259, and H. Yamashita. H. Sato, T. Suzuki, A. Takano (eds), *A Textual Companion to 'The Faerie Queene' 1590* (Tokyo: Kenyusha Books, 1993; electronic version, 1992).

THE FAIRY QUEEN

TO
THE MOST HIGH,
MIGHTY
And
MAGNIFICENT
EMPRESS RENOVV-
MED FOR PIETIE, VER-
TUE, AND ALL GRATIOUS
GOVERNMENT ELIZABETH BY
THE GRACE OF GOD QUEENE
OF ENGLAND FRAUNCE AND
IRELAND AND OF VIRGI-
NIA, DEFENDOUR OF THE
FAITH, &c. HER MOST
HUMBLE SERVAUNT
EDMUND SPENSER
DOTH IN ALL HU-
MILITIE DEDI-
CATE, PRE-
SENT
AND CONSECRATE THESE
HIS LABOURS TO LIVE
VVITH THE ETERNI-
TIE OF HER
FAME.

[Dedication to 1596 edition]

The First Book of *The Fairy Queen*, Containing the Legend of the Knight of the Red Cross, or, Of Holiness

1

Lo°, I the man, whose Muse whilom° did   *Behold formerly* *
   mask°   *conceal herself*‡
(As time her taught) in lowly shepherd's weeds,°   *clothes*
Am now enforced° (a far unfitter task)   *compelled*
For trumpets stern to change mine oaten reeds,
And sing of knights' and ladies' gentle° deeds, *noble; courteous*
Whose praises, having slept in silence long,
Me – all too mean° – the sacred Muse   *humble*
   areads°   *counsels*‡
To blazon broad° amongst her learned throng: *trumpet abroad*
Fierce wars and faithful loves shall
   moralise° my song.   *supply the moral subject of*†

2

Help then, O holy virgin, chief of nine,
   Thy weaker° novice to perform thy will: *too weak*
   Lay forth out of thine everlasting scrine°   *box for [holy] relics*
The antique rolls (which there lie hidden still)
Of fairy knights, and fairest Tanaquil,
Whom that most noble Briton Prince so long
Sought through the world and suffered so much
   ill°   *i.e., on her behalf*
That I must rue° his undeserved wrong: *pity*
O help thou my weak wit,° and sharpen my dull *understanding*
   tongue.

3

And thou, most dreaded imp° of highest Jove –   *child; demon*
   Fair Venus' son – that, with thy cruel dart°   *arrow*
   At that good knight so cunningly° didst   *cleverly*
   rove°   *randomly shoot*
That° glorious fire° it kindled in his   *so that ardour for glory*

heart –
Lay now thy deadly ebon'° bow apart°   *ebony   aside*
And, with thy mother mild, come to mine aid:
Come both, and with you bring triumphant Mart°   *Mars*
In loves and gentle jollities arrayed
After his murderous spoils and bloody rage allayed.

4

And with them eke,° O goddess heavenly bright –   *in addition*
Mirror of grace and majesty divine,
Great lady of the greatest isle, whose light
Like Phoebus' lamp throughout the world doth shine –
Shed thy fair beams into my feeble eyen,°   *eyes*
And raise my thoughts, too humble and too vile,°   *base*
To think of that true glorious type° of thine,   *emblem*
The argument of mine afflicted°   *humble†*
   style:°   *pen; poetic manner*
The which to hear, vouchsafe, O dearest dread, awhile.

CANTO 1

The patron of true holiness
   Foul Error doth defeat;
Hypocrisy him to entrap
   Doth to his home entreat.

1

A gentle° knight was pricking° on the plain,   *noble   spurring*
Yclad° in mighty arms° and silver shield,   *Clad*   armour*
Wherein old dints° of deep wounds did remain –   *dents†*
The cruel marks of many a bloody field°   *i.e., battlefield*
(Yet arms till that time did he never wield):
His angry steed did chide his foaming bit,
As much disdaining to the curb to yield:
Full jolly° knight he seemed, and fair°   *brave; splendid   nobly*
   did sit,
As one for knightly jousts and fierce encounters fit.

2

But on his breast a bloody cross he bore,
   The dear remembrance° of his dying Lord,   *memorial*
   For whose sweet sake that glorious badge he wore
   And, dead-as°-living, ever him adored.   *as if*
   Upon his shield the like was also scored°   *incised*[†]
   For sovereign° hope, which in his help he had.   *supreme*
   Right faithful true he was in deed and word,
   But of his cheer° did seem too solemn sad: *face; expression*
Yet nothing did he dread, but ever was ydrad.°   *dreaded*[*]

3

Upon a great adventure he was bound
   That greatest Gloriana to him gave –
   That greatest glorious Queen of Fairyland –
   To win him worship° and her grace° to have,   *esteem*[*] *favour*
   Which of all earthly things he most did crave.
   And ever as he rode his heart did yearn
   To prove his puissance° in battle brave   *power*
   Upon his foe, and his new force to learn:
Upon his foe, a dragon horrible and stern.°   *fierce; resolute*

4

A lovely lady rode him fair° beside,   *in comely fashion*
   Upon a lowly ass more white than snow:
   Yet she much whiter, but the same did hide
   Under a veil that wimpled° was full low;   *falling in folds*[†]
   And over all a black stole she did throw,
   As one that inly mourned: so was she sad,
   And heavy° sat upon her palfrey°   *sadly woman's light horse*
     slow.
   Seemed in her heart some hidden care she had;
And by her in a line° a milk-white lamb she lad.°   *on a lead led*

5

So pure an innocent° as that same lamb   *spotless, sinless person*
   She was in life and every virtuous lore,°   *teaching*
   And by descent from royal lineage came
   Of ancient kings and queens, that had of yore°   *old*
   Their sceptres stretched from east to western shore,
   And all the world in their subjection held

Till that infernal fiend with foul uproar°   *insurrection*
Forwasted° all their land and them expelled: *Devastated*
Whom to avenge she had this knight from far compelled.

6

Behind her far away° a dwarf did lag,   *Far behind her*
  That lazy seemed in being ever last,
  Or wearied with bearing of her bag
  Of needments° at his back. Thus as they passed,   *necessaries†*
  The day with clouds was sudden overcast,
  And angry Jove an hideous° storm of rain   *immense; terrifying*
  Did pour into his leman's° lap so fast   *beloved's*
  That every wight° to shroud° it did   *creature* take shelter*
    constrain,°   *force*
And this fair couple eke° to shroud themselves were   *also*
    fain.°   *obliged*

7

Enforced to seek some covert° nigh at hand,   *hiding place*
  A shady grove not far away they spied
  That promised aid the tempest to withstand,
  Whose lofty trees yclad° with summer's pride°   *clad* opulence*
  Did spread so broad that summer's light did hide,
  Not pierceable with power of any star;
  And all within were paths and alleys wide,
  With footing° worn, and leading inward far: *footprints‡*
Fair harbour° that them seems, so in they entered   *shelter; arbour*
    are.

8

And forth they pass, with pleasure forward led,
  Joying° to hear the birds' sweet harmony   *Rejoicing*
  Which, therein shrouded° from the tempest dread,   *sheltered*
  Seemed in their song to scorn the cruel sky.
  Much can° they praise the trees so straight   *did; knew how to*
    and high:
  The sailing° pine; the cedar proud and tall;   *tall; for sailing*
  The vine-prop elm; the poplar never dry;
  The builder° oak (sole king of forests all);   *for building*
The aspen good for staves; the cypress funeral;

9

The laurel, meed° of mighty conquerors   *reward*
  And poets sage; the fir that weepeth° still;°   *oozes[resin] always*
  The willow, worn of° forlorn°   *by abandoned*
    paramours;°   *lovers*
  The yew, obedient to the bender's will;
  The birch for shafts; the sallow for the mill;°   *mill-pond*
  The myrrh, sweet-bleeding in the bitter wound;
  The warlike beech; the ash for nothing ill;
  The fruitful olive; and the platan° round;   *plane tree*
The carver holm;° the maple, seldom ever   *holm oak for carving*
  inward sound.

10

Led with delight they thus beguile° the way   *pass pleasantly‡*
  Until the blustering storm is overblown,
  When, weening° to return whence they did stray,   *thinking*
  They cannot find the path which first was shown
  But wander to and fro in ways unknown,
  Furthest from end then when they nearest ween,
  That makes them doubt° their wits be not their   *also = fear*
    own:
  So many paths, so many turnings seen,
That which of them to take in diverse° doubt they   *distracting†*
  been.

11

At last resolving forward still to fare
  Till that some end they find or° in or out,   *either*
  That path they take that beaten seemed most bare
  And like to lead the labyrinth about,°   *through*
  Which, when by tract° they hunted had throughout,   *tracking*
  At length it brought them to a hollow cave
  Amid the thickest woods. The champion stout°   *brave*
  Eftsoons° dismounted from his courser   *Straight away*
    brave°   *handsome*
And to the dwarf awhile his needless spear he gave.

12

'Be well aware,' quoth then that lady mild,
　'Lest sudden mischief ye too rash provoke:
　The danger hid, the place unknown and wild,
　Breeds dreadful doubts.° Oft fire is without smoke,　　　*fears*
　And peril without show: therefore your stroke,
　Sir knight, withhold till further trial made.'
　'Ah, lady,' said he, 'shame were to revoke°　　　*withdraw*
　The forward footing for an hidden shade:°　　　*also: phantom*
Virtue gives herself light through darkness for to wade.'

13

'Yea, but,' quoth she, 'the peril of this place
　I better wot° than you, though now too late　　　*know*
　To wish you back return with foul disgrace.
　Yet wisdom warns, whilst foot is in the gate,°　*at the threshold*
　To stay° the step ere forced to retrait:°　　*stop withdraw it*[†]
　This is the wandering wood, this Error's den –
　A monster vile whom God and man does hate.
　Therefore, I rede° beware.' 'Fly, fly,' quoth then　　*advise*[*]
The fearful dwarf: 'This is no place for living men.'

14

But, full of fire and greedy hardiment,°　　　*daring*
　The youthful knight could not for aught be stayed,
　But forth into the darksome° hole he went,　　*gloomy*
　And looked in: his glistering° armour made　　*glittering*
　A little glooming° light, much like a shade,　　*gleaming*[‡]
　By which he saw the ugly monster plain –
　Half like a serpent horribly displayed,°　　*spread out*[*]
　But the other half did woman's shape retain,
Most loathsome, filthy, foul, and full of vile
　disdain.°　　　*loathsomeness*[†]

15

And as she lay upon the dirty ground
　Her huge long tail her den all overspread
　(Yet was in knots and many boughts° upwound)　*coils, folds*
　Pointed with mortal sting. Of her there bred
　A thousand young ones which she daily fed,
　Sucking upon her poisonous dugs, each one

Of sundry shapes, yet all ill-favoured:

Soon as that uncouth° light upon them shone,   *unfamiliar, strange*

Into her mouth they crept, and sudden all were gone.

16

Their dam upstart,° out of her den effrayed,°   *started up*
                                                              startled

And rushed forth, hurling° her hideous° tail   *thrashing*
                                                              huge; terrible

About her cursed head, whose folds displayed°   *unfolded to view*

Were stretched now forth at length without entrail.°   *coil†*

She looked about and, seeing one in mail

Armed to point,° sought back to turn again,   *fully armed*

For light she hated as the deadly bale,°   *injury [i.e., death]*

Aye wont° in desert° darkness to remain   *Always accustomed forsaken*

Where plain° none might her see, nor she see any plain;   *clearly†*

17

Which when the valiant elf perceived, he leaped,

As lion fierce, upon the flying prey,

And with his trenchant° blade her boldly kept   *sharp*

From turning back, and forced her to stay.

Therewith enraged she loudly 'gan to bray

And, turning fierce, her speckled tail advanced,

Threatening her angry sting him to dismay:°   *paralyse with fear*

Who, nought aghast, his mighty hand enhanced:°   *lifted up*

The stroke down from her head unto her shoulder glanced.°   *moved rapidly*

18

Much daunted° with that dint° her sense was dazed,°   *tamed* blow*
                                                              stupefied‡

Yet, kindling rage, herself she gathered° round   *coiled*

And, all at once, her beastly body raised

With doubled forces high above the ground;

Tho,° wrapping up her wreathed stern° around,   *Then tail*

Leaped fierce upon his shield, and her huge train°   *tail*

All suddenly about his body wound,

That° hand or foot to stir he strove in vain: *So that*
God help the man so wrapped in Error's endless train!

19

His lady, sad to see his sore° constraint,°   *extreme confinement*†
  Cried out, 'Now, sir knight, show what ye be;
  Add faith unto your force, and be not faint:
  Strangle her, else she sure will strangle thee.'
  That when he heard, in great
    perplexity,°   *entanglement;*† *trouble*
  His gall did grate° for grief and high disdain   *fret*†
  And, knitting° all his force, got one hand   *summoning*
    free,°   *extricated*†
  Wherewith he gripped her gorge with so great pain°   *effort*
That soon to loose her wicked bands did her constrain.°   *compel*

20

Therewith she spewed out of her filthy maw°   *womb;** *stomach*
  A flood of poison horrible and black,
  Full of great lumps of flesh and gobbets° raw,   *chunks*
  Which stunk so vilely that it forced him slack
  His grasping hold, and from her turn him back.
  Her vomit full of books and papers was,
  With loathly frogs and toads which eyes did lack
  And, creeping, sought way in the weedy grass;
Her filthy parbreak° all the place defiled has,   *vomit*‡ *

21

As when old father Nilus 'gins to swell
  With timely° pride° above the Egyptian   *seasonal abundance*
    vale,
  His fatty° waves do fertile slime outwell°   *fecund pour forth*†
  And overflow each plain and lowly dale;
  But, when his later spring° 'gins to   *flowing*
    avail,°   *withdraw;** *diminish*
  Huge heaps of mud he leaves, wherein there breed
  Ten thousand kind of creatures, partly male
  And partly female, of his fruitful seed
(Such ugly monstrous shapes elsewhere may no man
    read).°   *see*†

22

The same so sore° annoyed° has the knight   *extremely vexed*
  That, well nigh° choked with the deadly stink,   *very nearly*
  His forces fail,° ne can no° longer   *strength fails nor can he any*
    fight.
  Whose courage when the fiend perceived to shrink,
  She poured forth out of her hellish sink°   *womb as cesspit*[†]
  Her fruitful° cursed spawn of serpents small –   *multiple*
  Deformed monsters, foul and black as ink,
  Which swarming all about his legs did crawl
And him encumbered sore, but could not hurt at all:

23

As gentle shepherd in sweet eventide,
  When ruddy Phoebus 'gins to welk° in west,   *lose brightness**
  High on an hill his flock to viewen wide,
  Marks which do bite their hasty supper best,
  A cloud of cumbrous° gnats do him molest,   *annoying*
  All striving to infix their feeble stings,
  That from their 'noyance° he nowhere can rest,   *irritation*
  But with his clownish° hands their tender wings   *rustic*
He brusheth off, and oft doth mar° their murmurings;   *destroy*

24

Thus ill bestead,° and fearful more of   *surrounded;* harassed**
    shame
  Than of the certain peril he stood in,
  Half furious unto his foe he came –
  Resolved in mind all suddenly to win,
  Or soon to lose, before he once would lin° –   *desist*
  And struck at her with more than manly° force   *human*
  That,° from her body full of filthy sin,   *So that*
  He reft° her hateful head without   *hewed off*
    remorse:°   *scruple**
A stream of coal-black blood forth gushed from her
    corse.°   *body*

25

Her scattered brood, soon as their parent dear
  They saw so rudely° falling to the ground,   *violently*
  Groaning full deadly, all with troublous fear

Gathered themselves about her body round,
Weening° their wonted° entrance to have   *Thinking   accustomed*
    found
At her wide mouth. But, being there withstood,
They flocked all about her bleeding wound,
And sucked up their dying mother's blood,
Making her death their life, and eke° her hurt their good.   *also*

26

That detestable sight him much amazed,°   *bewildered; astonished*
    To see the unkindly° imps,° of°   *unnatural   offspring; devils   by*
        heaven accursed,
    Devour their dam: on whom, while so he gazed,
    Having all satisfied their bloody thirst,
    Their bellies swollen he saw with fulness burst,
    And bowels gushing forth: well worthy end
    Of such as drunk her life the which them nursed.
    Now needeth them no longer labour spend:
His foes have slain themselves, with whom he should contend.

27

His lady, seeing all that chanced° from far,   *happened*
    Approached, in haste to greet° his victory,   *congratulate him on†*
    And said: 'Fair° knight, born under happy°   *Excellent   fortunate*
        star,
    Who see your vanquished foes before you lie:
    Well worthy be you of that armory°   *armorial bearing; emblem*
    Wherein ye have great glory won this day,
    And proved your strength on a strong enemy,
    Your first adventure: many such, I pray,
And henceforth ever wish, that like succeed it may.'

28

Then mounted he upon his steed again,
    And with the lady backward sought to wend.°   *travel*
    That path he kept which beaten was most plain,
    Ne° ever would to any byway bend,   *Nor*
    But still° did follow one unto the end   *always*
    The which at last out of the wood them brought.
    So forward on his way (with God to° friend)   *as*
    He passeth forth, and new adventure sought;

Long way he travelled° before he heard of   *journeyed; travailed*
  aught.

29

At length they chanced to meet upon the way
  An aged sire in long black weeds° yclad,   *clothes*
  His feet all bare, his beard all hoary° grey,   *white; venerable*
  And by his belt his book he hanging had.
  Sober° he seemed, and very sagely°   *Serious wisely*
    sad,°   *melancholic*
  And to the ground his eyes were lowly bent:
  Simple in show, and void of malice° bad.   *evil*
  And all the way he prayed, as he went,
And often knocked his breast, as one that did repent.

30

He fair° the knight saluted,° louting   *courteously greeted*
    low,°   *bowing humbly*
  Who fair him quited,° as that courteous was;   *repaid*
  And after asked him if he did know
  Of strange adventures which abroad did pass.
  'Ah, my dear son,' quoth he, 'how should, alas,
  Silly° old man that lives in hidden cell,   *Innocent*
  Bidding his beads° all day for his trespass,° *Saying prayers* sin*
  Tidings of war and worldy trouble tell?
  With holy father sits not° with such things to   *is not fitting*
    mell.°   *meddle*

31

'But if of danger which hereby doth dwell,
  And homebred evil, ye desire to hear,
  Of a strange man I can you tidings tell
  That wasteth° all his country far and near.'   *ravages*
  'Of such,' said he, 'I chiefly do enquire,
  And shall you well reward to show the place
  In which that wicked wight° his days doth   *person**
    wear:°   *spend*
  For to all knighthood it is foul disgrace
That such a cursed creature lives so long a space.'

32

'Far hence,' quoth he, 'in wasteful° wilderness   *barren*
  His dwelling is, by which no living wight
  May ever pass, but through great distress.'
  'Now,' said the lady, 'draweth° toward night,   *it draws*
  And well I wote° that, of your later° fight,   *know   recent*
  Ye all forwearied° be: for what so strong   *tired out*
  But, wanting° rest, will also want of might?   *lacking*
  The sun, that measures° heaven all day long,   *traverses*
At night doth bait° his steeds the ocean waves among: *refresh*

33

'Then with the sun take, sir, your timely rest,
  And with new day new work at once begin:
  Untroubled night, they say, gives counsel best.'°   *best counsel*
  'Right well, sir knight, ye have advised been,'
  Quoth then that aged man: 'The way to win
  Is wisely to advise.° Now day is spent.   *take thought*
  Therefore with me ye may take up your inn
  For this same night.' The knight was well content,
So with the godly father to his home they went.

34

A little lowly hermitage it was,
  Down in a dale hard° by a forest's side,   *right*
  Far from resort° of people that did pass   *crowd*
  In travel to and fro: a little wide°   *short space away*
  There was an holy chapel edified,°   *built; spiritually wholesome*
  Wherein the hermit duly wont° to say   *was accustomed*
  His holy things° each morn and eventide;   *offices*
  Thereby a crystal stream did gently play,°   *ripple†*
Which from a sacred fountain welled forth alway.°   *always*

35

Arrived there the little house they fill,
  Ne° look for entertainment° where none was.   *Nor food*
  Rest is their feast, and all things at their will:
  The noblest mind the best contentment has.
  With fair° discourse° the evening so they *pleasing conversation*
      pass,
  For that old man of pleasing words had store,°   *abundance*

And well could file his tongue as smooth as glass:
  He told of saints and popes, and evermore
He strewed an *Ave Mary* after and before.

36

The drooping night thus creepeth on them fast,
  And the sad° humour,° loading their eyelids   *heavy dampness*
  As messenger of Morpheus, on them cast
  Sweet-slumbering dew, the which to sleep them bids.
  Unto their lodgings then his guests he rids°   *dispatches*
  Where, when all drowned in deadly sleep he finds,
  He to his study goes, and there, amids
  His magic books and arts of sundry kinds,
He seeks out mighty charms to trouble sleepy° minds.   *sleeping*

37

Then choosing out few words most horrible
  (Let none them read!), thereof did verses frame°   *fashion*
  With which, and other spells like terrible,
  He bade awake black Pluto's grisly° dame,   *terrifying*
  And cursed heaven, and spoke reproachful shame
  Of highest God, the lord of life and light:
  A bold, bad man that dared to call by name
  Great Gorgon, prince of darkness and dead night,
At which Cocytus quakes and Styx is put to flight.

38

And forth he called out of deep darkness dread
  Legions of sprites,° the which – like little flies   *spirits; demons*
  Fluttering about his ever-damned head –
  Await whereto their service he applies:
  To aid his friends, or fray° his enemies.   *attack*
  Of those he chose out two, the falsest two,
  And fittest for to forge true-seeming lies:
  The one of them he gave a message to,
The other by himself stayed, other work to do.

39

He making speedy way through spersed° air,   *dispersed*[t]
  And through the world of waters wide and deep,
  To Morpheus' house doth hastily repair:

Amid the bowels of the earth full steep,
And low, where dawning day doth never peep,
His dwelling is: there Tethys his wet bed
Doth ever wash, and Cynthia still° doth   *continually*
    steep°   *bathe†*
In silver dew his ever-drooping head,
Whiles sad Night over him her mantle black doth spread:

40

Whose double gates he findeth locked fast –
The one fair° framed° of burnished ivory,   *beautifully made*
The other all with silver overcast.
And wakeful dogs before them far do lie,
Watching to banish Care, their enemy,
Who oft is wont° to trouble gentle Sleep.   *accustomed*
By them the sprite doth pass in quietly,
And unto Morpheus comes, whom, drowned deep
In drowsy fit he finds: of nothing he takes keep.°   *notice*

41

And more to lull him in his slumber soft
A trickling stream from high rock tumbling down,
And ever-drizzling rain upon the
    loft,°   *from on high; from the sky*
Mixed with a murmuring wind (much like the soun'°   *sound*
Of swarming bees) did cast him in a swoon.
No other noise, nor people's troublous cries
(As still are wont to annoy the walled town)
Might there be heard, but careless° Quiet lies,   *free from care*
Wrapped in eternal silence, far from enemies.

42

The messenger, approaching, to him spake,
But his waste° words returned to him in vain: *wasted; empty*
So sound he slept that nought might him awake.
Then rudely he him thrust and pushed with
    pain,°   *roughly; forcefully*
Whereat he 'gan to stretch. But he again
Shook him so hard that forced him to speak:

As one then in a dream, whose dryer° brain   *too dry*
Is tossed with troublous sights and fancies° weak,   *imaginings*
He mumbled soft, but would not all° his silence   *completely*
    break.

43

The sprite then 'gan more boldly him to wake,
    And threatened unto him the dreaded name
    Of Hecate: whereat he 'gan to quake,
    And, lifting up his lumpish head, with blame
    Half-angry asked him for what he came.
    'Hither' (quoth he) 'me Archimago sent –
    He that the stubborn sprites can wisely° tame.   *skilfully*
    He bids thee to him send for his intent
A fit false dream that can delude the sleeper's sent.'° *will, assent*

44

The god obeyed and, calling forth straightway
    A diverse° dream out of the prison dark,   *diverting; distracting*†
    Delivered it to him, and down did lay
    His heavy head, devoid of careful° cark,°   *full of care burden*
    Whose senses were all straight° benumbed and   *straight away*
        stark.°   *rigid*
    He, back returning by the ivory door,
    Remounted up as light as cheerful lark,
    And on his little wings the dream he bore
In haste unto his lord, where he him left afore.°   *before*

45

Who, all this while, with charms and hidden° arts   *secret; occult*
    Had made a lady of that other sprite,
    And framed° of liquid° air her tender parts   *formed clear*†
    So lively,° and so like° in all men's sight,   *lifelike i.e., life*
    That weaker° sense it could have ravished   *weak*
        quite:°   *completely*
    The maker self,° for all his wondrous wit,°   *himself knowledge*
    Was nigh beguiled with so goodly sight.
    Her all in white he clad, and over it
Cast a black stole, most like to seem for Una fit.

46

Now when that idle° dream was to him brought, *insubstantial*
 Unto that elfin knight he bade him fly
 Where he slept soundly, void of evil thought,
 And with false shows abuse his fantasy
 In sort as° he him schooled privily.° *the manner that secretly*
 And that new creature, born without her due,° *unnaturally*
 Full of the maker's guile, with usage° sly *conduct, behaviour*
 He taught to imitate that lady true
Whose semblance she did carry under feigned hue.° *appearance*

47

Thus well instructed, to their work they haste
 And, coming where the knight in slumber lay,
 The one upon his hardy° head him placed *courageous*
 And made him dream of loves and lustful play,
 That° nigh his manly heart did melt away, *So that*
 Bathed in wanton bliss and wicked joy:
 Then, seemed him, his lady by him lay,
 And to him plained° how that false *lamented; complained*
  winged boy
Her chaste heart had subdued to learn Dame Pleasure's
  toy.° *games*

48

And she herself of beauty sovereign queen,
 Fair Venus, seemed unto his bed to bring
 Her whom he, waking, evermore did ween° *consider*
 To be the chastest flower that aye did spring
 On earthly branch – the daughter of a king –
 Now a loose leman° to vile service° bound. *mistress servitude*
 And eke° the Graces seemed all to sing *in addition*
 Hymen, io Hymen, dancing all around,
Whilst freshest° Flora her with ivy garland *most youthful*
  crowned.

49

In this great passion° of unwonted lust, *overpowering emotion*[1]
 Or wonted° fear of doing aught amiss, *customary*
 He started up, as seeming to mistrust° *suspect*
 Some secret ill or hidden foe of his:

Lo, there before his face his lady is,
Under black stole hiding her baited hook
And, as half blushing, offered him to kiss
With gentle blandishment° and lovely° look,   *cajolery† loving*
Most like that virgin true which for her knight him took.

50

All clean° dismayed to see so uncouth°   *completely   distasteful*
   sight,
And half enraged at her shameless guise,°   *manner; attire*
He thought have slain her in his fierce
   despite;°   *contempt; anger*
But, hasty heat tempering with sufferance° wise,   *forbearance*
He stayed his hand and 'gan himself advise
To prove° his sense and tempt her feigned truth.   *test*
Wringing her hands in women's piteous wise,°   *fashion*
Tho° can° she weep to stir up gentle ruth°   *Then did   pity*
Both for her noble blood and for her tender youth,

51

And said: 'Ah, sir, my liege lord and my love,
   Shall I accuse the hidden cruel fate
And mighty causes wrought in heaven above,
Or the blind god that doth me thus amate,°   *daunt*
For° hoped love to win me certain hate?   *Instead of*
Yet thus perforce° he bids me do, or die.   *through force*
Die is my due: yet rue my wretched state,
You, whom my hard avenging destiny
Hath made judge of my life or death indifferently.°   *alike*

52

'Your own dear sake forced me at first to leave
   My father's kingdom—'. There she stopped with tears
(Her swollen heart her speech seemed to bereave),°   *steal*
And then again begun: 'My weaker years,
Captived to Fortune and frail worldly fears,
Fly to your faith for succour and sure° aid: *certain*
Let me not die in languor° and long tears.'   *distress**
'Why, dame,' quoth he, 'what hath ye thus dismayed?
What frays° you that were wont° to comfort   *scares accustomed*
   me afraid?'

53

'Love of yourself,' she said, 'and dear°   *dire*
   constraint,°   *misfortune* *
Lets me not sleep, but waste the weary night
In secret anguish and unpitied plaint,°   *lament*
Whiles you in careless° sleep are drowned   *without care*
   quite'.°   *utterly*
Her doubtful° words made that   *fearful*
   redoubted° knight   *distinguished*
Suspect her truth: yet since no untruth he knew,
Her fawning love with foul disdainful° spite°   *scornful disgust*
He would not shend,° but said: 'Dear   *reprove; put to shame*
   dame, I rue
That for my sake unknown such grief unto you grew.

54

'Assure yourself it fell not all to ground,°   *i.e., was not ignored*
   For all so° dear as life is to my heart   *as*
I deem° your love, and hold me to you bound.   *esteem*
Ne° let vain fears procure° your needless   *Nor   cause*
   smart°   *grief*
Where cause is none, but to your rest depart.'
Not all content, yet seemed she to appease°   *soothe*
Her mournful plaints, beguiled of her
   art,°   *cheated of her deception*
And fed with words that could not choose but please:
So, sliding softly forth, she turned° as to her ease.   *returned*

55

Long after lay he musing at her mood,
   Much grieved to think that gentle dame so
     light°   *wanton; frivolous*
For whose defence he was to shed his blood.
At last, dull weariness of former fight
Having yrocked asleep his irksome°   *wearied; disgusted* *
   sprite,°   *mind*
Troublous dream 'gan freshly toss° his brain   *agitate* ‡
With bowers° and beds and ladies' dear delight: *bed chambers*
But when he saw his labour all was vain,°   *useless*
With that misformed° sprite he back returned again.   *misshapen* †

CANTO 2

The guileful great enchanter parts
    The Redcross knight from Truth,
Into whose stead° fair falsehood steps   *place*
And works° him woeful ruth.°   *causes   mischief*

1

By this the northern waggoner had set
    His sevenfold team behind the steadfast star
    That was in ocean waves yet never wet,
    But firm is fixed, and sendeth light from far
    To all that in the wide deep wandering are;
    And cheerful chanticleer,° with his note shrill,   *cockerel*
    Had warned once° that Phoebus' fiery car°   *once for all   chariot*
    In haste was climbing up the eastern hill,
Full° envious that night so long his room did fill,   *Extremely*

2

When those accursed messengers of hell,
    That feigning dream and that fair-
        forged° sprite,   *made beautiful and false*
    Came to their wicked master and 'gan tell
    Their bootless° pains° and ill-succeeding   *unsuccessful   efforts*
        night:
    Who, all in rage to see his skilful might
    Deluded° so, 'gan threaten hellish pain   *frustrated*
    And sad Proserpina's wrath, them to affright.
    But when he saw his threatening was but vain,°   *empty; idle*
He cast about and searched his baleful° books   *malign; harmful*
    again.

3

Eftsoons° he took that miscreated fair,   *Soon after*
    And that false other sprite, on whom he spread
    A seeming body of the subtle° air   *rarefied*
    Like a young squire, in loves and lustihead°   *vigour; lustfulness*
    His wanton days that ever loosely° led   *lasciviously*

Without regard of arms and dreaded fight:
Those two he took and, in a secret bed
Covered with darkness and misdeeming°   *causing suspicion*
  night,
Them both together laid to joy° in vain delight. *enjoy [themselves]*

4

Forthwith he runs with feigned faithful haste
  Unto his guest (who, after troublous sights
  And dreams, 'gan now to take more sound repast)
  Whom suddenly he wakes with fearful frights,
  As one aghast with fiends or damned sprites,
  And to him calls: 'Rise, rise, unhappy°   *unfortunate*
    swain,°   *youth*
  That here wex° old in sleep whiles wicked   *grow*
    wights°   *people**
  Have knit° themselves in Venus' shameful chain: *linked*
Come, see where your false lady doth her honour stain.'

5

All in amaze° he suddenly upstart   *bewilderment;† stupefaction**
  With sword in hand, and with the old man went;
  Who soon him brought into a secret part
  Where that false couple were full closely
    ment°   *joined together**
  In wanton lust and lewd embracement.
  Which, when he saw, he burned with jealous fire,
  The eye of reason was with rage yblent,°   *blinded**
  And would have slain them in his furious ire
But hardly° was restrained of° that aged sire.   *with difficulty by*

6

Returning to his bed in torment great
  And bitter anguish of his guilty sight,
  He could not rest, but did his stout° heart eat,   *brave*
  And waste his inward gall° with deep despite,° *anger outrage*
  Irksome° of life and too-long lingering night. *Bored;* wearied**
  At last fair Hesperus in highest sky
  Had spent his lamp and brought forth dawning light.
  Then up he rose and clad him hastily;
The dwarf him brought his steed: so both away do fly.

7

Now when the rosy-fingered morning fair,
 Weary of aged Tithon's saffron bed,
 Had spread her purple robe through dewy air,
 And the high hills Titan discovered,°   *revealed*
 The royal virgin shook off drowsihead°   *sleepiness*
 And, rising forth out of her baser°   *too humble*
  bower,°   *chamber*
 Looked for her knight, who far away was fled;
 And for her dwarf, that wont° to wait each *was accustomed*
  hour.
Then 'gan she wail and weep to see that woeful
  stour,°   *time of stress*†

8

And after him she rode with so much speed
 As her slow beast could make – but all in vain;
 For him so far had borne his light-foot steed,
 Pricked° with wrath and fiery fierce   *Spurred on*
  disdain,°   *anger* *
 That him to follow was but fruitless pain.° *effort; grief*
 Yet she her weary limbs would never rest,
 But every hill and dale, each wood and plain,
 Did search, sore° grieved in her gentle° breast *much noble*
He so ungently° left her, whom she loved best. *discourteously*

9

But subtle° Archimago, when his guests *insidious;*† *cunning*
 He saw divided into double parts,
 And Una wandering in the woods and forests –
 The end° of his drift° – he praised his devilish *goal designs*
  arts,
 That had such might over true-meaning hearts.
 Yet rests not so, but other means doth make° *plan*
 How he may work unto her further smarts:° *harm*
 For her he hated as the hissing snake,
And in her many troubles did most pleasure take.

10

He then devised himself how to disguise –
 For by his mighty science° he could take   *knowledge*
 As many forms and shapes in seeming wise°   *lifelike fashion*
 As ever Proteus to himself could make:
 Sometime a fowl, sometime a fish in lake,
 Now like a fox, now like a dragon fell° –   *fierce*
 That of himself he oft° for fear would quake,   *often*
 And oft would fly away. O, who can tell
The hidden° power of herbs, and might of magic spell? *occult*

11

But now seemed best the person° to put on°   *persona assume*
 Of that good knight, his late-beguiled guest.
 In mighty arms° he was yclad° anon,° *armour clad* forthwith*
 And silver shield: upon his coward breast
 A bloody cross, and on his craven crest°   *helmet*
 A bunch of hairs discoloured diversely.° *variously coloured*
 Full jolly° knight he seemed, and well   *fine*
  addressed;°   *accomplished†*
 And when he sat upon his courser free,°   *swift;† noble*
Saint George himself ye would have deemed° him to be. *judged*

12

But he the knight whose semblant° he did bear –   *appearance*
 The true Saint George – was wandered far away,
 Still flying from his thoughts and jealous fear:
 Will was his guide, and grief led him astray.
 At last him chanced to meet upon the way
 A faithless saracen,° all armed to point° *pagan fully armed*
 In whose great shield was writ with letters gay:° *brilliant*
 Sans foy. Full large of limb and every joint°   *member*
He was, and cared not for God or man a point.°   *at all*

13

He had a fair companion of his way° –   *journey*
 A goodly lady, clad in scarlet red
 Purfled° with gold and pearl of rich *edged; embroidered*
  assay,°   *value*
 And like a Persian mitre on her head
 She wore, with crowns and ouches°   *brooches*

garnished,°   *ornamented*
The which her lavish lovers to her gave.
Her wanton palfrey all was overspread
With tinsel trappings woven like a wave,
Whose bridle rung with golden bells and bosses°   *knobs*
   brave.°   *splendid*

14

With fair° disport° and courting dalliance   *innocent mirth; games*
   She entertained her lover all the way.
But when she saw the knight his spear advance
   She soon left off her mirth and wanton play,
And bade her knight address° him to the fray: *prepare*
His foe was nigh at hand. He, pricked° with pride   *goaded*
   And hope to win his lady's heart that day,
Forth spurred fast: adown his courser's side
The red blood trickling stained the way° as he did ride.   *track*

15

The knight of the Red Cross, when him he spied
   Spurring so hot with rage despiteous,°   *merciless*
'Gan fairly° couch° his spear and   *dexterously lower to attack*
   towards ride.
Soon meet they both, both fell° and furious,   *fierce*
That, daunted° with their forces   *stupefied; overcome*
   hideous,°   *huge*
Their steeds do stagger and amazed° stand;   *stupified*
And eke° themselves too rudely°   *also roughly*
   rigorous,°   *violent*
Astonied° with the stroke of their own hand,   *Dazed*
Do back rebut,° and each to other yieldeth°   *retreat surrenders†*
   land.

16

As when two rams, stirred with ambitious pride,
   Fight for the rule of the rich-fleeced flock,
Their horned fronts,° so fierce on either side   *foreheads*
Do meet that,° with the terror of the shock   *so that*
Astonied,° both stand senseless as a   *Stunned*
   block,°   *treee stump; blockhead*
Forgetful of the hanging° victory: *suspended in the balance*

So stood these twain, unmoved as a rock,
   Both staring fierce, and holding idly
The broken relics of their former cruelty.

17

The saracen, sore daunted° with the   *much dazed‡*
   buff,°   *blow, stroke*
   Snatcheth his sword and fiercely to him flies,
   Who well it wards and quiteth° cuff with cuff.   *repays*
   Each other's equal puissance° envies,°   *might seeks to rival**
   And through their iron sides with cruel spies°   *eyes*
   Does seek to pierce: repining° courage   *discontented; objecting*
      yields
   No foot to foe. The flashing fire flies,
   As from a forge, out of their burning shields,
And streams of purple blood new dyes the verdant fields.

18

'Curse on that cross,' quoth then the saracen,
   'That keeps thy body from the bitter fit:°   *i.e., death*
   Dead long ygo° I wote° thou haddest been   *ago* know*
   Had not that charm° from thee forwarned° *talisman forbidden*
      it.
   But yet I warn thee, now assured° sit,   *securely*
   And hide thy head.' Therewith upon his crest°   · *helmet*
   With rigour so outrageous he smit
   That a large share° it hewed out of the rest   *part*
And, glancing down his shield, from blame° him   *harm*
      fairly° blessed.°   *completely saved*

19

Who, thereat wondrous wrath, the sleeping spark
   Of native virtue° 'gan eftsoons° revive,   *courage straight away*
   And, at his haughty° helmet making mark,°   *tall aiming*
   So hugely° struck that it the steel did rive,   *forcefully*
   And cleft his head. He, tumbling down alive,
   With bloody mouth his mother earth did kiss,
   Greeting° his grave. His grudging° ghost *Welcoming† reluctant*
      did strive
   With the frail flesh; at last it flitted° is   *departed*
Whither the souls do fly of men that live amiss.

20

The lady, when she saw her champion fall
  Like the old ruins of a broken tower,
  Stayed not to wail his woeful° funeral,°   *lamentable   death‡*
  But from him fled away with all her power:
  Who after her as hastily 'gan scour,°   *run*
  Bidding the dwarf with him to bring away
  The saracen's shield, sign of the conqueror.
  Her soon he overtook and bade to stay,
For present cause was none of dread her to dismay.

21

She, turning back with rueful° countenance, *arousing compassion*
  Cried: 'Mercy, mercy, sir, vouchsafe to show
  On silly° dame, subject to hard   *helpless; humble*
    mischance°   *misfortune*
  And to your mighty will.' Her humblesse° low   *humility*
  In so rich weeds° and seeming-glorious show   *clothes*
  Did much inmove° his stout° heroic *affect with emotion‡   brave*
    heart,
  And said: 'Dear dame, your sudden overthrow
  Much rueth° me. But now put fear apart,° *rouses pity in   aside*
And tell both who ye be and who° that took your part.' *he was*

22

Melting in tears then 'gan she much lament:
  'The wretched woman – whom unhappy hour
  Hath now made thrall to your commandment° –   *authority‡*
  Before that angry heavens list° to lour,   *choose*
  And Fortune false betrayed me to your power,
  Was (O what now availeth that° I was!)   *what*
  Born the sole daughter of an emperor –
  He that the wide west under his rule has,
And high hath set his throne where Tiberis° doth *the River Tiber*
    pass.

23

'He in the first flower of my freshest age
  Betrothed me unto the only heir
  Of a most mighty king, most rich and sage:
  Was never prince so faithful and so fair;°   *handsome*

Was never prince so meek and debonair.°   *mild; courteous*
But, ere my hoped day of spousal shone,
My dearest lord fell from high honour's stair
Into the hands of his accursed fone,°   *foe*
And cruelly was slain – that shall I ever moan.°   *lament*

24

'His blessed body spoiled of lively° breath,   *despoiled living*
   Was afterward – I know not how – conveyed
   And from me hid: of whose most innocent death
   When tidings came to me, unhappy° maid,   *unfortunate*
   O how great sorrow my sad soul assayed!°   *assailed*
   Then forth I went his woeful corse° to find,   *body*
   And many years throughout the world I strayed,
   A virgin widow whose deep-wounded mind
With love did languish° as the stricken hind.   *pine; sicken*

25

'At last it chanced this proud saracen
   To meet me wandering, who perforce° me led   *forcibly*
   With him away, but yet could never win
   The fort° that ladies hold in sovereign dread.   *i.e., virginity*
   There lies he now with foul dishonour dead
   Who, whiles he lived, was called proud Sans foy –
   The eldest of three brethren, all three bred
   Of one bad sire, whose youngest is Sans joy;
And 'twixt them both was born the bloody, bold Sans loy.

26

'In this sad plight, friendless, unfortunate,
   Now miserable I, Fidessa, dwell,
   Craving of you, in pity of my state,
   To do none ill, if please ye not do well.'
   He in great passion° all this while did   *overpowering emotion*[†]
      dwell –
   More busying his quick eyes her face to view
   Than his dull ears to hear what she did tell –
   And said: 'Fair lady, heart of flint would rue
The undeserved woes and sorrows which ye show.

27

'Henceforth in safe assurance° may ye rest,   *security; betrothal*
  Having both found a new friend you to aid,
  And lost an old foe that did you molest:
  "Better new friend than an old foe", is said.'
  With change of cheer° the   *countenance*
    seeming°-simple maid   *having the specified appearance†*
  Let fall her eyen,° as shamefast,° to the earth,   *eyes modest*
  And yielding soft, in that she nought gainsaid.
  So forth they rode, he feigning seemly° mirth   *appropriate*
And she coy looks: so dainty,° they say, maketh   *fastidiousness†*
    dearth.°   *desirable*

28

Long time they thus together travelled
  Till, weary of their way, they came at last
  Where grew two goodly trees that fair° did spread   *splendidly*
  Their arms abroad,° with grey moss overcast,°   *afar covered*
  And their green leaves, trembling with every blast,
  Made a calm shadow far in compass° round.   *circumference*
  The fearful shepherd, often there aghast,
  Under them never sat, ne wont° there   *nor was accustomed*
    sound
His merry oaten pipe,° but shunned the unlucky ground.   *flute*

29

But this good knight, soon as he them can° spy,   *could*
  For the cool shade him thither hastily got,
  For golden Phoebus, now ymounted° high,   *mounted**
  From fiery wheels of his fair chariot
  Hurled his beam so scorching cruel hot
  That living creature mote° it not abide,°   *might tolerate*
  And his new lady it endured not.
  There they alight in hope themselves to hide
From the fierce heat and rest their weary limbs a tide.°   *while*

30

Fair seemly pleasance° each to other   *Apparent pleasing courtesy*
    makes
  With goodly purposes° there as they sit,   *conversation**
  And in his falsed° fancy° he her takes   *deceived imagination*

To be the fairest wight° that lived yit:°   *creature* yet*
Which to express he bends° his gentle°   *directs courteous*
    wit°   *mind*
And, thinking of those branches green to frame°   *fashion*
A garland for her dainty forehead fit,
He plucked a bough – out of whose rift°   *act of tearing;* split*
    there came
Small drops of gory° blood that trickled down the   *clotted**
    same.

31

Therewith a piteous yelling voice was heard,
    Crying: 'O spare with guilty hands to tear
    My tender sides in this rough rind°   *bark*
        embarred,°   *imprisoned†*
    But fly, ah fly far hence away, for fear
    Lest to you hap° that° happened to me   *chance to happen what*
        here,
    And to this wretched lady, my dear love –
    O too-dear love, love bought with death too dear.'
    Astoned° he stood, and up his hair did   *Astonished*
        hove,°   *rise†; lift†*
And with that sudden horror could no member° move.   *limb*

32

At last, whenas° the dreadful   *when*
    passion°   *powerful emotion† of dread*
    Was overpast and manhood° well awake,   *his rational self*
    Yet° musing° at the strange occasion,°   *Still marvelling event*
    And doubting much his sense, he thus bespake:°   *spoke*
    'What voice of damned ghost from Limbo lake,
    Or guileful° sprite° wandering in empty air –   *deceiving spirit*
    Both which frail men do oftentimes
        mistake° –   *take one for the other†*
    Sends to my doubtful ears these speeches rare°   *strange; thin*
And rueful° plaints,° me bidding guiltless blood   *pitiful laments*
    to spare?'

33

Then, groaning deep, 'Nor damned ghost,' quoth he,
  'Nor guileful sprite to thee these words doth speak,
  But once a man, Fradubio, now a tree:
  Wretched man, wretched tree, whose nature weak
  A cruel witch, her cursed will to wreak,°   *visit [on me]*
  Hath thus transformed, and placed in open plains
  Where Boreas doth blow full bitter bleak,°   *chillily*†
  And scorching sun does dry my secret° veins: *hidden*
For, though a tree I seem, yet cold and heat me pains.'

34

'Say on, Fradubio then, or° man or tree,'   *whether*
  Quoth then the knight, 'by whose mischievous arts
  Art thou misshaped thus as now I see?
  He oft finds medicine who his grief imparts,
  But double griefs afflict concealing hearts,
  As raging flames who striveth to suppress.'
  'The author, then,' said he, 'of all my smarts
  Is one Duessa, a false sorceress
That many an errant° knight hath brought to   *straying*
  wretchedness.

35

'In prime° of youthly years, when courage° hot   *spring nature*
  The fire of love and joy of chivalry
  First kindled in my breast, it was my lot
  To love this gentle° lady (whom ye see   *noble*
  Now not a lady but a seeming tree),
  With whom as once I rode accompanied,
  Me chanced of a knight encountered be
  That had a like fair lady by his side –
Like a fair lady, but did foul Duessa hide;

36

'Whose forged beauty he did take in hand°   *assert*
  All other dames to have exceeded far.
  I, in defence of mine, did likewise stand –
  Mine that did then shine as the morning star.
  So, both to battle fierce arranged are,
  In which his harder fortune was to fall

Under my spear: such is the die° of war.   *dice [i.e., chance]; death*
His lady, left as a prize martial,
Did yield her comely person to be at my call.

37

'So, doubly loved of° ladies unlike fair   *by*
  (The one seeming such, the other such indeed),
  One day in doubt I cast° for to compare   *resolved*
  Whether° in beauty's glory did exceed.   *Which*
  A rosy garland was the victor's meed;°   *reward*
  Both seemed to win, and both seemed won to be:°   *to be beaten*
  So hard the discord° was to be agreed.   *difference; disagreement*
  Fraelissa was as fair as fair mote° be,   *might*
And ever false Duessa seemed as fair as she.

38

'The wicked witch, now seeing all this while
  The doubtful balance equally to sway,
  What not by right she cast to win by guile,
  And by her hellish science° raised straightway   *art*
  A foggy mist that overcast the day,
  And a dull° blast° that,   *gloomy curse;‡ malignant wind‡*
    breathing on her face,
  Dimmed her former beauty's shining ray,
  And with foul ugly form did her disgrace:
Then was she fair alone, when none was fair in
    place.°   *by competition*

39

'Then cried she out: "Fie, fie, deformed wight°   *creature**
  Whose borrowed beauty now appeareth plain°   *plainly†*
  To have before bewitched all men's sight:
  O leave her soon, or let her soon be slain."
  Her loathly visage viewing with disdain,
  Eftsoons° I thought her such as she me told,   *Straight away*
  And would have killed her; but, with feigned pain,
  The false witch did my wrathful hand withhold:
So left her, where she now is turned to treën
    mould.°   *the shape of a tree*

40

'Thenceforth I took Duessa for my dame,°   *lady*
  And, in the witch unweeting,° joyed° long   *unaware⁺ rejoiced*
    time;
  Ne° ever wist° but that she was the   *Nor thought*
    same°   *as she seemed*
  Till on a day (that day is every prime,°   *spring*
  When witches wont do penance for their crime),
  I chanced to see her in her proper hue,°   *aspect; i.e. 'true colours'*
  Bathing herself in origan° and   *wild marjoram; penny royal*
    thyme:
  A filthy, foul old woman I did view
That ever to have touched her I did deadly rue.

41

'Her nether parts misshapen, monstrous,
  Were hid in water that° I could not see,   *so that*
  But they did seem more foul and hideous
  Than woman's shape man would believe to be.
  Thenceforth from her most beastly company°   *sexual contact**
  I 'gan refrain, in mind to slip away
  Soon as appeared safe opportunity;
  For danger great, if not assured° decay,°   *certain   death*
I saw before mine eyes, if I were known to stray.

42

'The devilish hag, by changes of my cheer,°   *countenance*
  Perceived my thought and, drowned in sleepy night,
  With wicked herbs and ointments did besmear
  My body all, through charms and magic might,
  That° all my senses were bereaved°   *So that   taken away*
    quite.°   *utterly*
  Then brought she me into this desert waste,
  And by my wretched lover's side she pight,°   *set; planted*
  Where now, enclosed in wooden walls full fast,
Banished from living wights, our weary days we
    waste.'°   *consume*

43

'But how long time,' then said the elfin knight,
  'Are you in this misformed° house to dwell?'   *ill-shaped*†
  'We may not change' (quoth he) 'this evil plight
  Till we be bathed in a living well:
  That is the term° prescribed by the spell.'   *condition; time limit*
  'O how' (said he) 'mote° I that well out find,°   *might   discover*
  That I may restore you to your wonted°   *accustomed*
    well?'°   *health; also: well*
  'Time and sufficed° Fates to former kind°   *satisfied   nature*
Shall us restore – none else from hence may us unbind.'

44

The false Duessa, now Fidessa hight,°   *named**†
  Heard how in vain Fradubio did lament,
  And knew well all was true. But the good knight,
  Full of sad° fear and ghastly°   *heavy   terrible*
    dreariment,°   *melancholy*†
  When all this speech the living tree had spent,°   *finished*
  The bleeding bough did thrust into the ground
  (That from the blood he might be innocent)
  And with fresh clay did close the wooden wound.
Then, turning to his lady, dead with fear her found:

45

Her seeming dead he found with feigned fear,
  As° all unweeting° of that well°   *As if   ignorant   what she well*
    she knew,
  And pained himself with busy care to rear°   *raise*
  Her out of careless° swoon. Her eyelids blue, *relieved from care*
  And dimmed sight with pale and deadly° hue,° *deathly aspect*
  At last she 'gan uplift: with trembling cheer°   *countenance*
  Her up he took (too simple° and too true)   *innocent; naive*
  And oft he kissed. At length, all past
    fear,°   *i.e., fear completely past*
He set her on her steed and forward forth did bear.

CANTO 3

Forsaken Truth long seeks her love
And makes the lion mild,
Mars blind Devotion's mart,° and falls   *market*[†]
In hand of lecher vild.°   *vile; base*

1

Nought is there under heaven's wide hollowness°   *convexity*
  That moves more dear° compassion of mind   *extreme; dire*
  Than beauty brought to unworthy° wretchedness *unwarranted*
  Through Envy's snares or Fortune's freaks° unkind.   *whims*
  I – whether lately° through her brightness blind,   *recently*
  Or through allegiance and fast° fealty°   *steadfast loyalty*
  Which I do owe unto all womenkind,
  Feel my heart pierced with so great agony
When such I see, that all for pity I could die.

2

And now it is impassioned° so deep –   *extremely moved*[†]
  For fairest Venus' sake, of whom I sing –
  That my frail eyes these lines with tears do steep°   *soak*
  To think how she, through guileful handling
  (Though true as touch,° though daughter of a   *a touchstone*
    king,
  Though fair as ever living wight° was fair,   *creature**
  Though nor in word nor deed ill meriting),
  Is from her knight divorced in despair
And her due loves derived° to that vile witch's share.   *transferred*

3

Yet she, most faithful lady, all this while
  Forsaken, woeful, solitary maid,
  Far from all people's press,° as in exile,   *throng*
  In wilderness and wasteful° deserts strayed   *desolate*
  To seek her knight: who, subtly betrayed
  Through that late vision which the enchanter wrought,
  Had her abandoned. She, of nought afraid,

Through woods and wasteness wide him daily sought;
Yet wished tidings none of him unto her wrought.

4

One day, nigh weary of the irksome° way,   *tiring; tedious*
   From her unhasty beast she did alight
   And on the grass her dainty limbs did lay
   In secret shadow, far from all men's sight.
   From her fair head her fillet° she   *headband*
      undight,°   *unfastened*[t]
   And laid her stole aside. Her angel's face
   As the great eye of heaven° shined bright   *i.e., sun*[t]
   And made a sunshine in the shady place:
Did never mortal eye behold such heavenly grace.

5

It fortuned out of the thickest wood
   A ramping° lion rushed   *on hind legs [a heraldic posture]*
      suddenly,
   Hunting full greedy° after salvage°   *very greedily   wild animal*
      blood.
   Soon as the royal virgin he did spy,
   With gaping mouth at her ran greedily,
   To have at once devoured her tender corse:°   *body*
   But to the prey whenas° he drew more nigh,   *when*
   His bloody rage assuaged with remorse
And, with the sight amazed, forgot his furious force.

6

Instead thereof he kissed her weary feet
   And licked her lily hands with fawning tongue,
   As° he her wrongèd innocence did weet°   *As if   know*
   (O, how can beauty master the most strong,
   And simple truth subdue avenging wrong?) –
   Whose yielded° pride and proud submission   *surrendered*[t]
   (Still dreading death) when she had marked° long,   *observed*
   Her heart 'gan melt in great compassion,
And drizzling tears did shed for pure affection.

7

'The lion, lord of every beast in field,'
  Quoth she, 'his princely puissance° doth abate,   *force*
  And mighty proud to humble weak does yield,
  Forgetful of the hungry rage which late
  Him pricked, in pity of my sad estate.°   *state*
  But he, my lion and my noble lord,
  How does he find in cruel heart to hate
  Her that him loved, and ever most adored,
As the god of my life? Why hath he me abhorred?'

8

Redounding° tears did choke the end of   *Overflowing;‡ echoing*
  her plaint,°   *lament*
  Which softly echoed from the neighbour wood;
  And, sad to see her sorrowful constraint,°   *distress**
  The kingly beast upon her gazing stood:
  With pity calmed, down fell his angry mood.
  At last, in close° heart shutting up her pain,   *inmost*
  Arose the virgin born of heavenly brood,°   *parentage†*
  And to her snowy palfrey got again
To seek her strayed champion, if she might
  attain.°   *catch up with him*

9

The lion would not leave her desolate,
  But with her went along, as a strong guard
  Of her chaste person and a faithful mate°   *companion*
  Of her sad° troubles and misfortunes hard. *heavy; melancholy*
  Still° when she slept he kept both watch and   *Ever*
  ward,°   *guard*
  And when she waked he waited diligent,
  With humble service to her will prepared:
  From her fair eyes he took commandment,
And ever by her looks conceived° her intent.   *imagined*

10

Long she thus travelled through deserts wide
  By which she thought her wandering knight should pass,
  Yet never show° of living wight° espied;   *sign creature**
  Till that at length she found the trodden grass

In which the tract° of people's footing° was   *track footsteps*‡
Under the steep foot of a mountain
   hoar.°   *venerable; white-capped*
The same she follows till at last she has
A damsel spied, slow footing her before,
That on her shoulders sad° a pot of water bore.   *weighed down*

11

To whom approaching she to her 'gan call
   To weet° if dwelling place were nigh at hand,   *know*
   But the rude° wench her answered nought at   *ignorant; uncivil*
      all:
   She could not hear, nor speak, nor understand;
   Till, seeing by her side the lion stand,
   With sudden fear her pitcher down she threw,
   And fled away; for never in that land
   Face° of fair lady she before did view,   *Appearance*
And that dread lion's look her cast in deadly hue.° *aspect; colour*

12

Full° fast she fled, ne° ever looked behind,   *Extremely nor*
   As if her life upon the wager lay;°   *i.e., were at stake*
   And home she came, whereas° her mother blind   *where*
   Sat in eternal night. Nought could she say
   But, sudden catching hold, did her dismay
   With quaking hands and other signs of fear;
   Who, full of ghastly° fright and cold affray,° *deathly*‡ *terror**
   'Gan shut the door. By this° arrived there   *i.e., time*
Dame Una, weary dame, and entrance did require.°   *beg*

13

Which, when none yielded, her unruly page
   With his rude° claws the wicket° open rent *violent small door*
   And let her in, where, of his cruel rage
   Nigh dead with fear and faint°   *fainting*
      astonishment,°   *insensibility*‡
   She found them both in darksome corner
      pent,°   *closely confined*
   Where that old woman day and night did pray
   Upon her beads° devoutly penitent: *rosary*

Nine hundred *Pater nosters*° every day,   *Our Fathers*
And thrice nine hundred *Aves*° she was   *Ave Marias [Hail Marys]*
   wont° to say.   *accustomed*

14

And to augment her painful penance more,
   Thrice every week in ashes she did sit,
   And next her wrinkled skin rough sackcloth wore,
   And thrice three times did fast from any bit.°   *morsel of food*
   But now for fear her beads she did forget;
   Whose needless dread° for to remove away   *fear*
   Fair Una framed° words and countenance   *formed*
      fit:°   *appropriate*
   Which hardly° done, at length she 'gan them   *with difficulty*
      pray
That in their cottage small that night she rest her may.

15

The day is spent, and cometh drowsy night,
   When every creature shrouded is in sleep:
   Sad Una down her lays in weary plight,
   And at her feet the lion watch doth keep.
   Instead of rest she does lament and weep
   For the late loss of her dear° loved knight,   *dearly*
   And sighs and groans, and evermore does steep°   *bathe*†
   Her tender breast in bitter tears all night:
All night she thinks too long, and often looks for light.

16

Now when Aldebaran was mounted high
   Above the shiny Cassiopeia's chair,
   And all in deadly° sleep did drowned lie,   *deathlike*
   One knocked at the door and in would fare.
   He knocked fast,° and often cursed and   *strongly**
      sware°°   *swore*
   That ready entrance was not at his call,
   For on his back a heavy load he bare°   *bore*
   Of nightly stealths° and pillage several,°   *thefts, stealing various*
Which he had got° abroad by purchase°   *obtained burglary*
      criminal.

17

He was to weet° a stout° and sturdy°   *for sure   resolute   intractable*
    thief,
    Wont° to rob churches of their ornaments,   *Accustomed*
    And poor men's boxes of their due relief,
    Which given was to them for good intents.°   *intentions*
    The holy saints of their rich vestments
    He did disrobe when all men careless° slept,   *free from care*
    And spoiled° the priests of their habiliments   *despoiled*
    Whiles none the holy things in safety kept:
Then he, by cunning° sleights,° in at the   *crafty† stratagems*
    window crept.

18

And all that he by right or wrong could find
    Unto this house he brought, and did bestow
    Upon the daughter of this woman blind –
    Abessa, daughter of Corceca slow,
    With whom he whoredom used (that few did know),
    And fed her fat with feast of offerings,°   *i.e., to God*
    And plenty, which in all the land did grow.
    Ne spared he° to give her gold and rings;   *Neither did he forbear*
And now he to her brought part of his stolen things.

19

Thus long the door with rage and threats he beat,
    Yet of those fearful women none durst rise:
    The lion frayed them° him in to let.   *made them afraid*
    He would no longer stay him to advise,°   *to reflect*
    But open breaks the door in furious wise,°   *manner*
    And entering is when, that disdainful° beast   *indignant *‡*
    Encountering fierce, him sudden doth surprise
    And, seizing° cruel claws on trembling breast,   *fastening†*
Under his lordly foot him proudly hath
    suppressed.°   *pushed down*

20

Him booteth° not resist, nor succour call: *It availed him*
    His bleeding heart is in the avenger's hand,
    Who straight him rent in thousand pieces small,
    And quite° dismembered hath: the thirsty land   *completely*

Drunk up his life; his corse left° on the   *body was left*
   strand.°   *ground*
His fearful friends wear out the woeful night,
Ne° dare to weep, nor seem to understand   *Neither [do they]*
The heavy hap° which on them is alight,   *misfortune*
Afraid lest to themselves the like mishappen might.

21

Now when broad day the world discovered° has,   *revealed*
   Up Una rose, up rose the lion eke,°   *also*
And on their former journey forward pass°   *proceed*
In ways unknown her wandering knight to seek,
With pains far passing° that long wandering Greek   *exceeding*
That for his love refused deity:
Such were the labours of this lady meek,
   Still° seeking him that from her still° did fly –   *Yet ever*
Then furthest from her hope when most she
     weened° nigh.   *believed to be*

22

Soon as she parted° thence the fearful twain –   *departed*
   That blind old woman and her daughter dear –
Came forth and, finding Kirkrapine there slain, *Robber*
For anguish great they 'gan to rend their hair,
And beat their breasts, and naked flesh to tear.
And when they both had wept and wailed their fill,
Then forth they ran like two amazed° deer,   *terrified*
   Half mad through malice and revenging
     will,°   *desire for revenge*
To follow her that was the causer of their ill:

23

Whom, overtaking, they 'gan loudly bray°   *cry out in grief**
   With hollow° howling and lamenting cry,   *dismal‡*
Shamefully at her railing all the way,
And her accusing of dishonesty
That was the flower of faith and chastity.
And still amidst her° railing she° did   *i.e., Abessa's i.e., Corececa*
   pray
That plagues and mischiefs and long misery

Might fall on her and follow all the way,
And that in endless error she might ever stray.

24

But, when she saw her prayers nought prevail,°   *have no success*
   She back returned with some labour lost,
   And in the way, as she did weep and wail,
   A knight her met in mighty arms°   *armour*
      embossed° –   *encased;*[t]*decorated*
   Yet knight was not, for all his bragging boast,°   *pomp**
   But subtle° Archimago, that Una sought   *cunning*
   By trains° into new troubles to have tossed.   *stratagems*
   Of that old woman tidings he besought,
If that of such a lady she could tellen aught.

25

Therewith she 'gan her passion° to renew,   *outburst of emotion*[t]
   And cry, and curse, and rail, and rend her hair,
   Saying, that harlot she too lately° knew   *recently*
   That caused her shed so many a bitter tear,
   And so forth told the story of her fear.
   Much seemed he to moan° her hapless   *lament*
      chance,°   *misfortune*
   And after for that lady did enquire
   Which, being taught, he forward 'gan advance
His fair enchanted steed, and eke° his charmed lance.   *also*

26

Ere long he came where Una travelled slow,
   And that wild champion waiting° her beside: *watching*
   Whom seeing such, for dread he durst° not show   *dared*
   Himself too nigh at hand, but turned wide
   Unto an hill, from whence, when she him spied,
   By his like-seeming shield her knight by name
   She weened° it was, and towards him 'gan ride.   *believed*
   Approaching nigh she wist° it was the same,   *thought*
And with fair° fearful humblesse° towards   *becoming humility*
      him she came,

27

And weeping said: 'Ah, my long-lacked lord,
  Where have ye been, thus long out of my sight?
  Much feared I to have been quite°   *utterly*
    abhorred,°   *regarded with disgust*†
  Or aught have done that ye displeasen might
  That should as death unto my dear° heart   *loving*
    light:°   *descend upon*
  For since mine eye your joyous sight did miss,
  My cheerful day is turned to cheerless night,
  And eke° my night of death the shadow° is: *in addition   image*
But welcome now, my light, and shining lamp of bliss.'

28

He thereto meeting,° said: 'My dearest dame,   *responding*†
  Far be it from your thought, and from my will,
  To think that knighthood I so much should shame
  As you to leave, that have me loved still°   *ever*
  And chose in fairy court of mere° goodwill   *absolute*
  Where noblest knights were to be found on earth:
  The earth shall sooner leave her kindly° skill° *natural   ability*
  To bring forth fruit, and make eternal dearth,°   *famine*
Than I leave you, my lief,° yborn° of heavenly *beloved   born**
    birth.'

29

'And, sooth° to say, why I left you so long   *truth*
  Was for to seek adventure in strange place,
  Where Archimago said a felon° strong   *villain*
  To many knights did daily work disgrace
  (But knight he now shall never more deface)° –   *destroy*
  Good cause of mine excuse. That mote° ye please *may*
  Well to accept, and evermore embrace
  My faithful service that by land and seas
Have vowed you to defend. Now then your plaint
    appease.'°   *allay*

30

His lovely° words her seemed due recompense   *loving*
  Of all her passed pains: one loving hour
  For many years of sorrow can dispense;°   *compensate*†

A dram of sweet is worth a pound of sour:
She has forgot how many a woeful stour°   *time of stress*†
For him she late endured; she speaks no more
Of past. True is, that true love hath no power
To looken back: his eyes be fixed before.
Before her stands her knight, for whom she toiled so
    sore.°   *greatly*

31

Much like as when the beaten mariner,
  That long hath wandered in the ocean wide –
  Oft soused in swelling Tethys' saltish tear,
  And long time having tanned his tawny hide
  With blustering breath of heaven, that none can bide,
  And scorching flames of fierce Orion's hound –
  Soon as the port from far he has espied,
  His cheerful whistle merrily doth sound,
And Nereus crowns with cups° (his mates him pledge   *libations*
  around):

32

Such joy made Una when her knight she found.
  And eke the enchanter joyous seemed no less
  Than the glad merchant that does view from ground
  His ship far come from watery wilderness:
  He hurls out vows, and Neptune oft doth bless.°   *praise*
  So forth they passed, and all the way they spent
  Discoursing of her dreadful late distress,
  In which he asked her, what the lion meant,
Who told her all that fell° in journey as she went.   *befell her*

33

They had not ridden far when they might see
  One pricking towards them with hasty heat
  Full strongly armed, and on a courser free°   *impetuous*
  That, through his fierceness, foamed all with sweat,
  And the sharp iron did for anger eat
  When his hot° rider spurred his chafed° side.   *choleric fretted*
  His look was stern° and seemed still to threat   *fierce*
  Cruel revenge which he in heart did hide,
And on his shield 'Sans loy' in bloody lines was dyed.

34

When nigh he drew unto this gentle° pair   *noble*
  And saw the red cross which the knight did bear,
  He burned in fire and 'gan eftsoons° prepare   *straight away*
  Himself to battle with his couched° spear.   *lowered for attack*
  Loath was that other, and did faint through fear
  To taste the untried dint° of deadly steel.   *blow*
  But yet his lady did so well him cheer
  That hope of new good hap° he 'gan to feel: *fortune*
So bent° his spear, and spurned° his horse with   *aimed struck*
    iron heel.

35

But that proud paynim° forward came so fierce   *pagan*
  And full of wrath that with his sharp-head spear
  Through vainly-crossed shield he quite° did pierce   *completely*
  And, had his staggering steed not shrunk for fear,
  Through shield and body eke he should him bear.°   *pierce**
  Yet so great was the puissance° of his push   *force*
  That from his saddle quite he did him bear:
  He tumbling rudely° down to ground did rush,   *forcefully*
And from his gored° wound a well of blood   *caused by piercing*†
    did gush.

36

Dismounting lightly° from his lofty steed   *swiftly*
  He to him leapt, in mind to reave° his life,   *take away**
  And proudly said: 'Lo, there the worthy° meed° *fitting reward*
  Of him that slew Sansfoy with bloody knife.
  Henceforth his ghost, freed from repining
    strife,°   *pain;* distress**
  In peace may passen over Lethe lake
  When mourning altars, purged with° enemy's life,   *purified by*
  The black infernal Furies doen° aslake.°   *do* appease*†
Life from Sansfoy thou tookest; Sansloy shall from thee take.'

37

Therewith in haste his helmet 'gan unlace
  Till Una cried: 'O hold that heavy° hand,   *angry; causing distress*
  Dear sir, whatever that thou be in place:°   *rank; before me*
  Enough is that thy foe doth vanquished stand

Now at thy mercy: mercy not withstand.°   *do not resist*
For he is one of the truest knights alive,
Though conquered now he lie on lowly
    land,°   *prostrate on the ground*
And, whilst him Fortune favoured, fair did thrive
In bloody field: therefore of life him not deprive.'

38

Her piteous words might not abate his rage
    But, rudely° rending° up his helmet, would   *violently tearing*
    Have slain him straight: but when he sees his age,
    And hoary head of Archimago old,
    His hasty hand he doth amazed hold
    And, half-ashamed, wondered at the sight
    (For that old man well knew he, though untold,
    In charm and magic to have wondrous might,
Ne° ever wont° in field, ne° in round lists,   *Neither was used nor*
    to fight),

39

And said: 'Why, Archimago, luckless sire,
    What do I see? What hard mishap° is this   *misfortune*
    That hath thee hither brought to taste mine ire?
    Or° thine the fault or mine the error is   *Either*
    Instead of foe to wound my friend amiss.'
    He answered nought, but in a trance still lay,
    And on those guileful dazed eyes of his
    The cloud of death did sit – which, doen° away,   *passed**
He left him lying so, ne° would no lenger° stay,   *nor any longer*

40

But to the virgin comes who, all this while,
    Amazed° stands herself so mocked to   *Astonished; bewildered*
        see
    By him who has the guerdon° of his guile   *reward*
    For so misfeigning° her true   *pretending in order to mislead†*
        knight to be.
    Yet is she now in more perplexity,°   *distraction; distress*
    Left in the hand of that same paynim bold

(From whom her booteth° not at all to flee)   *it avails her*
Who, by her cleanly° garment catching hold,   *pure*
Her from her palfrey plucked, her visage to behold.

41

But her fierce servant, full of kingly awe
  And high disdain,° whenas° his   *proud contempt when*
    sovereign dame
  So rudely handled by her foe he saw,
  With gaping jaws full greedy at him came
  And, ramping° on his shield, did   *raising his forepaws*
    ween° the same   *think*
  Have reft away° with his sharp rending claws: *split apart*
  But he was stout,° and lust did now inflame   *brave*
  His courage more, that° from his gripping paws   *so that*
He hath his shield redeemed, and forth his sword he draws.

42

O then too weak and feeble was the force
  Of salvage° beast his puissance to withstand;   *wild*
  For he was strong, and of so mighty corse°   *body*
  As ever wielded spear in warlike hand,
  And feats of arms did wisely° understand.   *skilfully*
  Eftsoons° he pierced through his chafed°   *Immediately angry*
    chest°   *breast*
  With thrilling° point of deadly iron brand,°   *piercing sword*
  And launched° his lordly heart: with death oppressed   *cut*
He roared aloud, whiles life forsook his stubborn breast.

43

Who now is left to keep the forlorn° maid   *forsaken*
  From raging spoil of lawless victor's will? –
  Her faithful guard removed, her hope dismayed,°   *destroyed*
  Herself a yielded° prey to save or spill.°   *surrendered† kill*
  He, now lord of the field, his pride to fill,
  With foul reproaches and disdainful spite
  Her vildly° entertains° and, will° or   *basely treats willing*
    nill,°   *unwilling*
  Bears her away upon his courser light.
Her prayers nought prevail: his rage is more of might.

44

And all the way with great lamenting pain
  And piteous plaints° she filleth his dull° ears,   *laments   deaf*
That stony heart could riven have in twain;
And all the way she wets with flowing tears,
But he, enraged with rancour, nothing hears.
Her servile beast yet would not leave her so,
But follows her far off: ne aught he fears
To be partaker of her wandering woe,
More mild in beastly kind° than that her beastly foe.   *nature*

Canto 4

To sinful house of Pride Duessa
    Guides the faithful knight
Where, brother's death to wreak,° Sansjoy   *avenge*
    Doth challenge him to fight.

1

Young knight whatever that dost arms profess,
  And through long labours huntest after fame,
Beware of fraud,° beware of fickleness,   *insincerity; deceit*
In choice and change of thy dear-loved dame,
Lest thou of her believe too lightly° blame°   *readily   accusation*
And rash misweening° do thy heart remove.   *mistrust**
For unto knight there is no greater shame
Than lightness° and inconstancy in love: *fickleness*
That doth this Redcross knight's example plainly prove.°   *attest*

2

Who, after that he had fair Una lorn°   *forsaken*
  (Through light° misdeeming° of her   *fickle   false judgement**
    loyalty),
  And false Duessa in her stead° had borne   *place*
  (Called Fidessa, and so supposed to be),
Long with her travelled till at last they see
A goodly° building, bravely   *fine*
    garnished°   *splendidly adorned**

(The house of mighty prince it seemed to be),
   And towards it a <u>broad highway</u> that led,
All bare through people's feet, which thither travelled.

3

Great troops of people travelled thitherward
   Both day and night, of each degree° and   *social station*
      place;°   *rank*
   But few returned, having 'scaped hard°   *with difficulty*
   With baleful° beggary or foul disgrace: *miserable**
   Which, ever after, in most wretched case,°   *situation; body*
   Like loathsome lazars° by the   *lepers; poor and diseased people*
      hedges lay.
   Thither Duessa bade him bend° his pace,°   *direct footsteps*
   For she is weary of the toilsome way,
And also nigh consumed is the lingering day.

4

A stately palace, built of squared brick,
   Which cunningly° was without mortar laid,   *skilfully*
   Whose walls were high but nothing strong nor thick,
   And golden foil all over them displayed°   *spread out**
   That purest sky with brightness they dismayed:
   High lifted up were many lofty towers,
   And goodly galleries far over° laid,   *high above*
   Full of fair° windows and delightful bowers;°   *fine chambers*
And on the top a dial told the <u>timely° hours</u>.   *of the day;† mortal*

concern wl this world materialism

5

It was a goodly heap° for to behold,   *random structure*
   And spake the praises of the workman's wit;°   *skill*
   But full great pity that so fair a mould°   *shape, form‡*
   Did on so <u>weak foundations</u> ever sit,
   For on a <u>sandy hill</u> (that still did flit°   *shift*
   And fall away) it mounted was full high
   That° every breath of heaven shaked it.   *So that*
   And all the <u>hinder parts</u>, that few could spy,
Were ruinous and old, but painted cunningly.

6

Arrived there they passed in forthright,°   *forthwith*
   For still° to all the gates stood open wide: *always*
   Yet charge of them was to a porter hight°   *committed**†*
   Called Malvenù, who entrance none denied.
   Thence to the hall, which was on every side
   With rich° array° and costly arras°   *festive display tapestry*
     dight:°   *adorned*
   Infinite sorts of people did abide
   There, waiting long to win the wished sight
Of her that was the lady of that palace bright.

7

By them they pass, all gazing on them round,°   *on all sides*
   And to the presence° mount, whose glorious   *presence chamber*
     view°   *aspect‡*
   Their frail amazed° senses did confound.   *dazed*
   In living prince's court none ever knew
   Such endless riches and so sumptuous show:
   Ne° Persia self° – the nurse of   *Not even herself*
     pompous° pride –   *showy*
   Like ever saw. And there a noble crew°   *company*
   Of lords and ladies stood on every side
Which, with their presence fair, the place much beautified.

8

High above all a cloth of state° was spread,   *canopy [over throne]*
   And a rich throne, as bright as sunny day,
   On which there sat, most brave° embellished   *splendidly†*
   With royal robes and gorgeous array,
   A maiden queen. That° shone as   *i.e., the throne*
     Titan's° ray   *the sun's*
   In glistering° gold and peerless precious stone: *glittering*
   Yet her bright blazing beauty did assay°   *attempt*
   To dim the brightness of her glorious throne,
As envying herself, that too exceeding shone.

9

Exceeding shone, like Phoebus' fairest child,
   That did presume° his father's fiery   *presumptuously aspire to*
     wain°   *chariot*

And flaming mouths of steeds unwonted° wild   *unusually*†
Through highest heaven with weaker° hand to   *too weak*
   rein:°   *direct*†
Proud of such glory and advancement vain,
While flashing beams do daze his feeble eyen,
He leaves the welkin way° most beaten   *[sun's] path in the sky*
   plain
And, rapt° with whirling wheels, inflames the   *carried off*
   skyen°   *skies*
With fire not made to burn but fairly for to shine.

10

So proud° she shined in her princely   *Thus proudly*
   state,°   *rank; throne*
Looking to heaven (for earth she did disdain)
And sitting high (for lowly° she did hate).   *lowliness*
Lo, underneath her scornful feet was lain
A dreadful dragon with an hideous° train,°   *huge; terrible tail*
And in her hand she held a mirror bright,
Wherein her face she often viewed fain°   *with pleasure*
And in her self-loved semblance took delight:
For she was wondrous fair as any living wight.°   *creature**

11

Of grisly° Pluto she the daughter was,   *terrifying*
And sad Proserpina the queen of hell:
Yet did she think her peerless worth to pass°   *surpass*
That parentage, with pride so did she swell.
And thundering Jove (that in high heaven doth dwell
And wield° the world) she claimed for her sire,   *govern*
Or if that any else did Jove excel:
For to the highest she did still aspire
Or, if aught higher were than that, did it desire.

12

And 'proud Lucifera' men did her call,
   That made herself a queen, and crowned to be –
Yet rightful kingdom she had none at all,
Ne° heritage of native sovereignty,°   *Nor by birthright*
But did usurp with wrong and tyranny
Upon the sceptre which she now did hold:

Ne ruled her realms with laws but policy,°   *political cunning*
And strong advisement° of six wizards° old,   *counsel wise men*
That with their counsels bad her kingdom did uphold.

13

Soon as the elfin knight in presence° came,   *to the royal presence*
    And false Duessa (seeming lady fair),
    A gentle° usher, Vanity by name,   *civil*
    Made room, and passage for them did prepare.
    So goodly° brought them to the lowest stair   *courteously*
    Of her high throne where they, on humble knee
    Making obeisance,° did the cause declare   *bow and curtsy*
    Why they were come: her royal state to see,
To prove the wide report of her great majesty.

14

With lofty eyes – half loath to look so low –
    She thanked them in her disdainful wise,°   *fashion*
    Ne° other grace vouchsafed them to show   *Nor*
    Of princess worthy – scarce them bade arise.
    Her lords and ladies all this while devise°   *prepare**
    Themselves to setten forth to strangers' sight:
    Some frounce° their curled hair in courtly guise,° *plait fashion*
    Some prank° their ruffs, and others   *fold**
        trimly dight°   *neatly arrange*
Their gay attire: each others'° greater pride does   *i.e., the others'*
    spite.

15

Goodly they all that knight do entertain,
    Right glad with him to have increased their crew.
    But to Duessa each one himself did pain°   *take trouble*
    All kindness° and fair courtesy to show,   *affection; kinship*
    For in that court whilom° her well they knew.   *formerly**
    Yet the stout° fairy 'mongst the   *resolute‡*
        middest° crowd   *very middle of the*
    Thought all their glory vain in knightly view,
    And that great princess too exceeding proud
That to strange° knight no better countenance° *alien demeanour*
    allowed.

16

Sudden° upriseth from her stately place   *Suddenly*
  The royal dame, and for her coach doth call.
  All hurtlen° forth, and she with princely pace,°   *rush step*
  As fair Aurora in her purple pall°   *robe*
  Out of the east the dawning day doth call,
  So forth she comes: her brightness broad doth blaze.
  The heaps of people thronging in the hall
  Do ride each other upon her to gaze:
Her glorious glitterand° light doth all men's eyes   *splendid*
  amaze.°   *dazzle*

17

So forth she comes, and to her coach does climb
  (Adorned all with gold, and garlands gay
  That seemed as fresh as Flora in her prime),°   *springtime youth*
  And strove to match, in royal rich array,°   *attire*
  Great Juno's golden chair,° the which (they say)   *chariot*
  The gods stand gazing on when she does ride
  To Jove's high house through heaven's brass-paved way
  Drawn of fair peacocks, that excel in pride,
And full of Argus' eyes their tails dispreaden° wide.   *spread out*†

18

But this was drawn of° six unequal° beasts,   *by differing*‡
  On which her six sage counsellors did ride –
  Taught to obey their bestial behests,
  With like conditions to their kinds° applied,   *natures*
  Of which the first, that all the rest did guide,
  Was sluggish Idleness, the nurse of sin.
  Upon a slothful ass he chose to ride,
  Arrayed in habit black and amice° thin   *hood*
Like to an holy monk, the service to begin.

19

And in his hand his portas° still° he   *portable breviary always*
  bare°   *bore*
That much was worn but therein little read,
  For of devotion he had little care.
  Still drowned in sleep, and most of his days dead,
  Scarce could he once uphold his heavy head

To looken whether it were night or day.
May° seem the wain was very evil° led   *It may   ill; evilly*
When such an one had guiding of the way
That knew not whether right he went, or else astray.

20

From worldly cares himself he did eloin,°   *remove*
   And greatly shunned manly exercise.
   From every work he challenged essoin°   *demanded exemption*
   For contemplation's sake: yet otherwise
   His life he led in lawless riotise,°   *riotous behaviour*[t]
   By which he grew to grievous malady,
   For in his listless limbs through evil guise°   *vicious behaviour*
   A shaking fever reigned continually:
Such one was Idleness, first of this company.

21

And by his side rode loathsome Gluttony,
   Deformed creature, on a filthy swine:
   His belly was upblown with luxury,°   *vicious self-indulgence*
   And eke° with fatness swollen were his eyen,   *also*
   And like a crane his neck was long and fine,°   *thin*
   With which he swallowed up excessive feast
   For want° whereof poor people oft did pine;°   *lack   starve*
   And all the way – most like a brutish beast –
He spewed° up his gorge, that° all did him   *vomited   so that*
   detest.

22

In green vine leaves he was right fitly clad
   (For other clothes he could not wear for heat),
   And on his head an ivy garland had,
   From under which fast trickled down the sweat.
   Still as he rode he somewhat° still did eat,   *something*
   And in his hand did bear a boozing can,°   *vessel*
   Of which he supped so oft that on his seat
   His drunken corse° he scarce upholden can –   *body*
In shape and life more like a monster than a man.

23

Unfit he was for any worldly thing,
  And eke° unable once° to stir or go:°   *also ever walk*
  Not meet to be of counsel to a king,
  Whose mind in meat and drink was drowned so
  That from his friends he seldom knew his foe.
  Full of diseases was his carcase blue,°   *bruised*
  And a dry° dropsy through his flesh did flow   *thirst-inducing*
  Which, by misdiet,° daily greater grew: *wrong diet*
Such one was Gluttony, the second of that crew.

24

And next to him rode lustful Lechery
  Upon a bearded goat, whose rugged° hair   *rough, shaggy*
  And wally° eyes (the sign of jealousy)   *glaring†*
  Was like the person self whom he did bear,
  Who rough, and black, and filthy did appear –
  Unseemly man to please fair lady's eye.
  Yet he of ladies oft was loved dear
  When fairer faces were bid standen by:
O, who does know the bent° of women's fantasy?   *inclination*

25

In a green gown he clothed was full fair°   *extremely finely*
  Which underneath did hide his filthiness;
  And in his hand a burning heart he bare,
  Full of vain follies and newfangledness:°   *novelty†*
  For he was false and fraught° with fickleness,   *filled*
  And learned had to love with secret looks,
  And well could dance, and sing with ruefulness,
  And fortunes tell, and read in loving books,°   *books of love*
And thousand other ways to bait his fleshly hooks.

26

Inconstant man, that loved all he saw,
  And lusted after all that he did love:
  Ne° would his looser° life be tied to law,   *Nor very loose*
  But joyed° weak women's hearts to tempt° and *rejoiced try*
    prove°   *test*
  If from their loyal loves° he might them move   *lovers*
  (Which lewdness filled him with reproachful° pain *shameful†*

Of° that foul evil° which all men   *From   illness*
    reprove,°   *censure*
That rots the marrow and consumes the brain):
Such one was Lechery, the third of all this train.

27

And greedy Avarice by him did ride
    Upon a camel laden all with gold:
    Two iron coffers hung on either side,
    With precious metal full as they might hold;
    And in his lap an heap of coin he told,°   *counted*
    For of his wicked pelf° his god he made,   *ill-gotten wealth*
    And unto hell himself for money sold:
    Accursed usury was all his trade,
And right and wrong alike in equal balance weighed.

28

His life was nigh° unto death's door yplaced,°   *next   situated**
    And threadbare coat and cobbled° shoes he   *roughly patched*
        wore,
    Ne° scarce good morsel all his life did taste,   *Nor*
    But both from back and belly still did spare°   *abstain*
    To fill his bags and richesse° to compare:°   *wealth   acquire**
    Yet child ne kinsman living had he none
    To leave them to, but through his daily care
    To get (and nightly fear to lose) his own,
He led a wretched life, unto himself
        unknown.°   *i.e, lacking self-knowledge*

29

Most wretched wight,° whom nothing might suffice,   *creature**
    Whose greedy lust did lack in greatest store°   *abundance*
    Whose need had end, but no end covetise;°   *covetousness*
    Whose wealth was want, whose plenty made him poor,
    Who had enough, yet wished ever more.
    A vile disease – and eke° in foot and hand   *in addition*
    A grievous gout – tormented him full sore°   *extremely*
    That° well he could not touch, nor go, nor stand: *So that*
Such one was Avarice, the fourth of that fair band.

30

And next to him malicious Envy rode
  Upon a ravenous wolf, and still° did chaw°   *ever chew*
  Between his cankered° teeth a venomous   *envious; malignant*
    toad,
  That° all the poison ran about his chaw:°   *So that jaw†*
  But inwardly he chawed° his own maw°   *devoured stomach*
  At neighbours' wealth,° that made him ever   *also: well-being*
    sad:
  For death it was when any good he saw,
  And wept that cause of weeping none he had;
But when he heard of harm, he waxed° wondrous glad.   *grew*

31

All in a kirtle° of discoloured° say° *coat multi-coloured silk cloth*
  He clothed was, ypainted full of eyes,
  And in his bosom secretly there lay
  An hateful snake, the which his tail upties°   *binds†*
  In many folds, and mortal sting implies.°   *enwraps*
  Still° as he rode he gnashed his teeth to see   *Ever*
  Those heaps of gold with gripple° covetise, *gripping; usurious*
  And grudged at° the great felicity   *envied;‡ grumbled*
Of proud Lucifera, and his own company.

32

He hated all good works and virtuous deeds,
  And him no less that any like° did use;° *suchs things perform*
  And who with gracious° bread the hungry *bestowing grace*
    feeds
  His alms for lack of faith he doth accuse:
  So every good to bad he doth abuse,°   *misrepresent*
  And eke the verse of famous poets' wit
  He does backbite, and spiteful poison spews
  From leprous mouth on all that ever writ:
Such one vile Envy was that fifth in row did sit.

33

And him beside rides fierce revenging Wrath
  Upon a lion, loath for to be led,
  And in his hand a burning brand° he hath,   *blade*
  The which he brandisheth about his head:

His eyes did hurl forth sparkles fiery red
And stared stern° on all that him beheld,   *fiercely*
As ashes pale of hue and seeming-dead;
And on his dagger still his hand he held,
Trembling through hasty rage when choler° in him   *yellow bile*
  swelled.

34

His ruffin° raiment° all was stained with blood   *villainous garb*
  Which he had spilt, and all to rags yrent
  Through unadvised° rashness waxen   *ill-considered*
    wood,°   *mad*
  For of° his hands he had no government,°   *over control*
  Ne°cared for° blood in his avengement.°   *Nor about vengeance*
  But when the furious fit was overpast
  His cruel facts° he often would repent: *deeds*
  Yet, wilful man, he never would forecast°   *consider beforehand*†
How many mischiefs° should ensue° his heedless   *ills follow*
  haste.

35

Full many mischiefs follow cruel Wrath:
  Abhorred Bloodshed and tumultuous Strife,
  Unmanly Murder and unthrifty° Scath,°   *wasteful Damage*
  Bitter Despite° with Rancour's rusty°   *Malice blood-red; foul*
    knife,
  And fretting Grief, the enemy of life:
  All these and many evils more haunt Ire:
  The swelling spleen° and frenzy raging rife,   *anger*
  The shaking palsy and Saint Francis' fire:°   *erysipelas?*
Such one was Wrath, the last of this ungodly tire.°   *band*

36

And after all, upon the wagon beam,°   *shaft*†
  Rode Satan, with a smarting whip in hand
  With which he forward lashed the lazy team
  So oft as Sloth still in the mire did stand.
  Huge routs of people did about them band,
  Shouting for joy, and still° before their way   *ever*
  A foggy mist had covered all the land:

And underneath their feet, all scattered, lay
Dead skulls, and bones, of men whose life had gone astray.

37

So forth they marchen in this goodly° sort°   fine company
  To take the solace° of the open air   pleasure
  And in fresh flowering fields themselves to sport.°   divert
  Amongst the rest rode that false lady fair –
  The foul Duessa – next unto the chair°   chariot
  Of proud Lucifera, as one of the train.
  But that good knight would not so nigh repair,°   make his way
  Himself estranging° from their joyance°   removing‡ rejoicing†
    vain
Whose fellowship seemed far unfit for warlike
    swain.°   youth; man

38

So, having solaced° themselves a space,°   entertained short while
  With pleasance° of the breathing° fields yfed,   delight fragrant
  They back returned to the princely place°   palace
  Whereas° an errant knight – in arms yclad   Where
  And heathenish shield (wherein with letters red
  Was writ 'Sans joy') – they new-arrived find.
  Inflamed with fury and fierce hardihead,°   audacity†
  He seemed in heart to harbour thoughts unkind,°   harmful
And nourish bloody vengeance in his bitter mind.

39

Who, when the shamed shield of slain Sansfoy
  He spied with that same fairy champion's page –
  Bewraying° him that did of late destroy   Revealing
  His eldest brother – burning all with rage
  He to him leaped, and that same envious gage°   envied pledge
  Of victor's glory from him snatched away.
  But the elfin knight – which ought° that warlike   owned
    wage° –   pledge
  Disdained to loose° the meed° he won in fray   yield prize
And, him rencountering° fierce, rescued the   engaging in battle
    noble prey.

40

Therewith they 'gan to hurtlen greedily° *dash forward eagerly*
 (Redoubted° battle ready to deraign),° *Dreadful engage*
 And clash their shields, and shake their swords on high,
 That° with their stir they troubled all the train; *So that*
 Till that great queen, upon eternal pain
 Of high displeasure that ensue might,
 Commanded them their fury to refrain,
 And if that either to that shield had right,
In equal lists° they should the morrow next it *impartial tilt-yard*
 fight.

41

'Ah, dearest dame,' quoth then the paynim bold,
 'Pardon the error of enraged wight°   *person**
 Whom great grief made forget the reins to hold
 Of reason's rule, to see this recreant° knight – *craven*
 No knight, but treacher° full of false *deceiver, traitor*
  despite°   *malice*
 And shameful treason who, through guile,° hath slain *trickery*
 The prowest° knight that ever field did fight – *most valiant*
 Even stout° Sansfoy (O who can then refrain?), *brave*
Whose shield he bears renversed° the more to heap *upside down*ᵗ
 disdain.

42

'And to augment the glory of his guile
 His dearest love, the fair Fidessa, lo
 Is there possessed of° the traitor vile,°   *by base*
 Who reaps the harvest sown by his foe –
 Sown in bloody field, and bought with woe:
 That brother's hand° shall dearly well requite° *action avenge*ᵗ
 So be, O queen, you equal° favour show.' *impartial*
 Him little answered the angry elfin knight:
He never meant with words but swords to plead his right;

43

But threw his gauntlet as a sacred pledge
 His cause in combat the next day to try.
 So been they parted both, with hearts on edge° *keen*
 To be avenged each on his enemy.

That night they pass in joy and jollity,
Feasting and courting both in bower° and hall: *bed chamber*
For steward was excessive Gluttony,
That of his plenty poured forth to all;
Which done, the chamberlain Sloth did to rest them call.

44

Now whenas° darksome° Night had all   *when   gloomy*
   displayed°   *unfolded* *
Her coal-black curtain over brightest sky
The warlike youths, on dainty couches laid,
Did chase away sweet sleep from sluggish eye
To muse on means of hoped victory.
But whenas Morpheus had, with leaden mace,
Arrested all that courtly company,
Uprose Duessa from her resting place
And to the paynim's lodging comes with silent pace,°   *step*

45

Whom broad awake she finds in troublous fit,
   Forecasting° how his foe he might annoy,°   *Considering   harm*
And him amoves° with speeches seeming   *stirs emotionally* *
   fit:°   *appropriate*
'Ah, dear Sansjoy, next dearest to Sansfoy —
Cause of my new grief, cause of my new joy:
Joyous to see his image in mine eye,
And grieved to think how foe did him destroy
That was the flower of grace and chivalry,
Lo his Fidessa: to thy secret faith I fly.'

46

With gentle words he can° her fairly° greet,   *did   courteously*
And bade say on the secret of her heart.
Then, sighing soft: 'I learn that little sweet
Oft tempered is' (quoth she) 'with muchel°   *much*
   smart;°   *pain*
For since my breast was launched° with   *pierced*
   lovely° dart   *of love*
Of dear Sansfoy I never 'joyed hour,
But in eternal woes my weaker° heart   *too weak*
Have wasted, loving him with all my power,

And for his sake have felt full many an heavy
    stour.°   *time of stress*†

47

'At last, when perils all I weened° past,   *believed*
  And hoped to reap the crop of all my care,
  Into new woes unweeting° I was cast   *unawares*
  By this false faitor,° who unworthy ware°   *impostor   wore*
  His worthy shield whom he, with guileful snare
  Entrapped, slew, and brought to shameful grave.
  Me, silly° maid, away with him he bare,   *innocent; helpless*
  And ever since hath kept in darksome cave
For that° I would not yield that° to Sansfoy I   *Because   that which*
  gave.

48

'But since fair sun hath 'spersed° that louring cloud   *dispersed*
  And to my loathed life now shows some light,
  Under your beams I will me safely shroud°   *shelter*
  From dreaded storm of his disdainful° spite:°   *scornful   anger*
  To you the inheritance belongs by right
  Of brother's praise; to you eke° 'longs° his love.   *also   belongs*
  Let not his love, let not his restless sprite,
  Be unrevenged, that calls to you above
From wandering Stygian shores where it doth endless°   *eternally*
  move.'

49

Thereto said he: 'Fair dame, be nought dismayed
  For sorrows past: their grief is with them gone.
  Ne° yet of present peril be afraid,   *Nor*
  For needless fear did never 'vantage°   *advantage*
    none,°   *anybody*
  And helpless° hap° it booteth°   *beyond help   misfortune   avails*
    not to moan.
  Dead is Sansfoy – his vital pains° are past,   *troubles of life*
  Though grieved ghost for vengeance deep do groan:
  He lives that shall him pay his duties° last,   *dues*
And guilty elfin blood shall sacrifice in haste.'

50

'Oh but I fear the fickle freaks'° (quoth she)   caprices‡
    'Of Fortune false, and odds° of arms in   chances
        field.'°   of battle
    'Why, dame,' (quoth he) 'what odds can ever be
    Where both do fight alike to win or yield?'
    'Yea, but' (quoth she) 'he bears a charmed shield,
    And eke enchanted arms that none can pierce –
    Ne none can wound the man that does them wield.'
    'Charmed or enchanted' (answered he then fierce)°   fiercely
'I no whit reck:° ne you the like need to rehearse.°   care   repeat

51

'But, fair Fidessa, sithence° Fortune's guile°   since trickery
    Or enemy's power hath now captived you,
    Return from whence ye came, and rest awhile
    Till morrow next that° I the elf subdue,   when
    And with Sansfoy's dead dowry you endue.'°   endow
    'Ay me, that is a double death,' she said,
    'With proud foe's sight my sorrow to renew:
    Wherever yet I be, my secret aid
    Shall follow you.' So, passing forth, she him obeyed.

CANTO 5

The faithful knight in equal field
    Subdues his faithless foe,
Whom false Fidessa saves, and for
    His cure to hell does go.

1

The noble heart that harbours virtuous thought
    And is with child of glorious° great intent   glory-seeking
    Can never rest, until it forth hath brought
    The eternal brood° of glory excellent:°   offspring   highest
    Such restless passion° did all night   overpowering emotion†
        torment
    The flaming courage° of that fairy knight,   heart

Devising how that doughty° tournament   *formidable*
 With greatest honour he achieven° might: *win; complete*
Still° did he wake, and still did watch for dawning light. *Ever*

2

At last the golden oriental° gate   *bright; eastern*
 Of greatest heaven 'gan to open fair,
 And Phoebus fresh, as bridegroom to his mate,° *consort*
 Came dancing forth, shaking his dewy hair,
 And hurled his glistering beams through the gloomy air –
 Which, when the wakeful elf perceived, straight way
 He started up and did himself prepare
 In sun-bright° arms and battailous *sun-bright*[†]
  array,°   *warlike attire*
For with that pagan proud he combat will that day;

3

And forth he comes into the common° hall, *communal*
 Where early wait him many a gazing eye
 To weet° what end to stranger knight may fall. *know*
 There many minstrels maken melody
 To drive away the dull melancholy,
 And many bards, that to the trembling chord
 Can tune their timely° voices *keeping time*[†]
  cunningly,°   *skilfully*
 And many chroniclers, that can° record *know how to*
Old loves, and wars for ladies done by many a lord.

4

Soon after comes the cruel saracen,
 In woven mail all armed warely,° *prudently*
 And sternly° looks at him, who not a pin *fiercely*
 Does care for look of living creature's eye.
 They bring them wines of Greece and Araby,
 And dainty° spices fetched from furthest Ind, *precious*
 To kindle heat of courage privily;° *within*
 And in the wine a solemn oath they bind
To observe the sacred laws of arms that are assigned.° *appointed*

5

At last comes forth that far-renowned queen
 With royal pomp and princely majesty.
 She is ybrought into a paled° green   *enclosed*
 And placed under stately canopy
 The warlike feats of both those knights to see.
 On the other side, in all men's open view,
 Duessa placed is, and on a tree
 Sansfoy his shield is hanged with bloody hue:° *colour*
Both those the laurel garlands° to the victor *i.e., prize of victory*
 due.

6

A shrilling° trumpet sounded from on high   *piercing*‡
 And unto battle bade themselves address:° *prepare*
 Their shining shields about their wrists they tie,
 And burning blades about their heads do bless° – *brandish*†
 The instruments of wrath and heaviness.° *anger*
 With greedy force each other doth assail
 And strike so fiercely that they do impress
 Deep-dinted° furrows in the battered mail: *dented*
The iron walls to ward° their blows are weak and frail. *fend off*

7

The saracen was stout° and wondrous strong, *fierce; powerful*
 And heaped blows like iron hammers great,
 For after blood and vengeance he did long;
 The knight was fierce° and full of youthly heat, *ardent; brave*
 And doubled strokes like dreaded thunder's threat,
 For all for praise and honour he did fight.
 Both stricken strike, and beaten both do beat,
 That° from their shields forth flieth fiery light, *So that*
And helmets hewn deep show marks of either's might.

8

So the one for wrong, the other strives for right:
 As when a griffin, seized of° his prey, *Epic simile* *who has seized*
 A dragon fierce encountereth in his flight
 (Through widest air making his idle° way) *aimless*
 That would his rightful ravin° rend away: *prey*
 With hideous° horror° both together smite *terrible shudder*

And souse° so sore° that they the heavens   *strike† hard*
    affray:°   *frighten*
The wise soothsayer, seeing so sad° sight,   *calamitous*
The amazed vulgar° tells of wars and mortal fight.   *populace*

9

So the one for wrong, the other strives for right,
    And each to deadly shame° would drive his   *i.e., shame of death*
    foe:
    The cruel steel so greedily doth bite
    In tender flesh that streams of blood down flow,
    With which the arms° – that erst° so bright   *weapons formerly*
    did show –
    In pure vermilion now are dyed.
    Great ruth in all the gazers' hearts did grow,
    Seeing the gored wounds gape so wide,
That victory they dare not wish to either side.

10

At last the paynim° chanced to cast his eye –   *pagan*
    His sudden° eye, flaming with wrathful fire –   *quick*
    Upon his brother's shield, which hung thereby.
    Therewith redoubled was his raging ire,
    And said: 'Ah, wretched son of woeful sire,
    Dost thou sit wailing by black Stygian lake
    Whilst here thy shield is hanged for victor's hire,°   *reward*
    And sluggish german° dost thy forces slake°   *kinsman abate*
To after-send his foe that him may overtake?

11

'Go, caitiff° elf, him quickly overtake,   *captive; cowardly*
    And soon redeem from his long wandering woe:
    Go, guilty ghost,° to him my message   *i.e., Redcross when dead*
    make,°   *be*
    That I his shield have quit° from dying foe.'   *regained*
    Therewith upon his crest° he struck him so   *helmet*
    That twice he reeled, ready twice to fall:
    End of the doubtful battle deemed tho°   *then*
    The lookers on, and loud to him 'gan call
The false Duessa: 'Thine the shield, and I, and all.'

12

Soon as the fairy heard his lady speak
  Out of his swooning dream he 'gan awake,
  And quickening° faith – that erst was   *enlivening*
    waxen° weak –   *had grown*
  The creeping deadly cold away did shake.
  Tho, moved with wrath, and shame, and lady's sake,° *regard*
  Of all at once he cast° avenged to be,   *resolved*
  And with so exceeding fury at him strake°   *struck*
  That forced him to stoop upon his knee
(Had he not stooped so, he should have cloven° *been split apart*
  be),

13

And said: 'Go now, proud miscreant,   *heretic; villain*[†]
  Thyself thy message do° to german° dear –   *be brother*
  Alone he, wandering, thee too long doth want:°   *lack*
  Go say, his foe thy shield with his doth bear.'
  Therewith his heavy hand he high 'gan rear
  Him to have slain when, lo, a darksome cloud
  Upon him fell: he nowhere doth appear,
  But vanished is. The elf him calls aloud,
But answer none receives: the darkness him does shroud.

14

In haste Duessa from her place arose,
  And, to him running, said: 'O prowest° knight   *most valiant*
  That ever lady to her love did choose,
  Let now abate the terror of your might
  And quench the flame of furious despite°   *outrage; anger*
  And bloody vengeance: lo, the infernal powers,
  Covering your foe with cloud of deadly night,
  Have borne him hence to Pluto's baleful bowers:°   *regions*
The conquest yours, I yours, the shield, and glory, yours.'

15

Not all so satisfied, with greedy eye
  He sought all round about his thirsty blade
  To bathe in blood of faithless enemy
  Who, all that while, lay hid in secret shade:

He stands amazed, how° he thence should   *as to how*
 fade.°   *disappear*
At last the trumpets triumph sound on high,° *also: loudly*
And running heralds humble homage made,
Greeting him goodly° with new victory,   *courteously*
And to him brought the shield, the cause of enmity,

16

Wherewith he goeth to thar sovereign queen
 And, falling her before on lowly knee,
 To her makes present of his service keen,
 Which she accepts with thanks and goodly° *courteous*
  gree,°   *goodwill*
 Greatly advancing° his gay° chivalry. *praising excellent*
So marcheth home, and by her takes the knight,
 Whom all the people follow with great glee,
 Shouting and clapping all their hands on height° *loudly*
That all the air it fills, and flies to heaven bright.

17

Home is he brought and laid in sumptuous bed,
 Where many skilful leeches° him abide° *doctors attend*
 To salve° his hurts, that yet still freshly bled. *anoint*
 In wine and oil they wash his wounds wide,
 And softly can embalm° on every side; *did anoint*
 And all the while most heavenly melody
 About the bed sweet music did divide,° *variously ornament*†
 Him to beguile of grief° and agony;   *pain*
And, all the while, Duessa wept full bitterly:

18

As when a weary traveller that strays
 By muddy shore of broad seven-mouthed Nile,
 Unweeting° of the perilous wandering ways, *Ignorant*
 Doth meet a cruel, crafty crocodile
 Which, in false grief hiding his harmful guile,
 Doth weep full sore,° and sheddeth tender tears: *extremely*
 The foolish man – that pities all this while
 His mournful plight – is swallowed up
  unwares,°   *without warning*
Forgetful of his own, that minds another's cares.

19

So wept Duessa until eventide,
  That° shining lamps in Jove's high house were lit.   *When*
  Then forth she rose, ne lenger° would abide,   *nor longer*
  But comes unto the place where the heathen knight
  In slumbering swoon (nigh void of vital sprite)°   *living spirit*
  Lay covered with enchanted cloud all day.
  Whom, when she found as she him left in
    plight,°   *in the same [bad] state*
  To wail his woeful case° she would not stay   *situation; body*
But to the eastern coast of heaven makes speedy way,

20

Where grisly° Night (with visage deadly° sad   *terrifying deathly*
  That Phoebus' cheerful face durst° never view,   *dared*
  And in a foul, black, pitchy mantle clad)
  She finds forth coming from her darksome°   *gloomy*
    mew°   *secret den*
  Where she all day did hide her hated hue.°   *aspect*
  Before the door her iron chariot stood,
  Already harnessed for journey new,
  And coal-black steeds, yborn of hellish brood,°   *parentage*†
That on their rusty° bits did champ as they were   *bloody*
    wood.°   *mad*

21

Who, when she saw Duessa – sunny bright,
  Adorned with gold and jewels shining clear° –   *brightly*
  She greatly grew amazed° at the sight,   *confounded*
  And the unacquainted° light began to fear   *unfamiliar*
  (For never did such brightness there appear),
  And would have back retired to her cave,
  Until the witch's speech she 'gan to hear,
  Saying: 'Yet, O thou dreaded dame, I crave
Abide, till I have told the message which I have.'

22

She stayed, and forth Duessa 'gan proceed:
  'O thou, most ancient grandmother of all –
  More old than Jove (whom thou at first did breed),
  Or that great house of gods celestial –

Which wast begot in Demogorgon's hall
And sawest the secrets of the world
   unmade,°   *before it was made*
Why sufferedest thou thy nephews° dear to fall   *grandsons*
With elfin sword, most shamefully betrayed?
Lo, where the stout° Sansjoy doth sleep in deadly   *valiant*
   shade;°   *shadow*

23

'And him before° I saw with bitter eyes   *before him*
   The bold Sansfoy shrink underneath his spear,
   And now the prey of fowls in field he lies,
   Nor° wailed of friends, nor laid on groaning bier,   *Neither*
   That whilom° was to me too dearly dear.   *formerly**
   O what of gods then boots° it to be born   *avails*
   If old Aveugle's sons so evil hear?°   *such ill is reported of*
   Or who shall not great Night's children scorn
When two of three her nephews are so foul°   *terribly*
   forlorn?°   *doomed*

24

'Up, then, up, dreary° dame, of darkness queen: *sad*
   Go, gather up the relics° of thy race;   *remains*
   Or else go them avenge, and let be seen
   That dreaded Night in brightest day hath place°   *precedence*†
   And can the children of fair light deface.'°   *abash;‡ extinguish*
   Her feeling speeches some compassion moved
   In heart, and change in that great mother's°   *grandmother's*
   face
   (Yet pity in her heart was never proved°   *experienced*
Till then, for evermore she hated, never loved),

25

And said: 'Dear daughter, rightly may I rue
   The fall of famous children born of me,
   And good successes which their foes ensue.°   *follow*
   But who can turn the stream of destiny,
   Or break the chain of strong Necessity,
   Which fast is tied to Jove's eternal seat?

The sons of Day he favoureth, I see,
  And by my ruin° thinks to make them great: *fall; destruction*
To make one great by other's loss is bad excheat.°   *levy, gain*‡

26

'Yet shall they not escape so freely° all,   *unpenalised*
  For some shall pay the price of others' guilt,
  And he – the man that made Sansfoy to fall –
  Shall with his own blood price° that he hath   *pay for* *
    spilt.°   *also: killed*
  But what art thou, that tellest of nephews killed?'
  'I that do seem not I, Duessa am,'
  Quoth she, 'however° now in garments gilt   *although*
  And gorgeous gold arrayed I to thee came:
Duessa I, the daughter of Deceit and Shame.'

27

Then, bowing down her aged back, she kissed
  The wicked witch, saying: 'In that fair face
  The false resemblance of Deceit (I wist)°   *knew*
  Did closely° lurk – yet so true-seeming grace   *secretly*
  It carried that I scarce in darksome place
  Could it discern, though I the mother be
  Of Falsehood, and root of Duessa's race.
  Oh, welcome, child whom I have longed to see,
And now have seen unwares:° lo, now I go with   *unexpectedly*
    thee.'

28

Then to her iron wagon she betakes,
  And with her bears the foul, well-favoured° witch: *beautiful*
  Through murksome° air her ready way she   *dark and thick*†
    makes.
  Her twifold team – of which two black as pitch,
  And two were brown, yet each to each unlich° –   *unlike*
  Did softly swim away, ne° ever stamp,   *nor*
  Unless she chanced their stubborn mouths to twitch;°   *tug*‡
  Then, foaming tar, their bridles they would champ
And, trampling the fine element,° would fiercely   *i.e., air*
    ramp.°   *rear up*

29

So well they sped that they be come at length
   Unto the place whereas° the paynim° lay,   *where pagan*
   Devoid of outward sense and native° strength,   *inborn*
   Covered with charmed° cloud from view of day   *magic*
   And sight of men since his late° luckless fray.°   *recent battle*
   His cruel wounds with cruddy° blood congealed   *clotted*
   They binden up so wisely° as they may,°   *as skilfully can*
   And handle softly till they can be healed:
So lay him in her chariot, close° in night concealed.   *secretly*

30

And all the while she stood upon the ground
   The wakeful dogs did never cease to bay,
   As giving warning of the unwonted° sound   *not often heard*
   With which her iron wheels did them affray,°   *scare*
   And her dark grisly° look them much dismay.°   *terrible daunt*
   The messenger of death, the ghastly° owl,   *terrifying*
   With dreary shrieks did also her bewray,°   *reveal*
   And hungry wolves continually did howl
At her abhorred face, so filthy and so foul.

31

Thence turning back, in silence soft° they stole,   *softly*
   And brought the heavy corse° with easy pace°   *body step*
   To yawning gulf of deep Avernus' hole.
   By° that same hole an entrance dark and base,°   *Through low*
   With smoke and sulphur hiding all the place,
   Descends to hell – there creature never passed
   That back returned without heavenly grace;
   But dreadful Furies, which their chains have brast,°   *burst*
And damned sprites sent forth to make ill° men   *evil*
     aghast.°   *terrified*

32

By that same way the direful dames do drive
   Their mournful chariot filed° with rusty° blood,   *defiled red*
   And down to Pluto's house are come belive:°   *swiftly*
   Which, passing through, on every side them stood

The trembling ghosts with sad, amazed° mood,   *bemused*
  Chattering their iron teeth, and staring wide
With stony eyes; and all the hellish brood
Of fiends infernal flocked on every side,
To gaze on earthly wight° that with the Night   *creature**
  durst° ride.   *dared*

33

They pass the bitter waves of Acheron,
  Where many souls sit wailing woefully,
And come to fiery flood° of Phlegethon,   *stream*
Whereas° the damned ghosts in torment fry   *Where*
And with sharp shrilling shrieks do bootless° cry, *without avail*
  Cursing high Jove, the which them thither sent.
The house of endless pain is built thereby,
  In which ten thousand sorts of punishment
The cursed creatures do eternally torment.

34

Before the threshold dreadful Cerberus
  His three deformed heads did lay along,
Curled with thousand adders venomous,
And lolled forth his bloody flaming tongue.
At them he 'gan rear his bristles strong
And felly° gnar° until Day's enemy   *fiercely snarl*
  Did him appease. Then down his tail he hung
And suffered them to passen quietly,
For she in hell and heaven had power equally.

35

There was Ixion turned on a wheel
  For daring tempt the queen of heaven to sin;
And Sisyphus an huge round stone did reel
Against an hill, ne° might from labour lin;°   *nor stop*
There thirsty Tantalus hung by the chin,
And Tityus fed a vulture on his maw;°   *innards*
Typhoeus' joints were stretched on a gin,°   *rack**
  Theseus condemned to endless sloth by law,
And fifty sisters water in leaky vessels draw.

36

They all, beholding worldly° wights in place,°   *from the upper world* / *there*
  Leave off their work, unmindful of their smart,°   *torment*
  To gaze on them, who forth by them do pace
  Till they be come unto the furthest part,
  Where was a cave ywrought by wondrous art –
  Deep, dark, uneasy,° doleful,° comfortless –   *disagreeable dreary*
  In which sad Aesculapius far apart
  Imprisoned was in chains remediless°   *without hope of rescue*
For that Hippolytus' rent corse he did redress.°   *restore*

37

Hippolytus a jolly° huntsman was   *splendid*
  That wont° in chariot chase the foaming boar: *used*
  He all his peers in beauty did surpass,
  But ladies' love as loss of time forbore.°   *shunned*
  His wanton stepdame loved him the more
  But, when she saw her offered sweets refused,
  Her love she turned to hate, and him before
  His father fierce of treason false accused,
And with her jealous° terms° his open ears abused;   *jealousy-inducing phrases*

38

Who, all in rage, his sea-god sire besought,°   *requested*
  Some cursed vengeance on his son to cast.
  From surging gulf two monsters straight° were brought,   *forthwith*
  With dread whereof his chasing steeds, aghast,°   *terrified*
  Both chariot swift and huntsman overcast.°   *overthrew*
  His goodly° corse,° on ragged cliffs yrent,   *beautiful body*
  Was quite° dismembered, and his members chaste   *completely*
  Scattered on every mountain as he went,
That° of Hippolytus was left no monument.°   *So that mark*[†]

39

His cruel stepdame, seeing what was done,
  Her wicked days with wretched knife did end,
  In death avowing the innocence of her son:

Which hearing, his rash sire began to rend
His hair, and hasty tongue that did offend.
Tho,° gathering up the relics° of his   *Then   remains*
  smart,°   *grief*
By Dian's means (who was Hippolyt's friend)
Them brought to Aesculape, that by his art
Did heal them all again, and joined every part.

40

Such wondrous science° in man's wit° to reign   *knowledge   mind*
  When Jove advised,° that could the dead revive,   *observed**
  And Fates expired could renew again,
  Of endless life he might him not deprive
  But unto hell did thrust him down alive,
  With flashing thunderbolt ywounded sore:
  Where, long remaining, he did always strive
  Himself with salves° to health for to restore,   *ointments*
And slake the heavenly fire that raged evermore.

41

There ancient Night, arriving, did alight
  From her nigh weary wain,° and in   *wagon and worn-out horses*
    her arms
  To Aesculapius brought the wounded knight
  Whom, having softly° disarrayed° of   *gently   disrobed*
    arms,°   *armour*
  Tho° 'gan to him discover all his harms,°   *Then   injuries*
  Beseeching him with prayer and with praise
  If either salves, or oils, or herbs, or charms
  A fordone° wight° from door of death   *shattered[†]   person**
    mote° raise,   *might*
He would at her request prolong her nephew's days.

42

'Ah, dame,' quoth he, 'thou temptest me in vain
  To dare the thing which daily yet I rue,
  And the old cause of my continued pain
  With like attempt to like end to renew.
  Is° not enough that, thrust from heaven due,°   *Is it   my due*
  Here endless penance for one fault I pay,
  But that redoubled crime with vengeance new

Thou biddest me to eke?° Can Night   *increase*
   defray°   *discharge‡*
The wrath of thundering Jove, that rules both night and day?'

43

'Not so,' quoth she, 'but sith° that heaven's king   *since*
   From hope of heaven hath thee excluded quite,°   *utterly*
   Why fearest thou, that canst not hope for thing,°   *anything*
   And fearest not that° more thee hurten might,   *that which*
   Now in the power of everlasting Night?
   Go to, then, O thou far-renowned son
   Of great Apollo: show thy famous might
   In medicine, that else° hath to thee won   *already*
Great pains, and greater praise, both never to be
   done.'°   *completed*

44

Her words prevailed, and then the learned leech°   *physician*
   His cunning° hand 'gan to his wounds to lay,   *skilful*
   And all things else the which his art did teach;
   Which having seen, from thence arose away
   The mother of dread darkness, and let stay
   Aveugle's son there in the leech's cure°   *care*
   And, back returning, took her wonted way
   To run her timely° race, whilst Phoebus   *temporal*
   pure°   *uncorrupted; bright*
In western waves his weary wagon did recure.°   *revive*

45

The false Duessa, leaving noyous° Night,   *harmful*
   Returned to stately palace of Dame Pride
   Where, when she came, she found the fairy knight
   Departed thence, albe° his wounds wide,   *although*
   Not thoroughly healed, unready were to ride.
   Good cause he had to hasten thence away,
   For on a day his wary dwarf had spied
   Where, in a dungeon deep, huge numbers lay
Of caitiff° wretched thralls that wailed night and day –   *captive*

46

A rueful sight° as could be seen with eye;   *i.e., As rueful a sight . . .*
    Of whom he learned had in secret wise°   *fashion*
    The hidden cause of their captivity –
    How, mortgaging° their lives to covetise,   *pledging to the death*
    Through wasteful pride and wanton riotise°   *riotous conduct*[†]
    They were, by law of that proud tyranness,°   *female tyrant*[†]
    Provoked with wrath and envy's false surmise,
    Condemned to that dungeon merciless,
Where they should live in woe and die in wretchedness.

47

There was that great proud king of Babylon,
    That would compel all nations to adore
    And him as only God to call upon,
    Till through celestial doom° thrown out of door   *judgement*
    (Into an ox he was transformed of yore);
    There also was King Croesus, that enhanced°   *lifted in pride*
    His heart too high through his great riches' store;°   *plenty*
    And proud Antiochus, the which advanced
His cursed hand against God and on his altars danced;

48

And them long time before great Nimrod was,
    That first the world with sword and fire
        warrayed;°   *ravaged by war**
    And after him old Ninus far did pass°   *surpass*
    In princely pomp, of all the world obeyed.
    There also was that mighty monarch – laid
    Low under all (yet above all in pride) –
    That name of native sire did foul upbraid,°   *censure*
    And would as Ammon's son be magnified
Till, scorned of God and man, a shameful death he died.

49

All these together in one heap were thrown,
    Like carcasses of beasts in butcher's stall.
    And in another corner wide were strewn
    The antique ruins of the Romans' fall:
    Great Romulus, the grandsire of them all,
    Proud Tarquin and too lordly Lentulus,

Stout° Scipio and stubborn Hannibal,   *Brave*
Ambitious Sylla and stern Marius,
High Caesar, great Pompey, and fierce Antonius.

50

Amongst these mighty men were women mixed –
    Proud women, forgetful of their yoke:
    The bold Semiramis (whose sides transfixed
    With son's own blade her foul reproaches spoke);
    Fair Sthenoboea (that herself did choke
    With wilful cord for wanting of° her will);   *failure to obtain*
    High-minded Cleopatra (that with stroke
    Of asp's sting herself did stoutly° kill),   *resolutely‡*
And thousands more the like, that did that dungeon fill,

51

Besides the endless routs of wretched thralls
    Which thither were assembled day by day
    From all the world, after their woeful falls
    Through wicked pride and wasted wealth's decay.°   *decline*
    But most of all which° in that dungeon lay   *those who*
    Fell from high princes' courts or ladies' bowers,°   *chambers*
    Where they in idle pomp° or wanton play   *splendour*
    Consumed had their goods and thriftless hours,
And lastly thrown themselves into these heavy
        stours.°   *death-struggles**

52

Whose case, whenas° the careful° dwarf had   *when full of care*
        told,
    And made example of their mournful sight
    Unto his master, he no lenger° would   *longer*
    There dwell in peril of like painful plight,
    But early rose and, ere that dawning light
    Discovered° had the world to heaven wide,   *Revealed*
    He by a privy postern° took his flight   *secret side door*
    That of° no envious° eyes he mote° be   *by spiteful might*
        spied:
For doubtless° death ensued if any him descried.   *certain*

53

Scarce could he footing find in that foul way
   For° many corses, like a great laystall°   *Because of burial place‡*
   Of murdered men (which therein strewed lay
   Without remorse or decent° funeral),   *seemly*
   Which all through that great princess's pride did fall
   And came to shameful end. And them beside,
   Forth riding° underneath the castle wall,   *As they rode forth*
   A dunghill of dead carcasses he spied –
The dreadful spectacle of that sad house of Pride.

Canto 6

From lawless lust by wondrous grace
   Fair Una is released;
Whom savage° nation does adore   *wild*
   And learns her wise behest.

1

As when a ship, that flies fair° under sail,   *well*
   An hidden rock escaped hath unwares
   That lay in wait her wreck for to bewail,
   The mariner, yet half-amazed, stares
   At peril past, and yet° in doubt° ne dares°   *still fear dares not*
   To joy° at his fool-happy° oversight: *rejoice lucky by chance*
   So doubly is distressed 'twixt joy and cares
   The dreadless courage of this elfin knight,
Having escaped so sad examples in his sight.

2

Yet sad he was that his too-hasty speed
   The fair Duessa had forced him leave behind,
   And yet more sad that Una, his dear dread,°   *revered one*
   Her truth had stained with treason so unkind°   *unnatural*
   (Yet crime° in her could never creature find).   *cause of blame*
   But, for his love and for her own self's sake,
   She wandered had from one to other Ind'

Him for to seek, ne ever would forsake,
Till her unwares the fierce Sansloy did overtake.

                                    3
Who, after Archimago's foul° defeat,   *ignominious*
   Led her away into a forest wild
And, turning wrathful fire to lustful heat,
   With beastly sin thought her to have defiled
   And made the vassal of his pleasures vild.°   *base*‡
Yet first he cast° by treaty,° and by   *resolved   entreaty*
      trains,°   *guile*
   Her to persuade that stubborn fort to yield
   (For greater conquest of hard love he gains
That works it to his will, than he that it constrains).°   *forces*

                                    4
With fawning words he courted her awhile
   And, looking lovely° and oft sighing sore,°   *lovingly   greatly*
   Her constant heart did tempt with diverse guile:
But words, and looks, and sighs she did abhor,
   As rock of diamond steadfast evermore.
Yet, for to° feed his fiery, lustful eye,   *in order to*
   He snatched the veil that hung her face before:
   Then 'gan her beauty shine as brightest sky
And burned his beastly heart to efforce° her   *vanquish with force*‡
      chastity.

                                    5
So, when he saw his flattering arts to fail,
   And subtle engines beat° from battery,   *beat back*
   With greedy force he 'gan the fort assail,°   *attack*
Whereof he weened possessed soon to be,
   And win rich spoil of ransacked chastity.
Ah heavens, that do this hideous act behold,
   And heavenly virgin thus outraged° see,   *violated*‡
   How can ye vengeance just so long withhold
And hurl not flashing flames upon that paynim bold?

6

The piteous maiden, careful,° comfortless,   *full of care*
  Does throw out thrilling° shrieks and shrieking   *piercing*
    cries –
  The last vain help of women's great distress –
  And, with loud plaints, importuneth the skies
  That° molten stars do drop like weeping eyes;   *so that*
  And Phoebus, flying so° most shameful sight,   *such a*
  His blushing face in foggy cloud implies,°   *enwraps*
  And hides for shame. What wit° of mortal   *mind*
    wight°   *person**
Can now devise to quit° a thrall from such a plight?   *liberate*

7

Eternal Providence, exceeding° thought,   *beyond*
  Where none appears, can make herself a way:
  A wondrous way it for this lady wrought
  From lion's claws to pluck the griped° prey.   *seized; embraced*
  Her shrill outcries and shrieks so loud did
    bray°   *sound in pain, terror*[†]
  That all the woods and forests did resound;
  A troop of fauns and satyrs, far away
  Within the wood, were dancing in a round
Whiles old Sylvanus slept in shady arbour sound;

8

Who, when they heard that piteous, strained° voice,   *extra-loud*[‡]
  In haste forsook their rural merriment
  And ran towards the far-rebounded° noise   *re-echoed*
  To weet° what wight so loudly did lament.   *discover*
  Unto the place they come incontinent° –   *forthwith*
  Whom, when the raging saracen espied
  (A rude,° misshapen, monstrous rabblement,   *barbaric*
  Whose like he never saw), he durst° not bide,°   *dared stay*
But got his ready steed and fast away 'gan ride.

9

The wild woodgods, arrived in the place,
  There find the virgin doleful, desolate,
  With ruffled raiments and fair, blubbered° face   *wet with tears*[‡]
  (As her outrageous° foe had left her late)°   *violent recently*

And trembling yet through fear of former hate.°   *object of hate*
All stand amazed at so uncouth° sight   *strange; marvellous*
And 'gin to pity her unhappy° state;   *unfortunate*
All stand astonished° at her beauty bright,   *dazed*
In their rude° eyes unworthy of so woeful plight.   *ignorant*

10

She, more amazed, in double dread doth dwell,
  And every tender part for fear does shake:
  As when a greedy wolf, through hunger fell,°   *severe*
  A silly° lamb far from the flock does take   *defenceless*‡
  Of whom he means his bloody feast to make,
  A lion spies fast running towards him,
  The innocent prey in haste he does forsake
  Which, quit from death, yet quakes in every limb
With change of fear, to see the lion look so grim.°   *fierce*

11

Such fearful fit assayed° her trembling heart,   *assailed*
  Ne° word to speak, ne° joint to move she had.   *Neither . . . nor*
  The savage nation° feel her secret smart,°   *wild race   injury*
  And read her sorrow in her countenance sad:
  Their frowning foreheads with rough horns yclad
  And rustic horror° all aside do lay   *roughness; bristliness*
  And, gently grinning, show a semblance° glad   *demeanour*
  To comfort her and, fear to put away,
Their backward-bent knees teach° her humbly to   *i.e., them*
    obey.

12

The doubtful° damsel dare not yet commit   *fearful*
  Her single person to their barbarous truth
  But still, 'twixt fear and hope, amazed does sit,
  Late-learned what harm to hasty trust ensueth.
  They, in compassion of her tender youth
  And wonder of her beauty sovereign,
  Are won° with pity and unwonted°   *overcome   unaccustomed*
    ruth
  And, all prostrate upon the lowly plain,
Do kiss her feet, and fawn on her with countenance fain.°   *glad*

13

Their hearts she guesseth by their humble guise,°   *attire; conduct*
  And yields her to extremity of time:° *the necessity of the moment*
  So, from the ground she fearless doth arise
  And walketh forth without suspect° of   *suspicion*
    crime.°   *wrong-doing*
  They, all as glad as birds of joyous prime,°   *spring; dawn*
  Thence lead her forth, about her dancing round,
  Shouting and singing all a shepherds' rhyme,
  And, with green branches strewing all the ground,
Do worship her as queen with olive garland crowned.

14

And all the way their merry pipes they sound
  That° all the woods with double echo ring,   *So that*
  And with their horned feet do wear the ground,
  Leaping like wanton kids in pleasant spring.
  So towards old Sylvanus they her bring,
  Who, with the noise awaked, cometh out
  To weet° the cause, his weak steps   *guiding*
    governing°   *guiding*
  (And aged limbs) on cypress stadle° stout,   *staff*[1]
And with an ivy twine his waist is girt about.

15

Far off he wonders what them makes so glad –
  Or° Bacchus' merry fruit they did invent,° *Whether discover*
  Or Cybele's frantic rites have made them mad.
  They, drawing nigh, unto their god present
  That flower of faith and beauty excellent;
  The god himself, viewing that mirror° rare,   *example*
  Stood long amazed, and burned in his intent:
  His own fair Dryope now he thinks not fair,
And Pholoe foul when her to this he doth compare.

16

The wood-born people fall before her flat,
  And worship her as goddess of the wood;
  And old Sylvanus self° bethinks not° *himself cannot imagine*
    what
  To think of wight° so fair, but gazing stood,   *creature**

In doubt to deem° her born of earthly   *judge*
   brood:°   *parentage†*
Sometimes Dame Venus self he seems to see
(But Venus never had so sober° mood);°   *temperate disposition*
Sometimes Diana he her takes to be
(But misseth bow and shafts, and buskins° to her knee).   *boots*

17

By view of her he 'ginneth to revive
  His ancient love and dearest Cypariss',
  And calls to mind his portraiture° alive –   *image [when]*
  How fair he was (and yet not fair to° this);   *compared to*
  And how he slew, with glancing dart amiss,
  A gentle hind, the which the lovely boy
  Did love as life, above all worldly bliss,
  For grief whereof the lad n'ould° after joy,   *would not*
But pined away in anguish and self-willed annoy.°   *harm*

18

The woody nymphs, fair hamadryads,
  Her to behold do thither run apace,
  And all the troop of light-foot naiads
  Flocked all about to see her lovely face.
  But when they viewed have her heavenly grace,
  They envy her in their malicious mind
  And fly away for fear of foul disgrace:
  But all the satyrs scorn their woody
    kind,°   *race born in the wood*
And henceforth nothing fair but her on earth they find.

oxymoron
    ↓
19

Glad of such luck the luckless lucky maid
  Did her content to please their feeble eyes,
  And long time with that savage people stayed
  To gather breath in many miseries;
  During which time her gentle° wit°   *courteous understanding*
    she plies
  To teach them truth which worshipped her in vain,°   *foolishly*
  And made her the image of idolatries.°   *idol of their idolatry*
  But when their bootless° zeal she did restrain   *fruitless*

From her own worship, they her ass would worship
    fain.°   *willingly; gladly*

20

It fortuned a noble warlike knight
  By just occasion to that forest came
  To seek his kindred, and the lineage right
  From whence he took his well-deserved name.
  He had in arms abroad won muchel° fame,   *much* *
  And filled far lands with glory of his might:
  Plain, faithful, true, and enemy of shame,
  And ever loved to fight for ladies' right,
But in vainglorious frays° he little did delight: *fights*

21

A satyr's son, yborn in forest wild
  By strange adventure,° as it did betide,°   *chance   happen*
  And there begotten of a lady mild,
  Fair Thyamis, the daughter of Labryde,
  That was in sacred bands of wedlock tied
  To Therion, a loose, unruly swain,
  Who had more joy to range the forest wide
  And chase the savage beast with busy pain,°   *toil*
Than serve his lady's love, and waste in pleasures vain.

22

The forlorn maid did with love's longing burn,
  And could not lack° her lover's company   *be without*
  But to the wood she goes, to serve her turn°   *fulfil her need*
  And seek her spouse, that from her still does fly
  And follows other game and
    venery.°   *hunting wild beasts; love-making*
  A satyr chanced her wandering for to find
  And, kindling coals of lust in brutish eye,
  The loyal links of wedlock did unbind,
And made her person thrall unto his beastly
    kind.°   *nature*

23

So long in secret cabin° there he held   *cave; hovel*
  Her captive to his sensual desire
  Till that with timely fruit her belly swelled,
  And bore a boy unto that savage sire.
  Then home he suffered her for to retire,°   *return*
  For ransom leaving him the late-born child
  Whom, till to riper years he 'gan aspire,°   *grow up*[†]
  He nursled° up in life and manners wild   *educated;*[†] *reared*
Amongst wild beasts and woods, from laws of men exiled.

24

For all he taught the tender imp° was but   *young child*
  To banish cowardice and bastard° fear: *contemptible*
  His trembling hand he would him force to put
  Upon the lion and the rugged° bear,   *shaggy*
  And from the she-bear's teats her whelps to tear;
  And eke° wild roaring bulls he would him make   *also*
  To tame, and ride their backs not made to bear;
  And the roebucks in flight to overtake,
That° every beast for fear of him did fly and quake.   *So that*

25

Thereby so fearless and so fell° he grew   *fierce, cruel*
  That his own sire and master° of his guise°   *teacher   conduct*
  Did often tremble at his horrid° view,°   *savage   aspect*
  And oft, for dread of hurt, would him advise
  The angry beasts not rashly to despise,
  Nor too much to provoke; for he would learn°   *teach*
  The lion stoop° to him in lowly° wise° *crouch*[†] *humble fashion*
  (A lesson hard), and make the leopard stern
Leave roaring when in rage he for revenge did yearn.

26

And for to make his power approved° more,   *esteemed;*[†] *tested*
  Wild beasts in iron yokes he would compel –
  The spotted panther and the tusked boar,
  The pardal° swift and the tiger cruel,   *leopard; panther*
  The antelope and wolf both fierce and fell –

And them constrain in equal team to draw.
Such joy he had their stubborn hearts to quell,
And sturdy courage tame with dreadful° awe,   *terrible*
That his behest they feared as a tyrant's law.

27

His loving mother came, upon a day,°   *one day*
Unto the woods to see her little son,
And chanced, unwares,° to meet him in the way   *suddenly*
After his sports and cruel pastime done,
When after him a lioness did run
That, roaring all with rage, did loud requere°   *beg*
Her children dear whom he away had won:
The lion whelps she saw how he did bear
And lull in rugged arms, withouten childish fear.

28

The fearful dame all quaked at the sight
And, turning back, 'gan fast to fly away
Until, with love revoked° from vain°   *called back   empty*
    affright,°   *fear*
She hardly° yet persuaded was to stay,   *with difficulty*
And then to him these womanish words 'gan say:
'Ah, Satyrane, my darling and my joy,
For love of me leave off this dreadful play.
To dally thus with death is no fit toy:
Go find some ther playfellows, mine own sweet boy.'

29

In these and like delights of bloody game
He trained was till riper years he raught,°   *reached*
And there abode, whilst any beast of name°   *no known beast*
Walked in that forest whom he had not taught
To fear his force; and then his courage haught°   *noble**
Desired of foreign foemen to be known,
And far abroad for strange adventures sought:
In which his might was never overthrown
But through all fairyland his famous worth was
    blown.°   *trumpeted*

30

Yet evermore it was his manner fair,
    After long labours and adventures spent,
    Unto those native woods for to repair°   *return*
    To see his sire and offspring° ancient.   *lineage*
    And now he thither came for like° intent   *that same*
    Where he unwares the fairest Una found –
    Strange° lady, in so strange habiliment,°   *Alien attire*
    Teaching the satyrs, which her sat around,
True sacred lore,° which from her sweet lips did *doctrine*
    redound.°   *issue*[†]

31

He wondered at her wisdom heavenly rare,
    Whose like in women's wit° he never knew;   *mind*
    And when her courteous deeds he did compare,
    'Gan her admire, and her sad sorrows rue,
    Blaming of Fortune, which such troubles threw,
    And joyed° to make proof of° her cruelty *rejoiced test*
    On gentle° dame, so hurtless° and so true. *noble innocent*
    Thenceforth he kept her goodly° company,   *gracious**
And learned her discipline° of faith and verity. *teaching*

32

But she, all vowed° unto the Redcross knight, *pledged*
    His wandering peril closely° did lament,   *secretly*
    Ne°in this new acquaintance could delight,   *Nor*
    But her dear° heart with anguish did torment, *loving;*[†] *heavy*
    And all her wit° in secret counsels spent *understanding*
    How to escape. At last, in privy° wise° *secret fashion*
    To Satyrane she showed her intent,
    Who, glad to gain such favour, 'gan devise
How with that pensive maid he best might thence arise.° *rebel*

33

So on a day, when satyrs all were gone
    To do their service to Sylvanus old,
    The gentle virgin, left behind alone,
    He led away with courage stout° and bold. *valiant*
    Too late it was to satyrs to be told,

Or ever hope recover her again:
In vain he seeks that° having cannot hold.   *what*
So fast he carried her with careful° pain°   *caring concern*
That they the woods are passed, and come now to the plain.

34

The better part now of the lingering day
They travelled had whenas° they far espied   *when*
A weary wight° forwandering° by the way,   *creature* straying*
And towards him they 'gan in haste to ride
To weet of° news that° did abroad   *discover of what*
    betide,°   *befall*
Or tidings of her knight of the Red Cross.
But he, them spying, 'gan to turn aside –
For fear as seemed, or for some feigned loss.
More greedy they of news fast towards him do cross:

35

A silly° man, in simple weeds° forworn,°   *simple clothes adorned*
And soiled with dust of the long-dried way;
His sandals were with toilsome travel torn,
And face all tanned° with scorching sunny ray,   *browned‡*
As° he had travelled many a summer's day   *As if*
Through boiling sands of Araby and Ind';
And in his hand a Jacob's staff, to stay°   *support*
His weary limbs upon; and eke° behind   *in addition*
His scrip° did hang, in which his needments°   *satchel necessities†*
    he did bind.

36

The knight, approaching nigh, of him enquired
Tidings of war and of adventures new,
But wars nor new adventures none he heard.°   *had heard of*
Then Una 'gan to ask if aught he knew,
Or heard abroad, of that her champion true,
That in his armour bare a crosslet° red.   *little cross*
'Aye me, dear dame' (quoth he), 'well may I rue
To tell the sad sight which mine eyes have read:°   *seen†*
These eyes did see that knight both living and eke dead.'

37

That cruel word her tender heart so thrilled°   *pierced*
　　That sudden cold did run through every vein,
　　And stony horror all her senses filled
　　With dying° fit° that down she fell for pain.   *deathly faint*
　　The knight her lightly° reared up again,   *swiftly*
　　And comforted with courteous kind relief;
　　Then, won from death, she bade him tellen plain
　　The further process° of her hidden grief: *story*
The lesser pangs can° bear who hath endured the   *he/she can . . .*
　　chief.

38

Then 'gan the pilgrim thus: 'I chanced this day,
　　This fatal day that shall I ever rue,
　　To see two knights (in travel on my way) –
　　A sorry sight – arranged in battle new,°   *renewed*
　　Both breathing vengeance, both of wrathful hue.
　　My fearful flesh did tremble at their strife
　　To see their blades so greedily imbrue°   *plunge†*
　　That, drunk with blood, yet thirsted after life:
What more? – the Redcross knight was slain with
　　paynim° knife.'   *pagan*

39

'Ah, dearest lord,' quoth she, 'how might that be,
　　And he the stoutest° knight that ever   *most valiant*
　　　　wone?'°   *lived*
　　'Ah, dearest dame,' quoth he, 'how might I see
　　The thing that might not be, and yet was done?'
　　'Where is' – said Satyrane – 'that paynim's son
　　That him of life, and us of joy, hath reft?'°   *deprived*
　　'Not far away,' quoth he, 'he hence doth wone,°   *remain*
　　Forby° a fountain, where I late him left   *Near*
Washing his bloody wounds, that through the steel were cleft.'

40

Therewith the knight thence marched forth in haste
　　Whiles Una, with huge heaviness oppressed,
　　Could not for sorrow follow him so fast.
　　And soon he came, as he the place had guessed,

Whereas° that pagan proud himself did rest   *Where*
In secret shadow by a fountain side
(Even he it was that erst° would have   *formerly*
    suppressed°   *violated*[†]
Fair Una) – whom, when Satyrane espied,
With foul° reproachful words he boldly him defied,   *harsh*

41

And said: 'Arise, thou cursed miscreant,°   *unbeliever*
    That hast, with knightless° guile and treacherous *unknightly*
    train,°   *deceit*
    Fair knighthood foully shamed, and dost vaunt
    That good knight of the Red Cross to have slain:
    Arise, and with like treason° now maintain°   *treachery defend*
    Thy guilty wrong, or else thee guilty yield.'
    The saracen, this hearing, rose amain°   *forthwith*
    And, catching up in haste his three-square shield
And shining helmet, soon him buckled° to the   *girded himself*[†]
    field,°   *battlefield*

42

And, drawing nigh him, said: 'Ah, misborn° elf,   *bastard*
    In evil hour thy foes thee hither sent
    Another's wrongs to wreak° upon thyself;   *revenge*
    Yet ill thou blamest me for having blent°   *contaminated*
    My name with guile and traitorous intent:
    That Redcross knight, perdy,° I never slew,   *by God*
    But had he been where erst his arms° were lent,   *armour*
    The enchanter vain° his error should not rue:° *foolish regret*
But thou his error shalt, I hope, now proven° true.'   *think*

43

Therewith they 'gan, both furious and fell,°   *fierce*
    To thunder blows and fiercely to assail,
    Each other bent° his enemy to quell°   *intent kill*
    That with their force they pierced both plate and mail,
    And made wide furrows in their fleshes° frail   *i.e., flesh*
    That it would pity° any living eye.   *cause pity in*
    Large floods of blood adown their sides did rail,°   *flow**
    But floods of blood could not them satisfy:
Both hungered after death; both chose to win or die.

44

So long they fight and fell° revenge pursue   *cruel*
  That, fainting each, themselves to breathen let
  And, oft refreshed, battle oft renew:
  As when two boars with rankling malice met
  Their gory sides fresh bleeding fiercely fret°   *tear*
  Till, breathless, both themselves aside retire
  Where, foaming wrath, their cruel tusks they whet,°   *sharpen*
  And trample the earth the whiles they may respire,
Then back to fight again, new breathed and entire.°   *fresh†*

45

So fiercely, when these knights had breathed once,
  They 'gan to fight return, increasing more
  Their puissant force and cruel rage at once
  With heaped strokes more hugely than before
  That, with their dreary° wounds and bloody gore   *gory;* dire*
  They, both deformed,° scarcely could be known.   *disfigured*
  By this sad Una, fraught° with anguish sore,°   *filled severe*
  Led with their noise (which through the air was thrown),
Arrived where they in earth their fruitless blood had sown.

46

Whom, all so soon as that proud saracen
  Espied, he 'gan revive the memory
  Of his lewd lust and late-attempted sin,
  And left the doubtful° battle hastily   *undecided*
  To catch her, newly offered to his eye.
  But Satyrane, with strokes him turning, stayed,
  And sternly bade him other business ply
  Than hunt° the steps of pure unspotted maid: *pursue*
Wherewith he, all enraged, these bitter speeches said:

47

'O foolish fairy's son, what fury mad
  Hath thee incensed to haste thy doleful fate?
  Were it not better I that lady had
  Than that thou hadst repented it too late?
  Most senseless man he, that himself doth hate,
  To love another! Lo, then, for thine aid
  Here take thy lover's token on thy pate.'°   *skull*

So they two fight, the whiles the royal maid
Fled far away, of that proud paynim° sore°   *pagan   extremely*
   afraid.

48

But that false pilgrim which that leasing° told,   *lie*
  Being indeed old Archimage, did stay
  In secret shadow all this to behold,
  And much rejoiced in their bloody fray.
  But, when he saw the damsel pass away,
  He left his stand° and her pursued apace   *place of cover*[t]
  In hope to bring her to her last decay.°   *downfall*[‡]
  But, for to tell her lamentable case,
And eke° this battle's end, will need another place.   *also*

CANTO 7

The Redcross knight is captive made,
  By giant proud oppressed;
Prince Arthur meets with Una great-
  ly with those news distressed.

1

What man so wise, what earthly wit° so ware,°   *mind   alert*
  As to descry the crafty, cunning train°   *trickery*
  By which deceit doth mask in visor fair
  And cast° her colours, dyed deep° in grain,   *order   fast*
  To seem like Truth, whose shape she well can feign
  (And fitting gestures to her purpose frame)
  The guiltless man with guile to entertain?
  Great mistress of her art was that false dame
The false Duessa, cloaked with Fidessa's name,

2

Who, when returning from the dreary Night
  She found not in that perilous house of Pride
  (Where she had left)° the Redcross knight,   *i.e. left him*
  Her hoped prey, would no lenger° bide°   *longer   wait*

But forth she went, to seek him far and wide.
Ere long she found whereas° he weary sat   *the place where*
To rest himself forby° a fountain side,   *close by*
Disarmed all of iron-coated plate;
And by his side his steed the grassy forage ate.

3
He feeds upon the cooling snade, and bathes
His sweaty forehead in the breathing wind
Which through the trembling leaves full gently plays,
Wherein the cheerful birds of sundry kind
Do chant° sweet music to delight his mind.   *sing*
The witch, approaching, 'gan him fairly° greet   *courteously*
And, with reproach of carelessness° unkind,   *negligence*
Upbraid for leaving her in place unmeet,°   *unfitting*
With foul° words tempering fair, sour gall with honey   *harsh*
    sweet.

4
Unkindness past they 'gan of solace treat,
And bathe in pleasance° of the joyous shade,   *delight*
Which shielded them against the boiling heat
And, with green boughs decking a gloomy glade,
About the fountain like a garland made –
Whose bubbling wave did ever freshly well,
Ne° ever would through fervent summer fade:°   *Nor diminish*
The sacred° nymph, which therein   *consecrated*
    wont° to dwell,   *was accustomed*
Was out of Dian's favour, as it then befell.°   *fell out*

5
The cause was this: one day, when Phoebe fair,
With all her band, was following the chase,
This nymph – quite° tired with heat of scorching air –   *utterly*
Sat down to rest in middest of the race.
The goddess, wroth, 'gan foully° her   *harshly*
    disgrace,°   *disfigure*
And bade the waters (which from her did flow)
Be such as she herself was then in place:°   *there*
Thenceforth her waters waxed dull and slow,
And all that drank thereof did faint and feeble grow.

6

| Hereof this gentle° knight unweeting° was | noble unaware |
| And, lying down upon the sandy grail,° | gravel |

Drank of the stream, as clear as crystal glass:

| Eftsoons° his manly forces 'gan to fail, | Forthwith |

And mighty strong was turned to feeble frail –

His changed powers at first themselves not felt,

Till crudled° cold his courage° 'gan assail,	congealed life force
And cheerful° blood in faintness chill did melt	animating
Which, like a fever fit, through all his body swelt.°	raged†

7

Yet goodly court he made still to his dame,

Poured out in looseness on the grassy ground,

| Both careless of his health and of his fame,° | reputation |
| Till at the last° he heard a dreadful sound | finally |

Which, through the wood loud bellowing, did rebound

| That° all the earth for terror seemed to shake, | So that |

And trees did tremble. The elf, therewith

| astound,° | confounded |
| Upstarted lightly° from his looser° make° | swiftly lewd mate |

And his unready weapons 'gan in hand to take.

8

| But ere he could his armour on him dight° | put on |

Or get his shield, his monstrous enemy

| With sturdy° steps came stalking° in | furious moving clumsily |

his sight –

| An hideous° giant, horrible and high, | huge; abominable |

That with his tallness seemed to threat the sky:

| The ground eke° groaned under him for dread. | also |

His living like saw never living eye,

| Ne durst° behold: his stature did exceed | Nor dared |

The height of three the tallest sons of mortal seed.

9

| The greatest Earth his uncouth° mother was, | rugged;† marvellous |

And blustering Æolus his boasted sire,

Who, with his breath – which through the world doth pass –

| Her hollow womb did secretly inspire,° | breathe into |
| And filled her hidden caves with stormy ire° | wrath [puns on 'air'] |

That° she conceived and, trebling the due time   *So that*
In which the wombs of women do expire,°   *reach fulfilment*[†]
Brought forth this monstrous mass of earthly slime,
Puffed up with wind and filled° with sinful   *also: 'filed' = defiled*
   crime.

10

So, grown great through arrogant delight
   Of the high descent whereof he was yborn,
     And through presumption° of his matchless might,   *pride*
   All other powers, and knighthood, he did scorn.
   Such now he marcheth on this man forlorn°   *alone*
   And left to loss:° his stalking steps are   *destruction*
     stayed°   *supported*
   Upon a snaggy° oak, which he had torn   *knotty*
   Out of his mother's bowels, and it made
His mortal° mace, wherewith his foemen he   *murderous*
   dismayed.°   *vanquished*

11

That,° when the knight he spied, he 'gan   *i.e. the mace*
   advance°   *raise*
   With huge force and insupportable main,°   *irresistible*[†] *strength*
   And towards him with dreadful fury prance,
   Who, hapless° and eke hopeless, all in vain   *luckless*
   Did to him pace sad battle to deraign,°   *engage*
   Disarmed, disgraced, and inwardly dismayed,°   *shamed*
   And eke so faint in every joint and vein
   Through that frail° fountain, which him feeble   *causing frailty*
   made,
That scarcely could he wield his bootless° single blade.   *useless*

12

The giant struck so mainly° merciless   *forcefully*
   That could have overthrown a stony tower
   And, were not° heavenly grace (that him did   *were it not for*
   bless),
   He had been powdered all as thin as flour.
   But he was wary of that deadly stour,°   *tumult; dust*
   And lightly° leapt from underneath the blow: *quickly*

Yet so exceeding was the villain's power
That with the wind it did him overthrow
And all his senses stunned, that° still he lay full low.　　*So that*

13

As when that devilish iron engine° – wrought　　*i.e., cannon*
  In deepest hell and framed° by Furies' skill –　　*fashioned*
  With windy nitre and quick° sulphur fraught°　*ignitable‡　filled*
  And rammed with bullet round (ordained to kill),
  Conceiveth° fire, the heavens it doth fill　　*Catches*
  With thundering noise, and all the air doth choke
  That° none can breathe, nor see, nor hear at will　*So that*
  Through smouldery° cloud of duskish,°　　*smothering†　black‡*
    stinking smoke,
That the only breath° him daunts who hath escaped　*breath alone*
    the stroke:

14

So daunted° when the giant saw the knight,　　*overcome**
  His heavy hand he heaved up on high
  And him to dust thought to have battered quite,°　*utterly*
  Until Duessa loud to him 'gan cry:
  'O great Orgoglio, greatest under sky,
  O hold thy mortal hand for lady's sake –
  Hold for my sake, and do him not to die
  But, vanquished, thine eternal bondslave° make,　*bondsman*
And me, thy worthy meed,° unto thy leman° take.'　*prize　lover*

15

He hearkened, and did stay° from further harms　　*desist*
  To gain so goodly guerdon° as she spake:°　*reward　said*
  So, willingly she came into his arms
  Who her as willingly to grace° did take,　　*[his] favour*
  And was possessed of his new-found make.°　　*mate*
  Then up he took the slumbered,° senseless　　*unconscious†*
    corse°　　*body*
  And, ere he could out of his swoon awake,
  Him to his castle brought with hasty force
And in a dungeon deep him threw without remorse.

16

From that day forth Duessa was his dear,
  And highly honoured in his haughty eye.
  He gave her gold and purple pall° to wear,   *mantle*
  And triple crown set on her head full high,
  And her endowed with royal majesty.
  Then, for to make her dreaded more of men,
  And people's hearts with awful terror tie,°   *constrain*
  A monstrous beast ybred in filthy fen
He chose, which he had kept long time in darksome den.

17

Such one it was as that renowned snake
  Which great Alcides in Stremona slew,
  Long fostered in the filth of Lerna lake,
  Whose many heads, out-budding° ever new,   *budding forth*†
  Did breed him endless labour to subdue:
  But this same monster much more ugly was,
  For seven great heads out of his body grew,
  An iron breast and back of scaly brass
And, all imbrued° in blood, his eyes did shine as glass.   *stained*

18

His tail was stretched out in wondrous length
  That° to the house of heavenly gods it raught° *So that* *reached*
  And, with extorted power and borrowed° strength, *assumed*‡
  The ever-burning lamps from thence it brought
  And proudly threw to ground, as things of nought;
  And underneath his filthy feet did tread
  The sacred things, and holy hests°   *commandments*
    foretaught.°   *taught before*‡
  Upon this dreadful beast with sevenfold head
He set the false Duessa for more awe and dread.

19

The woeful dwarf, which saw his master's fall
  While he had keeping of his grazing steed,
  And valiant knight become a caitiff° thrall,   *base*
  When all was past took up his forlorn°   *abandoned*
    weed° –   *covering*
  His mighty armour, missing most at need;° *when most needed*

His silver shield, now idle, masterless;
  His poinant° spear, that many made to bleed   *piercing*
  (The rueful° monuments of heaviness)° –   *pitiful sorrow*
And with them all departs to tell his great distress.

20

He had not travelled long when, on the way,
  He woeful lady, woeful Una, met,
  Fast-flying from the paynim's° greedy   *pagan's*
    prey°   *preying [on her]*
  Whilst Satyrane him from pursuit did let;°   *obstruct*
  Who, when her eyes she on the dwarf had set,
  And saw the signs that deadly tidings spake,
  She fell to ground for sorrowful regret,°   *upset at events*†
  And lively° breath her sad° breast did *living sorrowful; constant*
    forsake
(Yet might her piteous heart be seen to pant and quake).

21

The messenger of so unhappy news
  Would fain have died: dead was his heart within,
  Yet inwardly some little comfort shows.
  At last, recovering heart, he does begin
  To rub her temples and to chafe her chin,°   *cheek*
  And every tender part does toss and turn
  (So hardly° he the flitted° life does *with difficulty departed*†
    win°   *bid*
  Unto her native prison to return).
Then 'gins her grieved ghost° thus to lament and mourn: *spirit*

22

'Ye dreary instruments of doleful sight°   *i.e., her eyes*
  That do this deadly spectacle behold,
  Why do ye lenger° feed on loathed light,   *longer*
  Or liking° find to gaze on earthly   *pleasure* *
    mould°   *mortal bodies*
  Sith° cruel Fates the care-full threads unfold   *Since*
  The which my life and love together tied?
  Now let the stony dart of senseless cold°   *i.e, Death*
  Pierce to my heart and pass through every side,
And let eternal Night so sad sight from me hide.

23

'O lightsome day, the lamp of highest Jove,
    First made by him men's wandering ways to guide
When darkness he in deepest dungeon drove,
Henceforth thy hated face forever hide,
And shut up heaven's windows shining wide;
For earthly sight can nought but sorrow breed,
And late° repentance, which shall long abide.   *too late*
Mine eyes no more on vanity shall feed
But, seeled° up with death, shall have their deadly   *closed†*
    meed.'°   *reward*

24

Then down again she fell unto the ground,
    But he her quickly reared up again.
Thrice did she sink adown in deadly swound,°   *swoon*
And thrice he her revived with busy° pain.°   *solicitous care*
At last (when life recovered had the rein,
And over-wrestled his strong enemy),
With faltering tongue, and trembling every vein:
'Tell on' (quoth she) 'the woeful tragedy
The which these relics sad present unto mine eye.

25

'Tempestuous Fortune hath spent all her spite,
    And thrilling° Sorrow thrown his utmost dart: *piercing*
Thy sad tongue cannot tell more heavy plight
Than that I feel and harbour in mine heart:
Who hath endured the whole can bear each part.
If death it be, it is not the first wound
That launched° hath my breast with bleeding   *pierced*
    smart.°   *hurt*
Begin, and end the bitter, baleful stound:°   *time of trial**
If less than that I fear, more favour I have found.'

26

Then 'gan the dwarf the whole discourse° declare: *narrative*
    The subtle trains° of Archimago old;   *crafty tricks*
The wanton loves of false Fidesssa fair,
Bought with the blood of vanquished paynim bold;
The wretched pair transformed to treën mould;°   *shape of trees*

    The house of Pride, and perils round about;
    The combat which he with Sansjoy did hold;
    The luckless conflict with the giant stout,°   *terrible;* * *proud*
Wherein captived, of life or death he stood in doubt.

27

She heard with patience all unto the end
    And strove to master sorrowful assay,°   *tribulation*
    Which greater grew the more she did contend°   *struggle*
    And almost rent her tender heart in tway;°   *two*
    And love fresh coals unto her fire did lay,
    For greater love, the greater is the loss.
    Was never lady loved dearer day
    Than she did love the knight of the Red Cross,
For whose dear sake so many troubles her did toss.

28

At last, when fervent sorrow slaked° was,   *abated*
    She up arose, resolving him to find
    Alive or dead, and forward forth doth pass
    All as the dwarf the way to her assigned;
    And evermore, in constant care-full mind,
    She fed her wound with fresh renewed bale.°   *grief;* * *fire*
    Long tossed with storms and beat with bitter wind,
    High over hills and low down over dale,
She wandered many a wood, and measured many a vale.

29

At last she chanced by good hap° to meet   *fortune*
    A goodly° knight, fair° marching by the   *handsome* *splendidly*
      way
    Together with his squire, arrayed meet:°   *as was fitting*
    His glitterand° armour shined far away,   *sparkling*
    Like glancing° light of Phoebus' brightest ray.   *flashing* *
    From top to toe no place appeared bare
    That deadly dint° of steel endanger may;   *blow*
    Athwart° his breast a baldric brave°   *Across* *fine shoulder belt*
      he ware
That shined like twinkling stars with stones most precious° *very*
    rare.

30

And in the midst thereof one precious stone –
  Of wondrous worth, and eke° of wondrous   *also*
    mights,°   *magical powers*
  Shaped like a lady's head – exceeding shone,
  Like Hesperus among the lesser lights,
  And strove for to amaze the weaker sights.
  Thereby his mortal° blade full   *death-dealing*
    comely° hung   *handsomely*
  In ivory sheath ycarved with curious°   *ingenious*
    sleights° –   *designs*
  Whose hilts° were burnished gold, and handle   *hilt-guards*
    strong
Of mother pearl, and buckled with a golden tongue.

31

His haughty° helmet, horrid° all with gold,   *tall bristling*
  Both glorious brightness and great terror bred;
  For all the crest° a dragon did   *apex; heraldic device*
    enfold°   *embrace*†
  With greedy paws, and over all did spread
  His golden wings. His dreadful, hideous, head,
  Close couched° on the beaver,° seemed to throw   *lying visor*
  From flaming mouth bright sparkles fiery red
  That sudden horror to faint hearts did show,
And scaly tail was stretched adown his back full low.

32

Upon the top of all his lofty crest° –   *plume*
  A bunch of hairs, discoloured° diversely,   *many-coloured*
  With sprinkled° pearl and gold full richly dressed – *scattered*†
  Did shake, and seemed to dance for jollity,
  Like to an almond tree ymounted high
  On top of green Selinus all alone,
  With blossoms brave° bedecked daintily,   *splendid*
  Whose tender locks do tremble every one
At every little breath that under heaven is blown.

33

His warlike shield all closely covered was,
  Ne° might of° mortal eye be ever seen:°   *Nor by looked at*
  Not made of steel, nor of enduring brass
  (Such earthly metals soon consumed been),°   *are**
  But all of diamond, perfect, pure and clean°   *unmarked*
  It framed° was, one massy,° entire,°   *fashioned solid complete*
    mould,°   *form*
  Hewn out of adamant rock with engines
    keen,°   *sharp instruments*
  That° point of spear it never piercen could,   *So that*
Ne dint of dreadful sword divide the substance would.

34

The same to wight° he never wont°   *anybody* was accustomed to*
    disclose,
  But whenas° monsters huge he would°   *Except when wished to*
    dismay,°   *conquer*
  Or daunt° unequal armies of his foes,   *stupefy;‡ overcome*
  Or when the flying° heavens° he would   *moving stars*
    affray.°   *frighten*
  For so exceeding shone his glistering° ray   *glittering*
  That Phoebus' golden face it did attaint,°   *sully†*
  As when a cloud his beams doth overlay;
  And silver Cynthia waxed° pale and faint,   *grew*
As when her face is stained with° magic arts'   *by*
    constraint.°   *compulsion‡*

35

No magic arts hereof° had any might,°   *over it power; virtue*
  Nor bloody words of bold enchanter's
    call,°   *invocation [of spirits]*
  But all that was not such as seemed° in sight,   *it appeared*
  Before that shield did fade and sudden fall;
  And when him list° the rascal routs°   *it pleased base rabble*
    appal,
  Men into stones therewith he could transmew,°   *transmute*
  And stones to dust, and dust to nought at all.
  And when him list the prouder° looks subdue,   *too proud*
He would them, gazing, blind, or turn to other hue.°   *form*

36

Ne° let it seem that credence° this exceeds,   *Nor belief*
  For he that made the same was known right well
  To have done much more admirable° deeds: *wonderful*
  It Merlin was, which whilom° did excel   *formerly**
  All living wights° in might of magic spell.   *creatures**
  Both shield, and sword, and armour all he wrought
  For this young prince when first to arms he
    fell;°   *came of age to bear*
  But when he died, the Fairy Queen it brought
To fairyland, where yet it may be seen if sought.

37

A gentle° youth, his dearly-loved squire,   *noble; courteous*
  His spear of heben° wood behind him bare,   *ebony*
  Whose harmful head, thrice heated in the fire,
  Had riven many a breast with pike-head square.
  A goodly° person, and could manage fair°   *of fine bearing well*
  His stubborn steed with curbed° cannon   *strapped*
    bit,°   *tubular bit*[†]
  Who under him did trample as the air,
  And chafed that any on his back should sit:
The iron rowels° into frothy foam he bit.   *knobs on bit*[†]

38

Whenas° this knight nigh to the lady drew,   *When*
  With lovely° court° he 'gan her entertain;   *loving attention*
  But when he heard her answers loath, he knew
  Some secret sorrow did her heart distrain° –   *distress*
  Which to allay, and calm her storming pain,
  Fair-feeling words he wisely 'gan display,°   *express*
  And for her humour° fitting purpose°   *mood speech*
    feign°   *form**
  To tempt the cause itself for to bewray;°   *reveal*
Wherewith enmoved,° these bleeding words she   *much moved*[‡]
  'gan to say:

39

'What world's delight, or joy of living speech,
  Can heart, so plunged in sea of sorrows deep
  And heaped with so huge misfortunes, reach?

The care-full cold beginneth for to creep,
  And in my heart his iron arrow steep,°   *plunge [in blood]*†
  Soon as I think upon my bitter bale.°   *torment*
  Such helpless° harms it's better hidden   *beyond remedy*†
    keep°   *to keep*
  Than rip up° grief where it may not avail:° *rake up*‡ *help*
My last left comfort is, my woes to weep and wail.'

40

'Ah, lady dear,' quoth then the gentle knight,
  'Well may I ween° your grief is wondrous great,   *believe*
  For wondrous great grief groaneth in my sprite
  Whiles thus I hear you of your sorrows treat.
  But, woeful lady, let me you entreat
  For to unfold the anguish of your heart:
  Mishaps are mastered by advice discreet,
  And counsel mitigates the greatest smart:°   *hurt*
Found never help° who never would his   *He never found help*
  hurts impart.'

41

'O but,' quoth she, 'great grief will not be told,
  And can more easily be thought than said.'
  'Right so,' quoth he, 'but he that never would,
  Could never: will to might gives greatest aid.'
  'But grief,' quoth she, 'does greater grow
    displayed,°   *i.e, when revealed*
  If then it find not help, and breeds despair.'
  'Despair breeds not,' quoth he, 'where faith is
    staid.'°   *constant*‡
  'No faith so fast,' quoth she, 'but flesh does pair.'° *impair*
'Flesh may impair,' quoth he, 'but reason can repair.'

42

His goodly reason and well-guided speech
  So deep did settle in her gracious°   *enjoying grace*
    thought°   *grief**
  That her persuaded to disclose the breach
  Which Love and Fortune in her heart had wrought,
  And said: 'Fair sir, I hope good hap° hath brought *chance*
  You to inquire the secrets of my grief,

Or that° your wisdom will direct my thought,   *Either so that*
Or that your prowess can me yield relief.
Then hear the story sad, which I shall tell you brief:

43

'The forlorn° maiden, whom your eyes have seen   *forsaken*
  The laughing stock of Fortune's mockeries,
  Am the only daughter of a king and queen,
  Whose parents dear (whilst equal° destinies°   *impartial stars*
  Did run about,° and their felicities   *revolved*
  The favourable° heavens did not envy)   *auspicious*
  Did spread their rule through all the territories
  Which Pishon and Euphrates floweth by,
And Gihon's golden waves do wash continually.

44

'Till that their cruel, cursed enemy –
  An huge great dragon horrible in sight,
  Bred in the loathly lakes of Tartary –
  With murderous ravin° and devouring might   *voracity*
  Their kingdom spoiled,° and country wasted   *ravaged*
      quite.°   *utterly*
  Themselves, for fear into his jaws to fall,
  He forced to castle strong to take their flight
  Where, fast embarred° in mighty brazen   *imprisoned;† enclosed†*
      wall,
He has them now four years besieged to make them thrall.

45

'Full many knights adventurous and stout°   *brave*
  Have enterprised° that monster to subdue: *undertaken*
  From every coast° that heaven walks about°   *quarter visits*
  Have thither come the noble martial crew
  That famous hard achievements still pursue;
  Yet never any could that garland win,
  But all still shrunk, and still he greater grew.
  All they – for want° of faith or guilt of sin –   *lack*
The piteous prey of his fierce cruelty have been.

46

'At last, yled with far-reported praise
  Which flying Fame throughout the world had spread
  Of doughty knights whom Fairyland did raise –
  That noble Order hight° of Maidenhead –   *named*†*
  Forthwith to court of Glorian' I sped:
  Of Glorian', great queen of glory bright,
  Whose kingdom's seat Cleopolis is read,°   *called**
  There to obtain some such redoubted° knight   *dreaded; revered*
That parents dear from tyrant's power deliver might.

47

'It was my chance° (my chance was fair and good)   *luck*
  There for to find a fresh, unproved° knight,   *untried [in battle]*
  Whose manly hands imbrued in° guilty   *defiled by;* dyed with*
    blood
  Had never been, ne° ever by his might   *nor*
  Had thrown to ground the unregarded right.
  Yet of his prowess proof he since hath made
  (I witness am) in many a cruel fight:
  The groaning ghosts of many one dismayed°   *vanquished*
Have felt the bitter° dint° of his avenging blade.   *biting blow*

48

'And yet the forlorn° relics of his power –   *abandoned*
  His biting sword and his devouring spear,
  Which have endured many a dreadful stour° –   *battle*
  Can speak his prowess, that did erst° you   *formerly*
    bear,°   *i.e. the weapons*
  And well could rule.° Now he hath left you   *control, wield*
    here,
  To be the record° of his rueful loss   *testament*
  And of my doleful° disadventurous dear: *unfortunate*†
  O heavy° record° of the good Redcross,   *sad monument*
Where have you left your lord that could so well you
    toss?°   *wield*†

49

'Well hoped I, and fair beginnings had,
  That he my captive languor° should   *suffering* through captivity*
    redeem

Till, all unweeting,° an enchanter bad   *unknown [to Redcross]*
His sense abused, and made him to misdeem°   *misjudge*
My loyalty not such° as it did seem: *to be not such*
That rather death desire than such despite.°   *outrage*
Be judge, ye heavens, that all things right esteem,°   *value‡*
How I him loved, and love, with all my might:
So thought I eke° of him, and think I thought aright.   *too*

50

'Thenceforth me, desolate, he quite forsook,
  To wander where wild Fortune would me lead,
  And other byways he himself betook
  Where never foot of living wight° did tread   *creature**
  That brought not back the baleful° body dead;   *sinful*
  In which him chanced false Duessa meet –
  Mine only foe, mine only deadly dread,
  Who, with her witchcraft and misseeming°   *false*
    sweet,°   *sweetness*
Inveigled° him to follow her desires unmeet.° *Seduced‡ unworthy*

51

'At last by subtle sleights she him betrayed
  Unto his foe, a giant huge and tall,
  Who him disarmed, dissolute, dismayed,°   *fearful*
  Unwares surprised and, with mighty mall,°   *mace; mallet*
  The monster merciless him made to fall,
  Whose fall did never foe before behold.
  And now in darksome dungeon, wretched thrall,
  Remediless° for aye,° he doth him hold: *Beyond help eternally*
That is my cause of grief, more great than may be told.'

52

Ere she had ended all she 'gan to faint,
  But he her comforted and fair bespake:
  'Certes,° madam, ye have great cause of plaint   *Indeed*
  That stoutest heart, I ween,° could cause to quake.   *believe*
  But be of cheer, and comfort to you take,
  For, till I have acquit° your captive knight,   *rescued; ransomed*
  Assure yourself I will not you forsake.'
  His cheerful words revived her cheerless sprite,
So forth they went, the dwarf them guiding ever right.

Canto 8

Fair virgin, to redeem her dear,
   Brings Arthur to the fight,
Who slays the giant, wounds the beast,
   And strips Duessa quite.°   *utterly*

1

Aye me, how many perils do enfold
  The righteous man to make him daily fall,
  Were not that heavenly grace doth him uphold,
  And steadfast truth acquit him out of all!
  Her love is firm, her care continual,
  So oft as he through his own foolish pride
  Or weakness is to sinful bands° made thrall –   *the chains of sin*
  Else should this Redcross knight in bands have died,
For whose deliverance she this prince doth thither guide.

2

They sadly travelled thus until they came
  Nigh to a castle builded strong and high.
  Then cried the dwarf: 'Lo, yonder is the same
  In which my lord, my liege, doth luckless lie,
  Thrall to that giant's hateful tyranny:
  Therefore, dear sir, your mighty powers assay.'°   *prove*
  The noble knight alighted by and by°   *straight away*
  From lofty steed, and bade the lady stay,
To see what end of fight should him befall that day.

3

So with the squire, the admirer° of   *one who regards with wonder*†
    his might,
  He marched forth towards the castle wall,
  Whose gates he found fast shut, ne° living wight° *nor* *person**
  To ward° the same, nor answer comer's call.   *guard*
  Then took that squire a horn of bugle
    small,°   *made from small wild ox tusk*
  Which hung adown his side in twisted gold

And tassels gay. Wide wonders over all°   *everywhere*
Of that same horn's great virtues° weren told,   *powers*
Which had approved° been in uses manifold.°   *proved   many*

4

Was never wight that° heard that   *Nobody* ever*
   shrilling° sound   *piercing‡*
But trembling fear did feel in every vein:
Three miles it might be easy° heard around,   *easily*
And echoes three answered itself again.
No false enchantment nor deceitful train°   *stratagem*
Might once abide the terror of that blast
But presently° was void and wholly vain:°   *at once   futile*
No gate so strong, no lock so firm and fast,
But with that piercing noise flew open quite, or brast.°   *shattered*

5

The same before the giant's gate he blew
   That° all the castle quaked from the ground   *So that*
And every door of free will open flew.
The giant self,° dismayed with that sound   *himself*
Where he with his Duessa dalliance found,
In haste came rushing forth from inner bower°   *chamber*
With staring countenance stern° (as one   *fierce*
   astound)°   *confounded*
And staggering steps, to weet° what sudden   *discover*
   stour°   *tumult*
Had wrought that horror strange, and dared his dreaded
   power.

6

And after him the proud Duessa came,
   High mounted on her many-headed beast:
And every head with fiery tongue did flame,
And every head was crowned on his crest,°   *its apex*
And bloody-mouthed with late cruel feast.
That, when the mighty knight beheld, his mighty shield
Upon his manly arm he soon addressed,°   *prepared*
And at him fiercely flew, with courage filled,
And eager greediness through every member thrilled.°   *penetrated*

7

Therewith the giant buckled° him to fight,   *girded*‡
  Inflamed with scornful wrath and high° disdain,°   *great anger*
  And, lifting up his dreadful club on height
  (All armed with ragged snubs° and knotty grain),   *snags*‡
  Him thought at first encounter to have slain.
  But wise and wary was that noble peer°   *knight; equal*
  And, lightly leaping from so monstrous main,°   *force*
  Did fair° avoid the violence him near: *completely*
It booted° nought to think such thunderbolts to bear.   *availed*

8

Ne° shame he thought to shun so hideous°   *Nor such great*
  might:
  The idle stroke, enforcing furious way,
  Missing the mark of his misaimed sight,
  Did fall to ground and, with his heavy sway,°   *momentum*
  So deeply dinted in° the driven clay   *struck into*
  That three yards deep a furrow up did throw.
  The sad° Earth, wounded with so sore°   *heavy great*
  assay,°   *assault*
  Did groan full grievous underneath the blow
And, trembling with strange fear, did like an earthquake show:

9

As when almighty Jove, in wrathful mood,
  To wreak° the guilt of mortal sins is bent,   *punish*
  Hurls forth his thundering dart, with deadly feud,
  Enrolled in flames and smouldering°   *smoky*‡
  dreariment,°   *dreariness*‡
  Through riven clouds and molten firmament:
  The fierce, three-forked engine,° making way,   *instrument*
  Both lofty towers and highest trees hath rent,
  And all that might his° angry passage stay,°   *its prevent*
And, shooting in the earth, casts up a mound of clay.

10

His boisterous° club, so buried in the ground,   *huge*‡
  He could not rearen up again so light°   *quickly*
  But that the knight him at advantage found;
  And whiles he strove his cumbered° club to   *hampered*‡

quite°   *release*
Out of the earth, with blade all burning bright
He smote off his left arm which, like a block,
Did fall to ground, deprived of native might.
Large streams of blood out of the trunked°   *truncated*
    stock°   *stump*
Forth gushed, like fresh water stream from riven rock.

                                    11
Dismayed° with so desperate deadly wound,   *Overcome*
    And eke° impatient of unwonted° pain,   *also unaccustomed*
    He loudly brayed° with beastly, yelling   *cried out in pain**
        sound
    That° all the fields rebellowed° again: *So that re-echoed*†
    As great a noise as when, in Cymbrian plain,
    An herd of bulls, whom kindly° rage° doth   *natural craving*
        sting,
    Do for the milky mothers' want° complain   *lack*
    And fill the fields with troublous bellowing,
The neigbour woods around with hollow murmur°   *complaint*
    ring.

                                    12
That when his dear Duessa heard, and saw
    The evil stound° that dangered her estate,°   *blow state*
    Unto his aid she hastily did draw
    Her dreadful beast who, swollen with blood of late,
    Came ramping° forth with proud, presumptuous gait *raging*
    And threatened° all his heads like flaming   *i.e., harm with*
        brands.°   *swords*
    But him the squire made quickly to retreat,
    Encountering fierce with single sword° in hand,   *sword alone*
And 'twixt him and his lord did like a bulwark stand.

                                    13
The proud Duessa, full of wrathful spite
    And fierce disdain° to be   *anger*
        affronted° so,   *confronted;‡ attacked*†
    Enforced° her purple beast with all her might   *Forced*
    That stop° out of the way to overthrow,   *obstruction*

Scorning the let° of so unequal foe.   *hindrance*
But nathemore° would that courageous swain   *by no means**
To her yield passage 'gainst his lord to go,
But with outrageous strokes did him restrain,
And with his body barred the way atwixt them twain.

14

Then took the angry witch her golden cup
  Which still° she bore, replete with magic arts   *yet; always*
  (Death and despair did many thereof sup,
  And secret poison through their inner parts,
  The eternal bale° of heavy-wounded hearts),   *torment*
  Which, after charms and some enchantments said,
  She lightly sprinkled on his weaker° parts.   *too weak*
  Therewith his sturdy courage soon was quayed°   *subdued†*
And all his senses were with sudden dread dismayed.°   *overcome*

15

So down he fell before the cruel beast,
  Who on his neck his bloody claws did seize°   *fasten*
  That life nigh crushed out of his panting breast:
  No power he had to stir, nor will to rise.
  That when the careful° knight 'gan well   *full of care*
    advise,°   *observe*
  He lightly° left the foe with whom he fought   *quickly*
  And to the beast 'gan turn his enterprise° –   *bravery*
  For wondrous anguish in his heart it wrought
To see his loved squire into such thraldom brought –

16

And, high advancing° his bloodthirsty blade,   *raising*
  Struck one of those deformed heads so sore°   *hard*
  That of his puissance proud example made.
  His monstrous scalp° down to his teeth it tore,   *skull*
  And that misformed° shape misshaped more: *misshapen†*
  A sea of blood gushed from the gaping wound
  That her gay garments stained with filthy gore
  And overflowed all the field around,
That° over shoes in blood he waded on the ground.   *So that*

17

Thereat he roared for exceeding pain
  That, to have heard, great horror would have bred,
  And, scourging the empty air with his long train,°   *tail*
  Through great impatience of his grieved° head   *wounded*
  His gorgeous rider from her lofty stead°   *place*
  Would have cast down and trod in dirty mire,
  Had not the giant soon her succoured –
  Who, all enraged with smart° and frantic ire,   *hurt*
Came hurtling° in full fierce, and forced the knight   *clattering*
  retire.

18

The force, which wont° in two to be dispersed,   *was customarily*
  In one alone° left hand he now unites,   *remaining*
  Which is through rage more strong than both were
    erst:°   *formerly*
  With which his hideous° club aloft he dights°   *huge lifts†*
  And at his foe with furious rigour smites,
  That strongest oak might seem to overthrow.
  The stroke upon his shield so heavy lights
  That to the ground it doubleth° him full low: *bends*
What mortal wight° could ever bear so monstrous   *creature**
  blow?

19

And, in his fall, his shield – that covered was –
  Did loose his veil by chance, and open flew:
  The light whereof, that heaven's light did pass,°   *surpass*
  Such blazing brightness through the air threw
  That eye mote° not the same endure to view.   *might*
  Which, when the giant spied with staring eye,
  He down let fall his arm, and soft withdrew
  His weapon huge, that heaved was on high
For to have slain the man, that on the ground did lie.

20

And eke° the fruitful°-headed beast,   *in addition i.e., many*
  amazed°   *shocked*
  At flashing beams of that sunshiny shield,
  Became stark blind, and all his senses dazed,

That° down he tumbled on the dirty field,   *So that*
And seemed himself as conquered to yield:
Whom, when his mistress proud perceived to fall,
Whiles yet his feeble feet for faintness reeled,
Unto the giant loudly she 'gan call,
'O help, Orgoglio, help, or else we perish all!'

21

At her so piteous cry was much amoved°   *aroused*
  Her champion stout° and, for to aid his   *fierce; proud*
    friend,°   *lover*
Again his wonted angry weapon proved° –   *made trial of*
But all in vain. For he has read his end
In that bright shield, and all their forces spend
Themselves in vain; for, since that glancing° sight,   *dazzling*
He hath no power to hurt, nor to defend:
As, where the Almighty's lightning brand° does   *blade*
  light,°   *alight*
It dims the dazed° eyen and daunts the senses quite.   *dazzled*

22

Whom when the prince to battle new addressed
  And threatening high his dreadful stroke did see,
  His sparkling blade about his head he blessed°   *brandished*[t]
And smote off quite° his right leg by the knee,   *completely*
That° down he tumbled. As an aged tree,   *So that*
High-growing on the top of rocky clift,°   *cliff*
  Whose heart strings with keen steel hewen be,
The mighty trunk, half rent, with ragged rift°   *splitting*
Doth roll adown the rocks, and fall with fearful drift;°   *force*

23

Or as a castle, reared high and round,
  By subtle engines° and malicious sleight   *ingenious deceit*
  Is undermined from the lowest ground,
And her foundation forced° and   *overcome;*[‡] *broken open*[t]
  feebled quite,°   *utterly*
At last down falls, and with her heaped height
Her hasty ruin° does more heavy make,   *fall*
And yields itself unto the victor's might:

Such was this giant's fall, that seemed to shake
The steadfast globe of earth as° it for fear did shake.　　　*as if*

24

The knight, then lightly leaping to the prey,
　With mortal steel him smote again so sore°　　　　　　*hard*
　That headless his unwieldy° body lay,　　　*ponderous;‡ incapable*
All wallowed° in his own foul bloody gore,°　*lying blood; slime*
Which flowed from his wounds in wondrous
　　store.°　　　　　　　　　　　　　　　　　　*abundance*
　But, soon as breath out of his breast did pass,
　That huge great body, which the giant bore,
　Was vanished quite, and of that monstrous mass
Was nothing left, but like an empty bladder was.

25

Whose grievous fall when false Duessa spied,
　Her golden cup she cast unto the ground,
　And crowned mitre rudely° threw aside.　　　　　*roughly*
Such piercing grief her stubborn heart did wound
That she could not endure that doleful stound°　*time of pain**
　But, leaving all behind her, fled away.
　The lightfoot° squire her quickly turned around　*light-footed*
　And, by hard means° enforcing her to stay,　*with difficulty*
So brought unto his lord as his deserved prey.

26

The royal virgin, which beheld from far
　In pensive° plight and sad perplexity,°　　*anxious distress*
　The whole achievement° of this doubtful war,　　*process*
Came running fast to greet° his victory　　　*congratulate*
With sober° gladness and mild modesty,　　　　　*quiet*
　And with sweet joyous cheer° him thus　　　　*face*
　　bespake:°　　　　　　　　　　　　　　　*addressed†*
'Fair branch of noblesse,° flower of chivalry,　*nobleness*
　That with your worth the world amazed° make,　*astonished†*
How shall I quite° the pains ye suffer for my sake?　*requite*

27

'And you,° fresh bud of virtue springing fast,   *i.e., the squire*
   Whom these sad eyes saw nigh unto death's door,
   What hath poor virgin, for such peril past,
   Wherewith you to reward? Accept, therefore,
   My simple° self, and service evermore.   *innocent, humble*
   And He that high does sit, and all things see
   With equal° eyes, their merits to restore,°   *impartial reward*
   Behold° what ye this day have done for me   *i.e, may He behold*
And what I cannot quite, requite with usury.°   *interest*

28

'But sith° the heavens, and your fair   *since*
      handling,°   *management‡*
   Have made you master of the field this day,
   Your fortune master eke° with governing   *also*
   And, well begun, end all so° well, I pray.   *as*
   Ne° let that wicked woman 'scape away,   *Nor*
   For she it is that did my lord bethrall° –   *enslave†*
   My dearest lord – and deep in dungeon lay,
   Where he his better days hath wasted° all.   *consumed*
O hear, how piteous° he to you for aid does call.'   *piteously*

29

Forthwith he gave in charge unto his squire
   That scarlet whore to keepen carefully,
   Whiles he himself, with greedy great desire,
   Into the castle entered forcibly,
   Where living creature none he did espy.
   Then 'gan he loudly through the house to call,
   But no man cared to answer to his cry.
   There reigned a solemn silence over all,
Nor voice was heard, nor wight° was seen in bower or   *person**
      hall.

30

At last, with creeping crooked pace, forth came
   An old, old man, with beard as white as snow,
   That on a staff his feeble steps did frame°   *direct‡*
   And guide his weary gait both to and fro,
   For his eyesight him failed long ygo.°   *ago**

And on his arm a bunch of keys he bore,
The which, unused, rust did overgrow:
Those were the keys of every inner door,
But he could not them use, but kept them still in store.°   *laid by*

31

But very uncouth° sight was to behold   *strange*
　How he did fashion his untoward° pace,   *ungainly*[†]
　For, as he forward moved his footing° old,°   *walking*[‡] *aged*
　So backward still was turned his wrinkled face –
　Unlike to men, who, ever as they trace,°   *proceed*
　Both feet and face one way are wont° to lead.   *accustomed*
　This was the ancient keeper of that place,
　And foster father of the giant dead:
His name, Ignaro, did his nature right aread.°   *declare*

32

His reverend hairs and holy gravity
　The knight much honoured, as beseemed° well,   *befitted*
　And gently° asked, where all the people be,   *courteously*
　Which in that stately building wont to dwell;°   *usually lived*
　Who answered him full soft, he could not tell.
　Again he asked, where that same knight was laid
　Whom great Orgoglio in his puissance fell°   *fierce*
　Had made his caitiff° thrall.° Again he said   *wretched prisoner*
He could not tell, ne° ever other answer made.   *nor*

33

Then asked he, which way he in might pass:
　He could not tell, again he answered.
　Thereat the courteous knight displeased was,
　And said: 'Old sire, it seems thou hast not read°   *learned*
　How ill it sits with° that same silver head   *befits*
　In vain to mock, or mocked in vain to be:
　But if thou be, as thou art portrayed
　With Nature's pen, in age's grave
　　degree,°   *at the stage of aged gravity*
Aread° in graver wise what I demand° of thee.'   *Declare ask*

34

His answer likewise was, he could not tell –
  Whose senseless speech and doted° ignorance   *foolish*
  Whenas° the noble prince had marked well,   *When*
  He guessed his nature by his countenance,°   *demeanour*
  And calmed his wrath with goodly temperance.
  Then, to him stepping, from his arm did reach
  Those keys, and made himself free entrance.
  Each door he opened without any breach:°   *breaking down*
There was no bar to stop, nor foe him to impeach.°   *obstruct‡*

35

There all within full rich arrayed° he found   *very richly furnished**
  With royal arras° and resplendent gold,   *tapestries*
  And did with store° of everything abound   *abundance*
  That greatest prince's presence might behold.
  But all the floor (too filthy to be told)
  With blood of guiltless babes and innocents° true –   *martyrs*
  Which there were slain as sheep out of the fold –
  Defiled was, that dreadful was to view;
And sacred ashes° over it was strewed   *i.e., of burned martyrs*
  new.°   *newly*

36

And there beside, of marble stone, was built
  An altar carved with cunning° imagery°   *skilful; magic images*
  On which true Christian blood was often spilt,
  And holy martyrs often done° to die   *made*
  With cruel malice and strong tyranny:
  Whose blessed spirits from underneath the stone
  To God for vengeance cried continually,
  And with great grief were often heard to groan,
That° hardest heart would bleed to hear their piteous   *So that*
  moan.

37

Through every room he sought, and every bower,°   *chamber*
  But nowhere could he find that woeful thrall.
  At last he came unto an iron door
  That fast was locked, but key found not at all

Amongst that bunch to open it withal;
But in the same a little grate° was pight,°   *grating placed*
Through which he sent his voice, and loud did call
With all his power to weet° if living wight   *know*
Were housed there within, whom he enlargen° might.   *liberate*

38

Therewith an hollow, dreary, murmuring° voice   *lamenting*
These piteous plaints and dolours° did resound: *grievings*
'O who is that which brings me happy choice
Of death, that here lie dying every stound,°   *moment*
Yet live perforce° in baleful° darkness   *by compulsion deadly*
    bound?
For now three moons have changed thrice their
    hue,°   *aspect; colour*
And have been thrice hid underneath the ground,
Since I the heavens' cheerful face did view.
O welcome, thou, that dost of death bring tidings true.'

39

Which, when that champion heard, with piercing point
Of pity dear° his heart was thrilled°   *dire pierced*
    sore,°   *sharply*
And trembling° horror ran through every joint   *shuddering*
For ruth of gentle knight so foul° forlore;°   *appallingly lost*
Which, shaking off, he rent that iron door
With furious force and indignation fell:°   *fierce*
Where entered in, his foot could find no floor,
But all a deep descent as dark as hell,
That breathed ever forth a filthy, baneful° smell.   *poisonous*†

40

But neither darkness foul, nor filthy bands,°   *chains*
Nor noyous° smell, his purpose could   *noxious*
    withhold° –   *prevent*
Entire° affection hateth nicer° hands –   *Absolute squeamish*
But that, with constant zeal and courage bold,
After long pains and labours manifold,
He found the means that prisoner up to rear:°   *raise to his feet*†
Whose feeble thighs, unable to uphold

His pined° corse,° him scarce to light could   *wasted body*
  bear –
A rueful spectacle of death and ghastly drear.°   *wretchedness*

41

His sad° dull eyes, deep sunk in hollow pits,   *heavy*
  Could not endure the unwonted° sun to view;   *unaccustomed*
  His bare, thin cheeks, for want° of better°   *lack good*
    bits,°   *food*
  And empty sides deceived of their due,
  Could make a stony heart his hap° to rue;   *(mis)fortune*
  His raw-bone° arms, whose mighty brawned°   *gaunt brawny*
    bowers°   *muscles†*
  Were wont to rive steel plates, and helmets hew,
  Were clean° consumed, and all his vital powers   *completely*
Decayed, and all his flesh shrunk up like withered flowers.

42

Whom, when his lady saw, to him she ran
  With hasty joy: to see him made her glad,
  And sad to view his visage pale and wan,°   *pale; despairing*
  Who erst° in flowers of freshest youth was clad.   *formerly*
  Tho,° when her well of tears she wasted° had,   *Then spent*
  She said: 'Ah, dearest lord, what evil star
  On you hath frowned and poured his
    influence° bad,   *astrological power*
  That of your self ye thus berobbed are,
And this misseeming° hue° your manly   *inappropriate aspect*
  looks doth mar?

43

'But welcome now, my lord, in weal or
  woe,°   *in prosperity or misfortune*
  Whose presence I have lacked too long a day:
  And fie on Fortune, mine avowed foe,
  Whose wrathful wreaks° themselves do now allay,   *injuries*
  And for these wrongs shall treble penance pay
  Of treble good: good grows of evil's prief.'°   *proof; experience*
  The cheerless man, whom sorrow did dismay,°   *vanquish*
  Had no delight to treaten° of his grief: *discuss*
His long-endured famine needed more relief.

44

'Fair lady,' then said that victorious knight,
  'The things that grievous were to do or bear,
  Them to renew,° I wote,° breeds no delight: *rehearse know*
  Best music breeds delight in loathing ear,
  But the only° good that grows of passed fear   *main*
  Is to be wise, and ware° of like again.   *wary*
  This day's example hath this lesson dear°   *extreme*
  Deep written in my heart with iron pen:
That bliss may not abide in state of mortal men.

45

'Henceforth, sir knight, take to you wonted° strength,   *former*
  And master these mishaps with patient might:
  Lo, where your foe lies stretched in monstrous length,
  And lo, that wicked woman in your sight,
  The root of all your care and wretched plight,°   *trouble*
  Now in your power to let her live or die.'
  'To do her die' (quoth Una) 'were°   *would be*
    despite,°   *vindictive*
  And shame to avenge so weak an enemy:
But spoil° her of her scarlet robe, and let her fly.'   *despoil*

46

So as she bade that witch they disarrayed,°   *disrobed*
  And robbed of royal robes and purple pall,°   *mantle*
  And ornaments that richly were displayed:°   *laid out*
  Ne° spared they to strip her naked all.°   *Neither completely*
  Then when they had despoiled her, tiar'° and   *coronet*
    caul,°   *cap; net*
  Such as she was their eyes might her behold,
  That° her misshaped parts did them appall –   *So that*
  A loathly, wrinkled hag, ill-favoured, old,
Whose secret° filth good manners biddeth not be told.   *hidden*

47

Her crafty° head was altogether bald   *guileful*
  And, as in hate of honourable eld,°   *old age*
  Was overgrown with scurf and filthy scald;°   *scabs; ringworm*
  Her teeth out of her rotten gums were felled,
  And her sour breath abominably smelled;

Her dried dugs,° like bladders lacking wind,   *breasts*
Hung down, and filthy matter from them welled;
Her wrizzled° skin, as rough as maple   *wrinkled; shrivelled*
   rind,°   *bark*
So scabby was that would have loathed° all   *excited disgust in*
   womankind.

48

Her nether parts, the shame of all her kind,
  My chaster° Muse for shame doth blush to write;   *too chaste*
  But at her rump she growing had behind
  A fox's tail, with dung all foully dight;°   *smeared; befouled†*
  And eke° her feet most monstrous were in sight,   *in addition*
  For one of them was like an eagle's claw,
  With gripping talons armed to greedy fight,
  The other, like a bear's uneven° paw: *rugged*
More ugly shape yet never living creature saw.

49

Which, when the knights beheld, amazed they were,
  And wondered at so foul deformed wight.
  'Such, then,' said Una, 'as she seemeth here,
  Such is the face of Falsehood: such the sight
  Of foul Duessa when her borrowed light
  Is laid away, and counterfeisance° known.'   *fraud, deceit†*
  Thus, when they had the witch disrobed quite,°   *completely*
  And all her filthy feature° open shown,   *form*
They let her go at will, and wander ways unknown.

50

She, flying fast from heaven's hated face,
  And from the world that her discovered wide,°   *extensively*
  Fled to the wasteful° wilderness apace,   *desolate*
  From living eyes her open shame to hide,
  And lurked in rocks and caves long unespied.
  But that fair crew° of knights, and Una fair,   *band*
  Did in that castle afterwards abide
  To rest themselves, and weary powers repair,°   *restore*
Where store° they found of all that dainty° was   *plenty   choice*
   and rare.

Canto 9

His loves and lineage Arthur tells;
  The knights knit friendly bands;°   *bonds*
Sir Trevisan flies fron Despair,
  Whom Redcross knight withstands.

1

O goodly golden chain, wherewith yfere°   *together*
 The virtues linked are in lovely° wise,°   *loving fashion*
 And the noble minds of yore allied were
 In brave pursuit of chivalrous emprise,°   *enterprise*
 That° none did others' safety despise,°   *So that disregard*
 Nor aid envy° to him in need that stands,   *begrudge*
 But, friendly, each did others' praise devise
 How to advance with favourable hands,
As this good prince redeemed the Redcross knight from bands.

2

Who, when their powers (impaired through labour long)
 With due repast they had recured° well,   *restored*
 And that weak captive knight now waxed° strong,   *grew*
 Them list° no longer there at leisure dwell   *wished*
 But forward fare, as their adventures fell.
 But, ere they parted, Una fair besought
 That stranger knight his name and nation tell,
 Lest so great good as he for her had wrought
Should die unknown, and buried be in thankless thought.

3

'Fair virgin,' said the prince, 'ye me require°   *ask of*
 A thing without° the compass° of my   *beyond scope*
  wit,°   *knowledge*
 For both the lineage and the certain sire
 From which I sprang from me are hidden yet.
 For, all so soon as° life did me admit   *as soon as*
 Into this world, and showed heaven's light,
 From mother's pap° I taken was unfit,°   *breast unready*

And straight delivered to a fairy knight
To be upbrought in gentle° thews° and martial   *noble virtues*
   might.

4

'Unto old Timon he me brought belive° –   *straightway*
  Old Timon who, in youthly years, had been
  In warlike feats the expertest man alive,
  And is the wisest now on earth, I ween.°   *believe*
  His dwelling is low in a valley green,
  Under the foot of Rauran mossy hoar,°   *silvery with moss*
  From whence the river Dee, as silver clean,°   *bright*
  His tumbling billows rolls with gentle roar:
There all my days he trained me up in virtuous
   lore.°   *knowledge of virtue*

5

Thither the great magician, Merlin, came,
  As was his use,° oft-times to visit me;   *custom*
  For he had charge my discipline° to frame,° *education organise*
  And tutor's nouriture° to oversee.   *upbringing*
  Him oft and oft I asked, in privity,°   *secret*
  Of what loins and what lineage I did spring –
  Whose answer bade me still assured be
  That I was son and heir unto a king,
As Time in her just° term° the truth to light would *allotted span*
   bring.'

6

'Well worthy imp,'° then said the lady   *child*
  gent,°   *noble; courteously*
  And pupil fit for such a tutor's hand.
  But what adventure, or what high° intent,°   *noble undertaking*
  Hath brought you hither into Fairyland,
  Aread,° Prince Arthur, crown of martial   *Declare*
  band!'°   *company*
  'Full hard it is,' quoth he, 'to read° aright   *interpret*
  The course of heavenly cause, or understand
  The secret° meaning of the eternal might   *hidden*
That rules men's ways, and rules the thoughts of living
   wight.°   *creature**

7

'For whether He° through fatal deep   *God*
    foresight°   *ordained by fate*
    Me hither sent, for cause to me unguessed;
    Or that fresh, bleeding wound (which day and night
    Whilom° doth rankle in my riven breast)   *Constantly**
    With forced° fury° following his behest   *impelling frenzy*
    Me hither brought by ways yet never found,
    You to have helped, I hold myself yet° blessed.'   *even now*
    'Ah, courteous knight,' quoth she, 'what secret wound
Could ever find° to grieve the gentlest heart on   *contrive*
    ground?'°   *on earth*

8

'Dear dame,' quoth he, 'you sleeping sparks awake
    Which, troubled once, into huge flames will grow,
    Ne° ever will their fervent° fury slake   *Nor burning*
    Till living moisture° into smoke   *i.e., of the body's four humours**
    do flow,
    And wasted° life do lie in ashes low.   *consumed*
    Yet sithens° silence lesseneth not my fire   *since*
    But, told, it flames and, hidden, it does glow,
    I will reveal what ye so much desire:
Ah, Love,° lay down thy bow, the whiles I may   *Cupid*
    respire.°   *take breath*†

9

It was in freshest flower of youthly years,
    When courage° first does creep in manly   *the vital force*
    chest,°   *breast*
    Then first the coal of kindly° heat appears   *natural*
    To kindle love in every living breast:
    But me had warned old Timon's wise behest
    Those creeping flames by reason to subdue
    Before their rage grew to so great unrest
    As miserable° lovers use to° rue,   *wretched customarily*
Which still° wax° old in woe whiles woe still waxeth   *ever grow*
    new.

10

'That idle name of love, and lover's life,
 As loss of time and Virtue's enemy
 I ever scorned, and joyed° to stir up strife   *rejoiced*
 In middest of their mournful tragedy –
 Aye° wont° to laugh when them I heard to cry,   *Always used*
 And blow the fire which them to ashes burnt.
 Their god himself, grieved at my liberty,°   *freedom [from love]*
 Shot many a dart at me with fierce intent,
But I them warded all with wary
   government.'°   *conduct; control of passions*

11

'But all in vain: no fort can be so strong,
 Ne° fleshly breast can armed be so sound,   *Nor*
 But will at last be won with battery long,
 Or unawares at disadvantage found.
 Nothing is sure that grows on earthly ground,
 And who most trusts in arm of fleshly might,
 And boasts in beauty's chain not to be bound,
 Doth soonest fall in disadventurous° fight   *disastrous*†
And yields his caitiff° neck to victor's most   *coward's*
   despite.°   *malice*

12

'Example make of him your hapless° joy,   *luckless*‡
 And of myself now mated,° as you see;   *confounded*‡*
 Whose prouder° vaunt that proud avenging boy   *too proud*
 Did soon pluck down, and curbed my liberty.
 For, on a day,° pricked forth° with jollity   *one day spurred on*
 Of looser life and heat of hardiment,°   *daring*
 Ranging° the forest wide on courser   *Roaming*‡
   free,°   *unrestrained*
 The fields, the floods,° the heavens with one consent   *rivers*
Did seem to laugh on me, and favour mine intent.° *will; outlook*

13

'Forwearied° with my sports I did alight   *Tired out*‡
 From lofty steed, and down to sleep me laid:
 The verdant grass my couch did goodly° dight,° *well compose*
 And pillow was my helmet fair displayed.°   *laid out*

Whiles every sense the humour° sweet   *dew [of sleep]*
   embayed°   *bathed*
And, slumbering soft, my heart did steal away,
Me seemed by my side a royal maid
Her dainty limbs full softly down did lay:
So fair a creature yet saw never sunny day.

14

'Most goodly glee° and lovely° blandishment°   *joy loving*
   blandishment°   *flattery*†
She to me made, and bade me love her dear,
For dearly sure her love was to me bent°   *aimed*
As, when just time expired,° should appear.   *in due course*
But whether dreams delude, or true it were,
Was never heart so ravished with delight,
Ne living man like words did ever hear
As she to me delivered all that night,
And, at her parting, said she Queen of Fairies
   hight.°   *was called**†

15

'When I awoke and found her place devoid,°   *empty*
   And nought but pressed grass where she had lain,
I sorrowed all so° much as erst° I   *just as formerly*
   joyed,°   *rejoiced*
And washed all her place with watery eyen.°   *eyes*
From that day forth I loved that face divine;
From that day forth I cast° in careful° mind   *resolved troubled*
To seek her out with labour and long tine°   *difficulty*†
And never vow to rest till her I find:
Nine months I seek in vain, yet n'ill° that vow unbind.'   *will not*

16

Thus as he spake his visage waxed pale,
   And change of hue° great passion did bewray.°   *colour reveal*
Yet still he strove to cloak his inward bale,°   *fire; pain*
And hide the smoke that did his fire display,
Till gentle Una thus to him 'gan say:
'O happy Queen of Fairies, that hast found,
'Mongst many, one that with his prowess may

Defend thine honour, and thy foes confound:
True-loves° are often sown, but seldom grow on   *the herb Paris*
   ground.'°   *earth*

17

'Thine, O then,' said the gentle° Redcross   *noble; courteous*
   knight,
  'Next to that lady's love shall be the place,
  O fairest virgin, full of heavenly light,
  Whose wondrous faith,° exceeding earthly race,   *fidelity*
  Was firmest fixed in mine extremest case.
  And you, my lord, the patron° of my life,   *gaurdian; saint*
  Of that great queen may well gain worthy grace:
  For only worthy you° through   *For you alone are worthy*
   prowess' prief°   *test*
If living man mote° worthy be, to be her lief.'°   *might   beloved*

18

So, diversely° discoursing of their loves,   *variously*
  The golden sun his glistering° head 'gan show,   *glittering*
  And sad remembrance now the prince amoves°   *stirs**
  With fresh desire his voyage to pursue:
  Als'° Una yearned her travel° to renew.   *Also   journey; toil*
  Then those two knights, fast friendship for to bind
  And love establish each to other true,
  Gave goodly gifts – the signs of grateful mind –
And eke,° as pledges firm, right hands together joined.   *also*

19

Prince Arthur gave a box of diamond°   *(1) the gem; (2) adamant*
  sure,°   *pure*
  Embowed° with gold and gorgeous ornament,   *encircled*[†]
  Wherein were closed° few drops of liquor pure   *enclosed*
  Of wondrous worth and virtue excellent,°   *supreme power*
  That any wound could heal incontinent:°   *forthwith*
  Which, to requite,° the Redcross knight him gave   *repay*[‡]
  A book, wherein his Saviour's testament
  Was writ with golden letters rich and brave° –   *splendid*
A work of wondrous grace, and able souls to save.

20

Thus been they parted:° Arthur on his way   *i.e., Thus they parted*
   To seek his love, and the other for to fight
   With Una's foe, that all her realm did prey.°   *ravage*
   But she, now weighing the decayed plight
   And shrunken sinews of her chosen knight,
   Would not awhile her forward course pursue,
   Ne° bring him forth in face of dreadful fight,   *Nor*
   Till he recovered had his former hue° –   *aspect*
For him to be yet weak and weary well she knew.

21

So, as they travelled, lo, they 'gan espy
   An armed knight towards them gallop fast
   That seemed from some feared foe to fly,
   Or other grisly° thing that him aghast.°   *horrible terrified*
   Still° as he fled his eye was backward cast,   *Ever*
   As if his fear still followed him behind:
   Als' flew his steed as° he his bands° had   *as if reins*
     brast,°   *broken*
   And with his winged heels did tread the wind
As he had been a foal of Pegasus's kind.°   *race*

22

Nigh as he drew, they might perceive his head
   To be unarmed, and curled uncombed hairs
   Upstaring stiff,° dismayed with   *Standing on end†*
     uncouth° dread: *unknown*
   Nor drop of blood in all his face appears,
   Nor life in limb; and, to increase his fears,
   In foul reproach of knighthood's fair degree,
   About his neck an hempen rope he wears
   That with his glistering arms does ill agree –
But he of rope or arms has now no memory.

23

The Redcross knight toward him crossed fast
   To weet° what mister wight° was   *discover manner of person**
     so dismayed.
   There him he finds all senseless and aghast
   That° of himself he seemed to be afraid,   *So that*

Whom hardly° he from flying forward   *with difficulty*
   stayed,°   *prevented*
Till he these words to him deliver might:
'Sir knight, aread° who hath ye thus   *declare*
   arrayed,°   *afflicted**
And eke° from whom make ye this hasty flight;   *also*
For never knight I saw in such misseeming° plight.'   *unseemly**

24

He answered nought at all but, adding new
   Fear to his first amazement,° staring wide   *extreme fear†*
   With stony° eyes and heartless° hollow   *stupefied dejected*
     hue,°   *face*
   Astonished stood, as one that had espied
   Infernal furies with their chains untied.
   Him yet again, and yet again, bespake°   *addressed†*
   The gentle° knight; who nought to him replied   *courteous*
   But, trembling, every joint did inly quake,
And faltering tongue at last these words seemed forth to shake:

25

'For God's dear love, sir knight, do me not stay,°   *stop*
   For, lo, he comes – he comes fast after me.'
   Eft° looking back would fain have run away,   *Again*
   But he him forced to stay, and tellen free°   *freely*
   The secret cause of his perplexity:°   *distress*
   Yet nathemore° by his bold hearty°   *in no way courageous*
     speech
   Could his blood-frozen heart emboldened be
   But, through his boldness, rather fear did reach:°   *touch on*
Yet, forced, at last he made through silence sudden breach.

26

'And am I now in safety sure,' quoth he,
   'From him that would have forced me to die?
   And is the point of death now turned from me,
   That I may tell this hapless° history?'   *unfortunate*
   'Fear nought,' quoth he, 'no danger now is nigh.'
   'Then shall I you recount a rueful case,'°   *occurrence*
   Said he, 'the which with this unlucky eye

    I late beheld and, had not greater grace
Me reft° from it, had been partaker of the place.   *rescued*

27

'I lately chanced (would I had never chanced!)
  With a fair knight to keepen company,
    Sir Terwin hight,° that well himself advanced   *called**†
  In all affairs, and was both bold and free –
  But not so happy as mote° happy be: *might*
  He loved (as was his lot) a lady gent°   *gentle; noble*
    That him again° loved in the least degree;   *in return*
    For she was proud and of too high° intent,°   *ambitious mind*
And joyed° to see her lover languish and lament.   *rejoiced*

28

'From whom returning, sad and comfortless,°   *desolate*
  As on the way together we did fare,
    We met that villain (God from him me bless!),°   *protect*
  That cursed wight° from whom I 'scaped   *person**
    whilere° –   *a while before*
  A man of hell that calls himself "Despair":
  Who first us greets and, after, fair areads°   *tells*
    Of tidings strange and of adventures rare.°   *uncommon*
    So, creeping close as snake in hidden° weeds,   *hidden in*
Inquireth of our states and of our knightly deeds.

29

'Which, when he knew, and felt our feeble hearts
  Embossed with° bale° and bitter   *Driven to extremity*† *woe*
    biting grief
    Which Love had launched° with his deadly darts,   *pierced*
  With wounding words and terms of foul
    reprief°   *reproof; scorn*
  He plucked from us all hope of due relief
  That erst° us held in love of lingering° life.   *formerly remaining*
  Then, hopeless, heartless, 'gan the cunning thief
    Persuade us die to stint° all further strife: *stop*
To me he lent this rope, to him a rusty knife,

30

'With which sad instrument of hasty death
　　That woeful lover, loathing longer light,°　　*daylight any longer*
　　A wide way made to let forth living breath.
　　But I – more fearful, or more lucky, wight –
　　Dismayed with that deformed,° dismal°　　*hateful‡ dreadful‡*
　　　sight,
　　Fled fast away, half dead with dying fear:　　*fear of death*
　　Ne yet° assured° of life by you, sir　　*Nor am I yet secured*
　　　knight,
　　Whose like infirmity like chance may bear:
But God you never let° his charmed　　*may God never let you*
　　speeches hear.'

31

'How may a man,' said he, 'with idle° speech　　*empty*
　　Be won to spoil the castle° of his health?'°　　*body well-being*
　　'I wote',° quoth he, 'whom trial° late did　　*know experience*
　　　teach,
　　That like° would not for all this world's wealth:　　*same again*
　　His subtle tongue, like honey, melteth
　　Into the heart and searcheth every vein
　　That,° ere one be aware, by secret stealth　　*So that*
　　His power is reft° and weakness doth remain.　　*stolen*
O never, sir, desire to try his guileful train.'°　　*deceit*

32

'Certes,'° said he, 'hence° shall I never rest　*Certainly from now on*
　　Till I that treacher's° heart have heard and tried.　　*deceiver's*
　　And you, sir knight, whose name mote° I request,　　*may*
　　Of grace° do me unto his cabin° guide.'　　*courtesy cave*
　　'I, that hight° Trevisan,' quoth he, 'will ride –　　*am called*‡
　　Against my liking – back, to do you grace.
　　But for no gold nor glee° will I abide　　*entertainment; mirth*
　　By you when ye arrive in that same place;
For liefer had I° die than see his deadly face.'　　*I would rather*

33

Ere long they come where that same wicked wight
　　His dwelling has, low in a hollow cave,
　　Far underneath a craggy clift° ypight° –　　*cliff placed*

Dark, doleful, dreary, like a greedy grave
That still for carrion carcasses doth crave;
On top whereof aye° dwelled the ghastly° owl,   *ever   dreaded*
Shrieking his baleful note, which ever drave°   *drove*
Far from that haunt all other cheerful fowl.
And, all about it, wandering ghosts did wail and howl.

34

And, all about, old stocks° and stubs° of trees   *trunks   stumps*
(Whereon nor fruit nor leaf was ever seen)
Did hang upon the ragged, rocky knees;°   *crags†*
On which° had many wretches hanged   *i.e, on the tree trunks*
    been,
Whose carcasses were scattered on the green
And thrown about the cliffs. Arrived there
That bare-head knight, for dread and doleful teen,°   *grief*
Would fain have fled – ne° durst° approachen near   *nor   dared*
But the other forced him stay, and comforted in fear.°   *in his fear*

35

The darksome° cave they enter, where they find   *gloomy*
That cursed man low sitting on the ground,
Musing full sadly in his sullen mind:
His grisy° locks, long grown and unbound,   *grey, grizzled†*
Disordered hung about his shoulders round
And hid his face, through which his hollow°   *sunken*
    eyen°   *eyes*
Looked deadly dull, and stared as° astound;°   *as if stupefied**
His raw-bone° cheeks, through penury and   *gaunt*
    pine,°   *starvation‡*
Were shrunk into his jaws as he did never dine.

36

His garment, nought but many ragged clouts,°   *cloths*
With thorns together pinned and patched was,
The which his naked sides he wrapped abouts;°   *about*
And, him beside, there lay upon the grass
A dreary° corse,° whose life away did pass,   *bloody*   corpse*
All wallowed° in his own yet luke-warm blood   *lying*

That, from his wound, yet welled fresh, alas,
  In which a rusty° knife fast-fixed stood   *bloody*
And made an open passage for the gushing flood.

37

Which piteous spectacle – approving° true   *proving*
  The woeful tale that Trevisan had told –
  Whenas° the gentle° Redcross knight did   *When noble; kindly*
    view,
  With fiery zeal he burned in courage bold
  Him to avenge, before his blood were cold;
  And to the villain said: 'Thou damned wight,
  The author of this fact° we here behold,   *crime*‡
  What justice can but judge against thee right
With thine own blood to price° his blood, here shed in *pay for**
    sight?'

38

'What frantic fit,'° quoth he, 'hath thus   *moment of madness*‡
    distraught
  Thee, foolish man, so rash a doom° to give?   *judgement*
  What justice ever other judgement taught
  But he should die who merits not to live?
  None° else to death this man depairing drive° *Nothing drives*
  But his own guilty mind, deserving death.
  Is° then unjust to each his due to give,   *Is it*
  Or let him die that loatheth living breath,
Or let him die at ease that liveth here uneath?°   *in hardship*†

39

'Who travels by the weary, wandering way
  To come unto his wished home in haste,
  And meets a flood° that doth his passage stay,   *river*
  Is not great grace° to help him over past,   *favour; courtesy*
  Or free his feet that in the mire stick fast?
  Most envious man, that grieves at neighbour's good;
  And fond,° that joyest in the woe thou hast: *foolish*
  Why wilt not let him pass that long hath stood
Upon the bank, yet wilt thyself not pass the flood?

40

'He there does now enjoy eternal rest
  And happy ease, which thou dost want° and crave   *lack*
  And further from it daily wanderest:
  What if some little pain the passage have,
  That makes frail flesh to fear the bitter wave?
  Is not short pain well borne that brings long ease,
  And lays the soul to sleep in quiet grave? –
  Sleep after toil, port after stormy seas,
Ease after war, death after life does greatly please.'

41

The knight much wondered at his sudden wit°   *mental dexterity*
  And said: 'The term° of life is limited,   *span*
  Ne° may a man prolong nor shorten it: *Neither*
  The soldier may not move from watchful
     stead,°   *[his] watching place*
  Nor leave his stand,° until his captain bid.'   *post*
  'Who° life did limit by almighty   *He who*
     doom,'°   *judgement; sentence*
  Quoth he, 'knows best the terms° established;   *limits*
  And he that points° the sentinel his room° *appoints place*
Doth license him depart at sound of morning drum.

42

'Is not His deed what ever thing is done
  In heaven and earth? Did not He all create
  To die again? – all ends that was
     begun:°   *all that was begun has its end*
  Their times in His eternal book of fate
  Are written sure, and have their certain date.° *fixed times*
  Who, then, can strive with strong Necessity,
  That holds the world in his still-changing state,
  Or shun the death ordained by Destiny?
When hour of death is come, let none ask whence nor why.

43

'The longer life, I wote° the greater° sin; *know   the greater the*
  The greater sin, the greater punishment:
  All those great battles which thou boasts to win

Through strife, and bloodshed, and avengement,°   *vengeance*
Now praised, hereafter dear thou shalt repent,
For life must life, and blood must blood repay.
Is not enough thy evil life forespent°   *previously spent‡*
For he that once hath missed the right way,
The further he doth go, the further he doth stray.

44
'Then do no further go, no further stray,
  But here lie down and to thy rest betake,
  The ill to prevent that life ensuen may.°   *may follow from living*
  For what hath life, that may it loved make,
  And gives not rather cause it to forsake? –
  Fear, sickness, age, loss, labour, sorrow, strife,
  Pain, hunger, cold (that makes the heart to quake);
  And ever fickle Fortune rageth rife:
All which, and thousands mo',° do make a loathsome life.   *more*

45
'Thou, wretched man, of death hast greatest need
  If in true balance thou wilt weigh thy state;
  For never knight, that dared warlike deed,
  More luckless disaventures° did   *mischances*
    amate:°   *daunt; cast down*
  Witness the dungeon deep wherein of late
  Thy life, shut up, for death so oft did call;
  And, though good luck prolonged hath thy date,°   *lifespan*
  Yet death then would the like mishaps forestall
Into the which, hereafter, thou mayest happen fall.

46
'Why, then, dost thou, O man of sin, desire
  To draw thy days forth to their last degree?
  Is not the measure of thy sinful hire°   *reward for sinfulness*
  High heaped up with huge iniquity
  Against° the Day of Wrath to burden thee?   *In anticipation of*
  Is not enough that, to this lady mild,°   *gracious*
  Thou falsed° hast thy faith with perjury,   *betrayed*
  And sold thyself to serve Duessa vild,°   *vile, base*
With whom in all abuse thou hast thyself defiled?

47

'Is not He just that all this doth behold
  From highest heaven, and bears an equal° eye?   *impartial*
  Shall He thy sins up in His knowledge fold
  And guilty be of thine impiety?
  Is not His law, Let every sinner die;
  Die shall all flesh? What then must needs be done
  Is it not better to do willingly
  Than linger till the glass° be all outrun?   *i.e., hour-glass*
Death is the end of woes: die soon, O fairy's son.'

48

The knight was much inmoved with° his speech   *affected by*[t]
  That, as a sword's point, through his heart did pierce,
  And in his conscience made a secret breach,
  Well-knowing true all that he did rehearse,°   *recount*
  And to his fresh remembrance did reverse°   *bring back*
  The ugly view of his deformed crimes,
  That° all his manly powers it did disperse   *So that*
  As° he were charmed° with enchanted   *As if spellbound*
    rhymes,
That oftentimes he quaked, and fainted oftentimes.

49

In which amazement° when the   *extreme fear*[t]
  miscreant°   *misbeliever*
  Perceived him to waver, weak and frail,
  Whiles trembling horror did his conscience daunt,
  And hellish anguish did his soul assail
  To drive him to despair, and quite to quail,
  He showed him, painted in a table° plain,°   *picture clearly*[t]
  The damned ghosts that do in torments wail,
  And thousand fiends that do° them endless pain   *inflict on*
With fire and brimstone which for ever shall remain.

50

The sight whereof° so thoroughly him dismayed   *of which*
  That nought but death before his eyes he saw,
  And ever-burning wrath before him laid
  By righteous sentence of the Almighty's law.
  Then 'gan the villain him to overcraw,°   *exult over*[t]

And brought unto him swords, ropes, poison, fire,
And all that might him to perdition draw;
And bade him choose what death he would desire:
For death was due to him that had provoked God's ire.

51

But whenas none of them he saw him take
  He to him raught° a dagger sharp and keen,   *reached*
  And gave it him in hand. His hand did quake
  And tremble like a leaf of aspen green,
  And troubled blood through his pale face was seen
  To come and go with tidings° from the heart   *news; flowings*
  As° it a running messenger had been.   *As if*
  At last, resolved to work his final smart,°   *injury*
He lifted up his hand, that back again did start.

52

Which, whenas Una saw, through every vein
  The cruddled° brood ran to her well of life   *congealed*†
  As in a swoon. But, soon relived° again,   *revived*
  Out of his hand she snatched the cursed knife
  And threw it to the ground, enraged rife,°   *greatly*
  And to him said: 'Fie, fie, faint-hearted knight:
  What meanest thou by this reproachful strife?
  Is this the battle which thou vauntest° to fight   *boasted*
With that fire-mouthed dragon, horrible and bright?

53

'Come, come away, frail, seely,° fleshly   *miserable;* blessed**
  wight,°   *being**
  Ne° let vain words bewitch thy manly heart,   *Neither*
  Ne° devilish thoughts dismay° thy constant   *Nor vanquish*
    sprite.
  In heavenly mercies hast thou not a part?
  Why shouldst thou then despair, that chosen art?
  Where justice grows, there grows eke° greater grace,   *also*
  The which doth quench the brand of hellish smart,
  And that accursed hand-writing doth deface.
Arise, sir knight, arise, and leave this cursed place.'

54

So up he rose, and thence amounted°   *ascended*
    straight.°   *forthwith*
Which, when the carl° beheld, and saw his guest   *churl*
Would safe depart for all his subtle sleight,
He chose a halter from among the rest
And with it hung himself, unbid
    unblessed.°   *without prayer*[†] *or blessing*
But death he could not work himself thereby,
For thousand times he so himself had dressed,°   *prepared*
Yet nevertheless it could not do him die
Till he should die his last – that is, eternally.

Canto 10

Her faithful knight fair Una brings
To house of Holiness,
Where he is taught repentance and
The way to heavenly bliss.

1

What man is he, that boasts of fleshly might
    And vain assurance of mortality
Which, all so° soon as it° doth come to fight   *as   i.e., flesh*
Against spiritual foes, yields by and by,
Or from the field most cowardly doth fly?
Ne° let the man ascribe it to his skill   *Do not*
That through grace hath gained victory.
If any strength we have, it is to ill:°   *evil*
But all the good is God's, both power and eke° will.   *also*

2

By that which lately happened, Una saw
    That this her knight was feeble and too faint,
And all his sinews waxen weak and raw°   *painful*[†]
Through long imprisonment and hard
    constraint°   *confinement*[†]
Which he endured in his late° restraint,   *recent*

That yet he was unfit for bloody fight.
Therefore to cherish° him with diets daint'   *tend; encourage*
She cast° to bring him, where he cheeren might,   *resolved*
Till he recovered had his late decayed plight.°   *failing‡ condition*

3

There was an ancient house not far away,
Renowned throughout the world for sacred lore°   *doctrine*
And pure, unspotted life: so well, they say,
It governed was and guided evermore
Through wisdom of a matron grave and
    hoar,°   *white; venerable*
Whose only° joy° was to relieve the needs   *sole delight*
Of wretched souls, and help the helpless poor.
All night she spent in bidding of her beads,°   *saying her prayers* *
And all the day in doing good and godly deeds.

4

Dame Celia men did her call, as thought
From heaven to come, or thither to arise:
The mother of three daughters, well upbrought
In goodly thews° and godly exercise.°   *ordinances* * practice*
The eldest two – most sober, chaste and wise,
Fidelia and Speranza – virgins were:
Though spoused,° yet wanting° wedlock's   *espoused lacking*
    solemnise.
But fair Charissa to a lovely° fere°   *loving husband*
Was linked, and by him had many pledges° dear.   *i.e, children*

5

Arrived there, the door they find fast° locked,   *firmly*
For it was warily watched night and day
For fear of many foes. But when they knocked,
The porter opened unto them straightway:
He was an aged sire all hoary grey,
With looks full lowly cast, and gait full slow,
Wont° on a staff his feeble steps to stay,°   *Accustomed support*
Hight° Humiltà. They pass in, stooping low: *Called*†
For strait° and narrow was the way which he did   *confined*
    show.

6

Each goodly thing is hardest to begin,
   But, entered in, a spacious court° they see,   *courtyard*
   Both plain and pleasant to be walked in,
   Where them does meet a franklin° fair and free   *freeholder*
   And entertains with comely courteous glee.°   *joy*
   His name was Zeal, that him right became,°   *suited*
   For in his speeches and behaviour he
   Did labour lively to express the same,
And gladly them did guide till to the hall they came.

7

There fairly° them receives a gentle squire   *courteously*
   Of mild° demeanour and rare° courtesy,   *gracious extreme*
   Right cleanly° clad in comely sad° attire,   *wholly muted*
   In word and deed that showed great modesty,
   And knew his good to all of each degree,
   Hight Reverence. He them with speeches meet°   *fitting*
   Does fair entreat:° no courting nicety°   *treat courtly elegance*
   But simple true, and eke° unfeigned sweet,   *also*
As might become a squire so great persons to greet.

8

And afterwards them to his dame° he leads –   *mistress*
   That aged dame, the lady of the place,
   Who all this while was busy at her beads;°   *prayers*
   Which done, she up arose with seemly grace
   And toward them full matronly did pace.
   Where, when that fairest Una she beheld
   (Whom well she knew to spring from heavenly race),
   Her heart with joy unwonted° inly°   *unaccustomed inwardly*
     swelled
(As feeling wondrous comfort in her weaker
     eld),°   *the weakness of her age*

9

And, her embracing, said: 'O happy earth
   Whereon thy innocent feet do ever tread!
   Most virtuous virgin, born of heavenly birth,
   That, to redeem thy woeful parents' head

From tyrant's rage and ever-dying dread,° *fear of eternal death*
Hast wandered through the world now long a day
(Yet ceasest not thy weary soles to lead),
What grace hath thee now hither brought this way?
Or do thy feeble feet unweeting° hither stray? *unknowing*

10

'Strange thing it is an errant knight to see
 Here in this place – or any other wight° *person**
 That hither turns his steps: so few there be
 That choose the narrow path, or seek the right.
 All keep the broad highway, and take delight
 With many rather for to go astray
 And be partakers of their evil plight,
 Than with a few to walk the rightest way.
O foolish men, why haste ye to your own decay?'

11

'Thyself to see and tired limbs to rest,
 O matron sage,' quoth she, 'I hither came,
 And this good knight his way with me addressed,° *guided*
 Led with thy praises and broad-blazed fame,
 That up to heaven is blown.'° The *i.e., on Fame's trumpet*
  ancient dame
 Him goodly greeted in her modest guise,° *manner*
 And entertained them both, as best became,° *suited*
 With all the courtesies that she could devise,
Ne° wanted° aught° to show her *Nor lacked anything*
  bonteous or wise.

12

Thus as they 'gan of sundry things devise,° *to consider*
 Lo, two most goodly virgins came in place,
 Ylinked arm in arm in lovely wise.° *fashion*
 With countenance demure, and modest grace,
 They numbered even steps and equal pace;
 Of which the eldest, that Fidelia hight,
 Like sunny beams threw from her crystal face
 That could have dazed the rash beholder's sight,
And round about her head did shine like heaven's light.

13

She was arrayed all in lily white,
  And in her right hand bore a cup of gold
  With wine and water filled up to the height,
  In which a serpent did himself enfold°   *fold himself†*
  That horror made to all that did behold.
  But she no whit did change her constant mood,
  And in her other hand she fast did hold
  A book that was both signed and sealed with blood,
Wherein dark° things were writ, hard to be understood. *obscure*

14

Her younger sister, that Speranza hight,
  Was clad in blue, that her beseemed° well.   *suited*
  Not all so cheerful seemed she of sight°   *in appearance*
  As was her sister – whether dread did dwell,
  Or anguish, in her heart, is hard to tell.
  Upon her arm a silver anchor lay
  Whereon she leaned ever, as befell;°   *as was right*
  And ever up to heaven as she did pray
Her steadfast eyes were bent,° ne° swerved other *directed nor*
  way.

15

They, seeing Una, towards her 'gan wend,°   *move*
  Who them encounters with like courtesy:
  Many kind speeches they between them spend,
  And greatly joy° each other well to see.   *rejoice*
  Then to the knight with shamefast modesty
  They turn themselves, at Una's meek request,
  And him salute with well-beseeming glee,°   *joy*
  Who fair° them quits,° as him beseemed *courteously repays*
  best,
And goodly 'gan discourse of many a noble gest.° *deed*

16

Then Una thus: 'But she, your sister dear,
  The dear Charissa, where is she become° –   *gone*
  Or° wants° she health, or busy is elsewhere?' *Either lacks*
  'Ah, no,' said they, 'but forth she may not come,
  For she of late is lightened of her womb

And hath increased the world with one son more,
That° her to see should be but troublesome.'   *So that*
'Indeed,' quoth she, 'that should her trouble sore;°   *very much*
But thanked be God, and her increase so evermore.'

17

Then said the aged Celia: 'Dear dame,
And you, good sir, I wote° that of your toil   *understand*
And labours long, through which ye hither came,
Ye both forwearied° be. Therefore awhile   *wearied*
I read° you rest, and to your bowers°   *advise   bedrooms*
   recoil.'°   *retire*
Then called she a groom that forth him led
Into a goodly lodge,° and 'gan despoil°   *cell; lodging   relieve*
Of puissant° arms,° and laid in   *powerful   armour*
   easy° bed: *relaxing*
His name was meek Obedience, rightfully aread.°   *told*

18

Now when their weary limbs with kindly° rest,   *natural*
And bodies, were refreshed with due repast,
Fair Una 'gan Fidelia fair° request   *courteously*
To have her knight into her schoolhouse placed
That° of her heavenly learning he might taste,   *So that*
And hear the wisdom of her works divine.
She granted; and that knight so much aggraced°   *favoured*†
That she him taught celestial discipline,
And opened his dull eyes, that light mote° in them shine.   *might*

19

And that her sacred book, with blood ywrit,°   *written**
That none could read except she did them teach,
She unto him disclosed every whit,
And heavenly documents° thereout did preach –   *instruction*
That weaker° wit° of man could never   *too weak   understanding*
   reach
Of God, of grace, of justice, of free will,
That wonder was to hear her goodly speech.
For she was able with her words to kill,
And raise again to life, the heart that she did thrill.°   *pierce*

20

And when she list° pour out her larger°	*wished greater*
sprite°	*power*
She would command the hasty sun to stay,	
Or backward turn his course from heaven's height.	
Sometimes great hosts of men she could dismay;°	*conquer*
Dry-shod to pass, she parts the floods in tway;	
And eke huge mountains from their native seat	
She would command themselves to bear away	
And throw in raging sea with roaring threat:	
Almighty God her gave such power and puissance great.	

21

The faithful knight now grew in little space°	*short time*
By hearing her, and by her sisters' lore,°	*teaching*
To such perfection of all heavenly grace	
That wretched world he 'gan for to abhor,	
And mortal life 'gan loathe as thing forlore° –	*forsaken**
Grieved with remembrance of his wicked ways,	
And pricked with anguish of his sins so sore,°	*extreme*
That he desired to end his wretched days:	
So much the dart of sinful guilt the soul dismays.°	*overcomes*

22

But wise Speranza gave him comfort sweet,	
And taught him how to take assured° hold	*secure*
Upon her silver anchor as was meet:°	*fitting*
Else had his sins so great and manifold	
Made him forget all that Fidelia told.	
In this distressed, doubtful° agony	*apprehensive‡*
When him his dearest Una did behold	
Disdaining life, desiring leave to die,	
She found herself assailed with great perplexity,	

23

And came to Celia to declare her smart;°	*pain*
Who, well acquainted with that common plight	
Which sinful horror° works in wounded heart,	*horror of sin*
Her wisely comforted all that she might	
With goodly counsel and advisement° right,	*advice*

And straightway sent with careful diligence
  To fetch a leech,° the which had great insight   *physician*
  In that disease of grieved conscience,
And well could cure the same: his name was Patience.

24

Who, coming to the soul-diseased knight,
  Could hardly° him entreat° to tell his   *with difficulty induce‡*
    grief:
  Which known, and all that 'noyed° his heavy   *hurt*
    sprite°   *soul*
  Well-searched, eftsoons° he 'gan apply relief   *forthwith*
  Of salves° and medicines, which had   *ointments*
    passing° prief;°   *extreme power*
  And thereto added words of wondrous might
  By which to ease he him recured° brief,°   *restored quickly*
  And much assuaged the passion° of his plight,   *suffering*
That he his pain endured as seeming now more light.

25

But yet the cause and root of all his ill –
  Inward corruption and infected sin,
  Not purged nor healed – behind remained still
  And, festering sore,° did rankle° yet within,   *greatly fester*
  Close° creeping 'twixt the marrow and the skin.   *Furtively*
  Which to extirp° he laid him privily°   *uproot secretly*
  Down in a darksome° lowly place far in   *gloomy*
  Whereas° he meant his corrosives to apply,   *Where*
And with strict diet° tame his stubborn malady. *way of living*

26

In ashes and sackcloth he did array
  His dainty° corse,° proud humours to abate,   *weak‡* *body*
  And dieted with fasting every day
  The swelling of his wounds to mitigate,
  And made him pray both early and eke° late.   *also*
  And ever as superfluous° flesh did rot,   *swollen*
  Amendment ready still at hand did wait
  To pluck it out with pincers fiery hot,
That soon in him was left no one corrupted jot.

27

And bitter Penance with an iron whip
   Was wont him once to disple° every day;   *discipline*
   And sharp Remorse his heart did prick and nip
   That° drops of blood thence like a well did play;   *So that*
   And sad Repentance used° to   *was accustomed*
      embay°   *bathe;† drench†*
   His body in salt water smarting sore,
   The filthy blots of sin to wash away.
   So, in short space, they did to health restore
The man that would° not live, but erst° lay at   *wished   formerly*
   death's door.

28

In which his torment often was so great
   That like a lion he would cry and roar,
   And rend his flesh, and his own sinews eat.
   His own dear Una, hearing ever more
   His rueful shrieks and groanings, often tore
   Her guiltless garments and her golden hair
   For pity of his pain and anguish sore:
   Yet all with patience wisely did she bear,
For well she wist° his crime° could else be never clear. *knew   sin*

29

Whom, thus recovered by wise Patience
   And true Repentance, they to Una brought,
   Who, joyous of his cured conscience,
   Him dearly kissed, and fairly° eke° besought *courteously   also*
   Himself to cherish, and consuming thought
   To put away out of his care-full breast.
   By this,° Charissa (late in childbed brought) *By this time*
   Was waxen° strong, and left her fruitful nest: *growing*
To her fair Una brought this unacquainted° *unknown [to her]*
   guest.

30

She was a woman in her freshest° age,   *most blooming*
   Of wondrous beauty and of bounty° rare,° *goodness extreme*
   With goodly grace and comely personage,°   *appearance*
   That was on earth not easy to compare:°   *rival*

Full of great love, but Cupid's wanton snare
As hell she hated, chaste in work and will.
Her neck and breasts were ever open bare
That aye thereof her babes might suck their fill;
The rest was all in yellow robes arrayed still.

31

A multitude of babes about her hung,
  Playing their sports, that joyed° her to behold;   *it rejoiced*
  Whom still she fed whiles they were weak and young,
  But thrust them forth still° as they waxed old.   *ever*
  And on her head she wore a tiara of gold,
  Adorned with gems and ouches° wondrous fair,   *brooches*
  Whose passing° price° uneath° was   *surpassing value scarcely*
    to be told;
  And by her side there sate a gentle pair
Of turtle doves, she sitting in an ivory chair.

32

The knight and Una, entering, fair° her greet,   *courteously*
  And bid her joy of that her happy brood;
  Who them requites° with courtesies seeming   *repays*
    meet,°   *appropriate*
  And entertains with friendly cheerful mood.
  Then Una her besought to be so good
  As in her virtuous rules to school her knight,
  Now after all his torment well withstood
  In that sad house of Penance, where his sprite°   *soul*
Had passed° the pains of hell and long enduring   *passed through*
    night.

33

She was right joyous or her just request
  And, taking by the hand that fairy's son,
  'Gan him to instruct in every good behest°   *injunction*
  Of love, and righteousness, and well-to-done,°   *well-doing*
  And wrath and hatred warily to shun
  That drew on men God's hatred and His wrath,
  And many souls in dolours° had fordone.° *wretchedness ruined*
  In which, when she him well instructed hath,
From thence to heaven she teacheth him the ready° path: *direct*

34

Wherein his weaker wandering steps to guide
  An ancient matron she to her does call,
  Whose sober looks her wisdom well descried.°   *disclosed*
Her name was Mercy, well known over all
  To be both gracious and eke° liberal: *also*
To whom the careful charge of him she gave
  To lead aright, that he should never fall
  In all his ways through this wide world's wave,
That Mercy in the end his righteous soul might save.

35

The godly matron by the hand him bears
  Forth from her presence by a narrow way
  Scattered with bushy thorns and ragged briars,
  Which still° before him she removed away   *ever*
  That° nothing might his ready passage stay.° *So that* *prevent*
And ever when his feet encumbered° were,   *impeded*
  Or 'gan to shrink,° or from the right to stray, *draw back*
  She held him fast and firmly did upbear,
As careful nurse her child from falling oft does rear.°   *lift*

36

Eftsoons unto an holy hospital°   *hostel for pilgrims*
  That was forby° the way she did him bring,   *near†*
  In which seven beadsmen,° that had vowed all *men of prayer*
  Their life to service of high heaven's king,
  Did spend their days in doing godly thing.
  Their gates to all were open evermore
  That by the weary way were travelling,° *also: travailing, toiling*
  And one sat waiting° ever them before   *also: watching*
To call in comers-by that needy were and poor.

37

The first of them, that eldest was and best,°   *foremost*
  Of all the house had charge and government,
  As guardian and steward of the rest:
  His office° was to give   *function*
    entertainment°   *hospitable provision†*
  And lodging unto all that came and went –
  Not unto such as could him feast again,°   *in return*

And double quite for that° he on them   *doubly repay what*
  spent,
But such as want° of harbour° did   *lack refuge*
  constrain:°   *oppress*
Those for God's sake his duty was to entertain.°   *receive*

38

The second was the almoner° of the place: *alms-giver*
  His office was the hungry for to feed,
  And thirsty give to drink – a work of grace.
  He feared not once himself to be in need,
  Ne° cared to hoard for those whom he did breed.°   *Nor beget*
  The grace of God he laid up still in store,°   *abundance*
  Which as a stock° he left unto his seed:°   *capital offspring*
  He had enough, what need him care for more?
And had he less, yet some he would give to the poor.

39

The third had of their wardrobe custody,
  In which were not rich tires,° nor garments gay –   *clothes*
  The plumes of pride and wings of vanity –
  But clothes meet° to keep keen° cold away,   *suitable sharp*
  And naked nature seemly° to array,   *fittingly*
  With which bare wretched wights° he daily clad,   *people**
  The images of God in earthly clay;
  And if that no spare clothes to give he had,
His own coat he would cut, and it distribute glad.°   *gladly*

40

The fourth appointed by his office was
  Poor prisoners to relieve with gracious aid,
  And captives to redeem with price° of brass°   *sum money*†
  From Turks and Saracens which them had stayed.°   *captured*†
  And though they faulty° were, yet well he weighed   *sinful*
  That God to us forgiveth every hour
  Much more than that why° they in bonds°   *for which chains*
  were laid,
  And He that harrowed° hell with heavy°   *despoiled a great*
  stour°   *battle*
The faulty° souls from thence brought to His heavenly   *guilty*
  bower.

41

The fifth had charge sick persons to attend,
    And comfort those in point of death which lay –
    For them most needeth comfort in the end,
    When sin and hell and death do most dismay
    The feeble soul departing hence away.
    All is but lost that, living, we bestow,°   *give;‡ store up*
    If not well ended at our dying day:
    O man, have mind of that last, bitter throe,° *agony; death-throe*
For as the tree does fall, so lies it ever low.

42

The sixth had charge of them, now being dead,
    In seemly sort° their corses° to engrave,°   *manner bodies bury*
    And deck with dainty flowers their bridal bed
    That to their heavenly spouse both sweet and
        brave°   *finely-attired‡*
    They might appear, when He their souls shall save.
    The wondrous workmanship of God's own
        mould,°   *pattern; image*
    Whose face He made all beasts to fear, and gave
    All in his hand,° even dead we honour   *under his control*
        should:
Ah, dearest God, me grant I dead be not defouled.°   *defiled**

43

The seventh now, after death and burial done,
    Had charge the tender orphans of the dead
    And widows aid, lest they should be
        undone.°   *fall into misfortune*
    In face of judgement he their right would plead,
    Ne° aught° the power of mighty men did   *Neither at all*
        dread°   *fear*
    In their defence, nor would for gold or fee°   *bribe*
    Be won° their rightful causes down to tread: *won over*
    And when they stood in most necessity,
He did supply their want,° and gave them ever   *need*
    free.°   *liberally*

44

There when the elfin knight arrived was,
  The first and chiefest of the seven – whose care
  Was guests to welcome – towards him did pass,
  Where, seeing Mercy (that his steps upbore
  And always led), to her with reverence rare°   *particular*
  He humbly louted° in meek lowliness,   *bowed*
  And seemly welcome for her did prepare;
  For of their Order she was
    patroness,°   *founder; superior; protector*
Albe° Charissa were their chiefest foundress.   *Although*

45

There she awhile him stays° himself to rest,   *keeps*
  That to the rest more able he might be;
  During which time, in every good behest°   *commandment*
  And godly work of alms and charity,
  She him instructed with great industry.
  Shortly therein so perfect he became
  That from the first unto the last
    degree°   *step [on the ladder of virtue]*
  His mortal life he learned had to frame°   *fashion*
In holy righteousness, without° rebuke or blame.   *beyond*

46

Thence forward by that painful way they pass
  Forth to an hill that was both steep and high,
  On top whereof a sacred chapel was,
  And eke a little hermitage thereby,
  Wherein an aged holy man did lie°   *dwell*
  That day and night said his devotion,
  Ne° other worldly business did apply.°   *Nor apply himself to*
  His name was heavenly Contemplation: ~ a way to show him the way
Of God and goodness was his meditation.

47

Great grace that old man to him given had,
  For God he often saw from heaven's height,
  All° were his earthly eyen° both blunt°   *Although eyes dim*
    and bad
  And through great age had lost their kindly° sight;   *natural*

Yet wondrous quick° and pierceant° was his   *lively piercing*†
   sprite°   *soul*
As eagle's eye, that can behold the sun.
That hill they scale with all their power and might
That° his frail thighs, nigh weary and   *So that*
   fordone°   *exhausted*
'Gan fail; but by her help the top at last he won.°   *attained*

48

There they do find that goodly, aged sire,
   With snowy locks adown his shoulders shed
   As hoary frost with spangles doth attire
   The mossy branches of an oak half-dead.
   Each bone might through his body well be read,°   *seen*
   And every sinew seen through° his long fast: *because of*
   For nought he cared his carcase°   *He cared nothing for his body*
      long unfed.
   His mind was full of spiritual repast,
And pined° his flesh to keep his body low° and   *starved   weak*
   chaste;

49

Who, when these two approaching he espied,
   At their first presence grew aggrieved sore,°   *much*
   That forced him lay his heavenly thoughts aside;
   And had he not that dame respected more –
   Whom highly he did reverence and adore –
   He would not once have moved for the knight.
   They him saluted, standing far afore;°   *away [out of respect]*
   Who, well them greeting, humbly did requite,°   *salute, greet*†
And asked, to what end they clomb° that tedious   *climbed*
   height.

50

'What end,' quoth she, 'should cause us take such pain,
   But that same end which every living wight°   *person**
   Should make his mark,° high heaven to attain?   *goal*
   Is not from hence the way that leadeth right
   To that most glorious house that glistereth° bright   *glitters*
   With burning stars and everlasting fire,
   Whereof the keys are to thy hand behight°   *granted***†

By wise Fidelia? She doth thee require°   *request*
To show it to this knight, according his desire.'   *granting*

51

'Thrice happy man,' said then the father grave,
   'Whose staggering steps thy steady hand doth lead,
   And shows the way, his sinful soul to save.
   Who better can the way to heaven aread°   *show*
   Than thou thyself, that was both born and bred
   In heavenly throne, where thousand angels shine?
   Thou dost the prayers of the righteous seed
   Present before the majesty divine,
And his avenging wrath to clemency incline.

52

'Yet, since thou biddest, thy pleasure° shall be done.   *request*
   Then come, thou man of earth, and see the way
   That never yet was seen of fairy's son;
   That never leads the traveller° astray   *pilgrim; toiler*
   But, after labours long, and sad delay,
   Brings them to joyous rest and endless bliss.
   But first thou must a season° fast and pray,   *for a time*
   Till from her bands the sprite° assoiled° is,   *soul freed*
And have her strength recured° from frail infirmities.'   *restored*

53

That done, he leads him to the highest mount –
   Such one as that same mighty man of God
   (That blood-red billows like a walled front
   On either side disparted° with his rod   *parted asunder*†
   Till that his army dry-foot through them yode)°   *went**
   Dwelt forty days upon, where, writ in stone
   With bloody letters by the hand of God,
   The bitter doom° of death and baleful°   *sentence destructive*
      moan°   *grief*
He did receive, whiles flashing fire about him shone;

54

Or like that sacred hill, whose head full high –
   Adorned with fruitful olives all around –
   Is, as it were for endless memory°   *memorial*

Of that dear Lord who oft thereon was found,
For ever with a flowering garland crowned;
Or like that pleasant mount that is for aye
Through famous poets' verse each where°   *everywhere*
    renowned,
On which the thrice three learned ladies play
Their heavenly notes, and make full many a lovely lay.°   *song*

55

From thence far off he unto him did show
    A little path that was both steep and long
Which to a goodly city led his view,
    Whose walls and towers were builded high and strong
Of pearl and precious stone, that earthly tongue
Cannot describe, nor wit° of man can   *understanding*
    tell:°   *recount*
Too high a ditty° for my simple song.   *subject*
The 'City of the Great King' hight° it well,   *was called* *†
Wherein eternal peace and happiness doth dwell.

56

As he thereon stood gazing, he might see
    The blessed angels to and fro descend
From highest heaven in gladsome° company,   *joyful*
And with great joy into that city wend,°   *go*
As commonly° as friend does with his friend.   *familiarly* *†
Whereat he wondered much, and 'gan inquire
What stately building durst° so high extend   *dared*
Her lofty towers unto the starry sphere,
And what unkown nation there
    empeopled° were.   *established as the population†*

57

'Fair knight,' quoth he, 'Jerusalem that is,
    The New Jerusalem, that God has built
For those to dwell in that are chosen his:
    His chosen people, purged from sinful guilt
With precious blood, which cruelly was spilt
On cursed tree° of° that unspotted Lamb   *i.e., the cross from*
That for the sins of all the world was killed.

Now are they saints in all that city sam°   *together*
More dear unto their God than younglings to their dam.'

58

'Till now,' said then the knight, 'I weened° well°   *believed truly*
  That great Cleopolis – where I have been,
  In which that fairest Fairy Queen doth dwell –
  The fairest city was that might be seen;
  And that bright tower, all built of crystal
    clean° –
                        pure; completely
  Panthea – seemed the brightest thing that was.
  But now, by proof, all otherwise I ween,
  For this great city that does far surpass,
And this bright angels' tower quite dims that tower of glass.'

59

'Most true,' then said the aged holy man;
  'Yet is Cleopolis for earthly frame°   *manufacture; structure*
  The fairest piece° that eye beholden can;   *masterpiece*
  And well beseems° all knights of noble name,   *befits*
  That covet in the immortal book of fame
  To be eternised, that same to haunt,
  And do their service to that sovereign dame
  That glory does to them for guerdon° grant –   *reward*
For she is heavenly born, and heaven may justly vaunt.° *boast of*

60

'And thou, fair imp,° sprung out from English race   *child*
  (However now accounted elfin's son),
  Well worthy dost thy service for her grace°   *favour*
  To aid a virgin desolate, foredone.°   *exhausted*
  But when thou famous victory hast won,
  And high amongst all knights hast hung thy shield,
  Thenceforth the suit° of earthly conquest shun,   *pursuit*
  And wash thy hands from guilt of bloody field –
For blood can nought but sin, and wars but sorrows, yield.

61

'Then seek this path that I to thee presage°   *foretell*
  Which, after all, to heaven shall thee send;
  Then peaceably thy painful pilgrimage

To yonder same Jerusalem do bend,
    Where is for thee ordained a blessed end;
    For thou amongst the saints, whom thou dost see,
    Shalt be a saint, and thine own nation's friend
    And patron. Thou Saint George shalt called be –
Saint George of Merry England, the sign° of   *portent; signal*
    victory.'

62

'Unworthy wretch,' quoth he, 'of so great grace,
    How dare I think such glory to attain?'
    'These that have it attained were in like case'
    (Quoth he) 'as wretched, and lived in like pain.'
    'But deeds of arms must I at last be fain,°   *willing*
    And lady's love, to leave, so dearly bought?'
    'What need of arms, where peace doth aye° remain,'   *ever*
    Said he, 'and battles none are to be fought?
As for loose loves – they are vain, and vanish into nought.'

63

'O let me not' (quoth he) 'then turn again
    Back into the world, whose joys so fruitless are;
    But let me here for aye in peace remain,
    Or straight way on that last long voyage fare,
    That nothing may my present hope impair.'
    'That may not be,' said he, 'ne° mayest thou yet   *nor*
    Forgo that royal maid's bequeathed care,°   *i.e., Una's mission*
    Who did her cause into thy hand commit
Till from her cursed foe thou have her freely
    quit.'°   *completely freed*

64

'Then shall I soon,' quoth he, 'so God me grace,
    Abet° that virgin's cause disconsolate,   *Uphold†*
    And shortly back return unto this place
    To walk this way in pilgrim's poor estate.°   *condition*
    But now aread,° old father, why of late°   *tell recently*
    Didst thou behight° me born of English blood   *designate*†*
    Whom all a fairy's son do nominate?'°   *name*
    'That word shall I,' said he, 'avouchen° good,   *prove*

Sith° to thee is unknown the cradle of thy   *Since*
    brood.°   *nativity; parentage*[†]

65

'For well I wote° thou springest from ancient race   *know*
    Of Saxon kings that have, with mighty hand
    And many bloody battles fought in place,°   *on the spot*
    High reared their royal throne in Britain land,
    And vanquished them,° unable to withstand.   *i.e, the Britons*
    From thence a fairy thee unweeting°   *without [anyone] knowing*
        reft,°   *stole*
    There as thou slept in tender swaddling
        band,°   *infant binding-clothes*
    And her base elfin brood° there for thee left: *offspring*
Such, men do changelings call, so changed by fairies' theft.

66

'Thence she thee brought into this Fairyland
    And in an heaped furrow did thee hide,
    Where thee a ploughman, all unweeting,° found   *unsuspecting*
    As he his toilsome team that way did guide,
    And brought thee up in ploughman's state° to bide,   *condition*
    Whereof° *Georgos* he thee gave to° name;   *Wherefore as a*
    Till, pricked with° courage and thy   *spurred by*
        force's° pride,   *strength's*
    To fairy court thou camest to seek for fame
And prove° thy puissant arms, as seems thee best   *try*
    became.'°   *suited*

67

'O holy sire' (quoth he), 'how shall I quite°   *requite, repay*
    The many favours I with thee have found,
    That hast my name and nation read° aright,   *disclosed*
    And taught the way that does to heaven bound?'°   *lead*[†]
    This said, adown he looked to the ground
    To have returned,° but dazed were his eyen°   *i.e, his gaze eyes*
    Through passing° brightness, which did   *surpassing*
        quite° confound   *utterly*
    His feeble sense, and too exceeding shine:
So dark are earthly things compared to things divine.

68

At last, whenas° himself he 'gan to find,°   *when come to*
  To Una back he cast° him to retire,°   *resolved return*
  Who him awaited still with pensive° mind.   *apprehensive*
  Great thanks and goodly meed° to that good   *as best reward*
    sire
  He thence departing gave for his pain's hire;°   *wages*
  So came to Una, who him joyed° to see   *rejoiced*
  And, after little rest, 'gan him desire
  Of her adventures mindful for to be.
So leave they take of Celia and her daughters three.

CANTO 11

The knight with that old dragon fights
    Two days incessantly:
The third him overthrows and gains
    Most glorious victory.

1

High time now 'gan it wax° for Una fair   *grow*
  To think of those her captive parents dear,
  And their forwasted° kingdom to repair:°   *devastated restore*
  Whereto, whenas they now approached near,
  With hearty° words her knight she 'gan to cheer,   *bold; cheery*
  And in her modest manner thus bespake:
  'Dear knight – as dear as ever knight was dear –
  That all these sorrows suffer for my sake,
High heaven° behold the tedious toil ye for me   *i.e., may heaven*
  take.

2

'Now we are come unto my native soil,
  And to the place where all our perils dwell:
  Here haunts° the fiend and does° his daily   *frequents performs*
    spoil.
  Therefore henceforth be at your keeping
    well,°   *well on your guard*

And ever ready for your foeman fell.°   *terrible*
The spark of noble courage now awake,
And strive your excellent self to excel:
That shall ye evermore renowned make
Above all knights on earth that battle undertake.'

3

And, pointing forth, 'Lo, yonder is' (said she)
  'The brazen tower in which my parents dear
  For dread of that huge fiend imprisoned be,
  Whom I from far see on the walls appear,
  Whose sight my feeble soul doth greatly cheer.
  And on the top of all I do espy
  The watchman waiting tidings glad to hear,
  That, O my parents, might I happily
Unto you bring to ease you of your misery.'

4

With that they heard a roaring, hideous sound,
  That all the air with terror filled wide,
  And seemed uneath° to shake the   *almost;† distressingly*
    steadfast ground.
  Eftsoons° that dreadful dragon they espied,   *Soon after*
  Where stretched he lay upon the sunny side
  Of a great hill, himself like a great hill.
  But all so° soon as he from far descried   *as*
  Those glistering° arms that heaven with light did fill, *glittering*
He roused himself full blithe° and hastened them   *gladly*
    until.°   *unto*

5

Then bade the knight his lady yede° aloof°   *go* apart*
  And to an hill herself withdraw aside,
  From whence she might behold that battle's proof° *result*
  And eke° be safe from danger far descried: *also*
  She him obeyed, and turned a little wide.°   *away*
  Now, O thou sacred Muse, most learned dame,
  Fair imp° of Phoebus and his aged bride,   *child*
  The nurse of Time and everlasting Fame,
That warlike hands ennoblest with immortal name:

6

O, gently come into my feeble breast –
   Come gently, but° not with that mighty rage   *and*
   Wherewith the martial troops thou dost infest,°   *infect‡*
   And hearts of great heroes dost enrage
   That° nought their kindled courage may assuage   *So that*
   Soon as thy dreadful trump begins to sound:
   The god of war with his fierce equipage°   *armour†*
   Thou dost awake, sleep never he so sound,
And scared nations dost with horror stern° astound.   *terrible**

7

Fair goddess, lay that furious fit° aside   *mood;† [musical] strain*
   Till I of wars and bloody Mars do sing,
   And Britons' field with Saracen blood bedyed,
   'Twixt that great Fairy Queen and paynim° king,   *pagan*
   That with their horror heaven and earth did ring –
   A work of labour long, and endless praise.
   But now awhile let down° that haughty° string,   *loosen high*
   And to my tunes thy second tenor°   *string of tenor pitch‡*
     raise°   *sound†*
That° I this man of God his godly arms may   *So that*
     blaze.°   *proclaim*

8

By this the dreadful beast drew nigh to hand,
   Half-flying and half-footing° in his haste,   *half-walking*
   That with his largeness measured much land
   And made wide shadow under his huge waist,
   As mountain doth the valley overcast.
   Approaching nigh, he reared high afore
   His body monstrous, horrible and vast,
   Which, to increase his wondrous greatness more,
Was swollen with wrath, and poison, and bloody gore,

9

And, over all, with brazen scales was armed,
   Like plated coat of steel, so couched
     near°   *placed so close together*
   That nought mote° pierce, ne might his corse be   *might*
     harmed

With dint° of sword nor push of pointed spear;   *blow*
Which° – as an eagle, seeing prey appear,   *i.e., the scales*
His airy plumes doth rouse,° full rudely°   *ruffle† ruggedly†*
   dight° –   *placed*
So shaked he that horror was to hear
For, as the clashing of an armour bright,
Such noise his roused scales did send unto the knight.

10

His flaggy° wings, when forth he did   *drooping;‡ flag-like‡*
   display,°   *spread out*
Were like two sails in which the hollow°   *i.e., making hollow*
   wind
Is gathered full and worketh speedy way;
And eke° the pens° that did his pinions   *also skeletal bones**
   bind
Were like mainyards with flying canvas lined:
With which, whenas° him list° the air to beat,   *when wished*
And there by force unwonted° passage find,   *unaccustomed*
The clouds before him fled for terror great,
And all the heavens stood still, amazed with his threat.

11

His huge, long tail, wound up in hundred folds,
   Does overspread his long, brass-scaly back;
   Whose wreathed boughts,° whenever he unfolds,   *folds*
   And thick° entangled knots adown does   *thickly*
   slack° –   *loosen*
Bespotted as with shields of red and black –
It sweepeth all the land behind him far,°   *far behind him*
And of three furlongs does but little lack.°   *is little short of*
And at the point two stings infixed are,
Both deadly sharp that sharpest steel exceeden far.

12

But stings and sharpest steel did far exceed
   The sharpness of his cruel, rending
   claws:°   *i.e, the claws are sharper*
Dead was it sure, as sure as death in deed,°   *fact*
Whatever thing does touch his ravenous paws,
Or what within his reach he ever draws.

But his most hideous head my tongue to tell
Does tremble: for his deep, devouring jaws
Wide-gaped like the grisly° mouth of hell,   *terrible*
Through which into his dark abyss all ravin° fell.   *prey*

13

And that° more wondrous was, in either jaw   *what*
Three ranks of iron teeth enranged° were,   *arranged, ordered*†
In which yet-trickling blood, and gobbets° raw   *chunks*
Of late°-devoured bodies did appear,   *recently*
That sight thereof bred cold, congealed fear,
Which, to increase, and all at once to kill,
A cloud of smothering smoke and sulphur sear°   *scorching*†
Out of his stinking gorge forth steamed still,
That all the air about with smoke and stench did fill.

14

His blazing eyes, like two bright shining shields,
Did burn with wrath and sparkled living fire.
As two broad beacons, set in open fields,
Send forth their flames far off to every shire
And warning give that enemies conspire
With fire and sword the region to invade,
So flamed his eyen° with rage and rancorous ire: *eyes*
But far within, as in a hollow glade,
Those glaring lamps were set, that made a dreadful shade.

15

So° dreadfully he towards him did pace,   *Thus*
Forelifting° up aloft his speckled breast   *Raising in preparation*†
And often bounding on the bruised grass,
As for great joyance° of his new-come guest.   *delight*†
Eftsoons° he 'gan advance his   *Straight after*
    haughty° crest –   *tall; proud*
As chafed° boar his bristles doth uprear –   *vexed*
And shook his scales to battle ready dressed:°   *prepared*
That made the Redcross knight nigh quake for fear,
As bidding bold defiance to his foeman near.

16

The knight 'gan fairly° couch° his steady spear,   *skilfully level*
  And ran at him with rigorous° might: *extreme*
The pointed steel, arriving rudely° there,   *violently*
His harder hide would neither pierce nor bite,
But, glancing by, forth passed forward right.
Yet sore° amoved° with so puissant push   *greatly excited**
The wrathful beast about him turned light,°   *quickly*
And him, so rudely passing by, did brush
With his long tail that horse and man to ground did rush.

17

Both horse and man up lightly rose again,
  And fresh encounter towards him addressed;
But the idle° stroke yet back recoiled in vain,   *useless*
And found no place his deadly point to rest.
Exceeding rage inflamed the furious beast
To be avenged of so great despite;°   *insult*
For never felt his impierceable° breast   *unpierceable*
So wondrous force from hand of living wight,°   *person**
Yet had he proved° the power of many a puissant knight.   *tested*

18

Then, with his waving wings displayed wide,
  Himself up high he lifted from the ground,
And with strong flight did forcibly divide
The yielding air, which nigh° too feeble found   *almost*
Her flitting° parts and element unsound°   *changeable not solid†*
To bear so great a weight. He, cutting way
With his broad sails, about him soared round;
At last, low stooping with unwieldy sway,°   *power*
Snatched up both horse and man to bear them quite°   *utterly*
  away.

19

Long he them bore above the subject° plain   *lying beneath*
  So far as yewen° bow a shaft may send,   *yew*
Till struggling strong did him at last constrain°   *compel*
To let them down before his flight's end:
As haggard° hawk, presuming to contend   *untamed adult‡*
With hardy° fowl above his able might,°   *bold ability*

His weary pounces° all in vain doth spend   *anterior claws*
To truss° the prey too heavy for his flight   *seize and fly off with*†
Which, coming down to ground, does free itself by fight.

20

He so disseised° of his gripping gross,°   *dispossessed whole*† *prey*†
    The knight his thrillant° spear again assayed   *piercing*†
    In his brass-plated body to emboss,°   *plunge*†
    And three men's strength unto the stroke he laid.
    Wherewith the stiff beam° quaked, as afraid,   *spear shaft*
    And, glancing from his scaly neck, did glide
    Close under his left wing, then broad displayed.
    The piercing steel there wrought a wound full wide
That with the uncouth° smart° the monster   *unaccustomed pain*
    loudly cried.

21

He cried as raging seas are wont to roar
    When wintry storm his wrathful wreck° doth   *destruction*
        threat:
    The rolling billows beat the ragged shore
    As° they the earth would shoulder from her seat,   *As if*
    And greedy gulf° does gape as he   *mouth of oncoming wave*
        would eat
    His neighbour element° in his revenge.   *i.e., earth [or air]*
    Then 'gin the blustering brethren° boldly threat   *the winds*
    To move the world from off his steadfast hinge,°   *axis*
And boisterous° battle make, each other to avenge.   *savage*†

22

The steely head stuck fast still in his flesh
    Till with his cruel claws he snatched the wood
    And quite asunder broke. Forth flowed fresh
    A gushing river of black gory° blood,   *clotted**
    That drowned all the land whereon he stood –
    The stream thereof would drive a water mill.
    Trebly augmented was his furious mood
    With bitter sense° of his deep-rooted ill°   *pain*† *hurt; evil*
That° flames of fire he threw forth from his large nostril. *So that*

23

His hideous° tail then hurled° he about,   *huge   dashed*
  And therewith all enwrapped the nimble thighs
    Of his froth-foamy steed, whose courage stout,°   *brave*
    Striving to loose the knot that fast him ties,
    Himself in straiter° bands° too rash   *tighter   folds*
      implies°   *enfolds*
    That° to the ground he is perforce°   *So that   forcibly*
      constrained°   *compelled*
  To throw his rider – who can° quickly rise   *proceeded to*
  From off the earth, with dirty blood distained°   *sullied*
(For that reproachful fall right foully he disdained)° –   *scorned*

24

And freely took his trenchant° blade in hand,   *sharp*
  With which he struck so furious and fell°   *fiercely*
    That nothing seemed the puissance could withstand.
    Upon his crest the hardened iron fell,
    But his more hardened crest was armed so well
    That deeper dint° therein it would not make: *impression*
    Yet so extremely did the buff° him quell°   *blow   subdue*
    That from henceforth he shunned the like to take;
  But when he saw them come, he did them still°   *always*
    forsake.°   *avoid*

25

The knight was wroth to see his stroke beguiled,°   *foiled*
  And smote again with more outrageous might;
    But back again the sparkling steel recoiled,
    And left not any mark where it did light,
    As if in adamant rock it had been pight.°   *driven*
    The beast, impatient of his smarting wound
    And of so fierce and forcible° despite,°   *powerful‡   injury*
    Thought with his wings to sty° above the ground,   *rise*
But his late wounded wing unserviceable found.

26

Then, full of grief° and anguish vehement,   *pain*
  He loudly brayed,° that° like was never   *cried out*   so that*
    heard,
    And from his wide devouring oven sent

A flake° of fire that, flashing in his beard,   *[portion of] flame*†
Him all amazed° and almost° made   *alarmed in truth*‡
  affeared.°   *terrified*
The scorching flame sore swinged° all his   *scorched;*† *lashed*‡
  face,
And through his armour all his body seared,°   *burned*†
That he could not endure so cruel case,°   *plight; body*
But thought his arms to leave, and helmet to unlace.

27

Not that great champion of the antique° world –   *ancient*
  Whom famous poets' verse so much doth vaunt
  And hath for twelve huge labours high extolled° –   *praised*
  So many furies and sharp fits° did haunt   *paroxysms*
  When him the poisoned garment did enchant°   *bewitch*
  With Centaur's blood and bloody verses° charmed,   *magic*
  As did this knight twelve thousand dolours°   *pains*
  daunt,°   *overcome**
  Whom fiery steel now burned that erst° him armed: *formerly*
That° erst him goodly armed now most of all him   *That which*
  harmed.

28

Faint, weary, sore, emboiled,° grieved, burnt   *agitated*†
  With heat, toil, wounds, arms, smart° and inward fire   *pain*
  That never man such mischiefs did torment:
  Death better were, death did he oft desire;
  But death will never come when needs require.
  Whom, so° dismayed,° when that his foe   *thus overwhelmed*
  beheld,
  He cast° to suffer him no more respire,°   *resolved to live*
  But 'gan his sturdy stern° about to wield,   *tail*
And him so strongly struck that to the ground him felled.

29

It fortuned (as fair° it then befell)   *fortunately*
  Behind his back, unweeting,° where he stood,   *unknown to him*
  Of ancient time there was a springing well,
  From which fast trickled forth a silver flood,°   *stream*
  Full of great virtues,° and for medicine good.   *powers*
  Whilom,° before that cursed dragon got   *Once long ago**

That happy land, and all with innocent blood
  Defiled those sacred waves, it rightly hote°   *was named**†*
  'The Well of Life', ne° yet his virtues had forgot.   *nor*

30

For unto life the dead it could restore
  And guilt of sinful crimes clean° wash away;   *also: completely*
  Those that with sickness were infected sore°   *severely*
  It could recure,° and aged long decay   *restore*
  Renew, as one were° born that very   *as if the person had been*
    day.
  Both Silo this and Jordan did excel,
  And the English Bath, and eke° the German Spau;   *also*
  Ne° can Cephis' nor Hebrus match this well: *Neither*
Into the same the knight, back overthrown, fell.

31

Now 'gan the golden Phoebus for to steep°   *bathe†*
  His fiery face in billows° of the west,   *waves‡*
  And his faint° steeds watered in ocean deep   *weary*
  Whiles from their diurnal labours they did rest,
  When that infernal monster, having cast
  His weary foe into that living well,
  Can° high advance his broad discoloured°   *Did vari-coloured*
    breast
  Above his wonted° pitch,° with countenance   *its usual height*
    fell,°   *cruel*
And clapped his iron wings, as° victor he did   *as if*
    dwell.°   *remain*

32

Which, when his pensive° lady saw from far,   *anxious*
  Great woe and sorrow did her soul assay,°   *assail*
  As weening° that the sad end of the war,   *believing*
  And 'gan to highest God entirely° pray   *earnestly*
  That feared chance° from her to turn away.   *eventuality*
  With folded hands, and knees full lowly bent,
  All night she watched, ne° once adown would lay   *nor*
  Her dainty limbs in her sad dreariment,°   *dismal state†*
But praying still did wake, and waking did lament.

33

The morrow next 'gan early to appear
    That° Titan rose to run his daily race;   *When*
    But, early ere the morrow next 'gan rear
    Out of the sea fair Titan's dewy face,
    Up rose the gentle° virgin from her place,   *noble*
    And looked all about, if she might spy
    Her loved knight to move his manly pace,
    For that° she had great doubt° of his safety,   *Because fear*
Since late° she saw him fall before his enemy.   *recently*

34

At last she saw where he upstarted
    brave°   *courageously; finely attired*
    Out of the well wherein he drenched° lay,   *immersed*
    As eagle fresh out of the ocean wave
    Where he hath left his plumes all hoary grey,
    And decked himself with feathers youthly gay,
    Like eyas° hawk up mounts unto the skies   *young*
    His newly-budded pinions to assay,°   *try out*
    And marvels at himself still° as he flies: *ever*
So new this new-born knight to battle new did rise.

35

Whom when the damned fiend so fresh did spy,
    No wonder if he wondered at the sight,
    And doubted whether his late enemy
    It were, or other new supplied knight.
    He, now to prove his late renewed might,
    High brandishing his bright dew-burning°   *burning with dew*
        blade,
    Upon his crested° scalp° so sore° did smite *plumed head hard*
    That to the skull a yawning wound it made:
The deadly dint° his dulled senses all   *stroke*
    dismayed.°   *overcame*

36

I wote° not whether the revenging steel   *know*
    Were hardened with that holy water dew
    Wherein he fell, or sharper edge did feel,
    Or his baptised hands now greater° grew,   *stronger*

Or other secret virtue° did ensue° –   *power result*
Else never could the force of fleshly arm,
Ne° molten metal, in his blood imbrue:°   *Nor   stain itself*
For till that stound° could never wight° him *moment creature**
    harm
By subtlety, nor sleight, nor might, nor mighty charm.

37

The cruel wound enraged him so sore°   *extremely*
    That loud he yielded° for exceeding pain,   *uttered*
    As hundred ramping lions seemed to roar,
    Whom ravenous hunger did thereto constrain.°   *compel*
    Then 'gan he toss aloft his stretched train,°   *tail*
    And therewith scourge the buxom° air so sore   *yielding†*
    That to his force to yielden it was fain;°   *forced*
    Ne° aught° his sturdy° strokes might   *Nor anything violent*
       stand afore
That high trees overthrew, and rocks in pieces tore.

38

The same advancing high above his head
    With sharp intended sting so rude° him smote   *violently*
    That to the earth him drove, as stricken dead;
    Ne living wight would have him life behote.°   *held out hope of**
    The mortal sting his angry needle shot
    Quite through his shield, and in his shoulder seized,°   *fixed*
    Where fast it stuck, ne would thereout be got:
    The grief thereof him wondrous sore° diseased,°   *much troubled*
Ne might his rankling pain with patience be appeased.

39

But yet more mindful of his honour dear
    Than of the grievous smart° which him did   *wound*
       wring,°   *vex*
    From loathed soil he can° him lightly°   *proceeded to quickly*
       rear,°   *lift*
    And strove to loose the far-infixed sting:
    Which, when in vain he tried with struggling,
    Inflamed with wrath his raging blade he heft,°   *raised*
    And struck so strongly that the knotty string°   *cord*

Of his huge tail he quite asunder cleft:
Five joints thereof he hewed, and but the stump him left.

40

Heart cannot think what outrage° and what cries,   *outcry;**‡ *fury*
   With foul enfouldred° smoke and flashing fire,   *thunder-black*‡
   The hell-bred beast threw forth unto the skies,
   That° all was covered with darkness dire.   *So that*
   Then, fraught° with rancour and   *filled*
      engorged° ire,   *excessive;*‡ *greedy*‡
   He cast° at once him to avenge for all°   *resolved once for all*
   And, gathering up himself out of the mire
   With his uneven wings, did fiercely fall
Upon his sun-bright shield, and gripped it fast withal.°   *moreover*

41

Much was the man encumbered° with his   *hampered; entangled*
    hold,
   In fear to lose his weapon in his paw,
   Ne wist° yet how his talons to unfold: *Nor did he know*
   For harder was from Cerberus' greedy jaw
   To pluck a bone than from his cruel claw
   To reave° by strength the gripped gage° away.   *tear pledge*
   Thrice he assayed it from his foot to draw,
   And thrice in vain to draw it did assay:
It booted° nought to think to rob him of his prey.   *availed*

42

Tho° when he saw no power° might prevail,   *Then strength*
   His trusty sword he called to his last aid,
   Wherewith he fiercely did his foe assail,
   And double blows about him stoutly° laid   *forcefully*
   That° glancing fire out of the iron played,°   *So that flickered*‡
   As sparkles from the anvil use to° fly   *customarily*
   When heavy hammers on the wedge° are   *ingot*
      swayed:°   *swung*‡
   Therewith at last he forced him to untie
One of his grasping feet, him to defend thereby.

43

The other foot, fast fixed on his shield,
 Whenas° no strength nor strokes might him   *When*
  constrain°   *force*
To loose, ne° yet the warlike pledge to yield,   *nor*
He smote thereat with all his might and main,
That nought so° wondrous puissance might sustain. *such*
Upon the joint the lucky steel did light
And make such way that hewed it quite in twain:
The paw yet missed not his 'minished° might, *diminished*
But hung still on the shield, as it at first was pight.° *fixed in*

44

For grief thereof, and devilish despite,°   *pain; malice*
 From his infernal furnace forth he threw
Huge flames that dimmed all the heaven's light,
 Enrolled in duskish° smoke and brimstone blue – *blackish*‡
As burning Etna from his boiling stew°   *cauldron**
Doth belch out flames, and rocks in pieces broke,° *broken*
 And ragged ribs of mountains smolten new,
Enwrapped in coal-black clouds and filthy smoke,
That all the land with stench, and heaven with horror, choke.

45

The heat whereof, and harmful pestilence,
 So sore° him noyed° that forced him to retire *much vexed**
A little backward for his best defence,
 To save his body from the scorching fire
Which he from hellish entrails did expire.°   *breathe out*
It chanced (eternal God that chance did guide),
 As he recoiled backward, in the mire
His nigh° forwearied° feeble feet did slide, *almost   exhausted*
And down he fell, with dread of shame sore terrified.

46

There grew a goodly° tree him fair° beside – *beautiful   right*
 Loaden with fruit, and apples rosy red
As° they in pure vermilion had been dyed –   *As if*
 Whereof great virtues over all were
  read:°   *could be distinguished*
For happy life to all which thereon fed,

And life eke° everlasting did befall.   *also*
Great God it planted in that blessed stead°   *place*
With His almighty hand, and did it call
'The Tree of Life', the crime° of our first father's   *matter of guilt**
  fall.

47

In all the world like was not to be found,
    Save in that soil where all good things did grow,
    And freely sprang out of the fruitful ground
    As incorrupted Nature did them sow,
    Till that dread dragon all did overthrow.
    Another like fair tree eke grew thereby,
    Whereof whoso did eat eftsoons° did know   *forthwith*
    Both good and ill: O mournful memory° –   *memorial*
That tree through one man's fault hath done° us all to   *caused*
  die.

48

From that first tree forth flowed, as from a well,
    A trickling stream of balm, most sovereign°   *powerful*
    And dainty dear,° which on the ground   *very precious*
        still° fell,   *ever*
    And overflowed all the fertile plain
    As° it had dewed been with timely rain.   *As if*
    Life and long health that gracious° ointment gave, *full of grace*
    And deadly wounds could heal, and rear again
    The senseless corse° appointed for the grave.   *body*
Into that same he fell, which did from death him save.

49

For nigh° thereto the ever-damned beast   *Close by*
    Durst° not approach, for he was deadly   *Dared*
        made,°   *made for death*
    And all that life preserved did detest:
    Yet he it oft adventured° to invade.   *ventured*
    By this the drooping daylight 'gan to fade,
    And yield his room to sad, succeeding Night,
    Who with her sable mantle 'gan to shade
    The face of earth and ways of living wight,
And high her burning torch set up in heaven bright.

50

When gentle Una saw the second fall
  Of her dear knight – who, weary of long fight,
  And faint through loss of blood, moved not at all,
  But lay as in a dream of deep delight,
  Besmeared with precious balm whose virtuous
     might°   *healing power*
  Did heal his wounds and scorching heat allay –
  Again she stricken was with sore affright,
  And for his safety 'gan devoutly pray,
And watch the noyous° night, and wait for joyous   *troublesome*
  day.

51

The joyous day 'gan early to appear,
  And fair Aurora from the dewy bed
  Of aged Tithon' 'gan herself to rear
  With rosy cheeks, for shame as blushing red;
  Her golden locks for haste were loosely shed
  About her ears when Una her did mark
  Climb to her chariot, all with flowers spread,
  From heaven high to chase the cheerless dark:
With merry note her loud salutes the mounting lark.

52

Then freshly up arose the doughty° knight,   *valiant*
  All healed of his hurts and wounds wide,
  And did himself to battle ready dight;°   *prepare*
  Whose early foe – awaiting° him beside   *keeping watch*
  To have devoured so soon as day he spied –
  When now he saw himself so freshly rear,°   *rise*
  As if late fight had nought him damnified° – *hurt to damnation*
  He wox° dismayed,° and 'gan his   *grew faint-hearted**
    fate° to fear: *death*
Natheless,° with wonted° rage he him   *Nevertheless customary*
  advanced near,

53

And in his first encounter, gaping wide,
  He thought at once him to have swallowed quite,° *completely*
  And rushed upon him with outrageous° pride: *excessive; furious*

Who, him rencountering° fierce as hawk in flight,   *engaging*
Perforce° rebutted back. The weapon bright,   *Forcibly*
Taking advantage of his open jaw,
Ran through his mouth with so importune° might   *severe*
That deep empierced° his darksome hollow   *transfixed‡*
  maw°   *stomach*
And, back retired,° his life blood forth withal did   *withdrawn*
  draw.

                               54

So down he fell and forth his life did breathe,
  That vanished into smoke and clouds swift;
  So down he fell that° the earth him underneath   *so that*
  Did groan, as feeble so great load to lift;
  So down he fell, as an huge rocky clift,°   *cliff*
  Whose false° foundation waves have washed away,   *insecure‡*
  With dreadful poise° is from the mainland rift°   *force split‡*
  And, rolling down, great Neptune doth dismay:
So down he fell, and like an heaped mountain lay.

                               55

The knight himself even trembled at his fall,
  So huge and horrible a mass it seemed;
  And his dear lady, that beheld it all,
  Durst not approach for dread, which she
    misdeemed.°   *misjudged*
  But yet, at last, whenas the direful fiend
  She saw not stir, off-shaking vain affright,
  She nigher drew, and saw that joyous end.
  Then God she praised, and thanked her faithful knight,
That had achieved so great a conquest by his might.

Canto 12

Fair Una to the Redcross knight
        Betrothed is with joy,
Though false Duessa it to bar
        Her false sleights do employ.

1

Behold, I see the haven nigh at hand,
   To which I mean my weary course to bend:°   *aim*
Veer the main sheet and bear up with the land,
   The which afore° is fairly to be kenned,°   *before* *discerned*
And seemeth safe from storms that may offend.°   *harm*
There this fair virgin, weary of her way,
   Must landed be, now at her journey's end;
   There eke° my feeble bark a while may stay,   *also*
Till merry° wind and weather call her thence away.   *favourable*

2

Scarcely had Phoebus in the glooming° east   *gleaming;‡ twilit‡*
   Yet harnessed his fiery-footed team,
Ne° reared above the earth his flaming crest,°   *Nor* *rays*
   When the last deadly smoke aloft did steam
That sign of last-outbreathed life did seem
   Unto the watchman on the castle wall;
   Who thereby dead that baleful° beast did deem,° *malign* *judge*
And to his lord and lady loud 'gan call
To tell how he had seen the dragon's fatal° fall.   *deadly*

3

Up rose with hasty joy and feeble speed
   That aged sire, the lord of all that land,
And looked forth to weet° if true indeed   *discover*
   Those tidings were, as he did understand:
Which, whenas true by trial he out found,
   He bade° to open wide his brazen gate   *commanded*
   Which long time had been shut, and out of
      hand°   *straight away*

Proclaimed joy and peace through all his state:
For dead now was their foe which them forayed°   *ravaged*
   late.°   *of late*

4

Then 'gan triumphant trumpets sound on high,°   *aloft; loudly*
   That sent to heaven the echoed report
   Of their new joy, and happy victory
   'Gainst him that had them long oppressed with
      tort,°   *wrong; injury*
   And fast° imprisoned in sieged fort.   *firmly*
   Then all the people, as in solemn feast,
   To him assembled with one full consort,
   Rejoicing at the fall of that great beast
From whose eternal bondage now they were released.

5

Forth came that ancient lord and aged queen,
   Arrayed in antique robes down to the ground,
   And sad° habiliments right well   *dark*
      beseen;°   *as was appropriate*
   A noble crew° about them waited round   *company*
   Of sage and sober° peers all gravely gowned,   *solemn*
   Whom, far before, did march a goodly band
   Of tall° young men, all able arms to   *comely*
      sound° –   *i.e., to fight*
   But now they laurel branches bore in hand,
Glad sign of victory and peace in all their land.

6

Unto that doughty conqueror they came
   And, him before themselves prostrating low,
   Their lord and patron° loud did him proclaim,   *protector; saint*
   And at his feet their laurel boughs did throw.
   Soon after them, all dancing on° a row,   *in*
   The comely virgins came, with garlands dight,°   *adorned*
   As fresh as flowers in meadow green do grow
   When morning dew upon their leaves doth
      light,°   *alight; glisten*
And in their hands sweet timbrels° all upheld on   *tambourines*
   height.°   *high*

7

And them before the fry of° children young　　　　　crowd†
　　Their wanton° sports and childish mirth did play,　　playful
　　And to the maidens' sounding timbrels sung
　　In well-attuned notes a joyous lay,°　　　　　　　　song
　　And made delightful music all the way,
　　Until they came where that fair virgin stood.
　　As fair Diana in fresh summer's day
　　Beholds her nymphs enranged° in shady　　rambling;† ordered†
　　　wood –
Some wrestle, some do run, some bathe in crystal
　　　flood° –　　　　　　　　　　　　　　　　　　　stream

8

So she beheld those maidens' merriment
　　With cheerful view, who, when to her they came,
　　Themselves to ground with gracious humblesse° bent　humility
　　And her adored by honourable° name,°　　illustrious　title[s]‡*
　　Lifting to heaven her everlasting fame.
　　Then on her head they set a garland green
　　And crowned her 'twixt earnest and 'twixt game
　　Who, in her self-resemblance well
　　　beseen,°　　　　　　　　　appointed; open to view
Did seem such as she was – a goodly maiden queen.

9

And, after all, the rascal many° ran,　　　　　i.e. the rabble
　　Heaped together in rude° rabblement,°　　chaotic confusion†
　　To see the face of that victorious man,
　　Whom all admired° as from heaven sent,　　wondered at
　　And gazed upon with gaping wonderment.
　　But when they came where that dead dragon lay,
　　Stretched on the ground in monstrous large extent,
　　The sight with idle° fear did them dismay,　　groundless†
　　Ne durst° approach him nigh to touch or once　　dared
　　　assay.°　　　　　　　　　　　　　　　　　　feel*

10

Some feared and fled; some feared and well it feigned.°　disguised
　　One, that would wiser seem than all the rest,
　　Warned him not touch, for yet perhaps remained

Some lingering life within his hollow breast,
Or in his womb might lurk some hidden nest
Of many dragonets,° his fruitful seed;   *baby dragons*
Another said that in his eyes did rest°   *remain*
Yet sparkling fire, and bade thereof take heed;
Another said he saw him move his eyes indeed.

11

One mother, whenas° her foolhardy child   *when*
Did come too near and with his talons play,
Half dead through fear her little babe reviled,
And to her gossips° 'gan in counsel say: *friends*
'How can I tell but that his talons may
Yet scratch my son, or rend his tender hand?'
So diversely° themselves in vain they fray,°   *variously   scare*
Whiles some more bold to measure him nigh° stand,   *near*
To prove° how many acres he did spread of land.   *establish*

12

Thus flocked all the folk him round about,
The whiles the hoary° king, with all his train,   *venerable*
Being arrived where that champion stout°   *brave*
After his foe's defeasance° did remain,   *overthrow†*
Him goodly° greets, and fair° does entertain   *courteously   nobly*
With princely gifts of ivory and gold,
And thousand thanks him yields for all his pain.
Then, when his daughter dear he does behold,
Her dearly doth embrace, and kisses manifold.°   *many times*

13

And after to his palace he them brings,
With shawms° and trumpets and with   *oboes*
     clarions° sweet;   *high trumpets*
And all the way the joyous people sings,
And with their garments strews the paved street.
Whence mounting up, they find purveyance°   *provisions**
     meet°   *fitting*
Of all that prince's court became,°   *befitted*
And all the floor was, underneath their feet,

Bespread with costly scarlet° of great   *rich [red] cloth*
   name,°   *worth*
On which they lowly sit, and fitting purpose°   *discourse‡*
   frame.°   *express*

14

What needs me tell their feast and goodly° guise,°   *civil conduct*
   In which was nothing riotous nor vain?
   What needs of dainty dishes to devise,°   *narrate*
   Of comely services,° or courtly train?°   *food retinue*
   My narrow° leaves° cannot in them contain   *restricting pages*
   The large° discourse of royal princes' state. *important; extensive*
   Yet was their manner then but bare and plain,
   For the antique° world excess and pride did hate: *ancient*
Such proud luxurious° pomp is swollen up but late.   *excessive*

15

Then, when with meats and drinks of every kind
   Their fervent° appetites they quenched had,   *ardent*
   That ancient lord 'gan fit occasion find
   Of strange adventures and of perils sad°   *calamitous*
   Which in his travel° him befallen had   *journey; labour*
   For to demand of his renowned guest,
   Who then, with utterance grave and countenance
      sad,°   *serious*
   From point to point, as is before expressed,
Discoursed his voyage long, according° his request.   *consenting to*

16

Great pleasure mixed with pitiful regard
   That goodly° king and queen did   *gracious*
      passionate°   *fill with passion‡*
   Whiles they his pitiful adventures heard,
   That° oft they did lament his luckless state,   *So that*
   And often blame the too-importune° fate   *too-severe*
   That heaped on him so many wrathful wreaks;°   *injuries*
   For never gentle° knight, as he of late,   *noble*
   So tossed was in Fortune's cruel freaks:°   *whims‡*
And all the while salt tears bedewed the hearers' cheeks.

17

Then said the royal peer° in sober° wise:°	*father grave fashion*
'Dear son, great been° the evils which ye bore	*have been*
From first to last in your late enterprise,	
That I note° whether praise or pity more;	*know not*
For never living man, I ween,° so sore°	*believe hard*
In sea of deadly dangers was distressed.	
But since now safe ye seized° have the shore,	*gained*
And well arrived are (high God be blessed),	
Let us devise° of ease and everlasting rest.'	*talk*

18

'Ah, dearest lord,' said then that doughty knight,	
'Of ease or rest I may not yet devise;°	*imagine*
For, by the faith which I to arms have plight,°	*pledged*
I bounden° am straight after this	*compelled*
emprise° –	*enterprise*
As that your daughter can ye well advise –	
Back to return to that great Fairy Queen,	
And her to serve six years in warlike wise	
'Gainst that proud paynim° king that works°	*pagan causes*
her teen.°	*trouble*
Therefore I ought crave pardon till I there have been.'	

19

'Unhappy falls that hard necessity,'	
Quoth he, 'the troubler of my happy peace	
And vowed foe of my felicity:	
Ne° I against the same can justly press.°	*Nor contend**
But since that band° ye cannot now release,	*bond*
Nor done, undo (for vows may not be vain),°	*empty*
Soon as the term° of those six years shall cease,	*limit*
Ye then shall thither back return again,	
The marriage to accomplish vowed betwixt you twain.	

20

'Which, for my part, I covet to perform,	
In sort° as through the world I did proclaim,	*Exactly*
That whoso killed that monster most deform,	
And him in hardy° battle overcame,	*daring*
Should have mine only daughter to his dame,°	*for his wife*

And of my kingdom heir apparent be.
Therefore, since now to thee pertains the same
By due desert of noble chivalry,
Both daughter and eke° kingdom, lo, I yield to thee.'   *also*

21

Then forth he called that his daughter fair –
  The fairest Un', his only daughter dear,
  His only daughter and his only heir –
  Who, forth proceeding with sad,° sober°   *grave solemn*
    cheer,°   *aspect*
  As bright as doth the morning star appear
  Out of the east, with flaming locks bedight,°   *bedecked*
  To tell that dawning day is drawing near,
  And to the world does bring long-wished light,
So fair° and fresh° that lady showed herself in   *comely blooming*
    sight.

22

So fair and fresh, as freshest flower in May:
  For she had laid her mournful stole aside,
  And widow-like sad° wimple° thrown away,   *black veil*
  Wherewith her heavenly beauty she did hide
  Whiles on her weary journey she did ride;
  And on her now a garment she did wear
  All lily white, withouten spot° or pride,°   *blemish show*
  That seemed like silk or silver woven near,°   *to resemble*
But neither silk nor silver therein did appear.

23

The blazing brightness of her beauty's beam
  And glorious light of her sunshiny face
  To tell, were as to strive against the stream:
  My ragged rhymes are all too rude° and base   *dissonant*
  Her heavenly lineaments for to enchase.°   *enshrine†*
  No wonder; for her own dear, loved knight –
  All were she° daily with himself in   *Even though she was*
    place° –   *before him*
  Did wonder much at her celestial sight:°   *appearance*
Oft had he seen her fair, but never so fair dight:°   *adorned*

24

So fairly dight, when she in presence° came,   *to the royal presence*
  She to her sire made humble reverence,
  And bowed low, that her right well became,
  And added grace unto her excellence;
  Who, with great wisdom and grave eloquence,
  Thus 'gan to say — But ere° he thus had said,   *before*
  With flying speed, and seeming great pretence,°   *display; claim*
  Came running in, much like a man dismayed,
A messenger with letters, which his message said.

25

All in the open hall amazed° stood   *bewildered*
  At suddenness of that unwary° sight,   *unexpected†*
  And wondered at his breathless, hasty mood.
  But he for nought would stay° his passage right   *direct*
  Till fast° before the king he did alight,°   *right stop†*
  Where, falling flat, great humblesse° he did make,   *obeisance*
  And kissed the ground whereon his foot was pight;°   *placed*
  Then to his hands that writ° he did betake°   *letter* deliver*
Which he, disclosing,° read thus, as the paper spake: *unfolding**

26

'To thee, most mighty King of Eden fair,
  Her greeting sends, in these sad lines addressed,
  The woeful daughter and forsaken heir
  Of that great emperor of all the west;
  And bids thee be advised for the best,
  Ere thou thy daughter link in holy band
  Of wedlock to that new, unknown, guest:
  For he already plighted his right hand
Unto another love, and to another land.

27

'To me, sad maid, or, rather, widow sad,
  He was affianced long time before,
  And sacred pledges he both gave and had,
  False errant knight, infamous and forswore:°   *forsworn*
  Witness the burning altars which° he swore;   *by which*
  And guilty heavens° of his bold   *heavens guilty of receiving . . .*
     perjury

Which, though he hath polluted oft of yore,
  Yet I to them for judgement just do fly,
And them conjure° to avenge this shameful injury.   *call upon*

28

'Therefore, since mine he is, or° free or bond,°   *either serf; tied*
  Or false or true, or living or else dead,
  Withhold, O sovereign prince, your hasty hond°   *hand*
  From knitting league with him, I you aread;°   *advise*
  Ne ween° my right with strength adown to *And do not think*
    tread
  Through weakness of my widowhood or woe:
  For truth is strong her rightful cause to plead,
  And shall find friends if need requireth so:
So bid thee well to fare, Thy neither friend nor foe, Fidessa.'

29

When he these bitter, biting words had read,
  The tidings strange did him abashed make
  That still he sat long time astonished
  As in great muse,° ne word to creature spake. *fit of abstraction*
  At last his solemn silence thus he brake,
  With doubtful eyes fast fixed on his guest:
  'Redoubted° knight, that for mine only   *Distinguished*
    sake°   *sake alone*
  Thy life and honour late adventurest,°   *imperilled*
Let nought be hid from me that ought to be expressed.

30

'What mean these bloody vows and idle° threats, *incoherent*
  Thrown out from womanish, impatient mind?
  What heavens, what altars, what enraged heats
  Here heaped up with terms of love unkind°   *untoward*
  My conscience clear with guilty bands would bind?
  High God be witness that I guiltless am —
  But if yourself, sir knight, ye faulty° find,   *guilty*
  Or wrapped be in loves of former dame,
With crime° do not it cover, but disclose the same.' *wrongdoing*

31

To whom the Redcross knight this answer° sent: *[legal] defence*
  'My lord, my king, be nought thereat dismayed
  Till well ye wote° by grave°   *know   serious*
    intendiment°   *attention*[†]
  What woman, and wherefore,° doth me upbraid   *why*
  With breach of love and loyalty betrayed.
  It was in my mishaps, as hitherward
  I lately travelled, that unwares° I strayed *unknowingly; suddenly*
  Out of my way through perils strange and hard:
That day should fail me ere I had them all declared.

32

'There did I find (or rather, I was found
  Of)° this false woman that Fidessa hight:°   *By is called*[*†]
  Fidessa hight – the falsest dame on ground,
  Most false Duessa, royal richly
    dight,°   *dressed with royal richness*
  That° easy was to inveigle°   *So that trick; blind*
    weaker° sight –   *too weak*
  Who by her wicked arts and wily skill°   *cleverness*
  (Too false and strong for earthly skill° or   *discrimination*
    might)
  Unwares me wrought unto her wicked will,
And to my foe betrayed when least I feared ill.'

33

Then stepped forth the goodly° royal maid   *comely; admirable*
  And, to the ground herself prostrating low,
  With sober° countenance thus to him said: *serious*
  'O pardon° me, my sovereign lord, to show   *allow*
  The secret treasons which of late I know
  To have been wrought by that false sorceress.
  She, only she, it is that erst° did throw   *formerly*
  This gentle° knight into so great distress   *noble; courteous*
That death him did await in daily wretchedness.

34

'And now it seems that she suborned° hath   *craftily provided*
  This crafty messenger with letters vain°   *meaningless*
  To work new woe and improvided° scathe° *unforeseen*[†] *injury*

By breaking of the band betwixt us twain:
 Wherein she used hath the practic° pain°   *practical effort*
 Of this false footman,° cloaked with   *runner*
  simpleness,°   *innocence*
 Whom, if ye please for to discover°   *reveal by uncovering*
  plain,°   *clearly*†
 Ye shall him Archimago find, I guess –
The falsest man alive: who tries shall find no less.'

35

The king was greatly moved at her speech
 And, all with sudden indignation freight,°   *filled*
 Bade on that messenger rude hands to reach.
 Eftsoons° the guard, which on his state did wait, *Straight away*
 Attached° that faitour° false and bound him *Arrested impostor*
  strait;°   *tightly*
 Who, seeming sorely° chafed at° his *extremely injured, vexed by*
  band
 (As chained bear whom cruel dogs do bait),
 With idle° force did feign them to withstand,   *useless*
And often semblance made to 'scape out of their hand.

36

But they him laid° full low in dungeon deep   *deposited*
 And bound him hand and foot with iron chains,
 And with continual watch did warily keep.
 Who, then, would think that, by his subtle trains,° *stratagems*
 He could escape foul death or deadly pains?
 Thus, when that prince's wrath was pacified,
 He 'gan renew the late forbidden bans,
 And to the knight his daughter dear he tied
With sacred rites and vows for ever to abide.

37

His own two hands the holy knots did knit
 That none but death for ever can divide;
 His own two hands, for such a turn most fit,
 The houseling° fire did kindle and   *purifying;*† *sacramental*
  provide,
 And holy water thereon sprinkled wide.
 At which the bushy tead° a groom did light,   *torch*

And sacred lamp in secret chamber hide,
  Where it should not be quenched day nor night
For fear of evil fates, but burnen ever bright.

38

Then 'gan they sprinkle all the posts with wine
  And made great feast to solemnise that day –
  They all perfumed with frankincense divine
  And precious odours fetched from far away –
  That° all the house did sweat° with great   *So that condensate*
    array;°   *preparations*
  And all the while sweet Music did apply
  Her curious° skill° the warbling notes to   *ingenious expertise*
    play
  To drive away the dull Melancholy:
The whiles one sung a song of love and jollity.°   *festivity*

39

During the which there was an heavenly noise°   *music*
  Heard sound through all the palace pleasantly,°   *agreeably*
  Like as it had been many an angel's voice
  Singing before the eternal majesty
  In their trinal° triplicities° on high.   *three-part[†] sets of three[†]*
  Yet wist° no creature whence that heavenly sweet   *knew*
  Proceeded; yet each one felt secretly
  Himself thereby reft of his senses meet,°   *proper senses*
And ravished with rare° impression in his   *an exceptional*
    sprite.°   *soul*

40

Great joy was made that day of young and old
  And solemn feast proclaimed throughout the land,
  That° their exceeding mirth may not be told: *So that*
  Suffice it here by signs° to understand   *semblance[†]*
  The usual joys at knitting of love's band.
  Thrice happy man the knight himself did hold
  Possessed of his lady's heart and hand;
  And ever when his eyes did her behold,
His heart did seem to melt in pleasures manifold.

41

Her joyous presence and sweet company
  In full content he there did long enjoy,
  Ne° wicked envy, ne° vile jealousy   *Neither nor*
  His dear delights were able to annoy.
  Yet, swimming in that sea of blissful joy,
  He nought forgot how he whilom° had sworn –   *formerly**
  In case he should that monstrous beast destroy –
  Unto his Fairy Queen back to return:
The which he shortly did, and Una left to mourn.

42

Now strike your sails, ye jolly mariners,
  For we be come into a quiet road°   *sheltered water; anchorage*
  Where we must land some of our passengers,
  And light this weary vessel of her load.
  Here she awhile may make her safe abode
  Till she repaired have her tackles° spent   *rigging; gear*
  And wants° supplied. And then again abroad   *needs*
  On the long voyage whereto she is bent:°   *directed*
Well may she speed, and fairly finish her intent.

The Second Book of *The Fairy Queen*,
Containing the Legend of Sir Guyon,
or, Of Temperance

1

Right well I wote,° most mighty sovereign,   *know*
  That all this famous antique° history   *of ancient times‡*
  Of° some the abundance° of an idle brain   *By excess*
  Will judged be, and painted° forgery,   *counterfeit;‡ deceptive*
  Rather than matter° of just° memory,   *subject-matter true*
  Sith° none that breatheth living° air does   *Since giving life*
    know
  Where is that happy land of Fairy
  Which I so much do vaunt° yet nowhere show,   *praise*
But vouch° antiquities° which nobody can   *affirm ancient matters‡*
    know.

2

But let that man with better sense advise°   *reflect*
  That of the world least part to us is read,°   *declared**
  And daily how, through hardy° enterprise,°   *bold undertaking*
  Many great regions are discovered
  Which to° late° age were never mentioned.   *until recent*
  Whoever heard of the Indian Peru?
  Or who in venturous° vessel   *daring‡*
    measured°   *marked the course of*
    The Amazon's huge river, now found true?
Or fruitfullest Virginia who did ever view?

3

Yet all these were, when no man did them know –
  Yet have from wisest ages hidden been;
  And later times things more unknown shall show.°   *reveal*
  Why then should witless° man so much   *foolish*
    misween°   *wrongly hold‡*
  That nothing is but that which he hath seen?
  What if, within the moon's fair, shining sphere;

What if, in every star unseen,
Of other worlds he happily° should hear? –   *haply, by chance*
He wonder would much more: yet such to some appear.

4

Of Fairyland yet if he more inquire,°   *seek*
  By certain signs here set in sundry° place°   *various   places*
  He may it find: ne° let him then admire,°   *nor [merely] wonder*
  But yield° his sense to be° too blunt and   *deflect   from being‡*
    base
  That n'ote° without an hound fine°   *knows not   faint*
    footing° trace.°   *track‡   pursue‡*
  And thou, O fairest princess under sky,
  In this fair mirror mayest behold thy face,
  And shine own realms in land of Fairy,
And in this antique image° thy great   *image of antiquity*
    ancestry –

5

The which, O pardon° me thus to enfold   *permit*
  In covert° veil and wrap in shadows   *obscuring*
    light,°   *entertaining‡*
  That° feeble eyes your glory may behold   *So that*
  Which else° could not endure those beams bright,   *otherwise*
  But would be dazzled with exceeding light.
  O pardon; and vouchsafe with patient ear
  The brave adventures of this fairy knight,
  The good Sir Guyon, graciously to hear,
In whom great rule of temperance goodly doth appear.

CANTO I

Guyon, by Archimage abused,°   *deceived*
The Redcross knight awaits;°   *waylays*
Finds Mordant and Amavia slain
With Pleasure's poisoned baits.

1

That cunning° architect of cankered°   *crafty† spiteful; depraved*
  guile
  Whom prince's late displeasure left in bands
  For falsed° letters and suborned° wile° –   *false bribed deceit*
  Soon as the Redcross knight he understands
  To been departed out of Eden lands
  To serve again his sovereign elfin queen,
  His arts he moves,° and out of caitiff's° hands   *applies villain's*
  Himself he frees by secret means unseen:
His shackles empty left, himself escaped clean.°   *completely*

2

And forth he fares, full of malicious mind°   *intent*
  To worken mischief and avenging woe
  Wherever he that godly° knight may find –   *pious; devout*
  His° only° heart-sore° and his *i.e., Redcross's* *chief grief of heart*
  only foe,
  Sith° Una now he algates° must forgo   *Since altogether**
  Whom his victorious hands did erst restore
  To native crowns and kingdoms late° ygo',°   *recently gone**
  Where she enjoys sure peace for evermore,
As weather-beaten ship arrived on happy shore.

3

Him, therefore, now the object of his spite
  And deadly feud he makes: him to offend°   *harm*
  By forged° treason° or by open fight   *contrived treachery*
  He seeks, of all his drift° the aimed end.   *scheming*
  Thereto his subtle° engines° he does   *cunning devices*
  bend,°   *aim*

His practic° wit,° and his fair-   *practical   knowledge*
   filed° tongue,   *smooth*
With thousand other sleights.° For well he   *tricks*
   kenned°   *knew*
His credit° now in doubtful balance   *credibility;‡ reputation‡*
   hung:
For hardly° could be hurt who was already stung.   *with difficulty*

4

Still° as he went he crafty stales° did lay,   *Ever   decoys; ambushes*
   With cunning trains° him to entrap unawares,   *devices*
   And privy° spials° placed in all his way   *concealed   spies*
   To weet° what course he takes and how he fares,   *learn*
   To catch him at a vantage° in his   *at [Archimago's] advantage*
      snares.
   But now so wise and wary was the knight
   By trial of his former harms and cares
   That he descried, and shunned still, his sleight° –   *scheming*
The fish that once was caught new bait will hardly°   *not easily*
   bite.

5

Natheless° the enchanter would not spare his   *Nevertheless*
   pain°   *effort*
   In hope to win occasion° to his will;   *opportunity*
   Which, when he long awaited had in vain,
   He changed his mind from one to other ill,
   For to all good he enemy was still.
   Upon the way him fortuned° to meet –   *chanced*
   Fair° marching underneath a shady hill –   *Appropriately*
   A goodly° knight all armed in harness   *fine*
   meet,°   *seemly armour*
That from his head no place° appeared to his feet.   *chink*

6

His carriage° was full comely° and   *bearing   very handsome*
   upright,
   His countenance demure° and temperate: *grave*
   But yet so stern° and terrible in sight°   *fierce   appearance*
   That cheered his friends and did his foes amate.°   *dismay*
   He was an elfin born, of noble state°   *rank*

And mickle° worship° in his native   *much renown; prominence*
    land:
Well could he tourney and in lists debate,°   *contend*
And knighthood took of good Sir Huon's hand
When with King Oberon he came to Fairyland.

7

Him als' accompanied upon the way
    A comely° Palmer, clad in black attire,   *seemly*
    Of ripest years and hairs all hoary grey,
    That with his staff his feeble steps did steer°   *guide*
    Lest his long way his aged limbs should tire.
    And if by looks one may the mind aread,°   *know*
    He seemed to be a sage and sober° sire,   *temperate*
    And ever with slow pace the knight did lead,
Who taught his trampling steed with equal° steps to   *even*†
    tread.

8

Such, whenas Archimago them did view,
    He weened° well to work some uncouth°   *thought unexpected*
    wile.
    Eftsoons° untwisting his deceitful clue°   *Forthwith thread*
    He 'gan to weave a web of wicked guile
    And, with fair countenance and flattering
    style°
                                manner of speaking†
    To them approaching, thus the knight bespake:°   *addressed*†
'Fair son of Mars, that seek with warlike spoil
    And great achievements great yourself to make,
Vouchsafe to stay your steed for humble miser's° sake.'   *wretch's*

9

He stayed his steed for humble miser's sake
    And bade tell on the tenor of his plaint;°   *complaint; lament*
    Who, feigning then in every limb to quake
    Through inward fear, and seeming pale and faint,
    With piteous moan his piercing° speech 'gan   *distressing*
    paint:°   *deceive*
'Dear lady, how shall I declare thy case,
    Whom late I left in languorous°   *sorrowful**
    constraint?°   *affliction*

Would God thyself now present were in place°   *here; before us*
To tell this rueful tale: thy sight could win thee grace.

10

'Or, rather would – O would it had so chanced
  That you, most noble sir, had present been
  When that lewd ribald° with° vile lust   *debaucherer* by*
    advanced,°   *incited*
  Laid first his filthy hands on virgin clean°   *pure*
  To spoil° her dainty corse° so fair and   *despoil body*
    sheen°   *beautiful*
  As on the earth – great mother of us all –
  With living eye more fair was never seen
  Of chastity and honour virginal:
Witness, ye heavens, whom she in vain to help did call!'

11

'How may it be,' said then the knight half wroth,
  'That knight should knighthood ever so have
    shent?'°   *disgraced*
  'None but that saw,' quoth he, 'would ween for
    truth°   *truly believe*
  How shamefully that maid he did torment.
  Her looser° golden locks he rudely°   *loose violently*
    rent°   *wrenched*
  And drew her on the ground, and his sharp sword
  Against her snowy breast he fiercely bent,°   *aimed*
  And threatened death with many a bloody word:
Tongue hates to tell the rest that eye to see abhorred.

12

Therewith amoved° from his sober° mood,   *stirred* serious*
  'And lives he yet,' said he, 'that wrought this act,
  And do the heavens afford him vital° food?'   *life-bestowing*
  'He lives,' quoth he, 'and boasteth of the fact,'°   *deed*
  Ne° yet hath any knight his courage cracked.'° *Nor destroyed†*
  'Where may that treacher° then,' said he, 'be found, *deceiver*
  Or by what means may I his footing°   *footprints‡*
    tract?'°   *pursue‡*
  'That shall I show,' said he, 'as sure as hound

The stricken deer doth challenge° by the bleeding   scent†
    wound.'

13

He stayed not longer talk but, with fierce ire
    And zealous haste, away is quickly gone
To seek that knight where him that crafty squire
Supposed to be. They do arrive anon,°   together;* forthwith
Where sat a gentle° lady all alone,   noble
With garments rent and hair dishevelled,
Wringing her hands and making piteous moan:
Her swollen eyes were much disfigured,
And her fair face with tears was foully°   terribly
    blubbered.°   swollen‡

14

The knight, approaching nigh, thus to her said:
    'Fair lady, through foul sorrow ill bedight,°   adorned
Great pity is to see you thus dismayed,
And mar° the blossom of your beauty bright.   damaged
For-thy° appease° your grief and heavy   Therefore quieten
    plight,
And tell the cause of your conceived° pain.   inner; mental
For if he live that hath you done despite,°   injury
He shall you do due recompense again,
Or else his wrong with greater puissance° maintain.'   force

15

Which, when she heard, as° in despiteful°   as if malicious
    wise°   fashion
She wilfully her sorrow did augment,
And offered hope of comfort did despise:
Her golden locks most cruelly she rent,
And scratched her face with ghastly°   terrible
    dreariment,°   anguish†
Ne° would she speak, ne° see, ne yet be seen,   Neither nor
But hid her visage and her head down bent,
Either for grievous shame or for great teen,'°   injury; grief
As if her heart with sorrow had transfixed been,

16

Till that her squire bespake:° 'Madam, my   addressed [her]†
  lief,°   dear one
  For God's dear love be not so wilful bent,
  But do vouchsafe now to receive relief,
  The which good fortune doth to you present –
  For what boots° it to weep and to wayment°   avails wail
  When ill is chanced,° but doth the ill increase,   experienced
  And the weak mind with double woe torment?'
  When she her squire heard speak she 'gan appease
Her voluntary° pain, and feel some secret ease.   wilful

17

Eftsoon° she said: 'Ah, gentle trusty squire,   Forthwith
  What comfort can I, woeful wretch, conceive?°   imagine
  Or why should ever I henceforth desire
  To see fair heaven's face, and life not leave,
  Sith° that false traitor did my honour reave?'°   Since ravish
  'False traitor certes,'° said the fairy knight,   indeed
  'I read° the man that ever would deceive   reckon
  A gentle lady, or her wrong through might:°   force
Death were too little pain for such a foul despite.°   outrage

18

'But now, fair lady, comfort to you make,
  And read° who hath ye wrought this shameful plight,   declare
  That short° revenge the man may overtake   swift
  Whereso he be, and soon upon him light.'
  'Certes,' said she, 'I wote° not how he   know
  hight,°   what he is called*†
  But under him a grey steed did he wield,°   command
  Whose sides with dappled circles weren dight:°   adorned
  Upright he rode, and in his silver shield
He bore a bloody cross that quartered all the field.'°   surface

19

'Now by my head,' said Guyon, 'much I muse°   wonder
  How that same knight should do° so foul   perform
  amiss,°   misdeed
  Or ever gentle damsel so abuse;
  For, I may boldly say, he surely is

A right good knight, and true of word, I wis.°   *know*
  I present was, and can it witness well,
  When arms he swore and straight° did   *straight away*
    enterprise°   *venture upon*
  The adventure of the errant damsel,
In which he hath great glory won, as I hear tell.

20

'Natheless° he shortly shall again be tried,   *Nevermore*
  And fairly quit him° of the imputed   *prove himself innocent*
    blame;
  Else be ye sure he dearly shall abide,°   *endure punishment*
  Or make you good amendment° for the same: *reparation*
  All wrongs have mends,° but no amends of   *recompense*
    shame.
  Now therefore, lady, rise out of your pain
  And see the salving° of your blotted name.'   *healing*
  Full loath she seemed thereto, but yet did feign,
For she was inly glad her purpose so to gain.

21

Her purpose was not such as she did feign,
  Ne yet her person such as it was seen;
  But under simple show and semblant° plain   *appearance*
  Lurked false Duessa, secretly unseen,
  As a chaste virgin that had wronged been.
  So had false Archimago her disguised
  To cloak her guile with sorrow and sad teen,
  And eke° himself had craftily devised   *in addition*
To be her squire and do her service well aguised.°   *dressed*†

22

Her late forlorn° and naked he had found   *forsaken*
  Where she did wander in waste wilderness,
  Lurking in rocks and caves far underground,
  And with green moss covering her nakedness
  To hide her shame and loathly filthiness,
  Sith° her Prince Arthur of proud ornaments   *Since*
  And borrowed beauty spoiled.° Her natheless   *despoiled*
  The enchanter, finding fit for his intents,°   *purposes*

Did thus revest,° and decked with due° *reinstate*[†] *appropriate*
 habiliments.

23

For all he did was to deceive good knights,
 And draw them from pursuit of praise and fame
 To slug° in sloth and sensual delights,   *lie idly*
 And end their days with irrenowned° shame. *unrenowned*[†]
 And now exceeding grief him overcame
 To see the Redcross thus advanced° high: *raised*
 Therefore his crafty engine° he did frame° *plot devise*
 Against his praise to stir up enmity
Of° such as virtues like° mote° unto him *From similar might*
 ally.

24

So now he Guyon guides an uncouth° way *unknown; strange*
 Through woods and mountains till they came at last
 Into a pleasant dale that lowly lay
 Betwixt two hills, whose high heads
  overplaced,°   *overhanging*[†]
 The valley did with cool shade overcast;
 Through midst thereof a little river rolled,
 By which there sat a knight with helm unlaced,
 Himself refreshing with the liquid cold
After his travel° long and labours manifold. *journey; travail*

25

'Lo, yonder he,' cried Archimage aloud,
 'That wrought the shameful fact° which I did   *deed*
  show!°   *disclose*
 And now he doth himself in secret shroud
 To fly the vengeance for his outrage due –
 But vain:° for ye shall dearly do him   *in vain*
  rue,°   *make him repent*
 So God ye speed and send you good success,
 Which we, far off, will here abide to view.'
 So they him left, inflamed with wrathfulness,
That° straight against that knight his spear he did *So that*
 address.°   *raise*

26

Who, seeing him from far so fierce to prick,°   spur forward
  His warlike arms° about him 'gan embrace,°   armour put on
  And in the rest° his ready spear did stick;   spear-rest
  Tho,° whenas° still he saw him towards pace,   Then when
  He 'gan rencounter° him in equal race.   engage in battle
  They been ymet, both ready to affrap,°   strike†
  When suddenly that warrior 'gan abase°   lower
  His threatened spear, as if some new mishap
Had him betid,° or hidden danger did entrap,   befallen

27

And cried: 'Mercy, sir knight, and mercy, Lord,
  For mine offence° and heedless   impropriety
    hardiment,°   boldness
  That had almost committed crime abhorred
  And with reproachful shame mine honour shent°   disgraced
  Whiles cursed steel against that badge I bent° –   aimed
  The sacred badge of my redeemer's death
  Which on your shield is set for ornament.
  But his fierce foe his steed could stay uneath°   scarcely
Who, pricked° with courage keen,° did cruel   incited bold*
  battle breathe.

28

But when he heard him speak, straightway he knew
  His error and, himself inclining,° said: bowing
  'Ah, dear Sir Guyon, well becometh° you;   that befits
  But me behoveth rather to upbraid,
  Whose hasty hand so far from reason strayed
  That almost it did heinous violence
  On that fair image of that heavenly maid
  That decks° and arms° your shield with fair   adorns protects
  defence:
Your courtesy takes on you another's due offence.'

29

So been they both at one, and doen° uprear°   do raise
  Their beavers bright, each other for to greet.
  Goodly° comportance° each to other   courteous behaviour†
  bear,

And entertain themselves with courtesies meet.°   *fitting*
Then said the Redcross knight: 'Now mote° I   *must*
   weet,°   *know*
Sir Guyon, why with so fierce saliaunce°   *attack*[†]
And fell° intent ye did at erst° me meet;   *cruel first*
For sith° I know your goodly°   *since notable*
   governance,°   *self-control*
Great cause, I ween,° you guided, or some   *believe*
   uncouth° chance.'   *strange*

30

'Certes,'° said he, 'well mote° I shame to tell   *Indeed might*
   The fond° encheason° that me hither led.   *foolish occasion*
A false, infamous faitour° late befell°   *impostor chanced*
Me for to meet that seemed ill-bested,°   *in bad trouble*
And plained° of grievous outrage which he   *complained*
   read°   *stated*
A knight had wrought against a lady gent° –   *noble*
Which to avenge he to this place me led
Where you he made the mark of his intent,
And now is fled: foul shame him follow where he went':

31

So can° he turn his earnest unto game   *did*
   Through goodly handling and wise temperance.
By this his aged guide in° presence came –   *to his*
Who, soon as on that knight his eye did glance,
Eftsoons° of him had perfect   *Forthwith*
   cognizance°   *recognition*
Sith° him in fairy court he late°   *Since recently*
   avised° –   *observed**
And said: 'Fair son, God give you happy chance,
And that dear cross upon your shield devised,°   *painted**
Wherewith above all knights ye goodly seem aguised.°   *attired*[†]

32

'Joy may you have, and everlasting fame,
   Of late most hard achievement by you done,°   *performed*
For which enrolled is your glorious name
In heavenly registers above the sun,
Where you a saint with saints your seat have won.

But wretched we, where ye have left your mark,
  Must now anew begin like race°   *course in tournament; in life*
    to run:
  God guide thee, Guyon, well to end thy wark,°   *work**
And to the wished haven bring thy weary barque.'

33

'Palmer,' him answered the Redcross knight,
  'His be the praise that this achievement wrought,
  Who made my hand the organ of His might:
  More than goodwill attribute to me nought,
  For all I did, I did but as I ought.
  But you, fair sir, whose pageant next ensues,
  Well mote° ye thee° as well can wish your   *may thrive**
    thought,
  That home ye may report° thrice happy news –   *bring back*
For well ye worthy been for worth and gentle°   *noble*
    thews.'°   *qualities**

34

So courteous congé° both did give and take,   *leave*
  With right hands plighted, pledges of good will.
  Then Guyon forward 'gan his voyage make
  With his black Palmer, that him guided still:
  Still° he him guided, over vale and hill,   *Always*
  And with his steady staff did point his way.
  His race° with reason, and with words his will,   *journey**
  From foul intemperance he oft did stay,
And suffered not in wrath his hasty steps to stray.

35

In this fair wise° they travelled long yfere°   *manner together*
  Through many hard assays° which did   *afflictions**
    betide,°   *befall*
  Of which he honour still away did bear,
  And spread his glory through all countries wide.
  At last, as chanced them by a forest side
  To pass for succour° from the scorching ray,   *protection*
  They heard a rueful voice that dernly° cried   *dismally†*
  With piercing shrieks and many a doleful lay,°   *note*
Which, to attend, a while their forward steps they stay.

36

'But if that careless heavens,' quoth she, 'despise
  The doom° of just revenge, and take delight   *sentence*
  To see sad pageants of men's miseries,
  As bound by them to live in life's
     despite,°   *in spite of life's miseries*
  Yet can they not warn° death from wretched   *exclude**
     wight.°   *person**
  Come then, come soon, come sweetest death to me,
  And take away this long-lent loathed light:
  Sharp be thy wounds, but sweet the medicines be,
That long captived souls from weary thraldom free.

37

'But thou, sweet babe, whom frowning froward° fate   *adverse*
  Hath made sad witness of thy father's fall:
  Sith° heaven thee deigns to hold in living state,   *Since*
  Long mayest thou live, and better thrive withal
  Than to thy luckless parents did befall.
  Live thou, and to thy mother dead attest°   *bear witness*
  That clear she died from blemish criminal:
  Thy little hands imbrued in° bleeding breast,   *steeped in*[†]
Lo, I for pledges leave. So, give me leave to rest.'

38

With that a deadly shriek she forth did throw°   *utter*
  That through the wood re-echoed again,
  And after gave a groan so deep and low
  That seemed her tender heart was rent in twain,
  Or thrilled° with point of thorough-piercing pain,   *pierced*
  As gentle hind, whose sides with cruel steel
  Through-launched° forth her bleeding life does   *Penetrated*
     rain,
  Whiles the sad pang approaching she does feel,
Brays° out her latest° breath and up her eyes doth   *Cries* last*
  seel.°   *close*

39

Which, when that warrior heard, dismounting straight
  From his tall° steed, he rushed into the   *splendid*
    thick,°   *thicket**

And soon arrived where that sad portrait
Of death and dolour lay, half dead, half quick,   *alive*
In whose white alabaster breast did stick
A cruel knife that made a grisly° wound   *horrific*
From which forth gushed a stream of gore-
   blood° thick   *clotted blood‡*
That all her goodly° garments stained around   *fine*
And into a deep sanguine° dyed the grassy ground.   *blood red*

40

Pitiful spectacle° of deadly smart,°   *instance; exemplum   adversity*
Beside a bubbling fountain low she lay,
Which she increased with her bleeding heart
And the clean° waves with purple gore did ray.°   *pure   soil*
Als' in her lap a lovely babe did play
His cruel sport instead of sorrow due –
For in her streaming blood he did embay°   *immerse†*
His little hands, and tender° joints   *young*
   imbrue:°   *stain;‡ saturate‡*
Pitiful spectacle as ever eye did view!

41

Besides them both, upon the soiled° grass,   *defiled*
A dead corse° of an armed knight was spread,   *corpse*
Whose armour all with blood besprinkled was.
His ruddy lips did smile, and rosy red
Did paint his cheerful cheeks, yet° being dead: *just*
Seemed to have been a goodly
   personage°   *handsome figure of a man*
Now in his freshest flower of lustihead,°   *vigour; lustfulness*
Fit to inflame fair lady with love's rage,
But that fierce Fate did crop the blossom of his age.

42

Whom, when the good Sir Guyon did behold,
His heart 'gan wex° as stark° as marble stone   *grow   hard*
And his fresh blood did freeze with fearful° cold,   *apprehensive*
That° all his senses seemed bereft at one.°   *So that   together*
At last his mighty ghost° 'gan deep to groan –   *spirit*
As lion, grudging° in his great disdain,°   *murmuring   anger*
Mourns inwardly, and makes to himself moan –

Till ruth and frail° affection° did   *tender* *emotion*
   constrain°   *compel*
His stout° courage° to stoop and show his   *brave* *heart, mind*
   inward pain.

43

Out of her gored° wound the cruel steel   *pierced;*[‡] *bloody*[‡]
  He lightly° snatched, and did the floodgate°   *quickly* *torrent*
    stop
  With his fair garment; then 'gan softly feel
  Her feeble pulse to prove° if any drop   *test*
  Of living blood yet in her veins did hop° –   *leap; pulse*
  Which, when he felt to move, he hoped
    fair°   *with this good omen*[*]
  To call back life to her forsaken shop.°   *heart*
  So well he did her deadly wounds repair
That at the last she 'gan to breathe out living
    air.°   *the breath of life*

44

Which he, perceiving, greatly 'gan rejoice,
  And goodly counsel – that for wounded heart
  Is meetest° medicine – tempered with sweet voice: *fittest*
  'Aye me, dear lady, which the image art
  Of rueful° pity and impatient°   *lamentable* *intolerable*[†]
    smart,°   *wound*
  What direful chance armed with revenging fate,
  Or cursed hand, hath played his cruel part
  Thus foul to hasten your untimely date?° –   *death*
Speak, O dear lady, speak: help never comes too late.'

45

Therewith her dim eyelids she up 'gan rear,°   *raise*
  On which the dreary° death did sit, as sad   *heavy*
  As lump of lead, and made dark clouds appear.
  But, whenas° him all in bright armour clad   *when*
  Before her standing she espied had,
  As one out of a deadly dream affright°   *terrified*[†]

She weakly started, yet she nothing drad:°   *dreaded*
Straight down again herself in great
    despite°   *disdain [i.e., of life]*
She grovelling threw to ground, as hating life and light.

46

The gentle° knight her soon with   *noble; courteous*
    careful° pain   *full of care*
  Uplifted light,° and softly° did uphold   *swiftly   gently*
  (Thrice he her reared, and thrice she sunk again
  Till he his arms about her sides 'gan fold),
  And to her said: 'Yet if the stony cold
  Have not all seized on your frozen heart,
  Let one word fall that may your grief unfold,
  And tell the secret of your mortal smart:°   *wound*
He oft finds present° help who does his grief impart.'   *immediate*

47

Then, casting up a deadly look, full low
  She sighed from bottom of her wounded breast
  And, after many bitter throbs° did throw,°   *pulsations‡   beat*
  With lips full pale and faltering tongue oppressed,
  These words she breathed forth from riven chest:
  'Leave, ah leave off, whatever wight° thou be,   *person**
  To let° a weary wretch from her due rest   *Hindering*
  And trouble dying soul's tranquillity:
Take not away, now got, which° none would give to   *that which*
  me.'

48

'Ah far be it,' said he, 'dear dame, from me
  To hinder soul from her desired rest,
  Or hold sad life in long captivity;
  For all I seek is but to have redressed°   *removed*
  The bitter pangs that doth your heart infest.°   *trouble*
  Tell then, O lady, tell what fatal prief°   *trial*
  Hath with so huge misfortune you oppressed,
  That I may cast to° compass° your relief   *plan to effect*
Or die with you in sorrow and partake your grief.'

49

With feeble hands then stretched forth on high,
  As heaven accusing guilty of her death,
  And with dry drops congealed in her eye,
  In these sad words she spent her utmost° breath: *last*
  'Hear then, O man, the sorrows that uneath°   *with difficulty*
  My tongue can tell, so far all sense° they   *understanding*
    pass.°   *surpass*
  Lo, this dead corpse, that lies here underneath,
  The gentlest knight that ever on green grass
Gay steed with spurs did prick, the good Sir Mordant was:

50

'Was (aye the while that he is not so now)
  My lord, my love: my dear lord, my dear love,
  So long as heavens just with equal° brow   *impartial*
  Vouchsafed to behold us from above.
  One day, when him high courage did inmove° –   *move*
  As wont° ye knights to seek adventures wild –   *are accustomed*
  He pricked forth his puissant force to prove:°   *put to the test*
  Me then he left enwombed° of° this child –   *pregnant*† *with*
This luckless child, whom thus ye see with blood defiled.

51

Him fortuned (hard fortune, ye may guess)
  To come where vile Acrasia does wone° –   *dwell*
  Acrasia, a false enchantress
  That many errant knights hath foul fordone.°   *destroyed; ruined*
  Within a wandering island that doth run
  And stray in perilous gulf her dwelling is:
  Fair sir, if ever there ye travel, shun
  The cursed land where many wend° amiss,°   *go astray*
And know it by the name: it hight° the Bower of   *is called**†
  Bliss.

52

'Her bliss is all in pleasure and delight,
  Wherewith she makes her lovers drunken mad;
  And then, with words and deeds of wondrous might,
  On them she works her will to uses bad.
  My liefest° lord she thus beguiled had,   *most beloved*

For he was flesh (all flesh doth frailty breed).
Whom, when I heard to been so ill bested,°   *in such bad trouble*
Weak wretch, I wrapped myself in palmer's weed°   *attire*
And cast° to seek him forth through danger and great   *resolved*
   dread.

53

'Now had fair Cynthia by even turns
   Full measured three quarters of her year
   And thrice three times had filled her crooked horns,
   Whenas° my womb her burden would   *When*
      forbear°   *yield up**
   And bade me call Lucina to me near.
   Lucina came: a manchild forth I brought;
   The woods, the nymphs, my bowers,° my   *bedchambers*
      midwives were –
   Hard° help at need. So dear° thee, babe, I   *Cruel   dearly*
      bought,
Yet nought too dear I deemed° while so my dear I   *judged*
   sought.

54

Him so I sought, and so, at last, I found,
   Where him that witch had thralled° to her will   *captivated*
   In chains of lust and lewd desires ybound,
   And so transformed from his former
      skill°   *reason;*   discrimination**
   That me he knew not, neither his own ill;
   Till, through wise handling and fair governance,°   *control*
   I him recured° to a better will,   *restored*
   Purged from drugs of foul intemperance:
Then means I 'gan devise for his deliverance.

55

'Which, when the vile enchantress perceived
   How that my lord from her I would reprieve,°   *rescue‡*
   With cup thus charmed him parting she deceived:
   "Sad° verse, give death to him that death does give,   *Gloomy*
   And loss of love to her that loves to live,
   So soon as Bacchus with the nymph does link."
So parted we and on our journey drive°   *hastened*

Till, coming to this well, he stooped to drink:
The charm fulfilled, dead suddenly he down did sink.

56

'Which when I, wretch—.' Not one more word she said
  But, breaking off the end for want of breath,
  And sliding soft, as° down to sleep her laid,   *as if*
  And ended all her woe in quiet death.
  That seeing, good Sir Guyon could uneath°   *scarcely*
  From tears abstain, for grief his heart did grate° *fret; grieve*
  And from so heavy sight his head did wreathe,°   *turn*
  Accusing Fortune and too-cruel Fate
Which plunged had fair lady in so wretched state.

57

Then, turning to his Palmer, said: 'Old sire,
  Behold the image of mortality,
  And feeble nature clothed with fleshly tire,°   *apparel*
  When raging passion with fierce tyranny
  Robs reason of her due regality
  And makes it servant to her basest part:
  The strong it weakens with infirmity,
  And with bold fury arms the weakest heart;
The strong through pleasure soonest falls, the weak through
    smart.°   *pain*

58

'But temperance,' said he,° 'with golden   *i.e., the Palmer*
  squire°   *set-square*
  Betwixt them both can measure out a mean°   *middle way*
  Neither to melt in pleasure's hot desire,
  Nor fry° in heartless° grief and doleful   *burn¹ spiritless*
  teen.°   *trouble*
  Thrice happy man who fares° them both   *proceeds*
  atween;°   *between*
  But sith this wretched woman overcome
  Of° anguish rather than of crime° hath been,   *by sin*
  Reserve° her cause° to her eternal *Hold over case [legal]*
  doom,°   *judgement*
And in the mean° vouchsafe her honourable tomb.' *meantime*

59

'Palmer,' (quoth he) 'death is an equal doom°   *sentence*
  To good and bad, the common inn of rest.
  But after death the trial is to come,
  When best shall be to them that lived best.
  But both alike, when death hath both suppressed,°   *laid low*
  Religious reverence doth burial teen,°   *inspire; prescribe*
  Which whoso wants,° wants so much of his rest.   *lacks*
  For also° great shame after death, I ween,°   *just as believe*
As self to dien bad,° unburied bad to been.'   *i.e., commit suicide*

60

So both agree their bodies to engrave:°   *bury*
  The great Earth's womb they open to the sky,
  And with sad° cypress seemly° it   *dark; melancholy fittingly*
    embrace;°   *adorn*†
  Then, covering with a clod their closed eye,
  They lay therein those corses° tenderly,   *corpses*
  And bid them sleep in everlasting peace.
  But, ere° they did their utmost° obsequy,   *before last*
  Sir Guyon, more affection° to increase,   *emotion*
Benamed° a sacred vow which none should aye°   *Swore ever*
  release.°   *revoke*

61

The dead knight's sword out of his sheath he drew,
  With which he cut a lock of all° their hair   *both*
  Which, meddling° with their blood and earth, he   *mixing*
    threw
  Into the grave and 'gan devoutly swear:
  'Such and such evil God on Guyon rear,°   *direct*†
  And worse and worse, young orphan, be thy pain,
  If I or thou due vengeance do forbear°   *refrain from*
  Till guilty° blood her guerdon° do   *shed culpably reward*
    obtain.'
So shedding many tears, they closed the earth again.

From Canto 2

1

Thus when Sir Guyon, with his faithful guide,
    Had with due rites and dolorous lament
    The end of their sad tragedy uptied,
    The little babe up in his arms he hent,° –   *lifted*
    Who, with sweet pleasance° and bold   *pleasure*
        blandishment,°   *cajolery*[†]
    'Gan smile on them, that rather ought to weep,
    As careless of his woe, or innocent
    Of what was done, that ruth empierced° deep   *pierced sharply*[‡]
In that knight's heart, and words with bitter tears did
        steep:°   *bathe*[†]

2

'Ah, luckless babe, born under cruel star
    And in dead parents' baleful° ashes bred: *destructive; wretched*
    Full little weenest° thou what sorrows are   *suspect*
    Left thee for portion of thy livelihead.°   *life*[*]
    Poor orphan, in the wide world scattered
    As budding branch rent from the native tree,
    And thrown forth till it be withered –
    Such is the state of men: thus enter we
Into this life with woe, and end with misery.'

3

Then soft° himself inclining on his knee   *gently*
    Down to that well, did in the water ween°   *think*
    (So love does loathe disdainful nicety)°   *reserve*
    His guilty hands from bloody gore° to clean.   *blood*[‡]
    He washed them oft and oft, yet nought they been,
    For all his washing, cleaner. Still he strove;

Yet still the little hands were bloody seen –
The which him into great amazement drove,
And into diverse° doubt his wavering wonder   *distracting*[†]
    clove.°   *split*

4

He wist° not whether° blot of foul offence   *knew why*
  Might not be purged with water nor with bath:°   *bathing*
  Or° that high God, in lieu° of innocence,   *Either place*
  Imprinted had the token of His wrath
To show how sore° bloodguiltiness° he   *much inherited guilt*[†]
  hateth;
  Or that the charm and venom, which they drunk,
  Their blood with secret filth infected hath,
  Being diffused through the senseless trunk°   *body*
That through the great contagion direful deadly stunk.

5

Whom, thus at gaze,° the Palmer 'gan to   *gazing in bewilderment*
  board°   *address*
  With goodly reason and thus fair°   *courteously*
  bespake:°   *spoke*[†]
  'Ye been right hard° amated,° gracious   *greatly counfounded*
  lord,
  And of° your ignorance great marvell°   *because of astonishment*
  make,
  Whiles cause not well conceived° ye mistake.   *understood*
  But know that secret° virtues° are infused   *hidden powers*
  In every fountain and in every lake
  Which, who hath skill° them rightly to have   *knowledge*
  choosed,°   *chosen*
To proof of passing° wonders hath full often used. *surpassing*

6

'Of those, some were so from their source endued°   *invested*
  By great Dame Nature, from whose fruitful pap°   *nipple*
  Their wellheads spring and are with moisture dewed,
  Which feeds each living plant with liquid sap,
  And fills with flowers fair Flora's painted lap.
  But other some,° by gift of later   *some others*
  grace°   *more recent favour*

Or by good prayers, or by other hap,°   *chance*
Had virtue poured into their waters base,
And thenceforth were renowned, and sought from place to
      place.

                                    7
'Such is this well, wrought by occasion strange,
      Which to her nymph befell. Upon a° day,   *One*
      As she the woods with bow and shafts did range°   *roam*‡
      The heartless° hind and roebuck to dismay,°   *fearful* *vanquish*
      Dan° Faunus chanced to meet her by the way   *'Master'*
      And, kindling fire at her fair, burning eye,
      Inflamed was to follow beauty's chase,
      And chased her, that fast from him did fly:
As hind from her, so she fled from her enemy.

                                    8
'At last, when failing breath began to faint,°   *grow weak*
      And saw no means to escape, of shame afraid,
      She set her down to weep for sore° constraint°   *great* *affliction*
      And, to Diana calling loud for aid,
      Her dear° besought to let her die a maid.   *passionately*
      The goddess heard and, sudden, where she sat
      Welling out streams of tears, and quite dismayed°   *paralysed*
      With stony fear of that rude rustic mate,
Transformed her to a stone from steadfast virgin's state.

                                    9
'Lo, now she is that stone, from whose two heads,
      As from two weeping eyes, fresh streams do flow,
      Yet° cold through fear and old-conceived dreads.   *Still*
      And yet the stone her semblance seems to show,
      Shaped like a maid that such ye may her know:
      And yet her virtues in her water bide,
      For it is chaste and pure as purest snow,
      Ne° lets her waves with any filth be dyed,   *Nor*
But ever, like herself, unstained hath been tried.°   *found*

10

'From thence it comes that this babe's bloody hand
　　May not be cleansed with water of this well.
　　Ne certes,° sir, strive you it to withstand,　　　　　　*Nor indeed*
　　But let them still be bloody, as befell,°　　　　　　*has occurred*
　　That they his mother's innocence may tell
　　As she bequeathed in her last testament,
　　That as a sacred symbol° it may dwell　　　　　　　*token*
　　In her son's flesh to mind°　　　　　　　　*bring to mind*[†]
　　revengement°　　　　　　　　　　　　　*retribution*
And be for all chaste dames an endless°　　　　　　*eternal*
　　monument.'°　　　　　　　　　　　　*warning*[†]

11

He hearkened to his reason° and, the child　　　　　*statement*
　　Uptaking, to the Palmer gave to bear;
　　But his sad° father's arms,° with　　*valiant; lamentable armour*
　　blood defiled,
　　An heavy load, himself did lightly rear°　　　　　　　*lift*
　　And, turning to that place in which, whilere,°　　*previously*
　　He left his lofty° steed with golden sell°　　*noble saddle*
　　And goodly,° gorgeous barbs,° him found　*splendid coverings*[‡]
　　not there:
　　By other accident° that erst° befell　　　　*chance formerly*
He is conveyed, but how, or where, here fits not tell. . . .

Canto 3

　　Vain° Braggadocchio, getting Guyon's　　　　　*foolish*
　　　　Horse is made the scorn
　　Of° knighthood true, and is of fair　　　　　　　　*by*
　　　　Belphoebe foul° forlorn.°　　　*shamefully disgraced* *

1

Soon as the morrow fair with purple beams
　　Dispersed the shadows of the misty night,
　　And Titan, playing on the eastern streams,
　　　'Gan clear the dewy air with springing° light,　　*dawning*

Sir Guyon, mindful of his vow yplight,°   pledged*
Uprose from drowsy couch and him addressed
Unto the journey which he had behight:°   vowed*
His puissant° arms° about his noble breast   mighty armour
And many-folded shield he bound about his wrist.

2

Then, taking congé° of that virgin° pure,   leave i.e., Medina
  The bloody-handed babe unto her truth°   steadfastness
  Did earnestly commit, and her conjure°   made her swear
  In virtuous° lore to train his tender youth   doctrine
  And all that gentle° nouriture°   noble upbringing
    ensueth,°   follows from
  And that, so soon as riper years he raught,°   reached
  He might, for memory of that day's ruth,°   pity
  Be called Ruddimane, and thereby taught
To avenge his parents' death on them that had it
    wrought.°   caused

3

So forth he fared, as now befell,° on foot,   it turned out
  Sith° his good steed is lately from him gone –   Since
  Patience perforce!° Helpless, what may it   of necessity
    boot°   avail
  To fret for anger, or for grief to moan?
  His Palmer now shall foot no more alone.
  So Fortune wrought° as, under greenwood's side arranged that
  He lately heard that dying lady groan,
  He left his steed without,° and spear beside, outside [the forest]
And rushed in on foot to aid her ere she died.

4

The whiles° a losel,° wandering by the   Meanwhile worthless rogue
    way,
  One that to bounty° never cast° his   valour;* virtue applied
    mind,
  Ne° thought of honour ever did assay°   Nor test
  His baser° breast, but in his kestrel°   most base hawkish‡
    kind°   nature
  A pleasing vein of glory vain did find,
  To which his flowing° tongue and troublous   smooth

sprite°   *mind*
Gave him great aid and made him more inclined.
He that brave° steed there finding ready dight°   *fine prepared*
Purloined° both steed and spear, and ran away full   *Stole*
    light.°   *swiftly*

5

Now 'gan his heart all swell in jollity,°   *arrogance*
  And of himself great hope and help conceived
That,° puffed up with smoke of vanity,   *So that*
And with self-loved personage° deceived,   *image*
He 'gan to hope of° men to be received   *by*
For such as he him thought, or fain° would be: *gladly*
But for° in court gay portance° he perceived   *Because bearing†*
And gallant show to be in greatest gree,°   *favour**
Eftsoons° to court he cast° to advance his   *Forthwith resolved*
    first degree.

6

And by the way he chanced to espy
  One sitting idle on a sunny bank,
To whom avaunting° in great   *advancing; boasting*
    bravery°   *bravado*
As peacock that his painted plumes doth prank,°   *display*
He smote his courser in the trembling flank
And to him threatened his heart-thrilling° spear.   *-piercing*
The seely° man, seeing him ride so   *simple*
    rank,°   *haughtily; violently*
And aim at him, fell flat to the ground for fear,
And crying 'Mercy' loud,° his piteous hands 'gan   *loudly*
    rear.°   *raise*

7

Thereat the scarecrow° waxed° wondrous   *ridiculous figure† grew*
    proud
Through fortune of his first adventure fair,
And with big thundering voice reviled him loud:
'Vile caitiff,° vassal of dread and despair,   *captive; wretch*
Unworthy of the common-breathed air,
Why livest thou, dead dog, a longer day,
And dost not unto death thyself prepare?

Die, or thyself my captive yield for aye –
Great favour I thee grant for answer thus to stay.'

8

'Hold, O dear lord, hold your dead-doing° hand,'　　*death-dealing*
　　Then loud he cried, 'I am your humble thrall.'
　　'Ah, wretch,' (quoth he) 'thy destinies withstand
　　My wrathful will and do for mercy call.
　　I give thee life: therefore prostrated fall,
　　And kiss my stirrup – that thy homage be.'
　　The miser° threw himself, as an offal,°　　*wretch [piece of] refuse*‡
　　Straight at his foot in base humility,
And cleped° him his liege to hold of him in　　　　　　*called*
　　fee.°　　　　　　　　　　　　　　　　　　　*in servitude*‡

9

So, happy peace they made and fair accord.
　　Eftsoons° this liegeman 'gan to wax more bold,　　*Soon after*
　　And when he felt the folly of his lord,
　　In his own kind° he 'gan himself unfold –　　　　　*nature*
　　For he was wily-witted, and grown old
　　In cunning° sleights and practic knavery.　　*crafty*‡ *practised*‡
　　From that day forth he cast for to uphold
　　His idle° humour° with fine flattery　　　　*silly; worthless mood*
And blow the bellows to his swelling vanity.

10

Trompart – fit man for Braggadocchio
　　To serve at court in view of vaunting°　　*vainglorious; bragging*
　　eye.
　　Vainglorious man, when fluttering wind does blow
　　In his light° wings, is lifted up to sky –　　　　　　*fickle*
　　The scorn of knighthood and true chivalry,
　　To° think without desert° of°　　　　*[Which is] to reward by*
　　gentle° deed　　　　　　　　　　　　　　　　　*noble*
　　And noble worth to be advanced high:
　　Such praise is shame. But honour, virtue's meed,°　　*reward*
Doth bear the fairest flower in honourable seed.

11

So forth they pass, a well-consorted pair,
   Till that at length with Archimage they meet –
   Who, seeing one that shone in armour fair
   On goodly courser thundering with his feet,
   Eftsoons° suppposed him a person°   *Forthwith*
     meet°   *appropriate*
   Of his revenge to make the instrument;
   For since the Redcross knight he erst° did   *formerly*
     weet°   *believe*
   To been with Guyon knit in one consent° *in complete amity*
The ill which erst to him, he now to Guyon, meant.°   *intended*

12

And, coming close to Trompart, 'gan inquire
   Of him what mighty warrior that mote° be   *might*
   That rode in golden sell° with single° spear,   *saddle   only a*
   But wanted° sword to wreak his enmity.   *lacked*
   'He is a great adventurer,' said he,
   'That hath his sword through hard assay°   *trial*
     forgone,°   *lost* *
   And now hath vowed, till he avenged be
   Of that despite,° never to wearen none: *outrage*
That spear is him enough to doen° a thousand groan.'   *cause*

13

The enchanter greatly joyed° in the vaunt,°   *rejoiced boast*
   And weened° well ere long his will to win,   *thought*
   And both his foen° with equal foil° to   *foes   defeat*
     daunt.°   *overcome*
   Tho,° to him louting° lowly,° did begin *Then bowing humbly*
   To plain° of wrongs which had committed been   *complain*
   By Guyon and by that false Redcross knight,
   Which two, through treason° and deceitful   *treachery*
     gin,°   *cunning*
   Had slain Sir Mordant and his lady bright:
That mote° him honour bring to wreak° so foul   *might avenge*
     despite.

14

Therewith all suddenly he seemed enraged,
  And threatened death with dreadful countenance,
    As if their lives had in his hand been gaged;°   *pledged*
    And with stiff° force, shaking his mortal° lance *strong deadly*
    To let him weet° his doughty valiance,°   *know valour*
    Thus said: 'Old man, great sure shall be thy meed
    If, where those knights for fear of due vengeance
    Do lurk, thou certainly to me aread,°   *advise‡*
That I may wreak on them their heinous, hateful deed.'

15

'Certes,° my lord,' said he, 'that shall I soon,   *Indeed*
  And give you eke° good help to their decay;° *also destruction*
    But mote° I wisely you advise to   *may*
      doon:°   *undertake it sensibly*
    Give no odds to your foes, but do purvey° *equip*
    Yourself of sword before that bloody day;
    For they be two the prowest° knights on *most valiant*
      ground,°   *earth*
    And oft approved° in many hard assay:° *put to test trial*
    And eke° of surest steel that may be found *also*
Do arm yourself against that day them to confound.'

16

'Dotard'° (said he), 'let be thy deep° advice: *Old fool profound*
  Seems that through many years° thy wits thee fail, *i.e, age*
    And that weak eld° hath left thee nothing wise – *old age*
    Else never should thy judgement be so frail
    To° measure manhood by the sword or mail.   *As to*
    Is not enough four quarters of a man,
    Withouten sword or shield, an host to quail?
    Thou little wotest° what this right hand *knowest*
      can:°   *is capable of*
Speak they which have beheld the battles which it won.'

17

The man was much abashed at his boast;
  Yet well he wist° that whoso would contend *knew*
    With either of those knights on even° *equal*
      coast°   *attack;* footing*

Should need all of his arms him to defend –
Yet feared lest his boldness should offend;
When Braggadocchio said: 'Once° I did   *On the occasion when*
  swear,
When with one sword seven knights I brought to end,
Thenceforth in battle never sword to bear
But° it were that which noblest knight on earth doth   *Unless*
  wear.'

18

'Perdy, sir knight,' then said the enchanter belive,°   *swiftly*
  'That shall I shortly purchase° to your hand;   *obtain*
For now the best and noblest knight alive
Prince Arthur is, that wones° in Fairyland: *dwells*
He hath a sword that flames like burning brand.°   *torch*
The same, by my device,° I undertake   *ingenuity*
Shall by tomorrow by thy side be found.'
At which bold words the boaster 'gan to quake,
And wondered in his mind what mote° that   *might*
  monster° make.°   *prodigy   create*

19

He stayed not for more bidding, but away
  Was sudden vanished out of his sight:
The northern wind his wings did broad display°   *spread out*
At his command, and reared° him up light°   *lifted   lightly*
From off the earth to take his airy flight.
They looked about, but nowhere could espy
Tract° of his foot; then, dead through great   *Print*
  affright°   *terror†*
They both nigh were, and each bade other fly:
Both fled at once, ne° ever back returned eye,   *nor*

20

Till that they come unto a forest green,
  In which they shroud themselves from causeless fear.
Yet fear them follows still, whereso they been:
Each trembling leaf and whistling wind they hear
As ghastly° bug° their hair on end does   *terrifying   bugbear*
  rear;
Yet both do strive their fearfulness to feign.

At last they hear a horn that shrilled clear
Throughout the wood, that echoed again
And made the forest ring as it would rive in twain.

21

Eft° through the thick° they heard one   *After thicket**
    rudely° rush,   *violently*
    With noise whereof he from his lofty° steed   *noble*
    Down fell from ground and crept into a bush
    To hide his coward head from dying dread.°   *fear of death*
    But Trompart stoutly° stayed to taken heed   *bravely*
    Of what might hap. Eftsoon° there stepped forth   *Soon after*
    A goodly° lady clad in hunter's weed°   *fine garb*
    That seemed to be a woman of great worth°   *importance**
And, by her stately portance,° born of heavenly birth.   *carriage*†

22

Her face so fair as flesh it seemed not,
    But heavenly portrait of bright angel's hue° –   *face; complexion*
    Clear° as the sky, withouten blame° or   *Bright fault*
    blot°   *blemish*
    Through goodly mixture of complexions
    due;°   *appropriate humours*
    And in her cheeks the vermil° red did show   *vermilion*
    Like roses in a bed of lilies shed,
    The which ambrosial° odours from them threw   *celestial*†
    And gazer's sense with double pleasure fed,
Able to heal the sick and to revive the dead.

23

In her fair eyes two living lamps did flame,
    Kindled above at the heavenly Maker's light,
    And darted fiery beams out of the same
    So passing° pierceant,° and so wondrous *surpassingly piercing*†
    bright,
    That quite° bereaved° the rash beholder's sight: *utterly stole*
    In them the blinded god° his lustful fire   *i.e., Cupid*
    To kindle oft assayed, but had no might;°   *power [to do so]*
    For with dread majesty and awful° ire   *awe-inspiring*
She broke his wanton darts and quenched base desire.

24

Her ivory forehead, full of bounty° brave,°   *virtue excellent*
  Like a broad table° did itself dispread   *tablet*
  For Love his lofty triumphs to engrave
  And write the battles of his great godhead:
  All good and honour might therein be read,°   *discerned*
  For there their dwelling was. And when she spake,
  Sweet words, like dropping honey, she did shed,
  And 'twixt the pearls° and rubies° softly   *i.e., teeth lips*
    brake°   *broke*
A silver sound that heavenly music seemed to make.

25

Upon her eyelids many Graces sat
  Under the shadow of her even brows,
  Working belgards° and amorous retrait,°   *loving looks portrait†*
  And every one her with a grace° endows,   *virtue*
  And every one with meekness to her bows:
  So glorious° mirror of celestial grace,   *Such a brilliant*
  And sovereign° monument°   *queenly; supreme document; token*
    of mortal vows,
  How shall frail pen describe her heavenly face
For fear – through want of skill – her beauty to disgrace?

26

So fair, and thousand thousand times more fair,
  She seemed when she presented was to sight,
  And was yclad – for° heat of scorching air –   *because of [the]*
  All in a silken camus° lily white,   *loose dress, chemise†*
  Purfled upon° with many a folded   *Decorated; bordered*
    plight,°   *pleat*
  Which all above besprinkled was throughout
  With golden aiglets° that glistered°   *tags; pendants glittered*
    bright
  Like twinkling stars, and all the skirt about°   *around*
Was hemmed with golden fringe.

27

Below her ham° her weed° did somewhat   *knee   dress*
    train,°   *hang*
  And her straight legs most bravely were embailed°   *enclosed†*

In gilden° buskins° of costly   *gilded   boots*
    cordwain°   *Spanish leather*
All barred with golden bands which were
    entailed°   *ornamented*
With curious antics,° and full fair°   *grotesquerie   most finely*
    aumailed:°   *enamelled*†
Before° they fastened were under her knee   *In front*
In a rich jewel, and therein entrailed°   *Interlaced, gathered‡*
The ends of all their knots that none might see
How they within their foldings close enwrapped be.

                            28
Like two fair marble pillars they were seen
    Which do the temple of the gods support,
    Whom all the people deck with garlands green
    And honour in their festival resort.°   *gathering*
    Those same with stately grace and princely port°   *bearing*
    She taught to tread when she herself would
        grace;°   *lend grace to‡*
    But with the woody nymphs when she did play,
    Or when the fleeing leopard she did chase,
She could them nimbly move and after fly apace.

                            29
And in her hand a sharp boar spear she held,
    And at her back a bow, and quiver gay
    (Stuffed with steel-headed darts, wherewith she
        quelled°   *killed*
    The savage beasts in her victorious play),
    Knit° with a golden baldric°   *Made fast; joined   breast strap*
        which forelay
    Athwart° her snowy breast, and did divide   *Across*
    Her dainty paps° – which, like young fruit in May,   *breasts*
    Now little 'gan to swell and, being tied,
Through her thin weed° their places only signified.   *clothing*

                            30
Her yellow locks, crisped° like golden wire,°   *curled   thread*
    About her shoulders weren loosely shed,°   *dispersed*
    And when the wind amongst them did inspire°   *breathe*
    They waved like a pennant wide dispread°   *spread out†*

And low behind her back were scattered.
And whether art it were, or heedless hap,°   *pure chance*
As through the flowering forest rash° she fled,   *swiftly*
In her rude° hairs sweet flowers themselves did   *disordered*
   lap,°   *enfold*
And flourishing fresh leaves and blossoms did enwrap:

31

Such as Diana, by the sandy shore
   Of swift Eurotas, or on Cynthus green,
   Where° all the nymphs have her unwares°   *When suddenly*
      forlore,°   *forsaken*
   Wandereth alone with bow and arrows keen°   *sharp*
   To seek her game; or as that famous queen
   Of Amazons, whom Pyrrhus did destroy
   The day that first of Priam she was seen,
   Did show herself in great triumphant joy
To succour the weak state of sad° afflicted Troy.   *severely*

32

Such, whenas° heartless° Trompart her did view, *when cowardly*
   He was dismayed in his coward mind
   And doubted whether he himself should show,
   Or fly away, or bide alone behind:
   Both fear and hope he in her face did find;
   When she at last, him spying, thus bespake:
   'Hail, groom! Didst not thou see a bleeding hind,
   Whose right haunch erst° my steadfast°   *formerly steady‡*
      arrow strake?°   *struck*
If thou didst, tell me that I may her overtake.'

33

Wherewith revived, this answer forth he threw:
   'O goddess (for such I thee take to be,
   For neither doth thy face terrestrial show,
   Nor voice sound mortal) – I avow to thee,
   Such wounded beast as that I did not see
   Sith° erst° into this forest wild I came.   *Since first*
   But mote° thy goodlihead° forgive it me *may your excellency†*
   To weet° which of the gods I shall thee name   *inquire*
That unto thee due worship I may rightly frame.'°   *formulate*

34

To whom she thus:— but ere her words ensued,
  Unto the bush her eye did sudden glance
  In which vain Braggadocchio was mewed,°   *cooped up*
  And saw it stir. She lift her piercing lance
  And towards 'gan a deadly shaft advance,
    In mind to mark° the beast. At which sad°   *hit* serious*
      stour°   *danger†*
    Trompart forth stepped to stay° the mortal chance,   *prevent*
    Out crying: 'O whatever heavenly power
Or earthly wight thou be, withhold° this deadly hour –   *delay*

35

'O stay thy hand, for yonder is no game
  For thy fierce arrows, them to exercise;
  But lo, my lord, my liege, whose warlike name
  Is far-renowned through many bold emprise;° *chivalric exploit*
  And now in shade he shrouded° yonder lies.'   *concealed*
    She stayed. With that he crawled out of his nest,
    Forth creeping on his caitiff° hands and thighs,   *cowardly*
    And, standing stoutly° up, his lofty   *fiercely*
      crest°   *helmet plumes*
Did fiercely shake and rouse,° as coming late° *ruffle† recently*
    from rest.

36

As fearful fowl, that long in secret cave
  For dread of soaring hawk herself hath hid,
  Not caring how, her silly° life to save,   *defenceless*
  She her gay° painted plumes disordered,   *gaily*
  Seeing at last herself from danger rid,
    Peeps forth and soon renews her native° pride   *natural*
    (She 'gins her feathers foul° disfigured   *foully*
    Proudly to preen and set° on every side,   *settle*
So shakes off shame, ne° thinks how erst° she did *nor formerly*
    her hide;

37

So, when her goodly visage he beheld,
  He 'gan himself to vaunt.° But when he viewed   *praise**
  Those deadly tools which in her hand she held,

Soon into other fits° he was transmewed,°   moods changed
Till she to him her gracious speech renewed:
'All hail, sir knight, and well may thee befall,
As all the like which honour have pursued
Through deeds of arms and prowess martial:
All virtue merits praise, but such the most of all.'

38

To whom he thus: 'O fairest under sky,
True be thy words, and worthy of thy praise
That warlike feats dost highest glorify.
Therein have I spent all my youthly days,
And many battles fought, and many frays,°   fights
Throughout the world, whereso they might be found,
Endeavouring my dreaded name to raise
Above the moon, that Fame may it resound
In her eternal trump,° with laurel garland crowned.   trumpet

39

'But what art thou, O lady, which dost range°   roam‡
In this wild forest where no pleasure is,
And dost not it for joyous court exchange
Amongst thine equal peers, where happy bliss
And all delight does reign much more than this?
There thou mayest love, and dearly loved be,
And swim in pleasure which thou here dost miss.°   lack
There mayest thou best be seen and best mayest see:
The wood is fit for beasts, the court is fit for thee.'

40

'Whoso in pomp of proud estate,'° quoth she,   rank
'Does swim, and bathes himself in courtly bliss,
Does waste his days in dark obscurity
And in oblivion ever-buried is:
Where ease abounds, it's eath° to do amiss;   easy
But who his limbs with labours, and his mind
Behaves° with cares,° cannot so easy   Regulates concerns
    miss.°   go astray
Abroad in arms, at home in studious kind,°   fashion
Who° seeks with painful° toil shall Honour   He who painstaking
    soonest find.

41

'In woods, in waves, in wars she wonts° to dwell,   *is accustomed*
  And will be found with peril and with pain;
  Ne° can the man that moulds° in idle   *Nor rots;‡ buries himself*
    cell°   *room‡*
  Unto her happy mansion° attain.   *dwelling-place*
  Before her gate high God did sweat ordain,
  And wakeful watches, ever to abide:
  But easy is the way, and passage plain,
  To Pleasure's palace – it may soon be spied,
And day and night her doors to all stand open wide.

42

'In prince's court—' The rest she would have said,
  But that the foolish man, filled with delight
  Of her sweet words, that all his sense°   *reason*
    dismayed,°   *overcame*
  And with her wondrous beauty ravished quite,°   *completely*
  'Gan burn in filthy lust and, leaping light,°   *swiftly; wantonly*
  Thought in his bastard° arms her to embrace.   *base*
  With that she, swerving back, her javelin bright
  Against him bent° and fiercely did menace;   *aimed*
So turned she about, and fled away apace.

43

Which, when that peasant° saw, amazed he stood   *clown‡*
  And grieved at her flight, yet durst he not
  Pursue her steps through wild, unknown wood.
  Besides, he feared her wrath and threatened shot
  Whilst in the bush he lay, not yet forgot;
  Ne cared he greatly for her presence vain°   *worthless*
  But, turning, said to Trompart: 'What foul blot
  Is this to knight that lady should again
Depart to woods untouched, and leave so proud disdain?'

44

'Perdy,' said Trompart, 'let her pass at will
  Lest by her presence danger mote° befall;   *might*
  For who can tell – and sure I fear it ill –
  But that she is some power celestial?
  For whiles she spake her great words did appal

My feeble courage, and my heart oppress,
That yet I quake and tremble overall.'
'And I,' said Braggadocchio, 'thought no less
When first I heard her horn sound with such
    ghastliness.°   *dreadfulness†*

45

'For from my mother's womb this grace° I have   *power; favour*
  Me given by eternal destiny,
    That earthly thing may not my courage° brave   *spirit; heart*
  Dismay° with fear, or cause on foot to fly,   *Overcome*
  But either hellish fiends or powers on high –
  Which was the cause, when erst that horn I heard
  (Weening° it had been thunder in the sky),   *Thinking*
  I hid myself from it as one afeared;
But when I other° knew, myself I boldly reared.   *otherwise*

46

'But now, for fear of worse that may betide,
  Let us soon° hence depart.' They soon agree;   *quickly; readily*
  So to his steed he got and 'gan to ride
  As one unfit therefore,° that all might see   *for it*
  He had not trained been in chivalry:°   *horsemanship*
  Which well that valiant courser did discern,
  For he despised to tread in due degree,°   *with precise steps*
  But chafed° and foamed with courage fierce and stern,   *fretted*
And to be eased of that base burden still did yearn.

[In cantos 4–5, Guyon rescues the vengeful lover Phedon from Furor
(Anger), and binds him, defeating also his mother, Occasion. He is
immediately set upon by the wrathful knight Pyrochles, whom he also
defeats. At his request, Guyon releases Furor and Occasion, who,
however, turn against Pyrochles. Meanwhile Pyrochles's squire, Atin,
has gone to summon his brother Cymochles to his aid. Cymochles,
Acrasia's lover, is found in the Bower of Bliss. In canto 6, travelling to
aid Pyrochles, Cymochles is seduced by mirthful and lustful Phaedria
on her island in the Idle Lake. Guyon arrives at the lake side and,
unaccompanied by the Palmer (whom Phaedria refuses to allow into
her boat), rejects Phaedria's temptation to lust and sloth. Leaving

Cymochles on the island, he returns to the shore and rides away. Atin, also on the shore, watches his master, Pyrochles, arrive on fire and attempt, unsuccessfully, to quench himself in the lake. He is rescued by Archimago.]

Canto 7

Guyon finds Mammon in a delve°	den;† hollow†
Sunning his treasure hoar;°	ancient
Is by him tempted and led down	
To see his secret store.°	hoard

1

As pilot, well expert in perilous wave,	
That to a steadfast° star his course hath	steady‡*
bent,°	directed
When foggy mists or cloudy tempests have	
The faithful light of that fair lamp yblent°	blurred*
And covered heaven with hideous°	terrible
dreariment,°	gloom†
Upon his card° and compass firms° his eye	chart fixes†
(The masters° of his long experiment),°	teachers experience‡
And to them does the steady helm apply,°	adapt; conform
Bidding his winged vessel fairly forward fly:	

2

So Guyon, having lost his trusty guide –	
Late left beyond the Idle Lake – proceeds	
Yet° on his way, of none accompanied,	Still
And evermore himself with comfort° feeds	encouragement
Of his own virtues and praiseworthy deeds.	
So long he yode,° yet no adventure found	went
Which Fame of her shrill trumpet worthy reads° –	thinks
For still he travelled through wide, wasteful° ground	desolate
That nought but desert wilderness showed all around.	

3

At last he came unto a gloomy glade,
  Covered with boughs and shrubs from heaven's light,
  Whereas° he sitting found, in secret shade,   *Where*
  An uncouth,° savage and uncivil°   *strange rough;† barbarous‡*
    wight,°   *creature**
  Of grisly° hue and foul, ill-favoured sight.°   *terrifying aspect*
  His face with smoke was tanned, and eyes were
    bleared;°   *watery and inflamed*
  His head and beard with soot were ill bedight;°   *clothed*
  His coal-black hands did seem to have been seared° *scorched*
In smith's fire-spitting forge, and nails like claws appeared.

4

His iron coat,° all overgrown with rust,   *covering; coat-armour*
  Was underneath enveloped with gold,
  Whose glistering° gloss,° darkened with filthy *glittering lustre*
    dust,
  Well yet appeared to have been of old°   *formerly*
  A work of rich entail° and curious mould,°   *carving pattern*
  Woven with antics° and wild°   *grotesque figures*
    imagery.°   *images*
  And in his lap a mass of coin he told°   *counted*
  And turned upside down, to feed his eye
And covetous desire with his huge treasury.°   *treasure*

5

And round about him lay, on every side,
  Great heaps of gold that never could be spent,
  Of which some were rude° ore, not purified   *crude*
  Of° Mulciber's devouring element.°   *by i.e., fire*
  Some others were new driven° and distent° *beaten drawn out*
  Into great ingoes° and to wedges° square;   *ingots* ingots*
  Some in round plates withouten
    monument;°   *identifying mark;† inscription*
  But most were stamped, and in their metal bare
The antique° shapes of kings and caesars strange and *ancient‡*
  rare.

6

Soon as he Guyon saw, in great affright
   And haste he rose for to remove aside
   Those precious hills from stranger's envious sight,
   And down them poured through an hole full wide
   Into the hollow earth, them there to hide.
   But Guyon, lightly° to him leaping, stayed   *swiftly*
   His hand, that trembled as one terrified,
   And, though himself were at the sight dismayed,°   *overcome*
Yet him perforce° restrained and to him   *with force*
   doubtful° said: *afraid*

7

'What art thou, man (if man at all thou art),
   That here in desert hast shine habitance,°   *habitation*[†]
   And these rich heaps of wealth dost hide apart
   From the world's eye and from her right°   *correct*
   usance?'°   *use*
   Thereat, with staring° eyes fixed askance° *glaring mistrustfully*[†]
   In great disdain, he answered: 'Hardy° elf,   *foolhardy*
   That darest view my direful countenance,
   I read° thee rash and heedless of thyself   *perceive*
To trouble my still° seat° and heaps of precious *quiet abode*
   pelf.°   *booty;*[*] *riches*

8

'God of the world and worldlings I me call,
   Great Mammon, greatest god below the sky,
   That of my plenty pour out unto all,
   And unto none my graces° do envy:°   *favours begrudge*[‡]
   Riches, renown and principality,°   *high rank*
   Honour, estate° and all this world's good,°   *dignity goods*
   For which men swink° and sweat incessantly,   *toil*
   From me do flow into an ample flood,
And in the hollow earth have their eternal
   brood.°   *parentage;*[†] *nativity*[†]

9

'Wherefore, if me thou deign to serve and sue,°   *follow*
   At thy command, lo, all these mountains be;
   Or if to thy great mind or greedy view

All these may not suffice, there shall to thee
   Ten times so much be numbered frank° and   *unconditionally*
      free.'
   'Mammon,' said he, 'thy godhead's vaunt° is   *boast of godhead*
      vain,
   And idle offers° of thy golden   *the offers*
      fee:°   *reward; territories held in fee*
   To them that covet such eye-glutting gain
Proffer thy gifts, and fitter servants entertain.°   *retain*‡

10

Me ill besits,° that in der-   *[it] becomes**
   doing° arms   *performing daring deeds*†
   And honour's suit° my vowed days do spend,   *pursuit**
   Unto thy bounteous° baits° and   *munificent allurements*
      pleasing charms
   (With which weak men thou witchest)° to attend: *bewitch*†
   Regard of worldy muck° doth foully°   *filth; dross ill*
      blend°   *associate with*†
   And low abase the high, heroic°   *extraordinarily brave*
      sprite,°   *soul*
   That joys° for crowns and kingdoms to   *rejoices*
      contend.°   *strive for*
   Fair shields, gay steeds, bright arms be my delight:
Those be the riches fit for an adventurous knight.'

11

'Vainglorious elf' (said he), 'dost not thou weet°   *know*
   That money can thy wants at will supply?
   Shields, steeds and arms, and all things for thee meet°   *fitting*
   It can purvey° in twinkling of an eye,   *supply*
   And crowns and kingdoms to thee multiply.
   Do not I kings create, and throw the crown
   Sometimes to him that low in dust doth lie?
   And him that reigned, into his room° thrust down?   *place*
And whom I lust° do heap with glory and renown?'   *wish*

12

'All otherwise,' said he, 'I riches read,°   *consider*
   And deem° them root of all disquietness:°   *judge disturbance*‡
   First got with guile° and then preserved with   *deceit*

dread,°   fear
And after, spent with pride and lavishness,
Leaving behind them grief and heaviness.
Infinite mischiefs of° them do arise –   from
Strife and debate, bloodshed and bitterness,
Outrageous wrong and hellish covetise° –   avarice
That noble heart as great dishonour doth despise.

13

'Ne° thine be the kingdoms, ne° the sceptres   Neither . . . nor
   thine;
But realms and rulers thou dost both confound,°   vanquish
And loyal truth to treason° dost incline: treachery
Witness the guiltless blood poured oft on ground,
The crowned often slain, the slayer crowned;
The sacred diadem in pieces rent;
And purple robe gored° with many   smeared with blood;‡ pierced
   a wound;
Castles surprised, great cities sacked and burned:
So makest thou kings and gainest wrongful government.

14

'Long were to tell the troublous storms that toss
   The private state° and make the life unsweet: condition
Who° swelling sails in Caspian Sea doth cross   He who
And in frail wood on Adrian° gulf doth   Adriatic
   fleet,°   float; sail
Doth not, I ween,° so many evils meet.'   believe
Then Mammon, waxing° wrath: 'And why then'   growing
   (said)
'Are mortal men so fond° and indiscreet   foolish
So evil thing to seek unto their aid
And having not, complain, and having, it upbraid?'

15

'Indeed,' quoth he, 'through foul intemperance
   Frail men are oft captived to covetise.
But would they think with how small allowance
Untroubled Nature doth herself suffice,
Such superfluities they would despise

Which with sad° care impeach° our native joys: *heavy harm‡*
    At the well head the purest streams arise,
    But mucky filth his branching arms annoys,°   *infects*
And with uncomely weeds the gentle wave accloys:°   *chokes*

16

'The antique° world in his first flowering youth   *ancient‡*
    Found no defect in his Creator's grace,
    But with glad thanks and unreproved° truth°   *faultless loyalty*
    The gifts of sovereign bounty did embrace:
    Like angels' life was then men's happy case;°   *state*
    But later ages' pride, like corn-fed steed,
    Abused her plenty and fat swollen increase
    To all licentious lust, and 'gan exceed
The measure of her mean° and natural first   *temperate balance*
    need.

17

'Then 'gan a cursed hand the quiet womb
    Of his great grandmother with steel to wound
    And the hid treasures in her sacred tomb
    With sacrilege° to dig. Therein he   *theft from a sacred place*
        found
    Fountains of gold and silver to abound,
    Of which the matter° of his huge desire   *extent‡*
    And pompous pride eftsoons° he did compound: *soon after*
    Then avarice 'gan through his veins inspire°   *breathe over; fan*
His greedy flames, and kindled life-devouring fire.'

18

'Son,' said he then, 'let be thy bitter scorn,
    And leave the rudeness° of that antique age   *barbarity*
    To them that lived therein in state
        forlorn:°   *abandoned; ignorant*
    Thou that dost live in later times must wage°   *hire out*
    Thy works for wealth, and life for gold engage.°   *pledge*
    If, then, thee list° my offered grace° to use,   *wish favour*
    Take what thou please of all this surplusage.°   *superabundance*
    If thee list not, leave have thou to refuse –
But thing refused do not afterwards accuse.'°   *censure*

19

'Me list not,' said the elfin knight, 'receive
   Anything offered till I know it well be got;
   Ne wote I° but thou didst these goods   *I do not know*
     bereave°   *steal*
   From rightful owner by unrighteous lot,°   *chance; prize*
   Or that blood-guiltiness° or guile them blot.'° *bloodshed   defile*
   'Perdy,'° quoth he, 'yet never eye did view,   *Indeed; By God*
   Ne° tongue did tell, ne hand these handled not,   *Nor*
   But safe I have them kept in secret mew°   *hiding place*
From heaven's sight and power of all which them pursue.'

20

'What secret place,' quoth he, 'can safely hold
   So huge a mass° and hide from heaven's eye?   *treasure*‡
   Or where hast thou thy wone,° that so much gold   *dwelling**
   Thou canst preserve from wrong and robbery?'
   'Come thou,' quoth he, 'and see.' So, by and by,
   Through that thick covert he him led, and found
   A darksome way which no man could descry
   That deep descended through the hollow ground,
And was with dread and horror compassed around.

21

At length they came into a larger space
   That stretched itself into an ample plain,
   Through which a beaten broad highway did trace°   *lead*
   That straight did lead to Pluto's grisly°   *terrifying*
     reign.°   *kingdom*
   But that way's side there sat infernal Pain,°   *Punishment*
   And fast beside him sat tumultuous Strife:
   The one in hand an iron whip did strain,°   *grip*†
   The other brandished a bloody knife;
And both did gnash their teeth, and both did threaten life.

22

On the other side, in one consort,° there sat   *group*
   Cruel Revenge and rancorous Despite,°   *Malice*
   Disloyal Treason, and heart-burning Hate;
   But gnawing Jealousy, out of their sight,

Sitting alone his bitter lips did bite;
And trembling Fear still to and fro did fly,
And found no place where safe he shroud° him might.   *hide*
Lamenting Sorrow did in darkness lie,
And Shame his ugly face did hide from living eye.

23

And over them sad Horror with grim hue°   *aspect*
    Did always soar, beating his iron wings;
    And after him owls and night-ravens flew,
    The hateful messengers of heavy° things,   *sad*
    Of death and dolour° telling sad tidings;   *grief; pain*
    Whiles sad Celeno, sitting on a clift,°   *cliff*
    A song of bale° and bitter sorrow sings   *death*
    That heart of flint asunder could have rift° –   *riven*
Which, having ended, after him she flieth swift.

24

All these before the gates of Pluto lay,
    By whom they, passing, spake unto them nought.
    But the elfin knight with wonder all the way
    Did feed his eyes and filled his inner thought.
    At last him to a little door he brought
    That to the gate of hell, which gaped wide,
    Was next adjoining, ne° them parted°   *nor separated‡*
        aught:°   *anything*
    Betwixt them both was but a little stride
That did the house of Richesse° from hell-mouth divide.   *Wealth*

25

Before the door sat self-consuming Care,
    Day and Night keeping wary watch and ward°   *guard*
    For fear lest Force or Fraud should unaware°   *unseen*
    Break in and spoil the treasure there in guard:
    Ne would he suffer Sleep once thitherward
    Approach, albe° his drowsy den were next;° *although adjacent*
    For next to Death is Sleep to be compared,
    Therefore his house is unto his annexed:
Here Sleep, there Richesse – and hell-gate them both betwixt.

26

So soon as Mammon there arrived, the door
  To him did open and afforded way.
  Him followed eke° Sir Guyon evermore,   *also*
  Ne darkness him, ne danger might dismay.°   *overcome*
  Soon as he entered was, the door straightway
  Did shut, and from behind it forth there leaped
  An ugly fiend, more foul than dismal day,°   *unlucky, evil day*
  The which with monstrous stalk° behind him stepped   *stride*†
And, ever as he went, due watch upon him kept.

27

Well hoped he ere long° that hardy° guest –   *soon daring*
  If ever covetous hand, or lustful eye,
  Or lips he laid on thing that liked him° best,   *he liked*
  Or ever sleep his eye-strings did untie –
  Should be his prey. And therefore still on high
  He over him did hold his cruel claws,
  Threatening with greedy grip to do him° die   *cause him to*
  And rend in pieces with his ravenous paws,
If ever he transgressed the fatal° Stygian°   *deadly underworld*
  laws.

28

That house's form within was rude° and strong,   *rough*
  Like a huge cave hewn out of rocky clift,
  From whose rough vault the ragged°   *irregular*
    breaches° hung   *fissures*
  Embossed° with massy° gold of   *Swelling heavy*
    glorious° gift°   *splendid nature*
  And with rich metal loaded every rift,°   *seam*
  That heavy ruin° they did seem to threat.   *collapse*
  And over them Arachne high did lift
  Her cunning web and spread her subtle°   *artful; finely woven*
    net,
Enwrapped in foul smoke and clouds more black than jet.

29

Both roof, and floor, and walls were all of gold,
  But overgrown with dust and old decay,
  And hid in darkness that° none could behold   *so that*

The hue thereof; for view of cheerful day
 Did never in that house itself display,°   *make manifest*‡
But a faint shadow of uncertain light
Such as a lamp, whose life does fade away,
Or as the moon clothed with cloudy night
Does show to him that walks in fear and sad°   *heavy*
 affright.°   *terror*†

30

In all that room was nothing to be seen
 But huge great iron chests and coffers strong,
 All barred with double bands that° none could *so that*
  ween°   *think*
 Them to efforce° by violence or wrong: *force open*†
On every side they placed were along.
But all the ground with skulls was scattered,
And dead men's bones, which round about were flung,
 Whose lives, it seemed, whilom° there were shed *once* *
And their vile carcases now left unburied.

31

They forward pass, ne Guyon yet spoke word
 Till that they came unto an iron door
 Which to them opened of his own accord,
 And showed of riches such exceeding store° *abundance*
As eye of man did never see before,
Ne ever could within one place be found,
 Though all the wealth which is, or was of yore,
 Could gathered be through all the world around
And that above were added to that underground.

32

The charge thereof° unto a covetous sprite° *of it* *demon*
 Commanded° was, who thereby did attend,° *Committed* *wait*
 And warily awaited° day and night   *kept watch*
 From other covetous fiends it to defend
Who it to rob and ransack did intend.
Then Mammon, turning to the warrior, said:
 'Lo, here the world's bliss, lo, here the end° *target*
 To which all men do aim: rich to be made.
Such grace° now to be happy is before thee laid.' *fortune* *

33

'Certes,'° said he, 'I n'ill° thine offered grace,   *Indeed   do not wish*
  Ne to be made so° happy do intend: *in such a way*
  Another bliss° before mine eyes I place,   *blessing, joy*
  Another happiness, another end.
  To them that list° these base regards° I   *wish   objects of sight*‡
    lend,
  But I in arms and in achievements brave
  Do rather choose my flitting° hours to spend,   *transitory*
  And to be lord of those that riches have,
Than them to have myself, and be their servile slave.'

34

Thereat the fiend his gnashing teeth did grate,
  And grieved so long to lack his greedy
    prey;°   *a prey that was greedy*
  For well he weened° that so glorious° bait   *thought   splendid*
  Would tempt his guest to take thereof assay.°   *trial*
  Had he so done, he had him snatched away
  More light° than culver° in the falcon's fist: *swiftly   dove*
  Eternal God thee save from such decay.°   *death*
  But whenas° Mammon saw his purpose missed,   *when*
Him to entrap unwares° another way he   *by surprise*
    wist.°   *thought up*

35

Thence forward he him led, and shortly brought
  Unto another room, whose door forthright°   *immediately*
  To him did open as it had been taught.
  Therein an hundred ranges° weren   *cooking ranges*
    pight,°   *placed*
  And hundred furnaces, all burning bright.
  By every furnace many fiends did bide,
  Deformed creatures, horrible in sight;
  And every fiend his busy pains° applied   *labours*
To melt the golden metal ready to be tried.°   *refined*

36

One with great bellows gathered filling air,
  And with forced wind the fuel did inflame;
  Another did the dying brands° repair°   *logs   renew*

With iron tongs, and sprinkled oft the same
With liquid waves fierce Vulcan's rage to tame –
Who, mastering them, renewed his former heat.
Some scummed° the dross that from the metal came;   *skimmed*
Some stirred the molten ore with ladles great;
And every one did swink,° and every one did sweat.   *toil*

37

But whenas° earthly wight° they present saw,   *when creature**
  Glistering° in arms° and battailous° *Glittering armour warlike*
    array,
  From their hot work they did themselves withdraw
  To wonder at the sight; for till that day
  They never creature saw that came that way.
  Their staring eyes sparkling with fervent° fire,   *glowing*
  And ugly shapes, did nigh the man dismay°   *overwhelm*
  That,° were it not for shame, he would   *So that*
    retire;°   *withdraw*
Till that him thus bespake° the sovereign lord and *addressed†*
  sire:

38

'Behold, thou fairy's son, with mortal eye
  That° living eye before did never see: *That which*
  The thing that thou didst crave so earnestly
  To weet° – whence all the wealth late° showed *know recently*
    by me
  Proceeded – lo, now is revealed to thee:
  Here is the fountain° of the world's good.   *origin*
  Now, therefore, if thou wilt enriched be,
  Advise° thee well and change thy wilful mood *Consider*
Lest thou perhaps hereafter wish,° and be withstood.' *wish it*

39

'Suffice it, then, thou money god,' quoth he,
  'That all thine idle° offers I refuse.   *worthless*
  All that I need I have; what needeth me
  To covet more than I have cause to use?
  With such vain shows thy wordlings vile abuse,° *impose on*
  But give me leave to follow mine emprise."° *enterprise*
  Mammon was much displeased, yet n'ote° he *could not*

    choose
  But bear the rigour of his bold mesprise,°   *contempt†*
And thence him forward led him further to entice.

40

He brought him through a darksome,° narrow strait   *gloomy‡*
  To a broad gate all built of beaten gold.
  The gate was open, but therein did wait
  A sturdy° villain, striding stiff° and bold,   *fierce resolutely*
  As if that highest God defy he would:
  In his right hand an iron club he held,
  But he himself was all of golden mould,°   *body‡*
  Yet had both life and sense, and well could wield
That cursed weapon when his cruel° foes he   *fierce*
    quelled.°   *killed*

41

Disdain he called was, and did disdain
  To be so called, and whoso did him call.
  Stern was his look and full of stomach° vain,   *pride*
  His portance° terrible and his stature tall,   *bearing†*
  Far passing the height of men terrestrial,
  Like an huge giant of the Titans' race,
  That made him scorn all creatures great and small
  And with his pride all other power deface:° *outface;‡ outshine†*
More fit amongst black fiends than men to have his place.

42

Soon as those glitterand° arms he did espy,   *glittering*
  That with their brightness made that darkness light,
  His harmful club he 'gan to hurtle° high   *brandish forcibly†*
  And threaten battle to the fairy knight,
  Who likewise 'gan himself to battle dight;°   *prepare*
  Till Mammon did his hasty hand withhold
  And counselled him abstain from perilous fight:
  For nothing might abash° the villain bold,   *discomfit*
Ne mortal steel empierce° his miscreate°   *transfix‡ unnatural†*
    mould.°   *body‡*

43

So, having him with reason pacified,
    And the fierce carl° commanding to forbear,   *churl*
    He brought him in. The room was large and wide
    As° it some guild° or solemn°   *As if guild hall imposing;* sacred*
      temple were:
    Many great golden pillars did upbear
    The massy roof, and riches huge sustain,
    And every pillar decked was full dear°   *gloriously*
    With crowns and diadems and titles° vain   *inscriptions*
Which mortal princes wore whiles they on earth did reign.

44

A rout° of people there assembled were   *company*
    Of every sort and nation under sky,
    Which with great uproar pressed to draw near
    To the upper part, where was advanced high
    A stately° siege° of sovereign majesty;   *royal throne*
    And thereon sat a woman gorgeous gay,°   *brilliant**
    And richly clad in robes of royalty
    That° never earthly prince in such array   *Such that*
His glory did enhance and pompous° pride   *stately; arrogant*
    display.

45

Her face right wondrous fair did seem to be
    That her broad beauty's beam great brightness threw
    Through the dim shade that all men might it see;
    Yet was not that same her own native hue,°   *aspect*
    But wrought by art and counterfeited show
    Thereby more lovers unto her to call.
    Natheless,° most heavenly fair in deed and view *Nevertheless*
    She by creation was till she did fall:
Thenceforth she sought for helps° to cloak her crime *aids*
    withal.

46

There, as in glistering° glory she did sit,   *glittering*
    She held a great gold chain, ylinked well,
    Whose upper end to highest heaven was knit,° *fastened*
    And lower part did reach to lowest hell.

And all that press° did about her swell   *crowd*
To catchen hold of that long chain, thereby
To climb aloft and others to excel:
That was Ambition, rash desire to sty,°   *elevate*
And every link thereof a step of dignity.°   *social rank*

47

Some thought to raise themselves to high degree°   *rank*
   By riches and unrighteous reward;
   Some by close shouldering;° some by flattery;   *thrusting aside*
   Others through friends; others for base regard;°   *bribes*
   And all by wrong ways for themselves prepared.
   Those that were up themselves kept others low;
   Those that were low themselves held others hard,
   Ne° suffered them to rise or greater grow,   *Nor*
But every one did strive his fellow down to throw.

48

Which, whenas Guyon saw, he 'gan inquire
   What meant that press about that lady's throne,
   And what she was that did so high aspire.
   Mammon him answered: 'That goodly one,
   Whom all that folk with such contention
   Do flock about, my dear, my daughter, is:
   Honour and dignity from her alone
   Derived are, and all this world's bliss
For which ye men do strive: few get, but many miss.

49

'And fair Philotime she rightly hight,°   *is named**†*
   The fairest wight that woneth° under sky,   *dwells*
   But that this darksome nether world her light
   Doth dim with horror and deformity:
   Worthy of heaven and high felicity,
   From whence the gods have her for envy thrust.
   But sith° thou hast found favour in mine eye,   *since*
   Thy spouse I will her make, if that thou lust,°   *desire*
That she may thee advance for works and merits just.

50

'Gramercy,° Mammon,' said the gentle° *Thank you courteous*
 knight,
 'For so great grace° and offered high estate.   *favour*
 But I, that am frail flesh and earthly wight,
 Unworthy match for such immortal mate
 Myself well wote,° and mine unequal fate.° *know destiny*†
 And were I not, yet is my troth yplight° *pledged**
 And love avowed to other lady late,° *recently*
 That to remove the same I have no might:° *power*
To change love causeless° is reproach to warlike *causelessly*
 knight.'

51

Mammon inmoved° was with inward wrath *affected*‡
 Yet, forcing it to feign, him forth thence led
 Through grisly° shadows° by a beaten *terrifying also: ghosts*
  path
 Into a garden goodly° garnished° *splendidly furnished; adorned*
 With herbs and fruits, whose kinds mote° not be *might*
  read:°   *told*
 Not such as earth, out of her fruitful womb,
 Throws forth to men, sweet and well-
  savoured;° *pleasingly scented*
 But direful, deadly black, both leaf and bloom,
Fit to adorn the dead and deck the dreary tomb.

52

There mournful cypress grew in greatest store,° *abundance*
 And trees of bitter gall and ebon' sad,
 Dead-sleeping poppy and black hellebore,
 Cold coloquintida and tetra mad,
 Mortal samnitis and cicuta bad –
 With which the unjust Athenians made to die
 Wise Socrates, who, thereof quaffing glad,
 Poured out his life and last philosophy
To the fair Critias, his dearest belamy.° *friend*

53

The Garden of Proserpina this hight,
  And in the midst thereof a silver seat
  With a thick arbour goodly overdight,°   *covered*†
  In which she often used from open heat
  Herself to shroud° and pleasures to   *shelter*
    entreat.°   *occupy herself with*†
  Next thereunto did grow a goodly° tree   *splendid*
  With branches broad dispread and body great,
  Clothed with leaves that° none the wood mote° *so that might*
    see
And loaden all with fruit as thick as it might be.

54

Their fruit were golden apples, glistering bright,
  That° goodly was their glory to behold.   *So that*
  On earth like never grew, ne° living wight   *nor*
  Like ever saw, but they from hence were sold:°   *derived*
  For those which Hercules with conquest bold
  Got from great Atlas' daughters hence began
  And, planted there, did bring forth fruit of gold;
  And those with which the Euboean young man wan° *won*
Swift Atalanta, when through craft he her outran.

55

Here also sprung that goodly golden fruit
  With which Acontius got his lover true,
  Whom he had long time sought with fruitless suit;
  Here eke° that famous golden apple grew   *also*
  The which amongst the gods false Ate threw,
  For which the Idaean ladies disagreed,
  Till partial° Paris deemed° it Venus due *fond;*† *biased judged*
  And had of her fair Helen for his meed,°   *reward*
That many noble Greeks and Trojans made to bleed.

56

The warlike elf much wondered at this tree
  So fair and great that shadowed all the ground;
  And his broad branches, laden with rich fee,° *offerings; wealth*
  Did stretch themselves without° the utmost   *beyond*
    bound°   *boundary*

Of this great garden, compassed° with a   surrounded
  mound,°   embankment;‡ boundary†
Which, overhanging, they themselves did steep°   bathe†
In a black flood which flowed about it round:
That is the river of Cocytus deep
In which full many souls do endless° wail and weep.   ever

57
Which to behold he clomb° up to the bank   climbed
  And, looking down, saw many damned wights
  In those sad waves (which direful deadly stank),
  Plunged continually of° cruel sprites   by
  That, with their piteous cries and yelling shrights,°   shrieks*
  They made the further shore resounden wide.°   afar
  Amongst the rest of those same rueful° sights   pitiful
  One cursed creature he by chance espied
That drenched° lay full deep under the garden side.   submerged*

58
Deep was he drenched to the upmost° chin,   very top of [his]
  Yet gaped still, as° coveting to drink   as if
  Of the cold liquor which he waded in,
  And, stretching forth his hand, did often think
  To reach the fruit which grew upon the brink;
  But both the fruit from hand and flood° from mouth   water
  Did fly aback and made him vainly swink:°   labour
  The whiles he starved with hunger and with drouth°   thirst
He daily died, yet never thoroughly dien couth.°   was able to die

59
The knight, him seeing labour so in vain,
  Asked who he was and what he meant° thereby: signified
  Who, groaning deep, thus answered him again:°   in response
  'Most cursed of all creatures under sky,
  Lo, Tantalus, I here tormented lie,
  Of whom high Jove wont° whilom° feasted   used to formerly*
    be!
  Lo, here I now for want° of food do die –   lack
  But if that thou be such as I thee see,
Of grace I pray thee, give to eat and drink to me.'

60

'Nay, nay, thou greedy Tantalus,' quoth he,
  'Abide° the fortune of thy present fate,°   *Endure   destiny*
  And unto all that live in high degree°   *rank*
  Example be of mind intemperate,
  To teach them how to use their present state.'
  Then 'gan the cursed wretch aloud to cry,
  Accusing highest Jove and gods ingrate,°   *ungrateful*
  And eke blaspheming heaven bitterly,
As author of injustice, there to let him die.

61

He looked a little further and espied
  Another wretch, whose carcase deep was drent°   *submerged*
  Within the river, which the same did hide;
  But both his hands, most filthy feculent,°   *excrement-besmeared*[†]
  Above the water were on high extent°   *extended*
  And fained° to wash themselves   *compelled, obliged*
    incessantly –
  Yet nothing cleaner were for such intent,°   *assiduity*
  But rather fouler seemed to the eye;
So lost his labour vain and idle° industry.   *pointless*

62

The knight, him calling, asked who he was;
  Who, lifting up his head, him answered thus:
  'I Pilate am, the falsest judge, alas,
  And most unjust, that by unrighteous
  And wicked doom,° to Jews   *sentence*
    despiteous°   *contemptuous*
  Delivered up the Lord of Life to die,
  And did acquit a murderer felonous:°   *wicked*
  The whiles° my hands I washed in purity,   *While*
The whiles° my soul was soiled with foul   *During that time*
  iniquity.'

63

Infinite more, tormented in like pain,
  He there beheld, too long here to be told;°   *recounted*
  Ne Mammon would there let him long remain
  For terror of the tortures manifold

In which the damned souls he did behold,
But roughly him bespake:° 'Thou fearful fool,   *addressed*†
Why takest not of that same fruit of gold,
Ne sittest down on that same silver stool
To rest thy weary person in the shadow° cool?'   *shade*

64

All which he did to do° him deadly° fall   *cause   mortally*
  In frail intemperance through sinful bait,°   *temptation*
  To which, if he inclined had at all,
  That dreadful fiend – which did behind him wait° –   *watch*
  Would him have rent in thousand pieces
    straight.°   *straight away*
  But he was wary wise in all his way,°   *ways*
  And well perceived his deceitful sleight,
  Ne suffered lust° his safety to betray –   *desire*
So goodly° did beguile the guiler° of the prey.   *cleverly   beguiler**

65

And now he has so long remained there
  That vital powers 'gan wax° both weak and wan°   *grow   sickly*
  For want° of food and sleep, which two upbear,   *lack*
  Like mighty pillars, this frail life of man
  That° none without the same enduren can.   *So that*
  For now three days of men were full outwrought°   *completed*
  Since he this hardy° enterprise began;   *brave*
  For-thy° great Mammon fairly° he   *Therefore   respectfully*†
    besought
Into the world to guide him back as he him brought.

66

The god, though loath, yet was constrained to obey,
  For longer time than that no living wight
  Below the earth might suffered be to stay;
  So back again him brought to living° light.   *of the living*
  But all so° soon as his enfeebled sprite°   *as   life-force*
  'Gan suck this vital air into his breast,
  As° overcome with too exceeding might   *As if*
  The life did flit° away out of her nest,   *pass*
And all his senses were with deadly° fit°   *deathly   crisis*‡
    oppressed.

Canto 8

Sir Guyon, laid in swoon, is by
   Acrates' sons despoiled,°   *violated; plundered*
Whom Arthur soon hath rescued
   And paynim° brethren foiled.   *pagan*

1

And is there care in heaven? And is there love
  In heavenly spirits to these creatures base
  That may compassion of their evils° move?   *ills*
  There is: else much more wretched were the case
  Of men than beasts. But O, the exceeding grace
  Of highest God, that loves His creatures so,
  And all his works with mercy doth embrace,
  That blessed angels he sends to and fro
To serve to° wicked man to serve° his wicked *attend upon assail**
  foe.

2

How oft do they their silver bowers° leave   *chambers*
  To come to succour° us that succour want?°   *reinforce lack*
  How oft do they with golden pineons cleave
  The flitting° skies, like flying   *shifting*
    pursuivant,°   *royal messenger*
  Against foul fiends to aid us militant?°   *warring*
  They for us fight, they watch and duly ward,°   *protect*
  And their bright squadrons round about us plant,
  And all for love, and nothing for reward.
O why should heavenly God to men have such regard?

3

During the while that Guyon did abide
  In Mammon's house, the Palmer (whom whilere° *a while since*
  That wanton maid° of passage had   *i.e., Phaedria in canto 6*
    denied),
  By further search, had passage found elsewhere

And, being on his way, approached near
Where Guyon lay in trance; when suddenly
He heard a voice that called loud and clear:
'Come hither, come hither, O come hastily' –
That° all the fields resounded with the rueful° cry.   *So that*   *pitiful*

4

The Palmer lent his ear unto the noise
To weet° who called so importunely:°   *know*   *urgently*
Again he heard a more efforced° voice   *compelling*†
That bade him come in haste. He by and by°   *straight away*
His feeble feet directed to the cry
Which to that shady delve° him brought at last   *hollow*†
Where Mammon erst did sun his treasury.
There the good Guyon he found slumbering fast
In senseless dream – which sight at first him sore°   *greatly*
        aghast.°   *terrified*

5

Beside his head there sat a fair° young man,   *handsome*
Of wondrous beauty and of freshest° years,   *most youthful*
Whose tender bud to blossom new began
And flourish fair above his equal peers.°   *those of the same rank*
His snowy front° curled with golden hairs   *forehead*
Like Phoebus' face adorned with sunny rays
Divinely shone, and two sharp, winged
        shears,°   *scissor-shaped wings*†
Decked with diverse° plumes like painted jays,   *vari-coloured*
Were fixed at his back to cut his airy ways:

6

Like as Cupido on Idaean hill
When, having laid his cruel bow away,
And mortal arrows (wherewith he doth fill
The world with murderous spoils and bloody prey),
With his fair mother he him dights° to play   *prepares*
And with his goodly sisters, Graces three;
The goddess, pleased with his wanton play,
Suffers herself through sleep beguiled to be
The whiles the other ladies mind° their merry glee.   *pursue*

7

Whom, whenas the Palmer saw, abashed° he was   *confounded*
  Through fear and wonder that° he nought could say,   *so that*
  Till him the child° bespoke:° 'Long   *noble youth addressed*[†]
    lacked, alas,
  Hath been thy faithful aid in hard assay°   *affliction*
  Whiles deadly fit thy pupil doth dismay.°   *overcome*
  Behold this heavy sight, thou reverend sire;
  But dread of death and dolour° do away:°   *grief do away with*
  For life ere long shall to her home retire,°   *return*
And he that breathless° seems shall courage° cold   *dead life*
    respire.°   *breathe again*

8

The charge, which God doth unto me aret,°   *deliver*[†]
  Of his dear safety I to thee commend;°   *entrust*
  Yet will I not forgo ne° yet forget   *nor*
  The care thereof myself unto the end,
  But evermore him succour and defend
  Against his foe and mine. Watch thou, I pray,
  For evil is at hand him to offend.'°   *harm*
  So having said, eftsoons° he 'gan display°   *forthwith spread*
His painted, nimble wings and vanished quite° away.   *utterly*

9

The Palmer, seeing his left empty place
  And his slow eyes beguiled of their sight,
  Wox° sore° afraid and, standing still a space,   *Grew greatly*
  Gazed after him as fowl escaped by flight.
  At last, him turning to his charge behight,°   *ordained;*[†] *delivered*[†]
  With trembling hand his troubled pulse 'gan try
  Where, finding life not yet dislodged quite,
  He much rejoiced and covered it tenderly,
As chicken newly hatched, from dreaded destiny.

10

At last he spied where towards him did pace
  Two paynim° knights, all armed as bright as sky;   *pagan*
  And them beside an aged sire did trace,°   *tread*
  And far before a lightfoot page did fly,
  That breathed strife and troublous enmity:

Those were the two sons° of   *i.e., Cymochles and Pyrochles*
  Acrates old
Who, meeting erst° with Archimago sly   *formerly*
Forby° that Idle strand,° of°   *Near shore of the Idle Lake by*
  him were told
That he, which erst them combated, was Guyon bold.

11

Which to avenge on him they dearly° vowed,   *fervently*
  Wherever that on ground° they mote° him find. *earth might*
  False Archimage provoked their courage° proud,   *spirit*
  And strifeful Atin in their stubborn° mind   *unyielding*
  Coals of contention and hot vengeance tined.°   *kindled*
  Now been they come whereas the Palmer sat,
  Keeping° that slumbered corse° *Guarding unconscious*† *body*
    to him assigned:
  Well knew they both his person, sith° of late   *since*
With him in bloody arms they rashly did debate.°   *contend*

12

Whom when Pyrochles saw, inflamed with rage
  That sire he foul° bespake:° 'Thou dotard *rudely addressed*†
    vile,
  That with thy bruteness° shendest° thy   *folly shames*
    comely° age;   *what befits*
  Abandon soon,° I rede,° the   *straightway advise*
    caitiff°spoil   *worthless*
  Of that same outcast carcase that erewhile
  Made itself famous through false treachery,
  And crowned his coward crest° with knightly *helmet; head*
    style.°   *title*
  Lo where he now, inglorious, doth lie
To prove he lived ill that did thus foully die.'

13

To whom the Palmer fearless° answered: *fearlessly*
  'Certes,° sir knight, ye been too much to blame *Indeed*
  Thus for to blot the honour of the dead,
  And with foul cowardice his carcase shame
  Whose living hands immortalised his name.
  Vile is the vengeance on the ashes cold,

And envy base to bark at sleeping fame:°   *reputation*
  Was never wight° that treason° of him told; *person* treachery*
Yourself his prowess proved° and found him fierce and *tested*
  bold.'

14

Then said Cymochles: 'Palmer, thou dost dote;°   *talk stupidly*
  Ne° canst of prowess, ne° of knighthood   *Neither nor*
    deem,°   *judge*
  Save as thou seest or hearest – but well I wote° *know*
  That of his puissance trial made extreme.
  Yet gold all is not that° doth golden seem, *that which*
  Ne all good knights that shake° well spear and *brandish*
    shield.
  The worth of all men by their end esteem,
  And then due praise or due reproach them yield:
Bad therefore I him deem that thus lies dead on field.'

15

'Good or bad' ('gan° his brother fierce reply)   *did*
  'What do I reck,° sith° that he died   *care since*
    entire?°   *unmutilated*
  Or what doth his bad death now satisfy
  The greedy hunger of revenging ire
  Sith wrathful hand wrought not her own desire?
  Yet since no way is left to wreak° my spite, *avenge*
  I will him reave° of arms, the victor's hire,° *deprive reward*
  And of that shield, more worthy of good knight:
For why should a dead dog be decked in armour bright?'

16

'Fair sir,' said then the Palmer, suppliant,°   *beseechingly*
  'For knighthood's love, do not so foul a deed;
  Ne blame° your honour with so shameful *discredit†*
    vaunt°   *boast*
  Of vile revenge. To spoil° the dead of *despoil*
    weed°   *equipment*
  Is sacrilege, and doth all sins exceed;
  But leave these relics of his living might
  To deck his hearse° and trap° his tomb-black *corpse‡ bedeck*
    steed.'

'What hearse or steed' (said he) 'should he have
   dight,°   *adorned*
But be entombed in the raven or the kite?'

17

With that, rude° hand upon his shield he laid,   *violent*
   And the other brother 'gan his helmet unlace,
   Both fiercely bent° to have him   *resolved*
     disarrayed;°   *stripped of clothing*
   Till that they spied where towards them did pace
   An armed knight of bold and bounteous°   *favourable*
     grace,°   *aspect*
   Whose squire bore after him an ebon° lance   *ebony*
   And covered shield. Well kenned° him so far   *knew*
     space°   *at such a distance*
   The enchanter by his arms° and   *armour*
     amenance°   *bearing;† conveyance†*
When under him he saw his Lybian steed to prance,

18

And to those brethren said: 'Rise, rise, belive,°   *forthwith*
   And unto battle do yourselves address.
   For yonder comes the prowest° knight alive,   *most valiant*
   Prince Arthur, flower of grace and nobilesse,°   *nobleness*
   That hath to paynim° knights wrought great distress   *pagan*
   And thousand saracens foully° done to die.'   *terribly caused*
   That word so deep did in their heart impress°   *imprint*
   That both eftsoons° upstarted furiously   *at once*
And 'gan themselves prepare to battle greedily.

19

But fierce Pyrochles, lacking his own sword,
   The want° thereof now greatly 'gan to plain,°   *lack lament*
   And Archimage besought him that afford
   Which he had brought for Braggadocchio vain.
   'So would I,' said the enchanter, 'glad° and   *gladly*
     fain°   *willingly*
   Beteem° to you this sword, you° to defend,   *Accord† yourself*
   Or aught that else your honour might maintain,
   But that this weapon's power I well have kenned°   *discovered*
To be contrary to the work which ye intend.

20

'For that same knight's own sword this is of
    yore°   *formerly; from long ago*
  Which Merlin made by his almighty art
  For that his nursling when he knighthood swore,
  Therewith to doen° his foes eternal smart.   *cause*
  The metal first he mixed with meadwort
  That° no enchantment from his dint° might   *So that blow*
    save;
  Then it in flames of Etna wrought apart°   *separately*
  And seven times dipped in the bitter wave
Of hellish Styx, which hidden virtue° to it gave.   *power*

21

'The virtue is, that neither steel nor stone
  The stroke thereof from entrance may defend,
  Ne° ever may be used by his foen,°   *Neither foes*
  Ne° forced his rightful owner to offend,°   *Nor harm*
  Ne ever will it break, ne ever bend:
  Wherefore Mordure° it rightfully is   *Hard-biter*
    hight.°   *named**†
  In vain therefore, Pyrochles, should I lend
  The same to thee against his lord to fight,
For sure it would deceive thy labour and thy might.'

22

'Foolish old man,' said then the pagan, wroth,
  'That weenest° words or charms may force withstand: *believe*
  Soon shalt thou see, and then believe for truth,
  That I can carve with this enchanted brand
  His lord's own flesh.' Therewith out of his hand
  That virtuous steel he rudely° snatched away,   *violently*
  And Guyon's shield about his wrist he bound;
  So° ready dight° fierce battle to assay° *Thus prepared venture*
And match his brother in battailous° array.° *warlike equipment*

23

By this that stranger knight in presence° came   *before them*
  And goodly° salued° them; who nought *courteously greeted*‡
    again°   *in return*
  Him answered, as courtesy became,

But with stern looks and stomachous° disdain   *bitter‡*
Gave signs of grudge° and   *reluctance*
   discontentment° vain.°   *dissatisfaction‡ foolish*
Then, turning to the Palmer, he 'gan spy
Where at his feet, with sorrowful demean'°   *demeanour*
And deadly hue,° an armed corse° did lie   *aspect body*
In whose dead face he read° great magnanimity.   *perceived*

24

Said he then to the Palmer: 'Reverend sire,
   What great misfortune hath betid° this knight?   *befallen*
Or did° his life her fateful date° expire,   *Did either death*
Or did he fall by treason or by fight?
However,° sure° I rue his piteous plight.'   *Whatever indeed*
'Not one nor other,' said the Palmer grave,
Hath him befallen, but clouds of deadly night
A while his heavy eyelids covered have,
And all his senses drowned in deep senseless wave.

25

'Which those his cruel foes, that stand hereby,
   Making advantage to revenge their spite,
Would him disarm and treaten shamefully –
Unworthy usage of redoubted knight.
But you, fair sir, whose honourable sight°   *appearance*
Doth promise hope of help and timely grace,°   *divine aid*
Mote° I beseech to succour his sad plight,   *May*
And by your power protect his feeble case:°   *condition; body*
First praise of knighthood is foul outrage to deface.'°   *erase*

26

'Palmer,' said he, 'no knight so rude,° I ween,°   *barbaric believe*
As to doen outrage to a sleeping ghost;°   *spirit*
Ne° was there ever noble courage seen   *Nor*
That in advantage would his puissance boast:
Honour is least where odds appeareth most.
Maybe that better reason will assuage
The rash revengers' heat: words well disposed
Have secret power to appease inflamed rage;
If not, leave unto me thy knight's last patronage.'°   *protection‡*

27

Tho,° turning to those brethren, thus bespoke:°   *Then spoke*
  'Ye warlike pair, whose valorous great might
  It seems just wrongs to vengeance do provoke
  To wreak your wrath on this dead-seeming knight,
  Mote° aught allay the storm of your despite   *Might*
  And settle patience in so furious heat?
  Not to debate° the challenge° of your right,   *dispute claim*
  But for this carcase pardon I entreat,
Whom Fortune hath already laid in lowest seat.'

28

To whom Cymochles said: For what art thou
  That makest thyself his daysman° to prolong   *mediator*
  The vengeance prest?° Or who shall let° me   *at hand hinder*
    now
  On this vile body from to wreak my wrong,
  And make his carcase as the outcast dung?
  Why should not that dead carrion satisfy
  The guilt which, if he lived had thus long,
  His life for due revenge should dear aby?°   *pay the penalty for*
The trespass still doth live, albe° the person die.'   *although*

29

'Indeed,' said then the Prince, 'the evil done
  Dies not when breath the body first doth leave,
  But from the grandsire to the nephew's° son   *grandson's*
  And all his seed the curse doth often cleave,
  Till vengeance utterly the guilt bereave:°   *remove*
  So straitly° God doth judge. But gentle knight   *strictly*
  That doth against the dead his hand uprear
  His honour stains with rancour° and   *ill-feeling*
    despite,°   *disdain*
And great disparagement° makes to his former   *disgrace; discredit*
  might.'

30

Pyrochles 'gan reply the second time,
  And to him said: 'Now, felon,° sure I read°   *wretch perceive*
  How that thou art partaker of his crime;
  Therefore, by Termagant, thou shalt be dead.'

With that his hand, more sad° than lump of lead,   *heavy*
Uplifting high, he weened° with Mordure –   *thought*
His own good sword Mordure – to cleave his head.
The faithful steel such treason° n'ould°   *treachery would not*
    endure
But, swerving from the mark, his lord's life did assure.°   *secure**

31
Yet was the force so furious and so fell°   *fierce*
That horse and man it made to reel aside.
Natheless° the Prince would not forsake his   *Nevertheless*
    sell°   *saddle*
(For well of yore he learned had to ride)
But, full of anger, fiercely to him cried:
'False traitor° miscreant,° thou broken   *treacherous unbeliever*
    hast
The law of arms to strike foe undefied!°   *unchallenged*
But thou thy treason's fruit, I hope, shalt taste
Right sour, and feel the law which thou hast
    defaced.'°   *discredited*

32
With that his baleful° spear he fiercely bent°   *deadly aimed*
Against the pagan's breast, and therewith thought
His cursed life out of her lodge to have rent.
But ere the point arrived where it ought,
That sevenfold shield which he from Guyon brought
He cast between to ward the bitter stound:°   *shock*
Through all those folds the steel head passage wrought
And through his shoulder pierced, wherewith to ground
He grovelling° fell all gored° in his   *face down‡ soaking‡*
    gushing wound.

33
Which, when his brother saw, fraught° with great grief   *filled‡*
And wrath, he to him leaped furiously
And foully said: 'By Mahoun,° cursed   *Muhammad*
    thief,°   *villain*
That direful stroke thou dearly shalt aby'.°   *pay for*
Then, hurling up° his harmful blade on high,   *brandishing*
Smote him so hugely° on his haughty   *hideously*

crest°　　　　　　　　　　　　　　*lofty head; proud plume*
That from his saddle forced him to fly –
Else mote° it needs down to his manly breast　　　　　*must*
Have cleft his head in twain and life thence dispossessed.

34

Now was the Prince in dangerous distress,
  Wanting° his sword when he on foot should°　　*Lacking　had to*
    fight:
  His single spear° could do him small　　　　　　　*spear alone*
    redress°　　　　　　　　　　　　　*compensation; aid*
  Against two foes of so exceeding might,
  The least of which was match for any knight.
  And now the other, whom he erst° did　　　　　*previously*
    daunt,°　　　　　　　　　　　　　　　　*overcome*
  Had reared himself again to cruel fight,
  Three times more furious and more puissant,
Unmindful° of his wound, of his fate ignorant.　　　　*careless*

35

So both at once° him charge on either side　　　　　*together*
  With hideous strokes and importable° power　　*unendurable*
  That forced him his ground to traverse wide
  And wisely watch to ward that deadly stour;°　　　*attack*
  For in° his shield as thick as stormy shower　　　　　*on*
  Their strokes did rain, yet did he never quail,
  Ne° backward shrink, but as a steadfast tower,　　　*Nor*
  Whom foe with double battery doth assail,
Them on her bulwark bears and bids them nought avail.

36

So stoutly° he withstood their strong assay°　　*bravely　attack*
  Till that at last, when he advantage spied,
  His poignant° spear he thrust with puissant　　　*piercing*
    sway°　　　　　　　　　　　　　　　　　*force*
  At proud Cymochles whiles his shield was wide,
  That° through his thigh the mortal steel did　　　*So that*
    gride.°　　　　　　　　　　　　　　　　*pierce†*
  He, swerving with the force, within his flesh

Did break the lance and let the head abide:
  Out of the wound the red blood flowed fresh°   *strongly*
That underneath his feet soon made a purple plesh.°   *puddle*

37

Horribly then he 'gan to rage and rail,
  Cursing his gods and himself damning deep.
  Also, when his brother saw the red blood rail°   *flow* *
  Adown so fast and all his armour steep,°   *soak*
  For very fellness° loud he 'gan to weep,   *angry pain* *
  And said: 'Caitiff,° curse on thy cruel hand   *Wretch*
  That twice hath sped.° Yet shall it not thee   *accomplished its end*
    keep
  From the third brunt° of this my fatal   *sharp blow* *
    brand:°   *blade*
Lo, where the dreadful Death behind thy back doth stand.'

38

With that he struck, and the other struck withal,°   *as well*
  That nothing seemed mote° bear so monstrous   *[as if] it might*
    might:
  The one upon his covered shield did fall
  And, glancing down, would not his owner bite.
  But the other did upon his truncheon° smite   *broken spear-shaft*
  Which, hewing quite° asunder, further way   *completely*
  It made and on his haqueton° did light,   *mail-plated jacket*
  The which dividing with importune° sway°   *violent   momentum*
It seized in his right side, and there the dint° did stay.   *blow*

39

Wide was the wound, and a large lukewarm flood,
  Red as the rose, thence gushed grievously
  That,° when the paynim spied the streaming blood,   *So that*
  Gave° him great heart° and hope of victory.   *It gave   courage*
  On the other side, in huge perplexity,
  The Prince now stood, having his weapon broke:
  Nought could he hurt, but still at ward° did lie –   *on guard*
  Yet with his truncheon he so rudely° struck   *violently*
Cymochles twice that twice him forced his foot
    revoke.°   *draw back*†

40

Whom, when the Palmer saw in such distress,
 Sir Guyon's sword he lightly° to him raught° *swiftly handed*
 And said: 'Fair son, great God thy right hand bless
 To use that sword so wisely as it ought.'° *deserves*
 Glad was the knight, and with fresh courage
  fraught,° *equipped‡*
 Whenas° again he armed felt his hand. *When*
 Then – like a lion which hath long time sought
 His robbed° whelps and, at the last, them found *stolen*
Amongst the shepherd swains, then waxeth wood° and *mad*
 yond° – *savage†*

41

So fierce° he laid about him and dealt blows *fiercely*
 On either side, that neither mail could hold
 Ne° shield defend the thunder of his throws.° *Nor blows*
 Now to Pyrochles many strokes he told;° *counted out*
 Eft° to Cymochles twice so many *Likewise*
  fold.° *many times*
 Then, back again turning his busy hand,
 Them both at once compelled with courage bold
 To yield wide way to his heart-thrilling° brand: *piercing*
And, though they both stood stiff,° yet could not both *firm*
 withstand.

42

As savage bull, whom two fierce mastiffs bait,
 When rancour doth with rage him once engore° *infuriate†*
 Forgets with wary ward° them to await, *guard*
 But with his dreadful horns them drives afore,
 Or flings aloft, or treads down in the floor,
 Breathing out wrath and bellowing disdain
 That° all the forest quakes to hear him roar: *So that*
 So raged Prince Arthur 'twixt his foemen twain
That neither could his mighty puissance sustain.

43

But ever at Pyrochles when he smit –
 Who Guyon's shield cast ever him before,
 Whereon the Fairy Queen's portait was writ° – *inscribed*

His hand relented and the stroke forbore,
And his dear° heart the picture 'gan adore,   *noble*
Which oft the paynim saved from deadly stour.°   *death**
But him henceforth the same can save no more,
For now arrived is his fatal hour
That n'ote° avoided be by earthly skill or power.   *may not*

44

For when Cymochles saw the foul reproach
  Which them impeached, pricked with guilty shame
  And inward grief he fiercely 'gan approach
  (Resolved to put away that loathly blame,
  Or die with honour and desert° of fame),   *merit*
  And on the hauberk° struck the Prince so   *mail tunic*
    sore°   *severely*
  That quite disparted° all the linked frame   *split open†*
  And pierced to the skin, but bit no more,
Yet made him twice to reel that never moved afore.°   *before*

45

Whereat renfierced° with wrath and sharp   *made fierce again†*
    regret°   *anguish*
  He struck so hugely with his borrowed blade
  That it empierced° the pagan's   *pierced through‡*
    burgonet°   *visored helmet*
  And, cleaving the hard steel, did deep invade
  Into his head, and cruel passage made
  Quite° through his brain. He, tumbling down on   *Completely*
    ground,
  Breathed out his ghost° which, to the infernal shade   *spirit*
  Fast flying, there eternal torment found
For all the sins wherewith his lewd life did abound.

46

Which when his german° saw, the stony fear   *brother*
  Ran to his heart and all his sense dismayed:
  Ne° thenceforth life ne° courage did appear   *Neither nor*
  But, as a man whom hellish fiends have frayed,°   *frightened*
  Long trembling still he stood; at last thus said:
  'Traitor, what hast thou done? However may
  Thy cursed hand so cruelly have swayed°   *attacked†*

Against that knight? Harrow° and   *[a cry of alarm]*
    wellaway,°   *alas*
After so wicked deed why livest thou longer day?"°   *a day longer*

47

With that, all desperate, as° loathing light,°   *as if daylight*
    And with revenge desiring soon to die,
    Assembling all his force and utmost might,
    With his own sword he fierce at him did fly,
    And struck, and foined,° and lashed outrageously,   *lunged*
    Withouten reason or regard.° Well knew   *heeding anything*
    The Prince, with patience and sufferance
      sly,°   *knowing forbearance*
    So hasty heat soon cooled to subdue.
Tho,° when this breathless wox,° that°   *Then grew i.e., Arthur*
    battle 'gan renew.

48

As when a windy tempest bloweth high
    That° nothing may withstand his stormy   *So that*
      stour,°   *commotion*
    The clouds, as things afraid, before him fly;
    But all so soon as his outrageous° power   *violent*
    Is laid,° they fiercely then begin to shower   *diminished*
    And, as in scorn of his spent, stormy spite,
    Now all at once their malice° forth do pour –   *virulence*
    So did Prince Arthur bear himself in fight
And suffered rash Pyrochles waste his idle° might.   *useless*

49

At last, whenas° the saracen perceived   *when*
    How that strange° sword refused to serve his need,   *alien*
    But, when he struck most strong, the dint°   *blow*
      deceived,°   *cheated*
    He flung it from him and, devoid of dread,
    Upon him lightly° leaping without heed,   *swiftly*
    'Twixt his two mighty arms engrasped fast,
    Thinking to overthrow and down him tread:
    But him in strength and skill the Prince surpassed
And, through his nimble sleight,° did under him   *adroitness*
    down cast.

50

Nought booted° it the paynim then to strive;   *availed*
  For, as a bittern in the eagle's claw,
  That may not hope by flight to 'scape alive,
  Still waits for death with dread and trembling awe,°   *terror*
  So he, now subject to the victor's law,
  Did not once move nor upward cast his eye
  For vile disdain and rancour, which did gnaw
  His heart in twain with sad° melancholy,°   *weary anger**
As one that loathed life and yet despised to die.

51

But, full of princely bounty° and great mind,°   *virtue purpose*
  The conqueror nought cared him to slay
  But, casting wrongs and all revenge behind,
  More glory thought to give life than decay,°   *death*
  And said: 'Paynim, this is thy dismal day;°   *death-day*
  Yet, if thou wilt renounce thy miscreance,°   *false faith*
  And my true liegeman yield thyself for aye,
  Life will I grant thee for thy valiance
And all thy wrongs will wipe out of my sovenance.'°   *memory*

52

'Fool,' said the pagan, 'I thy gift defy,
  But use thy fortune as it doth befall,
  And say that I not overcome do die,
  But, in despite° of life, for death do call.'   *disdain*
  Wroth was the Prince, and sorry yet withal
  That he so wilfully refused grace.
  Yet, sith° his fate so cruelly did fall,   *since*
  His shining helmet he 'gan soon unlace,
And left his headless body bleeding all the place.

53

By this Sir Guyon, from his trance awaked –
  Life having mastered her senseless foe –
  And, looking up, whenas his shield he lacked
  And sword saw not, he waxed wondrous°   *extremely*
    woe.°   *woeful*
  But when the Palmer, whom he long ago
  Had lost, he by him spied, right glad he grew,

And said: 'Dear sir, whom, wandering to and fro,
  I long have lacked, I joy° thy face to view: *rejoice*
Firm is thy faith whom danger never from me drew.

54

'But rede° what wicked hand hath robbed me   *inform me*
  Of my good sword and shield.' The Palmer, glad
  With so fresh° hue° uprising him to see,   *lively colour*
  Him answered: 'Fair son, be no whit sad
  For want° of weapons, they shall soon be had.'   *lack*
  So 'gan he to discourse the whole debate°   *battle*
  Which that strange knight for him sustained had
  And those two saracens confounded late,
Whose carcases on ground were horribly prostrate.

55

Which, when he heard and saw the tokens true,
  His heart with great affection was embathed,
  And to the Prince, bowing with reverence due
  As to the patron° of his life, thus said: *protector*
  'My lord, my liege, by whose most gracious aid
  I live this day and see my foes subdued,
  What may suffice to be for meed° repaid   *recompense*
  Of so great graces° as ye have me showed,   *favours*
But to be ever bound—'

56

To whom the Infant° thus: 'Fair sir, what need   *noble youth*
  Good turns be counted as a servile bond
  To bind their doers to receive their meed?
  Are not all knights by oath bound to withstand
  Oppressor's power by arms and puissant hand?
  Suffice that I have done my due° in   *duty*
    place.'°   *in this instance*
  So goodly purpose they together found
  Of kindness and of courteous aggrace° –   *favour*†
The whiles false Archimage and Atin fled apace.

Canto 9

The house of Temperance, in which
   Doth sober° Alma dwell,   *temperate; serious*
Besieged of many foes, whom stranger
   Knights to flight compel.

1

Of all God's works which do this world adorn,
  There is no one more fair and excellent
  Than is man's body, both for power and form,
  Whiles it is kept in sober° government.°   *temperate control*
  But none than it more foul and indecent°   *unseemly*
  Distempered° through misrule and passions   *[When] disordered*
    base:
   It grows a monster, and incontinent°   *forthwith; intemperately*
  Doth lose his dignity and native
    grace:°   *attractiveness; divine influence*
Behold, who list,° both one and other in this place.   *wishes*

2

After the paynim° brethren conquered were,   *pagan*
  The Briton Prince, recovering his stolen sword
  And Guyon his lost shield, they both yfere°   *together*
  Forth passed on their way in fair accord,
  Till him the Prince with gentle° court°   *courteous attention†*
    did board:
   'Sir knight, mote° I of you this courtesy read°   *might be told*
  To weet° why on your shield so goodly   *know*
    scored°   *delineated*
  Bear ye the picture of that lady's head? –
Full lively° is the semblant,° though the substance *lifelike image*
    dead.'

3

'Fair sir,' said he, 'if in that picture dead
  Such life ye read,° and virtue in vain show,   *discern*
  What mote ye ween° if the true livelihead° *think living form‡**

Of that most glorious visage ye did view?
But if the beauty of her mind ye knew,
That is her bounty° and imperial power   *virtue; excellence*
Thousand times fairer than her mortal hue,°   *aspect*
O how great wonder would your thoughts devour,
And infinite desire into your spirit pour!

4

'She is the mighty Queen of Fairy,
    Whose fair retrait° I in my shield do bear: *portrait*†
    She is the flower of grace and chastity,
    Throughout the world renowned far and near –
    My lief,° my liege, my sovereign, my dear,   *beloved*
    Whose glory shineth as the morning star
    And with her light the earth enlumines° clear: *illuminates**
    Far reach her mercies, and her praises far,
As well in state of peace as puissance in war.'

5

'Thrice happy man,' said then the Briton knight,
    'Whom gracious lot° and thy great valiance°   *chance valour*
    Have made thee soldier of that princess bright,
    Which with her bounty and glad° countenance   *beautiful**
    Doth bless her servants and them high advance.
    How may strange knight hope ever to aspire,
    By faithful service and meet° amenance,°   *fitting conduct*†
    Unto such bliss? – sufficient were that hire°   *reward*
For loss of thousand lives to die at her leisure.'

6

Said Guyon: 'Noble lord, what meed° so great,   *reward*
    Or grace of earthly prince so sovereign,°   *supreme*
    But by your wondrous worth and warlike feat
    Ye well may hope and easily attain?
    But were your will her sold° to entertain,° *pay for service take*‡
    And numbered be amongst Knights of Maidenhead,
    Great guerdon,° well I wote,° should you   *recompense know*
        remain,°   *await*
    And in her favour high be reckoned
As Artegall and Sophy now been honoured.'

7

'Certes,'° then said the Prince, 'I God avow   *Indeed*
    That sith° I arms and knighthood first did   *since*
      plight,°   *pledge*
    My whole desire hath been, and yet is now,
    To serve that queen with all my power and might.
    Now hath the Sun with his lamp-burning light
    Walked round about the world, and I no less,
    Sith of that goddess I have sought the sight,
    Yet nowhere can her find: such happiness
Heaven doth me envy,° and Fortune favour less.'   *begrudge*‡

8

'Fortune, the foe of famous° chevisance,°   *renowned   chivalry*†
    Seldom' (said Guyon) 'yields to Virtue aid,
    But in her way throws mischief and mischance,
    Whereby her course is stopped and passage stayed.
    But you, fair sir, be not herewith dismayed,
    But constant keep the way in which ye stand –
    Which, were it not that I am else delayed
    With hard° adventure which I have in hand,   *laborious*
I labour would to guide you through all Fairyland.'

9

'Gramercy, sir,' said he, 'but mote I weet°   *know*
    What strange adventure do ye now pursue?
    Perhaps my succour° or advisement meet°   *aid   suitable advice*
    Mote stead° you much your purpose to   *help*‡
      subdue.'°   *achieve*†
    Then 'gan Sir Guyon all the story show°   *disclose*
    Of false Acrasia and her wicked wiles,
    Which to avenge the Palmer him forth drew
    From fairy court. So talked they, the whiles
They wasted had much way and measured many miles.

10

And now fair Phoebus 'gan decline in haste
    His weary wagon to the western vale
    Whenas° they spied a goodly castle, placed   *When*
    Forby° a river in a pleasant dale,   *Beside*
    Which, choosing for that evening's hospital,°   *hostel for pilgrims*

They thither marched. But when they came in sight,
And from their sweaty coursers did avail,°　　　　　*dismount**
They found the gates fast barred long ere night,
And every loop° fast locked, as fearing foes'　　　　*loophole*
　　despite.°　　　　　　　　　　　　　　　　　　　*injury*

11

Which, when they saw, they weened° foul　　　　*believed*
　　reproach°　　　　　　　　　　　　　　　　　　*insult*
Was to them done their entrance to forestall,°　　*obstruct‡*
Till that the squire 'gan nigher to approach
And wind° his horn under the castle wall,　　　　*blow*
That° with the noise it shook as it would fall.　　*So that*
Eftsoons° forth looked from the highest spire　*Straight away*
The watch, and loud unto the knights did call
To weet° what they so rudely°　*know forcefully; discourteously*
　　did require:
Who gently° answered, they entrance did desire.　*courteously*

12

'Fly, fly, good knights,' said he, 'fly fast away
If that your lives ye love as meet° ye should.　　*is fitting*
Fly fast, and save yourselves from near°　　　*imminent*
　　decay:°　　　　　　　　　　　　　　　　　　*death*
Here may ye not have entrance though we
　　would.°　　　　　　　　　　　　　　　*would wish it*
We would and would again, if that we could;
But thousand enemies about us rave,°　　　*rove;* rage‡*
And with long siege us in this castle hold:
Seven years this wise° they us besieged have,　*in this fashion*
And many good knights slain that have us sought to save.'

13

Thus as he spoke, lo with outrageous° cry　　　*furious*
A thousand villains° round about　*deformed creatures; serfs*
　　them swarmed
Out of the rocks and caves adjoining nigh,
Vile caitiff° wretches, ragged, rude,　*enslaved;* miserable*
　　deformed,
All threatening death, all in strange manner armed,
Some with unwieldy clubs, some with long spears,

Some rusty knives, some staves in fire warmed.
Stern was their look like wild amazed°   *bewildered; stupefied*
    steers,
Staring with hollow eyes and stiff, upstanding hairs.

14

Fiercely at first those knights they did assail,°   *attack*
    And drove them to recoil. But when again
    They gave fresh charge, their forces 'gan to fail,
    Unable their encounter to sustain:
    For with such puissance and impetuous main°   *strength*
    Those champions broke on them that forced them fly
    Like scattered sheep, whenas the shepherd's swain°   *when*
    A lion and a tiger doth espy
With greedy pace forth rushing from the forest nigh.

15

A while they fled, but soon returned again
    With greater fury than before was found,
    And evermore their cruel captain
    Sought with his rascal° routs° to enclose them   *riotous rabble*
        round
    And, overrun, to tread them to the ground.
    But soon the knights with their bright-burning blades
    Broke their rude° troops and orders° did   *barbaric ranks*
        confound,
    Hewing and slashing at their idle°   *insubstantial**
        shades,°   *phantoms*
For though they bodies seem, yet substance from them fades:

16

As when a swarm of gnats at eventide
    Out of the fens of Allan do arise,
    Their murmuring small trumpets sounden wide
    Whiles in the air the clustering army flies
    That, as a cloud, doth seem to dim the skies:
    Ne° man nor beast may rest or take repast   *Neither*
    From their sharp wounds and noyous° injuries   *vexing*
    Till the fierce northern wind with blustering blast
Doth blow them quite° away, and in the ocean cast.   *completely*

17

Thus when they had that troublous crowd dispersed,
   Unto the castle gate they came again
     And entrance craved which was denied erst.°   *formerly*
     Now, when report of that their perilous pain°   *difficulty*
     And cumbrous° conflict which they did sustain,   *troublesome*
   Came to the lady's ear which° there did   *ear of the lady who*
     dwell,
   She forth issued with a goodly train
     Of squires and ladies equipaged° well,   *arrayed*[t]
And entertained° them right fairly, as   *received*[t]
     befell.°   *was appropriate*

18

Alma she called was, a virgin bright°   *beautiful*
   That had not yet felt Cupid's wanton rage:
     Yet was she wooed of° many a gentle° knight   *by noble*
     And many a lord of noble parentage,
   That sought with her to link in marriage:
     For she was fair as fair mote° ever be,   *might*
     And in the flower now of her freshest age;
     Yet full of grace° and goodly modesty,   *comeliness; divine virtue*
That° even heaven rejoiced her sweet face to see.   *So that*

19

In robe of lily white she was arrayed
   That from her shoulder to her heel down raught,°   *reached*
   The train whereof loose far behind her strayed,
   Branched with gold and pearl most richly wrought,
   And borne of two fair damsels which were taught
   That service well. Her yellow golden hair
     Was trimly° woven and in tresses° wrought,   *neatly plaits*
     Ne° other tire° she on her head did wear,   *Nor head-dress*
But crowned with a garland of° sweet rosier.°   *from [a] rose bush*

20

Goodly° she entertained those noble knights   *Courteously*
   And brought them up into her castle hall,
     Where gentle° court° and gracious°   *courteous attention*[t] *kindly*
     delight
   She to them made with mildness virginal,

Showing herself both wise and liberal.°   *bountiful*
There when they rested had a season due°   *fitting period*
They her besought, of favour special,
Of that fair castle to afford them view:
She granted, and, them leading forth, the same did show.

21

First she them led up to the castle wall,
That was so high as foe might not it climb,
And also fair and fencible° withal: *well-fortified*†
Not built of brick, ne yet of stone and lime,
But of thing like to that Egyptian slime°   *bitumen*
Whereof King Nine° whilom° built Babel   *Ninus formerly**
   tower.
But O, great pity, that no longer time
So goodly workmanship should not endure:
Soon it must turn to earth: no earthly thing is sure.

22

The frame° thereof seemed partly circular   *structure*
And part triangular: O work divine!
Those two the first and last proportions° are –   *shapes; figures*
The one imperfect, mortal, feminine;
The other immortal, perfect, masculine.
And 'twixt them both a quadrate was the base,
Proportioned equally by seven and nine:
Nine was the circle set in heaven's place,
All which, compacted,° made a goodly   *combined*
   diapase.°   *octave*

23

Therein two gates were placed seemly° well: *appropriately*
The one before,° by which all in did pass,   *i.e., the mouth*
Did the other° far in workmanship excel;   *i.e., the rectum*
For not of wood, nor of enduring brass,
But of more worthy substance framed° it was.   *formed*
Doubly disparted,° it did lock and close   *divided*†
That,° when it locked,° none might   *So that   was locked*†
   through pass
And, when it opened, no man might it close –
Still° open to their friends and closed to their foes.   *Ever*

24

Of hewn stone the porch° was fairly°   *i.e., lower face   beautifully*
    wrought –
Stone of more value, and more smooth and fine,
Than jet or marble far from Ireland brought;
Over the which was cast a wandering vine°   *i.e., beard*
Enchased° with a wanton° ivy twine.   *Adorned†   luxuriant*
And over it a fair portcullis° hung   *i.e., nose*
Which to the gate directly did incline,
With comely compass° and   *fine curve; extent*
    compacture° strong,   *compactness†*
Neither unseemly short, nor yet exceeding long.

25

Within the barbican° a   *loophole;† watch-tower [i.e., the mouth]*
    porter° sat,   *i.e., the tongue*
Day and night duly keeping watch and ward:°   *guard*
Nor wight° nor word mote° pass out of the gate   *thing*   might*
But in good order and with due regard.°   *attention*
Utterers of secrets he from thence debarred,
Babblers of folly and blazers° of crime.°   *broadcasters   evil*
His alarm bell might loud and wide be heard
When cause required, but never out of time:°   *at the wrong time*
Early and late it rang, at evening and at prime.°   *dawn*

26

And round about the porch on every side
Twice sixteen warders° sat, all armed bright   *i.e., the teeth*
In glistering° steel and strongly fortified: *glittering*
Tall° yeomen seemed they, and of great   *Handsome; strong*
    might,
And were enranged° ready still° for   *arranged in ranks†   ever*
    fight.
By them as Alma passed with her guests
They did obeisance, as beseemed° right,   *befitted*
And then again returned to their rests.
The porter eke° to her did lout° with humble   *also   bow*
    gests.°   *gestures*

27

Thence she them brought into a stately hall°   *i.e., the throat*
 Wherein were many tables fair dispread°   *spread out*
 And ready dight° with drapets° festival   *prepared cloths*†
 Against° the viands should be   *In preparation for when*
  ministered.
 At the upper end there sat, yclad in red
 Down to the ground, a comely personage
 That in his hand a white rod managed:
 He, steward, was hight° Diet – ripe of age,   *called**†
And in demeanour sober, and in counsel sage.

28

And through the hall there walked to and fro
 A jolly° yeoman, marshall of the same,   *handsome; jovial*
 Whose name was Appetite. He did bestow
 Both guests and meat° whenever in they came,   *food*
 And knew them how to order° without   *i.e., according to rank*
  blame
 As him the steward bade. They both at one°   *together*
 Did duty to their lady, as became:°   *was fitting*
 Who, passing by, forth led her guests anon
Into the kitchen room, ne° spared for niceness°   *nor delicacy*‡
 none.°   *anything*

29

It was a vault° ybuilt for great dispence° *i.e., the stomach storage*
 With many ranges reared° along the wall   *placed upright*
 And one great chimney, whose long tunnel thence
 The smoke forth threw. And in the midst of all
 There placed was a cauldron wide and tall
 Upon a mighty furnace, burning hot –
 More hot than Etna or flaming Mongiball.
 For day and night it burned, ne ceased not,
So long as anything it in the cauldron got.

30

But to delay the heat – lest by mischance
 It might break out and set the whole on fire –
 There added was by goodly° ordinance°   *excellent decree*
 A huge great pair of bellows, which did stir°   *move*

Continually, and cooling breath inspire.°   *breathe*
About the cauldron many cooks accoiled°   *assembled*[†]
With hooks and ladles as need did require.
The whiles the viands in the vessel boiled
They did about their business sweat, and sorely° toiled.   *greatly*

31

The master cook was called Concoction –
  A careful man and full of comely guise.°   *behaviour*
  The kitchen clerk, that hight Digestion,
  Did order all the achates° in seemly°   *provisions appropriate*
    wise,°   *fashion*
  And set them forth as well he could devise.
  The rest had several° offices° assigned –   *various duties*
  Some to remove the scum as it did rise;
  Others to bear the same away did mind;
And others it to use according to his kind.°   *its nature*

32

But all the liquor which was foul and waste –
  Not good nor serviceable else for aught –
  They in another great round vessel placed
  Till by a conduit pipe it thence were brought.
  And all the rest, that noyous° was and nought,   *troublesome*
  By secret ways, that none might it espy,
  Was close° conveyed and to the back gate brought   *secretly*
  That cleped° was Port Esquiline, whereby   *called*
It was avoided° and thrown out   *emptied*
    privily.°   *secretly [and: to the privy]*

33

Which goodly order and great workman's skill
  Whenas° those knights beheld, with rare°   *When exquisite*
    delight
  And gazing wonder they their minds did fill;
  For never had they seen so strange a sight.
  Thence back again fair Alma led them right,
  And soon into a goodly parlour° brought   *i.e., the heart*
  That was with royal arras° richly dight,°   *tapestry adorned*
  In which was nothing portrayed, nor wrought,
Not wrought, nor portrayed, but easy to be thought.

34

And in the midst thereof, upon the floor,
 A lovely bevy° of fair ladies sat   *company*
 Courted of° many a jolly° paramour,   *by handsome*
 The which them did in modest wise° amate,° *fashion woo†*
 And each one sought his lady to aggrate.°   *gratify†*
 And eke amongst them little Cupid played
 His wanton° sports, being returned late° *lively recently*
 From his fierce wars and having from him laid
His cruel bow, wherewith he thousands hath
 dismayed.°   *vanquished*

35

Diverse delights they found themselves to please:
 Some sang in sweet consort,° some *fellowship; harmony*
  laughed for joy,
 Some played with straws, some idly sat at ease.
 But other some could not abide to toy:
 All pleasance° was to them grief and annoy: *delight*
 This frowned, that fawned,° the third for shame did *cringed‡*
  blush;
 Another seemed envious or coy;
 Another in her teeth did gnaw a rush.
But at these strangers' presence, every one did hush.

36

Soon as the gracious° Alma came in *comely; kindly; full of grace*
 place°   *before them*
 They all at once out of their seats arose
 And to her homage made with humble grace:°   *duty‡*
 Whom, when the knights beheld, they 'gan dispose
 Themselves to court, and each a damsel chose.
 The Prince by chance did on a lady light
 That was right fair and fresh as morning rose,
 But somewhat sad, and solemn eke in sight,° *appearance*
As if some pensive° thought constrained° her *anxious oppressed*
 gentle sprite.°   *mind*

37

In a long purple pall,° whose skirt with gold   *robe*
   Was fretted° all about, she was arrayed,   *interlaced*
   And in her hand a poplar branch did hold:
   To whom the Prince, in courteous manner, said:
   'Gentle° madam, why been ye thus dismayed   *Noble; courteous*
   And your fair beauty do with sadness spill?°   *spoil*
   Lives any that you hath thus ill apaid?°   *pleased*
   Or doen you love, or doen you lack your will?
Whatever be the cause, it sure beseems° you ill.'   *befits*

38

'Fair sir,' said she in half disdainful wise,°   *manner*
   'How is it that this word° in me ye blame,   *i.e., sadness*
   And in yourself do not the same advise?°   *observe*
   Him ill beseems another's faults to name
   That may unwares be blotted with the same.
   Pensive I yield I am, and sad in mind,
   Through great desire of glory and of fame –
   Ne aught, I ween,° are ye therein behind   *think*
That have twelve months sought one, yet nowhere can her
    find.'

39

The Prince was inly° moved at her speech,   *inwardly; extremely*
   Well weeting° true what she had rashly°   *knowing impetuously*
    told,
   Yet with fair semblant° sought to hide the   *appearance*
    breach°   *inroad⁺*
   Which change of colour did perforce° unfold,   *necessarily*
   Now seeming flaming hot, now stony cold.
   Tho,° turning soft° aside, he did inquire   *Then gently*
   What wight° she was that poplar branch did hold: *person**
   It answered was, her name was Praise-desire,
That by well doing sought to honour to aspire.

40

The whiles,° the fairy knight did   *During which time*
   entertain°   *speak to⁺*
   Another damsel of that gentle° crew°   *noble company*
   That was right fair and modest of demean,°   *demeanour*

But that too oft she changed her native° hue:°   *natural   colour*
Strange was her attire, and all her garments blue,
Close round about her tucked with many a plight.°   *pleat*
Upon her fist the bird which shunneth view,
And keeps in coverts° close° from   *hiding places   concealed*
    living wight,
Did sit, as yet° ashamed how rude Pan did her   *still*
    dight.°   *mistreat*

41

So long as Guyon with her communed°   *conversed*
    Unto the ground she cast her modest eye,
    And ever and anon with rosy red
    The bashful blood her snowy cheeks did dye,
    That her became as polished ivory
    Which cunning° craftsman's hand hath overlaid   *skilful*
    With fair vermilion or pure castory.°   *reddish-brown oil*
    Great wonder had the knight to see the maid
So strangely passioned,° and to her   *affected with passion*
    gently° said: *courteously*

42

'Fair damsel, seemeth by your troubled cheer°   *countenance*
    That either me too bold ye ween,° this wise°   *think   manner*
    You to molest, or other ill to fear
    That in the secret of your heart close lies,
    From whence it doth, as cloud from sea, arise.
    If it be I, of pardon I you pray;
    But if aught else that I mote° not devise,°   *may   conjecture*
    I will, if please you it discure,° assay°   *reveal*   attempt*
To ease you of that ill so° wisely as I may.'   *as*

43

She answered nought but, more abashed for shame,
    Held down her head the whiles her lovely face
    The flashing blood with blushing did inflame,
    And the strong passion marred her modest grace
    That° Guyon marvelled at her uncouth°   *So that   strange*
    case,°   *plight*
    Till Alma him bespake:° 'Why wonder ye,   *addressed*†
Fair sir, at that which ye so much embrace?

She is the fountain of your modesty:
You shamefast are, but Shamefastness itself is she.'

44

Thereat the elf did blush in privity°   *secretly*
  And turned his face away; but she the same
  Dissembled fair, and feigned to oversee.°   *disregard*
  Thus they awhile with court° and goodly   *attention*[†]
    game°   *sport*
  Themselves did solace, each one with his dame,
  Till that great lady thence away them sought°   *requested*
  To view her castle's other wondrous frame.°   *structure*
  Up to a stately turret° she them brought,   *i.e., the head*
Ascending by ten steps° of alabaster wrought.   *i.e., vertebrae*

45

That turret's frame most admirable° was,   *wonderful*
  Like highest heaven compassed° around,   *vaulted*[‡]
  And lifted high above this earthly mass,
  Which it surviewed° as hills doen lower ground.   *overlooked*[‡]
  But not on ground° mote like to this be found –   *earth*
  Not that which antique° Cadmus whilom°   *ancient*[‡] *once*[*]
    built
  In Thebes, which Alexander did confound;°   *destroy*
  Nor that proud tower of Troy, though richly gilt,
From which young Hector's blood by cruel Greeks was spilt.

46

The roof hereof was arched overhead,
  And decked with flowers and
    herbars° daintily: *flower gardens;*[*†] *arbours*[*†]
  Two goodly beacons,° set in watches'°   *i.e., eyes   watchmen's*
    stead,°   *place*
  Therein gave light and flamed continually,
  For they of living fire most subtly°   *skilfully*
  Were made, and set in silver sockets bright,
  Covered with lids devised of substance sly°   *cleverly made*
  That° readily they shut and open might: *So that*
O, who can tell the praises of that Maker's might!

47

Ne° can I tell, ne° can I stay to tell,   *Neither   nor*
  This part's great workmanship and wondrous power
  That all this other world's work doth excel,
  And likest is unto that heavenly tower
  That God hath built for his own blessed bower.°   *dwelling*
  Therein° were diverse rooms and diverse stages;   *i.e., the brain*
  But three the chiefest and of greatest power,
  In which there dwelt three honourable sages –
The wisest men, I ween,° that lived in their ages.   *believe*

48

Not he, whom Greece (the nurse of all good arts),
  By Phoebus' doom,° the wisest thought alive,   *judgement*
  Might be compared to these by many parts;°   *times*
  Nor that sage Pylian sire, which did survive
  Three ages such as mortal men contrive,°   *manage*
  By whose advice old Priam's city fell,
  With these in praise of policies° mote strive.   *public affairs*
  These three in these three rooms did sundry° dwell, *separately*
And counselled fair Alma how to govern well.

49

The first of them could things to come foresee;
  The next could of things present best advise;
  The third things past could keep in memory:
  So that no time, nor reason, could arise
  But that the same could one of these comprise.°   *comprehend*
  For-thy° the first did in the forepart sit,   *Therefore*
  That nought mote hinder his quick prejudice:°   *presaging*[†]
  He had a sharp° foresight and working°   *keen   lively*
    wit°   *understanding*
That never idle was, ne once could rest a whit.

50

His chamber was dispainted° all within   *variously painted*[†]
  With sundry° colours, in the which were writ°   *several   painted*
  Infinite shapes of things dispersed° thin:°   *scattered   sparsely*
  Some such as in this world were never yet,
  Ne can devised be of° mortal wit;°   *by   mind*
  Some daily seen, and known by their names,

Such as in idle° fantasies° do flit:°   *vain   fancies   shift about*
Infernal hags, centaurs, fiends, hippodames,°   *hippopotamuses*
Apes, lions, eagles, owls, fools, lovers, children, dames.

51
And all the chamber filled was with flies,
   Which buzzed all about and made such sound
   That they encumbered° all men's ears   *inconvenienced; impeded*
     and eyes,
   Like many swarms of bees assembled round
   After their hives with honey do abound:
   All those were idle thoughts and fantasies,
   Devices,° dreams, opinions unsound,   *desires; notions*
   Shows, visions, soothsays° and prophecies,   *predictions‡*
And all that feigned is, as leasings,° tales and lies.   *falsehoods*

52
Amongst them all sat he which woned° there,   *dwelled*
   That hight° Phantastes by his nature true –   *was called*†
   A man of years yet fresh,° as mote° appear,   *young   might*
   Of swart° complexion and of crabbed°   *livid;* dark   churlish*
     hue,°   *aspect*
   That him full of melancholy did show;
   Bent, hollow, beetle brows, sharp staring eyes,
   That mad or foolish seemed: one by his view°   *appearance*
   Mote deem° him born with ill-disposed skies   *judge*
When oblique Saturn sat in the house of agonies.

53
Whom Alma, having showed to her guests,
   Thence brought them to the second room, whose walls
   Were painted fair° with memorable gests°   *splendidly   exploits*
   Of famous wizards,° and with picturals°   *sages   pictures†*
   Of magistrates, of courts, of tribunals,
   Of commonwealths, of states, of policy,°   *statecraft*
   Of laws, of judgements, and of decretals,°   *decrees‡*
   All arts, all science, all philosophy,
And all that in the world was aye° thought   *ever*
     wittily.°   *wisely; cleverly*

54

Of those that room was full, and them among
 There sat a man of ripe and perfect° age   *mature; middle*
 Who did them meditate all his life long,
 That° through continual practice and usage° *So that habit*
 He now was grown right wise and wondrous sage.
 Great pleasure had those stranger knights to see
 His goodly° reason and grave personage° *excellent appearance*
 That° his disciples both desired to be;   *So that*
But Alma thence them led to the hindmost room of three.

55

That chamber seemed ruinous and old,
 And therefore was removed far behind;
 Yet were the walls, that did the same uphold,
 Right firm and strong, though somewhat they
  declined.°   *leaned‡*
 And therein sat an old, old man, half blind
 And all decrepit in his feeble corse:°   *body*
 Yet lively vigour rested° in his mind   *remained*
 And recompensed him with a better scorse:° *exchange†*
Weak body well is changed for mind's redoubled force.

56

This man of infinite remembrance° was,   *memory*
 And things foregone through many ages held,
 Which he recorded still as they did pass,
 Ne suffered them to perish through long eld° *age*
 (As all things else the which this world doth
  wield),°   *command*
 But laid them up in his immortal scrine° *box [of immortality]*
 Where they for ever incorrupted dwelled:
 The wars he well remembered of King Nine,
Of old Assaracus, and Inachus divine.

57

The years of Nestor nothing were to his,
 Ne yet Methuselah, though longest lived,
 For he remembered both their infancies.
 Ne° wonder, then, if that he were deprived *No*
 Of native strength now that he them survived.

His chamber all was hanged about with rolls
And old records from ancient times derived –
Some made in books, some in long parchment scrolls
That were all worm-eaten and full of canker holes.

58

Amidst them all he in a chair was set,°   *sat*
  Tossing and turning them withouten end;
    But, for he was unable them to fet,°   *fetch*
    A little boy did on him still° attend,   *always*
    To reach whenever he for aught did send;
    And oft, when things were lost or laid amiss,
    That boy them sought and unto him did lend.°   *give**
    Therefore he Anamnestes° cleped° is,   *i.e., the Recaller called*
And that old man Eumnestes,° by their   *i.e., Good Memory*
    properties.

59

The knights, there entering, did him reverence due,
  And wondered at his endless exercise;
  Then, as they 'gan his library to view
  And antique° registers for to advise,°   *ancient‡ look at**
  There chanced to the Prince's hand to rise°   *come to hand†*
  An ancient book hight *Briton Monuments*°   *Records*
  That of this land's first conquest did devise,°   *recount**
  And old division into regiments,°   *kingdoms**
Till it reduced was to one man's governments.°   *control*

60

Sir Guyon chanced eke° on another book   *also*
  That hight *Antiquity of Fairyland*,
  In which, whenas° he greedily did look,   *when*
  The offspring° of elves and fairies there he found   *origin*
  As it delivered was from hand to hand.
  Whereat they, burning both with fervent fire
  Their country's ancestry to understand,
  Craved leave of Alma and that aged sire
To read those books – who gladly granted their desire.

[In canto 10 Arthur reads, in *Briton Monuments*, of the early history of Britain from its conquest and settlement by Aeneas's great-grandson Brutus through the Roman occupation to the reign of Uther Pendragon (st. 68). As well as being a history of the realm it is also a list of Arthur's and Queen Elizabeth's reputed ancestors. Meantime, Guyon reads a complementary, mythological history of the queen and her kingdom in terms of fairy lore (st. 70–6), which brings things up to date with Henry VIII (Oberon) and Elizabeth herself (Glorian).]

Canto 11

The enemies of Temperance
Besiege her dwelling place;
Prince Arthur them repels, and foul
Maleger doth deface.°   *destroy*

1

What war so cruel, or what siege so sore,°   *difficult*
  As that which strong affections° do apply   *passions*
  Against the fort of reason evermore
  To bring the soul into captivity:
  Their force is fiercer through infirmity
  Of the frail flesh, relenting° to their rage,   *giving way*
  And exercise most bitter tyranny
  Upon the parts brought into their bondage:
No wretchedness is like to sinful villeinage.°   *servitude to sin*

2

But in a body which doth freely yield
  His parts to Reason's rule obedient,
  And letteth her that ought the sceptre wield,
  All happy peace and goodly government
  Is settled there in sure establishment.°   *stability*
  There Alma, like a virgin queen most bright,°   *beautiful*
  Doth flourish in all beauty excellent,
  And to her guests doth bounteous° banquet   *liberal*
    dight,°   *prepare*
Attempered° goodly well for health and for delight.   *Regulated*

3

Early before the morn with crimson ray
  The windows of bright heaven opened had,
  Through which into the world the dawning day
  Might look, that maketh every creature glad,
  Uprose Sir Guyon, in bright armour clad,
  And to his purposed journey him prepared.
  With him the Palmer eke, in habit sad,°   *dark*
  Himself addressed to that adventure hard:
So to the river's side they both together fared,

4

Where them awaited, ready at the ford,
  The ferryman, as Alma had behight,°   *promised*
  With his well-rigged boat. They go aboard,
  And he eftsoons° 'gan launch his bark   *at once*
    forthright.°   *straight ahead*
  Ere long they rowed were quite° out of sight,   *completely*
  And fast the land behind them fled away:
  But let them pass, whiles weather right
  Do serve their turns. Here I awhile must stay
To see a cruel° fight done° by the Prince this   *fierce   undertaken*
  day.

5

For all so° soon as Guyon thence was gone   *as*
  Upon his voyage with his trusty guide,
  That wicked band of villains° fresh   *depraved creatures; serfs*
    begun
  That castle to assail on every side
  And lay strong siege about it far and wide.
  So huge and infinite their number were
  That all the land they under them did hide;
  So foul and ugly, that exceeding fear
Their visages impressed° when they approached near.   *imprinted*

6

Them in twelve troops their captain did dispart°   *segregate*†
  And round about in fittest steads° did place,   *situations*

Where each might best offend° his proper part   *attack*
And his contrary object most deface°   *lay waste*
As every one seemed meetest in° that case.   *best fitted for*
Seven of the same against the castle gate
In strong entrenchments he did closely° place,   *densely; hidden*
Which with incessant force and endless hate
They battered day and night and entrance did await.

7

The other five, five sundry ways he set
Against the five great bulwarks of that pile,°   *building*
And unto each a bulwark did aret°   *entrust†*
To assail with open force or hidden guile
In hope thereof to win victorious spoil.
They all that charge° did fervently apply°   *duty   comply with**
With greedy malice and importune° toil,   *persistent; demanding*
And planted there their huge artillery,
With which they daily made most dreadful battery.

8

The first troop was a monstrous rabblement°   *mob;‡ swarm‡*
Of foul, misshapen wights,° of which some were   *creatures**
Headed like owls with beaks uncomely bent,
Others like dogs, others like griffins drear,°   *terrible*
And some had wings, and some had claws to tear,
And every one of them had lynx's eyes,
And every one did bow and arrows bear:
All those were lawless lusts, corrupt envies,°   *maliciousness*
And covetous aspects,° all cruel enemies.   *glances†*

9

Those same against the bulwark of the Sight
Did lay strong siege and battailous° assault,   *pugnacious*
Ne° once did yield it respite day nor night;   *Nor*
But soon as Titan 'gan his head exalt,°   *raise‡*
And soon again as he his light with
     hault,°   *withheld [pseudo-archaism]*
Their wicked engines° they against it bent:°   *machines   directed*

That is, each thing by which the eye may fault;°   *do wrong; sin*
But two than all more huge and violent –
Beauty and money – they that bulwark sorely°   *severely*
    rent.°   *damaged*

10

The second bulwark was the Hearing sense,
   'Gainst which the second troop designment°   *a plan, design[t]*
     makes:
   Deformed creatures in° strange difference,°   *of dissimilarity*
   Some having heads like harts, some like to snakes,
   Some like wild boars late roused out of the
     brakes.°   *ferns; bushes*
   Slanderous reproaches and foul infamies,
   Leasings,° backbitings and vainglorious cracks,°   *Lies boasts*
   Bad counsels, praises and false flatteries –
All those against that fort did bend their batteries.

11

Likewise that same third fort, that is the Smell,
   Of° that third troop was cruelly   *By*
     assayed,°   *assaulted; tempted*
   Whose hideous shapes were like to fiends of hell:
   Some like to hounds, some like to apes dismayed,°   *frightened*
   Some like to puttocks° all in plumes arrayed,   *kites; buzzards*
   All shaped according their conditions;°   *dispositions*
   For by those ugly forms weren portrayed
   Foolish delights and fond° abusions°   *foolish impostures*
Which do that sense besiege with light°   *wanton; frivolous*
     illusions.

12

And that fourth band which cruel battery bent
   Against the fourth bulwark, that is the Taste,
   Was as the rest, a grisy° rabblement,   *horrible*
   Some mouthed like greedy ostriches, some faced
   Like loathly toads, some fashioned in the waist
   Like swine: for so deformed is luxury,°   *over-indulgence*
   Surfeit, misdiet and unthrifty waste,
   Vain feasts and idle superfluity:
All those this sense's fort assail incessantly.

13

But the fifth troop most horrible of hue°   aspect
   And fierce of force was dreadful to report:
   For some like snails, some did like spiders show,
   And some like ugly urchins thick and short.   hedgehogs
   Cruelly they assailed that fifth fort,
   Armed with darts of sensual delight,
   With stings of carnal lust, and strong effort°   drive
   Of feeling° pleasures, with which,   belonging to the sense of feel
      day and night,
Against that same fifth bulwark they continued fight.

14

Thus these twelve troops with dreadful puissance
   Against that castle restless siege did lay,
   And evermore their hideous ordinance°   array; missiles
   Upon the bulwarks cruelly did play
   That° now it 'gan to threaten near decay.°   So that   ruin‡
   And evermore their wicked captain
   Provoked them the breaches to assay,°   attack
   Sometimes with threats, sometimes with hope of gain,
Which by the ransack of that piece° they   piece of work [i.e., body]
      should attain.

15

On the other side the assieged° castle's ward°   besieged   garrison
   Their steadfast stands did mightily maintain,
   And many bold repulse and many hard
   Achievements wrought with peril and with pain
   That goodly° frame° from ruin to sustain.   excellent   structure
   And those two brethren giants did defend
   The walls so stoutly° with their sturdy°   valiantly   violent
      main°   force
   That never entrance any durst° pretend°   dared   attempt
But they to direful death their groaning ghosts did send.

16

The noble virgin, lady of the place,°   castle
   Was much dismayed with that dreadful sight,
   For never was she in so evil case;°   situation
   Till that the Prince, seeing her woeful plight,

'Gan her recomfort° from so sad   *encourage; console*
    affright,°   *terror*[t]
Offering his service and his dearest life
For her defence, against that carl° to fight   *churl*
Which was their chief, and the author of that strife.
She him remercied° as the patron° of her life. *thanked* protector*

17

Eftsoons° himself in glitterand° arms he   *Straight away glittering*
    dight,°   *dressed*
And his well-proved weapons to him hent.°   *seized*
So, taking courteous congé,° he behight°   *leave ordered*[*t]
Those gates to be unbarred, and forth he went:
Fair mote° he thee,° the prowest and most   *may thrive**
    gent°   *noble*
That ever brandished bright steel on high.
Whom, soon as that unruly rabblement
With his squire issuing did espy,
They reared a most outrageous,° dreadful, yelling cry,   *furious*

18

And therewith all at once at him let fly
    Their fluttering arrows thick as flakes of snow,
    And round about him flock impetuously
    Like a great water flood that, tumbling low
    From the high mountains, threats to overflow
    With sudden fury all the fertile plain,
    And the sad husbandman's long hope doth throw
Adown the stream, and all his vows° make   *prayers*
    vain:°   *useless*
Nor bounds° nor banks his headlong ruin° may   *boundaries fall*
    sustain.

19

Upon his shield their heaped hail he bore,
    And with his sword dispersed the rascal flocks,
    Which fled asunder and him fell before,
    As withered leaves drop from their dried stocks°   *stems*
    When the wroth western wind does reave° their   *plunder*
    locks.
    And underneath him his courageous steed,

The fierce Spumador, trod them down like docks° –   weeds
The fierce Spumador, born of heavenly seed,
Such as Laomedon of° Phoebus' race did breed.   from

20

Which sudden horror and confused cry
  Whenas their captain heard, in haste he yode°   went
  The cause to weet° and fault to remedy.   know
  Upon a tiger swift and fierce he rode
  That as the wind ran underneath his load,
  Whiles his long legs nigh raught° unto the ground: reached
  Full large he was of limb, and shoulders broad,
  But of such subtle° substance and   rarefied
    unsound°   light; not solid
That like a ghost he seemed whose grave-clothes were
  unbound.

21

And in his hand a bended bow was seen,
  And many arrows under his right side,
  All deadly dangerous, all cruel keen,°   sharp
  Headed with flint and feathers bloody dyed,
  Such as the Indians in their quivers hide.
  Those could he well direct, and straight as line,
  And bid them strike the mark which he had eyed –
  Ne° was there salve, ne° was there medicine,   Neither nor
That mote° recure° their wounds, so inly they did   might cure
  tine.°   sting†

22

As pale and wan as ashes was his look,
  His body lean and meagre° as a   emaciated
    rake,°   also: raiker = vagabond*
  And skin all withered like a dried ruck° –   hayrick
  Thereto° as cold and dreary° as a   Also melancholy; dire
    snake –
  That seemed to tremble evermore and quake.
  All in a canvas thin he was bedight,°   dressed
  And girded with a belt of twisted brake;°   bracken
  Upon his head he wore an helmet light

Made of a dead man's skull, that seemed a ghastly°   *horrifying*
    sight.

23

Maleger was his name, and after him
  There followed fast° at hand two wicked hags,   *close*
  With hoary locks all loose and visage grim,
  Their feet unshod, their bodies wrapped in rags,
  And both as swift on foot as chased stags:
  And yet the one her other leg° had lame,   *one of her legs*
  Which with a staff all full of little snags°   *knots*
  She did support, and Impotence her name;
But the other was Impatience, armed with raging flame.

24

Soon as the carl° from far the Prince espied,   *churl*
  Glistering in arms and warlike ornament,
  His beast he felly° pricked on either° side   *fiercely each*
  And his mischievous° bow full ready bent,°   *destructive aimed*
  With which at him a cruel shaft he sent.
  But he was wary and it warded well
  Upon his shield that° it no further went,   *so that*
  But to the ground the idle quarrel° fell: *square-headed arrow*
Then he another and another did expel.°   *discharge*[†]

25

Which to prevent the Prince his mortal° spear   *deathly*
  Soon to him raught° and fierce at him did ride,   *reached*
  To be avenged of that shot whilere;°   *former*
  But he was not so hardy° to abide   *rash; foolhardy*
  That bitter stound° but, turning quick aside   *attack*
  His lightfoot beast, fled fast away for fear:
  Whom to pursue the Infant° after hied°   *noble youth sped*
  So fast as his good courser could him bear –
But labour lost it was to ween° approach him near;   *think to*

26

For as the winged wind his tiger fled
  That° view of eye could scarce him overtake,   *So that*
  Ne scarce° his feet on ground were seen to tread.   *Nor scarcely*
  Through hills and dales he speedy way did make,

Ne hedge ne ditch his ready passage brake,°   *hindered*
And in his flight the villain turned his face
(As wonts° the Tartar by the Caspian lake   *customarily does*
Whenas the Russian him in fight does chase)
Unto his tiger's tail, and shot at him apace.°   *immediately*

27

Apace he shot, and yet he fled apace°   *swiftly*
  Still° as the greedy knight nigh to him drew;   *Ever*
  And oftentimes he would relent° his pace   *slacken‡ **
  That° him his foe more fiercely should pursue –   *So that*
  Who, when his uncouth° manner he did   *unknown; strange*
    view,
  He 'gan advise° to follow him no more,   *resolve*
  But keep his standing° and his shafts   *place; footing†*
    eschew°   *avoid*
Until he had quite° spent his perilous store,°   *completely   hoard*
And then assail him fresh ere° he should shift for more.   *before*

28

But that lame hag, still as abroad he strew
  His wicked arrows, gathered them again
  And to him brought, fresh battle to renew –
  Which he, espying, cast° her to restrain   *determined*
  From yielding succour to that cursed swain,
  And, her attaching,° thought her hands to tie.   *seizing*
  But soon as him dismounted on the plain
  The other hag did far away espy,
Binding her sister, she to him ran hastily

29

And, catching hold of him as down he leant,
  Him backward overthrew and down him stayed
  With their rude hands and grisy°   *grim*
    grapplement,°   *grappling†*
  Till that the villain, coming to their aid,
  Upon him fell and load upon him laid.
  Full little wanted° but he had him slain   *lacked*
  And of the battle baleful end had made,
  Had not his gentle squire beheld his pain
And comen to his rescue ere his bitter bane.°   *death*

30

So, greatest and most glorious thing on ground°   *earthly*
 May often need the help of weaker hand:
 So feeble is man's state, and life unsound,°   *unstable*
 That in assurance° it may never stand   *security*
 Till it dissolved be from earthly band.
 Proof be thou, Prince, the prowest° man alive *most valiant*
 And noblest born of all in Britain land:
 Yet thee fierce Fortune did so nearly° drive° *hard press*
That had not grace thee blessed,° thou shouldest not *guarded*
 survive.

31

The squire, arriving, fiercely in his arms
 Snatched first the one and then the other jade –
 His chiefest lets° and authors of his harms – *hindrances*
 And them perforce° withheld with threatened *with force*
  blade,
 Lest that his lord they should behind invade:
 The whiles the Prince, pricked with reproachful shame,
 As one awaked out of long slumbering shade,° *darkness*
 Reviving thoughts of glory and of fame,
United all his powers to purge himself from blame.

32

Like as a fire, the which in hollow cave
 Hath long been underkept° and down *kept in subjection*[†]
  suppressed,
 With murmurous° disdain doth inly° *grumbling*[†] *extremely*
  rave,°   *rage*[‡]
 And grudge° in so strait° prison to be *complain constricting*
  pressed,
 At last breaks forth with furious unrest
 And strives to mount unto his native seat:
 All that did erst° it hinder and molest   *previously*
 It now devours with flames and scorching heat,
And carries into smoke with rage and horror great:

33

So mightily the Briton Prince him roused
  Out of his hold and broke his caitiff°   *imprisoning; demanding*
    bands
  And, as a bear whom angry curs have toused,°   *worried*
  Having off-shaken them and escaped their hands,
  Becomes more fell,° and all that him withstands   *fierce*
  Treads down and overthrows. Now had the carl
  Alighted from his tiger, and his hands
  Discharged° of his bow and deadly quarrel,°   *Emptied   arrows*
To seize upon his foe flat lying on the marl° –   *earth*[†]

34

Which now him turned to disadvantage dear,°   *extreme*
  For neither can he fly, nor other° harm,   *the other [Arthur]*
  But trust unto his strength and manhood mere,
  Sith° now he is far from his monstrous swarm   *since*
  And of his weapons did himself disarm.
  The knight, yet wrathful for his late disgrace,
  Fiercely advanced his valorous right arm
  And him so sore° smote with his iron mace   *grievously*
That grovelling° to the ground he fell and   *prostrate*[‡]
    filled° his place.°   *measured   length*

35

Well weened° he that field° was then his own,   *thought   victory*
  And all his labour brought to happy end;
  When sudden up the villain overthrown
  Out of his swoon arose, fresh to contend,
  And 'gan himself to second battle bend°   *apply*
  As° hurt he had not been. Thereby there lay   *As though*
  An huge great stone which stood upon one end
  And had not been removed many a day:
Some landmark seemed to be, or sign of sundry°   *different*
    way.°   *paths*

36

The same he snatched and, with exceeding sway,°   *force*
  Threw at his foe, who was right well aware°   *alert*
  To shun the engine° of his meant°   *instrument   intended*
    decay:°   *death*

It booted° not to think that throw to bear,   *availed*
But ground he gave and lightly° leapt   *quickly*
   arrear,°   *backwards**
Eft° fierce returning, as a falcon fair   *Again*
That once hath failed of her souse° full   *swooping on prey*
   near,°   *only just*
Remounts again into the open air
And unto better fortune doth herself prepare.

37

So, brave returning with his brandished blade,
   He to the carl himself again addressed,
   And struck at him so sternly° that he made   *fiercely*
   An open passage through his riven breast
That° half the steel behind his back did rest: *So that*
   Which, drawing back, he looked evermore
   When the heart blood should gush out of his chest
Or his dead corse° should fall upon the floor –   *body*
But his dead corse upon the floor fell nathemore,°   *not at all*

38

Ne° drop of blood appeared shed to be,   *Nor*
   All° were the wound so wide and wondrous   *Although*
   That through his carcase one might plainly see.
Half in amaze° with horror hideous,°   *terror† terrible*
   And half in rage to be deluded thus,
   Again through both the sides he struck him quite,°   *thoroughly*
That made his sprite° to groan full piteous: *spirit; life-force*
   Yet nathemore forth fled his groaning sprite,
But freshly, as at first, prepared himself to fight.

39

Thereat he smitten was with great affright,°   *fear*
   And trembling terror did his heart appall;°   *shock; terrify*
   Ne wist he° what to think of that same   *Neither did he know*
     sight,
Ne° what to say, ne what to do at all.   *Nor*
   He doubted° lest it were some magical   *was afraid*
   Illusion that did beguile° his sense,   *deceive*

Or wandering ghost that wanted° funeral,   *lacked*
Or airy spirit under false pretence,°   *guise*
Or hellish fiend raised up through devilish
   science.°   *skill; knowledge*

40

His wonder far exceeded reason's reach
   That° he began to doubt his dazzled°   *So that   confounded*[‡]
    sight,
   And oft of error did himself appeach:°   *accuse*
   Flesh without blood, a person without sprite,°   *soul; breath*
   Wounds without hurt, a body without might°   *power*
   That could do harm yet could not harmed be,
   That could not die yet seemed a mortal wight,°   *creature**
   That was most strong in most infirmity –
Like did he never hear, like did he never see.

41

Awhile he stood in this astonishment,
   Yet would he not, for all his great dismay,
   Give over° to effect his first intent   *Give up*
   And the utmost means of victory assay,°   *attempt*
   Or the utmost issue of his own decay.°   *death*
   His own good sword, Mordure, that never failed
   At need till now, he lightly° threw away,   *quickly*
   And his bright shield that nought him now availed,
And with his naked hands him forcibly assailed.

42

'Twixt his two mighty arms him up he snatched,
   And crushed his carcase so against his breast
   That the disdainful soul he thence dispatched
   And the idle° breath all utterly expressed.° *vain   squeezed out*
   Tho,° when he felt him dead, adown he cast   *Then*
   The lumpish° corse unto the senseless ground: *cumbersome*[‡]
   Adown he cast it with so puissant
    wrest°   *powerful a straining;*[†] *turn*
   That back again it did aloft rebound,
And gave against his mother earth a groanful sound,

43

As when Jove's harness-bearing bird° from high   *i.e., the eagle*
  Stoops° at a flying heron with proud disdain,   *swoops†*
  The stone-dead quarry° falls so forcibly   *hawk's prey*
  That it rebounds against the lowly plain,
  A second fall redoubling back again.
  Then thought the Prince all peril sure° was past   *surely*
  And that he victor only° did remain: *alone*
  No sooner thought, than that the carl as fast
'Gan heap huge strokes on him as ere he down was cast.   *before*

44

Nigh his wits' end then wox° the amazed knight,   *grew*
  And thought his labour lost and travail vain°   *pointless*
  Against this lifeless shadow so to fight:
  Yet life he saw, and felt his mighty main°   *strength*
  That, whiles he marvelled still, did still him pain.
  For-thy° he 'gan some other ways advise°   *Therefore consider*
  How to take life from that dead-living swain
  Whom still he marked° freshly to arise   *noted*
From the Earth, and from her womb new spirits to
    reprise.°   *gain anew†*

45

He then remembered well that° had been said,   *what*
  How the Earth his mother was and first him bore:
  She eke° so° often as his life decayed   *moreover as*
  Did life with usury° to him restore,   *interest*
  And raised him up much stronger than before
  So° soon as he unto her womb did fall.   *As*
  Therefore to ground he would him cast no more,
  Ne° him commit to grave terrestrial,   *Nor*
But bear him far from hope of succour usual.

46

Tho° up he caught him 'twixt his puissant hands   *Then*
  And, having scruzed° out of his carrion corse   *squeezed†*
  The loathful° life, now loosed from sinful   *hateful*
    bands,°   *bands of sin*
  Upon his shoulders carried him perforce°   *forcibly*

Above three furlongs, taking his full course,°   extent
Until he came unto a standing° lake.   non-tidal; stagnant
Him thereinto he threw without remorse,
Ne stirred° till hope of life did him forsake: moved
So end of that carl's days and his own pains did make.

47

Which, when those wicked hags from far did spy,
  Like two mad dogs they ran about the lands,
  And the one of them, with dreadful yelling cry
  Throwing away her broken chains and bands,
  And having quenched her burning fire brands,
  Headlong herself did cast into that lake.
  But Impotence, with her own skilful hands,
  One of Maleger's cursed darts did take,
So rived° her trembling heart and wicked end did make.   split

48

Thus now, alone, he conqueror remains.
  Tho,° coming to his squire, that kept his steed,   Then
  Thought him to have mounted; but his feeble veins
  Him failed thereto and served not his need
  Through loss of blood which from his wounds did bleed,
  That° he began to faint and life decay.   So that
  But his good squire, him helping up with speed,
  With steadfast° hand upon his horse did   firm; constant
    stay°   support
And led him to the castle by the beaten way,

49

Where many grooms and squires ready were
  To take him from his steed full tenderly;
  And eke° the fairest Alma met him there   also
  With balm and wine and costly spicery°   spices
  To comfort him in his infirmity.
  Eftsoons° she caused him up to be conveyed   soon after
  And of his arms despoiled° easily:°   relieved gently
  In sumptuous bed she made him to be laid
And, all the while his wounds were dressing, by him stayed.

Canto 12

Guyon, by Palmer's governance°   *guidance*
 Passing through perils great,
 Doth overthrow the Bower of Bliss
 And Acrasia defeat.

1

Now 'gins this goodly frame° *structure [of Book 2 and human body]*
 of Temperance
 Fairly° to rise, and her adorned head   *Beautifully*
 To prick° of highest praise forth to advance, *the point; summit*
 Formerly° grounded and fast settled   *First*†
 On firm foundation of true bountihead;° *virtue*†
 And this brave knight, that for virtue fights,
 Now comes to point° of that same perilous *centre*
  stead°   *place*
 Where Pleasure dwells in sensual delights
'Mongst thousand dangers and ten thousand magic
  mights.°   *powers; forces*

2

Two days now in that sea he sailed has,
 Ne° ever land beheld, ne° living wight,° *Neither nor creature**
 Ne ought save peril, still° as he did pass. *always*
 Tho,° when appeared the third morrow bright *Then*
 Upon the waves to spread her trembling light,
 An hideous roaring far away they heard
 That all their senses filled with affright,° *terror*
 And straight they saw the raging surges reared
Up to the skies, that them of drowning made
  afeared.°   *frightened*

3

Said then the Boatman: 'Palmer, steer aright
 And keep an even course; for yonder way
 We needs must pass (God do us well acquit!).° *deliver*

That is the Gulf of Greediness, they say,
That deep engorgeth all this world's prey –
Which, having swallowed up excessively,
He soon in vomit up again cloth lay°   *deposit*
And belcheth forth his superfluity,
That° all the seas for fear do seem away to fly. *So that*

4
'On the other side an hideous° rock is pight° *immense placed*
 Of mighty magnes-stone,° whose craggy clift° *loadstone cliff*
Depending° from on high, dreadful to sight, *Hanging down*
Over the waves his rugged arms doth lift
And threateneth down to throw his ragged° rift° *jagged rocks*
On whoso cometh nigh: yet nigh it draws
 All passengers, that none from it can shift,
 For whiles they fly that Gulf's devouring jaws
They on this rock are rent and sunk in helpless waves'.

5
Forward they pass and strongly he them rows
 Until they nigh unto that Gulf arrive,
Where stream° more violent and greedy grows. *the water*
Then he with all his puissance doth strive
To strike his oars, and mightily doth drive
The hollow vessel through the threatful wave
 Which, gaping wide to swallow them alive
 In the huge abyss of his engulfing grave,
Doth roar at them in vain, and with great terror rave.° *rage*

6
They, passing by, that grisly° mouth did see *terrifying*
 Sucking the seas into his entrails deep
That seemed more horrible than hell to be,
Or that dark dreadful hole of Tartar'° steep *Tartarus*
Through which the damned ghosts do often creep
Back to the world, bad livers to torment –
 But nought that falls into this direful deep,
 Ne° that approacheth nigh the wide descent, *Nor*
May back return, but is condemned to be drent.° *drowned*

7

On the other side they saw that perilous rock
    Threatening itself on them to ruinate,°   *fall in pieces*‡
    On whose sharp cliffs the ribs of vessels broke,°   *broken*
    And shivered° ships which had been wrecked late,   *shattered*‡
    Yet stuck, with carcases exanimate°   *dead*‡
    Of such as, having all their substance spent
    In wanton joys and lusts intemperate,
    Did afterwards make shipwreck violent
Both of their life and fame, for ever foully blent.°   *tarnished*

8

For-thy° this hight° the Rock of Vile   *Therefore was named**†
    Reproach –
    A dangerous and detestable place
    To which nor fish nor fowl did once approach
    But° yelling mews° with seagulls hoarse and   *Except gulls*
        base,
    And cormorants with birds of ravenous race,
    Which still sat waiting° on that wasteful°   *watching desolate*
        clift°   *cliff*
    For spoil° of wretches, whose unhappy   *goods; harm*
        case° –   *plight; body*
    After lost credit° and consumed thrift –   *savings*
At last them driven hath to this despairful drift.°   *course*

9

The Palmer, seeing them in safety passed,
    Thus said: 'Behold the examples in our sights
    Of lustful luxury and thriftless waste.
    What now is left of miserable° wights   *wretched*
    Which spent their looser° days in lewd delights   *too lustful*
    But shame and sad reproach, here to be read°   *perceived*
    By these rent° relics speaking their ill plights?   *torn*
    Let all that live hereby be counselled
To shun Rock of Reproach, and it as death to dread.'

10

So forth they rowed, and that ferryman
    With his stiff° oars did brush the sea so strong   *resolute*
    That the hoar° waters from his frigate ran   *foaming*

And the light bubbles danced all along
Whiles the salt brine out of the billows sprang.
At last, far off, they many islands spy
On every side, floating the floods among.
Then said the knight: 'Lo, I the land descry;
Therefore, old sire, thy course do thereunto apply.'°   direct†

11

'That may not be,' said then the ferryman,
   'Lest we unweeting° hap° to be   unknowingly chance
     fordone;°   wrecked
   For those same islands, seeming° now and then,   appearing
   Are not firm land, nor any certain° wone,°   stable habitation
   But straggling° plots which to and fro do run   wandering
   In wide waters: therefore are they hight
   The Wandering Islands. Therefore do them shun,
   For they have oft drawn many a wandering wight
Into most deadly danger and distressed plight.

12

'Yet well they seem to him that far doth view –
   Both fair and fruitful, and the ground dispread°   covered†
   With grassy green of delectable hue,
   And the tall trees, with leaves apparelled,
   Are decked with blossoms dyed in white and red
   That mote° the passengers thereto allure.   may
   But whosoever once hath fastened
   His foot thereon may never it recure,°   retrieve
But wandereth ever more uncertain and unsure:

13

'As the Isle of Delos whilom,° men report,   long ago*
   Amid the Aegean Sea long time did stray,
   Ne made for shipping any certain port
   Till that Latona, travelling° that way   [puns on travail = labour]
   Flying from Juno's wrath and hard° assay,°   fierce assault
   Of her fair twins was there delivered
   Which afterwards did rule the night and day:
   Thenceforth it firmly was established,
And for° Apollo's honour highly heried.'°   in worshipped

14

They to him hearken as beseemeth meet,°   *was fitting*
  And pass on forward: so their way does lie
  That one of those same islands which do fleet°   *float*
  In the wide sea they needs must passen by –
  Which seemed so sweet and pleasant to the eye
  That it would tempt a man to touchen° there.   *call at in passing*
  Upon the bank they sitting did espy
  A dainty° damsel dressing of her hair,   *delightful*
By whom a little skippet° floating did appear.   *small boat, skiff*[†]

15

She, them espying, loud to them can° call,   *did*
  Bidding them nigher draw unto the shore,
  For she had cause to busy them withal;°   *with*
  And therewith loudly laughed. But nathemore°   *not at all*
  Would they once turn, but kept on as afore;°   *before*
  Which, when she saw, she left her locks undight°   *disordered*[‡]
  And, running to her boat withouten oar,
  From the departing land it launched light°   *quickly; wantonly*
And after them did drive with all her power and might.

16

Whom, overtaking, she in merry sort°   *fashion*
  Them 'gan to board° and purpose°   *come alongside; accost*   *talk*[†]
    diversely,°   *on various topics*
  Now feigning dalliance and wanton sport,
  Now throwing forth lewd words immodestly,
  Till that the Palmer 'gan full bitterly
  Her to rebuke for being loose and light:
  Which not abiding,° but more scornfully   *enduring*
  Scoffing at him that did her justly wite,°   *blame*
She turned her boat about and from them rowed
    quite.°   *completely away*

17

That was the wanton Phaedria, which late
  Did ferry him over the Idle Lake;
  Whom, nought regarding, they kept on their gate°   *course**
  And all her vain allurements did forsake,
  When them the wary boatman thus bespake:°   *addressed*[†]

'Here now behoveth us well to advise°   consider
And of our safety good heed to take;
For here before a perilous passage lies
Where many mermaids haunt, making false melodies.

                          18
'But by the way there is a great quicksand
    And whirlpool of hidden jeopardy:
    Therefore, Sir Palmer, keep an even° hand,   steady
    For 'twixt them both the narrow way doth lie.'
    Scarce had he said when, hard at hand, they spy
    That quicksand nigh with water covered;
    But by the checked° wave° they did descry   checkered   water
    It plain, and by the sea discoloured.
It called was the Quicksand of Unthriftihead.°   Extravagance†

                          19
They, passing by, a goodly° ship did see,   handsome
    Laden from far° with precious merchandise   distant lands
    And bravely° furnished° as ship might   as splendidly   equipped†
      be,
    Which, through great disadventure° or   misfortune
      misprize,°   mistake†
    Herself had run into that hazardise;°   hazardous situation†
    Whose mariners and merchants, with much toil,
    Laboured in vain to have recured° their prize   recovered
    And the rich wares to save from piteous spoil.
But neither toil nor travail might her back recoil.°   force back

                          20
On the other side they see that perilous pool
    That called was the Whirlpool of Decay
    (In which full many had with hapless° dole°   luckless   destiny
    Been sunk, of whom no memory did stay),
    Whose circled° waters, rapt° with swirling   circling   impelled
      sway°   might
    Like to a restless wheel, still running round,
    Did covet, as they passed by that way,
    To draw their boat within the utmost bound
Of his wide labyrinth, and then to have them drowned.

21

But the heedful boatman strongly forth did stretch
  His brawny arms and all his body strain
  That° the utmost° sandy breach° they   *So that furthest bay*†
    shortly fetch,°   *reach*‡
  Whiles the dread danger does behind remain.
  Sudden they see, from midst of all the main,
  The surging waters like a mountain rise,
  And the great sea puffed up with proud disdain
  To swell above the measure of his guise°   *habit; practice*
As threatening to devour all that his power despise.

22

The waves came rolling, and the billows roar
  Outrageously,° as° they enraged were,   *Violently as though*
  Or wrathful Neptune did them drive before
  His whirling chariot, for exceeding
    fear°   *[i.e., the waves are afraid]*
  (For not one puff of wind there did appear);
  That° all the three thereat wox° much afraid,   *So that grew*
  Unweeting° what such horror° strange did *Ignorant of ruffling*
    rear.°   *cause*
  Eftsoons° they saw an hideous host arrayed   *Soon after*
Of huge sea monsters, such as living sense dismayed.

23

Most ugly shapes and horrible aspects,°   *appearances*
  Such as Dame Nature self° mote° fear to see,   *herself might*
  Or shame° that ever should so foul defects   *be ashamed*
  From her most cunning° hand escaped be –   *skilful*
  All dreadful portraits° of deformity: *images*
  Spring-headed hydras and sea-shouldering whales;
  Great whirlpools° (which all fishes make to   *spouting whales*
    flee);
  Bright scolopendras° armed with silver scales;   *sea centipedes*
Mighty monoceroses° with immeasured° *narwhals unmeasurable*
    tails;

24

The dreadful fish that hath deserved the name
  Of Death,° and like him looks in dreadful   *the morse [walrus]*
    hue;°   *aspect*
The grisly° wasserman,° that makes his   *terrifying   merman*
    game
The flying ships with swiftness to pursue;
The horrible sea-satyr, that doth show
His fearful face in time of greatest storm;
Huge ziffius,° whom mariners eschew   *the xiphias, or sword-fish*[†]
No less than rocks (as travellers inform);
And greedy rosmarines° with visages   *walruses*[†]
    deform.°   *deformed*

25

All these and thousands thousands many more,
  And more deformed monsters thousand fold,
  With dreadful noise and hollow rumbling roar
  Came rushing in the foamy waves enrolled,
  Which seemed to fly for fear them to behold:
  No wonder if these did the knight appall;°   *terrify*
  For all that here on earth we dreadful hold
  Be but as bugs° to fearen° babes   *bugbears   frighten*
    withal°   *with*
Compared to the creatures in the sea's entrail.

26

'Fear nought,' then said the Palmer well-advised,°   *cautious* *
  'For these same monsters are not these indeed,
  But are into these fearful shapes disguised°   *tranformed*
  By that same wicked witch to work us dread,
  And draw° from on this journey to proceed.'   *divert*
  Tho,° lifting up his virtuous° staff on   *Then   potent; magical*
    high,
  He smote the sea, which calmed was with speed;
  And all that dreadful army fast 'gan fly
Into great Tethys' bosom, where they hidden lie.

27

Quit from that danger forth their course they kept,
  And as they went they heard a rueful° cry   *pitiful*
  Of one that wailed and pitifully wept
  That° through the sea the resounding plaints did fly.   *So that*
  At last they in an island did espy
  A seemly° maiden, sitting by the shore,   *lovely*
  That with great sorrow and sad agony
  Seemed some great misfortune to deplore,
And loud to them for succour called evermore:

28

Which Guyon, hearing, straight the Palmer bade
  To steer the boat towards that doleful maid
  That he might know, and ease, her sorrow sad;
  Who him, advising better, to him said:
  'Fair sir, be not displeased if disobeyed,
  For ill it were to hearken to her cry;
  For she is inly° nothing ill apaid,°   *inwardly distressed*
  But only womanish fine° forgery°   *skilful‡ shamming*
Your stubborn heart to affect with frail infirmity.

29

'To which, when she your courage hath inclined
  Through foolish pity, then her guileful bait
  She will embosom° deeper in your mind   *plunge‡*
  And for your ruin at the last await.'
  The knight was ruled, and the boatman straight
  Held on his course with staid° steadfastness,   *unchanging‡*
  Ne ever shrunk, ne ever sought to bate°   *abate; rest*
  His tired arms for toiled weariness,
But with his oars did sweep the watery wilderness.

30

And now they nigh approached to the stead°   *place*
  Whereas° those mermaids dwelt. It was a still   *Where*
  And calmy bay, on the one side sheltered
  With the broad shadow of an hoary° hill;   *ancient*
  On the other side an high rock towered still,
  That° 'twixt them both a pleasant°   *So that delightful*
    port° they made   *opening*

And did like an half theatre fulfil.°   complete
There those five sisters had continual trade°   occupation
And used to bathe themselves in that deceitful shade.

31

They were fair° ladies till they fondly° strived   beautiful foolishly
  With the Heliconian maids for mastery –
  Of° whom they, overcomen, were deprived   By
  Of their proud beauty and the one moiety°   half
  Transformed to fish for their bold surquedry,°   arrogance
  But the upper half their hue° retained still   shape
  And their sweet skill in wonted° melody,   customary
  Which ever after they abused to ill°   evil
To allure weak travellers whom, gotten, they did kill.

32

So now to Guyon, as he passed by,
  Their pleasant tunes they sweetly thus applied:°   addressed†
  'O thou, fair son of gentle° fairy,   noble
  That art in mighty arms most magnified°   praised
  Above all knights that ever battle tried,
  O turn thy rudder hitherward awhile.
  Here may thy storm-beat vessel safely ride –
  This is the port of rest from troublous toil,
The world's sweet inn from pain and wearisome turmoil.'

33

With that the rolling sea, resounding soft,°   gently
  In his big° bass them fitly° answered;   loud appropriately
  And on the rock the waves, breaking aloft,
  A solemn mean° unto them measured,°   middle part adjusted†
  The whiles sweet Zephyrus loud whistled
  His treble – a strange kind of harmony
  Which Guyon's senses softly tickled
  That° he the boatman bade row easily   So that
And let him hear some part of their rare° melody.   exquisite

34

But him the Palmer from that vanity°   trifle
  With temperate advice discounselled°   dissuaded
  That° they it passed, and shortly 'gan descry   So that

The land to which their course they levelled;°   *directed*
When suddenly a gross° fog overspread,   *massive*
With his dull vapour, all that desert has,°   *i.e., has overspread*
And heaven's cheerful face enveloped,
That° all things one, and one as nothing, was,   *So that*
And this great universe seemed one confused mass.

35

Thereat they greatly were dismayed, ne wist°   *nor knew*
How to direct their way in darkness wide,
But feared to wander in that wasteful° mist   *desolate*
For° tumbling into mischief unespied:°   *For fear of unnoticed*
Worse is the danger hidden than descried.
Suddenly an innumerable flight
Of harmful fowls, about them fluttering, cried,
And with their wicked wings them oft did smite
And sore° annoyed,° groping in that   *greatly troubled*
    grisly° night.   *terrible*

36

Even all the° nation° of   *Absolutely every race*†
    unfortunate°   *inauspicious*
And fatal° birds about them flocked were,   *deathly; prophetic*
Such as, by nature, men abhor and hate:
The ill-faced owl, death's dreadful messenger;
The hoarse night-raven, trump° of doleful   *trumpet*
    drear;°   *gloom*‡
The leather-winged bat, day's enemy;
The rueful stritch,° still waiting on the bier;   *screech-owl*‡ *
The whistler° shrill, that whoso hears doth   *a bird of ill omen*†
    die;
The hellish harpies, prophets of sad destiny.

37

All those, and all that else doth horror breed,
About them flew, and filled their sails with fear.
Yet stayed they not, but forward did proceed,
Whiles the one did row and the other stiffly° steer,   *steadfastly*
Till that at last the weather 'gan to clear
And the fair land itself did plainly show.

Said then the Palmer: 'Lo, where does appear
  The sacred° soil where all our perils grow: *accursed*‡
Therefore, sir knight, your ready arms° about you   *armour*
    throw.'

38

He hearkened, and his arms about him took,
  The whiles the nimble boat so well her sped
  That with her crooked° keel the land she struck.   *curved*
  Then forth the noble Guyon sallied,°   *set out*†
  And his sage Palmer that him governed;°   *guided*
  But the other by his boat behind did stay.
  They marched fairly° forth, of nought   *positively, firmly*†
    ydread,°   *afraid**
  Both firmly armed for every hard assay°   *attack*
With constancy and care 'gainst danger and dismay.°   *conquest*

39

Ere long they heard an hideous bellowing
  Of many beasts that roared outrageously°   *furiously*
  As if that hunger's point, or Venus' sting,
  Had them enraged with fell° surquedry.°   *fierce pride*
  Yet nought they feared, but passed on hardily°   *boldly*
  Until they came in view of those wild beasts
  Who, all at once, gaping full greedily,
  And rearing fiercely their upstarting crests,°   *heads*
Ran towards° to devour those unexpected guests.   *to them*

40

But soon as they approached with deadly threat
  The Palmer over them his staff upheld –
  His mighty° staff that could all charms defeat.   *powerful*
  Eftsoons° their stubborn courages were quelled   *Straight away*
  And high-advanced crests down meekly felled.°   *lowered**
  Instead of fraying,° they themselves did   *attacking;* frightening*
    fear,
  And trembled as them passing they beheld,
  Such wondrous power did in that staff appear
All monsters to subdue to him that did it bear.

41

Of that same wood it framed° was cunningly° *made with skill*
 Of which Caduceus whilom° was made –   *formerly**
 Caduceus, the rod of Mercury,
 With which he wonts° the Stygian realms *it is his custom to*
  invade
 Through ghastly° horror and eternal shade.   *terrifying*
 The infernal fiends with it he can assuage,
 And Orcus tame, whom nothing can persuade,
 And rule the Furies when they most do rage:
Such virtue° in his staff had eke° this *[magical] power indeed*
 Palmer sage.

42

Thence passing forth, they shortly do arrive
 Whereas° the Bower of Bliss was situate –   *Where*
 A place picked out by choice of best alive
 That Nature's work by art can imitate;°   *i.e., artists*
 In which whatever in this worldly state
 Is sweet and pleasing unto living sense,
 Or that may daintiest° fantasy° *most discriminating‡ fancy*
  aggrate,°   *gratify*
 Was poured forth with plentiful dispence° *liberality†*
And made there to abound with lavish affluence.° *profusion*

43

Goodly° it was enclosed round about,   *Firmly*
 As well their entered guests to keep within
 As those unruly beasts to hold without° –   *outside*
 Yet was the fence thereof but weak and thin:
 Nought feared° their force that fortalage° *was afraid fortress*
  to win,
 But wisdom's power and temperance's might,
 By which the mightiest things efforced°   *forced open†*
  been.°   *have been*
 And eke° the gate was wrought of substance light, *in addition*
Rather for pleasure than for battery or fight:

44

It framed° was of precious ivory,   *formed*
  That seemed a work of admirable° wit.°   *wonderful ingenuity*
  And therein all the famous history
  Of Jason and Medea was ywrit:°   *depicted**
  Her mighty charms, her furious loving fit;°   *lunacy‡*
  His goodly conquest of the golden fleece,
  His falsed° faith and love too lightly°   *broken swiftly*
    flit;°   *fleeting†*
  The wondered° Argo, which in   *marvellous‡*
    venturous° piece°   *risky‡; daring‡; task‡*
First through the Euxine seas bore all the flower of Greece.

45

Ye might have seen the frothy billows fry°   *seethe†*
  Under the ship as through them she went,
  That° seemed the waves were into ivory –   *So that it*
  Or ivory into the waves – were sent;
  And otherwhere° the snowy substance   *elsewhere‡*
    sprent°   *sprinkled*
  With vermil, like the boy's blood therein shed,
  A piteous spectacle did represent;
  And otherwhiles,° with gold besprinkled,   *at other times*
It seemed the enchanted flame which did Creusa wed.

46

All this, and more, might from that goodly° gate   *splendid*
  Be read,° that ever open stood to all   *discerned*
  Which thither came. But in the porch there sat
  A comely personage, of stature tall
  And semblance pleasing more than natural,
  That travellers to him seemed to entice:
  His looser° garment to the ground did fall   *very loose*
  And flew about his heels in wanton wise,°   *fashion*
Not fit for speedy pace or manly exercise.

47

They in that place him Genius did call:
  Not that celestial power to whom the care
  Of life and generation of all
  That lives pertains in charge particular

(Who wondrous things concerning our welfare,
And strange phantoms doth let us oft foresee,
And oft of secret ills bids us beware:
That is ourself, whom, though we do not see,
Yet each doth in himself it well perceive to be;

48

Therefore a god him sage antiquity
   Did wisely make, and good Agdistis call);
   But this same was to that quite contrary –
   The foe of life, that good envies° to all,   *begrudges*
   That secretly doth us procure to fall
   Through guileful° semblants° which he   *deceptive   phantoms*
      makes us see.
   He of the garden had the governail,°   *control*
   And Pleasure's porter was devised° to be,   *assigned*
Holding a staff for more
     formality.°   *propriety;† outward appearance†*

49

With diverse flowers he daintily was decked
   And strewed about, and by his side
   A mighty mazer° bowl of wine was set   *maple**
   As if it had been sacrified,°   *offered as a sacrifice*
   Wherewith all new-come guests he gratified.
   So did he eke° Sir Guyon, passing by;   *too*
   But he his idle courtesy defied,
   And overthrew his bowl disdainfully,
And broke his staff, with which he charmed° semblants *conjured*
   sly.°   *cleverly made*

50

Thus being entered, they behold around
   A large and spacious plain, on every side
   Strewed with pleasances,° whose fair grassy *pleasure-grounds‡*
     ground,
   Mantled° with green, and goodly   *Covered*
     beautified°   *made beautiful‡*
   With all the ornaments of Flora's pride,° *plenty [i.e., flowers]*
   Wherewith her mother, Art, as half in scorn

Of niggard Nature, like a pompous° bride   *splendid*
Did deck her and too lavishly adorn,
When forth from virgin bower she comes in the early morn.

51

Thereto° the heavens, always jovial,   *In addition*
  Looked on them lovely,° still° in steadfast   *lovingly always*
    state,
  Ne° suffered storm nor frost on them to fall,   *Neither*
  Their tender buds or leaves to violate;°   *spoil*
  Nor scorching heat, nor cold intemperate
  To afflict the creatures which therein did dwell;
  But the mild air with season moderate
  Gently attempered° and disposed so well   *moderated; ordered*
That still it breathed forth sweet
    spirit° and wholesome smell: *breath*

52

More sweet and wholesome than the pleasant hill
  Of Rhodope, on which the nymph that bore
  A giant babe herself for grief did kill;
  Or the Thessalian Tempe, where of yore
  Fair Daphne Phoebus' heart with love did gore;°   *pierce*
  Or Ida, where the gods loved to repair
  Wherever they their heavenly bowers forlore;°   *left*
  Or sweet Parnass', the haunt of Muses fair;
Or Eden self, if aught with Eden mote° compare.   *might*

53

Much wondered Guyon at the fair aspect
  Of that sweet place, yet suffered no delight
  To sink into his sense nor mind affect,
  But passed forth and looked still° forward   *ever*
    right,°   *right ahead*
  Bridling his will and mastering his might,
  Till that he came unto another gate –
  No gate, but like one, being goodly dight°   *made*
  With boughs and branches, which did broad dilate°   *spread*
Their clasping arms in wanton wreathings intricate,

54

So° fashioned a porch with rare°   *Thus   exquisite*
   device,°   *invention*
   Arched overhead with an embracing vine,
   Whose bunches, hanging down, seemed to entice
   All passers by to taste their luscious wine,
   And did themselves into their hands incline,
   As freely offering to be gathered:
   Some deep empurpled,° as the hyacinth;   *made purple*†
   Some as the rubine, laughing sweetly red;
Some like fair emeralds, not yet well ripened.

55

And them amongst some were of burnished gold –
   So made by art to beautify the rest –
   Which did themselves amongst the leaves enfold,
   As lurking from the view of covetous guest
   That° the weak boughs, with so rich load oppressed,   *So that*
   Did bow adown as over-burdened.
   Under that porch a comely dame did rest,
   Clad in fair° weeds° but foul° disordered,   *fine clothes badly*
And garments loose° that seemed unfit for   *wanton*
   womanhead.°   *womanliness*

56

In her left hand a cup of gold she held,
   And with her right the riper fruit did reach,
   Whose sappy liquor – that with fulness swelled –
   Into her cup she scruzed° with dainty   *squeezed*†
   breach°   *separation*
   Of her fine fingers, without foul impeach,°   *sullying [them]*
   That so fair wine press made the wine more sweet:
   Thereof she used to give° to drink to each   *customarily gave*
   Whom, passing by, she happened to meet:
It was her guise° all strangers goodly° so to   *habit liberally; kindly*
   greet.

57

So she to Guyon offered it to taste,
   Who, taking it out of her tender hand,
   The cup to ground did violently cast

That all in pieces it was broken found,
And with the liquor stained all the land.
Whereat Excess exceedingly was wroth,
Yet n'ote° the same amend,° ne° yet　　　　*could not change nor*
　　withstand,
But suffered him to pass, all were she loath –
Who, nought regarding her displeasure, forward goeth.

58

There the most dainty° paradise on ground°　　　*delightful earth*
　　Itself doth offer to his sober° eye,　　　　*temperate; serious*
　　In which all pleasures plenteously abound,
　　And none does other's happiness envy:
　　The painted flowers, the trees upshooting high,
　　The dales for shade, the hills for breathing space,
　　The trembling groves, the crystal° running by,　　　*water*[†]
　　And that which all fair works doth most
　　　　aggrace,°　　　　　　　　　　　　　　*add grace to*[†]
That Art, which all that wrought, appeared in no place.

59

One would have thought (so cunningly° the　　　　*skilfully*
　　rude°　　　　　　　　　　　　　　　　　*rough*
　　And scorned parts were mingled with the fine)
　　That Nature had, for wantonness,°　　　　*capriciousness*
　　　　ensued°　　　　　　　　　　　　　*followed*
　　Art, and that Art at Nature did repine:°　　　*complain*
　　So striving each the other to undermine,
　　Each did the other's work more beautify;
　　So, differing both in wills, agreed in fine;°　　　*in the end*
　　So all agreed through sweet diversity
This garden to adorn with all variety.

60

And in the midst of all a fountain stood,
　　Of richest substance that on earth might be,
　　So pure and shiny that the silver flood°　　　*water*
　　Through every channel running one might see.
　　Most goodly° it with curious°　　　*beautifully　ingenious*
　　　　imagery°　　　　　　　　　*images*
　　Was overwrought, and shapes of naked boys –

Of which some seemed with lively jollity°   lust;* mirth
To fly about, playing their wanton° toys,°   lustful sports
While others did themselves embay° in liquid joys.   bathe†

                              61
And, over all, of purest gold, was spread
    A trail of ivy in his native° hue;°   natural colour
    For the rich metal was so coloured
    That wight° who did not well-advised° it   person* carefully*
        view,
    Would surely deem it to be ivy true:
    Low his lascivious arms adown did creep
    That,° themselves dipping in the silver dew,   So that
    Their fleecy flowers they tenderly did steep,°   bathe†
Which drops of crystal seemed for wantonness° to   lust; fun
        weep.

                              62
Infinite streams continually did well
    Out of this fountain, sweet and fair to see,
    The which into an ample laver° fell   bowl
    And shortly grew to so great quantity
    That like a little lake it seemed to be,
    Whose depth exceeded not three cubits height,
    That through the waves one might the bottom see
    All paved with jasper shining bright,
That° seemed the fountain in that sea did sail upright.   So that it

                              63
And all the margent° round about was set   margin‡
    With shady laurel trees, thence to defend°   ward off
    The sunny beams which on the billows beat
    And those which therein bathed mote° offend.°   might harm
    As Guyon happened by the same to wend,
    Two naked damsels he therein espied
    Which, therein bathing, seemed to contend
    And wrestle wantonly, ne cared to hide
Their dainty parts from view of any which them eyed.

64

Sometimes the one would lift the other quite° *completely*
 Above the waters, and then down again
 Her plunge, as overmastered by might,
 Where° both awhile would covered remain, *Whereupon*
 And each the other from to rise restrain –
 The whiles their snowy limbs, as through a veil,
 So through the crystal waves appeared plain;
 Then suddenly both would themselves unhele° *uncover**
And the amorous° sweet spoils to greedy eyes reveal. *lovely*

65

As that fair star, the messenger of morn,
 His dewy face out of the sea doth rear;
 Or as the Cyprian goddess, newly born
 Of the ocean's fruitful froth, did first appear:
 Such seemed they; and so their yellow hair
 Crystalline humour° dropped down apace. *moisture*
 Whom such, when Guyon saw, he drew him near
 And somewhat 'gan relent° his earnest pace: *slacken‡*
His stubborn breast 'gan secret pleasance° to embrace. *delight*

66

The wanton maids, him espying, stood
 Gazing awhile at his unwonted° guise.° *unusual conflict*
 Then the one herself low ducked in the flood,
 Abashed that her a stranger did advise;° *look at**
 But the other rather higher did arise
 And her two lily paps° aloft displayed, *breasts*
 And all that might his melting heart entice
 To her delights she unto him bewrayed° *revealed‡*
(The rest, hid underneath, him more desirous made).

67

With that the other likewise thus uprose,
 And her fair locks – which formerly were bound
 Up in one knot – she low adown did loose,
 Which, flowing long and thick, her clothed around
 And the ivory in golden mantle gowned.
 So that fair spectacle from him was reft,° *stolen*
 Yet that which reft it no less fair was found.

So, hid in locks and waves from looker's theft,
Nought but her lovely face she for his looking left.

68

Withal° she laughed, and she blushed withal,° *With that at it*
 That° blushing to her laughter gave more grace, *So that*
 And laughter to her blushing, as did fall.° *happen*
 Now, when they spied the knight to slack his pace
 Them to behold, and in his sparkling° *flaming; gleaming [eyes]*
  face
 The secret signs of kindled lust appear,
 Their wanton merriments they did increase
 And to him beckoned to approach more near,
And showed him many sights that courage° cold could *lust*
  rear.° *raise*

69

On which when gazing him the Palmer saw,
 He much rebuked those wandering eyes of his
 And, counselled well, him forward thence did draw.
 Now are they come nigh to the Bower of Bliss –
 Of her fond° favourites so named amiss – *besotted*
 When thus the Palmer: 'Now, sir, well advise,° *reflect*
 For here the end of all our travail° *[punning on travel = journey]*
  is;
 Here wones° Acrasia, whom we must surprise *dwells*
Else she will slip away, and all our drift° *scheme*
  despise.'° *frustrate*†

70

Eftsoons° they heard a most melodious sound *Soon after*
 Of all that mote° delight a dainty° ear – *might discriminating*‡
 Such as at once° might not on living ground° *together earth*
 (Save in this paradise) be heard elsewhere.
 Right hard it was for wight which did it hear
 To read° what manner music that mote be; *discern*
 For all that pleasing is to living ear
 Was there consorted° in one *combined harmoniously*
  harmony –
Birds, voices, instruments, winds, waters, all agree.

71

The joyous birds, shrouded° in cheerful shade,   *sheltered*
  Their notes unto the voice attempered°   *blended; harmonised*[†]
    sweet;°   *sweetly*
  The angelical, soft° trembling voices made   *softly*
  To the instruments divine respondence°   *response*[†]
    meet;°   *fitting*
  The silver-sounding instruments did meet°   *unite*
  With the bass murmur of the water's fall;
  The water's fall, with difference discrete° –   *distinct*
  Now soft, now loud, unto the wind did call;
The gentle, warbling wind low answered to all.

72

There, whence that music seemed heard to be,
  Was the fair witch, herself now solacing
  With a new lover whom, through sorcery
  And witchcraft, she from far did thither bring.
  There she had him now laid slumbering
  In secret shade after long wanton joys,
  Whilst round about them pleasantly did sing
  Many fair ladies and lascivious boys,
That ever mixed their song with light licentious toys.°   *games*

73

And all that while right over him she hung
  With her false° eyes fast fixed in his sight,   *treacherous*
  As seeking medicine° whence she was stung,   *remedy;* * *physic*
  Or greedily depasturing° delight;   *consuming;*[†] *grazing*[†]
  And, oft inclining down, with kisses light
  (For fear of waking him) his lips bedewed,
  And through his humid° eyes did suck his sprite,°   *moist soul*
  Quite° molten into lust and pleasure lewd –   *Utterly*
Wherewith° she sighed oft as if his case she rued –   *At which*

74

The whiles someone did chant this lovely° lay:°   *love song*
  'Ah, see – who so fair thing dost fain° to see –   *rejoice* *
  In springing flower the image of thy day;
  Ah, see the virgin rose, how sweetly she
  Doth first peep forth with bashful modesty,

That fairer seems the less ye see her may.
Lo, see soon after how more bold and free
Her bared bosom she doth broad° display;   *openly*
Lo, see soon after how she fades and falls away.

75

'So passeth, in the passing of a day,
   Of mortal life the leaf, the bud, the flower,
   Ne° more doth flourish after first decay   *Nor*
   That erst° was sought to deck both bed and   *formerly*
      bower°   *chamber*
   Of many a lady and many a paramour:°   *lover*
   Gather, therefore, the rose whilst yet is prime,°   *youth; spring*
   For soon comes age that will her pride deflower;
   Gather the rose of love whilst yet is time,
Whilst loving thou mayest loved be with equal crime.'°   *guilt*

76

He ceased, and then 'gan all the choir of birds
   Their diverse notes to attune° unto his lay   *harmonise*†
   As in approvance° of his pleasing words.   *approval*†
   The constant° pair heard all that he did say,   *resolute*
   Yet swerved not but kept their forward way
   Through many covert° groves and thickets   *secret*
      close,°   *dense*
   In which they, creeping, did at last display°   *get sight of*†
   The wanton lady with her lover loose,
Whose sleepy head she in her lap did soft dispose.°   *place*

77

Upon a bed of roses she was laid,
   As faint through heat, or dight to°   *prepared for**
      pleasant° sin,   *pleasing*
   And was arrayed – or, rather, disarrayed –
   All in a veil of silk and silver thin
   That hid no whit her alabaster skin,
   But rather showed more white, if more might be.
   More subtle web Arachne cannot spin,
   Nor the fine nets which oft we woven see
Of scorched° dew, do not in the air more lightly   *sun-lit*†
      flee.°   *float*

78

Her snowy breast was bare to ready spoil
 Of hungry eyes, which n'ote° therewith be filled,   *could not*
 And yet, through languor of° her late°   *lassitude† from recent*
  sweet toil,
 Few° drops, more clear than nectar, forth distilled   *A few*
 That like pure orient° pearls adown it trilled,°   *brilliant flowed*
 And her fair eyes, sweet smiling in delight,
 Moistened their fiery beams, with which she thrilled°   *pierced*
 Frail hearts, yet quenched not: like starry light
Which, sparkling on the silent waves, does seem more bright.

79

The young man sleeping by her seemed to be
 Some goodly° swain° of honourable   *handsome young man*
  place°   *rank*
 That° certes° it great pity was to see   *So that indeed*
 Him his nobility so foul deface:°   *mar; destroy*
 A sweet regard° and amiable grace,   *appearance*
 Mixed with manly sternness, did appear,
 Yet sleeping,° in his well-proportioned face,   *Even while he slept*
 And on his tender lips the downy hair
Did now but freshly spring and silken blossoms bear.

80

His warlike arms – the idle° instruments   *useless*
 Of sleeping praise – were hung upon a tree,
 And his brave° shield, full of old   *fine*
  monuments,°   *identifying marks; scars*
 Was foully° razed° that° none the   *shockingly erased† so that*
  signs° might see.   *emblems*
 Ne° for them ne° for honour cared he,   *Neither nor*
 Ne aught that did to his advancement tend,
 But in lewd loves and wasteful luxury°   *lust; profligacy*
 His days, his goods, his body he did spend:
O horrible enchantment that him so did blend.°   *blind*

81

The noble elf and careful Palmer drew
 So nigh to them (minding nought but lustful game)
 That sudden forth they on them rushed, and threw

A subtle° net which only for the same   *fine; skilfully contrived*
The skilful Palmer formally° did frame.°   *handsomely* fashion*
So held them under fast, the whiles the rest
Fled all away for fear of fouler shame.
The fair enchantress, so unwares oppressed,
Tried all her arts, and all her sleights, thence out to
   wrest.°   *twist*

82

And eke° her lover strove, but all in vain: *too*
   For that same net so cunningly° was wound   *skilfully*
   That neither guile nor force might it distrain.°   *tear off**
   They took them both, and both them strongly bound
   In captive bands which there they ready found;
   But her in chains of adamant he tied,
   For nothing else might keep her safe and sound;
   But Verdant (so he hight)° he soon untied,   *was called*†*
And counsel sage instead thereof to him applied.°   *directed*

83

But all those pleasant bowers and palaces brave°   *splendid*
   Guyon broke down with rigour pitiless,
   Ne aught° their goodly workmanship might   *Nor in any way*
     save
   Them from the tempest of his wrathfulness
   But that their bliss° he turned to balefulness.°   *joy   distress†*
   Their groves he felled, their gardens did deface,°   *destroy*
   Their arbours spoil,° their cabinets°   *ravage   bowers†*
     suppress,°   *throw down*
   Their banquet houses° burn, their buildings   *banqueting halls*
     raze,
And of the fairest late° now made the foulest place.   *until recently*

84

Then led they her away, and eke that knight
   They with them led, both sorrowful and sad.
   The way they came, the same returned they right,°   *directly*
   Till they arrived where they lately had
   Charmed those wild beasts that raged with fury mad –
   Which, now awaking, fierce at them 'gan fly
   As° in their mistress's rescue, whom they led;   *As if*

But them the Palmer soon did pacify.
Then Guyon asked, what meant those beasts which there did
    lie.

85

Said he: 'These seeming beasts are men indeed
  Whom this enchantress hath transformed thus –
  Whilom° her lovers which her lusts did feed,   *Formerly* *
  Now turned into figures hideous
  According to their minds like° monstrous.'°   *similarly bestial*
  'Sad end' (quoth he) 'of life intemperate,
  And mournful meed° of joys   *reward*
    delicious:°   *voluptuous; exquisite*
  But, Palmer, if it mote° thee so aggrate,°   *might please*†
Let them returned be unto their former state.'

86

Straightway he with his virtuous° staff them   *powerful; magic*
  struck,
  And straight of° beasts they comely men became: *from*
  Yet, being men, they did unmanly look,
  And stared ghastly,° some for inward   *terribly; terrifyingly*
    shame,
  And some for wrath to see their captive dame.
  But one above the rest in special,
  That had an hog been late – hight Grill by name –
  Repined° greatly, and did him miscall°   *Complained*‡ *abuse*
That had from hoggish form him brought to
    natural.°   *his natural shape*

87

Said Guyon: 'See the mind of beastly man
  That hath so soon forgot the excellence
  Of his creation when he life began,
  That now he chooseth, with vile°   *base*
    difference,°   *disagreement; distinguishing mark*
  To be a beast and lack intelligence.'
  To whom the Palmer thus: 'The dunghill kind
  Delights in filth and foul incontinence:°   *intemperance*
  Let Grill be Grill and have his hoggish mind;
But let us hence depart whilst weather serves, and wind.'

The Third Book of *The Fairy Queen*,
Containing the Legend of Britomartis,
or, Of Chastity

1

It falls° me here to write of Chastity –   *befalls*
   That fairest virtue, far above the rest;
   For which what needs me fetch from fairy
   Foreign examples it to have expressed,
   Sith° it is shrined in my sovereign's breast,   *Since*
   And formed° so lively° in each perfect part   *expressed† lifelike*
   That to all ladies which have it professed
   Need but behold the portrait° of her heart,   *image‡*
If portrayed it might be by any living art.

2

But living art may not least part express,°   *portray*
   Nor life-resembling° pencil it can paint,   *life-depicting*
   All° were it Zeuxis or Praxiteles: *Even though*
   His daedal° hand would fail and greatly   *skilful†*
      faint,°   *weaken*
   And her perfections with his error taint.
   Ne° poets' wit – that passeth° painter far   *Nor surpasses*
   In picturing the parts of beauty daint° –   *excellent*
   So hard a workmanship° adventure°   *labour undertake; risk*
      dare
For fear, through want° of words, her excellence to mar.   *lack*

3

How then shall I, apprentice of the skill
   That whilom° in divinest wits did reign,   *formerly**
   Presume so high to stretch mine humble quill?
   Yet now my luckless lot° doth me constrain   *fortune*
   Hereto perforce.° But, O dread sovereign,   *To this of necessity*
   Thus far forth pardon, sith° that choicest°   *since the finest*
      wit°   *skill*
   Cannot your glorious portrait figure°   *represent*

plain°   *absolutely, purely*‡
That I in coloured shows may shadow° it,   *represent*
And antique° praises unto present persons fit.°   *ancient*‡ *apply*

4

But if in living colours and right hue°   *form*
  Yourself you covet to see pictured°   *depicted; described in words*‡
  Who can it do more lively° or more true   *lifelike*
  Than that sweet verse, with nectar sprinkled,
  In which a gracious° servant   *courteous; enjoying [royal] favour*
    pictured
  His Cynthia, his heaven's fairest light –
  That with his melting sweetness ravished,
  And with the wonder of her beams bright,
My senses lulled are in slumber of delight.

5

But let that same delicious° poet lend   *pleasing*
  A little leave unto a rustic muse
  To sing his mistress's praise, and let him mend°   *rectify*
  If aught amiss her liking may abuse;°   *injure*
  Ne° let his fairest Cynthia refuse   *And do not*
  In mirrors more than one herself to see,
  But either Gloriana let her choose,
  Or in Belphoebe fashioned to be:
In the one her rule, in the other, her rare° chastity.   *exquisite*

Canto I

Guyon encountereth Britomart,
    Fair Florimell is chased;
    Duessa's trains° and Malecasta's   *stratagems*
      Champions are defaced.°   *overcome; discredited*

1

The famous Briton Prince and fairy knight,
  After long ways and perilous pains endured,
  Having their weary limbs to perfect plight°   *condition*

Restored, and sorry° wounds right well   *grievous*
  recured,°   *healed*
Of° the fair Alma greatly were procured°   *By urged*
To make there longer sojourn and abode.
But when thereto they might not be allured
From seeking praise and deeds of arms abroad,
They courteous congé° took and forth together   *leave*
  yode.°   *went*

2

But the captived Acrasia he sent,
  Because of travel° long, a nigher° way,   *journey shorter*
With a strong guard, all rescue to prevent,
And her to fairy court safe to convey
That° her for witness of his hard assay°   *So that endeavour*
Unto his Fairy Queen he might present.
But he himself betook another way,
To make more trial of his hardiment°   *courage*
And seek adventures as he with Prince Arthur went.

3

Long so they travelled through wasteful° ways,   *desolate*
  Where dangers dwelt and perils most did wone,°   *dwell*
To hunt for glory and renowned praise.
Full many countries they did overrun°   *traverse*
From the uprising to the setting sun,
And many hard adventures did achieve,°   *accomplish*
Of all the which they honour ever won,
Seeking the weak oppressed to relieve,
And to recover right for such as wrong did grieve.

4

At last, as through an open plain they yode,°   *proceeded*
  They spied a knight that towards°   *in their direction*†
  pricked° fair,   *spurred*
And him beside an aged squire there rode
That seemed to couch° under his shield three-   *stoop*
  square°   *i.e., equilateral*
As if that age bade him that burden spare
And yield it those that stouter could it wield.
He, them espying, 'gan himself prepare

And on his arm address° his goodly shield,   *arrange*
That bore a lion passant° in a golden field.°   *walking background*

5

Which seeing, good Sir Guyon dear° besought   *urgently*
  The Prince of grace° to let him run that turn.   *as a favour*
  He granted: then the fairy quickly raught°   *seized*
  His poignant° spear and sharply 'gan to   *sharp-pointed*
    spurn°   *spur‡*
  His foamy steed, whose fiery feet did burn
  The verdant grass as he thereon did tread.
  Ne° did the other back his foot return,°   *Neither withdraw*
  But fiercely forward came withouten dread
And bent° his dreadful spear against the other's head.   *aimed*

6

They been ymet, and both their points
    arrived;°   *i.e., reached their targets*
  But Guyon drove so furious and fell°   *fiercely*
  That seemed both shield and plate it would have rived:°   *split*
  Natheless° it bore his foe not from his   *Nevertheless*
    sell,°   *saddle*
  But made him stagger as he were not well.
  But Guyon self,° ere well he was aware,   *himself*
  Nigh° a spear's length behind his crupper fell –   *Nearly*
  Yet in his fall so well himself he bare
That mischievous° mischance his life and limbs did   *harmful*
  spare.

7

Great shame and sorrow of that fall he took,
  For never yet, sith° warlike arms he bore   *since*
  And shivering° spear in bloody field first   *quivering*
    shook,°   *launched*
  He found himself dishonoured so sore.°   *severely*
  Ah, gentlest knight that ever armour bore,
  Let not thee grieve dismounted to have been
  And brought to ground that never was before –
  For not thy fault, but secret power unseen:
That spear enchanted was which laid thee on the green.

8

But weenedest° thou what wight° thee   *had you known   person**
    overthrew,
    Much greater grief and shamefuller regret
    For thy hard fortune then thou wouldst renew,
    That of a single damsel° thou wert met   *maid alone*
    On equal plain and there so hard beset:
    Even the famous Britomart it was,
    Whom strange adventure° did from Britain fet°   *chance   fetch*
    To seek her lover (love far-sought, alas),
Whose image she had seen in Venus' looking glass.

9

Full of disdainful° wrath he fierce uprose   *indignant‡*
    For to revenge that foul, reproachful shame
    And, snatching his bright sword, began to close
    With her on foot and stoutly° forward came: *bravely*
    Die rather would he than endure that same.
    Which, when his Palmer saw, he 'gan to fear
    His toward° peril and untoward°   *impending*   unfortunate*
      blame°   *hurt**
    Which by that new rencounter° he should   *encounter*
      rear° –   *bring about**
For death sat on the point of that enchanted spear.

10

And, hasting towards him, 'gan fair° persuade   *gently*
    Not to provoke misfortune, nor to ween°   *think*
    His spear's default° to mend with cruel blade;   *defect*
    For by his mighty science° he had seen   *knowledge*
    The secret virtue° of that weapon keen,°   *power   sharp*
    That mortal puissance mote° not withstand: *might*
    Nothing on earth mote always happy° been;   *fortunate*
    Great hazard were it, and adventure°   *undertaking*
      fond,°   *foolish*
To lose long-gotten honour with one evil hand.°   *action*

11

By such good means he him discounselled°   *dissuaded*
    From prosecuting his revenging rage;
    And eke° the Prince like treaty°   *also   persuasion*

handled°   *undertook*
His wrathful will with reason to assuage,
And laid the blame not to his carriage°   *conduct*
But to his starting steed that swerved aside,
And to the ill purveyance° of his page   *management**
That had his furniture° not firmly tied: *harness; equipment*
So is his angry courage° fairly° pacified.   *spirit suitably†*

12

Thus reconcilement was between them knit
    Through goodly temperance and affection chaste,
    And either vowed with all their power and wit°   *skill*
    To let not other's honour be defaced°   *discredited*
    Of° friend or foe – whoever it embased° –   *By degraded‡*
    Ne° arms to bear against the other's side;   *Nor*
    In which accord° the Prince was also placed   *agreement*
    And with that golden chain of concord tied.
So, goodly all agreed, they forth yfere° did ride.   *together*

13

O goodly usage° of those antique° times,   *custom ancient‡*
    In which the sword was servant unto right;
    When not for malice and contentious° crimes   *quarrelsome*
    But all for praise and proof° of manly might   *trial*
    The martial brood° accustomed to fight.   *race‡*
    Then honour was the meed° of victory,   *reward*
    And yet the vanquished had no despite.°   *suffered no outrage*
    Let later age that nobler use envy°   *rival**
Vile rancour to avoid, and cruel surquedry.°   *arrogance*

14

Long they thus travelled in friendly wise°   *manner*
    Through countries waste° and eke well   *desolate*
        edified,°   *built on**
    Seeking adventures hard, to exercise
    Their puissance, whilom° full dernly°   *at times* grievously**
        tried.
    At length they came into a forest wide
    Whose hideous horror and sad trembling sound

Full grisly° seemed. Therein they long did ride   *terrifying*
  Yet tract° of living creature none they found,   *track; print*
Save bears, lions and bulls, which roamed them around.

15

All suddenly, out of the thickest brush,°   *undergrowth*
  Upon a milk-white palfrey,° all alone,   *woman's light horse*
  A goodly° lady did forby° them rush,   *beautiful past*
  Whose face did seem as clear° as crystal stone,   *pure*
  And eke through fear was white as whale's bone.
  Her garments all were wrought of beaten gold,
  And all her steed with tinsel° trappings shone –   *glittering*
  Which fled so fast that nothing mote him hold,
And scarce them leisure gave her passing to behold.

16

Still° as she fled her eye she backward threw,   *Ever*
  As° fearing evil that pursued her fast;   *As if*
  And her fair yellow locks behind her flew,
  Loosely dispersed° with puff of every blast –   *scattered‡*
  All as a blazing star° doth far outcast   *i.e., comet*
  His hairy beams, and flaming locks dispread,°   *spread out†*
  At sight whereof the people stand aghast;
  But the sage wizard° tells, as he has read,°   *wise man forecast*
That it importunes° death and doleful   *portends†*
    drearihead.°   *sorrow*

17

So as they gazed after her a while,
  Lo where a grisly foster° forth did rush,   *forester*
  Breathing out beastly lust her to defile.
  His tireling° jade he fiercely forth did push   *tired†*
  Through thick and thin both over bank and bush
  In hope her to attain by hook or crook,
  That° from his gory° sides the blood   *So that spurred; bloody*
    did gush.
  Large were his limbs and terrible his look,
And in his clownish° hand a sharp boar spear he shook.   *peasant*

18

Which outrage, when those gentle knights did see,
    Full of great envy° and fell° jealousy,°   *hostility fierce anger*
    They stayed not to advise° who first should be,   *consider*
    But all spurred after fast, as they mote° fly,   *might*
    To rescue her from shameful villainy.°   *degradation;* evil*
    The Prince and Guyon equally belive°   *eagerly; quickly*
    Herself pursued, in hope to win thereby
    Most goodly meed,° the fairest dame alive;   *reward*
But after the foul foster Timias did strive.

19

The whiles° fair Britomart, whose constant mind   *Meantime*
    Would not so lightly° follow   *wantonly; swiftly; frivolously*
        beauty's chase,
    Ne° recked of° lady's love, did stay behind,   *Nor cared for*
    And them awaited there a certain space°   *i.e., of time*
    To weet° if they would turn back to that place.   *see*
    But when she saw them gone she forward went,
    As lay her journey, through that perilous pace,°   *passage*
    With steadfast courage and stout°   *resolute*
        hardiment° –   *daring*
Ne evil thing she feared, ne evil thing she meant.°   *thought; pitied*

20

At last, as nigh out of the wood she came,
    A stately castle far away she spied,
    To which her steps directly she did frame.°   *direct*
    That castle was most goodly edified,°   *built*
    And placed for pleasure nigh that forest side;
    But fair° before the gate a spacious plain,   *beautifully*
    Mantled° with green, itself did spreaden wide,   *Coated*
    On which she saw six knights that did deraign°   *engage in*
Fierce battle against one with cruel might and main.

21

Mainly° they all at once° upon him laid   *Violently together*
    And sore° beset on every side around   *grievously*
    That nigh° he breathless grew; yet nought°   *soon not at all*
        dismayed,
    Ne ever to them yielded foot of ground

(All° had he lost much blood through many a   *Although*
  wound)
But stoutly° dealt his blows, and every way   *bravely*
To which he turned in his wrathful stound,°   *attack*
Made them recoil and fly from dread decay,°   *death*
That° none of all the six before,° him   *So that in front [of him]*
  durst assay,

22

Like dastard curs that, having at a bay°   *at bay*
  The savage beast embossed° in weary   *driven to extremity*[t]
  chase,
  Dare not adventure on° the stubborn°   *risk approaching fierce*
  prey,
  Ne bite before, but roam from place to place
  To get a snatch when turned is his face.
  In such distress and doubtful jeopardy
  When Britomart him saw she ran apace
  Unto his rescue, and with earnest cry
Bade those same six forbear° that single enemy.   *release**

23

But to her cry they list° not lenden ear,   *choose*
  Ne aught the more their mighty stroke surcease;°   *cease*
  But, gathering him round about more near,
  Their direful rancour rather did increase;
  Till that she, rushing through the thickest press,°   *crowd*
  Perforce° disparted° their   *Forcibly separated*[t]
  compacted gyre°   *tight circle*
  And soon compelled to hearken unto peace.
  Tho° 'gan she mildly of them to inquire   *Then*
The cause of their dissension and outrageous° ire: *extreme*

24

Whereto that single knight did answer frame:
  'These six would me enforce by odds° of might   *inequality*[t]
  To change my lief° and love another dame –   *beloved*
  That death me liefer° were than such   *preferable*
  despite,°   *shameful outrage*
  So unto wrong to yield my wrested° right;   *taken by force*[‡]*
  For I love one, the truest one on ground,°   *earth*

Ne list° me change: she the Errant Damsel   *Nor wish*
    hight,°   *is called**†
For whose dear sake full many a bitter stound°   *attack*
I have endured and tasted many a bloody wound.'

25

'Certes,'° said she, 'then been ye six to blame   *Indeed*
    To ween° your wrong by force to justify: *think*
    For knight to leave his lady were great shame,
    That faithful is, and better were to die.
    All loss is less, and less the infamy,
    Than loss of love to him that loves but one;
    Ne may love be compelled by mastery,°   *greater force; subjection*
    For soon as mastery comes, sweet Love anon
Taketh his nimble wings and soon away is gone.'

26

Then spake one of those six: 'There dwelleth here,
    Within this castle wall, a lady fair,
    Whose sovereign° beauty hath no living peer,   *queenly; supreme*
    Thereto so bounteous° and so debonair°   *generous gracious*
    That never any mote° with her compare.   *may*
    She hath ordained this law, which we
        approve,°   *sanction; demonstrate*‡
    That every knight which doth this way repair,
    In case he have no lady nor no love,
Shall do unto her service never to remove.

27

'But if he have a lady or a love,
    Then must he her forgo with foul defame;°   *disgrace*
    Or else with us by dint° of sword approve   *blow*
    That she is fairer than our fairest dame –
    As did this knight, before ye hither came.'
    'Perdy,'° said Britomart, 'the choice is hard;   *Indeed*
    But what reward had he that overcame?'
    'He should advanced be to high regard'
(Said they) 'and have our lady's love for his reward.

28

'Therefore aread,° sir, if you have a love.'   *declare*
  'Love have I sure,' quoth she, 'but lady none.
  Yet will I not fro' mine own love remove,
  Ne to your lady will I service doen,
  But wreak° your wrongs wrought to this knight   *avenge*
    alone,°   *single*
  And prove° his cause.' With that her   *make good*
    mortal° spear   *deadly*
  She mightily aventred° towards one   *thrust†*
  And down him smote ere well aware he were;
Then to the next she rode, and down the next did bear.

29

Ne did she stay° till three on ground she laid   *stop*
  That° none of them himself could rear again.   *So that*
  The fourth was by that other knight dismayed° –   *vanquished*
  All were he° weary of his former pain –   *He was completely*
  That now there do but two of six remain;
  Which two did yield before she did them smite.
  'Ah' (said she them), 'now may ye all see plain
  That truth is strong and true love most of might,
That for his trusty servants doth so strongly fight.'

30

'Too well we see' (said they) 'and prove° too well   *demonstrate*
  Our faulty weakness and your matchless might:
  For-thy,° fair sir, yours be the damosel   *Therefore*
  Which, by her own law, to your lot doth light;
  And we, your liegemen, faith unto you plight.'
  So underneath her feet their swords they
    marred,°   *spoiled [by disgracing]*
  And after her besought, well as they might,
  To enter in and reap the due reward:
She granted, and then in they all together fared.

31

Long were it to describe the goodly° frame°   *excellent structure*
  And stately port° of Castle Joyous   *appearance*
  (For so that castle hight by common name),
  Where they were entertained with courteous

And comely° glee° of° many   *appropriate rejoicing; mirth by*
   gracious
Fair ladies and of many a gentle knight,
Who through a chamber long and spacious
Eftsoons° them brought unto their lady's sight,   *Soon after*
That of them cleped° was the 'Lady of Delight'.   *called*

32

But for to tell the sumptuous array
   Of that great chamber should be labour lost,
   For living wit,° I ween,° cannot display°   *mind believe exhibit*‡
   The royal riches and exceeding cost
   Of every pillar and of every post,
   Which all of purest bullion° framed°   *gold and/or silver made*
     were,
   And with great pearls and precious stones embossed°   *adorned*
   That° the bright glitter of their beams clear   *So that*
Did sparkle forth great light, and glorious° did   *brightly shining*
   appear.

33

These stranger knights, through passing,° forth   *passing through*
   were led
   Into an inner room whose royalty°   *magnificence*
   And rich purveyance° might uneath° be   *arrangement scarcely*
   read:°   *told*
   Mote° prince's palace beseem° so decked to   *Well might it befit*
   be.
   Which stately manner° whenas° they did see –   *mode when*
   The image of superfluous° riotise°   *excessive riotous living*†
   Exceeding much the state of mean°   *median [i.e., temperate]*
     degree –
   They greatly wondered whence so sumptuous
     guise°   *style of living*
Might be maintained, and each 'gan diversely devise.°   *conjecture*

34

The walls were round about apparelled
   With costly cloths of Arras and of Tours,
   In which with cunning hand was portrayed
   The love of Venus and her paramour,

The fair Adonis, turned to a flower –
A work of rare device° and wondrous wit.°   *ingenuity skill*
First did it show the bitter baleful°   *grievous*
 stour°   *time of stress*†
Which her assayed° with many a fervent   *assailed*
 fit°   *access of emotion*
When first her tender heart was with his beauty smit;

35

Then with what sleights and sweet allurements she
 Enticed the boy (as well that art she knew),
 And wooed him her paramour to be –
 Now making garlands of each flower that grew,
 To crown his golden locks with honour due;
 Now leading him into a secret shade
From his beauperes° and from bright heaven's *companions**
 view,
 Where him to sleep she gently would persuade,
Or bathe him in a fountain by some covert° glade. *secret*

36

And whilst he slept she over him would spread
 Her mantle, coloured like the starry skies,
 And her soft arm lay underneath his head,
 And with ambrosial kisses bathe his eyes.
 And whilst he bathed, with her two crafty spies
 She secretly would search each dainty limb,
 And throw into the well sweet rosemaries,
 And fragrant violets and pansies trim,°   *beautiful*
And ever with sweet nectar she did sprinkle him.

37

So did she steal his heedless heart away,
 And joyed his love in secret unespied.
 But for° she saw him bent to cruel play   *because*
 To hunt the savage beast in forest wide,
 Dreadful of° danger that mote° him betide, *Fearful at might*
 She oft and oft advised him to refrain
 From chase of greater° beasts, whose brutish pride *very large*
 Mote breed him scathe° unawares. But all in vain – *hurt*
For who can shun the chance that destiny doth ordain?

38

Lo where, beyond, he lieth languishing,°   *growing weak*
  Deadly engored° of° a great wild boar,   *deeply wounded[†] by*
  And, by his side, the goddess, grovelling,°   *lying face down*
  Makes for him endless moan, and evermore
  With her soft garment wipes away the gore
  Which stains his snowy skin with hateful hue.
  But, when she saw no help might him restore,
  Him to a dainty flower she did transmew,°   *transmute*
Which in that cloth was wrought as if it lively° grew.   *living*

39

So was that chamber clad in goodly° wise,°   *splendid   fashion*
  And round about it many beds were dight°   *arranged*
  As whilom° was the antique° world's   *formerly[*] ancient[‡]*
    guise:°   *manner*
  Some for untimely ease, some for delight,
  As pleased them to use that use it might.
  And all was full of damsels and of squires
  Dancing and revelling both day and night,
  And swimming deep in sensual desires –
And Cupid still° amongst them kindled lustful fires.   *always*

40

And all the while sweet Music did
    divide°   *add a descant, or variations, to[†]*
  Her looser° notes with Lydian harmony,   *most wanton*
  And all the while sweet birds thereto applied
  Their dainty lays° and dulcet melody,   *songs*
  Aye° carolling of love and jollity,°   *Ever   mirth; pleasure*
  That° wonder was to hear the trim°   *So that   beautiful*
    consort.°   *harmony; band*
  Which, when those knights beheld, with scornful eye
  They 'sdained such lascivious disport°   *diversion*
And loathed the loose demeanour of that wanton
    sort.°   *company*

41

Thence they were brought to that great lady's view,
  Whom they found sitting on a sumptuous bed
  That glistered all with gold and glorious show

As the proud Persian queens accustomed.° *practised habitually*
 She seemed a woman of great bountihead,° *liberality*†
 And of rare° beauty – saving that askance *exceptional*
 Her wanton eyes – ill signs of womanhood –
 Did roll too lightly,° and too often glance *wantonly*
Without regard of grace or comely amenance.° *mien; conduct*†

42

Long work it were, and needless, to devise° *describe* *
 Their goodly entertainment and great glee:° *sport*
 She caused them to be led in courteous wise° *manner*
 Into a bower,° disarmed for to be, *chamber*
 And cheered well with wine and spicery.
 The Redcross knight was soon disarmed there,
 But the brave maid would not disarmed be,
 But only vented up° her umbrere,° *raised for air visor*
And so did let her goodly° visage to appear. *beautiful*

43

As when fair Cynthia, in darksome night,
 Is in a noyous° cloud enveloped, *troublesome*
 Where she may find the substance thin and light
 Breaks forth her silver beams, and her bright head
 Discovers° to the world discomfited° – *Reveals perplexed*
 Of the poor travelller that went astray
 With thousand blessings she is heried:° *praised* *
 Such was the beauty and the shining ray
With which fair Britomart gave light unto the day.

44

And eke° those six, which lately with her fought, *in addition*
 Now were disarmed, and did themselves present
 Unto her view and company unsought:
 For they all seemed courteous and gent,° *noble*
 And all six brethren born of one parent,
 Which had them trained in all civility
 And goodly° taught to tilt and tournament. *well*
 Now were they liegemen to this lady free,
And her knights' service ought° to hold of her in *owed*
  fee.° *as her right*

45

The first of them by name Gardante°   *i.e., Gazer*
   hight,°   *was named**†
  A jolly person and of comely° view;°   *handsome   appearance*
  The second was Parlante,° a bold knight,   *Talker; Flatterer*
  And next to him Jocante° did ensue;°   *Jovial Play   follow*
  Basciante° did himself most courteous show,   *Kissing*
  But fierce Bacchante° seemed too fell° and   *Drinking   fierce*
   keen;°   *bold**
  And yet in arms Noctante° greater grew: *Night-dweller*
  All were fair knights and goodly° well beseen,   *handsome*
But to fair Britomart they all but shadows been.°   *were*

46

For she was full of amiable° grace,   *kindly*
  And manly terror mixed therewithal
  That,° as the one stirred up affection° base,   *So that   passion*
  So the other did men's rash desire appal,
  And hold them back that would in error fall –
  As he that hath espied a vermeil° rose,   *vermilion*
  To which sharp thorns and briars the way forstall,°   *obstruct*
  Dare not, for dread, his hardy° hand expose   *bold*
But, wishing it far of, his idle° wish doth lose.   *empty*

47

Whom when the lady saw so fair a wight,°   *person**
  All ignorant of her contrary sex
  (For her she weened° a fresh° and lusty   *believed to be   young*
   knight),
  She greatly 'gan enamoured to wex°   *grow*
  And with vain thoughts her falsed°   *deceived*
   fancy° vex.   *imagination*
  Her fickle heart conceived hasty fire –
  Like sparks of fire which fall in slender flex° –   *flax*
  That shortly burned into extreme desire
And ransacked all her veins with passion entire.°   *inward;*† *earnest*

48

Eftsoons° she grew to great impatience   *Soon after*
  And into terms° of open outrage° burst   *a condition   passion*
  That plain° discovered° her   *clearly*† *revealed*

    incontinence° –   *intemperance*
Ne° recked° she who her meaning did mistrust;   *Nor cared*
For she was given all to fleshly lust,
And poured forth in sensual delight
That all regard of shame she had discussed,°   *shaken off‡**
And meet° respect of honour put to flight: *fitting*
So shameless beauty soon becomes a loathly sight.

49

Fair ladies that to love captived are,
    And chaste desires do nourish in your mind,
Let not her fault your sweet affections mar,
Ne blot the bounty° of all womankind,   *virtue*
'Mongst thousands good one wanton dame to find:
Amongst the roses grow some wicked weeds;
For this was not to love but lust inclined,
For love does always bring forth bounteous° deeds,   *excellent*
And in each gentle° heart desire of honour breeds.   *noble*

50

Not so of love this looser° dame did   *too wanton*
    skill,°   *understood*
But as a coal to kindle fleshly flame,
Giving the bridle to her wanton will
And treading underfoot her honest name:
Such love is hate, and such desire is shame.
Still did she rove at her with crafty glance
Of her false° eyes that at her heart did aim,   *faithless; deceiving*
And told her meaning in her countenance;
But Britomart dissembled it with ignorance.

51

Supper was shortly dight,° and down they sat,   *ready*
    Where they were served with all sumptuous fare,
Whiles fruitful Ceres and Lyaeus fat
Poured out their plenty without spite° or   *grudging*
    spare:°   *frugality‡*
Nought wanted there that dainty° was and   *choice*
    rare,°   *exotic*
And aye° the cups their banks° did   *ever benches; tables*
    overflow,

And aye between the cups she did prepare
Way to her love, and secret darts did throw –
But Britomart would not such guileful message know.

52

So when they slaked had the fervent heat
    Of appetite with meats° of every sort,   *food*
    The lady did fair Britomart entreat
    Her to disarm, and with delightful sport
    To loose her warlike limbs and strong effort.°   *power*
    But when she mote° not thereunto be won   *might*
    (For she her sex under that strange purport° *outward bearing*†
    Did use° to hide, and plain appearance shun), *Was accustomed*
In plainer wise° to tell her grievance she began,   *fashion*

53

And all at once discovered° her desire   *revealed*
    With sighs and sobs and plaints and piteous grief –
    The outward sparks of her in-burning fire;
    Which, spent in vain, at last she told her brief
    That but if° she did lend her short relief   *unless*
    And do her comfort, she mote algates° die.   *altogether**
    But the chaste damsel – that had never prief° *experience*
    Of such malengin° and fine° forgery°   *guile subtle deception*
Did easily believe her strong extremity.

54

Full easy was for her to have belief
    Who, by self-feeling of her feeble sex,
    And by long trial of the inward grief
    Wherewith imperious love her heart did vex,°   *afflict*
    Could judge what pains do loving hearts perplex.° *plague*†
    Who means no guile beguiled soonest shall,
    And to fair semblance doth light° faith   *quickly*
      annex;°   *attach to*
The bird that knows not the false fowler's call
Into his hidden net full easily doth fall.

55

For-thy° she would not, in discourteous wise,°   *Therefore fashion*
  Scorn the fair offer of good will professed,
  For great rebuke° it is love to despise,   *disgrace* *
  Or rudely° disdain a gentle° heart's   *roughly noble; courteous*
    request;
  But with fair° countenance,° as   *courteous demeanour*
    beseemed best,
  Her entertained (natheless° she inly°   *nevertheless inwardly*
    deemed°   *judged*
  Her love too light° to woo a wandering°   *wanton travelling*
    guest):
  Which she, misconstruing, thereby esteemed
That from like inward fire that outward smoke had steamed.

56

Therewith a while she her fleet° fancy fed   *swiftly changing*
  Till she mote win fit time for her desire;
  But yet her wound still inward freshly bled,
  And through her bones the false° instilled fire   *falsely*
  Did spread itself and venom close° inspire.   *secretly; inwardly*
  Tho° were the tables taken all away   *Then*
  And every knight, and every gentle squire,
  'Gan choose his dame with 'basciomani'° gay   *hand-kissing*
With whom he meant° to make his sport and courtly   *intended*
    play.

57

Some fell to dance, some fell to hazardry,°   *dicing* *
  Some to make love, some to make merriment,
  As diverse wits to diverse things apply;
  And all the while fair Malecasta bent°   *aimed*
  Her crafty engines° to her close° intent.   *ruses secret*
  By this° the eternal lamps,° wherewith high *And now i.e., stars*
    Jove
  Doth light the lower world, were half yspent,
  And the moist daughters of huge Atlas strove
Into the ocean deep to drive their weary drove.

58

High time it seemed then for every wight
 Them to betake unto their kindly° rest.   *natural*
 Eftsoons° long waxen torches weren lit   *Straight away*
 Unto their bowers° to guiden every guest: *bed chambers*
 Tho, when the Britoness saw all the rest
 Avoided° quite° she 'gan herself   *Withdrawn completely*
  despoil°   *undress*
 And safe commit to her soft feathered nest
 Where, through long watch and late day's weary toil,
She soundly slept and careful° thoughts did quite *troublesome*
  assoil.°   *dispel*[†]

59

Now whenas° all the world in silence deep   *when*
 Yshrouded° was, and every mortal wight   *covered**
 Was drowned in the depth of deadly sleep,
 Fair Malecasta – whose engrieved° sprite° *troubled soul*
 Could find no rest in such perplexed plight –
 Lightly° arose out of her weary bed   *Wantonly; quickly*
 And, under the black veil of guilty Night,
 Her with a scarlet mantle covered
That was with gold and ermine fair° enveloped. *well; beautifully*

60

Then, panting soft and trembling every joint,
 Her fearful feet towards the bower she moved
 Where she for secret purpose did appoint
 To lodge the warlike maid unwisely loved;
 And, to her bed approaching, first she proved°   *checked*
 Whether she slept or waked: with her soft hand
 She softly felt if any member moved,
 And lent her wary ear to understand°   *discover*
If any puff of breath, or sign of sense,° she found. *consciousness*

61

Which, whenas none she found, with easy shift° – *movement*
 For fear lest her unwares she should abraid° – *startle;*[†] *arouse*[†]
 The embroidered quilt she lightly up did lift
 And by her side herself she softly laid,

Of every finest finger's touch afraid;
Ne° any noise she made, ne° word she spake,   *Neither nor*
But inly sighed. At last the royal maid
Out of her quiet slumber did awake,
And changed her weary side the better ease to take.

62

Where, feeling one close couched by her side,
She lightly° leaped out of her filed° bed   *quickly defiled*
And to her weapon ran, in mind to gride°   *run through; wound*
The loathed lecher. But the dame, half dead
Through sudden fear and ghastly° drearihead,°   *fearful*[†] *terror*
Did shriek aloud that° through the house it rang,   *so that*
And the whole family,° therewith adread,   *household*
Rashly° out of their roused couches sprung,   *In haste*
And to the troubled chamber all in arms did throng.

63

And those six knights – that lady's champions –
And eke° the Redcross knight ran to the stound,°   *also uproar*
Half armed, half unarmed, with them at once:°   *together*
Where, when confusedly they came, they found
Their lady lying on the senseless ground.
On the other side they saw the warlike maid,
All in her snow-white smock, with locks unbound,
Threatening the point of her avenging blade
That with so troublous terror they were all dismayed.

64

About their lady first they flocked around,
Whom, having laid in comfortable couch,
Shortly they reared out of her frozen swound.°   *swoon*
And afterwards they 'gan with foul reproach
To stir up strife and troublous conteck°   *quarrelling*
    broach.°   *cause*[‡]
But by example of the last day's loss
None of them rashly durst to her approach,
Ne° in so glorious spoil themselves emboss:°   *Nor adorn*
Her succoured° eke the champion of the bloody cross.   *aided*

65

But one of those six knights, Gardante hight,
　　Drew out a deadly bow, and arrows keen,°　　　　　　*sharp*
　　Which forth he sent with felonous° despite°　　*cruel** *contempt*
　　And fell° intent against the virgin sheen:°　　*malicious radiant*
　　The mortal steel stayed° not till it was seen　　　*stopped*
　　To gore° her side – yet was the wound not deep,　　*pierce*
　　But lightly razed° her soft silken skin　　　　　　*grazed*
　　That° drops of purple blood thereout did weep　　*So that*
Which did her lily smock with stains of vermeil steep.°　*soak*

66

Wherewith enraged, she fiercely at them flew,
　　And with her flaming sword about her laid
　　That° none of them foul mischief° could　　*So that injury*
　　　eschew,°　　　　　　　　　　　　　　　　　　*avoid*
　　But with her dreadful strokes were all dismayed.°　*overcome*
　　Here, there, and everywhere about her swayed°　*swung*
　　Her wrathful steel that° none mote it abide;　　*so that*
　　And eke° the Redcross knight gave her good aid,　*in addition*
　　Aye° joining foot to foot and side to side,　　　*Ever*
That° in short space their foes they have quite terrified.　*So that*

67

Tho,° whenas° all were put to shameful flight,　　*Then when*
　　The noble Britomartis her arrayed
　　And her bright arms about her body dight:°　　*prepared*
　　For nothing would she longer there be stayed
　　Where so loose life and so ungentle° trade　　*ignoble*
　　Was used of knights and ladies seeming gent.°　*noble*
　　So, early, ere the gross earth's griesy° shade　　*grey†*
　　Was all dispersed out of the firmament,
They took their steeds and forth upon their journey went.

[In canto 2 Britomart talks with the Redcross knight about Artegall –
the knight of Justice of Book 5 – with whom she has fallen in love.
Stanzas 17–26 describe in flashback how she first saw him in Merlin's
magic mirror, while the rest of the canto is devoted to Britomart's love
melancholy and arguments with her nurse, Glaucè, over her condition.

In canto 3 Britomart and her nurse seek out Merlin, who reveals to them the 'famous progeny' springing from 'ancient Trojan blood' (st. 22), culminating in Elizabeth I, that will derive from her union with Artegall. At the end of the canto Britomart sets out on her quest dressed in the recently captured armour of 'Angela, the Saxon queen' (st. 58) and accompanied by Glaucè as her squire.]

Canto 4

Bold Marinell of° Britomart   *by*
   Is thrown on the rich strond:°   *shore*
Fair Florimell of Arthur is
   Long followed but not found.

1

Where is° the antique° glory now   *What has become of ancient‡*
   become
   That whilom° wont° in women to appear?   *formerly* used*
   Where be the brave achievements done by some?
   Where be the battles, where the shield and spear,
   And all the conquests, which them high did rear,
   That matter° made for famous poets' verse,   *subject*
   And boastful men so oft abashed to hear?
   Been they all dead and laid in doleful°   *grievous*
   hearse,°   *coffin†*
Or doen they only sleep, and shall again reverse?°   *return*

2

If they be dead, then woe is me therefore.
   But if they sleep, O let them soon awake,
   For all too long I burn with envy sore°   *extreme*
   To hear the warlike feats which Homer spake
   Of bold Penthesilea, which made a lake
   Of Greekish blood so oft in Trojan plain.
   But when I read how stout° Deborah strake°   *brave struck*
   Proud Sisera, and how Camilla hath slain
The huge Orsilochus, I swell with great disdain.°   *indignation*

3

Yet these, and all that else had puissance,
  Cannot with noble Britomart compare,
  As well for glory of great valiance
  As for pure chastity and virtue rare,°   *exceptional*
  That all her goodly deeds do well declare.
  Well worthy stock, from which the branches sprung,
  That in late years so fair a blossom bare
  As thee, O queen, the matter of my song,
Whose lineage from this lady I derive along:°   *in a straight line*

4

Who when, through speeches with the Redcross knight,
  She learned had the estate° of Artegall,   *condition; rank*
  And in each point herself informed aright,
  A friendly league of love perpetual
  She with him bound and congé° took withal.   *leave*
  Then forth he on his journey did proceed
  To seek adventures which mote° him befall,   *might*
  And win him worship° through his warlike   *honour; renown*
    deed
Which always of his pains he made the chiefest meed.° *reward*

5

But Britomart kept on her former course,
  Ne° ever doffed her arms, but all the way   *Nor*
  Grew pensive through that amorous discourse
  By which the Redcross knight did erst° display   *formerly*
  Her lover's shape and chivalrous array.°   *attire*
  A thousand thoughts she fashioned in her mind,
  And in her feigning fancy did portray
  Him such as fittest she for love could find:
Wise, warlike, personable, courteous and kind.

6

With such self-pleasing thoughts her wound she fed
  And thought so to beguile° her grievous   *cheat; divert*
    smart.°   *wound*
  But so her smart was° much more   *i.e., the wound was so*
    grievous bred,
  And the deep wound more deep engorged° *excessively filled*

her heart,
That naught but death her dolour° mote   sorrow
    depart.°   banish
So forth she rode without repose or rest,
Searching all lands and each remotest part,
Following the guidance of her blinded guest,°   i.e., Cupid
Till that to the sea-coast at length she her
    addressed.°   directed herself

7

There she alighted from her light-foot beast
    And, sitting down upon the rocky shore,
    Bade her old squire unlace her lofty crest.°   helmet
    Tho,° having viewed awhile the surges hoar°   Then foamy
    That 'gainst the craggy cliffs did loudly roar,
    And in their raging surquedry° disdained°   pride were angry
    That the fast° earth affronted° them so   firm defied‡
      sore°   much
    And their devouring covetise° restrained,   greed
Thereat she sighed deep, and after thus complained:

8

'Huge sea of sorrow and tempestuous grief,
    Wherein my feeble bark is tossed along
    Far from the hoped haven of relief,
    Why do thy cruel billows beat so strong,
    And thy moist mountains each on others throng,
    Threatening to swallow up my fearful life?
    O do thy cruel wrath and spiteful wrong
    At length allay and stint° thy stormy strife,   cease
Which in these troubled bowels reigns and rageth rife:

9

'For else my feeble vessel, crazed° and cracked°   damaged broken
    Through thy strong buffets and outrageous° blows,   violent
    Cannot endure, but needs it must be wracked°   wrecked
    On the tough rocks or on the sandy shallows
    The whilst that Love it steers and Fortune rows:
    Love, my lewd° pilot, hath a restless mind,   unskilled; bungling
    And Fortune boatswain no assurance° knows,   steadiness

But sail withouten stars 'gainst tide and wind:
How can they other do, sith° both are bold and blind?   *since*

10

'Thou god of winds that reignest in the seas,
 That reignest also in the continent,°   *land*
 At last blow up some gentle gale of ease
 The which may bring my ship, ere it be rent,
 Unto the gladsome port of her intent;
 Then, when I shall myself in safety see,
 A table° for eternal monument   *tablet*
 Of thy great grace, and my great jeopardy,
Great Neptune, I avow to hallow° unto thee.'   *dedicate*

11

Then sighing softly sore° and inly°   *with pain   inwardly; profoundly*
 deep,
 She shut up all her plaint° in privy° grief,   *lament   secret*
 For her great courage would not let her weep;
 Till that old Glaucè 'gan with sharp reprief°   *reproof*
 Her to restrain and give her good relief
 Through hope of those which Merlin had her told
 Should of her name and nation be chief,
 And fetch their being from the sacred mould
Of her immortal womb, to be in heaven enrolled.

12

Thus, as she her recomforted,° she spied   *consoled*
 Where, far away, one all in armour bright
 With hasty gallop towards her did ride.
 Her dolour° soon she ceased, and on her dight°   *grief   placed*
 Her helmet, to her courser mounting light,°   *swiftly*
 Her former sorrow into sudden wrath –
 Both cousin passions of distroubled°   *disturbed**
  sprite° –   *mind*
 Converting, forth she beats the dusty path:
Love and despite° at once her courage kindled hath.   *disdain*

13

As when a foggy mist hath overcast
   The face of heaven and the clear air engrossed,°   *made dense‡*
   The world in darkness dwells till that at last
   The watery south wind, from the seaboard coast
   Upblowing, doth disperse the vapour loosed,
   And pours itself forth in a stormy shower:
   So the fair Britomart, having disclosed°   *hatched [as a bird]*
   Her cloudy care into a wrathful stour,°   *storm†*
The mist of grief dissolved, did into vengeance pour.

14

Eftsoons° her goodly° shield addressing   *Forthwith splendid*
   fair°   *making well ready*
   That mortal spear she in her hand did take
   And unto battle did herself prepare.
   The knight, approaching, sternly her bespake:°   *addressed†*
   'Sir knight, that dost thy voyage rashly make
   By this forbidden way in my despite,°   *contempt of me*
   Ne° dost by other's death example take,   *Nor*
   I rede° thee soon retire° whiles thou hast   *advise withdraw‡*
   might,
Lest afterwards it be too late to take thy flight.'

15

Ythrilled° with deep disdain° of his   *Deeply moved*† contempt*
   proud threat
   She shortly thus: 'Fly they that need to fly:
   Words fearen° babes. I mean not thee entreat   *frighten*
   To pass but, maugre° thee, will pass or die':   *in spite of*
   Ne longer stayed for the other to reply,
   But with sharp spear the rest made dearly known.
   Strongly the strange knight ran, and sturdily°   *ruthlessly*
   Struck her full on the breast, that made her down
Decline her head, and touch her crupper with her crown.

16

But she again° him on the shield did smite   *in return*
   With so fierce fury and great puissance
   That, through his three-square scutcheon° piercing   *shield*
   quite,°   *utterly*

And through his mailed hauberk,° by   *coat of mail*
   mischance°   *[his] bad luck*
The wicked steel through his left side did glance.°   *hit obliquely*
Him so° transfixed she before her bore   *thus*
Beyond his croup° the length of all her lance   *crupper, rump*
Till, sadly° sousing° on the sandy shore,   *heavily falling*†
He tumbled in a heap and wallowed in his gore.

17

Like as the sacred° ox, that careless°   *consecrated   without care*
   stands
  With gilded horns and flowery garlands crowned,
  Proud of his dying honour and dear bands,
  Whiles the altars fume° with frankincense around,   *smoke*
  All suddenly with mortal stroke astound,°   *stunned**
  Doth grovelling fall, and with his streaming gore
  Distains° the pillars and the holy ground,   *Stains*
  And the fair flowers that decked him afore:
So fell proud Marinell upon the precious shore.

18

The martial maid stayed not him to lament
  But forward rode and kept her ready° way   *direct*
  Along the strand which, as she overwent,
  She saw bestrewed all with rich array
  Of pearls and precious stones of great assay,°   *worth*
  And all the gravel mixed with golden ore –
  Whereat she wondered much, but would not stay
  For gold, or pearls, or precious stones an
    hour,°   *more than a short time*
But them despised all; for all was in her power.

19

Whiles thus he lay in deadly° 'stonishment,°   *deathly shock**
  Tidings hereof came to his mother's ear.
  His mother was the black-browed Cymoent –
  The daughter of great Nereus – which did bear
  This warlike son unto an earthly peer,°   *mate*
  The famous Dumarin,° who, on a day,   *i.e., Of the sea*
  Finding the nymph asleep in secret where°   *place*

As he by chance did wander that same way,
Was taken with her love and by her closely° lay.   *secretly*

20

There he this knight of her begot whom, born,
    She of his father 'Marinell' did name,
    And in a rocky cave, as wight° forlorn,°   *creature* abandoned*
Long time she fostered up till he became
A mighty man at arms, and mickle° fame   *much*
Did get through great adventures by him done:
For never man he suffered by that same
Rich Strand to travel whereas° he did wone,°   *where dwell*
But that he must do battle with the sea nymph's son.

21

An hundred knights of honourable name
    He had subdued, and them his vassals made,
    That° through all Fairyland his noble fame   *So that*
Now blazed° was, and fear did all invade   *proclaimed*
That none durst° passen through that perilous glade.   *dared*
And, to advance his name and glory more,
Her sea-god sire she dearly° did persuade   *earnestly*
To endow her son with treasure and rich
    store,°   *abundant riches*
'Bove all the sons that were of earthly wombs ybore.°   *born**

22

The god did grant his daughter's dear° demand   *earnest*
    To doen° his nephew° in all riches flow: *make grandson*
    Eftsoons° his heaped waves he did command   *Forthwith*
Out of their hollow bosom forth to throw
All the huge treasure which the sea below
Had in his greedy gulf devoured deep
And him enriched through the overthrow
And wrecks of many wretches, which did weep
And often wail their wealth which he from them did keep.

23

Shortly upon that shore there heaped was
    Exceeding riches and all precious things,
    The spoil of all the world, that° it did pass°   *so that surpass*

The wealth of the East and pomp of Persian kings:
Gold, amber, ivory, pearls, ouches,° rings,   *brooches*
And all that else was precious and dear,
The sea unto him voluntary brings
That shortly he a great lord did appear,
As was in all the land of Fairy or elsewhere.

24

Thereto° he was a doughty, dreaded knight,   *In addition*
 Tried° often to the scathe° of many   *Proved injury*
  dear°   *bold men**
 That° none in equal arms him matchen might –   *So that*
 The which his mother, seeing, 'gan to fear
 Lest his too haughty hardiness° might rear°   *boldness cause*
 Some hard mishap in hazard of his life.
 For-thy° she oft him counselled to forbear   *Therefore*
 The bloody battle, and to stir up strife,
But, after all his war, to rest his weary knife.

25

And, for his more assurance,° she inquired   *security‡*
 One day of Proteus by his mighty spell
 (For Proteus was with prophecy inspired)
 Her dear son's destiny to her to tell,
 And the sad end of her sweet Marinell.
 Who, through foresight of his eternal
  skill,°   *knowledge of things eternal*
 Bade her from womankind to keep him well,
 For of a woman he should have much ill:
A virgin strange° and stout° him should   *alien brave*
  dismay,° or kill.   *vanquish*

26

For-thy she gave him warnings every day
 The love of women not to entertain –
 A lesson too, too hard for living clay
 From love in course of nature to refrain.
 Yet he his mother's lore° did well retain,   *instruction*

And ever from fair ladies' love did fly:
Yet many ladies fair did oft complain
That they for love of him would algates° die –   *come what may*
Die whoso list° for him, for he was love's enemy.   *wishes*

27

But ah, who can deceive his destiny,
  Or ween° by warning to avoid his fate? –   *think*
  That° when he sleeps in most   *Destiny*
    security,°   *freedom from care;‡ safety*
  And safest seems, him soonest doth amate°   *cast down*
  And findeth due effect or soon or late:°   *sooner or later*
  So feeble is the power of fleshly arm.
  His mother bade him women's love to hate,
  For she of woman's force did fear no harm –
So, weening to have armed him, she did quite disarm.

28

This was that woman, this that deadly wound,
  That Proteus prophesied should him dismay,
  The which his mother vainly did expound
  To be heart-wounding love which should assay°   *try*
  To bring her son unto his last decay.°   *death*
  So tickle° be the terms° of mortal state,   *fickle limits; conditions*
  And full of subtle sophisms, which do play
  With double senses and with false°   *misleading*
    debate°   *argument*
To approve° the unknown purpose of eternal fate.   *demonstrate*

29

Too true the famous Marinell it found
  Who, through late° trial, on that wealthy Strand   *recent*
  Inglorious now lies in senseless swound°   *swoon*
  Through heavy stroke of Britomartis' hand.
  Which, when his mother dear did understand,
  And heavy tidings heard – whereas° she played   *where*
  Amongst her watery sisters by a pond,
  Gathering sweet daffadillies to have made
Gay garlands from the sun their foreheads fair to shade –

30

Eftsoons° both flowers and garlands far away	*Straight away*
She flung, and her fair dewy locks yrent.°	*tore**
To sorrow huge she turned her former play,	
And gamesome mirth to grievous dreariment.°	*sadness†*
She threw herself down on the continent,°	*earth†*
Ne° word did speak, but lay, as in a swoon,	*Nor*
Whiles all her sisters did for her lament	
With yelling outcries and with shrieking sound,	
And every one did tear her garland from her crown.°	*head*

31

Soon as she up out of her deadly fit°	*crisis‡**
Arose, she bade her chariot be brought,	
And all her sisters that with her did sit	
Bade eke° at once their chariots be sought.	*also*
Tho,° full of bitter grief and pensive° *Then*	*melancholy; anxious*
thought,	
She to her wagon clomb;° clomb all the rest,	*climbed*
And forth together went with sorrow fraught.°	*weighed down*
The waves, obedient to their behest,	
Them yield ready passage and their rage surceased.°	*stopped*

32

Great Neptune stood amazed at their sight°	*the sight of them*
Whiles on his broad round back they softly slid,	
And eke himself mourned at their mournful plight;	
Yet wist° not what their wailing meant; yet did	*knew*
For great compassion of their sorrow bid	
His mighty waters to them buxom° be.	*compliant*
Eftsoons the roaring billows still abid,°	*remained still*
And all the grisly° monsters of the sea	*terrifying*
Stood gaping at their gate° and wondered	*manner of proceeding*
them to see.	

33

A team of dolphins ranged in array
  Drew the smooth chariot of sad Cymoent:
  They were all taught by Triton to obey
  To the long reins at her commandment.
  As swift as swallows on the waves they went

That° their broad flaggy fins no foam did rear,   *So that*
Ne bubbling roundel° they behind them sent.   *circle of bubbles*
The rest of° other fishes drawen were,   *by*
Which with their finny oars the swelling sea did shear.

34

Soon as they been arrived upon the brim°   *edge*
  Of the Rich Strand their chariots they forlore,°   *left**
  And let their teamed fishes softly swim
  Along the margent° of the foamy shore,   *margin*
  Lest they their fins should bruise, and surbate°   *bruise†*
    sore°   *grievously*
  Their tender feet° upon the stony ground.   *extremities*
  And, coming to the place where, all in gore
  And cruddy° blood enwallowed° they   *clotted   wallowing†*
    found
The luckless Marinell lying in deadly swound,

35

His mother swooned thrice, and the third time
  Could scarce recovered be out of her pain:
  Had she not been devoid of mortal slime°   *clay; flesh*
  She should not then have been relived° again.   *revived*
  But soon as life recovered had the rein,
  She made so piteous moan and dear°   *grievous*
    wayment°   *lamentation*
  That the hard rocks could scarce from tears refrain;
  And all her sister nymphs with one consent
Supplied her sobbing breaches° with sad   *intervals of her sobbing*
    complement.

36

'Dear image of myself' (she said) 'that is,
  The wretched son of wretched mother born,
  Is this thine high advancement? O is this
  The immortal name with which thee, yet unborn,
  Thy grandsire Nereus promised to adorn?
  Now liest thou of life and honour reft;°   *bereaved*
  Now liest thou a lump of earth forlorn –
  Ne° of thy late life memory is left;   *Neither*
Ne° can thy irrevocable destiny be weft?°   *Nor avoided;† waived*

37

'Fond° Proteus, father of false prophecies,   *Foolish*
   And they more fond that credit° to thee give: *credence*
   Not this the work of woman's hand, I wis,°   *know*
   That so deep wound through these dear members drive.
   I feared love – but they that love do live;
   But they that die do neither love nor hate.
   Natheless° to thee thy folly I forgive,   *Nevertheless*
   And to myself, and to accursed Fate,
The guilt I do ascribe – dear° wisdom bought too late.   *grievous*

38

'O what avails it of immortal seed
   To been ybred° and never born to die?   *have been bred**
   Far better I it deem to die with speed
   Than waste in woe and wailful misery.
   Who° dies the utmost dolour° doth   *He who   sorrow*
     aby,°   *suffer**
   But who that lives is left to wail his loss:
   So life is loss, and death felicity.
   Sad life worse than glad death; and greater cross°   *misfortune‡*
To see friend's grave than, dead, the grave self to engross.° *fill†*

39

'But if the heavens did his days envy
   And my short bliss malign,° yet mote° they well   *envy† might*
   Thus much afford me ere that° he did die,   *before*
   That the dim eyes of my dear Marinell
   I mote have closed, and him bade farewell,
   Sith° other offices° for mother meet°   *Since duties fitting*
   They would not grant.
   Yet, maugre° them, farewell, my sweetest sweet: *despite*
Farewell my sweetest son, sith we no more shall meet.'

40

Thus, when they all had sorrowed their fill,
   They softly 'gan to search° his grisly° wound,   *examine terrible*
   And, that° they might him handle more at   *so that*
     will,°   *as they wished*
   They him disarmed and, spreading on the ground

Their watchet° mantles fringed with silver round,　　　*pale blue*
They softly wiped away the jelly-blood°　　　*clotted blood*
From the orifice – which, having well upbound,
They poured in sovereign° balm and nectar good:　　　*precious*
Good both for earthly medicine and for heavenly food.

41

Tho,° when the lily-handed Liagore　　　*Then*
　(This Liagore whilom° had learned skill　　　*formerly* *
　In leech's° craft by great Apollo's lore,°　　　*doctor's teaching*
　Sith her whilom upon high Pindus hill
　He loved, and at last her womb did fill
　With heavenly seed, whereof wise Paeon sprung)
　Did feel his pulse, she knew there stayed still
　Some little life his feeble sprites° among –　　　*vital spirits*
Which to his mother told, despair she from her flung.

42

Tho up him taking in their tender hands,
　They easily° unto her chariot bear.　　*quietly; without causing pain*
　Her team at her commandment quiet stands
　Whiles they the corse° into her wagon rear°　　　*body　lift*
　And strew with flowers the lamentable bier.°　　　*stretcher*
　Then all the rest into their coaches climb,
　And through the brackish° waves their passage shear:　　*salty*†
　Upon great Neptune's neck they softly swim
And to her watery chamber swiftly carry him.

43

Deep in the bottom of the sea her bower
　Is built of hollow billows heaped high,
　Like to thick clouds that threat a stormy shower;
　And vaulted all within like to the sky
　In which the gods do dwell eternally.
　There they him laid in easy couch well dight,°　　　*prepared*
　And sent in haste for Tryphon to apply
　Salves to his wounds and medicines of might° –　　　*powerful*
For Tryphon of° sea gods the sovereign leech is　　　*by*
　　hight° –　　　*called* *†

44

The whiles the nymphs sit all about him round,
   Lamenting his mishap° and heavy plight.   *misfortune*
   And oft his mother, viewing his wide wound,
   Cursed the hand that did so deadly smite
   Her dearest son, her dearest heart's delight.
   But none of all those curses overtook
   The warlike maid, the example of that might,
   But fairly° well she thrived, and well did   *very*
     brook°   *use; enjoy*
Her noble deeds, ne her right course for aught forsook.

45

Yet did false Archimage her still pursue
   To bring to pass his mischievous intent,
   Now that he had her singled from the crew°   *company*
   Of courteous knights, the Prince, and fairy gent,°   *noble*
   Whom late° in chase of beauty excellent   *recently*
   She left, pursuing that same foster° strong –   *forester*
   Of whose foul outrage° they, impatient,   *violence*
   And full of fiery zeal, him followed long
To rescue her from shame and to revenge her wrong.

46

Through thick and thin, through mountains and through
    plains,
   Those two great champions did at once° pursue   *together*
   The fearful damsel with incessant pains –
   Who from them fled, as lightfoot hare from view
   Of hunter swift and scent of hounds true.°   *trusty*
   At last they came unto a double way
   Where, doubtful which to take her to rescue,
   Themselves they did dispart,° each to assay°   *separate† try*
Whether more happy were° to win so   *Which would be the luckier*
   goodly prey.

47

But Timias, the Prince's gentle squire,
   That lady's love unto his lord forelent,°   *yielded†*
   And° with proud envy° and indignant ire   *Both enmity*
   After that wicked foster fiercely went:

So been they three sundry ways ybent.°   *directed**
But fairest fortune to the Prince befell,
Whose chance it was – that soon he did repent –
To take that way in which that damosel
Was fled afore, afraid of him as fiend of hell.

48

At last of her, far off, he gained view.
   Then 'gan he freshly° prick° his foamy steed,   *eagerly   spur*
   And, ever as he nigher to her drew,
   So evermore he did increase his speed
   And of each turning still kept wary heed.
   Aloud to her he oftentimes did call,
   To do away vain doubt and needless° dread: *uncalled for*
   Full mild to her he spake, and oft let fall
Many meek words to stay° and comfort her   *stop [her]*
   withal.°   *besides*

49

But nothing might relent° her hasty flight,   *abate‡**
   So deep the deadly fear of that foul swain
   Was erst° impressed in her gentle sprite.°   *formerly   mind*
   Like as a fearful dove which, through the reign
   Of the wide air, her way does cut amain°   *at full speed‡*
   Having far off espied a tercel-gent°   *peregrine falcon*
   Which after her his nimble wings doth strain,
   Doubleth her haste for fear to be forhent°   *overtaken and seized†*
And with her pinions cleaves the liquid° firmament: *transparent†*

50

With no less haste, and eke with no less dread,
   That fearful lady fled from him that meant°   *intended*
   To her no evil thought nor evil deed.
   Yet former fear of being foully shent°   *violated; shamed*
   Carried her forward with her first intent;
   And, though oft looking backward well she viewed
   Herself freed from that foster insolent,°   *intemperate*
   And that it was a knight which now her sued,°   *pursued*
Yet she no less the knight feared than that villain rude.°   *barbaric*

51

His uncouth° shield and strange arms° her   *mysterious   armour*
    dismayed
    (Whose like in Fairyland were seldom seen)
    That° fast she from him fled, ne° less afraid   *So that   nor*
    Than of wild beasts if she had chased been.
    Yet he her followed still with
        courage° keen –   *bravery; sexual excitement*
    So long that now the golden Hesperus
    Was mounted high in top of heaven sheen,°   *bright*
    And warned his other brethren joyous
To light their blessed lamps in Jove's eternal house.

52

All suddenly dim wox° the dampish air   *grew*
    And grisly° shadows covered heaven bright,   *terrifying; dark*
    That now with thousand stars was decked fair:
    Which, when the Prince beheld – a loathful sight –
    And that perforce,° for want° of longer light,   *of necessity   lack*
    He mote° surcease° his suit and lose the hope   *must   cease*
    Of his long labour, he 'gan foully° wite°   *terribly   blame*
    His wicked fortune that had turned aslope,°   *askew*
And cursed night that reft from him so goodly scope.°   *goal; end*

53

Tho,° when her ways he could no more descry,   *Then*
    But to and fro at disadventure° strayed –   *random†*
    Like as a ship, whose loadstar, suddenly
    Covered with clouds, her pilot hath dismayed –
    His wearisome pursuit perforce he stayed
    And, from his lofty steed dismounting low,
    Did let him forage. Down himself he laid
    Upon the grassy ground to sleep a throw:°   *short while**
The cold earth was his couch, the hard steel his pillow.

54

But gentle Sleep envied° him any rest: *begrudged*
    Instead thereof sad sorrow and disdain°   *indignation*
    Of his hard hap° did vex his noble breast,   *fortune*
    And thousand fancies beat his idle brain
    With their light wings, the sights of semblants°   *images*

vain.°   *empty*
  Oft did he wish that lady fair mote° be   *might*
  His Fairy Queen for whom he did complain;°   *lament*
  Or that his Fairy Queen were such as she;
And ever hasty Night he blamed bitterly:

55

'Night, thou foul mother of annoyance sad,°   *oppressive trouble*
  Sister of heavy Death and nurse of Woe,
  Which was begot in heaven, but for thy bad
  And brutish shape thrust down to hell below
  Where, by the grim flood° of Cocytus slow,   *waters*
  Thy dwelling is, in Herebus' black house
  (Black Herebus, thy husband, is the foe
  Of all the gods), where thou,
    ungracious,°   *wicked; lacking divine grace*
Half of thy days dost lead in horror hideous:

56

'What had the eternal Maker need of thee
  The world in his continuous course to keep,
  That dost all things deface, ne lettest see
  The beauty of His work? Indeed,° in sleep   *Truly*
  The slothful body that doth love to steep°   *bathe†*
  His listless limbs and drown his baser° mind   *too base*
  Doth praise thee oft, and oft from Stygian deep
  Calls thee his goddess (in his error blind)
And great Dame Nature's handmaid, cheering every
    kind.°   *species*

57

'But well I wote° that to an heavy heart   *know*
  Thou art the root and nurse of bitter cares,
  Breeder of new, renewer of old smarts.°   *wounds*
  Instead of rest thou lendest railing° tears;   *flowing;† angry*
  Instead of sleep thou sendest troublous fears
  And dreadful visions, in the which, alive,
  The dreary° image of sad Death appears.   *terrible;* melancholy*
  So from the weary spirit thou dost drive
Desired rest, and men of happiness deprive.

58

'Under thy mantle black there hidden lie
   Light-shunning theft and traitorous° intent,   *treacherous*
   Abhorred bloodshed and vile felony,°   *wrath**
   Shameful deceit and danger° imminent,   *harm*
   Foul horror and eke° hellish dreariment:°   *in addition terrors*
   All these, I wote,° in thy protection be,   *know*
   And light do shun for fear of being shent.°   *shamed*
   For light alike is loathed of them and thee,
And all that lewdness° love do hate the light to see.   *wickedness*

59

'For Day discovers° all dishonest ways,   *reveals*
   And showeth each thing as it is indeed:
   The praises of high God he fair displays,
   And His large° bounty rightly doth aread.°   *generous declare*
   Day's dearest children be the blessed seed
   Which darkness shall subdue and heaven win:
   Truth is his daughter; he her first did breed,
   Most sacred virgin, without spot of sin.
Our life is day, but death with darkness doth begin.

60

'O when will day then turn to me again,
   And bring with him his long-expected° light?   *long-awaited*
   O Titan, haste to rear° thy joyous wain:°   *raise chariot*
   Speed thee to spread abroad thy beams bright,
   And chase away this too long-lingering Night.
   Chase her away from whence she came, to hell.
   She, she it is that hath me done
     despite:°   *behaved maliciously to me*
   There let her with the damned spirits dwell,
And yield her room to Day that it can govern well.'

61

Thus did the Prince that weary night outwear
   In restles anguish and unquiet pain;
   And early, ere the morrow did uprear
   His dewy head out of the ocean main,

He up arose, as half in great disdain,°   *indignation*
And clomb° onto his steed. So forth he went   *climbed*
With heavy look and lumpish pace that plain°   *plainly†*
In him bewrayed° great grudge and   *displayed*
   maltalent:°   *ill-will*
His steed eke seemed to apply° his steps to his   *adapt*
   intent.°   *mood*

Canto 5

Prince Arthur hears of Florimell:
  Three fosters° Timias wound;   *foresters*
Belphoebe finds him almost dead
  And reareth out of swound.°   *swoon*

1

Wonder it is to see in diverse° minds   *different*
  How diversely° Love doth his pageants play,   *variously*
And shows his power in variable° kinds:°   *different natures*
The baser wit (whose idle thoughts alway
Are wont to cleave unto the lowly clay)°   *i.e., body*
It stirreth up to sensual desire,
And in lewd sloth to waste his careless day;
  But in brave sprite° it kindles goodly fire   *soul*
That to all high desert and honour doth aspire.

2

Ne° suffereth it uncomely idleness   *Neither*
  In his free thought to build her sluggish nest;
Ne° suffereth it thought of ungentleness°   *Nor   discourtesy*
Ever to creep into his noble breast:
But to the highest and the worthiest
Lifteth it up that else would lowly fall.
It lets not fall, it lets it not to rest,
  It lets not scarce this Prince to breathe at all,
But to his first pursuit him forward still doth call –

3

Who long time wandered through the forest wide
  To find some issue° thence, till that at last   *happening*
  He met a dwarf that seemed terrified
  With some late peril which he hardly°   *with difficulty*
    passed,°   *escaped*
  Or other accident which him aghast;°   *terrified*
  Of whom he asked whence he lately came,
  And whither now he travelled so fast?
  For sore° he swat° and, running through that   *greatly perspired*
    same
Thick forest, was bescratched, and both his feet nigh lame.

4

Panting for breath, and almost out of heart,°   *spirit; life*
  The dwarf him answered: 'Sir, ill mote I°   *it might harm me to*
    stay
  To tell the same. I lately did depart
  From fairy court, where I have many a day
  Served a gentle° lady of great sway°   *noble power*
  And high account throughout all elfin land,
  Who lately left the same and took this way.
  Her now I seek, and if ye understand°   *know*
Which way she fared hath, good sir tell out of
    hand.'°   *immediately*

5

'What mister wight,'° said he, 'and how   *kind of person**
    arrayed?'
  'Royally clad,' quoth he, 'in cloth of gold,
  As meetest° may beseem° a noble   *most befittingly become*
    maid.
  Her fair locks in rich circlet be enrolled –
  A fairer wight did never sun behold;
  And on a palfrey rides more white than snow –
  Yet she herself is whiter many fold.°   *times*
  The surest sign whereby ye may her know
Is, that she is the fairest wight alive, I trow.'°   *believe; affirm*

6

'Now certes,° swain,' said he, 'such one, I ween,°   *indeed think*
 Fast flying through this forest from her foe –
 A foul, ill-favoured foster – I have seen.
  Herself, well as I might, I rescued tho,°   *then; on that occasion*
  But could not stay – so fast she did forego,°   *go on ahead*
  Carried away with wings of speedy fear.'
  'Ah, dearest God,' quoth he, 'that is great woe,
  And wondrous ruth° to all that shall it hear.   *cause of sorrow*
But can ye read,° sir, how I may her find, or where?'   *inform*

7

'Perdy,° me liever were to weeten°   *Indeed I would rather know*
   that'
 (Said he) 'than ransome of the richest knight,
 Or all the good that ever yet I got;
  But froward° Fortune and too-forward Night   *adverse*
  Such happiness did – maugre° – to me   *curse them†*
   spite,°   *evilly deprive*
  And from me reft° both life and light at one.°   *stole together*
  But, dwarf, aread° what is that lady   *inform[me]*
   bright°   *beautiful*
  That through this forest wandereth thus alone,
For of her error° strange I have great ruth and moan.'   *wandering*

8

'That lady is,' quoth he, 'whereso° she be,   *wherever*
 The bountiest° virgin, and most   *most virtuous*
  debonair,°   *gracious*
 That ever living eye, I ween,° did see.   *believe*
  Lives none this day that may with her compare
  In steadfast° chastity and virtue rare° –   *resolute extreme*
  The goodly ornaments of beauty bright –   *splendid*
  And is ycleped° Florimell the Fair: *called**
  Fair Florimell, beloved of many a knight;
Yet she loves none but one, that Marinell is hight.°   *named*†*

9

'A sea-nymph's son, that Marinell is hight,
 Of° my dear dame is loved dearly° well.   *By extremely*
 In other none° but him she sets delight –   *no other*

All her delight is set on Marinell;
But he sets nought at all by Florimell:
For lady's love his mother long ago
Did him, they say, forewarn through
    sacred° spell.   *divine [i.e., from a god]*
But fame° now flies that of a foreign foe   *the rumour*
He is yslain – which is the ground° of all our woe. *basis; cause*

10

'Five days there be since he (they say) was slain,
  And four since Florimell the court forwent°   *left*
  And vowed never to return again
  Till him alive or dead she did invent.°   *discover*
  Therefore, fair sir, for love of knighthood gent°   *noble*
  And honour of true ladies, if ye may,
  By your good counsel or bold hardiment°   *bravery*
  Or° succour her or me direct the way: *Either*
Do one or other good, I you most humbly pray.

11

'So may ye gain to you full great renown
  Of all good ladies through the world so wide,
  And haply° in her heart find highest room°   *with luck* *place*
  Of whom ye seek to be most magnified:°   *glorified; praised*
  At least eternal meed° shall you abide.'°   *reward* *be left to**
  To whom the Prince: 'Dwarf, comfort to thee take,
  For till thou tidings learn what her betide,°   *befall*
  I here avow thee never to forsake:
Ill wears he arms that n'ill° them use for lady's sake.' *will not*

12

So with the dwarf he back returned again
  To seek his lady where he mote° her find.   *might*
  But by the way he greatly 'gan complain°   *lament*
  The want° of his good squire late left behind,   *lack*
  For whom he wondrous° pensive° grew in *extremely* *anxious*
    mind
  For doubt° of danger which mote him betide;   *fear*
  For him he loved above all mankind,
  Having him true and faithful ever tried,°   *proved*
And bold as ever squire that waited by knight's side –

13

Who, all this while, full hardly° was   *to the greatest extreme*
   assayed°   *assailed*
   Of° deadly danger which to him betid.°   *By   befell*
   For whiles his noble lord pursued that noble maid,
   After that foster° foul he fiercely rid°   *forester   rode*
   To been avenged of the shame he did
   To that fair damsel. Him he chased long
   Through the thick woods, wherein he would have hid
   His shameful head from his avengement° strong,   *revenge*
And oft him threatened death for his outrageous wrong.

14

Natheless° the villain sped himself so well –   *Nevertheless*
   Whether through swiftness of his speedy beast,
   Or knowledge of those woods, where he did dwell –
   That shortly he from danger was released
   And out of sight escaped at the least;°   *last*
   Yet not escaped from the due reward
   Of his bad deeds, which daily he increased,
   Ne° ceased not till him oppressed hard   *Nor*
The heavy plague° that for such lechers is   *blow; affliction*
   prepared.

15

For, soon as he was vanished out of sight,
   His coward courage 'gan emboldened be,
   And cast° how to avenge him of that foul   *considered*
   despite°   *injury*
   Which he had borne of his bold enemy;
   Tho° to his brethren came – for they were three   *Then*
   Ungracious° children of one graceless   *evil [lacking divine grace]*
   sire –
   And unto them complained how that he
   Had used been of that foolhardy squire:
So them with bitter words he stirred to bloody ire.

16

Forthwith themselves with their sad°   *sorrow-inducing*
   instruments
   Of spoil and murder they 'gan arm belive,°   *swiftly*

And with him forth into the forest went
　To wreak the wrath which he did erst° revive　　　　*just*
　In their stern° breasts on him which late did drive　　*fierce*
　Their brother to reproach and shameful flight:
　For they had vowed that never he alive
　Out of that forest should escape their might –
Vile rancour their rude hearts had filled with such
　　despite.°　　　　　　　　　　　　　　　　　*malice*

17

Within that wood there was a covert° glade　　　　*secret*
　Forby° a narrow ford, to them well known,　　　　*Near*
　Through which it was uneath° for wight°　*difficult anyone**
　　to wade;
　And now by fortune it was overflown.°　　　　*flooded*
　By that same way they knew that squire unknown°　*i.e., to him*
　Mote algates° pass; for-thy°　　*whatever else** *therefore*
　　themselves they set
　There in await,° with thick woods overgrown,　　*ambush*
　And all the while their malice they did whet°　　*sharpen*
With cruel threats his passage through the ford to let.°　*hinder*

18

It fortuned, as they devised° had,　　　　　　*planned*
　The gentle° squire came riding that same way,　*noble; courteous*
　Unweeting° of their wile and treason° bad,　*Ignorant treachery*
　And through the ford to passen did assay.°　　*attempt*
　But that fierce foster° which late° fled away,　*forester recently*
　Stoutly° forth stepping on the further shore,　　*Boldly*
　Him boldly bade his passage there to stay
　Till he had made amends and full restore°　　*reparation*
For all the damage° which he had him done afore.°　*harm before*

19

With that, at him a quivering dart he threw
　With so° fell° force and villainous despite°　*such fierce hatred*
　That through his habergeon° the fork –　*sleeveless coat of mail*
　　head flew
　And through the linked mails empierced°　　*pierced through*‡
　　quite° –　　　　　　　　　　　　　　　　*completely*
　But had no power in his soft flesh to bite.

That stroke the hardy° squire did sore°　　　　　*bold greatly*
　displease,°　　　　　　　　　　　　　　　　　　*vex*
But more that him he could not come to smite;
For by no means the high bank he could seize,°　　　*attain*
But laboured long in that deep ford with vain°　　　*profitless*
　disease,°　　　　　　　　　　　　　　　　　　*difficulty*

20

And still the foster with his long boar-spear
　Him kept from landing at his wished will.°　　　*as he wanted*
Anon one sent out of the thicket near
A cruel shaft, headed with deadly ill,°　　　　　　*evil; harm*
And feathered with an unlucky° quill:　　　*causing misfortune*
The wicked steel stayed not till it did light
In his left thigh, and deeply did it thrill.°　　　　*pierce*
Exceeding grief° that wound in him　　　　　　　*pain*
　empight° –　　　　　　　　　　　　　　　　*implanted*
But more that with his foes he could not come to fight.

21

At last, through wrath and vengeance making way,
　He on the bank arrived with mickle°　　　　　　*much*
　pain,°　　　　　　　　　　　　　　　*also: difficulty*
Where the third brother did him sore° assay°　*grievously assail*
And drove at him, with all his might and main,
A forest bill° which both his hands did　　　　　*scythe*
　strain.°　　　　　　　　　　　　　　*tightly grasp*†
But warily he did avoid the blow
And with his spear requited him again
That° both his sides were thrilled° with the　*So that pierced*
　throw
And a large stream of blood out from the wound did flow.

22

He, tumbling down, with gnashing teeth did bite
　The bitter earth and bade to let him in
Into the baleful° house of endless night　*malignant; wretched*
Where wicked ghosts do wail their former sin.
Tho° 'gan the battle freshly to begin,　　　　　*Then*
For nathemore for° that spectacle bad　*not at all, because of*
Did the other two their cruel vengeance blin,°　　*cease**

But both at once on both sides him bestad,°   *beset*
And load upon him laid, his life for to have had.

23

Tho, when that villain he advised,° which late   *observed**
  Affrighted had the fairest Florimell,
  Full of fierce fury and indignant hate
  To him he turned and, with rigour° fell,°   *harshness   pitiless*
  Smote him so rudely° on the pannicle°   *roughly   skull*[†]
  That to the chin he cleft his head in twain.
  Down on the ground his carcase grovelling fell;
  His sinful soul with desperate° disdain°   *despairing   scorn*
Out of her fleshly firm° fled to the place of pain.   *earth; body*

24

That seeing now, the only° last of three   *very*
  Who with that wicked shaft him wounded had,
  Trembling with horror (as that did foresee
  The fearful end of his avengement sad°   *causing sorrow*
  Through which he follow should his brethren bad),
  His bootless° bow in feeble hand upcaught   *worthless*
  And therewith shot an arrow at the lad –
  Which, faintly fluttering, scarce his helmet raught°   *reached*
And glancing fell to ground, but him annoyed nought.

25

With that he would have fled into the wood,
  But Timias him lightly° overhent°   *swiftly   overtook**
  Right as he entering was into the flood,
  And struck at him with force so violent
  That headless him into the ford he sent:
  The carcase with the stream was carried down,
  But the head fell backward on the continent.°   *ground*
  So mischief fell upon the meaner's
    crown:°   *head of the one intending it*
They three be dead with shame; the squire lives with renown.

26

He lives, but takes small joy of his renown,
  For of that cruel wound he bled so sore
  That from his steed he fell in deadly swoon;

Yet still the blood forth gushed in so great store°   *abundance*
That he lay wallowed° all in his own gore.   *prostrate*
Now God thee keep, thou gentlest squire alive,
Else shall thy loving lord thee see no more
But both of comfort him thou shalt deprive
And eke° thyself of honour, which thou didst achieve.   *also*

27

Providence heavenly passeth living thought,
    And doth for wretched men's relief make way;
    For lo! great grace, or Fortune, hither brought
    Comfort° to him that comfortless now lay.   *Aid*
    In those same woods, ye well remember may
    How that a noble huntress did wone° –   *dwell*
    She that base Braggadocchio did affray°   *frighten*
    And made him fast out of the forest run:
Belphoebe was her name, as fair as Phoebus' sun.

28

She, on a day,° as she pursued the chase   *one day*
    Of some wild beast which, with her arrows keen,°   *sharp*
    She wounded had, the same along did trace°   *track*
    By track of blood which she had freshly seen
    To have besprinkled all the grassy green.
    By the great persue° which she there perceived   *track of blood*
    Well hoped she the beast engored° had been,   *deeply wounded*†
    And made more haste the life to have bereaved –
But ah! her expectation greatly was deceived.

29

Shortly she came whereas° that woeful squire,   *to where*
    With blood deformed,° lay in deadly   *disfigured*
        swound;°   *swoon*
    In whose fair eyes (like lamps of quenched fire)
    The crystal humour° stood congealed round: *moisture*
    His locks, like faded leaves fallen to ground,
    Knotted with blood in bunches rudely ran,
    And his sweet lips, on which before that stound°   *time of trial**
    The bud of youth to blossom fair began,
Spoiled° of their rosy red, were woxen° pale   *Despoiled   grown*
        and wan:

30

Saw never living eye more heavy° sight,   *sad*
  That could have made a rock of stone to rue°   *feel pity*
  Or rive° in twain. Which, when that lady bright,   *split*
  Besides° all hope, with melting eyes did view,   *Beyond*
  All suddenly abashed° she changed hue°   *confounded   aspect*
  And, with stern horror, backward 'gan to start.
  But when she better him beheld, she grew
  Full of soft passion and unwonted° smart:°   *unaccustomed   pain*
The point of pity pierced through her tender heart.

31

Meekly she bowed down to weet° if life   *discern*
  Yet in his frozen members did remain;
  And, feeling by his pulse's beating rife°   *readily*
  That the weak soul her seat did yet retain,
  She cast° to comfort° him with busy   *resolved   succour*
    pain.°   *trouble*
  His double-folded neck she reared upright,
  And rubbed his temples and each trembling vein;
  His mailed habergeon she did undight,°   *unfasten†*
And from his head his heavy burgonet° did light.°   *helmet‡   lift*

32

Into the woods thenceforth in haste she went
  To seek for herbs that mote° him remedy,°   *might   cure*
  For she of herbs had great intendiment,°   *understanding‡ **
  Taught of° the nymph which from her infancy   *by*
  Her nursed had in true nobility.
  There, whether it divine Tobacco were,
  Or Panacea, or Polygony,
  She found and brought it to her patient dear
Who, all this while, lay bleeding out his heart-blood
    near.°   *almost*

33

The sovereign° weed betwixt two marbles   *powerful*
  plain°   *smooth*
  She pounded small and did in pieces bruise,°   *pound*
  And then atween° her lily hands twain   *between*

Into his wound the juice thereof did scruze;°   squeeze†
And round about, as she could well it use,
The flesh therewith she suppled° and did   anointed; softened
   steep°   bathe†
To abate all spasm and soak the swelling bruise;
And after having searched the intuse° deep,   bruise†
She with her scarf did bind the wound from cold to keep.

34

By this he had sweet life recured° again   regained
   And, groaning inly° deep,° at last his eyes –   extremely deeply
   His watery eyes, drizzling like dewy rain –
   He 'gan uplift toward the azure skies,
   From whence descend all hopeless° remedies.   unhoped-for†
   Therewith he sighed and, turning him aside,
   The goodly maid full of divinities
   And gifts of heavenly grace he by him spied,
Her bow and golden quiver lying him beside.

35

'Mercy, dear Lord,' said he, 'what grace° is this   favour
   That thou hast showed to me, sinful wight,°   creature*
   To send thine angel from her bower of bliss
   To comfort me in my distressed plight?
   Angel or goddess do I call thee right?
   What service may I do unto thee meet°   fitting
   That hast from darkness me returned to light,
   And with thy heavenly salves and medicines sweet
Hast dressed my sinful wounds? I kiss thy blessed feet.'

36

Thereat she, blushing, said: 'Ah, gentle squire,
   Nor goddess I, nor angel, but the maid
   And daughter of a woody° nymph, desire   woodland†
   No service but thy safety and aid –
   Which, if thou gain, I shall be well apaid.°   repaid; pleased
   We mortal wights, whose lives and fortunes be
   To common accidents still open laid,
   Are bound with common bond of frailty
To succour wretched wights whom we captived see.'

37

By this her damsels, which the former chase
   Had undertaken after her, arrived –
   As did Belphoebe – in the bloody place,
   And thereby deemed the beast had been deprived
   Of life, whom late their lady's arrow rived.°   *pierced*
   For-thy° the bloody track they followed fast,   *Therefore*
   And every one to run the swiftest strived;
   But two of them the rest far overpassed,
And where their lady was arrived at the last.

38

Where, when they saw that goodly° boy with blood   *handsome*
   Defouled,° and their lady dress his wound,   *defiled**
   They wondered much, and shortly understood
   How him in deadly case° their lady found,   *plight*
   And rescued out of the heavy stound.°   *trial**
   Eftsoons° his warlike courser – which was strayed *Soon after*
   Far in the woods whiles that he lay in swound° – *swoon*
   She made those damsels search:° which, being stayed, *seek*
They did him set thereon, and forth with them conveyed.

39

Into that forest far they thence him led,
   Where was their dwelling in a pleasant glade,
   With mountains round about environed,
   And mighty woods, which did the valley shade
   And like a stately theatre it made,
   Spreading itself into a spacious plain.
   And in the midst a little river played
   Amongst the pumice stones, which seemed to plain° *lament*
With gentle murmur that his course they did restrain.

40

Beside the same a dainty° place there lay,   *delightful*
   Planted with myrtle trees and laurels green,
   In which the birds sang many a lovely lay°   *song*
   Of gods' high praise and of their loves' sweet teen,° *grief*
   As° it an earthly paradise had been –   *As if*
   In whose enclosed shadow there was pight° *erected; pitched*
   A fair pavilion,° scarcely to be seen,   *tent**

The which was all within most richly dight°   *equipped*
That greatest princes living it mote well delight.

41

Thither they brought the wounded squire, and laid
 In easy couch his feeble limbs to rest.
 He rested him a while, and then the maid
 His ready wound with better salves new dressed:° *prepared*
 Daily she dressed him and did the best
 His grievous hurt to guarish° that she might,   *cure**
 That° shortly she his dolour° hath   *So that pain*
  redressed°   *relieved*
 And his foul sore reduced to fair plight° –   *condition*
It she reduced,° but himself destroyed quite.° *healed‡ utterly*

42

O foolish physic, and unfruitful pain,
 That heals up one, and makes another, wound:
 She his hurt thigh to him recured° again,   *restored*
 But hurt his heart – the which before was sound –
 Through an unwary° dart which did rebound *unexpected†*
 From her fair eyes and gracious countenance.
 What boots° it him from death to be unbound   *avails*
 To be captived in endless durance°   *constraint*
Of sorrow and despair without allegeance?° *alleviation**

43

Still as his wound did gather and grow whole,
 So still his heart wox° sore and health decayed – *grew*
 Madness to save a part and lose the whole.
 Still° whenas° he beheld the heavenly maid *Always when*
 Whiles daily plasters to his wound she laid,° *applied*
 So still his malady the more increased
 The whiles her matchless beauty him dismayed.° *vanquished*
 Ah God, what other could he do at least°   *last*
But love so fair a lady that his life released?° *freed [from death[*

44

Long while he strove in his courageous breast
 With reason due the passion to subdue,
 And love for to dislodge out of his nest:

Still when her excellencies he did view,
Her sovereign bounty° and celestial   *virtue; kindness*
  hue,°   *countenance*
The same to love he strongly was constrained.
But when his mean estate he did review
He from such hardy° boldness was restrained,   *daring*
And of his luckless lot and cruel love thus plained:° *complained*

45

'Unthankful wretch,' said he, 'is this the meed°   *repayment*
  With which her sovereign mercy thou does quite?°   *reward*
Thy life she saved by her gracious deed,
But thou dost ween° with villainous°   *think base*
  despite°   *contempt*
To blot her honour and her heavenly light.
Die, rather, die, than so disloyally
Deem° of her high desert,° or seem so   *Judge merit*
  light.°   *wanton; fickle*
Fair death it is to shun more shame, to
  die:°   *To die to shun shame is . . .*
Die, rather, die, than ever love disloyally.

46

'But if to love disloyalty it be,
  Shall I then hate her that from death's door
Me brought? – ah, far be such reproach from me.
What can I less do than her love therefore
Sith° I her due reward cannot restore?   *Since*
Die, rather, die, and dying do her serve –
Dying her serve, and living her adore.
Thy life she gave, thy life she doth deserve:
Die, rather, die, than ever from her service swerve.

47

'But, foolish boy, what boots° thy service base   *signifies*
  To her to whom the heavens do serve and sue?° –   *woo*[†]
Thou a mean squire of meek and lowly place;
She heavenly born and of celestial hue.
How then? Of all, Love taketh equal view;

And doth not highest God vouchsafe to take
The love and service of the basest crew?
If she will not, die meekly for her sake:
Die, rather, die, than ever so fair love forsake.'

48

Thus warrayed° he long time against his will,°   *made war   desire*
  Till that, through weakness, he was forced at last
  To yield himself unto the mighty ill° –   *i.e., love melancholy*
  Which, as a victor proud, 'gan ransack fast
  His inward parts and all his entrails waste
  That° neither blood in face, nor life in heart,   *So that*
  It left, but both did quite dry up and blast,°   *shrivel*
  As piercing levin,° which the inner part   *lightning*
Of everything consumes, and calcineth by
    art.°   *powders through its power*

49

Which seeing, fair Belphoebe 'gan to fear
  Lest that his wound were inly well not healed,
  Or that the wicked steel empoisoned were:
  Little she weened° that love he close°   *thought   secretly*
    concealed.
  Yet still he wasted, as the snow congealed°   *turned to ice*
  When the bright sun his beams thereon doth beat,
  Yet never he his heart to her revealed,
  But rather chose to die for sorrow great
Than with dishonourable terms her to entreat.

50

She, gracious lady, yet no pains did spare
  To do him ease or do him remedy:
  Many restoratives of virtues rare,°   *extreme power*
  And costly cordials° she did apply   *medicines for the heart*
  To mitigate his stubborn malady;
  But that sweet cordial, which can restore
  A love-sick heart, she did to him envy° –   *deny; begrudge*
  To him and to all the unworthy world forlore°   *deserted**
She did envy that sovereign salve in secret store.° *place; receptacle*

51

That dainty rose, the daughter of her morn,
   More dear than life she tendered,° whose flower   *esteemed*
   The garland of her honour did adorn.
   Ne° suffered she the midday's scorching power,   *Neither*
   Ne° the sharp northern wind, thereon to shower,°   *Nor fall*
   But lapped° up her silken leaves most   *wrapped; folded*
      chaire°   *carefully‡ **
   When so the froward° sky began to lour;   *adverse*
   But soon as calmed was the crystal air
She did it fair dispread° and let to flourish fair.   *display†*

52

Eternal God, in his almighty power,
   To make example of his heavenly grace,
   In paradise whilom° did plant this flower,   *formerly **
   Whence he it fetched out of her native place
   And did in stock of earthly flesh enrace°   *implant‡ **
   That° mortal men her glory should admire: *So that*
   In gentle lady's breast and bounteous° race *virtuous; excellent*
   Of womankind it fairest flower doth spire,°   *shoot*
And beareth fruit of honour and all chaste desire.

53

Fair imps° of beauty – whose bright shining beams   *offspring*
   Adorn the world with like to heavenly light,
   And to your wills both royalties and realms
   Subdue through conquest of your wondrous might –
   With this fair flower your goodly garlands dight°   *adorn*
   Of chastity and virtue virginal,
   That shall embellish more your beauty bright
   And crown your heads with heavenly coronal° *garland;† circlet*
Such as the angels wear before God's tribunal.°   *judgement seat‡*

54

To your fair selves a fair example frame°   *make*
   Of this fair virgin, this Belphoebe fair,
   To whom in perfect love and spotless fame
   Of chastity none living may compare;

Ne° poisonous envy justly can impair   *Neither*
The praise of her fresh flowering maidenhead.
For-thy° she standeth on the highest stair°   *Therefore   step*
Of the honourable stage° of   *platform*
   womanhead°   *womanhood*
That ladies all may follow her example dead.°   *when [she is] dead*

55

In so° great praise° of steadfast chastity   *such   merit*
   Natheless° she was so courteous and kind,   *Nevertheless*
   Tempered° with grace and goodly modesty,   *Balanced*
   That seemed° those two virtues strove to find   *it seemed*
   The higher place in her heroic mind.
   So striving, each did other more augment,
   And both increased the praise of womankind,
   And both increased her beauty excellent:
So all did make in her a perfect complement.°   *fulfilment*

CANTO 6

The birth of fair Belphoebe and
   Of Amoret is told.
The Garden of Adonis fraught°   *filled*
   With pleasures manifold.

1

Well may I ween,° fair ladies, all this while   *believe*
   Ye wonder how this noble damosel°   *damsel; maiden*
   So great perfections did in her compile,°   *assemble‡*
   Sith° that in savage° forests she did dwell,   *Since   wild*
   So far from court and royal citadel,
   The great schoolmistress of all courtesy:
   Seemeth that such wild woods should far expel
   All civil° usage° and gentility,   *orderly;† refined‡ conduct*
And gentle° sprite° deform with rude°   *noble   soul   rough*
   rusticity.

2

But to this fair Belphoebe in her birth
   The heavens so favourable were and free,°   *liberal*
   Looking with mild aspect upon the earth,
   In the horoscope of her nativity,
   That all the gifts of grace and chastity
   On her they poured forth of° plenteous   *from*
      horn:°   *cornucopia [horn of plenty]*
   Jove laughed on Venus from his sovereign see,°   *throne*
   And Phoebus with fair beams did her adorn,
And all the Graces rocked her cradle, being° born.   *when she was*

3

Her birth was of the womb of morning dew,
   And her conception of the joyous prime,°   *spring*
   And all her whole creation did her show
   Pure and unspotted from all loathly crime°   *sin; blame*
   That is ingenerate° in fleshly slime.   *inborn*
   So was this virgin born, so was she bred,
   So was she trained up from time to time°   *constantly‡*
   In all chaste virtue and true bountihead° *virtue; goodness*
Till to her due perfection she was ripened.

4

Her mother was the fair Chrysogone,
   The daughter of Amphisa, who by race
   A fairy was, yborn of high degree:
   She bore Belphoebe; she bore in like case° *same body; fashion*
   Fair Amoretta in the second place.
   These two were twins, and twixt them two did share
   The heritage of all celestial grace
   That all the rest it seemed they robbed bare
Of bounty,° and of beauty, and all virtues rare.   *goodness*

5

It were a goodly story to declare
   By what strange accident° fair Chrysogone   *chance*
   Conceived these infants, and how them she bare
   In this wild forest, wandering all alone,
   After she had nine months fulfilled and gone.

For not as other women's common brood
   They were enwombed in the sacred throne
   Of her chaste body, nor with common food,
As other women's babes, they sucked vital° blood.   *of life*

6

But wondrously they were begot and bred
   Through influence of the heavens' fruitful ray,
   As it in antique° books is mentioned: *ancient‡*
   It was upon a summer's shiny day,
   When Titan fair his beams did display,
   In a fresh fountain, far from all men's view,
   She bathed her breast the boiling heat to allay.
   She bathed with roses red, and violets blue,
And all the sweetest flowers that in the forest grew.

7

Till, faint through irksome weariness, adown
   Upon the grassy ground herself she laid
   To sleep, the whiles a gentle slumbering swoon
   Upon her fell, all naked bare displayed.
   The sunbeams bright upon her body played,
   Being through former bathing mollified,°   *softened*
   And pierced into her womb, where they
      embayed°   *bathed;† enveloped‡*
   With so sweet sense° and secret power unspied   *sensation*
That in her pregnant flesh they shortly fructified.

8

Miraculous may° seem to him that reads   *it may*
   So strange example of conception;
   But reason teacheth that the fruitful seeds
   Of all things living, through impression
   Of the sunbeams in moist complexion,°   *a body of moist humour*
   Do life conceive and quickened° are by
      kind:°   *brought to life*
               nature
   So, after Nilus' inundation,
   Infinite shapes of creatures men do find
Informed° in the mud on which the sun hath   *Shaped;† formed†*
   shined.

9

Great father, he, of generation
  Is rightly called, the author of life and light;
  And his fair sister for creation
  Ministereth° matter fit which, tempered°   *Supplies mixed*
    right°   *correctly*
  With heat and humour,° breeds the living   *moisture*
    wight.°   *creature**
  So sprang these twins in womb of Chrysogone;
  Yet wist° she nought thereof but, sore°   *knew extremely*
    affright,°   *afraid*
  Wondered to see her belly so upblown,
Which still increased till she her term° had full outgone.   *time*

10

Whereof conceiving shame and foul disgrace
  (Albe° her guiltless conscience her cleared),   *Albeit; even though*
  She fled into the wilderness a space°   *for a time*
  Till that the unwieldy burden she had reared,°   *borne**†
  And shunned dishonour, which as death she feared;
  Where, weary of long travail,° down to rest   *also: travel*
  Herself she set,° and comfortably° cheered.   *sat consolingly†*
  There a sad° cloud of sleep her overcast   *heavy; melancholy*
And seized every sense with sorrow sore oppressed.   *grievously*

11

It fortuned° fair Venus, having lost   *chanced*
  Her little son, the winged god of love
  (Who, for some light° displeasure° which him   *trifling offence*
    crossed,
  Was from her fled as flit° as airy dove,   *nimbly†*
  And left her blissful bower of joy above –
  So from her often had he fled away
  When she for aught him sharply did reprove,
  And wandered in the world in strange array,
Disguised in many shapes that none might him
    bewray),°   *disclose*

12

Him for to seek she left her heavenly house –
  The house of goodly forms and fair aspects
  Whence all the world derives the glorious
  Features of beauty, and all shapes select,°   *fine*
  With which high God his workmanship hath decked –
  And searched every way through which his wings
  Had borne him or his track she mote° detect: *might*
  She promised kisses sweet, and sweeter things
Unto the man that of him tidings to her brings.

13

First she him sought in court, where most he
    used°   *was accustomed*
  Whilom° to haunt, but there she found him not; *Formerly**
  But many there she found which sore° accused   *greatly*
  His falsehood, and with foul, infamous blot
  His cruel deeds and wicked wiles did spot:°   *blame*
  Ladies and lords she everywhere mote hear
  Complaining how, with his empoisoned° shot, *poisonous*†
  Their woeful hearts he wounded had whilere,° *previously*
And so had left them languishing° 'twixt hope and *suffering*
  fear.

14

She then the cities sought° from gate to gate,   *searched*
  And everyone did ask, did he him see?
  And everyone her answered that too late
  He had him seen, and felt the cruelty
  Of his sharp darts and hot artillery;
  And everyone threw forth reproaches rife
  Of his mischievous° deeds, and said that he   *harmful*
  Was the disturber of all civil° life, *orderly; communal*
The enemy of peace, and author of all strife.

15

Then in the country she abroad him sought,
  And in the rural cottages inquired,
  Where also many plaints° to her were *formal complaints*
    brought
  How he their heedless° hearts with love had fired, *unaware*

And his false venom through their veins inspired.°　　*infused*
And eke° the gentle shepherd swains, which sat　　*also*
Keeping their fleecy flocks, as they were hired,
She sweetly heard complain both how and what
Her son had to them done – yet she did smile thereat.

16

But when in none of all these she him got,
　　She 'gan advise° where else he mote him hide.　　*consider*
At last she her bethought that she had not
　　Yet sought the savage° woods and forests wide　　*wild*
In which full° many lovely nymphs abide,　　*very*
　　'Mongst whom might be that he did closely° lie,　　*secretly*
Or that the love of some of them him tied:
　　For-thy° she thither cast° her course to apply　　*Therefore resolved*
To search the secret haunts of Dian's company.

17

Shortly unto the wasteful° woods she came,　　*desolate*
　　Whereas° she found the goddess with her crew,°　　*Where company*
After late chase of their imbrued° game,　　*bloody*
　　Sitting beside a fountain in a row –
Some of them washing with the liquid dew
From off their dainty limbs the dusty sweat
　　And soil which did deform° their lively° hue;°　　*disfigure natural colour*
Others lay shaded from the scorching heat;
The rest upon her person gave attendance great.

18

She, having hung upon a bough on high
　　Her bow and painted quiver, had unlaced
Her silver buskins° from her nimble thigh,　　*knee-high boots*
　　And her lank° loins° ungirt, and breasts unbraced,°　　*slim waist loosened*
After her heat the breathing cold to taste.
Her golden locks – that late° in tresses bright　　*recently*
　　Embraided° were for hindering of° her haste –　　*Plaited** *in order not to impede*

Now loose about her shoulders hung undight,°   *disarrayed*
And were with sweet ambrosia all besprinkled light.°   *lightly*

19

Soon as she Venus saw behind her back
  She was ashamed to be so loose° surprised,   *ungirt*
  And wox° half wroth against her damsels slack   *grew*
  That had not her thereof before advised,
  But suffered her so carelessly disguised°   *transformed*
  Be overtaken. Soon her garments loose
  Upgathering in her bosom she comprised°   *laid hold of**
  Well as she might, and to the goddess rose,
Whiles all her nymphs did like a garland her enclose.

20

Goodly° she 'gan fair Cytherea greet,   *Pleasantly*
  And shortly° asked her what cause her   *quickly; concisely*
    brought
  Into that wilderness, for her unmeet,°   *unsuited*
  From her sweet bowers° and beds with pleasures   *chambers*
    fraught° –   *filled*
  That sudden change she strange adventure°   *occurrence*
    thought.
  To whom, half-weeping, she thus answered
  That she her dearest son Cupido sought
  Who, in his frowardness,° from her was fled;   *perverseness*
That she repented sore to have him angered.

21

Thereat Diana 'gan to smile in scorn
  Of her vain° plaint,° and to her, scoffing, said: *idle lament*
  'Great pity, sure, that ye be so forlorn°   *forsaken*
  Of° your gay° son that gives ye so good   *By immoral;† merry*
    aid
  To your disports: ill mote ye been
    apaid.'°   *i.e., you must be badly displeased*
  But she was more engrieved,° and replied: *vexed*
  'Fair sister, ill beseems it° to upbraid   *it is inappropriate*
  A doleful heart with so disdainful pride:
The like that mine, may be your pain another tide.°   *time*

22

'As you in woods and wanton° wilderness   *luxuriant*
  Your glory set° to chase° the savage°   *place in chasing wild*
    beasts,
  So my delight is all in joyfulness –
  In beds, in bowers, in banquets and in feasts;
  And ill becomes you, with your lofty° crests,°   *proud heads*
  To scorn the joy that Jove is glad to seek.
  We both are bound to follow heaven's behests,
  And tend our charges with obeisance° meek: *obedience*
Spare, gentle sister, with reproach my pain to eke,°   *augment*

23

'And tell me if that ye my son have heard
  To lurk amongst your nymphs in secret wise,°   *fashion*
  Or keep° their cabins.° Much am I   *dwell in rooms;*† *huts*
    afeared
  Lest he like one of them himself disguise
  And turn his arrows to their exercise –
  So may he long himself full easy° hide,°   *very easily*
  For he is fair and fresh in face and guise°   *aspect*
  As any nymph (let it not be envied).'°   *begrudged*
So saying, every nymph full narrowly she eyed.

24

But Phoebe therewith sore° was angered,   *grievously*
  And sharply said: 'Go, dame – go seek your boy
  Where you him left, in Mars's bed.
  He comes not here – we scorn his foolish joy,
  Ne° lend we leisure to his idle toy.°   *Neither love-games*
  But if I catch him in this company,
  By Stygian lake I vow – whose sad° annoy°   *great discomfort*
  The gods do dread – he dearly shall aby:°   *endure**
I'll clip his wanton wings that° he no more shall fly.'   *so that*

25

Whom whenas Venus saw so sore displeased,
  She inly° sorry was and 'gan relent   *inwardly; extremely*
  What she had said: so her she soon appeased

With sugared words and gentle blandishment°   *flattery*
Which, as a fountain, from her sweet lips went
And welled goodly forth that,° in short space,   *so that*
She was well pleased and forth her damsels sent
Through all the woods to search from place to place
If any track of him or tidings they mote° trace.   *might*

26

To search° the god of love her nymphs she sent   *seek*
  Throughout the wandering forest everywhere;
  And after them herself eke with her went
  To seek the fugitive both far and near.
  So long they sought till they arrived were
  In that same shady covert whereas° lay   *where*
  Fair Chrysogone in slumbery trance whilere° –   *previously*
  Who, in her sleep (a wondrous thing to say),
Unwares had born two babes as fair as springing° day. *dawning*

27

Unwares she them conceived, unwares she bore:
  She bore withouten pain that° she conceived   *that which*
  Withouten pleasure – ne her° need implore   *neither did she*
  Lucina's aid. Which, when they both perceived,
  They were through wonder nigh° of sense bereaved   *almost*
  And, gazing each on other, nought bespake.°   *spoke†*
  At last they both agreed, her seeming grieved,
  Out of her heavy swoon not to awake
But from her loving side the tender babes to take.

28

Up they them took – each one a babe uptook –
  And with them carried to be fostered.
  Dame Phoebe to a nymph her babe betook
  To be upbrought in perfect maidenhead,°   *maidenhood*
  And of herself her name Belphoebe read;°   *named**
  But Venus hers thence far away conveyed
  To be upbrought in goodly womanhead,°   *womanhood*
  And in her little love's stead, which was strayed,
Her Amoret called, to comfort her dismayed.

29

She brought her to her joyous paradise
  Where most she wones° when she on earth does   *inhabits*
    dwell –
  So fair a place as Nature can devise:
  Whether in Paphos, or Cytheron hill,
  Or it in Gnidus be, I wote° not well.   *know*
  But well I wote by trial that this same
  All other pleasant° places doth excel,   *delightful*
  And called is by her lost lover's name
The Garden of Adonis, far renowned by fame.

30

In that same garden all the goodly° flowers   *lovely*
  Wherewith Dame Nature doth her
      beautify,°   *adorn; make beautiful*
  And decks the garlands of her paramours,°   *lovers*
  Are fetched. There is the first seminary°   *seed-plot*†
  Of all things that are born to live and die
  According to their kinds.° Long work it were   *natures; species*
  Here to account° the endless progeny   *recount*
  Of all the weeds° that bud and blossom there: *plants*
But so much as doth need must needs be counted° here.   *related*

31

It sited was in fruitful soil of old,°   *long ago*
  And girt in with two walls on either side,
  The one of iron, the other of bright gold,
  That° none might through break nor overstride.   *So that*
  And double gates it had which opened wide
  By which both in and out men moten° pass –   *might*
  The one fair and fresh, the other old and dried.
  Old Genius the porter of them was –
Old Genius, the which a double nature has.

32

He letteth in, he letteth out to wend°   *travel*
  All that to come into the world desire:
  A thousand thousand naked babes attend
  About him day and night, which do require°   *request*

That he with fleshly weeds° would them   *clothing [i.e., flesh]*
      attire.
Such as him list,° such as eternal Fate   *pleases*
Ordained hath, he clothes with sinful mire
And sendeth forth to live in mortal state
Till they again return back by the hinder gate.

33

After that they again returned been,
      They in that garden planted be again
      And grow afresh, as° they had never seen   *as if*
      Fleshly corruption nor mortal pain.
      Some thousand years so° doen° they there remain,   *thus do*
      And then of° him are clad with other hue,°   *by shape*
      Or° sent into the changeful world again   *Before [being]*
      Till thither they return where first they grew:
So like a wheel around they run from old to new.

34

Ne° needs there gardener to set or sow,   *Nor*
      To plant or prune for, of their own accord,
      All things as they created were do grow,
      And yet remember well the mighty word
      Which first was spoken by the Almighty Lord
      That bade them to increase and multiply.
      Ne do they need with water of the ford°   *stream*
      Or of the clouds to moisten their roots dry,
For in themselves eternal moisture they imply.°   *are full up with†*

35

Infinite shapes of creatures there are bred,
      And uncouth° forms which none yet ever knew,   *strange*
      And every sort is in a sundry° bed   *separate*
      Set by itself and ranked in comely° row: *decorous; seemly*
      Some fit for reasonable° souls to endue,°   *rational put on†*
      Some made for beasts, some made for birds to wear,
      And all the fruitful spawn of fishes' hue°   *shape*
      In endless ranks along enranged° were   *arranged†*
That seemed the ocean could not contain them there.

36

Daily they grow, and daily forth are sent
  Into the world it to replenish more:
  Yet is the stock° not lessened, nor spent,   *source; store*
  But still remains in everlasting store°   *abundance*
  As it at first created was of yore.
  For in the wide womb of the world there lies,
  In hateful darkness and in deep horror,
  An huge eternal Chaos which supplies
The substances of Nature's fruitful progenies.

37

All things from thence do their first being fetch
  And borrow matter, whereof they are made,
  Which, whenas° form and feature° it does   *when shape*
    catch,°   *assume*
  Becomes a body and doth then invade°   *enter*†
  The state of life out of the grisly° shade.   *horrible*
  That substance is etern', and bideth° so;   *remains*
  Ne when the life decays and form does fade
  Doth it consume° and into nothing go,   *evaporate*
But changed is, and often altered to and fro.

38

The substance is not changed nor altered,
  But the only° form and outward fashion;°   *only the shape*
  For every substance is conditioned°   *given the nature*†
  To change her hue° and sundry forms to don,° *aspect assume*
  Meet° for her temper° and   *Suitable disposition*
    complexion.°   *constitution*
  For forms are variable, and decay
  By course of kind° and by occasion,   *nature*
  And that fair flower of beauty fades away
As doth the lily fresh before the sunny ray.

39

Great enemy to it and to all the rest
  That in the Garden of Adonis springs°   *grows*
  Is wicked Time, who, with his scythe addressed,° *equipped*
  Does mow the flowering herbs and goodly° things *splendid*
  And all their glory to the ground down flings,

Where they do wither and are foully marred.
He flies about and, with his flaggy° wings,   *drooping;‡ flaglike‡*
Beats down both leaves and buds without regard,
Ne ever pity may relent° his malice hard.   *make relent*

40

Yet pity often did the gods relent
   To see so° fair things marred and spoiled quite,   *such*
   And their great mother, Venus, did lament
   The loss of her dear brood,° her dear delight: *offspring*
   Her heart was pierced with pity at the sight
   When, walking through the garden, them she spied,
   Yet n'ote° she find redress for such   *knew not how to*
     despite.°   *malice*
For all that lives is subject to that law:
All things decay in time, and to their end do draw.

41

But were it not that Time their troubler is,
   All that in this delightful garden grows
   Should happy be and have immortal bliss:
   For here all plenty and all pleasure flows,
   And sweet love gentle fits° amongst them   *moments of passion*
     throws
   Without fell° rancour or fond° jealousy.   *cruel   foolish*
   Frankly° each paramour his leman°   *Freely   beloved*
     knows,°   *possesses*
   Each bird his mate, ne any does envy°   *neither does any begrudge*
Their goodly merriment and gay° felicity.   *merry*

42

There is continual spring, and harvest° there   *i.e., autumn*
   Continual, both meeting at one time;
   For both the boughs do° laughing   *i.e., the boughs do both*
     blossoms bare
   And with fresh colours deck the wanton°   *frolicsome*
     prime;°   *spring*
   And eke° at once° the heavy trees they   *also   at the same time*
     climb
   Which seem to labour under their fruits' load –
   The whiles the joyous birds make their pastime

Amongst the shady leaves (their sweet abode)
And their true loves without suspicion tell abroad.

43

Right in the middest of that paradise
  There stood a stately mount, on whose round top
  A gloomy grove of myrtle trees did rise,
  Whose shady boughs sharp steel did never lop,
  Nor wicked beasts their tender buds did crop,
  But, like a garland, compassed° the height   *encircled*
  And, from their fruitful sides, sweet gum did drop
  That° all the ground, with precious dew   *So that*
    bedight,°   *bedecked*
Threw forth most dainty odours and most sweet delight.

44

And in the thickest covert of that shade
  There was a pleasant arbour – not by art,
  But of the trees' own inclination° made,   *bending; disposition*
  Which, knitting their rank° branches part to part,   *crowded*
  With wanton° ivy twine entrailed°   *dense; lustful entwined*‡
    athwart°   *across*
  And eglantine and caprifole° among,   *honeysuckle*
  Fashioned above within their inmost part,
  That° neither Phoebus' beams could through them   *So that*
    throng°   *press*
Nor Aeolus' sharp blast could work them any wrong.

45

And all about grew every sort of flower
  To which sad lovers were transformed of yore:
  Fresh° Hyacinthus (Phoebus' paramour   *Young*
  And dearest love);
  Foolish Narciss' that likes the watery shore;
  Sad Amaranthus, made a flower but late –
  Sad Amaranthus, in whose purple gore
  Meseems I see Amintas' wretched fate,
To whom sweet poet's verse hath given endless
    date.°   *immortality*

46

There wont° fair Venus often to enjoy   *was accustomed*
  Her dear Adonis' joyous company,
  And reap sweet pleasure of the wanton boy:
  There yet, some say, in secret he does lie,
  Lapped° in flowers and precious spicery,°   *Enclosed spices*
  By her hid from the world, and from the skill°   *knowledge*
  Of Stygian gods, which do her love envy:
  But she herself, whenever that she will,
Possesseth him and of his sweetness takes her fill.

47

And sooth° it seems they say – for he may not   *truth*
  For ever die and ever buried be
  In baleful° night, where all things are forgot: *deadly*
  Albe he° subject to mortality,   *Although he is*
  Yet is etern' in mutability
  And by succession made perpetual –
  Transformed oft, and changed diversely;°   *variously*
  For him the Father of all Forms they call:
Therefore needs mote° he live, that living gives to all.   *must*

48

There now he liveth in eternal bliss,
  Joying° his goddess and of her enjoyed,   *Enjoying*
  Ne feareth he henceforth that foe of his
  Which with his cruel tusk him deadly cloyed;°   *pierced;† gored†*
  For that wild boar, the which him once annoyed,°   *injured*
  She firmly hath imprisoned for aye
  (That° her sweet love his malice mote° avoid)   *So that may*
  In a strong rocky cave which is, they say,
Hewn underneath that mount, that none him loosen may.

49

There now he lives in everlasting joy
  With many of the gods in company
  Which thither haunt, and with the winged boy°   *i.e., Cupid*
  Sporting himself in safe felicity –
  Who, when he hath with spoils and cruelty
  Ransacked the world, and in the woeful hearts
  Of many wretches set his triumphs high,

Thither resorts and, laying his sad° darts   *sorrow-inducing*
Aside, with fair Adonis plays his wanton parts.

50

And his true love, fair Psyche, with him plays –
 Fair Psyche, to him lately° reconciled   *recently*
 After long troubles and unmeet°   *inappropriate*
  upbrays°   *upbraidings†*
 With which his mother Venus her reviled
 And eke himself her cruelly exiled.
 But now in steadfast love and happy state
 She with him lives, and hath him born a child,
 Pleasure, that doth both gods and men aggrate° –   *gratify†*
Pleasure, the daughter of Cupid and Psyche
  late.°   *i.e., recent daughter*

51

Hither great Venus brought this infant fair,
 The younger daughter of Chrysogone,
 And unto Psyche with great trust and care
 Committed her yfostered to be,
 And trained up in true femininity:
 Who no less carefully her tendered°   *cherished*
 Than her own daughter, Pleasure, to whom she
 Made her companion, and her lessoned°   *instructed‡*
In all the lore° of love and goodly   *doctrine*
  womanhead.°   *womanhood*

52

In which, when she to perfect ripeness grew
 Of grace and beauty noble paragon,°   *pattern‡*
 She brought her forth into the world's view
 To be the example of true love alone,
 And loadstar of all chaste affection,
 To all fair ladies that do live on ground.°   *earth*
 To fairy court she came, where many one
 Admired her goodly haviour,° and found   *bearing*
His feeble heart wide-launched° with love's cruel   *deeply pierced*
  wound.

53

But she to none of them her love did cast°   *bestow*†
  Save to the noble knight Sir Scudamour,
  To whom her loving heart she linked fast°   *firmly*
  In faithful love to abide for evermore,
  And for his dearest sake endured sore°   *extremely*
  Sore° trouble of° an heinous enemy   *Severe from*
  Who her would forced have to have forlore°   *deserted**
  Her former love and steadfast loyalty,
As ye may elsewhere read that rueful history.

54

But well I ween° ye first desire to learn   *believe*
  What end unto that fearful damosel
  (Which fled so fast from that same foster° stern° *forester cruel*
  Whom with his brethren Timias slew)° *overcame with affliction**
    befell:
  That was to weet° the goodly Florimell   *indeed*
  Who, wandering for to seek her lover dear –
  Her lover dear, her dearest Marinell –
  Into misfortune fell, as ye did hear,
And from Prince Arthur fled with wings of idle° *unnecessary*
    fear.

Canto 7

The witch's son loves Florimell:
    She flies, he fains° to die.   *wishes*
Satyrane saves the Squire of Dames
    From giant's tyranny.

1

Like as an hind forth singled from the herd,
  That hath escaped from a ravenous beast,
  Yet flies away, of her own feet affeared,°   *frightened*
  And every leaf that shaketh with the least
  Murmur of wind her terror hath increased –
  So fled fair Florimell from her vain° fear   *foolish*

Long after she from peril was released:
Each shade° she saw, and each noise she did hear,　　　*shadow*
Did seem to be the same which she escaped whilere.°　　*formerly*

2

All that same evening she in flying spent,
　　And all that night her course continued.
　　Ne° did she let dull sleep once to relent,°　　　*Neither lessen*‡
　　Nor weariness to slack her haste; but fled
　　Ever alike, as if her former dread
　　Were hard° behind, her ready to arrest.°　　　　*close capture*
　　And her white palfrey, having conquered°　*succeeded in gaining**
　　The mastering reins out of her weary wrist,
Perforce° her carried wherever he thought best.　　　*Forcibly*

3

So long as breath and able° puissance°　　　*sufficient strength*
　　Did native courage unto him supply,
　　His pace he freshly° forward did advance　　*eagerly; briskly*
　　And carried her beyond all jeopardy –
　　But nought that wanteth° rest can long aby:°　*lacks endure**
　　He, having through incessant travel spent
　　His force, at last perforce° adown did lie,　　　*of necessity*
　　Ne° foot could further move. The lady gent°　　*Nor noble*
Thereat was sudden struck with great
　　astonishment°　　　　　　　　　　　　　　*consternation*‡

4

And, forced to alight, on foot mote°　　　　　　　　*must*
　　algates° fare,　　　　　　　　　　　　　　*continually**
　　A traveller unwonted° to such way.　　　　*unaccustomed*
　　Need teacheth her this lesson hard and rare,°　　*exceptional*
　　That Fortune all in equal launce° doth sway°　*balance*‡ *incline*‡
　　And mortal miseries doth make her play.
　　So long she travelled till at length she came
　　To an hillside, which did to her bewray°　　　　*disclose*
　　A little valley, subject to° the same,　　　　*lying under*‡
All covered with thick woods that quite it overcame.°　*covered*

5

Through the tops of the high trees she did descry
    A little smoke, whose vapour thin and light,
    Reeking° aloft, uprolled to the sky —   *Emanating**
    Which cheerful sign did send unto her sight
    That in the same did wone° some living
        wight.°   *dwell*
                                                              *creature**
    Eftsoons° her steps she thereunto applied,°   *At once   directed*
    And came at last in weary, wretched plight
    Unto the place, to which her hope did guide,
To find some refuge there and rest her weary side.

6

There in a gloomy hollow glen she found
    A little cottage built of sticks and reeds
    In homely wise,° and walled with sods around,   *fashion*
    In which a witch did dwell, in loathly weeds°   *clothes*
    And wilful° want,° all careless of her   *deliberate   deprivation*
        needs,
    So choosing solitary to abide
    Far from all neighbours that° her devilish deeds   *So that*
    And hellish arts from people she might hide,
And hurt far off unknown whomever she
        envied.°
                                                    had a grudge against

7

The damsel, there arriving, entered in,
    Where, sitting on the floor, the hag she found,
    Busy (as seemed) about some wicked gin;°   *stratagem*
    Who, soon as she beheld that sudden°   *stupefying*
        stound,°
                                                              arrival
    Lightly° upstarted from the dusty ground,   *Quickly*
    And with fell° look and hollow, deadly gaze,   *fierce*
    Stared on her awhile as one astound° —   *stunned**
    Ne° had one word to speak for great   *Nor*
        amaze,°
                                                              astonishment
But showed by outward signs that dread her sense did daze.

8

At last, turning her fear to foolish wrath,
　She asked what devil had her thither brought,
　　And who she was, and what unwonted° path　　　　*unused*
　　Had guided her, unwelcomed, unsought?
　　To which the damsel, full of doubtful°　　　　*fearful; doubting*
　　　thought,
　　Her mildly answered: 'Beldame,° be not wroth　*Good mother*
　　With silly° virgin, by adventure° brought　　*helpless‡　chance*
　　Unto your dwelling, ignorant° and loath,°　*innocent　reluctant*
That crave but room to rest while° tempest overbloweth.'　*until*

9

With that, adown out of her crystal eyen,°　　　　　　*eyes*
　Few° trickling tears she softly forth let fall　　　*A few*
　　That like two orient° pearls did purely shine　　*brilliant*
　　Upon her snowy cheek. And therewithal°　*along with them*
　　She sighed soft that none so bestial,
　　Nor savage heart, but ruth° of her sad plight　　*pity*
　　Would make to melt or piteously appal:°　*dismay with pity*
　　And that vile hag – all were her whole delight
In mischief° – was much moved at so piteous sight,　　*harm*

10

And 'gan recomfort° her in her rude°　　　　*comfort　rough*
　　wise°　　　　　　　　　　　　　　　　　　　*fashion*
　With womanish compassion of her plaint,°　　　*lament*
　　Wiping the tears from her suffused° eyes　*filled with water‡*
　　And bidding her sit down to rest her faint
　　And weary limbs a while. She, nothing quaint°　　*dainty*
　　Nor 'sdainful° of so homely fashion　　　　*disdainful*
　　(Sith° brought she was now to so hard　　　*Since*
　　　constraint)°　　　　　　　　　　　　　　*distress**
　　Sat down upon the grassy ground anon,°　*immediately**
As glad of that small rest as bird of tempest gone.

11

Tho° 'gan she gather up her garments rent,　　　　*Then*
　And her loose locks to dight° in order due　*prepare; dress*
　　With golden wreath and gorgeous ornament;
　　Whom such whenas the wicked hag did view,

She was astonished at her heavenly hue,°   *appearance*
And doubted her to deem° an earthly wight,   *to judge her*
But or° some goddess or of Diana's crew,°   *either company*
And thought her to adore with humble sprite:°   *spirit; mind*
To adore thing so divine as beauty were but right.

12

This wicked woman had a wicked son,
The comfort of her age and weary days,
A lazy lourd,° for nothing good to done,°   *lout† do*
But stretched forth in idleness always,
Ne° ever cast° his mind to covet praise,   *Nor set*
Or ply° himself to any honest trade;   *apply*
But all the day before the sunny rays
He used to slug° or sleep in slothful shade: *lie idly*
Such laziness both lewd° and poor at once him   *ignorant; lustful*
    made.

13

He, coming home at undertime,° there found   *midday**
The fairest creature that he ever saw,
Sitting beside his mother on the ground,
The sight whereof did greatly him adaw,°   *daunt†*
And his base thought with terror and with awe
So inly smote that – as one which had gazed
On the bright sun unwares doth soon withdraw
His feeble eyen,° with too much brightness dazed –   *eyes*
So stared he on her, and stood long while amazed.

14

Softly at last he 'gan his mother ask
What mister wight° that was, and whence   *manner of creature**
    derived,
That in so strange disguisement° there did   *disguise†*
  mask,°   *conceal herself†*
And by what accident° she there arrived.   *chance*
But she, as one nigh of her wits deprived,
With nought but ghastly° looks him answered,   *terrified*
Like to a ghost that lately° is revived   *recently*
From Stygian shores where late it wandered:
So both at her, and at each other, wondered.

15

But the fair virgin was so meek and mild
    That she to them vouchsafed to embase°   *humble*
    Her goodly° port,° and to their senses   *fine bearing*
        vild°   *vile; base*
    Her gentle speech applied that° in short space   *so that*
    She grew familiar° in that   *part of family; witch's companion*
        desert place.
    During which time the churl, through her so kind
    And courteous use,° conceived affection   *treatment [of him]*
        base,
    And cast° to love her in his brutish mind: *determined*
No love, but brutish lust that was so beastly tined.°   *kindled*

16

Closely° the wicked flame his bowels brent,°   *Secretly burnt*
    And shortly grew into outrageous° fire;   *violent*
    Yet had he not the heart, nor hardiment,°   *boldness*
    As unto her to utter his desire.
    His caitiff° thought durst not so high aspire,   *base*
    But with soft sighs and lovely semblances°   *shows of love*
    He weened° that his affection entire°   *believed heartfelt*
    She should aread.° Many   *guess*
        resemblances°   *shows of affection*‡
To her he made, and many kind°   *loving*
        remembrances.°   *keepsakes*

17

Oft from the forest wildings° he did bring,   *wild fruit*‡
    Whose sides empurpled° were with smiling red;   *reddened*†
    And oft young birds, which he had taught to sing
    His mistress' praises, sweetly carolled;
    Garlands of flowers sometimes for her fair head
    He fine° would dight,° sometimes the   *delicately prepare*
        squirrel wild
    He brought to her in bands,° as   *cage?; lead and collar?*
        conquered
    To be her thrall, his fellow servant vild:°   *lowly*
All which she of him took with countenance meek and mild.

18

But past awhile,° when she fit season° saw — *after a while   time*
  To leave that desert mansion,° she cast° — *dwelling   resolved*
  In secret wise° herself thence to withdraw, — *manner*
  For fear of mischief° which she did forecast° — *harm   anticipate*
  Might be by the witch or by her son compassed.° — *devised*
  Her weary palfrey closely° as she might — *secretly*
  (Now well recovered after long repast)° — *rest‡*
  In his proud furniture° she freshly dight,° — *trappings   dressed*
His late miswandered° ways now to — *gone astray†*
  remeasure° right, — *retrace†*

19

And early, ere the dawning day appeared,
  She forth issued and on her journey went.
  She went in peril, of each noise afeared,° — *frightened*
  And of each shade° that did itself present; — *shadow*
  For still° she feared to be overhent° — *ever   overtaken**
  Of° that vile hag or her uncivil° son, — *By rough;†   barbarous‡*
  Who when, too late awaking, well they kent° — *knew*
  That their fair guest was gone, they both begun
To make exceeding moan, as° they had been undone. — *as if*

20

But that lewd lover did the most lament
  For her depart° that ever man did hear: — *departure*
  He knocked his breast with desperate intent,
  And scratched his face, and with his teeth did tear
  His rugged° flesh, and rent his ragged hair, — *shaggy; rough*
  That° his sad mother, seeing his sore° plight, — *So that   grievous*
  Was greatly woebegone, and 'gan to fear
  Lest his frail senses were emperished° quite, — *enfeebled‡**
And love to frenzy turned, sith° love is frantic — *since*
  hight.° — *called*†*

21

All ways she sought, him to restore to plight,° — *health*
  With herbs, with charms, with counsel, and with tears;
  But tears, nor charms, nor herbs, nor counsel might
  Assuage the fury° which his entrails tears: — *possession by love*
  So strong is passion, that no reason hears.° — *i.e., it will hear no*

Tho,° when all other helps she saw to fail,   *Then*
  She turned herself back to her wicked lears,°   *doctrines*
  And by her devilish arts thought to prevail
To bring her back again, or work her final bale.°   *death*

22

Eftsoons° out of her hidden cave she called   *Forthwith*
  An hideous beast of horrible aspect
  That could the stoutest° courage have   *bravest*
    appalled,°   *dismayed*
  Monstrous° misshaped, and all his back was   *Monstrously*
    specked
  With thousand spots of colours quaint°   *cunningly*
    elect;°   *chosen*
  Thereto° so swift that it all beasts did   *In addition*
    pass.°   *surpass*
  Like never yet did living eye detect,
  But likest it to an hyena was
That feeds on women's flesh as others feed on grass.

23

It forth she called, and gave it straight° in charge   *strictly*
  Through thick and thin her to pursue apace,
  Ne° once to stay and rest, or breathe at large,°   *Nor at leisure*
  Till her he had attained and brought in place°   *thither*
  Or quite devoured her beauty's scornful grace.
  The monster, swift as word that from her went,
  Went forth in haste, and did her footing°   *footprints*
    trace°   *track*
  So sure and swiftly through his perfect scent
And passing speed, that shortly he her overhent.°   *overtook**

24

Whom when the fearful damsel nigh espied,
  No need to bid her fast away to fly –
  That ugly shape so sore her terrified
  That it she shunned no less than dread to die,
  And her flit° palfrey did so well apply°   *swift adapt*
  His nimble feet to her conceived° fear   *understood*
  That, whilst his breath did strength to him supply,

From peril free he her away did bear.
But when his force 'gan fail, his pace 'gan wex
    arrear;°   *lag behind*

25

Which, whenas° she perceived, she was dismayed   *when*
    At that same last extremity full° sore,°   *most grievously*
    And of her safety greatly grew afraid.
    And now she 'gan approach to the sea shore
    As it befell, that° she could flee no more   *so that*
    But yield herself to spoil° of greediness.   *spoliation*
    Lightly° she leaped, as a wight°   *Swiftly   creature**
      forlore,°   *ruined; lost**
    From her dull° horse in desperate distress,   *sluggish*
And to her feet betook her doubtful sickerness.° *safety;* security**

26

Not half so fast the wicked Myrrha fled
    From dread of her revenging father's hond;°   *hand*
    Nor half so fast to save her maidenhead
    Fled fearful Daphne on the Aegean strond,°   *strand*
    As Florimell fled from that monster yond°   *furious;[†] yonder*
    To reach the sea, ere she of him were raught,°   *seized; raped*
    For in the sea to drown herself she fond°   *intended*
    Rather than of° the tyrant to be caught: *by*
Thereto fear gave her wings, and need her courage taught.

27

It fortuned (high God did so ordain),
    As she arrived on the roaring shore
    In mind to leap into the mighty main,
    A little boat lay hoving° her before,   *at anchor;[‡]* floating**
    In which there slept a fisher old and poor
    The whiles his nets were drying on the sand.
    Into the same she leaped, and with the oar
    Did thrust the shallop° from the floating   *boat[†]*
      strand° –   *shore where it floated*
So safety found at sea which she found not at land.

28

The monster, ready on the prey to seize,
  Was of his forward° hope deceived°   *almost achieved cheated*
    quite,°   *utterly*
  Ne durst° assay° to wade the perilous seas   *dared attempt*
  But, greedily long gaping at the sight,
  At last in vain was forced to turn his flight
  And tell the idle° tidings to the dame.   *useless; unwelcome*
  Yet, to avenge his devilish despite,°   *malice*
  He set upon her palfrey tired, lame,
And slew him cruelly ere any rescue came.

29

And after having him embowelled°   *disembowelled*
  To fill his hellish gorge, it chanced a knight
  To pass that way as forth he travelled.
  It was a goodly swain, and of great might
  As ever man that bloody field did fight;
  But in vain shows (that wont° young knights   *customarily*
    bewitch)
  And courtly service took no delight,
  But rather joyed° to be, than seemen, such,   *rejoiced*
For both to be and seem to him was labour like.°   *equal*

30

It was, to weet,° the good Sir Satyrane   *indeed*
  That ranged abroad to seek adventures wild,
  As was his wont° in forest and in plain: *custom*
  He was all armed in rugged° steel unfiled   *rough*
  As in the smoky forge it was compiled,°   *constructed†*
  And in his scutcheon° bore a satyr's head.   *shield*
  He, coming present where the monster vild°   *brutish*
  Upon that milk-white palfrey's carcase fed,
Unto his rescue ran and greedily him sped.°   *dispatched*

31

There well perceived he that it was the horse
  Whereon fair Florimell was wont° to ride   *accustomed*
  That of° that fiend was rent without remorse: *by*
  Much feared he lest aught did ill betide°   *befall*
  To that fair maid, the flower of women's pride;

For he her dearly loved, and in all
  His famous conquests highly magnified.°   *glorified; praised*
Besides, her golden girdle, which did fall
From her in flight, he found, that did him sore°   *grievously*
    appall.°   *dismay*

32

Full of sad° fear and doubtful° agony   *heavy fearful*
  Fiercely he flew upon that wicked fiend,
  And with huge strokes and cruel battery
  Him forced to leave his prey for to° attend   *in order to*
  Himself from deadly danger to defend:
  Full many wounds in his corrupted flesh
  He did engrave,° and muchell° blood did   *cut much**
    spend° –   *spill*
  Yet might not do him° die, but aye more fresh   *cause him to*
And fierce he still appeared the more he did him thresh.° *thrash*

33

He wist° not how him to despoil of life,   *knew*
  Ne how to win the wished victory,
  Sith° him he saw still stronger grow through strife   *Since*
  And himself weaker through infirmity.
  Greatly he grew enraged and, furiously
  Hurling his sword away, he lightly° leaped   *swiftly*
  Upon the beast that with great cruelty
  Roared and raged to be underkept:
Yet he perforce° him held, and strokes upon him   *forcibly*
    heaped.

34

As he that strives to stop a sudden flood,
  And in strong banks his violence enclose,
  Forceth it swell above his wonted°   *customary*
    mood°   *disposition*
  And largely overflow the fruitful plain
  That° all the country seems to be a main,°   *So that sea*
  And the rich furrows float,° all quite°   *flood utterly*
    fordone:°   *desolate*
  The woeful husbandman doth loud complain

To see his whole year's labour lost so soon,
For which to God he made so many an idle boon;°   *prayer*

35

So him he held, and did thtough right amate.°   *cast down*
  So long he held him, and him beat so long,
  That at the last his fierceness 'gan abate
  And meekly stoop° unto the victor strong –   *yield*
  Who, to avenge the implacable° wrong   *unappeasable*
  Which he supposed done to Florimell,
  Sought by all means his dolour° to prolong   *pain*
Sith° dint° of steel his carcase could not quell° *Since blow kill*
(His maker with her charms had framed° him so well).   *made*

36

The golden riband which that virgin wore
  About her slender waist he took in hand,
  And with it bound the beast, that loud did roar
  For great despite° of that unwonted°   *disdain unaccustomed*
    band,
  Yet dared not his victor to withstand,
  But trembled like a lamb fled from the prey,°   *capture*
  And all the way him followed on the strand°   *shore*
  As he had long been learned° to obey –   *taught*
Yet never learned he such service till that day.

37

Thus as he led the beast along the way
  He spied far off a mighty giantess,
  Fast flying on a courser dappled grey
  From a bold knight that, with great hardiness,°   *bravery*
  Her hard pursued and sought for to suppress.°   *vanquish*
  She bore before her lap a doleful squire
  Lying athwart her horse in great distress,
  Fast bounden hand and foot with cords of wire,
Whom she did mean to make the thrall of her desire.

38

Which, whenas Satyrane beheld, in haste
  He left his captive beast at liberty,
  And crossed the nearest way by which he cast°   *determined*

Her to encounter ere she passed by:
But she the way shunned nathemore for-
   thy°   *not at all because of that*
But forward galloped fast; which, when he spied,
His mighty spear he couched° warily,   *levelled*
And at her ran. She, having him descried,
Herself to fight addressed and threw her load aside.

39

Like as a goshawk that in foot doth bear
  A trembling culver,° having spied on height°   *dove high*
  An eagle that with plumy wings doth shear°   *cleave*
  The subtle° air, stooping with all his might   *thin*
  The quarry° throws to ground with fell° despite *prey fierce*
  And to the battle doth herself prepare:
  So ran the giantess unto the fight –
  Her fiery eyes with furious sparks did stare°   *glare*
And with blasphemous bans° high God in pieces tear.   *curses*[†]

40

She caught in hand an huge great iron mace,
  Wherewith she many had of life deprived;
  But ere the stroke could seize his° aimed place   *its*
  His spear amids° her sun-broad shield arrived, *in the centre of*
  Yet nathemore° the steel asunder rived° *not at all split*
  (All were the beam° in bigness like *Even though the shaft was*
    a mast),
  Ne° her out of the steadfast saddle drived° *Nor drove*
  But, glancing on the tempered metal, brast°   *broke*
In thousand shivers,° and so forth beside her passed. *splinters*

41

Her steed did stagger with that puissant stroke,
  But she no more was moved with that might°   *force*
  Than it had lighted on an aged oak,
  Or on the marble pillar that is pight°   *erected*
  Upon the top of Mount Olympus' height
  For the brave youthly champions to assay°   *attempt*
  With burning chariot wheels it nigh° to smite *nearly*
  (But who that smites it mars his joyous play
And is the spectacle of ruinous decay).°   *destruction*

42

Yet therewith sore° enraged, with stern°   *extremely   fierce*
   regard°   *look*
  Her dreadful weapon she to him addressed,°   *aimed*
  Which on his helmet martelled° so hard   *hammered*[t]
  That made him low incline his lofty crest
  And bowed his battered visor to his breast:
  Wherewith he was so stunned that he n'ote° ride,   *could not*
  But reeled to and fro from east to west;
  Which, when his cruel enemy espied,
She lightly° unto him adjoined side to side   *swiftly; wantonly*

43

And, on his collar laying puissant hand,
  Out of his wavering seat him plucked perforce° –   *forcibly*
  Perforce him plucked, unable to withstand
  Or help himself – and, laying thwart her horse
  In loathly wise like to a carrion corse,°   *dead body used as prey*
  She bore him fast away. Which, when the knight
  That her pursued, saw, with great remorse°   *pity*
  He near° was touched in his noble sprite°   *closely   mind*
And 'gan increase his speed as she increasd her flight.

44

Whom, whenas° nigh approaching she espied,   *when*
  She threw away her burden angrily;
  For she list° not the battle to abide°   *wished   await*
  But made herself more light, away to fly.
  Yet her the hardy° knight pursued so nigh°   *brave   close*
  That almost in the back he oft her strake;°   *struck*
  But still when him at hand she did espy,
  She turned, and semblance of fair fight did make;
But when he stayed, to flight again she did her take.

45

By this the good Sir Satyrane 'gan wake
  Out of his dream that did him long entrance,
  And, seeing none in place,° he 'gan to make   *before him*
  Exceeding moan, and cursed that cruel chance
  Which reft from him so fair a
    chevisance.°   *chivalric undertaking*[t]

At length he spied whereas° that woeful squire   *where*
Whom he had rescued from captivance°   *captivity*†
Of° his strong foe, lay tumbled in the mire,   *From*
Unable to arise, or hand or foot to stir.

46

To whom approaching, well he mote° perceive   *might*
In that foul plight a comely° personage°   *handsome body*
And lovely face made fit for to deceive
Frail lady's heart with love's consuming rage,
Now in the blossom of his freshest age.
He reared him up and loosed his iron bands,
And after 'gan enquire his parentage,
And how he fell into that giant's hands,
And who that was who chased her along the lands.°   *ground*

47

Then, trembling yet through fear, the squire bespake:°   *spoke*†
'That giantess Argante is behight,°   *called**†
A daughter of the Titans which did make
War against heaven, and heaped hills on height°   *high*
To scale the skies and put Jove from his right.
Her sire Typhoeus was, who, mad through mirth
And drunk with blood of men slain by his might,
Through incest her of his own mother, Earth,
Whilom° begot, being but half twin of that birth.   *Formerly**

48

'From that birth another babe she bore,
To weet° the mighty Ollyphant, that wrought   *So to say*
Great wreak° to many errant knights of yore,   *injury*
And many hath to foul° confusion° brought.   *terrible ruin*
These twins, men say (a thing for passing°   *surpassing*
  thought),
Whiles in their mother's womb enclosed they were,
Ere they into the lightsome° world were   *bright with light*
  brought
In fleshly lust were mingled° both yfere,°   *conjoined together*
And in that monstrous wise° did to the world appear.   *manner*

49

'So lived they ever after in like sin
  'Gainst Nature's law and good behaviour;
  But greatest shame was to that maiden twin
  Who, not content so foully to devour
  Her native flesh and stain° her brother's   *defile*
    bower,°   *bedchamber*
  Did wallow in all other fleshly mire,
  And suffered beasts her body to deflower:
  So hot she burned in that lustful fire,
Yet all that might not slake her sensual desire,

50

But over all the country she did range
  To seek young men to quench her flaming thirst
  And feed her fancy° with delightful change.   *imagination*
  Whom so she fittest finds to serve her lust,
  Through her main° strength (in which she most doth   *mighty*
    trust),
  She with her brings into a secret isle
  Where in eternal bondage° die he must,   *captivity*
  Or be the vassal of her pleasures vile
And all in shameful sort° himself with her defile.   *fashion*

51

'Me, seely° wretch, she so at vantage°   *miserable   her advantage*
    caught
  After she long in wait for me did lie,
  And meant unto her prison to have brought,
  Her loathsome pleasure there to satisfy,
  That thousand deaths me liever were° to   *I would [much] prefer*
    die
  Than break the vow that to fair Columbell
  I plighted have, and yet keep steadfastly –
  As for my name, it mistereth not° to tell: *is unnecessary**
Call me the Squire of Dames; that me beseemeth° well.   *suits*

52

'But that bold knight, whom ye pursuing saw,
  That giantess, is not such as she seemed,
  But a fair virgin that in martial law

And deeds of arms above all dames is deemed,°   *judged*
And above many knights is eke° esteemed   *in addition*
For her great worth. She Palladine is hight;°   *called**†
She you from death, you me from dread redeemed.
Ne any may that monster match in fight
But she, or such as she that is so chaste a wight.'°   *person**

53
'Her well beseems that quest,' quoth Satyrane,
    'But read,° thou Squire of Dames, what vow is this   *tell*
Which thou upon thyself hast lately taken?'
    'That shall I you recount,' quoth he, 'ywis,°   *indeed*
So be ye pleased to pardon all amiss.
    That gentle° lady whom I love and serve,   *noble*
After long suit and weary services
    Did ask me how I could her love deserve,
And how she might be sure that I would never swerve.°   *deviate*

54
'I, glad by any means her grace° to gain,   *favour*
    Bade her command my life to save° or spill.°   *spare   destroy*
Eftsoons° she bade me, with incessant pain   *Soon after*
    To wander through the world abroad at will,
And everywhere where, with my power or skill,
    I might do service unto° gentle dames,   *become lover to*
That I the same should faithfully fulfil,
    And at twelve months' end should bring their names
And pledges° as the spoils of my victorious   *signs of favour*
    games.

55
'So well I to fair ladies' service did,
    And found such favour in their loving hearts,
That ere the year his course has compassed,°   *completed*
    Three hundred pledges for my good deserts,
And thrice three hundred thanks for my good
    parts,°   *qualities; genitals*
I with me brought and did to her present:
    Which when she saw, more bent° to eke°   *intending   increase*
    my smarts°   *pains*

Than to reward my trusty true intent,
She 'gan for me devise a grievous punishment,

56

'To weet,° that I my travel° should resume,   *Namely   also: travail*
  And with like labour walk the world around,
  Ne ever to her presence should presume
  Till I so many other dames had found
  The which, for all the suit I could propound,
  Would me refuse their pledges to afford,
  But did abide for ever chaste and sound.'
  'Ah, gentle squire,' (quoth he) 'tell at one word,
How many foundest thou such to put in thy record?'

57

'Indeed, sir knight,' said he, 'one word may tell
  All that I ever found so wisely staid,°   *constant*
  For only three they were disposed so well;
  And yet three years I now abroad have strayed
  To find them out.' 'Mote° I,' then laughing said   *Might*
  The knight, 'enquire of thee what were those three
  The which thy proffered courtesies denied? –
  Or° ill they seemed, sure, advised to be,   *Either*
Or brutishly brought up, that never did fashions see.'

58

'The first which then refused me,' (said he)
  'Certes° was but a common courtesan –   *Truly*
  Yet flat refused to have ado with me
  Because I could not give her many a jane'°   *silver coin*
  (Thereat full heartily laughed Satyrane);
  'The second was an holy nun to choose,°   *if you please*
  Which would not let me be her chaplain
  Because she knew, she said, I would disclose°   *reveal*
Her counsel if she should her trust in me repose.

59

'The third a damsel was of low degree
  Whom I in country cottage found by chance.
  Full little weened° I that chastity   *thought*
  Had lodging in so mean a maintenance:°   *means of subsistence*

Yet was she fair, and in her countenance
Dwelt simple truth in seemly fashion.
Long thus I wooed her with due observance,
In hope unto my pleasure to have won –
But was as far at last as when I first begun.

60

'Save her I never any woman found
    That chastity did for itself embrace,
    But were for other causes firm and sound:
    Either for want° of handsome° time and   *lack convenient*
        place,
    Or else for fear and shame of foul disgrace.
    Thus am I hopeless ever to attain
    My lady's love in such a desperate case;
    But all my days am like to waste in vain,
Seeking to match the chaste with the unchaste ladies'
        train.'°   *procession*

61

'Perdy,'° said Satyrane, 'thou Squire of Dames,   *Truly*
    Great labour fondly° hast thou hent° in hand   *foolishly taken*
    To get small thanks, and therewith many blames,
    That may amongst Alcides' labours stand.'
    Thence back returning to the former land°   *region*
    Where late he left the beast he overcame,
    He found him not, for he had broke his band,
    And was returned again unto his dame
To tell what tidings of fair Florimell became.

Canto 8

The witch creates a snowy lady
  Like to Florimell,
Who, wronged by carl,° by Proteus saved,   *churl*
  Is sought by Paridell.

1

So oft as I this history record,
  My heart doth melt with mere° compassion   *utter*
  To think how, causeless° of her own   *not because*
    accord,°   *agreement*
  This gentle° damsel, whom I write upon,°   *noble about*
  Should plunged be in such affliction°   *distress*†
  Without all hope of comfort or relief,
  That° sure, I ween,° the hardest heart of stone   *So that think*
  Would hardly find° to aggravate her grief: *find it within itself*
For misery craves rather mercy than reprief.°   *reproof*

2

But that accursed hag, her hostess late,
  Had so enrankled° her malicious heart   *pained*†
  That she desired the abridgement° of her   *shortening*
    fate,°   *allotted life*
  Or long enlargement of° her painful   *release from*
    smart.°   *injury*
  Now, when the beast (which, by her wicked art,
  Late forth she sent) she back returning spied,
  Tied with her broken girdle, it a part
  Of her rich spoils whom he had erst° destroyed   *previously*
She weened,° and wondrous gladness to her heart   *thought*
    applied.

3

And with it running hastily to her son,
  Thought with that sight him much to have relieved;
  Who, thereby deeming° sure the thing as done,   *judging*
  His former grief with fury fresh revived,

Much more than erst, and would have algates° 　　altogether
　　rived° 　　　　　　　　　　　　　　　　　　torn
The heart out of his breast. For sith° her dead 　　since
He surely deemed, himself he thought deprived
Quite° of all hope, wherewith he long had fed 　　Completely
His foolish malady, and long time had misled;

4

With thought whereof exceeding mad he grew,
　　And in his rage his mother would have slain
　　Had she not fled into her secret mew° 　　　　den
Where she was wont° her sprites° to 　　accustomed　demons
　　entertain° – 　　　　　　　　　　　　　　　receive‡
The masters° of her art. There was she 　　　　instruments
　　fain° 　　　　　　　　　　　　　　　　　accustomed
To call them all in order to her aid,
And them conjure° upon eternal pain 　　　　　swear
To counsel her, so carefully° dismayed,° 　with care　overcome
How she might heal her son whose senses were decayed.

5

By their advice, and her own wicked wit,° 　　　　skill
　　She there devised a wondrous work to frame° 　　fashion
　　Whose like on earth was never framed yet,
That° even Nature self° envied the same, 　　So that　herself
And grudged to see the counterfeit should shame
The thing itself. In hand she boldly took° 　　undertook
To make another like the former dame –
Another Florimell, in shape and look
So lively° and so like° that many it mistook. 　　alive　lifelike

6

The substance whereof she the body made
　　Was purest snow in massy° mould° congealed, 　solid　shape
　　Which she had gathered in a shady glade
Of the Riphoean hills, to her revealed
By errant° sprites but from all men 　　　wicked; wandering
　　concealed.
The same she tempered with fine mercury
And virgin wax that never yet was sealed,° 　impressed upon
And mingled° them with perfect° 　　　　mixed　pure

  vermily°   *vermilion*
That like a lively sanguine° it seemed to the eye. *blood red*

7

Instead of eyes two burning lamps she set
 In silver sockets, shining like the skies,
 And a quick-moving spirit did arret°   *entrust*†
 To stir and roll them like a woman's eyes;
 Instead of yellow locks she did devise°   *contrive*
 With golden wire to weave her curled head –
 Yet golden wire was not so yellow thrice
 As Florimell's fair hair; and in the stead°   *place*
Of life she put a sprite to rule the carcase dead:

8

A wicked sprite yfraught° with fawning guile   *filled**
 And fair resemblance° above all the rest,   *appearance*
 Which with the Prince of Darkness fell
  somewhile°   *once upon a time*
 From heaven's bliss and everlasting rest.
 Him needed not instruct° which way were best *teaching*
 Himself to fashion likest Florimell,
 Ne° how to speak, ne how to use° his gest,° *Nor hold bearing*
 For he in counterfeisance° did excel,   *deceit*†
And all the wiles of women's wits knew passing° well. *extremely*

9

Him shaped thus she decked in garments gay
 Which Florimell had left behind her late,°   *recently*
 That° whoso then her saw would surely say *So that*
 It was herself whom it did imitate,
 Or fairer than herself – if aught algate°   *by any means*
 Might fairer be. And then she forth her brought
 Unto her son, that lay in feeble state –
 Who, seeing her, 'gan straight upstart, and thought
She was the lady self whom he so long had sought;

10

Tho,° fast her clipping° 'twixt his arms twain, *Then clasping*
 Extremely joyed° in so happy sight   *rejoiced*
 And soon forgot his former sickly pain.

But she, the more to seem such as she hight,°　　　*was called**†
Coyly rebutted° his embracement light,°　　　*rejected*‡* *wanton*
Yet still with gentle countenance retained,
Enough to hold a fool in vain° delight:　　　*empty*
Him long she so with shadows entertained,
As her creatress had in charge to her ordained.

11

Till on a day, as he disposed was
　　To walk the woods with that his idol fair,
　　Her to disport° and idle time to pass　　　*divert; amuse*
　　In the open freshness of the gentle air,
　　A knight that way there chanced to repair:
　　Yet knight he was not, but a boastful swain
　　That deeds of arms had ever in despair° –　　*despaired to perform*
　　Proud Braggadocchio, that in vaunting vain
His glory did repose, and credit° did maintain.　　*credibility*‡

12

He, seeing with that churl so fair a wight,°　　　*creature**
　　Decked with many a costly ornament,
　　Much marvelled thereat, as well he might;
　　And thought that match a foul°　　　*disgraceful*
　　　disparagement.°　　　*inequality*
　　His bloody spear eftsoons° he boldly bent°　　*forthwith aimed*
　　Against the silly° clown,° who, dead through　　*ignorant*‡ *rustic*
　　　fear,
　　Fell straight to ground in great astonishment.
　　'Villain,'° said he, 'this lady is my dear:　　　*Base creature*
Die if thou it gainsay. I will away her bear.'

13

The fearful churl durst not gainsay, nor do,°　　　*act*
　　But trembling stood and yielded him the prey –
　　Who, finding little leisure her to woo,
　　On Trompart's steed her mounted without stay,°　　*delay*
　　And without rescue led her quite° away.　　*completely*
　　Proud man himself then Braggadocchio deemed,
　　And next to none after that happy day,
　　Being possessed of that spoil, which seemed
The fairest wight on ground° and most of men esteemed.　　*earth*

14

But when he saw himself free from pursuit,
    He 'gan make gentle° purpose°   *tender‡ conversation‡*
      to his dame
    With terms of love and lewdness dissolute;
    For he could well his glozing° speeches   *coaxing*
      frame°   *fashion*
    To such vain uses that him best became.°   *best suited*
    But she thereto would lend but light regard,
    As seeming sorry that she ever came
    Into his power that used her so hard
To reave° her honour, which she more than life   *despoil*
    preferred.

15

Thus as they two of kindness° treated long,   *love*
    There them by chance encountered on the way
    An armed knight upon a courser strong
    Whose trampling feet upon the hollow lay°   *lea; ground; land*
    Seemed to thunder, and did nigh affray
    That capon's° courage: yet he looked grim   *eunuch's*
    And feigned to cheer his lady in dismay,
    Who seemed for fear to quake in every limb,
And her to save from outrage° meekly prayed him.   *violence*

16

Fiercely that stranger forward came, and nigh
    Approaching, with bold words and bitter threat
    Bade that same boaster, as he mote,° on high,°   *must loudly*
    To leave to him that lady for escheat,°   *forfeit**
    Or bid° him battle without further treat.°   *challenge‡ parley**
    That challenge did too peremptory seem
    And filled his senses with abashment great –
    Yet seeing nigh him jeopardy extreme,
He it dissembled well, and light° seemed to esteem,   *lightly*

17

Saying: 'Thou foolish knight, that weenest° with words   *think*
    To steal away that° I with blows have won   *what*
    And brought through points of many perilous swords.
    But if thee list° to see thy courser run,   *wish*

Or prove thyself, this sad° encounter shun   *demanding; heavy*
And seek else° without hazard of thy head.'   *elsewhere*
At those proud words that other knight begun
To wax exceeding wroth, and him aread°   *advised*
To turn his steed about, or sure he would be dead.

18

'Sith,° then,' said Braggadocchio, 'needs thou wilt   *Since*
   Thy days abridge through proof° of puissance,°   *trial   might*
   Turn we our steeds that both in equal tilt°   *combat*‡
   May meet again and each take happy chance.'
   This said, they both a furlong's mountenance°   *distance*
   Retired° their steeds to run in even   *Withdrew*‡
     race;°   *equal space, interval*
  But Braggadocchio with his bloody lance,
   Once having turned, no more returned his face,
But left his love to loss and fled himself apace.

19

The knight, him seeing fly, had no regard°   *concern*
   Him to pursue, but to the lady rode
   And, having her from Trompart lightly° reared,°   *easily   lifted*
   Upon his courser set the lovely load
   And with her fled away without abode.°   *delay**
   Well weened° he that fairest Florimell   *believed*
   It was with whom in company he yode,°   *went*
  And so herself did always to him tell:
So made him think himself in heaven that was in hell.

20

But Florimell herself was far away
   (Driven to great distress by Fortune strange),°   *alien*
   And taught the careful° mariner to play   *watchful*
   Sith° late mischance had her compelled to change   *Since*
   The land for sea, at random there to range.°   *roam*‡
   Yet there that cruel queen° avengeress,   *i.e., Fortune*
   Not satisfied so far her to estrange
  From courtly bliss and wonted° happiness,   *customary*
Did heap on her new waves of weary wretchedness.

21

For, being fled into the fisher's boat
  For refuge from the monster's cruelty,
  Long so she on the mighty main° did float   *ocean*
  And with the tide drove forward carelessly,° *at will; heedlessly*‡
  For the air was mild, and cleared was the sky,
  And all his winds Dan° Aeolus did keep   *'Lord'*
  From stirring up their stormy enmity,
  As° pitying to see her wail and weep –   *As if*
But all this while the fisher did securely sleep.

22

At last when, drunk° with drowsiness,° he   *replete heavy sleep*‡
  woke
  And saw his drover° drive along the   *fishing boat*
  stream,°   *current*
  He was dismayed, and thrice his breast he struck
  For marvel of that accident extreme.
  But when he saw that blazing beauty's beam
  Which, with rare° light, his boat did   *exquisite*
  beautify,°   *ornament*
  He marvelled more, and thought he yet did dream,
  Not well awaked, or that some ecstasy
Assotted° had his senses, or dazed was his eye.   *Infatuated*

23

But when, her well advising,° he perceived° *observing understood*
  To be no vision, nor fantastic sight,°   *product of his fantasy*
  Great comfort of her presence he conceived,
  And felt in his old courage° new delight   *sexual power*
  To 'gin awake and stir his frozen sprite;°   *vital spirits*
  Tho° rudely° asked her, how she thither came. *Then roughly*
  'Ah,' said she, 'father, I n'ote° read° aright *cannot declare*
  What hard misfortune brought me to the same;
Yet am I glad that here I now in safety am.

24

'But, thou good man, sith° far in° sea we be,   *since out to*
  And the great waters 'gin apace to swell
  That° now no more we can the mainland see,   *So that*

Have care, I pray, to guide the cock-boat° well　　*small boat*
Lest worse on sea than us on land befell.'
Thereat the old man did nought but fondly°　　*stupidly; lovingly*†
　grin,
And said his boat the way could wisely° tell;　　*ingeniously**
But his deceitful eyes did never lin°　　*cease*
To look on her fair face, and mark° her　　*observe; stain with lust*
　snowy skin.

25

The sight whereof, in his congealed flesh,
　Infixed such secret sting of greedy lust
　That the dry, withered stock° it 'gan refresh,　　*stump*
　And kindled heat that soon in flames forth burst:
　The driest wood is soonest burnt to dust.
　Rudely to her he leaped and his rough hand,
　Where ill became him, rashly would have thrust,
　But she with angry scorn did him withstand,
And shamefully reproved for his rudeness° fond.°　　*violence　mad*

26

But he, that never good nor manners knew,
　Her sharp rebuke full° little did esteem:　　*very*
　Hard is to teach an old horse amble true.
　The inward smoke, that did before but steam,
　Broke into open fire and rage extreme;
　And now he strength 'gan add unto his will,°　　*lust*
　Forcing to do that did him foul
　　misseem:°　　*what was most inappropriate*
　Beastly he threw her down, ne cared to
　　spill°　　*nor cared if he ruined*
Her garments gay with scales of fish that all° did fill.　　*everywhere*

27

The silly° virgin strove him to withstand　　*helpless*‡
　All that she might, and him in vain reviled:
　She struggled strongly both with foot and hand
　To save her honour from that villain vild,°　　*depraved*
　And cried to heaven, from human help exiled.
　O ye brave knights, that boast this lady's love,

Where be ye now when she is nigh defiled
  Of° filthy wretch? Well may she you reprove   *By*
Of falsehood or of sloth when most it may
    behove.°   *you were needed*

28

But if that thou, Sir Satyrane, didst weet,°   *know*
  Or thou, Sir Peridure, her sorry state,
  How soon would ye assemble many a fleet
  To fetch from sea that° ye at land lost late:°   *what recently*
  Towers, cities, kingdoms ye would ruinate°   *destroy*
  In your avengement° and dispiteous° rage, *revenge merciless*
  Ne° aught your burning fury mote° abate.   *Neither might*
  But if Sir Calidore could it presage,° *have a presentiment of*†
No living creature could his cruelty assuage.

29

But sith° chat none of all her knights is nigh,   *since*
  See how the heavens, of voluntary grace
  And sovereign° favour towards chastity,   *supreme*
  Do succour send to her distressed case:
  So much high God doth innocence embrace.
  It fortuned, whilst thus she stiffly° strove,   *resolutely*
  And the wide sea importuned° long *troubled; petitioned urgently*
    space°   *time*
  With shrilling shrieks, Proteus abroad did rove
Along the foamy waves driving his finny drove.

30

Proteus is shepherd of the seas of yore,°   *anciently*
  And hath the charge of Neptune's mighty herd –
  An aged sire with head all frowy° hoar°   *mustily aged*
  And sprinkled frost upon his dewy beard,
  Who, when those pitiful outcries he heard
  Through all the seas so ruefully resound,
  His chariot swift in haste he thither steered
  Which, with° a team of scaly phocas°   *by seals*
    bound,°   *united together*
Was drawn upon the waves that foamed him around.

31

And, coming to that fisher's wandering boat,
   That went at will withouten card° or sail,   *chart*
   He therein saw that irksome° sight, which smote   *distressing*
   Deep indignation and compassion frail°   *tender*†
   Into his heart at once.° Straight did he hale   *simultaneously*
   The greedy villain from his hoped prey,
   Of which he now did very little fail,
   And, with his staff that drives his herd astray,°   *forward*
Him beat so sore that life and sense did much
     dismay° –   *overcome*

32

The whiles the piteous lady up did rise,
   Ruffled,° and foully 'rayed° with filthy   *disordered defiled*
     soil,°   *stains*
   And blubbered° face with tears of her fair eyes.   *disfigured*
   Her heart nigh broken was with weary toil
   To save herself from that outrageous spoil;
   But when she looked up to weet° what   *discover*
     wight°   *creature**
   Had her from so infamous fact° assoiled,°   *deed liberated*
   For shame (but more for fear of his grim sight)
Down in her lap she hid her face, and loudly shright.°   *shrieked*

33

Herself not saved yet from danger dread
   She thought, but changed from one to other fear.
   Like as a fearful partridge, that is fled
   From the sharp° hawk which her attached°   *hungry seized*
     near,°   *nearly*
   And falls to ground to seek for succour there,
   Whereas° the hungry spaniel she does spy   *Where*
   With greedy jaws her ready for to tear:
   In such distress and sad perplexity
Was Florimell, when Proteus she did see thereby.

34

But he endeavoured, with speeches mild,
   Her to recomfort° and encourage bold,   *comfort*
   Bidding her fear no more her foeman vild,°   *base*

Nor doubt himself – and who he was, her told.
　　Yet all that could not from affright° her hold,　　　　　fear
　　Ne° to recomfort° her at all prevailed,　　　　Nor comfort
　　For her faint heart was with the frozen cold
　　Benumbed so inly° that her wits nigh failed　　　　extremely
And all her senses with abashment° quite were　　　　confusion
　　　　quailed.°　　　　　　　　　　　　　　　overpowered

35

Her up betwixt his rugged° hands he reared°　　　rough lifted
　　And with his frory° lips full softly kissed,　　　　　frozen
　　Whiles the cold icicles from his rough beard
　　Dropped adown upon her ivory breast –
　　Yet he himself so busily addressed°　　　　　　　applied
　　That her out of astonishment° he wrought°　　dismay brought
　　And, out of that same fisher's filthy nest
　　Removing her, into his chariot brought,
And there with many gentle terms her fair besought.°　entreated

36

But that old lecher which, with bold assault,
　　That beauty durst presume to violate,
　　He cast° to punish for his heinous fault:　　　　　resolved
　　Then took he him, yet trembling sith° of late,　　　since
　　And tied behind his chariot to aggrate°　　　　　gratify†
　　The virgin whom he had abused so sore.
　　So dragged him through the waves in scornful state,
　　And after cast him up upon the shore;
But Florimell with him unto his bower° he bore.　　　chamber

37

His bower is at the bottom of the main°　　　　　　ocean
　　Under a mighty rock, 'gainst which do rave
　　The roaring billows in their proud disdain
　　That,° with the angry working of the wave,　　　So that
　　Therein is eaten out an hollow cave
　　That seems rough mason's hand with engines°　　　tools
　　　　keen°　　　　　　　　　　　　　　　　sharp
　　Had long laboured it to engrave °　　　　　　　cut†
　　There was his wone,° ne° living wight°　dwelling nor creature*

was seen
Save one old nymph, hight° Panope, to keep it clean.   *named**†*

38

Thither he brought the sorry° Florimell   *grieving;* distressed**
And entertained° her the best he might;   *showed hospitality to*
And Panope her entertained eke° well,   *in addition*
As an immortal mote° a mortal wight,   *might*
To win her liking unto his delight.
With flattering words he sweetly wooed her,
And offered fair gifts to allure her sight;
But she both offers and the offerer
Despised, and all the fawning of the flatterer.

39

Daily he tempted her with this or that,
And never suffered her to be at rest.
But evermore she him refused flat°   *absolutely‡*
And all his feigned kindness did detest,
So firmly she had sealed up her breast.°   *heart*
Sometimes he boasted that a god he hight:
But she a mortal creature loved best;
Then he would make himself a mortal wight:
But then she said she loved none but a fairy knight.

40

Then like a fairy knight himself he dressed,
For every shape on him he could endue;°   *assume*
Then like a king he was to her expressed,°   *portrayed*
And offered kingdoms unto her in view
To be his leman,° and his lady true.   *beloved*
But when all this he nothing saw prevail,
With harder means he cast° her to subdue,   *determined*
And with sharp threats her often did assail
So thinking for to make her stubborn courage quail.

41

To dreadful shapes he did himself transform,
Now like a giant, now like to a fiend,
Then like a centaur, then like to a storm
Raging within the waves: thereby he weened°   *thought*

Her will to win unto his wished end.
But when with fear, nor favour, nor with all
He else could do, he saw himself esteemed,
Down in a dungeon deep he let her fall,
And threatened there to make her his eternal thrall.°   *prisoner*

42

Eternal thraldom was to her more lief°   *preferable*
Than loss of chastity or change of love:
Die had she rather in tormenting grief
Than° any should of falseness her reprove,   *Than that*
Or looseness – that she lightly° did remove.   *swiftly*
Most virtuous virgin, glory be thy meed,°   *reward*
And crown of heavenly praise with saints above
Where most° sweet hymns of this thy famous deed   *mostly*
Are still amongst them sung, that far my rhymes exceed.

43

Fit song of° angels carolled to be –   *by*
But yet what so my feeble Muse can frame°   *compose*
Shall be to advance° thy goodly chastity,   *praise*
And to enrol thy memorable name
In the heart of every honourable dame,
That° they thy virtuous deeds may imitate   *So that*
And be partakers of thy endless fame.
It irks me leave thee in this woeful state,
To tell of Satyrane, where I him left of late –

44

Who, having ended with that Squire of Dames
A long discourse of his adventures vain,
The which himself, than ladies, more defames,°   *disgraces*
And finding not the hyena to be slain,
With that same Squire returned back again
To his first way. And as they forward went
They spied a knight fair° pricking° on the plain   *fast spurring*
As if he were on some adventure bent,
And in his port° appeared manly hardiment.°   *bearing boldness*

45

Sir Satyrane him towards did address,°   *make his way*
   To weet° what wight he was and what his quest;   *know*
   And coming nigh, eftsoons° he 'gan to guess,   *soon after*
   Both by the burning heart which on his breast
   He bore, and by the colours in his crest,
   That Paridell it was. Tho° to him yode,°   *Then went*
   And him saluting, as beseemed best,
   'Gan first enquire of tidings far abroad,
And afterwards on what adventure now he rode.

46

Who, thereto answering, said: 'The tidings bad
   Which now in fairy court all men do tell,
   Which turned hath great mirth to mourning sad,
   Is the late° ruin° of proud Marinell   *recent fall*
   And sudden parture of fair Florimell   *departure*
   To find him forth:° and after her are   *continually search for him*
     gone
   All the brave knights that do in arms excel
   To safeguard her, ywandered all alone:
Amongst the rest my lot (unworthy) is to be one.'

47

'Ah, gentle° knight,' said then Sir Satyrane,   *noble*
   'Thy labour all is lost, I greatly dread,
   That hast a thankless service on thee taken
   And offerest sacrifice unto the dead –
   For dead, I surely doubt,° thou mayest aread°   *fear declare*
   Henceforth for ever Florimell to be,
   That° all the noble Knights of Maidenhead   *So that*
   (Which her adored) may sore° repent°   *greatly mourn*
     with me,
And all fair ladies may for ever sorry be.'

48

Which words when Paridell heard, his hue°   *aspect*
   'Gan greatly change and seemed dismayed to be;
   Then said: 'Fair sir, how may I ween° it true   *know*

That ye do tell in such uncertainty?
　　Or° speak ye of report, or did ye see   *Either*
　　Just cause of dread that makes ye doubt so sore?
　　For, perdy,° else how mote° it ever be   *indeed   might*
　　That ever hand should dare for to engore°   *stain itself with*†
Her noble blood? – the heavens such cruelty abhor.'

49

'These eyes did see that° they will ever rue   *what*
　　To have seen,' quoth he, 'whenas° a monstrous beast   *when*
　　The palfrey, whereon she did travel, slew,
　　And of his bowels made a bloody feast:
　　Which speaking token showeth at the least
　　Her certain loss if not her sure decay.°   *death*
　　Besides, that° more suspicion increased,   *what*
　　I found her golden girdle cast astray,
Distained° with dirt and blood, as relic of the prey.'   *Discoloured*

50

'Ay me,' said Paridell, 'the signs be sad,
　　And but° God turn the same to good soothsay,°   *Unless   omen*
　　That lady's safety is sore° to be drad.°   *greatly   feared*
　　Yet will I not forsake my forward way
　　Till trial° do more certain truth bewray.'°   *proof   disclose*
　　'Fair sir,' quoth he, 'well may it you succeed,
　　Ne long shall Satyrane behind you stay,
　　But to the rest which in this quest proceed
My labour add, and be partaker of their
　　speed.'°   *success; swiftness*

51

'Ye noble knights,' said then the Squire of Dames,
　　'Well may ye speed in so praiseworthy pain;°   *effort*
　　But sith° the sun now 'gins to slake his beams   *since*
　　In dewy vapours of the western main,°   *ocean*
　　And loose the team out of his weary wain,°   *chariot*
　　Mote not mislike° you also to abate   *May it not displease*
　　Your zealous haste till morrow next again
　　Both light of heaven, and strength of men, relate?° –   *restore*†
Which, if ye please, to yonder castle turn your gait.'

52

That counsel pleased well; so all yfere°   *together*
  Forth marched to a castle them before,
  Where, soon arriving, they restrained were
  Of ready entrance, which ought evermore
  To errant knights be common. Wondrous sore°   *Extremely*
  Thereat displeased they were, till that young Squire
  'Gan them inform the cause why that same door
  Was shut to all which lodging did desire:
The which to let you weet° will further time require.   *know*

CANTO 9

> Malbecco will no strange knights host
>   For peevish° jealousy;   *perverse; foolish*
> Paridell jousts with Britomart –
>   Both show their ancestry.

1

Redoubted° knights, and honourable dames,   *Revered*
  To whom I level° all my labour's end,   *direct*
  Right sore I fear lest, with unworthy blames,
  This odious argument my rhymes should shend,°   *disgrace*
  Or aught your goodly patience offend,
  Whiles of a wanton lady I do write
  Which, with her loose incontinence,° doth   *intemperance*
    blend°   *dim**
  The shining glory of your sovereign light,
And knighthood foul defaced by a faithless knight.

2

But never let the example of the bad
  Offend the good: for good by paragon°   *comparison†*
  Of evil may more notably be read,°   *discerned*
  As white seems fairer matched with black at one.°   *together*
  Ne° all are shamed by the fault of one –   *Nor*
  For lo, in heaven, whereas° all goodness is,   *where*
  Amongst the angels a whole legion

Of wicked sprites° did fall from happy bliss: *spirits*
What wonder, then, if one of women all° did   *all women*
    miss?°   *err*

3

Then listen, lordings, if ye list° to weet°   *wish know*
  The cause why Satyrane and Paridell
  Mote° not be entertained, as seemed meet,° *Might appropriate*
  Into that castle, as the Squire does tell:
  'Therein a cankered,° crabbed carl° does *ill-tempered churl*
    dwell
  That has no skill° of court nor courtesy,   *knowledge*
  Ne cares what men say of him ill or well –
  For all his days he drowns in privity,°   *seclusion*
Yet has full large° to live and spend at liberty. *largesse; riches*

4

'But all his mind is set on mucky° pelf°   *filthy money*
  To hoard up heaps of evil-gotten° mass,° *ill-gotten treasure*[†]
  For which he others wrongs, and wrecks° himself. *destroys*
  Yet is he linked to a lovely lass
  Whose beauty doth her bounty° far surpass,   *virtue*
  The which to him both far unequal years
  And also far unlike conditions° has, *personal qualities*
  For she does joy° to play amongst her peers, *rejoice*
And to be free from hard restraint and jealous fears.

5

'But he is old and withered like hay,
  Unfit fair lady's service to supply;
  The privy° guilt whereof makes him alway   *secret*
  Suspect her truth and keep continual spy
  Upon her with his other, blinked,° eye; *constantly glancing*[†]
  Ne° suffereth he resort° of living *Neither assembly*
    wight°   *creature*[*]
  Approach to her, ne° keep her company,   *nor*
  But in close° bower° her mews° from *secret chamber imprisons*
    all men's sight,
Deprived of kindly° joy and natural delight.   *friendly*

6

'Malbecco he, and Hellenore she hight,   *is called**†
  Unfitly yoked together in one team:
  That is the cause why never any knight
  Is suffered here to enter, but° he seem   *except*
  Such as no doubt of him he need misdeem.'°   *suspect*
Thereat Sir Satyrane 'gan smile and say:
'Extremely mad the man, I surely deem,°   *judge*
That weens° with watch and hard restraint to   *thinks*
  stay°   *obstruct*
A woman's will, which is disposed to go astray.

7

'In vain he fears that which he cannot shun;
  For who wotes° not that woman's subtleties   *knows*
  Can guilen° Argus when she list°   *beguile   wishes*
    misdone?°   *to do wrong*
  It is not iron bands, nor hundred eyes,
  Nor brazen walls, nor many wakeful spies
  That can withhold° her wilful, wandering feet; *restrain*
  But fast° good will with gentle° courtesies, *firm   civil*
  And timely service to her pleasures meet°   *fitting*
May her perhaps contain that else would algates° *always**
  flit.'°   *deviate**

8

'Then is he not more mad,' said Paridell,
  'That hath himself unto such service sold
  In doleful thraldom all his days to dwell?
  For, sure, a fool I do him firmly hold
  That loves his fetters, though they were of gold.
  But why do we devise° of others' ill   *converse*
  Whiles thus we suffer this same dotard old
  To keep us out in scorn, of° his own will,   *by*
And rather do not ransack all and himself kill?'

9

'Nay, let us first,' said Satyrane, 'entreat
  The man by gentle° means to let us in,   *courteous*
  And afterwards affray° with cruel threat,   *frighten*
  Ere that we efforce° it do begin.   *to gain by force*†

Then, if all fail, we will by force it win
And eke° reward the wretch for his misprize°   *also contempt*‡
As may be worthy of his heinous sin.'
That counsel pleased. Then Paridell did rise,
And to the castle gate approached in quiet wise,°   *fashion*

10

Whereat, soft knocking, entrance he desired.
The goodman self,° which then the porter played,   *himself*
Him answered that all were now retired
Unto their rest and all the keys conveyed
Unto their master, who in bed was laid
That° none him durst awake out of his dream,   *So that*
And therefore them of patience gently prayed.
Then Paridell began to change his theme
And threatened him with force and punishment extreme:

11

But all in vain, for nought mote° him relent.   *might*
And now so long before the wicket° fast°   *gate locked*
They waited that the night was forward spent,
And the fair welkin,° foully overcast,   *sky*
'Gan blowen up a bitter, stormy blast
With shower and hail so horrible and dread
That this fair many° were compelled at last   *company*
To fly for succour° to a little shed   *shelter*
The which beside the gate for swine was ordered.°   *appointed*

12

It fortuned, soon after they were gone,
Another knight whom tempest thither brought
Came to that castle and, with earnest moan,°   *lament*
Like as the rest, late entrance dear° besought –   *earnestly*
But like so as the rest he prayed for nought,
For flatly he of entrance was refused.
Sorely° thereat he was displeased, and thought   *Extremely*
How to avenge himself, so sore abused;
And evermore the carl of courtesy°   *in the name of courtesy*
   accused.

13

But to avoid the intolerable stour°   storm†
  He was compelled to seek some refuge near,
  And to that shed to shroud him from the shower
  He came, which full of guests he found whilere,°   already
  So as he was not let to enter there:
  Whereat he 'gan to wax exceeding wroth,
  And swore that he would lodge with them yfere,°   together
  Or them dislodge, all were they lief or
    loath;°   whether they wanted or not
And so defied them each, and so defied them both.

14

Both were full loath to leave that needful° tent,°   necessary   abode
  And both full loath in darkness to debate;°   fight
  Yet both full lief° him lodging to have lent,   willing
  And both full lief his boasting to abate.
  But chiefly Paridell his heart did grate°   fret
  To hear him threaten so despitefully,°   scornfully
  As if he did a dog to kennel rate°   scold†
  That durst° not bark; and rather had he die   dare
Than when he was defied, in coward corner lie.

15

Tho,° hastily remounting to his steed,   Then
  He forth issued, like as a boistrous wind
  Which in the earth's hollow cave hath long been hid
  And, shut up fast within her prison's
    blind,°   place of concealment†
  Makes the huge element against her kind°   nature
  To move, and tremble as it were aghast,
  Until that it an issue forth may find;
  Then forth it breaks and, with his furious blast,
Confounds both land and seas, and skies doth overcast.

16

Their steel-head spears they strongly couched,° and met lowered
  Together with impetuous rage and force
  That,° with the terror of their fierce affret,° So that onslaught†
  They rudely° drove to ground both man and horse,   forcibly
  That each awhile lay like a senseless corse.°   corpse

But Paridell, sore° bruised with the blow,   *extremely*
  Could not arise the countercharge to scorse°   *exchange*
  Till that young squire him reared° from below: *raised*
Then drew he his bright sword and 'gan about him
    throw.°   *wave*

17

But Satyrane, forth stepping, did them stay,
  And with fair treaty° pacified their ire.   *entreaty; discussion*
  Then, when they were accorded° from the fray,   *reconciled*‡
  Against that castle's lord they 'gan conspire
  To heap on him due vengeance for his hire.°   *reward*
  They been agreed, and to the gates they go
  To burn the same with unquenchable fire
  And that uncourteous carl, their common foe,
To do° foul death to die,° or wrap in grievous woe.   *cause   kill*

18

Malbecco, seeing them resolved indeed
  To flame the gates, and hearing them to call
  For fire in earnest, ran with fearful speed,
  And, to them calling from the castle wall,
  Besought them humbly him to bear°   *put up with*
    withal,°   *nevertheless*
  As ignorant of servant's bad abuse
  And slack attendance unto strangers' call.
  The knights were willing all things to excuse
(Though nought believed) and entrance late did not refuse.

19

They been ybrought° into a comely°   *brought*   *handsome*
    bower°   *chamber*
  And served of° all things that mote° needful be.   *with   might*
  Yet secretly their host did on them lour,°   *scowl*
  And welcomed more for fear than charity:
  But they dissembled° what they did not   *pretended not to notice*
    see,
  And welcomed themselves. Each 'gan undight°   *remove*

Their garments wet, and weary armour free,
To dry themselves by Vulcan's flaming light,
And eke° their lately° bruised parts to bring in   *also   recently*
   plight,°   *to health*

20

And eke that stranger knight amongst the rest
  Was for like need enforced to disarray.
    Tho,° whenas° vailed° was her lofty   *Then   when   taken off*
    crest,°   *helmet*
    Her golden locks, that were in trammels° gay   *braids*
    Upbounden, did themselves adown display°   *spread out*
    And raught° unto her heels, like sunny beams   *reached*
    That in a cloud their light did long time stay,°   *restrain‡*
    Their vapour vaded,° show their golden gleams,   *departed‡*
And through the azure air shoot forth their pierceant streams.

21

She also doffed her heavy habergeon°   *coat of mail*
  Which the fair feature° of her limbs did hide,   *shape*
    And her well pleated frock – which she did wont
    To tuck about her short when she did ride –
    She low let fall, that flowed from her lank° side *slim*
    Down to her foot with careless modesty.
    Then of them all she was espied
    To be a woman wight° (unwist° to   *female person*   unkown*
    be) –
The fairest woman wight that ever eye did see:

22

Like as Minerva, being late returned
  From the slaughter of the giants conquered
    (Where proud Encelad', whose wide nostrils burned
    With breathed flames like to a furnace red,
    Transfixed with the spear, down tumbled dead
    From top of Haemus, by him heaped high),
    Hath loosed her helmet from her lofty head
    And her Gorgonian shield 'gins to untie
From her left arm to rest in glorious victory.

23

Which whenas° they beheld, they smitten were   *when*
  With great amazement of so wondrous sight,
  And each on other, and they all on her,
  Stood gazing, as if sudden great affright
  Had them surprised. At last, advising° right   *perceiving*
  Her goodly° personage° and glorious   *splendid appearance*
    hue,°   *form*
  Which they so much mistook, they took delight
  In their first error; and yet still anew
With wonder of her beauty fed their hungry view.

24

Yet n'ote° their hungry view be satisfied   *could not*
  But, seeing, still the more desired to see,
  And ever firmly fixed did abide
  In contemplation of divinity.
  But most they marvelled at her chivalry° *knightly prowess*
  And noble prowess, which they had approved,° *experienced*
  That° much they fained° to know who she *So that longed*
    mote° be;   *might*
  Yet none of all them her thereof amoved,° *stirred emotionally**
Yet everyone her liked, and everyone her loved.

25

And Paridell, though partly discontent
  With his late fall and foul° indignity,   *shameful*
  Yet was soon won his malice to relent°   *soften*
  Through gracious regard of her fair eye
  And knightly worth, which he too late° did try,   *recently*
  Yet tried, did adore. Supper was dight.°   *prepared*
  Then they Malbecco prayed, of courtesy,
  That of his lady they might have the sight
And company at meat,° to do them more delight.   *their meal*

26

But he, to shift their curious° request,   *inquisitive*
  'Gan causen° why she could not come in   *give reasons*
    place:°   *appear before them*
  Her crazed° health, her late°   *broken recent*
    recourse° to rest,   *retirement*

And humid evening ill for sick folks' case –
But none of those excuses could take place,°   *find acceptance*
Ne° would they eat till she in presence came.   *Nor*
She came in presence with right comely grace
And fairly° them saluted,° as   *courteously greeted*
  became,°   *was fitting*
And showed herself in all a gentle° courteous dame.   *well-born*

27

They sat to meat, and Satyrane his chance°   *Satyrane's fortune*
  Was her before,° and Paridell beside;   *opposite*
But he° himself sat looking still askance   *i.e., Malbecco*
'Gainst Britomart, and ever closely° eyed°   *secretly watched*
Sir Satyrane that glances might not glide.°   *slip [between them]*
But his blind eye, that sided Paridell,
All his demeanour° from his sight did hide –   *conduct*
On her fair face so° did he feed his fill   *thus*
And sent close° messages of love to her at will.   *secret*

28

And ever and anon, when none was ware,°   *vigilant*
  With speaking looks that close embassage° bore,   *message*
He roved° at her and told his secret   *shot erotic looks*
  care,°   *passion*
For all that art he learned had of yore.
Ne° was she ignorant of that lewd lore,°   *Neither doctrine*
But in his eye his meaning wisely°   *knowledgeably*
  read,°   *discovered*
And with the like him answered evermore:
She sent at him one fiery dart whose head
Empoisoned was with privy° lust and jealous   *secret; genital*
  dread.

29

He from that deadly throw made no defence,
  But to the wound his weak heart opened wide –
The wicked engine,° through false influence,   *instrument*
Passed through his eyes and secretly did glide
Into his heart, which it did sorely° gride.°   *extremely pierce†*
But nothing new to him was that same pain,
Ne° pain at all; for he so oft had tried°   *Nor tested*

The power thereof, and loved so oft in vain,
That thing of course° he counted, love to   *as a matter of course*
   entertain.

30

Thenceforth to her he sought to intimate
  His inward grief by means to him well known:
  Now Bacchus' fruit° out of the silver plate   *i.e., wine*
  He on the table dashed (as overthrown°   *knocked over*
  Or of the fruitful liquor overflown),°   *overfilled; drunk*
  And by the dancing bubbles did divine,°   *prophesy*
  Or therein write to let his love be shown;
  Which well she read° out of the learned line   *discerned*
A sacrament profane in mystery of wine.

31

And when so° of his hand the pledge she raught,° *thus received**
  The guilty cup she feigned to mistake°   *take clumsily*
  And in her lap she shed her idle draught,
  Showing desire her inward flame to slake.°   *moderate*
  By such close° signs they secret way did make   *secret*
  Unto their wills and one eye's watch escape:
  Two eyes him needeth for to watch and wake°   *guard**
  Who lovers will deceive. Thus was the ape,
By their fair° handling, put into Malbecco's cape.   *clever*

32

Now when of meats and drinks they had their fill,
  Purpose° was moved by that gentle° dame   *A proposal noble*
  Unto those knights adventurous, to tell
  Of deeds of arms which unto them became,°   *befell*
  And everyone his kindred and his name.
  Then Paridell, in whom a kindly° pride   *natural*
  Of gracious speech, and skill his words to frame,°   *order*
  Abounded, being glad of so fit tide°   *occasion*
Him to commend to her, thus spake, of all well eyed.

33

'Troy, that art now nought but an idle° name,   *empty*
  And in thine ashes buried now dost lie
  (Though whilom° far much greater than thy fame,   *once**

Before that angry gods and cruel sky°   *heaven*
Upon thee heaped a direful destiny),
What boots° it boast thy glorious descent,   *avails*
And fetch from° heaven thy great genealogy,   *trace to*
Sith° all thy worldy praises being   *Since the fact of*
    blent°   *obscured†*
Their offspring hath embased° and later glory   *made base*
    shent.°   *disgraced*

34
'Most famous worthy of the world – by whom
    That war was kindled which did Troy inflame,°   *set on fire*
    And stately towers of Ilium whilom
    Brought unto baleful° ruin – was by name   *deadly; wretched*
    Sir Paris, far renowned through noble fame,
    Who, through great prowess and bold hardiness,°   *bravery*
    From Lacedaemon fetched the fairest dame
    That ever Greece did boast or knight possess,
Whom Venus to him gave for meed° of worthiness: *reward*

35
'Fair Helen, flower of beauty excellent
    And garland of the mighty conquerors,
    That madest many ladies dear° lament   *grievously*
    The heavy loss of their brave° paramours   *handsome*
    Which they far off beheld from Trojan towers,
    And saw the fields of fair Scamander strewn
    With carcases of noble warriors
    Whose fruitless lives were under furrow sown,
And Xanthus' sandy banks with blood all overflown.°   *flooded*

36
'From him my lineage I derive aright°   *directly*
    Who, long before the ten years' siege of Troy,
    Whiles yet on Ida he a shepherd hight,°   *was designated*†
    On fair Oenone got° a lovely boy   *begot*
    Whom, for remembrance of her passed joy,
    She, of° his father, Parius did name;   *after*
    Who, after Greeks did Priam's realm destroy,
    Gathered the Trojan relics saved from flame
And, with them sailing thence, to the isle of Paros came

37

'(That was by him called Paros which before
　　Hight Nausa). There he many years did reign
　　And built Nausicle by the Pontic shore,
　　The which he, dying, left next in remain°　　*as the remaining heir*†
　　To Paridas his son,
　　From whom I, Paridell, by kin descend –
　　But, for fair lady's love and glory's gain,
　　My native soil have left, my days to spend
In suing° deeds of arms, my life's and labour's end.'　　*following*

38

Whenas° the noble Britomart heard tell　　　　　　　　　*When*
　　Of Trojan wars and Priam's city sacked –
　　The rueful° story of Sir Paridell –　　　　　　　　*lamentable*
　　She was impassioned° at that piteous act　　*deeply stirred*†
　　With zealous envy of° the Greeks' cruel fact°　*ill will at deed*
　　Against that nation from whose race of old,
　　She heard, that she was lineally extract:°　　　　*descended*
　　For noble Britons sprang from Trojans bold,
And Troynovant was built of old Troy's ashes cold.

39

Then, sighing soft awhile, at last she thus:
　　'O lamentable fall of famous town,
　　Which reigned so many years victorious
　　And of all Asia bore the sovereign crown,
　　In one sad night consumed and thrown down.
　　What stony heart, that hears thy hapless° fate,　　*unfortunate*
　　Is not empierced° with deep compassion　　　　*transfixed*‡
　　And makes example of man's wretched state,
That flowers so fresh at morn and fades at evening late?

40

'Behold, sir, how your pitiful complaint°　　　　　　*lament*
　　Hath found another partner of your pain;
　　For nothing may impress so dear°　　　　　*such extreme*
　　　　constraint°　　　　　　　　　　　　　*distress*
　　As country's cause and common foe's disdain.°　*contempt*
　　But, if it should not grieve you back again

To turn your course, I would to hear desire
  What to Aeneas fell,° sith° that men sayen°   *befell   since   say*
  He was not in the city's woeful fire
Consumed, but did himself to safety retire."°   *withdraw*†

41

'Anchises' son, begot of Venus fair,'
  Said he, 'out of the flames for safeguard° fled,   *safety*
  And with a remnant did to sea repair
  Where he, through fatal° error,° long   *fate-ordained   wandering*
    was led
  Full many years, and weetless° wandered   *in ignorance*†
  From shore to shore amongst the Lybic
    sands°   *i.e., north African shores*
  Ere rest he found. Much there he suffered,
  And many perils passed in foreign lands,
To save his people sad from victors' vengeful hands.

42

'At last in Latium he did arrive,
  Where he with cruel war was entertained°   *greeted*
  Of° the inland folk, which sought him back to drive   *By*
  Till he with old Latinus was constrained
  To contract wedlock (so the Fates ordained) –
  Wedlock contract° in blood and eke° in blood   *contracted   also*
  Accomplished, that° many dear°   *so that   grievously*
    complained.
  The rival slain, the victor through the flood°   *i.e., of blood*
Escaped hardly,° hardly praised his wedlock good.   *with difficulty*

43

'Yet, after all, he victor did survive,
  And with Latinus did the kingdom part.°   *divide*
  But after, when both nations 'gan to strive
  Into their names the title to convert,°   *direct; claim*
  His son, Iulus, did from thence depart
  With all the warlike youth of Trojan blood,
  And in long Alba° placed his throne apart,   *Alba Longa*
  Where fair it flourished and long time stood
Till, Romulus renewing it, to Rome removed.'

44

'There – there,' said Britomart, 'afresh appeared
  The glory of the later world to spring,
  And Troy again out of her dust was reared°   *raised*
  To sit in second seat of° sovereign king *i.e., for a second time as*
  Of all the world under her governing.
  But a third kingdom yet is to arise
  Out of the Trojans' scattered offspring
  That, in all glory and great enterprise,
Both first and second Troy shall dare to equalise.°   *rival*[‡]

45

'It Troynovant is hight, that with the waves
  Of wealthy Thames washed is along,
  Upon whose stubborn neck (whereat he raves
  With roaring rage, and sore° himself does   *extremely*
    throng°   *press*
  That° all men fear to tempt° his *So that risk the dangers of*[†]
    billows strong)
  She fastened hath her foot, which stands so high
  That it a wonder of the world is sung
  In foreign lands, and all which passen by –
Beholding it from far – do think it threats the sky.

46

'The Trojan Brut did first that city found,
  And Highgate made the mere° thereof by west,   *boundary*
  And Overtgate by north: that is the bound°   *boundary*
  Toward the land; two rivers bound the rest.
  So huge a scope° at first him seemed best   *extent*[†]
  To be the compass° of his kingdom's seat;   *circumference*
  So huge a mind could not in lesser rest,
  Ne° in small meres° contain his glory great *Nor confines;*[†] *limits*[†]
That Albion had conquered first by warlike feat.'

47

'Ah fairest lady knight,' said Paridell,
  'Pardon, I pray, my heedless oversight
  Who had forgot that° whilom° I heard tell   *what once*[*]
  From aged Mnemon;° for my wits   *He who remembers*
    been light.°   *frail*

Indeed, he said – if I remember right –
That "of the antique Trojan stock° there grew   *race*
Another plant that raught° to wondrous height   *reached*
And far abroad his mighty branches threw
Into the utmost angle° of the world   *corner [punning on England]*
   he knew.

48

' "For that same Brut, whom much he did advance°   *praise*
In all his speech, was Sylvius his son
Whom, having slain through luckless arrow's glance,
He fled for fear of that° he had misdone,   *what*
Or else for shame so foul reproach to shun,
And with him led to sea a youthly train°   *company*
Where, weary wandering, they long time did wone,°   *remain*
And many fortunes° proved° in the ocean   *misfortunes suffered*
   main°   *sea*
And great adventures found that now were long to sayen.°   *tell*

49

' "At last by fatal course° they driven were   *directed by Fate*
Into an island spacious and broad
The furthest north that did to them appear;
Which, after rest, they seeking far abroad
Found it the fittest soil for their abode,
Fruitful of all things fit for living food,
But wholly waste° and void of people's trod°   *desolate track**
Save an huge nation of the giants' brood,°   *offspring*
That fed on living flesh and drunk men's vital blood.

50

' "Whom he, through weary wars and labours long,
Subdued with loss of many Britons bold:
In which the great Gogmagot of° strong   *By*
Corineus, and Coulin of Debon old
Were overthrown and laid in earth full cold,
Which quaked under their so hideous° mass –   *huge*
A famous history, to be enrolled
In everlasting monuments of brass
That all the antique° worthies' merits far did   *ancient‡*
   pass.°   *surpass*

51

' "His work great Troynovant; his work is eke°   *in addition*
   Fair Lincoln, both renowned far away
   That° who from east to west will   *So that*
     endlong° seek   ·   *from end to end*
   Cannot two fairer cities find this day,
   Except Cleopolis." So heard I say
   Old Mnemon. Therefore, sir, I greet you well,
   Your country kin,° and you entirely°   *countryman earnestly*
     pray
   Of pardon for the strife which late befell
Betwixt us both unknown.' So ended Paridell.

52

But all the while that he these speeches spent,
   Upon his lips hung fair Dame Hellenore
   With vigilant regard and due attent,°   *attention*
   Fashioning worlds of fancies° evermore   *imaginings*
   In her frail° wit° that now her quite left.° *feeble mind forsook*
   The whiles,° unwares,° away her   *Meanwhile unknowingly*
     wandering eye
   And greedy ears her weak heart from her bore:
   Which he, perceiving, ever privily°   *secretly*
In speaking many false° belgards° at her *treacherous loving looks*
     let fly.

53

So long these knights discoursed diversely°   *variously*
   Of strange affairs and noble hardiment°   *bravery*
   Which they had passed with mickle° jeopardy,   *much*
   That now the humid° night was farforth° *dewy very far* *
     spent,
   And heavenly lamps were halfendeal° ybrent;° *half* *burnt* *
   Which the old man, seeing well (who too long thought
   Every discourse and every argument,
   Which by the hours he measured), besought
Them to go to rest. So all unto their bowers° were *chambers*
     brought.

Canto 10

Paridell rapeth° Hellenore: *abducts*
  Malbecco her pursues,
Finds amongst satyrs, whence with him
  To turn° she doth refuse.   *return*

1

The morrow next, so soon as Phoebus' lamp
  Bewrayed° had the world with early light,   *Revealed*
And fresh Aurora had the shady damp
  Out of the goodly heaven amoved° quite,°   *removed completely*
Fair Britomart and that same fairy knight
  Uprose, forth on their journey for to wend;°   *go*
But Paridell complained that his late fight
  With Britomart so sore° did him offend°   *grievously hurt*
That ride he could not, till his hurts he did amend.

2

So forth they fared, but he behind them stayed
  Maugre° his host, who grudged° grievously *Despite grumbled*
To house a guest that would be needs obeyed,
  And of his own him left not at liberty:
Might wanting° measure° moveth°   *lacking control causes*
  surquedry.°   *pride*
Two things he feared, but the third was death:
  That fierce young man's unruly mastery;°   *superior force*
His money, which he loved as living breath;
And his fair wife, whom honest° long he kept   *chaste*
  uneath.°   *with difficulty*

3

But patience, perforce: he must aby°   *endure**
  What Fortune and his fate will on him lay:
Fond° is the fear that finds no remedy.   *Foolish*
  Yet° warily he watcheth every way   *Always*
By which he feareth evil happen may,
  So the evil thinks by watching to prevent:

Ne° doth he suffer her nor night nor day   *Neither*
   Out of his sight herself once to absent;
So doth he punish her and eke° himself torment.   *in addition*

4

But Paridell kept better watch than he,
   A fit occasion for his turn to find:
False Love, why do men say thou canst not see,
And in their foolish fancy feign thee blind,
That with thy charms the sharpest sight dost bind
And to thy will abuse? Thou walkest free
And seest every secret of the mind:
   Thou seest all, yet none at all sees thee:
All that is by the working of thy deity.

5

So perfect in that art was Paridell
   That he Malbecco's halfen° eye° did   *half**† *eyesight*
      wile° –   *deceive*
His halfen eye he wiled wondrous well,
And Hellenore's both eyes did eke beguile
(Both eyes and heart at once) during the while
That he there sojourned his wounds to heal –
   That° Cupid self,° it seeing, close°   *So that himself secretly*
      did smile
To weet° how he her love away did steal,   *perceive*
And bade that none their joyous treason° should   *treachery*
   reveal.

6

The learned lover lost no time nor tide°   *opportunity*
   That least advantage mote° to him afford,   *might*
   Yet bore so fair a sail that none espied
His secret drift till he her laid aboard.°   *approached to board*
When so in open place and common board°   *table*
He fortuned her to meet, with common°   *ordinary*
   speech°   *discourse*
He courted her, yet bated° every word   *moderated*
That his ungentle° host n'ote° him   *uncivil   could not*
   appeach°   *charge*
Of vile° ungentleness or hospitage's° breach.   *base hospitality's*†

7

But when apart (if ever her apart)
  He found, then his false° engines° fast   *treacherous   devices*
    he plied,
  And all the sleights unbosomed in his
    heart.°   *tricks in his heart he . . .*
  He sighed, he sobbed, he swooned, he perdy
    died,°   *would certainly die*
  And cast himself on ground her fast beside.
  Tho,° when again he him bethought to live,   *Then*
  He wept and wailed and false laments belied,°   *faked†*
  Saying, but if° she mercy would him give   *unless*
That he mote algates° die, yet did his death forgive. *otherwise*

8

And otherwhiles° with amorous delights   *at other times*
  And pleasing toys° he would her entertain,   *games of love*
  Now singing sweetly to surprise her sprites,°   *spirits; humour*
  Now making lays° of love and lovers' pain: *songs*
  Bransles, ballads, virelays, and verses vain.°   *idle*
  Oft purposes,° oft riddles he   *question-and-answer games**
    devised,
  And thousands like which flowed in his brain,
  With which he fed her fancy,° and enticed   *imagination*
To take to his new love, and leave her old despised.

9

And everywhere he might, and every while,°   *whenever [he could]*
  He did her service dutiful, and sued°   *did homage*
  At hand with humble pride and pleasing guile
  So closely° yet° that none but she it viewed,°   *secretly   still*
  Who well perceived all, and all indued.°   *absorbed†*
  Thus finely° did he his false nets   *cunningly*
    dispread,°   *spread out*
  With which he many weak hearts had subdued
  Of yore, and many had ylike° misled: *alike**
What wonder, then, if she were likewise carried?

10

No fort so fencible,° no walls so strong,   *well-fortified*
  But that continual battery will rive,°   *split asunder*
  Or daily siege through dispurveyance° long   *lack of provisions*†
  And lack of rescues° will to parley drive;   *aid*
  And piece° that unto parley ear will give   *fortress*
  Will shortly yield itself, and will be made
  The vassal of the victor's will belive:°   *straight away*
  That stratagem had oftentime assayed°   *put to the proof*
This crafty paramour,° and now it plain displayed.   *lover*

11

For through his trains° he her entrapped hath   *stratagems*
  That° she her love and heart hath wholly sold   *So that*
  To him without regard of gain, or scathe,°   *hurt*
  Or care of credit,° or of husband old   *reputation*
  Whom she hath vowed to dub a fair° cuckhold.   *fine*
  Nought wants° but time and place, which   *Nothing is wanting*
    shortly she
  Devised hath and to her lover told.
  It pleased well; so well they both agree:
So ready ripe to° ill, ill women's counsels be.   *to perform*

12

Dark was the evening, fit for lovers' stealth,
  When chanced Malbecco busy be elsewhere,
  She to his closet went where all his wealth
  Lay hid. Thereof she countless sums did rear°   *collect**
  The which she meant away with her to bear:
  The rest she fired for sport or for° despite,°   *through malice*
  As Helen – when she saw aloft appear
  The Trojan flames, and reach to heaven's height,
Did clap her hands, and joyed° at the doleful sight.   *rejoiced*

13

This second Helen, fair Dame Hellenore,
  The whiles her husband ran with sorry° haste   *pitiful*
  To quench the flames which she had tined° before,   *ignited*
  Laughed at his foolish labour spent in waste,°   *vain*
  And ran into her lover's arms right fast –
  Where, strait° embraced, she to him did cry   *tightly*

And call aloud for help ere help were
    past;°   *before it was too late*
For lo! that guest would bear her forcibly,
And meant to ravish her that rather had° to die.   *would rather*

14

The wretched man, hearing her call for aid,
  And ready seeing him with her to fly,
  In his disquiet mind was much dismayed;
  But when again he backward cast his eye,
  And saw the wicked fire so furiously
  Consume his heart and scorch his idol's face,
  He was therewith distressed diversely,°   *in all directions*
  Ne wist° he how to turn nor to what place: *Neither knew*
Was never wretched man in such a woeful case.

15

Aye° when to him she cried to her he turned,   *Ever*
  And left the fire: love money overcame;
  But when he marked how his money burned,
  He left his wife: money did love disclaim.°   *discount*†
  Both was he loath to lose his loved dame,
  And loath to leave his liefest° pelf°   *most beloved wealth*
    behind –
  Yet sith° he n'ote° save both, he saved that   *since could not*
    same
  Which was the dearest to his dunghill mind,
The god of his desire, the joy of misers blind.

16

Thus whilst all things in troublous uproar were,
  And all men busy to suppress the flame,
  The loving couple need no rescue fear,
  But leisure had, and liberty, to frame°   *organise*
  Their purposed° flight free from all men's   *planned*
    reclaim;°   *recall*
  And Night, the patroness of love-stealth fair,
  Gave them safe conduct till to end they came.
  So been they gone yfere° – a wanton pair   *together*
Of lovers loosely knit, where list° them to repair.° *it pleased go*

17

Soon as the cruel flames yslaked were,
　Malbecco, seeing how his loss did lie,
　　Out of the flames which he had quenched whilere°   *previously*
　Into huge waves of grief and jealousy
　Full deep emplunged° was, and drowned nigh   *plunged†*
　'Twixt inward dole° and felonous°   *grief   violent**
　　despite.°   *outrage*
　He raved, he wept, he stamped, he loud did cry,
　And all the passions that in man may light
Did him at once oppress and vex his caitiff° sprite.°   *base   soul*

18

Long thus he chewed the cud of inward grief,
　And did consume his gall with anguish sore:°   *extreme*
　Still° when he mused on his late   *Ever*
　　mischief,°   *misfortune; hurt*
　Then still the smart° thereof increased more   *wound*
　And seemed more grievous than it was before.
　At last, when sorrow, he saw, booted° nought,   *availed*
　Ne° grief might not his love to him restore,   *Nor*
　He 'gan devise how her he rescue mought° –   *might*
Ten thousand ways he cast° in his confused thought.   *deliberated*

19

At last, resolving like a pilgrim poor
　To search her forth whereso she might be found,
　　And bearing with him treasure in close° store,°   *secret   hoard*
　The rest he leaves in ground: so takes in hand
　To seek her endlong° both by sea and   *from one end to the other*
　　land.
　Long he her sought – he sought her far and near,
　And everywhere that he mote° understand   *might*
　Of knights and ladies any meetings were,
And of each one he met he tidings° did enquire.   *news*

20

But all in vain; his woman was too wise
　Ever to come into his clutch again,
　And he too simple ever to surprise
　The jolly° Paridell for all his pain.°   *amorous; handsome   labour*

One day, as he forepassed° by the plain   passed along‡
With weary pace, he far away espied
A couple, seeming well to be his twain,
Which hoved° close under a forest side   lingered*
As if they lay in wait or else themselves did hide.

21

Well weened° he that those the same mote° be,   thought might
    And as he the better did their shape advise°   discern
    Him seemed more their manner did agree:
    For the one was armed all in warlike wise,
    Whom to be Paridell he did devise;°   presume
    And the other, all yclad in garments light,°   wanton
    Discoloured° like to womanish disguise,   Vari-coloured; feigned
    He did resemble° to his lady bright:°   compare beautiful
And ever his faint heart much yearned at the sight.

22

And ever fain° he towards them would go,   desirous
    But yet durst not for dread approachen nigh,
    But stood aloof, unweeting° what to do;   unsure
    Till that, pricked forth° with love's extremity,   spurred on by
    That is the father of foul jealousy,
    He closely nearer crept the truth to weet°   know
    But, as he nigher drew, he easily
    Might 'scern° that it was not his sweetest sweet,   discover‡
Ne° yet her belamour,° the partner of his sheet.   Nor lover

23

But it was scornful Braggadocchio
    That with his servant Trompart hovered there
    Sith° late he fled from his too earnest° foe: Since determined
    Whom such whenas Malbecco spied clear,
    He turned back and would have fled
        arrear°   into the background*
    Till Trompart, running hastily, him did stay
    And bade before his sovereign lord appear:
    That was him loath, yet durst he not gainsay
And, coming him before, low louted° on the   bowed
    lay.°   ground; lea

24

The boaster at him sternly° bent his brow,   *fiercely*
  As if he could have killed him with his look,
  That to the ground him meekly made to bow
  And awful terror deep into him struck
  That° every member° of his body   *So that limb*
    quook.°   *quaked*
  Said he: 'Thou man of nought, what dost thou here,
  Unfitly furnished with thy bag and book,
  Where I expected one with shield and spear
To prove some deeds of arms upon an equal peer.'°   *knight*

25

The wretched man at his imperious speech
  Was all abashed and, low prostrating, said:
  'Good sir, let not my rudeness be no breach
  Unto your patience, ne be ill apaid;°   *pleased*
  For I unwares this way by fortune strayed,
  A silly° pilgrim driven to distress   *simple*
  That seek a lady – .' There he sudden stayed,°   *stopped*
  And did the rest with grievous sighs suppress
While tears stood in his eyes, few° drops of bitterness.   *some*

26

'What lady, man?', said Trompart; 'Take good heart
  And tell thy grief, if any hidden lie:
  Was never better time to show° thy smart°   *reveal hurt*
  Than now that noble succour is thee by –
  That is the whole world's common remedy.'
  That cheerful word his weak heart much did cheer,
  And with vain hope his spirits faint supply,
  That bold he said: 'O most redoubted° peer,   *revered*
Vouchsafe with mild regard a wretch's case to hear.'

27

Then, sighing sore,° 'It is not long' (said he)   *grievously*
  'Sith° I enjoyed the gentlest° dame alive,   *since most noble*
  Of whom a knight – no knight at all, perdy,°   *indeed*
  But shame of all that do for honour strive –
  By treacherous deceit did me deprive.

Through open outrage° he her bore   presumption;* insolence
   away,
And with foul force unto his will° did drive –   passion
Which all good knights that arms do bear this day
Are bound for to revenge and punish if they may.

28

'And you, most noble lord, that can and dare
   Redress the wrong of miserable wight,°   creature*
Cannot employ your most victorious spear
In better quarrel than defence of right,
And for a lady 'gainst a faithless knight.
So shall your glory be advanced° much,   extolled
And all fair ladies magnify° your might   glorify
And eke° myself, albe I simple such,°   also humble as I am
Your worthy pain° shall well reward with   toil
   guerdon° rich.'   recompense

29

With that out of his budget° forth he drew   pouch
   Great store of treasure therewith him to tempt;
But he on it looked scornfully askew°   sidelong†
As much disdaining to be so misdeemed,°   misjudged
Or a warmonger° to be basely named,   mercenary
And said: 'Thy offers base I greatly loathe,
And eke thy words uncourteous and unkempt.°   rude†
I tread in dust thee and thy money both,
That, were it not for shame – .' So turned from him, wroth.

30

But Trompart, that his master's humour° knew   disposition
   In lofty looks to hide an humble° mind,   lowly
Was inly tickled with that golden view,
And in his ear him rounded° close behind.   whispered*
Yet stooped° he not, but lay still in the wind,   swooped‡
Waiting advantage on the prey to seize,
Till Trompart, lowly to the ground inclined,
Besought him his great courage° to appease°   anger quieten
And pardon simple man that rash° him did displease.   rashly

31

Big looking like a doughty doucepeer,°   *noble knight*
    At last he thus: 'Thou clod of vilest clay,
    I pardon yield, and with thy rudeness bear.
    But weet° henceforth that all that golden prey,°   *know booty*
    And all that else the vain world vaunten° may,   *boast of*
    I loathe as dung, ne° deem° my due reward: *nor judge*
    Fame is my meed,° and glory virtue's prey.   *reward*
    But minds of mortal men are muchel°   *much*
        marred,°   *corrupted*
And moved amiss with massy° muck's°   *heavy gold's*
        unmeet° regard.°   *unsuitable aspect*

32

'And more, I grant to thy great misery
    Gracious respect: thy wife shall back be sent,
    And that vile° knight, whoever that he be,   *base*
    Which hath thy lady reft, and knighthood shent,°   *disgraced*
    By Sanglamort my sword (whose deadly dent°   *blow*
    The blood hath of so many thousands shed),
    I swear, ere long shall dearly it repent:
    Ne he 'twixt heaven and earth shall hide his head,
But soon he shall be found and shortly done be dead.'°   *killed*

33

The foolish man thereat wox° wondrous blithe   *grew*
    As if the word so spoken were half done,
    And humbly thanked him a thousand sith°   *times*
    That had from death to life him newly won.
    Tho° forth the boaster marching, brave° begun   *Then showily‡*
    His stolen steed to thunder furiously
    As if he heaven and hell would overrun
    And all the world confound° with cruelty   *vanquish*
That° much Malbecco joyed° in his   *So that rejoiced*
        jollity.°   *gallantry**

34

Thus long they three together travelled
    Through many a wood and many an uncouth° way   *unknown*
    To seek his wife that was far wandered;
    But those two sought not but the present prey –

To weet,° the treasure which he did bewray,°   *Namely disclose*
On which their eyes and hearts were wholly set
With purpose how they might it best
   betray.°   *cheat‡ [out of him]*
For sith° the hour that first he did them let   *since*
The same behold, therewith their keen desires were
   whet.°   *whetted*

35

It fortuned, as they together fared,
   They spied where Paridell came pricking° fast   *spurring*
   Upon the plain, the which himself prepared
   To joust with that brave stranger knight a cast° *throw; defeat*
   As on adventure by the way he passed.
   Alone he rode, without his paragon,°   *companion‡*
   For, having filched° her bells, her up he cast   *stolen‡*
   To the wide world and let her fly alone:
He n'ould° be clogged.° So had he served   *would not impeded*
   many one.

36

The gentle° lady, loose at randon° left,   *well-born neglected‡*
   The greenwood long did walk and wander wide
   At wild adventure,° like a forlorn   *to chance in the wilderness*
   weft,°   *waif‡*
   Till on a day° the satyrs her espied   *one day*
   Straying alone withouten groom° or guide. *male attendant*
   Her up they took and with them home her led,
   With them as housewife ever to abide
   To milk their goats and make them cheese and bread,
And everyone as common good° her handled,   *goods; property*

37

That shortly she Malbecco has forgot,
   And eke° Sir Paridell, all were he° dear,   *also although he was*
   Who from her went to seek another lot°   *prize‡*
   And now by Fortune was arrived here,
   Where those two guilers° with Malbecco were.   *deceivers**
   Soon as the old man saw Sir Paridell
   He fainted, and was almost dead with fear;

Ne word he had to speak his grief to tell,
But to him louted° low and greeted goodly well,   *bowed*

38

And after asked him for Hellenore.
  'I take no keep of her,' said Paridell,
  'She woneth° in the forest there before.'°   *dwells   in front*
  So forth he rode, as his adventure
    fell;°   *to face whatever awaited him*
  The whiles the boaster from his lofty sell°   *saddle*
  Feigned to alight something amiss to mend.
  But the fresh swain° would not his leisure   *young man [Paridell]*
    dwell°   *wait*
  But went his way – whom, when he passed kenned,°   *knew*
He up remounted light° and after feigned to wend.°   *swiftly   go*

39

'Perdy, nay,' said Malbecco, 'shall ye not,
  But let him pass as lightly as he came;
  For little good of him is to be got,
  And mickle° peril to be put to shame.   *much*
  But let us go to seek my dearest dame,
  Whom he hath left in yonder forest wild;
  For of her safety in great doubt° I am   *fear*
  Lest savage beasts her person have despoiled° –   *violated*
Then all the world is lost and we in vain have toiled.'

40

They all agree, and forward them addressed.°   *proceeded*
  'Ah, but' (said crafty Trompart) 'weet° ye well   *know*
  That yonder in that wasteful° wilderness   *desolate*
  Huge monsters haunt and many dangers dwell:
  Dragons, and minotaurs, and fiends of hell,
  And many wild woodmen° which rob and rend   *wild men*
  All travellers. Therefore advise° ye well   *consider*
  Before ye enterprise° that way to wend: *undertake*
One may his journey bring too soon to evil end.'

41

Malbecco stopped in great astonishment°   *dread*‡
   And, with pale eyes fast fixed on the rest,
   Their counsel craved in danger imminent.
   Said Trompart: 'You, that are the most oppressed
   With burden of great treasure, I think best
   Here for to stay in safety behind:
   My lord and I will search the wide forest.'
   That counsel pleased not Malbecco's mind,
For he was much afraid himself alone to find.

42

'Then it is best' (said he) 'that ye do leave
   Your treasure here in some security,°   *safe place*‡
   Either fast° closed° in some hollow   *firmly enclosed*
     greave,°   *thicket*
   Or buried in the ground from jeopardy
   Till we return again in safety.
   As for us two, lest doubt of us ye have,
   Hence far away he will blindfolded lie –
   Ne privy be unto your treasure's grave.'
It pleased: so he did. Then they march forward
     brave.°   *in splendour*

43

Now when amid the thickest woods they were,
   They heard a noise° of many bagpipes shrill,   *sound; band*
   And shrieking hubbubs, them approaching near,
   Which all the forest did with horror fill.
   That dreadful sound the boaster's heart did thrill°   *pierce*
   With such amazement that in haste he fled,
   Ne ever looked back for good or ill;
   And after him eke fearful Trompart sped.
The old man could not fly, but fell to ground half dead:

44

Yet afterwards, close° creeping as he might,   *stealthily*
   He in a bush did hide his fearful head.
   The jolly° satyrs, full of fresh° delight,   *lustful; joyous youthful*
   Came dancing forth, and with them nimbly led
   Fair Hellenore with garlands all bespread,°   *covered*

Whom their May-lady they had newly made.
    She, proud of that new honour which they read,°   *declared*
    And of their lovely° fellowship full glad,   *loving*
Danced lively, and her face did with a laurel shade.

45

The silly° man that in the thicket lay   *simple; wretched*
    Saw all this goodly sport, and grieved sore;°   *extremely*
    Yet durst he not against it do or say,
    But did his heart with bitter thoughts engore°   *pierce deeply*†
    To see the unkindness° of his Hellenore.   *unnatural behaviour*
    All day they danced with great lustihead,°   *lustfulness; vigour*
    And with their horned feet the green grass wore
    The whiles their goats upon the browses° fed,   *young shoots*
Till drooping Phoebus 'gan to hide his golden head.

46

Tho° up they 'gan their merry pipes to truss°   *Then pack away*
    And all their goodly herds did gather round;
    But every satyr first did give a buss°   *kiss*‡
    To Hellenore – so busses did abound.
    Now 'gan the humid° vapour shed°   *damp cover[with drops]*†
       the ground
    With pearly dew, and the earth's gloomy shade
    Did dim the brightness of the welkin° round   *sky*
    That every bird and beast awarned° made   *aware*†
To shroud° themselves whiles sleep their senses did   *shelter*
    invade.

47

Which, when Malbecco saw, out of his bush
    Upon his hands and feet he crept full light,   *speedily*
    And like a goat amongst the goats did rush
    That, through the help of his fair horns on height°   *high*
    And misty damp of misconceiving° *causing misunderstanding*†
       night,
    And eke through likeness of his goatish beard,
    He did the better counterfeit aright:
    So home he marched amongst the horned herd,
That° none of all the satyrs him espied or heard.   *So that*

48

At night, when all they° went to sleep, he viewed   *they all*
  Whereas° his lovely wife amongst them lay   *Where*
  Embraced of° a satyr rough and rude,   *by*
  Who all the night did mind his joyous play:
  Nine times he heard him come aloft ere day,
  That° all his heart with jealousy did swell;   *So that*
  But yet that night's example did bewray°   *reveal*
  That not for nought his wife them loved so well
When one so oft a night did ring his matins bell.

49

So closely as he could he to them crept
  When, weary of their sport, to sleep they fell;
  And to his wife, that now full soundly slept,
  He whispered in her ear and did her tell
  That it was he which by her side did dwell,
  And therefore prayed her wake to hear him
    plain.°   *clearly;† lament*
  As one out of a dream not waked well
  She turned her, and returned back again:
Yet her for to awake he did the more constrain.°   *urge*

50

At last, with irksome° trouble, she abraid;°   *wearied awoke**
  And then perceiving that it was indeed
  Her old Malbecco which did her upbraid
  With looseness of her love and loathly deed,
  She was astonished° with exceeding dread   *overcome*
  And would have waked the satyr by her side;
  But he her prayed for mercy or for meed°   *reward*
  To save his life, ne° let him be descried,°   *nor discovered*
But hearken to his lore° and all his counsel hide.   *lesson*

51

Tho 'gan he her persuade° to leave that lewd   *urge*
  And loathsome life, of god and man abhorred,
  And home return where all should be renewed
  With perfect peace and bands of fresh° accord,°   *new harmony*
  And she received again to bed and board°   *table*
  As if no trespass ever had been done.

But she it all refused at one word,°   *immediately*
And by no means would to his will be won,
But chose amongst the jolly satyrs still to wone.°   *dwell*

52
He wooed her till dayspring° he espied,   *dawn*
    But all in vain, and then turned to the herd,
    Who butted him with horns on every side
    And trod down in the dirt, where his hoar beard
    Was foully dight° and he of death afeared.°   *dirtied*[t] *afraid*
    Early, before the heaven's fairest light
    Out of the ruddy east was fully reared,°   *risen*
    The herds out of their folds were loosed quite,°   *completely*
And he amongst the rest crept forth in sorry plight.

53
So soon as he the prison door did pass
    He ran as fast as both his feet could bear,
    And never looked who behind him was,
    Ne scarcely who before: like as a bear
    That, creeping close° amongst the hives to   *secretly*
        rear°   *gather* *
    An honeycomb, the wakeful dogs espy
    And, him assailing, sore° his carcase tear   *severely*
    That° hardly° he with life away does fly, *So that with difficulty*
Ne stays till safe himself he sees from jeopardy.

54
Ne stayed he till he came unto the place
    Where late his treasure he entombed had –
    Where, when he found it not (for Trompart base
    Had it purloined for his master bad),
    With extreme fury he became quite mad,
    And ran away – ran with himself away –
    That who so strangely had him seen bestad,°   *situated*
    With upstart hair and staring eyes' dismay,
From Limbo lake him late escaped sure would say.

55

High over hills and over dales he fled
   As if the wind him on his wings had borne,
   Ne° bank nor bush could stay° him when he   *Neither stop*
     sped
   His nimble feet, as° treading still on thorn.   *as if*
   Grief, and Despite,° and Jealousy, and Scorn   *Contempt; Anger*
   Did all the way him follow hard behind,
   And he himself himself loathed so forlorn° –   *abandoned*
   So shamefully forlorn – of° womankind: *by*
That as a snake still lurked in his wounded mind.

56

Still he fled forward looking backward still,°   *ever*
   Ne stayed° his flight nor fearful agony   *halted*
   Till that he came unto a rocky hill
   Over the sea suspended dreadfully,°   *terrifyingly*
   That living creature it would terrify
   To look adown, or upward to the height.
   From thence he threw himself despiteously,°   *pitilessly*
   All desperate° of his fore-damned°   *despairing already damned*†
     sprite°   *soul*
That seemed no help for him was left in living sight.

57

But, through long anguish and self-murdering thought,
   He was so wasted and forpined° quite°   *emaciated utterly*
   That all his substance was consumed to nought,
   And nothing left but like an airy sprite,°   *spirit*
   That° on the rocks he fell so flit° and light   *So that airy*†
   That he thereby received no hurt at all,
   But chanced on a craggy cliff to light,
   Whence he with crooked claws so long did crawl
That at the last he found a cave with entrance small.

58

Into the same he creeps and thenceforth there
   Resolved to build his baleful° mansion°   *wretched dwelling*
   In dreary darkness and continual fear
   Of that rock's fall, which ever and anon
   Threats with huge ruin° him to fall   *great destruction; large fall*

upon
That° he dare never sleep but that one eye   *So that*
Still ope he keeps for that occasion;
Ne ever rests he in tranquillity:
The roaring billows beat his bower° so boisterously.°   *chamber*

59

Ne ever is he wont° on aught to feed   *accustomed*
But toads and frogs, his pasture° poisonous,   *food*
Which in his cold complexion° do breed   *temperament*
A filthy blood or humour rancorous,
Matter° of doubt and dread suspicious,   *Substance*
That doth with cureless° care consume the heart,   *incurable‡*
Corrupts the stomach with gall vicious,°   *noxious; malignant*
Crosscuts° the liver with internal smart°   *Cuts across† wound*
And doth transfix the soul with Death's eternal dart.

60

Yet can he never die but, dying, lives,
And doth himself with sorrow new sustain
That death and life at once unto him gives,
And painful pleasure turns to pleasing pain.
There dwells he ever, miserable swain –
Hateful both to himself and every wight° –   *creature**
Where he through privy° grief and horror   *private*
vain,°   *pointless*
Is woxen° so deformed that he has quite   *grown*
Forgot he was a man, and Jealousy is hight.°   *called*†*

Britomart chaseth Ollyphant,
    Finds Scudamour distressed;
    Assays° the house of Busirane,   *Attacks*
    Where Love's spoils are expressed.°   *portrayed*

I

O hateful, hellish snake: what Fury first
    Brought thee from baleful° house of   *noxious; deadly*
      Proserpine
    Where, in her bosom, she thee long had nursed
    And fostered up with bitter milk of tine° –   *affliction*†
    Foul Jealousy, that turnest love divine
    To joyless dread, and makest the loving heart
    With hateful thoughts to languish and to pine,°   *waste away*
    And feed itself with self-consuming smart?°   *hurt*
Of all the passions in the mind thou vilest art.

2

O let him far be banished away,
    And in his stead let Love for ever dwell:
    Sweet Love, that doth his golden wings embay°   *bathe*†
    In blessed nectar and pure Pleasure's well,
    Untroubled of° vile fear or bitter fell.°   *by gall;*† *rancour*†
    And ye, fair ladies, that your kingdoms make
    In the hearts of men, them govern wisely well,
    And of fair Britomart example take
That was as true in love as turtle° to her make:°   *dove mate*

3

Who with Sir Satyrane, as erst° ye read,   *formerly*
    Forth riding from Malbecco's hostless house,
    Far off espied a young man, the which fled
    From an huge giant that with hideous
    And hateful outrage° long him chased thus.   *exertion;* * *fury*
    It was that Ollyphant, the brother dear
    Of that Argante vile and vicious

From whom the Squire of Dames was reft°   *taken*
    whilere:°   *formerly*
This all so bad as she, and worse, if worse aught were.

4

For as the sister did in feminine
    And filthy lust exceed all womankind,
    So he surpassed his sex masculine
    In beastly use° that I did ever find.   *custom*
    Whom, whenas Britomart beheld behind   *when*
    The fearful boy so greedily pursue,
    She was enmoved° in her noble mind   *stirred*‡
    To employ her puissance to his rescue,
And pricked° fiercely forward where she did him view.   *spurred*

5

Ne° was Sir Satyrane her far behind,   *Nor*
    But with like firmness did ensue° the chase: *follow*
    Whom when the giant saw he soon resigned
    His former suit and from them fled apace.
    They after both and boldly bade him base,°   *chased him*
    And each did strive the other to outgo;
    But he them both outran a wondrous space,
    For he was long,° and swift as any roe,   *tall*
And made much better speed to escape his feared foe.

6

It was not Satyrane whom he did fear
    But Britomart, the flower of chastity,
    For he the power of chaste hands might not bear,
    But always did their dread encounter fly.
    And now so fast his feet he did apply
    That he has gotten to a forest near,
    Where he is shrouded in security.°   *safety*
    The wood they enter and search everywhere:
They searched diversely,° so both divided   *in different directions*
    were.

7

Fair Britomart so long him followed
  That she at last came to a fountain sheer°   *pure*
  By which there lay a knight all wallowed°   *prostrate*
  Upon the grassy ground, and by him near
  His habergeon,° his helmet and his spear;   *coat of mail*
  A little off° his shield was rudely° thrown, *way off roughly*
  On which the winged boy° in colours clear *i.e., Cupid*
  Depicted was full easy to be known,
And he thereby, wherever it in field° was shown.   *battle*

8

His face upon the ground did grovelling lie
  As if he had been slumbering in the shade
  That° the brave maid would not for courtesy   *So that*
  Out of his quiet slumber him abraid,°   *arouse*†
  Nor seem too suddenly him to invade.°   *intrude upon*
  Still° as she stood she heard with grievous throb° *Ever pulse*
  Him groan, as if his heart were pieces made,
  And with most painful pangs to sigh and sob
That pity did the virgin's heart of patience° rob.   *composure*

9

At last, forth breaking into bitter plaints,°   *laments*
  He said: 'O sovereign lord that sittest on high
  And reignest in bliss among thy blessed saints,
  How sufferest thou such shameful cruelty
  So long unwreaked of° thine enemy?   *unavenged on*
  Or hast thou, lord, of good men's cause no heed?
  Or doth thy justice sleep, and silent lie?
  What booteth° then the good and righteous deed *avails*
If goodness find no grace, nor righteousness no meed?° *reward*

10

'If good find grace, and righteousness reward,
  Why then is Amoret in caitiff° band,   *imprisoning*
  Sith° that more bounteous° creature never   *Since virtuous*
    fared
  On foot upon the face of living land?
  Or if that heavenly justice may withstand
  The wrongful outrage of unrighteous men,

Why then is Busirane with wicked hand
Suffered these seven months' day° in secret   *seven full months*
  den
My lady and my love so cruelly to pen?

11

'My lady and my love is cruelly penned
  In doleful darkness from the view of day
  Whiles deadly torments do her chaste breast rend
  And the sharp steel doth rive° her heart in tway°   *split   two*
  All for° she Scudamour will not deny.   *All because*
  Yet thou, vile man, vile Scudamour, art sound,
  Ne° canst her aid, ne° canst her foe   *Neither   nor*
    dismay:°   *overcome*
  Unworthy wretch to tread upon the ground,
For whom so fair a lady feels so sore° a wound.'   *grievous*

12

There an huge heap of singults° did oppress   *sobs†*
  His struggling soul, and swelling throbs impeach°   *impede*
  His faltering tongue with pangs of dreariness,°   *grief*
  Choking the remnant of his plaintive speech,
  As if his days were come to their last reach –
  Which, when she heard, and saw the ghastly fit
  Threatening into his life to make a breach,
  Both with great ruth° and terror she was smit,   *pity*
Fearing lest from her cage the weary soul would flit.°   *fly*

13

Tho,° stooping down, she him amoved°   *Then   aroused†*
    light,°   *gently*
  Who therewith somewhat starting up, 'gan look
  And, seeing him behind a stranger knight,
  Whereas no living creature he
    mistook,°   *Which he mistook for a ghost*
  With great indignance° he that sight forsook   *indignation†*
  And, down again himself disdainfully
  Abjecting,° the earth with his fair forehead   *Throwing down‡*
    struck:
  Which the bold virgin seeing 'gan apply
Fit medicine to his grief, and spake thus courteously:

14

'Ah, gentle° knight, whose deep-conceived°   *noble   engendered*
   grief
  Well seems to exceed the power of patience,°   *endurance*
  Yet if that heavenly grace some good relief
  You send, submit you to high providence,
  And ever in your noble heart prepense°   *consider beforehand*
  That all the sorrow in the world is less
  Than virtue's might and valour's confidence.°   *boldness*
  For who n'ill° bide° the burden of distress   *will not   abide*
Must not here think to live, for life is wretchedness.

15

'Therefore, fair sir, do comfort to you take,
  And freely read° what wicked felon° so   *declare   villain*
  Hath outraged you and thralled° your   *imprisoned*
   gentle° make.   *beloved*
  Perhaps this hand may help to ease your woe
  And wreak° your sorrow on your cruel foe: *avenge*
  At least it fair endeavour will apply.'
  Those feeling words so near the quick did go
  That up his head he reared° easily   *raised*
And, leaning on his elbow, these few words let fly:

16

'What boots° it plain° that° cannot be   *avails   to lament   what*
  redressed,
  And sow vain sorrow in a fruitless ear
  Sith° power of hand, nor skill° of learned   *Since   knowledge*
   breast,
  Ne worldly prize, cannot redeem my dear
  Out of her thraldom and continual fear?
  For he the tyrant, which her hath in ward°   *under guard*
  By strong enchantments and black magic lere,°   *lore*
  Hath in a dungeon deep her close embarred,
And many dreadful fiends hath 'pointed° to her   *appointed*
  guard.

17

'There he tormenteth her most terribly,
  And day and night afflicts with mortal° pain,   *deathly*
  Because to yield him love she doth deny –
  Once to me yold° not to be yold again.   *yielded**
  But yet by torture he would her constrain
  Love to conceive in her disdainful breast:
  Till so she do she must in dool° remain,   *pain;** sorrow*
  Ne may by living means be thence released –
What boots it then to plain that cannot be redressed?'

18

With this sad hersall° of his heavy stress°   *rehearsal*[†] *affliction**
  The warlike damsel was impassioned°   *deeply moved*
    sore,°   *extremely*
  And said: 'Sir knight, your cause is nothing less
  Than is your sorrow, certes° – if not more;   *indeed*
  For nothing so much pity doth implore
  As gentle lady's helpless misery.
  But yet, if please ye listen to my lore,°   *instruction*
  I will with proof° of last extremity°   *evidence death*
Deliver her fro' thence, or with her for you die.'

19

'Ah, gentlest knight alive,' said Scudamour,
  What huge heroic magnanimity°   *fortitude*
  Dwells in thy bounteous° breast? What couldest thou *virtuous*
    more
  If she were thine, and thou as now am I?
  Oh spare thy happy days, and them apply
  To better boot,° but let me die that ought: *advantage*
  More is more loss – one is enough to die.'
  'Life is not lost,' said she, 'for which is bought
Endless renown: that more than death is to be sought.'

20

Thus she at length persuaded him to rise
  And with her wend, to see what new success°   *chance*
  Mote° him befall upon new enterprise.°   *Might undertaking*
  His arms – which he had vowed to disprofess° –   *renounce*[†]
  She gathered up and did about him dress,°   *place*

And his forwandered° steed unto him got.   wandered away
So forth they both yfere° make their progress   together
And march not past the mountenance° of a   distance
    shot°   bow shot
Till they arrived whereas° their purpose they did   where
    plot.°   plan

21

There they, dismounting, drew their weapons bold
    And stoutly° came unto the castle gate,   boldly
    Whereas no gate they found them to withhold,°   hold back
    Nor ward° to wait° at morn and evening late;   guard watch
    But in the porch, that did them sore amate,°   dismay
    A flaming fire ymixed with smouldery° smoke   suffocating†
    And stinking sulphur that, with grisly°   terrifying
        hate°   abhorrence
    And dreadful horror, did all entrance choke,
Enforced° them their forward footing to   Compelled
    revoke.°   draw back

22

Greatly thereat was Britomart dismayed,
    Ne° in that stound° wist° how herself to   Nor moment knew
        bear —
    For danger vain it were to have assayed°   assailed
    That cruel element which all things fear,
    Ne none can suffer to approachen near —
    And, turning back to Scudamour, thus said:
    'What monstrous enmity provoke° we here,   summon up
    Foolhardy as the Earth's children, the which made
Battle against the gods? — so we a god invade.

23

'Danger without discretion to attempt
    Inglorious and beastlike is. Therefore, sir knight,
    Aread° what course of° you is safest   Declare by
        dempt,°   judged
    And how we with our foe may come to fight.'
    'This is,' quoth he, 'the dolorous° despite°   grievous malice
    Which erst° to you I plained;° for neither   previously lamented
        may

This fire be quenched by any wit° or might,   *intelligence*
 Ne yet by any means removed away,
So mighty be the enchantments which the same do
  stay.°   *maintain*

24

'What is there else but cease these fruitless pains
 And leave me to my former languishing?
 Fair Amoret must dwell in wicked chains,
 And Scudamour here die with sorrowing.'
 'Perdy° not so'(said she), 'for shameful thing *Indeed*
 It were to abandon noble chevisance° *assistance; prowess*[†]
 For show of peril, without venturing.
 Rather let try extremities of chance
Than enterprised° praise for dread to   *undertaken*
  disadvance.'°   *retreat*[†]

25

Therewith resolved to prove her utmost might,
 Her ample shield she threw before her face
 And, her sword point directing forward right,
 Assailed the flame – the which eftsoons gave place
 And did itself divide with equal space
 That° through she passed: as a thunderbolt *So that*
 Pierceth the yielding air, and doth displace
 The soaring clouds into sad° showers ymolt,° *heavy melted**
So to her yold° the flames and did their force *yielded**
  revolt.°   *turn back*[†]

26

Whom, whenas Scudamour saw past the fire,
 Safe and untouched, he likewise 'gan assay° *make the attempt*
 With greedy will and envious desire,
 And bade the stubborn flames to yield him way.
 But cruel Mulciber would not obey
 His threatful pride, but did the more augment
 His mighty rage and, with imperious sway,
 Him forced (maugre)° his fierceness to relent *in spite of himself*
And back retire, all scorched and pitifully brent.° *burned*

27

With huge impatience he inly° swelt° –   *inwardly; greatly burned*[†]
   More for great sorrow that he could not pass
   Than for the burning torment which he felt –
   That° with fell° woodness° he   *So that fierce fury*
      effierced° was   *maddened*[†]
   And, wilfully him throwing on the grass,
   Did beat and bounce° his head and breast full   *bang*[‡]
      sore,°   *extremely*
   The whiles the championess now entered has
   The utmost° room and passed the foremost door –   *outermost*
The utmost room, abounding with all precious
     store.°   *abundance*

28

For round about the walls yclothed were
   With goodly arras° of great majesty,   *tapestries*
   Woven with gold and silk so close and near°   *tightly*
   That the rich metal lurked privily,°   *craftily*
   As faining° to be hid from envious eye.   *desiring; also: feigning*
   Yet here and there and everywhere unwares°   *suddenly*
   It showed itself, and shone unwillingly:
   Like a discoloured° snake, whose hidden snares *vari-coloured*
Through the green grass his long, bright-burnished back
     declares.

29

And in those tapets° were fashioned   *tapestries*
   Many fair portraits° and many a fair° feat,   *pictures*[‡] *fine*
   And all of love and all of lustihead°   *lust; youthful vigour*
   (As seemed by their semblant)° did   *appearance*
      entreat;°   *treat of*
   And eke° all Cupid's wars they did repeat,°   *also rehearse*
   And cruel battles which he whilom fought
   'Gainst all the gods to make his empire great;
   Besides the huge massacres which he wrought
On mighty kings and caesars, into thraldom brought.

30

Therein was writ° how often thundering Jove   *inscribed*
   Had felt the point of his heart-piercing dart
   And, leaving heaven's kingdom, here did rove
   In strange disguise to slake his scalding smart:°   *wound*
   Now like a ram, fair Helle to pervert;°   *ruin; corrupt*
   Now like a bull, Europa to withdraw:
   Ah, how the fearful lady's tender heart
   Did lively° seem to tremble when she saw   *lifelike*
The huge seas under her to obey her servant's° law.   *lover's*

31

Soon after that into a golden shower
   Himself he changed fair Danaë to view,
   And through the roof of her strong brazen tower
   Did rain into her lap an honey dew,
   The whiles her foolish guard – that little knew
   Of such deceit – kept the iron door fast barred,
   And watched that none should enter nor issue:
   Vain was the watch and bootless° all the   *pointless*
      ward°   *guarding*
Whenas° the god to golden hue° himself   *When   shape*
   transferred.°   *changed†*

32

Then was he turned into a snowy swan
   To win fair Leda to his lovely° trade:°   *loving dealings†*
   O wondrous skill and sweet wit° of the man   *ingenuity*
   That her in daffadillies sleeping made,
   From scorching heat her dainty limbs to shade,
   Whiles the proud bird, ruffling his feathers wide,°   *widely*
   And brushing° his fair breast, did her invade.   *preening*
   She slept, yet 'twixt her eyelids closely° spied   *secretly*
How towards her he rushed, and smiled at his
      pride.°   *splendour; arousal**

33

Then showed it how the Theban Semele,
   Deceived of° jealous Juno, did require°   *by   ask*
   To see him in his sovereign majesty,
   Armed with his thunderbolts and lightning fire,

Whence dearly she with death bought her desire.
But fair Alcmena better match did make,
Joying° his love in likeness more entire:°   *Enjoying perfect*
Three nights in one, they say, that for her sake
He then did put, her pleasure longer to partake.

34

Twice was he seen in soaring eagle's shape
  And with wide wings to beat the buxom air:
  Once when he with Asterie did 'scape,
  Again whenas° the Trojan boy so fair   *when*
  He snatched from Ida hill and with him bare.
  Wondrous delight it was there to behold
  How the rude° shepherds after him did stare,   *ignorant*
  Trembling through fear lest down he fallen should,
And often to him calling to take surer hold.

35

In satyr's shape Antiopa he snatched,
  And like a fire when he Aegina assayed;°   *assaulted*
  A shepherd when Mnemosyne he catched;°   *caught*
  And like a serpent to the Thracian maid.
  Whiles thus on earth great Jove these pageants played,
  The winged boy did thrust into his throne
  And, scoffing, thus unto his mother said:
  'Lo, now the heavens obey to me alone
And take me for their Jove whiles Jove to earth is gone.'

36

And thou, fair Phoebus, in thy colours bright
  Was there inwoven, and the sad distress
  In which that boy° thee plunged for   *i.e., Cupid*
    despite,°   *malice*
  That thou bewrayedest° his mother's wantonness   *disclosed‡*
  When she with Mars was meynt° in joyfulness: *combined*
  For-thy° he thrilled° thee with a leaden dart *Therefore pierced*
  To love fair Daphne which thee loved less:
  Less she thee loved than was thy just desert,
Yet was thy love her death, and her death was thy smart.°   *hurt*

37

So lovedest thou the lusty Hyacinth;
 So lovedest thou the fair Coronis dear:
 Yet both are of° thy hapless° hand extinct:°   *by unlucky dead*
 Yet both in flowers do live, and love thee bear,
 The one a paunce,° the other a sweet briar;   *pansy*
 For grief whereof ye mote° have lively° seen *might as if alive*
 The god himself rending his golden hair
 And breaking quite° his garland ever green,   *utterly*
With other signs of sorrow and impatient teen.°   *grief*

38

Both for those two, and for his own dear son –
 The son of Climene – he did repent
 Who, bold to guide the chariot of the sun,
 Himself in thousand pieces fondly° rent   *foolishly*
 And all the world with flashing fire brent:°   *burned*
 So like, that all the walls did seem to flame.
 Yet cruel Cupid, not herewith content,
 Forced him eftsoons° to follow other game   *soon after*
And love a shepherd's daughter for his dearest dame –

39

He loved Isse for his dearest dame,
 And for her sake her cattle fed awhile,
 And for her sake a cowherd vile° became   *lowly*
 (The servant of Admetus, cowherd vile)
 Whiles that from heaven he suffered exile.
 Long were to tell each other lovely fit:°   *frenzy of love*
 Now like a lion, hunting after spoil,
 Now like a stag, now like a falcon flit,°   *swift*†
All which in that fair arras was most lively writ.°   *portrayed*

40

Next unto him was Neptune pictured°   *depicted*
 In his divine resemblance wondrous like:
 His face was rugged,° and his   *shaggy; wrinkled*
  hoary° head   *white; venerable*
 Dropped with brackish° dew. His three-forked   *salty*†
  pike°   *trident*
 He sternly shook, and therewith fierce did strike

The raging billows, that° on every side   *so that*
They trembling stood and made a long broad dike
That his swift chariot might have passage wide,
Which four great hippodames° did draw in   *hippopotamuses*
    teamwise° tied.   *as a team*

41

His sea-horses did seem to snort amain,°   *with full force‡*
And from their nostrils blow the briny steam
That made the sparkling waves to smoke again
And flame with gold; but the white, foamy cream
Did shine with silver and shoot forth his beam.
The god himself did pensive seem and sad,
And hung adown his head as° he did dream,   *as if*
For privy° love his breast empierced° had: *secret transfixed‡*
Ne° aught but dear Bisaltis aye° could make him glad. *Nor ever*

42

He loved eke Iphimedia dear,
    And Aeolus' fair daughter, Arne hight,°   *called*†
For whom he turned himself into a steer,
    And fed on fodder to beguile° her sight.   *deceive*
Also, to win Deucalion's daughter bright°   *beautiful*
He turned himself into a dolphin fair;
And like winged horse he took his flight
To snaky-locked Medusa to repair,
On whom he got° fair Pegasus that flitteth° in *begot flies swiftly*
    the air.

43

Next Saturn was (but who would ever ween°   *believe*
    That sullen Saturn was ever weened°   *also: weaned = trained to‡*
    to love? –
Yet love is sullen and Saturnlike seen,
As he did for Erigone it prove),
That to a centaur did himself transmove.°   *transform†*
So proved it eke that gracious° god of wine   *handsome*
When, for to compass° Philliras' hard love,   *win;‡ accomplish‡*
He turned himself into a fruitful vine
And into her fair bosom made his grapes decline.

44

Long were to tell the amorous assays°   *assaults*
  And gentle pangs with which he maked° meek   *made*
  The mighty Mars to learn his wanton plays:
  How oft for Venus, and how often eke
  For many other nymphs he sore° did shriek   *grievously*
  With womanish tears and with unwarlike smarts°   *wounds*
  Privily° moistening his horrid° cheek.   *Secretly bristling*
  There was he painted full of burning darts
And many wide wounds launched° through his inner   *pierced*
  parts.

45

Ne did he spare (so cruel was the elf)°   *little devil*
  His own dear mother (ah, why should he so?);
  Ne did he spare° sometime to prick himself   *forbear*
  That he might taste the sweet consuming woe
  Which he had wrought to many others mo'.°   *more*
  But to declare the mournful tragedies
  And spoils wherewith he all the ground° did strew,   *earth*
  More eath° to number with how many eyes   *It would be easier*
High heaven beholds sad lovers' nightly thieveries:

46

Kings, queens, lords, ladies, knights and damsels gent°   *noble*
  Were heaped together with the vulgar° sort°   *common crowd*
  And mingled with the rascal rabblement°   *rabble‡*
  Without respect of person or of port°   *social standing*
  To show Dan° Cupid's power and great effort.°   *Lord strength*
  And round about a border was entrailed°   *interlaced‡*
  Of broken bows and arrows shivered° short;   *shattered*
  And a long bloody river through them railed,°   *flowed**
So lively° and so like that living sense it
    failed.°   *lifelike [only] lacked*

47

And at the upper end of that fair room
  There was an altar built of precious stone
  Of passing° value and of great renown,   *surpassing*
  On which there stood an image, all alone,
  Of massy° gold which with his own light shone;   *solid*

And wings it had with sundry colours dight° –   bedecked
    More sundry colours than the proud pavone°   peacock
    Bears in his boasted fan, or Iris bright
When her discoloured° bow she spreads through   vari-coloured
    heaven bright.

48

Blindfold he was, and in his cruel fist
    A mortal° bow and arrows keen° did hold   deadly   sharp
    With which he shot at random when him list,°   wished
    Some headed with sad° lead, some with pure   melancholy; heavy
        gold
    (Ah man, beware how thou those darts behold).
    A wounded dragon under him did lie
    Whose hideous° tail his left foot did enfold,   huge; terrible
    And with a shaft was shot through either eye
That no man forth might draw, ne no man remedy.

49

And underneath his feet was written thus:
    'Unto the victor of the gods this be.'
    And all the people in that ample house
    Did to that image bow their humble knee
    And oft committed foul idolatry.
    That wondrous sight fair Britomart amazed,
    Ne, seeing, could her wonder satisfy,
    But ever more and more upon it gazed,
The whiles the passing° brightness her frail senses   exceeding
    dazed.

50

Tho° as she backward cast her busy eye   Then
    To search each secret of that goodly stead,°   place
    Over the door thus written she did spy:
    'Be bold'. She oft and oft it over-read,°   read over
    Yet could not find what sense it figured;
    But what so were therein or° writ or meant,   either
    She was no whit thereby discouraged
    From prosecuting of her first intent,
But forward with bold steps into the next room she went.

51

Much fairer than the former was that room,
 And richlier by many parts° arrayed;   *much more*
 For not with arras made in painful° looms   *laborious*
 But with pure gold it all was overlaid,
 Wrought with wild antics° which their follies   *grotesques*
  played
 In the rich metal as° they living were: *as if*
 A thousand monstrous forms therein were made,
 Such as false Love doth oft upon him wear;
For Love in thousand monstrous forms doth oft appear.

52

And, all about, the glistering walls were hung
 With warlike spoils and with victorious preys°   *booty*
 Of mighty conquerors and captains strong,
 Which were whilom° captived° in their *formerly* made captive*
  days
 To cruel love, and wrought° their own   *caused*
  decays.°   *ruin; death*
 Their swords and spears were broke and hauberks° *mail coats*
  rent,
 And their proud garlands of triumphant bays
 Trodden in dust with fury insolent
To show the victor's might and merciless intent.

53

The warlike maid, beholding earnestly
 The goodly ordinance° of this rich   *arrangement; equipment*
  place,
 Did greatly wonder, ne could satisfy
 Her greedy eyes with gazing a long space;°   *while*
 But more she marvelled that no footing's°   *footprint's‡*
  trace,°   *track; print*
 Nor wight,° appeared, but wasteful°   *creature* desolate*
  emptiness
 And solemn silence over all that place.
 Strange thing it seemed that none was to possess° *inhabit*
So rich purveyance,° ne them keep with   *trappings; provision**
  carefulness.

54

And as she looked about she did behold
  How over that same door was likewise writ
  'Be bold, be bold,' and everywhere, 'Be bold,'
  That° much she mused, yet could not　　　　*So that*
    construe° it　　　　　　　　　　　　　*interpret*
  By any riddling skill, or common wit.°　　　*sense*
  At last she spied, at that room's upper end,
  Another iron door, on which was writ:
  'Be not too bold' – whereto, though she did bend°　*apply*
Her earnest mind, yet wist° not what it might　　*knew*
  intend.°　　　　　　　　　　　　　　　*signify*

55

Thus she there waited until eventide,
  Yet living creature none she saw appear.
  And now sad° shadows 'gan the world to　　*dark; melancholy*
    hide
  From mortal view, and wrap in darkness drear;
  Yet n'ould° she doff° her weary arms, for　*would not remove*
    fear
  Of secret danger, ne let sleep oppress
  Her heavy eyes with nature's burden dear;
  But drew herself aside in sickerness,°　　　*security*
And her well-pointed° weapons did about her　*sharp; ready*
  dress.°　　　　　　　　　　　　　　*prepare*

Canto 12

The masque of Cupid and the enchanted
  Chamber are displayed,
Whence Britomart redeems fair
  Amoret, through charms° decayed.°*spells wasted away*

1

Tho,° whenas° cheerless Night ycovered had　*Then when*
  Fair heaven with an universal cloud
  That° every wight,° dismayed°　*So that creature* overcome*

with darkness sad,
In silence and in sleep themselves did shroud,
She heard a thrilling° trumpet sound aloud –   *piercing*
Sign of nigh battle, or got victory.
Nought therewith daunted was her courage proud,
But rather stirred to cruel° enmity,   *fierce*
Expecting° ever° when some foe she might   *Awaiting always*
    descry.

                                    2

With that an hideous° storm of wind arose,   *terrible; immense*
    With dreadful thunder and lightning atwixt,°   *in between**
    And an earthquake, as if it straight would loose
    The world's foundations from his centre fixed.°   *fixed centre*
    A direful° stench of smoke and sulphur mixed   *dreadful‡*
    Ensued, whose noyance° filled the fearful   *nuisance*
        stead°   *place*
    From the fourth hour of night until the sixth;
    Yet the bold Britomart was nought ydred,°   *afraid**
Though much inmoved,° but steadfast still   *affected inwardly‡ **
    persevered.

                                    3

All suddenly a stormy whirlwind blew
    Throughout the house that clapped° every door;   *slammed*
    With which that iron wicket° open flew   *door*
    As° it with mighty levers had been tore,°   *As if wrenched*
    And forth issued – as on the ready floor
    Of some theatre – a grave personage
    That in his hand a branch of laurel bore,
    With comely haviour° and countenance   *deportment; manner*
        sage,
Yclad in costly garments, fit for tragic stage.

                                    4

Proceeding to the midst he still did stand,
    As if in mind he somewhat° had to say   *something*
    And, to the vulgar° beckoning with his hand   *crowd*
    In sign of silence, as to hear a play,
    By lively° actions he 'gan bewray°   *vigorous unfold*
    Some argument° of matter°   *theme subject matter*

passioned.°   *passionate*‡
  Which done, he back retired soft away
  And, passing by, his name discovered° –   *revealed*
Ease – on his robe in golden letters ciphered.°   *written*‡

5

The noble maid, still standing, all this viewed,
  And marvelled at his strange°   *unknown*
    intendiment.°   *intention*†
  With that a joyous fellowship issued
  Of minstrels making goodly°   *excellent*
    merriment,°   *merry-making*‡
  With wanton bards and rhymers impudent,
  All which together sung full° cheerfully   *very*
  A lay° of love's delight with sweet concent;°   *song   harmony*
  After whom marched a jolly company,
In manner of a masque, arranged orderly.

6

The whiles,° a most delicious harmony   *Meantime*
  In full strange notes was sweetly heard to sound,
  That° the rare sweetness of the melody   *So that*
  The feeble senses wholly did confound°   *confuse*
  And the frail soul in deep delight nigh drowned.
  And when it ceased shrill trumpets loud did bray,
  That their report did far away rebound;°   *re-echo*
  And when they ceased, it 'gan again to play,
The whiles° the maskers marched forth in trim°   *While   correct*
  array.°   *order*

7

The first was Fancy,° like a lovely boy   *Imagination*
  Of rare° aspect° and beauty without peer –   *finest   appearance*
  Matchable either to that imp° of Troy   *youth*‡
  Whom Jove did love and chose his cup to bear,
  Or that same dainty° lad which was so dear   *handsome*
  To great Alcides that, whenas° he died,   *when*
  He wailed womanlike with many a tear,
  And every wood and every valley wide
He filled with Hylas' name: the nymphs eke° 'Hylas' cried.   *also*

8

His garment neither was of silk nor say°   *fine-textured wool*
  But painted plumes, in goodly order dight,°   *arranged*
  Like as the sunburnt Indians do array°   *dress*
  Their tawny bodies in their proudest plight.°   *dress†*
  As those same plumes, so seemed he vain and light;° *frivolous*
  That by his gait might easily appear;
  For still he fared° as° dancing in delight,   *moved as if*
  And in his hand a windy° fan did bear   *to produce wind*
That in the idle air he moved still here and there.

9

And him beside marched amorous Desire,
  Who seemed of riper years than the other swain –
  Yet was that other swain this elder's sire
  And gave him being, common to them twain.
  His garment was disguised° very   *ostentatiously made*
    vain,°   *frivolously*
  And his embroidered bonnet sat awry;
  'Twixt both his hands few sparks he close did strain°   *clasp*
  Which still he blew and kindled busily
That° soon they life conceived and forth in flames did   *So that*
  fly.

10

Next after him went Doubt, who was yclad
  In a discoloured° coat of strange   *vari-coloured*
    disguise°   *fashion**
  That at his° back a broad capuccio° had,   *its hood†*
  And sleeves dependent° Albanese   *hanging*
    wise.°   *in the Scots fashion*
  He looked askew° with his mistrustful   *aslant;† unfavourably‡*
    eyes
  And nicely° trod, as° thorns lay in his way,   *carefully as if*
  Or that the floor to shrink° he did advise;°   *give way† perceive*
  And on a broken reed he still did stay°   *support*
His feeble steps, which shrunk° when hard thereon he *collapsed†*
  lay.

11

With him went Danger, clothed in ragged weed°   *attire*
  Made of bearskin that him more dreadful made:
  Yet his own face was dreadful, ne° did need   *nor*
  Strange° horror to deform his grisly°   *Added terrifying*
    shade.°   *darkness*
  A net in one hand and a rusty blade
  In the other was, this Mischief,° that   *Harm*
    Mishap:°   *Misfortune*
  With the one his foes he threatened to invade,°   *attack*
  With the other he his friends meant° to enwrap;   *intended*
For whom he could not kill he practised° to entrap.   *schemed*‡

12

Next him was Fear, all armed from top to toe,
  Yet thought himself not safe enough thereby,
  But feared each shadow moving to and fro;
  And his own arms when glittering he did spy
  Or clashing heard, he fast away did fly,
  As ashes pale of hue and wingy-heeled;
  And evermore on Danger fixed his eye,
  'Gainst whom he always bent° a brazen shield   *inclined*
Which his right hand unarmed fearfully did wield.

13

With him went Hope in rank,° a handsome maid   *in line*
  Of cheerful look and lovely to behold.
  In silken samite° she was light° arrayed,   *rich silk fabric lightly*
  And her fair locks were woven up° in gold;   *plaited*
  She always smiled, and in her hand did hold
  An holy water sprinkle° dipped in dew,   *sprinkler*
  With which she sprinkled favours manifold
  On whom she list,° and did great liking show –   *wished*
Great liking unto many, but true love to few.

14

And after them Dissemblance and
    Suspect°   *Dissimulation Suspicion*
  Marched in one rank,° yet an unequal pair;   *row*
  For she was gentle and of mild aspect,
  Courteous to all and seeming debonair,°   *gracious; mild*

Goodly adorned and exceeding fair –
Yet was that all but painted and purloined,°   *stolen*‡
And her bright brows were decked with borrowed hair,
Her deeds were forged, and her words false coined,
And always in her hand two clues° of silk she twined.   *balls*

15

But he was foul° ill-favoured and grim,   *extremely*
    Under his eyebrows looking still askance;
And ever as Dissemblance laughed on him,
He loured on her with dangerous eye-glance,
Showing his nature in his countenance.
His rolling eyes did never rest in place
But walked° each where,° for fear of hid   *shifted   everywhere*
    mischance,
Holding a lattice still before his face
Through which he still° did peep as forward he did pace.   *ever*

16

Next him went Grief and Fury matched yfere:°   *together*
    Grief all in sable sorrowfully clad
Down hanging his dull head with heavy cheer,°   *face*
Yet inly being more than seeming sad.
A pair of pincers in his hand he had,
With which he pinched people to the heart
That° from thenceforth a wretched life they led   *So that*
In wilful languor° and consuming smart,°   *sickness   hurt*
Dying each day with inward wounds of Dolour's° dart.   *Grief's*

17

But Fury was full ill apparelled
    In rags that° naked nigh she did appear,   *so that*
With ghastly looks and dreadful drearihead° –   *gloominess*‡
For from her back her garments she did tear,
And from her head oft rent her snarled° hair.   *knotted; matted*
In her right hand a firebrand she did toss°   *wave*
About her head, still roaming here and there
As a dismayed deer, in chase embossed,°   *pursued to extremity*‡
Forgetful of his safety hath his right way lost.

18

After them went Displeasure and Pleasance° –   *Delight*
   He looking lumpish° and full sullen sad,   *melancholy*
   And hanging down his heavy countenance;
   She cheerful fresh and full of joyance° glad,   *delight†*
   As if no sorrow she ne° felt nor drad° –   *neither   dreaded*
   That° evil°-matched pair they seemed to be: *So that   ill*
   An angry wasp the one in a vial had;
   The other in hers a honey-lady° bee.   *laden*
Thus marched these six couples forth in fair
    degree.°   *with comely steps*

19

After all these there marched a most fair dame
   Led of two greasy° villains, the one Despite,°   *horrible   Malice*
   The other cleped° Cruelty by name.   *called*
   She, doleful lady, like a dreary sprite°   *spirit*
   Called by strong charms out of eternal night,
   Had Death's own image figured in her face,
   Full of sad signs,° fearful to living sight;   *marks; symbols*
   Yet in that horror showed a seemly grace,
And with her feeble feet did move a comely° pace.   *pleasing*

20

Her breast all naked (as net° ivory   *unadorned; simple*
   Without adorn° of gold or silver bright   *adornment†*
   Wherewith the craftsman wonts° it   *is accustomed*
    beautify)°   *adorn*
   Of her due honour° was despoiled quite,°   *ornament   completely*
   And a wide wound therein (oh rueful° sight)   *pitiful*
   Entrenched deep with knife accursed keen,°   *sharp*
   Yet freshly bleeding forth her fainting sprite°   *soul*
   (The work of cruel hand), was to be seen
That dyed in sanguine red her skin all snowy clean.

21

At that wide orifice her trembling heart
   Was drawn forth and in silver basin laid,
   Quite° through-transfixed with a deadly dart,   *Completely*
   And in her blood yet steaming fresh embayed;°   *plunged†*
   And those two villains which her steps upstayed

When her weak feet could scarcely her sustain,
And fading vital powers 'gan to fade,
Her forward still with torture did constrain°   *compel*
And evermore increased her consuming pain.

22

Next after her the winged god himself
  Came riding on a lion ravenous,
  Taught to obey the manege° of that   *horsemanship*‡
    elf°   *mischievous boy*‡
  That man and beast with power imperious
  Subdueth to his kingdom tyrannous.
  His blindfold eyes he bade a while unbind
  That° his proud spoil of that same dolorous   *So that*
  Fair dame he might behold in perfect kind:°   *fashion*
Which seen, he much rejoiced in his cruel mind

23

Of which full proud, himself uprearing high,
  He looked round about with stern disdain
  And did survey his goodly company;°   *companions; band*
  And, marshalling the evil°-ordered train,   *ill-*
  With that° the darts which his right hand did   *Thereupon*
    strain°   *clasp*
  Full dreadfully he shook° that° all did quake,   *waved so that*
  And clapped on high his coloured wings twain
  That all his many° it afraid did make;   *company*
Tho,° blinding him° again, his way he forth did   *Then himself*
  take.

24

Behind him was Reproach, Repentance, Shame:
  Reproach the first, Shame next, Repent behind:
  Repentance feeble, sorrowful and lame;
  Reproach despiteful,° careless and unkind;   *malicious*
  Shame most ill-favoured, bestial and blind.
  Shame loured, Repentance sighed, Reproach did scold;
  Reproach sharp stings, Repentance whips entwined,
  Shame burning brandirons° in her hand did hold: *swords*‡
All three to each unlike, yet all made in one
  mould.°   *form;*‡ *pattern*‡

25

And after them a rude,° confused rout   *rough*
  Of persons flocked whose names is° hard to   *it is*
   read.°   *discern†*
  Amongst them was stern Strife and Anger stout,°   *fierce*
  Unquiet Care and fond° Unthriftihead,°   *foolish Thriftlessness†*
  Lewd° Loss of Time, and Sorrow, seeming   *Worthless; lustful*
   dead,
  Inconstant Change and false Disloyalty,
  Consuming Riotise° and guilty Dread   *Riotousness†*
  Of heavenly vengeance, faint Infirmity,
Vile° Poverty and, lastly, Death with infamy.   *Lowly; demeaning*

26

There were full° many more like maladies   *very*
  Whose names and natures I n'ote° readen°   *cannot declare*
   well:
  So many mo' (as there be fantasies
  In wavering women's wit) that none can tell,
  Or° pains in love, or punishments in hell: *Either*
  All which disguised marched in masquing wise°   *fashion*
  About the chamber with that damosel°   *damsel*
  And then returned, having marched thrice,
Into the inner room from whence they first did rise.°   *come forth*

27

So soon as they were in, the door straightway
  Fast° locked,° driven with that stormy   *Firmly was locked†*
   blast
  Which first it opened, and bore all away.
  Then the brave maid, which all this while was placed
  In secret shade and saw both first and last,
  Issued forth, and went unto the door
  To enter in, but found it locked fast.
  It vain she thought with vigorous° uproar°   *forceful violence‡*
For to efforce° when charms had closed it afore.   *force open†*

28

Where force might not avail, there sleights° and   *wiles*
   art°   *cunning*
  She cast° to use, both fit for hard   *resolved*

    emprise;°   *undertaking*
For-thy° from that same room not to depart   *Therefore*
Till morrow next she did herself advise,
When that same masque again should forth arise.°   *issue*
The morrow next appeared with joyous cheer,
Calling men to their daily exercise;
Then she, as morrow fresh, herself did rear
Out of her secret stand° that day for to outwear.   *guard-post*

29

All that day she outwore in wandering
    And gazing on that chamber's ornament,°   *furnishings*
Till that again the second evening
Her covered with her sable vestment,
Wherewith the world's fair beauty she hath blent.°   *obscured*
Then, when the second watch was almost past,
That brazen door flew open, and in went
Bold Britomart as she had late forecast,°   *anticipated*
Neither of idle shows nor of false charms aghast.°   *frightened*

30

So soon as she was entered, round about
    She cast her eyes to see what was become
Of all those persons which she saw without:°   *outside*
But lo, they straight were vanished all and some,°   *one and all*
Ne° living wight° she saw in all that room   Nor *creature**
Save that same woeful lady, both whose hands
Were bounden fast (that did her ill become),
And her small waist girt round with iron bands
Unto a brazen pillar, by the which she stands.

31

And her before the vile Enchanter sat,
    Figuring strange characters of his art:
With living blood he those characters wrote,
Dreadfully dropping from her dying heart
Seeming° transfixed by his cruel dart,   *Which appeared to be*
And all perforce° to make her him to love –   *indeed; forcibly*
Ah, who can love the worker° of her smart?°   *cause hurt*

A thousand charms° he formerly did prove,°   spells try
Yet thousand charms could not her steadfast heart
    remove.°   move

32

Soon as that virgin knight he saw in place,°   there; before him
    His wicked books in haste he overthrew,
    Not caring his long labours to deface,°   destroy
    And, fiercely running to that lady true,
    A murderous knife out of his pocket drew,
    The which he thought (for villainous despite)°   malice
    In her tormented body to imbrue.°   plunge†
    But the stout° damsel, to him leaping light,°   brave swiftly
His cursed hand withheld, and mastered his might.

33

From her — to whom his fury first he meant° —   intended
    The wicked weapon rashly° he did wrest   quickly‡
    And, turning to herself his fell° intent,   cruel
    Unwares° it struck into her snowy chest   Suddenly
    That° little drops empurpled° her fair   So that reddened†
      breast.
    Exceeding wroth therewith the virgin grew,
    Albe° the wound were nothing° deep   Although not at all
      impressed,
    And fiercely forth her mortal blade she drew
To give him the reward for such vile outrage due.

34

So mightily she smote him that to ground
    He fell half dead: next stroke him should have slain,
    Had not the lady (which by him stood bound)
    Dernly° unto her called to abstain   Secretly*
    From doing° him to die; for else her pain   causing
    Should be remediless, sith° none but he   since
    Which wrought it could the same recure° again.   heal
    Therewith she stayed her hand, loath stayed to be
(For life to him she envied,° and longed revenge to   begrudged
      see),

35

And to him said: 'Thou wicked man, whose meed°   *reward*
  For so huge mischief and vile villainy
  Is death, or, if that aught do death exceed,
  Be sure, that nought may save thee from to die
  But if° that thou this dame do presently°   *Unless forthwith*
  Restore unto her health and former state.
  This do, and live: else die, undoubtedly.'
  He, glad of life, that looked for death but late,°   *recently*
Did yield himself right willing to prolong his date°   *life-span*

36

And, rising up, 'gan straight to overlook°   *peruse*
  Those cursed leaves, his charms back to reverse:
  For dreadful things out of that baleful° book   *malign; deadly*
  He read, and measured° many a sad° verse,   *read through evil*
  That° horror 'gan the virgin's heart to pierce,   *So that*
  And her fair locks up stared stiff on end
  Hearing him those same bloody lines rehearse.
  And all the while he read she did extend
Her sword high over him if aught° he did offend.   *in any way*

37

Anon she 'gan perceive the house to quake
  And all the doors to rattle round about.
  Yet all that did not her dismayed make,
  Nor slack her threatful hand for danger's doubt,°   *fear*
  But still with steadfast eye and courage stout°   *brave*
  Abode,° to weet° what end would come of all. *Stayed know*
  At last that mighty chain, which round about
  Her tender waist was wound, adown 'gan fall,
And that great brazen pillar broke in pieces small.

38

The cruel steel which thrilled° her dying heart   *pierced*
  Fell softly forth as of his° own accord,   *its*
  And the wide wound (which lately° did   *recently*
    dispart°   *cleave*
  Her bleeding breast, and riven bowels gored),°   *pierced*
  Was closed up as it had not been bored,
  And every part to safety full sound –

As° she were never hurt – was soon°   *As if straight away*
   restored.
Tho,° when she felt herself to be unbound   *Then*
And perfect whole, prostrate she fell unto the ground.

39

Before fair Britomart she fell prostrate,
   Saying: 'Ah, noble knight, what worthy meed°   *reward*
   Can wretched lady, quit° from woeful state,   *relieved*
   Yield you in lieu of° this your gracious deed?   *in recompense for*
   Your virtue self° her own reward shall breed –   *itself*
   Even immortal praise and glory wide,°   *far-spread*
   Which I, your vassal, by your prowess freed,
   Shall through the world make to be notified,
And goodly well advance,° that° goodly well was   *praise what*
   tried.'°   *proved*

40

But Britomart, uprearing her from ground,
   Said: 'Gentle° dame, reward enough, I ween,°   *Noble think*
   For many labours more than I have found,
   This: that in safety now I have you seen
   And mean° of your deliverance have been.   *means*
   Henceforth, fair lady, comfort to you take,
   And put away remembrance of late teen:°   *suffering; hurt*
   Instead thereof, know that your loving make°   *consort; lover*
Hath no less grief endured for your gentle sake.'

41

She was much cheered to hear him mentioned
   Whom, of all living wights,° she loved best.   *creatures**
   Then laid the noble championess° strong   *female champion†*
   hand
   Upon the Enchanter which had her distressed
   So sore° and with foul outrages°   *grievously injury; violence*
   oppressed:
   With that great chain wherewith, not long ago,
   He bound that piteous lady prisoner, now released,
   Himself she bound (more worthy to be so)
And captive with her led to wretchedness and woe.

42

Returning back, those goodly° rooms (which   splendid
   erst°   formerly
  She saw so rich and royally arrayed)
  Now vanished utterly and clean° subversed° completely upset†
  She found, and all their glory quite°   utterly
   decayed,°   destroyed
  That° sight of such a change her much dismayed.   So that
  Thence forth descending to that perilous porch,
  Those dreadful flames she also found delayed°   put out
  And quenched quite, like a consumed torch,
That erst° all enterers wont° so cruelly to scorch.   formerly used

43

More easy issue° now than entrance late°   exit recent
  She found; for now that feigned° dreadful flame,   imaginary
  Which choked the porch of that enchanted gate,
  And passage barred to all that thither came,
  Was vanished quite, as° it were not the same,   as if
  And gave her leave at pleasure forth to pass.
  The enchanter self,° which all that fraud° did   himself deceit
   frame°   create
  To have efforced° the love of that fair lass,   compelled†
Seeing his work now wasted,° deep°   destroyed deeply
   engrieved° was.   vexed*

44

But when the victoress° arrived there   female victor†
  Where late she left the pensive° Scudamour   anxious
  With her own trusty squire, both full of fear,
  Neither of them she found where she them lore.°   left
  Thereat her noble heart was 'stonished sore;°   greatly
  But most fair Amoret – whose gentle sprite°   mind; soul
  Now 'gan to feed on hope (which she before
  Conceived had) to see her own dear knight –
Being beguiled° thereof, was filled with new   cheated
  affright.°   fear†

45

But he, sad° man, when he had long in dread°   *also: weary   fear*
    Awaited there for Britomart's return,
    Yet saw her not nor sign of her good speed,°   *success*
    His expectation to despair did turn,
    Misdeeming° sure° that her those   *Wrongly judging   indeed*
        flames did burn;
    And therefore 'gan advise° with her old squire   *discuss*
    (Who her dear nursling's loss no less did mourn)
    Thence to depart for further aid to enquire:
Where let them wend° at will, whilst here I do   *travel*
    respire.°   *take breath*

[NOTE: in the first edition of Books 1–3 (1590), the following stanzas appeared instead of stanzas 43–5 above:

At last she came unto the place where late
    She left Sir Scudamour in great distress
    'Twixt dolour° and despite° half desperate   *grief   anger*
    Of his love's succour,° of his own
        redress,°   *aid*
                                      reparation; assistance
    And of the hardy° Britomart's success.   *bold*
    There on the cold earth him now thrown she found
    In wilful anguish and dead° heaviness,°   *utter   grief; melancholy*
    And to him called: whose voice's known sound,
Soon as he heard, himself he reared light° from   *lightly; swiftly*
    ground.

There did he see, that° most on earth him   *what*
    joyed,°   *made rejoice*
    His dearest love, the comfort of his days,
    Whose too long absence him had sore°   *greatly*
        annoyed°   *vexed*
    And wearied his life with dull delays.
    Straight he upstarted from the loathed lays°   *ground; leas*
    And to her ran with hasty eagerness,
    Like as a deer that greedily embays°   *bathes;† plunges†*
    In the cool soil° after long thirstiness   *pool*
Which he in chase endured hath, now nigh breathless.

Lightly° he clipped° her 'twixt his arms twain   *Swiftly embraced*
  And straitly° did embrace her body bright° –   *tightly fair*
  Her body, late the prison of sad pain,
  Now the sweet lodge of love and dear delight.
  But she, fair lady, overcomen quite°   *completely*
  Of° huge affection, did in pleasure melt   *With*
  And in sweet ravishment° poured out her   *ecstasy*
    sprite.°   *spirit*
  No word they spake, nor earthly thing they felt,
But like two senseless stocks° in long embracement   *blocks*
  dwelt.

Had ye them seen ye would have surely thought
  That they had been that fair hermaphrodite
  Which that rich Roman of white marble wrought
  And in his costly bath caused to be site:°   *sited*
  So seemed those two, as° grown together   *as if*
    quite,°   *completely*
  That Britomart, half envying their bliss,
  Was much impassioned° in her gentle°   *inflamed*[t] *noble*
    sprite°   *mind*
  And to herself oft wished like happiness:
In vain she wished, that° Fate n'ould° let her yet   *what would not*
  possess.

Thus do those lovers with sweet countervail°   *reciprocation*
  Each other of love's bitter fruit despoil.
  But now my team begins to faint and fail,
  All woxen° weary of their diurnal° toil: *grown daily*
  Therefore I will their sweaty yokes assoil°   *release*
  At this same furrow's end, till a new day.
  And ye, fair swains, after your long turmoil,
  Now cease your work and at your pleasure play:
Now cease your work: tomorrow is an holy day.°   *also: holiday*]

From The Fourth Book of *The Fairy Queen*, Containing the Legend of Cambel and Telamond, or, Of Friendship

[Book 4 is closely linked to Book 3: from chaste love the narrative moves to friendship. Many of the characters from Book 3 have important parts to play in Book 4, and here, in canto 10, Scudamour, still questing for Amoret, speaks at Britomart's request, telling her and others how he first won her love.]

CANTO 10

> Scudamour doth his conquest tell
> Of virtuous Amoret:
> Great Venus' temple is described,
> And lover's life forth set.°   *set forth; portrayed*

1

'True he it said – whatever man it said –
  That love with gall and honey doth abound:
  But if the one be with the other weighed,
  For every dram of honey therein found,
  A pound of gall doth over it redound.°   *exceed‡*
  That I too true by trial° have approved;°   *experience proved*
  For since the day that first with deadly wound
  My heart was launched° and learned° to have   *pierced taught*
    loved,
I never joyed° hour but still° with care was moved.   *enjoyed ever*

2

'And yet such grace is given them° from above   *i.e., lovers*
  That all the cares and evil which they meet
  May nought at all their settled° minds   *steadfast; dedicated*
    remove,
  But seem, 'gainst common sense, to them most sweet,

As° boasting in their martyrdom   *As if*
    unmeet.°   *excessive;* * *improper*
So all that ever yet I have endured
I count as nought, and tread down under feet,
Since of my love at length I rest assured
That to disloyalty she will not be allured.°   *enticed*

3

'Long were to tell the travail° and long toil   *also: travel*
    Through which this shield of love I late° have won   *recently*
And purchased this peerless beauty's spoil,°   *plunder*
That harder may be ended than begun –
But since ye so desire, your will be done.
    Then hark, ye gentle° knights and ladies free,°   *noble   free-born*
My hard mishaps that ye may learn to shun;
    For though sweet Love to conquer glorious be,
Yet is the pain thereof much greater than the fee.°   *reward*

4

'What time° the fame of this renowned prize   *At the time when*
    Flew first abroad and all men's ears possessed
I, having arms then taken, 'gan advise°   *counsel [myself]*
To win me honour by some noble gest°   *deed*
And purchase me some place among the best.
    I boldly thought (so young men's thoughts are bold)
That this same brave emprise° for me did   *chivalric undertaking*
    rest,
And that both shield and she whom I behold
Might be my lucky lot,° sith° all by lot° we   *prize   since   chance*
    hold.

5

'So on that hard adventure forth I went
    And to the place of peril shortly came:
That was a temple fair and ancient
    Which of great mother Venus bare the name,
    And far renowned through exceeding fame
(Much more than that which was in Paphos built,
    Or that in Cyprus, both long since° this same,   *post-dating*
Though all the pillars of the one were gilt
And all the other's pavement were with ivory spilt).°   *overlaid†*

6

'And it was seated in an island strong,
   Abounding all with delices° most rare,°   *delights   exquisite*
   And walled by Nature 'gainst invaders wrong
   That none mote° have access nor inward   *might*
      fare,°   *passage; go*
   But by one way that passage did prepare:°   *furnish*
   It was a bridge, ybuilt in goodly° wise°   *handsome   fashion*
   With curious corbs,° and pendants°   *corbels† columns; posts*
      graven fair
   And arched all with porches, did arise°   *i.e., which did arise*
On stately pillars framed° after the Doric   *fashioned*
      guise.°   *mode; pattern*

7

'And for defence thereof, on the other end
   There reared° was a castle fair and strong   *raised*
   That warded° all which in or out did wend,°   *guarded go*
   And flanked° both the bridge's sides along   *protected†*
   'Gainst all that would it fain° to force or wrong.   *wish*
   And therein woned° twenty valiant knights   *dwelled*
   (All twenty tried° in war's experience long)   *proved*
   Whose office° was against all manner°   *duty all sorts of*
      wights°   *people**
By all means to maintain that castle's ancient rights.

8

'Before that castle was an open plain,
   And in the midst thereof a pillar placed
   On which this shield, of° many sought in vain –   *by*
   The Shield of Love, whose guerdon° me hath   *reward*
      graced –
   Was hanged on high with golden ribbons laced.
   And in the marble stone was written this,
   With goodly golden letters well° enchased:°   *finely engraved*
   "Blessed be the man that well can use his bliss:
Whose ever be the shield, fair Amoret be his."

9

'Which, when I read, my heart did inly° yearn   *extremely*
   And pant with hope of that adventure's hap,°   *success*
   Ne° stayed further news thereof to learn,   *Nor*
   But with my spear upon the shield did rap
   That° all the castle ringed with the clap.°   *So that   noise*
   Straight forth issued a knight all armed to
      proof,°   *impenetrably*[†]
   And bravely mounted to his most°   *greatest*
      mishap° –   *misfortune*
   Who, staying nought to question from aloof,°   *a distance*[‡]
Ran fierce at me that° fire glanced from his horse's hoof. *so that*

10

'Whom boldly I encountered as I could,
   And by good fortune shortly him unseated.
   Eftsoons° outsprung two more of equal   *Straight away*
      mould,°   *build*
   But I them both with equal hap defeated –
   So all the twenty I likewise entreated,°   *handled*
   And left them groaning there upon the plain.
   Then, pressing° to the pillar, I repeated°   *hurrying   said over*[‡]
   The rede° thereof for guerdon of° my pain,   *inscription   for*
And, taking down the shield, with me did it retain.

11

'So forth without impediment I passed
   Till to the bridge's outer gate I came,
   The which I found sure° locked and chained fast.   *securely*
   I knocked, but no man answered me by name;
   I called, but no man answered to my clame:°   *call;*[†] *also: claim*
   Yet I persevered still to knock and call
   Till at the last I spied within the same
   Where one stood peeping through a crevice small;
To whom I called aloud, half angry herewithal.

12

'That was, to weet,° the porter of the place,   *assuredly*
   Unto whose trust the charge thereof was lent:
   His name was Doubt, that had a double face –
   The one forward looking, the other backward bent,

Therein resembling Janus ancient
Which hath in charge the ingate° of the year.   *entrance*†
And evermore his eyes about him went
As if some proved° peril he did fear,   *evident*
Or did misdoubt° some ill whose cause did not appear.   *suspect*

13
'On the one side he, on the other sat Delay,
Behind the gate that none her might espy;
Whose manner° was all passengers° to stay   *habit wayfarers*
And entertain with her occasions° sly,   *pretexts*
Through which some lost great hope unheedily°   *heedlessly*†
Which never they recover might again;
And others, quite° excluded forth,° did   *utterly from proceeding*
    lie
Long languishing° there in unpitied pain,   *pining; growing feeble*
And seeking often entrance afterwards, in vain.

14
'Me whenas° he had privily° espied   *when secretly*
Bearing the shield which I had conquered°   *won in battle*
    late,°   *recently*
He kenned° it straight and to me opened wide.   *knew*
So in I passed, and straight° he closed the gate.   *straight away*
But, being in, Delay in close° await°   *secret ambush*
Caught hold on me and thought my steps to stay,
Feigning full many a fond° excuse to prate°   *trivial*† *babble*
And time to steal, the treasure of man's day,
Whose smallest minute lost no riches render° may.   *recompense**

15
'But by no means my way I would forslow°   *slacken*‡
For aught that ever she could do or say
But, from my lofty steed dismounting low,
Passed forth on foot, beholding all the way
The goodly works, and stones of rich assay,°   *value*
Cast° into sundry shapes by wondrous skill   *Formed*
That° like on earth nowhere I reckon° may;   *So that allege**
And underneath, the river rolling still°   *constantly*
With murmur soft, that seemed to serve the workman's will.

16

'Thence forth° I passed to the second gate,   *forward*
  The Gate of Good Desert,° whose goodly   *Merit*
    pride°   *splendour*
  And costly frame° were long here to relate.   *structure*
  The same to all stood always open wide,
  But in the porch did evermore abide
  An hideous° giant, dreadful to behold,   *terrible; immense*
  That stopped the entrance with his spacious° stride   *vast*
  And, with the terror of his countenance bold,
Full many did affray° that else fain° enter   *frighten   desire to*
  would.

17

'His name was Danger, dreaded over all,
  Who by day and night did watch and duly ward°   *protect*
  From fearful cowards entrance to forestall,°   *obstruct‡*
  And faint-heart fools, whom show of peril hard
  Could terrify from Fortune's fair award.
  For oftentimes faint hearts at first espial
  Of his grim face were from approaching scared:
  Unworthy they of grace whom one denial
Excludes from fairest hope withouten further trial.°   *attempt*

18

'Yet many doughty warriors – often tried°   *proved*
  In greater perils to be stout° and bold –   *brave*
  Durst not the sternness of his look abide°   *endure*
  But, soon as they his countenance did behold,
  Began to faint and feel their courage° cold.°   *also: lust   cool*
  Again some other, that in hard assays°   *assaults*
  Were cowards known and little count° did   *esteem; account*
    hold,°   *have*
  Either through gifts, or guile, or suchlike ways,
Crept in by stooping low or stealing of the keys.

19

'But I, though meanest man° of° many   *lower in social degree   than*
  more,
  Yet, much disdaining unto him to lout°   *bow*
  Or creep between his legs so in to go,

Resolved him to assault with manhood stout,°   bold
And either beat him in or drive him out.
Eftsoons° advancing that enchanted shield,   Forthwith
With all my might I 'gan to lay about –
Which, when he saw, the glaive° which he did   sword; lance
     wield
He 'gan forthwith to avale° and way unto me yield.   submit*

20

'So° as I entered I did backward look,   Thus
For fear of harm that might lie hidden there.
And lo, his hindparts, whereof heed I took,
Much more deformed, fearful, ugly were
Than all his former parts did erst° appear;   formerly
For hatred, murder, treason, and despite,°   malice
With many more, lay in ambushment° there,   ambush
Awaiting to entrap the wareless° wight°   unwary‡ creature*
Which did not them prevent° with vigilant foresight.   anticipate

21

'Thus, having passed all peril, I was come
Within the compass of that island's space,
The which did seem unto my simple°   humble
     doom°   judgement
The only° pleasant and delightful place   supreme
That ever trodden was of° footing's°   by foot[print]'s‡
     trace.°   step
For all that Nature by her mother wit
Could frame in° earth and form of substance°   make on matter
     base
Was there, and all that Nature did omit,
Art, playing second Nature's part, supplied it.

22

'No tree that is of count° in greenwood grows,   account
From lowest juniper to cedar tall;
No flower in field that dainty odour throws,
And decks his branch with blossoms over all,
But there was planted, or grew natural;°   naturally
Nor sense of man so coy° and curious   reserved‡
     nice°   over-delicate

But there mote° find to please itself withal;°   *might   with*
No heart could wish for any quaint° device,   *skilful*
But there it present was and did frail sense entice.

23

'In such luxurious° plenty of all pleasure   *extravagant*
  It seemed a second paradise to guess,°   *as one might guess*
So lavishly enriched with Nature's treasure
  That if the happy° souls, which do possess   *blessed*
  The Elysian fields and live in lasting bliss,
  Should happen this with living eyes to see,
  They soon would loathe their lesser happiness
  And wish to life returned again to be
That in this joyous place they mote have joyance° free.   *delight*

24

'Fresh° shadows, fit to shroud° from sunny ray;   *Cool   shelter*
  Fair launds,° to take the sun in season due;   *glades*
Sweet springs, in which a thousand nymphs did play;
  Soft-rumbling brooks that gentle slumber drew;
  High-reared mounts, the lands about to view;
  Low-looking dales, disloigned° from common gaze;   *far off*†
  Delightful bowers to solace lovers true;
  False° labyrinths,° fond° runners'   *Deceiving mazes loving*†
    eyes to daze –
All which, by Nature made, did Nature self amaze.   *herself*

25

'And all without were walks and alleys, dight°   *adorned*
  With diverse trees enranged° in even ranks,°   *arranged*† *rows*
And here and there were pleasant arbours pight,°   *placed*
  And shady seats and sundry flowering banks
  To sit and rest the walkers' weary shanks;
  And therein thousand pairs of lovers walked,
  Praising their god and yielding him great thanks,
  Ne° ever aught but of their true loves talked,   *Neither*
Ne° ever for rebuke or blame of any balked.°   *Nor   stopped*

26

'All these together by themselves did sport
   Their spotless pleasures and sweet loves' content.
     But far away from these, another sort°   *company*
     Of lovers linked in true hearts' concent,°   *harmony*‡
     Which loved not as these for like intent,°   *intention*
     But on chaste virtue grounded° their desire,   *founded*
     Far from all fraud or feigned
        blandishment,°   *cajolery;*† *allurement*†
   Which, in their spirits kindling zealous fire,
Brave thoughts and noble deeds did evermore aspire.

27

'Such were great Hercules, and Hylas dear;
   True Jonathan and David, trusty tried;°   *proved*
     Stout° Theseus and Pirithous his fere;°   *Brave* *comrade*
     Pylades, and Orestes by his side;
     Mild° Titus, and Gisippus without pride;   *Gracious*
     Damon and Pythias, whom death could not sever:
   All these, and all that ever had been tied
   In bands of friendship, there did live for ever,
Whose lives, although decayed,° yet loves decayed never.   *dead*

28

'Which whenas° I, that never tasted bliss   *when*
   Nor happy hour, beheld with gazeful° eye,   *intently gazing*†
     I thought there was none other heaven than this,
     And 'gan their endless happiness envy
     That, being free from fear and jealousy,
     Might frankly° there their love's desire possess,   *freely*
     Whilst I, through pains and perilous jeopardy,
   Was forced to seek my life's dear patroness:
Much dearer be the things which come through hard distress.

29

'Yet all those sights, and all that else I saw,
   Might not my steps withhold but that forthright
     Unto that purposed° place I did me draw   *intended*
     Whereas° my love was lodged day and night: *Where*
     The temple of great Venus – that is hight°   *called**†
     The Queen of Beauty, and of Love the mother,

There worshipped of° every living wight° –   *by creature* *
Whose goodly workmanship far passed° all other   *surpassed*
That ever were on earth, all° were they   *although they*
    set° together.   *brought*

30

'Not that same famous temple of Dian',
    Whose height all Ephesus did oversee,°   *overlook*
    And which all Asia sought with vows profane –
    One of the world's seven wonders said to be –
    Might match with this by many a degree;
    Nor that which that wise king of Jewry framed,°   *made*
    With endless cost, to be the Almighty's see;°   *dwelling*
    Nor all that else through all the world is named°   *dedicated*
To all the heathen gods might like this be clamed.°   *proclaimed* *

31

'I, much admiring that so goodly° frame,°   *splendid structure*
    Unto the porch approached, which open stood;
    But therein sat an amiable° dame   *lovely* ‡
    That seemed to be of very sober mood,
    And in her semblant° showed great   *demeanour;* * *appearance* *
    womanhood.
    Strange was her tire;° for on her head a crown   *attire*
    She wore much like unto a Danish hood,
    Powdered° with pearl and stone, and all her gown   *sprinkled*
Enwoven was with gold, that raught° full low adown.   *reached*

32

'On either side of her two young men stood,
    Both strongly armed, as fearing one another:
    Yet were they brethren both of half the blood,
    Begotten by two fathers of one mother,
    Though of contrary natures each to other.
    The one of them hight Love, the other Hate:
    Hate was the elder, Love the younger brother,
    Yet was the younger stronger in his state
Than the elder, and him mastered still° in all   *ever*
    debate.°   *disputes*

33

'Natheless that dame so well them tempered°   *ruled; harmonised*
  both
  That she them forced hand to join in hand,
  Albe that° Hatred was thereto full loath   *Although*
  And turned his face away as he did stand,
  Unwilling to behold that lovely band.°   *bond of love*
  Yet she was of such grace and virtuous might
  That her commandment° he could not   *bidding; authority*†
    withstand,
  But bit his lip for felonous° despite°   *fierce* * *scorn*
And gnashed his iron tusks at that displeasing sight.

34

'Concord she cleped° was in common rede,°   *called speech*†
  Mother of blessed Peace and Friendship true:
  They both her twins, both born of heavenly seed,
  And she herself likewise divinely grew –
  The which right well her works divine did show,
  For strength, and wealth,° and happiness she   *well-being*
    lends,°   *bestows*
  And strife, and war, and anger does subdue;
  Of little, much; of foes she maketh friends,
And to afflicted minds sweet rest and quiet sends.

35

'By her the heaven is in his course contained,
  And all the world in state unmoved° stands,   *steadfast*
  As their almighty maker first ordained
  And bound them with inviolable bands:
  Else would the waters overflow the lands
  And fire devour the air, and hell them quite,°   *release*
  But that she holds them with her blessed hands.
  She is the nurse of pleasure and delight,
And unto Venus' grace the gate doth open right.

36

'By her I, entering, half dismayed was,
  But she in gentle° wise° me   *courteous fashion*
    entertained,°   *greeted*
  And 'twixt herself and Love did let me pass.

But Hatred would my entrance have restrained,
And with his club me threatened to have brained,
Had not the lady with her powerful speech
Him from his wicked will uneath°   *with difficulty*
  refrained.°   *restrained*
And the other eke° his malice did impeach°   *also obstruct*
Till I was throughly° past the peril of his reach. *completely*

37

'Into the inmost temple thus I came
  Which fuming° all with frankincense I   *smoking;‡ aromatic†*
    found,
  And odours rising from the altar's flame.
  Upon an hundred marble pillars round
  The roof high up was reared° from the ground,   *raised*
  All decked with crowns, and chains,° and garlands gay, *swags*
  And thousand precious gifts worth may a pound,
  The which sad lovers for their vows did pay;
And all the ground was strewed with flowers as fresh as May.

38

'An hundred altars round about were set,°   *placed*
  All flaming with their sacrifices' fire,
  That° with the steam° thereof the   *So that   smoke; vapour*
    temple sweat
  Which, rolled in clouds, to heaven did aspire
  And in them bore true lovers' vows entire.°   *intact†*
  And eke° an hundred brazen cauldrons bright,   *in addition*
  To bathe in joy and amorous desire,
  Every of which was to a damsel hight;°   *allocated*†*
For all the priests were damsels in soft linen dight.° *attired*

39

'Right in the midst the goddess self° did stand   *herself*
  Upon an altar of some costly mass°   *material*
  Whose substance was uneath° to understand: *difficult*
  For neither precious stone, nor dureful° brass, *durable†*
  Nor shining gold, nor mouldering° clay it   *crumbling to decay†*
    was,
  But much more rare and precious to esteem° –   *judgement‡*
  Pure in aspect and like to crystal glass,

Yet glass was not, if one did rightly deem,°   *judge*
But, being fair and brittle, likest glass did seem.

40

'But it in shape and beauty did excel
   All other idols which the heathen adore,
   Far passing° that which, by surpassing skill,   *surpassing*
   Phidias did make in Paphos isle of yore,
   With which the wretched Greek, that life forlore,°   *abandoned*
   Did fall in love; yet this much fairer shined,
   But covered with a slender° veil afore;°   *thin in front*
   And both her feet and legs together twined°   *encircled*†
Were with a snake, whose head and tail were fast°   *firmly*
   combined.

41

'The cause why she was covered with a veil
   Was hard to know, for that° her priests the same   *because*
   From people's knowledge laboured to conceal.
   But sooth° it was not sure° for womanish   *truly certainly*
     shame,
   Nor any blemish which the work mote°   *might*
     blame,°   *discredit*†
   But for (they say) she hath both kinds° in one,   *natures; genders*
   Both male and female, both under one name:
   She sire and mother is herself alone,
Begets and eke conceives, ne° needeth other   *nor*
   none.°   *any other*

42

'And all about her neck and shoulders flew
   A flock of little loves, and sports, and joys,
   With nimble wings of gold and purple hue,
   Whose shapes seemed not like to terrestrial boys
   But like to angels playing heavenly toys.°   *games*
   The whiles° their eldest brother was away –   *Meantime*
   Cupid, their elder brother: he enjoys°   *possesses with delight*
   The wide kingdom of love with lordly sway,
And to his law compels all creatures to obey.

43

'And all about her altar scattered lay
   Great sorts° of lovers piteously complaining –   *companies*
   Some of their loss; some of their love's delay;
   Some of their pride; some paragons° disdaining;   *lovers*†
   Some fearing fraud,° some fraudulently feigning,   *deceit*
   As everyone had cause of good or ill.
   Amongst the rest, some one, through love's constraining
   Tormented sore, could not contain it still,
But thus broke forth that° all the temple it did fill: *so that*

44

' "Great Venus, Queen of Beauty and of Grace,
   The joy of gods and men, that under sky°   *heaven*
   Dost fairest shine and most adorn thy place;
   That with thy smiling looks dost pacify
   The raging seas and makest the storms to fly:
   Thee, goddess, thee the winds, the clouds do fear;
   And when thou spreadest thy mantle forth on high,
   The waters play and pleasant° lands appear,   *delightful*
And heavens laugh, and all the world shows joyous cheer.

45

' "Then doth the daedal° earth show   *variously adorned;*† *skilful*†
   forth to thee
   Out of her fruitful lap abundant flowers;
   And then all living wights,° soon as they see   *creatures**
   The spring break forth out of his lusty° bowers,   *vigorous*
   They all do learn to play the paramours.
   First do the merry birds – thy pretty pages,
   Privily° pricked with thy lustful   *Secretly; in their genitals*
   powers –
   Chirp loud to see thee out of their leafy cages,
And thee, their mother, call to cool their kindly° rages.   *natural*

46

' "Then do the savage beasts begin to play
   Their pleasant frisks,° and loathe their   *capers*
   wonted° food: *customary*
   The lions roar, the tigers loudly bray,°   *cry out**
   The raging bulls rebellow through the wood,

And, breaking forth, dare tempt° the deeepest flood   risk
To come where thou dost draw them with desire.
So all things else that nourish° vital°   are sustained by   life giving
   blood,
Soon as with fury thou dost them inspire,
In generation seek to quench their inward fire.

47

'"So all the world by thee at first was made,
   And daily yet thou dost the same repair;°   restore
Ne aught on earth that merry is and glad,
Ne aught on earth that lovely is and fair,
But thou the same for pleasure dost prepare.
Thou art the root of all that joyous is,
   Great god of men and women, queen of the air,
Mother of laughter and well-spring of bliss:
O grant that of my love at last I may not miss."

48

'So did he say; but I, with murmur° soft   lament
   (That° none might hear the sorrows of my heart),   So that
Yet inly° groaning deep and sighing oft,   inwardly
Besought her to grant ease unto my smart,°   hurt
And to my wound her gracious help impart.
Whilst thus I spake, behold, with happy eye
   I spied where, at the idol's feet apart,°   a little away from
A bevy of fair damsels close° did lie   together
Waiting whenas° the anthem should be sung on   for when
   high.°   also: loudly

49

'The first of them did seem of riper years
   And graver countenance than all the rest;
Yet all the rest were eke her equal peers,
Yet unto her obeyed all the best.°   to the utmost
Her name was Womanhood, that° she expressed   which
By her sad° semblant° and demeanour wise;   grave aspect
For steadfast still her eyes did fixed rest,
Ne roved at random after gazer's guise,°   fashion
Whose luring baits oft-times do heedless hearts entice.

50

'And next to her sat goodly Shamefastness,
  Ne ever durst° her eyes from ground uprear,°   *dared raise*
  Ne ever once did look up from her dais,
  As if some blame of evil she did fear,
  That in her cheeks made roses oft appear.
  And her against° sweet Cheerfulness was placed,   *opposite*
  Whose eyes like twinkling stars in evening clear
  Were decked with smiles that all sad humours° chased *moods*
And darted forth delights, the which her goodly°   *excellently*
    graced.

51

'And next to her sat sober Modesty,
  Holding her hand upon her gentle° heart;   *mild; noble*
  And her against sat comely Courtesy,
  That unto every person knew her part.°   *role; what she owed*
  And her before was seated overthwart°   *diagonally opposite*
  Soft Silence and submiss° Obedience,   *submissive*
  Both linked together never to dispart,°   *separate*[†]
  Both gifts of God not gotten° but from thence,   *begotten*
Both garlands of his saints against their foes' offence.

52

'Thus sat they all around in seemly°   *fitting*
  rate,°   *manner; mode; proportion, ratio*[†]
  And in the midst of them a goodly° maid –   *beautiful*
  Even in the lap of Womanhood – there sat,
  The which was all in lily white arrayed,
  With silver streams amongst the linen strayed:°   *strewn*
  Like to the morn when first her shining face
  Hath to the gloomy world itself bewrayed.°   *revealed*
  That same was fairest Amoret in place,
Shining with beauty's light and heavenly virtues' grace.

53

'Whom, soon as I beheld, my heart 'gan throb,
  And wade in doubt what best were to be done;
  For sacrilege me seemed the church to rob,
  And folly seemed to leave the thing undone

Which with so strong attempt I had begun.
  Tho,° shaking off all doubt and shamefast fear   *Then*
  (Which lady's love, I heard, had never won
  'Mongst men of worth), I to her stepped near
And by the lily hand her laboured up to rear.°   *raise*

54

'Thereat the foremost matron did me blame
  And sharp rebuke for being over bold,
  Saying it was to knight's unseemly shame
  Upon a recluse° virgin to lay hold   *secluded [as a religious]*
  That unto Venus' services was sold.°   *delivered up*
  To whom I thus: "Nay, but it fitteth° best   *suits*
  For Cupid's man with Venus' maid to hold,
  For ill your goddess' services are dressed°   *ordered; tended*
By virgins, and her sacrifices let° to rest."°   *permitted cease*

55

'With that my shield I forth to her did show
  Which all that while I closely° had concealed,   *secretly*
  On which, when Cupid with his killing bow
  And cruel shafts emblazoned she beheld,
  At sight thereof she was with terror quelled°   *overcome*
  And said no more. But I, which all that while
  The pledge of faith, her hand, engaged held,
  Like wary hind within the weedy° soil,°   *rushy pool*
For no entreaty would forgo so glorious spoil;

56

'And evermore upon the goddess' face
  Mine eye was fixed, for fear of her offence,°   *disfavour**
  Whom, when I saw with amiable° grace°   *kindly favour*
  To laugh at me and favour my pretence,°   *claim*
  I was emboldened with more confidence
  And, nought for niceness° nor for envy sparing,   *shyness*
  In presence of them all forth led her thence –
  All looking on and like° astonished staring,   *equally*
Yet to lay hand on her not one of all them daring.

57

'She often prayed and often me besought,
  Sometime with tender tears, to let her go,
  Sometime with witching smiles: but yet for nought
  That ever she to me could say or do
  Could she her wished freedom from me woo.
  But forth I led her through the temple gate,
  By which I hardly passed with much
    ado°   *would have passed with great difficulty*
  But° that same lady, which me friended   *Except that*
    late°   *recently*
In entrance, did me also friend in my retreat.

58

'No less did Danger threaten me with dread
  When he saw me – maugre° all his power –   *despite*
  That glorious spoil of beauty with me lead,
  Than Cerberus when Orpheus did recover
  His leman° from the Stygian prince's   *beloved*
    bower.°   *chamber*
  But evermore my shield did me defend
  Against the storm of every dreadful stour:°   *fight*
  Thus safely with my love I thence did wend.'°   *go*
So ended he his tale, where I this canto end.

From CANTO 11

    Marinell's former wound is healed,
      He comes to Proteus' hall,
    Where Thames doth the Medway wed
      And feasts the sea gods all.

1

But ah, for pity that I have thus long
  Left a fair lady languishing in pain:
  Now well away° that I have done such wrong   *alas*
  To let fair Florimell in bands remain –
  In bands of love and in sad thraldom's chain,

From which, unless some heavenly power her free
   By miracle (not yet appearing plain),
   She longer yet is like° captived to be   *likely*
That° even to think thereof, it inly° pities   *So that profoundly*
   me.°   *makes me pity her*

2

Here needs you to remember how, erewhile,°   *a while since*
   Unlovely° Proteus, missing to° his   *Ugly failing in*
      mind°   *intention*
   That virgin's love to win by wit or wile,
   Her threw into a dungeon deep and blind,°   *windowless*
   And there in chains her cruelly did bind
   In hope thereby her to his bent° to draw.   *inclination‡*
   For whenas° neither gifts nor graces° kind   *when favours*
   Her constant mind could move at all he saw,
He thought her to compel by cruelty and awe.

3

Deep in the bottom of an huge great rock
   The dungeon was in which her bound he left,
   That neither iron bars nor brazen lock
   Did need to guard from force or secret theft
   Of all her lovers which would her have reft;°   *carried away*
   For walled it was with waves which raged and roared
   As° they the cliff in pieces would have cleft.   *As if*
   Besides,° ten thousand monsters foul   *Close by;* *in addition‡*
      abhorred
Did wait about it, gaping grisly° all begored.°   *terrifyingly bloody*

4

And in the midst thereof did horror dwell,
   And darkness dread that never viewed day,
   Like to the baleful° house of lowest hell   *deadly*
   In which old Styx her aged bones alway
   (Old Styx, the grand-dame° of the gods) doth   *grandmother*
      lay.
   There did this luckless maid seven months abide,
   Ne° ever evening saw, ne° morning ray,   *Neither nor*
   Ne ever from the day the night descried,°   *detected*
But thought it all one night that did no hours divide.

5

And all this was for love of Marinell,
   Who her despised (ah, who would her despise?),
   And women's love did from his heart expel,
   And all those joys that weak mankind entice.
   Natheless° his pride full dearly he did   *Nevertheless*
      price,°   *value*
   For of° a woman's hand it was ywroke°   *by* *punished; expelled**
   That° of the wound he yet in languor° lies,   *So that* *distress*
   Ne can be cured of that cruel stroke
Which Britomart him gave when he did her provoke.

6

Yet far and near the nymph his mother sought,
   And many salves did to his sore° apply,   *wound*
   And many herbs did use. But whenas° nought   *when*
   She saw could ease his rankling° malady,   *festering‡*
   At last to Tryphon she for help did hie°   *hasten*
   (This Tryphon is the sea gods' surgeon hight),°   *known as**‡*
   Whom she besought to find some remedy,
   And, for his pains, a whistle° him behight° *flute; pipe* *promised*
That of a fish's shell was wrought with rare° delight.   *exquisite*

7

So well that leech° did hearken to her request,   *physician*
   And did so well employ his careful° pain,° *painstaking* *trouble*
   That in short space his hurts he had redressed°   *cured*
   And him restored to healthful state again,
   In which he long time after did remain
   There with the nymph his mother, like her thrall,
   Who, sore° against his will, did him retain   *greatly*
   For fear of peril which to him mote° fall   *might*
Through his too venturous° prowess proved° *adventurous‡* *tested*
   over all.

8

It fortuned then a solemn feast was there
   To all the sea gods and their fruitful seed
   In honour of the spousals which then were
   Betwixt the Medway and the Thames agreed.
   Long had the Thames (as we in records read)

Before that day her wooed to his bed;
But the proud nymph would for no worldy meed°   *reward*
Nor no entreaty to his love be led,
Till now, at last relenting, she to him was wed.

9

So both agreed that this their bridal feast
  Should for the gods in Proteus' house be made,
  To which they all repaired, both most° and least,   *greatest*
  As well which in the mighty ocean trade°   *resort‡*
  As that in rivers swim or brooks do wade –
  All which, not if an hundred tongues to tell,
  And hundred mouths, and voice of brass I had,
  And endless memory that mote excel,
In order as they came could I recount them well. . . .

[The catalogue of rivers follows.]

CANTO 12

> Marin for love of Florimell
>   In languor° wastes his life: *distressed condition*
> The nymph his mother getteth her
>   And gives to him for wife.

1

O what an endless work I have in hand
  To count the seas' abundant progeny,
  Whose fruitful seed far passeth° those in land,   *surpasses*
  And also those which wone° in the azure sky!   *dwell*
  For much more eath° to tell° the stars on high   *easy count*
  (Albe° they endless seem in estimation)   *Although*
  Than to recount the sea's posterity:
  So fertile be the floods in generation,
So huge their numbers, and so numberless their nation.

2

Therefore the antique° wizards° well   *ancient⁺ sages*
   invented°   *devised*
  That Venus of the foamy sea was bred,
  For that° the seas by her are most augmented: *Because*
  Witness the exceeding° fry which there are fed, *large number of*
  And wondrous shoals which may of none be read.°   *counted*
  Then blame me not if I have erred in count
  Of gods, of nymphs, of rivers yet unread;°   *untold*
  For though their numbers do much more surmount,°   *surpass*
Yet all those same were there which erst° I did   *previously*
   recount.

3

All those were there, and many other more
  Whose names and nations° were too long to tell,   *kinds⁺*
  That° Proteus' house they filled even to the door;   *So that*
  Yet were they all in order, as befell,°   *it turned out*
  According to their degrees° disposed well.   *ranks*
  Amongst the rest was fair Cymodoce,
  The mother of unlucky Marinell,
  Who thither with her came to learn and see
The manner° of the gods when they at banquet be.   *conduct*

4

But for° he was half mortal (being bred   *because*
  Of mortal sire, though of immortal womb),
  He might not with immortal food be fed,
  Ne° with the eternal gods to banquet come;   *Nor*
  But walked abroad, and round about did roam
  To view the building of that uncouth° place, *strange; unknown*
  That seemed unlike unto his earthly home:
  Where, as he to and fro by chance did trace,°   *tread*
There unto him betid° a disadventurous°   *befell unfortunate⁺*
   case.°   *event*

5

Under the hanging of an hideous cliff
  He heard the lamentable° voice of one   *doleful*
  That piteously complained her careful° grief,   *full of care*
  Which never she before disclosed to none

But to herself her sorrow did bemoan.
So feelingly her case she did complain°　　　　　*lament*
That ruth it moved in the rocky stone,
And made it seem to feel her grievous pain,
And oft to groan with billows beating from the main:°　　*ocean*

6

'Though vain I see my sorrows to unfold
　And count° my cares when none is nigh to hear,　　*recount*
Yet, hoping grief may lessen, being told,
I will them tell, though unto no man near:
For heaven, that unto all lends equal° ear,　　　*impartial*
Is far from hearing of my heavy plight;
And lowest hell, to which I lie most near,
Cares not what evils hap° to wretched　　　　　*happen*
　wight;°　　　　　　　　　　　　　　　*creature**
And greedy seas do in the spoil° of life delight.　　*despoliation*

7

'Yet lo, the seas, I see, by often beating
　Do pierce the rocks, and hardest marble wears.
But his hard rocky heart for no entreating
Will yield; but, when my piteous plaints° he hears,　*laments*
Is hardened more with my abundant tears.
Yet, though he never list° to me relent,　　　*wishes*
But let° me waste in woe my wretched years,　　*lets*
Yet will I never of my love repent,
But joy° that for his sake I suffer prisonment.　　*rejoice*

8

'And when my weary ghost,° with grief outworn,　*life; spirit*
　By timely° death shall win° her wished rest,　*opportune gain*
Let then this plaint° unto his ears be borne,　　*complaint*
That blame it is to him that arms professed
To let her die whom he might have
　redressed'.°　　　　　*delivered;** restored**
There did she pause, enforced° to give place　　*compelled*
Unto the passion that her heart oppressed;
And after she had wept and wailed a space,
She 'gan afresh thus to renew° her wretched case:　*repeat*

9

'Ye gods of seas – if any gods at all
   Have any care of right, or ruth of° wretches' wrong –   *pity on*
   By one or other way me, woeful thrall,
   Deliver hence out of this dungeon strong
   In which I, daily dying, am too long.
   And if ye deem° me death for loving one   *adjudge*
   That loves not me, then do it not prolong,
   But let me die and end my days at one,°   *once for all*
And let him live unloved, or love himself alone.

10

'But if that life ye unto me decree,
   Then let me live as lovers ought to do
   And of my life's dear love beloved be.
   And if he shall through pride your doom° undo,   *judgement*
   Do you by duress him compel thereto
   And in this prison put him here with me:
   One prison fittest is to hold us two.
   So had I rather to be thrall than free:
Such thraldom or such freedom let it surely be.

11

'But oh, vain judgement and conditions vain,
   The which the prisoner points° unto the free,   *appoints*
   The whiles I him condemn and deem° his   *decide*
      pain,°   *punishment*
   He where he list° goes loose° and laughs at me.   *wishes free*
   So ever loose, so ever happy, be:
   But whereso loose or happy that thou art,
   Know, Marinell, that all this is for thee.'
   With that she wept and wailed as if her heart
Would quite° have burst through great abundance of her   *utterly*
      smart.°   *pain*

12

All which complaint° when Marinell had heard,   *lament*
   And understood the cause of all her care
   To come of him for using her so hard,
   His stubborn heart (that never felt misfare)°   *misfortune**

Was touched with soft remorse and pity rare,°   *extreme*
That° even for grief of mind he oft did groan   *So that*
And inly° wish that in his power it were   *inwardly*
Her to redress. But since he means found none,
He could no more but her great misery bemoan.

13

Thus while his stony heart with tender ruth
　Was touched, and mighty courage mollified,°   *softened*
Dame Venus' son, that tameth stubborn youth
　With iron bit and maketh him abide°   *remain; suffer*
　Till like a victor on his back he ride,
　Into his mouth his mastering bridle threw
　That made him stoop till he did him bestride.
　Then 'gan he make him tread his steps anew
And learn to love by learning lovers' pains to rue.

14

Now 'gan he in his grieved mind devise
　How from that dungeon he might her enlarge:°   *liberate*
　Some while he thought by fair and humble wise°   *manner*
　To Proteus self° to sue for her discharge;   *himself*
　But then he feared his mother's former charge°   *precept*
　'Gainst women's love, long given him in vain.
　Then 'gan he think perforce° with sword and   *by force*
　　targe°   *shield*
　Her forth to fetch and Proteus to constrain;°   *imprison*
But soon he 'gan such folly to forethink° again.   *rethink*[†]

15

Then did he cast° to steal her thence away   *determine*
　And might him bear where none of her might know –
　But all in vain, for why° he found no way   *because*
　To enter in or issue forth below,
　For all about that rock the sea did flow.
　And though° unto his will she given were,   *even if*
　Yet without ship or boat her thence to row
　He wist° not how her thence away to bear;   *knew*
And danger well he wist long to continue there.

16

At last, whenas° no means he could invent,°   *when   discover*
　　Back to himself he 'gan return the blame
　　That was the author of her punishment,
　　And with vile curses and reproachful shame
　　To damn himself by every evil name,
　　And deem° unworthy or° of love or life   *judge [himself]   either*
　　That had despised so chaste and fair a dame
　　Which him had sought through trouble and long strife,
Yet had refused a god that her had sought to° wife.   *as his*

17

In this sad plight he walked here and there,
　　And roamed round about the rock in vain
　　As° he had lost himself he wist not where,   *As if*
　　Oft listening if he mote° her hear again,   *might*
　　And still° bemoaning her unworthy° pain: *ever   unmerited*
　　Like as an hind, whose calf is fallen unwares
　　Into some pit, where she him hears complain,°   *lament*
　　And hundred times about the pit side fares,
Right sorrowfully mourning her
　　　　bereaved° cares.   *of which she is deprived*

18

And now by this° the feast was throughly°   *this time   completely*
　　　　ended
　　And everyone 'gan homeward to resort:
　　Which seeing, Marinell was sore°   *extremely*
　　　　offended°   *displeased*
　　That his departure thence should be so short°   *imminent*
　　And leave his love in that sea-walled fort.
　　Yet durst° he not his mother disobey,   *dared*
　　But, her attending° in full seemly°   *accompanying   fitting*
　　　　sort,°   *fashion*
　　Did march amongst the many° all the way: *company*
And all the way did inly mourn like one astray.°   *lost*

19

Being returned to his mother's bower,
　　In solitary silence far from wight°   *creature**
　　He 'gan record° the lamentable stour°   *revolve   distress†*

In which his wretched love lay day and night
For his dear sake, that ill deserved that plight:
The thought whereof empierced° his heart so deep   *pierced*‡
That of no worldly thing he took delight,
Ne° daily food did take, ne° nightly sleep,   *Neither nor*
But pined, and mourned, and languished, and alone did weep;

20

That° in short space his wonted cheerful hue°   *So that colour*
  'Gan fade and lively° spirits deaded quite:°   *vital completely*
His cheek-bones raw° and eye-   *showing through the skin*†
  pits° hollow grew,   *eye-sockets*
And brawny arms had lost their known might,
That nothing like himself he seemed in sight.°   *in appearance*
Ere long so weak of limb and sick of love
He wox° that longer he n'ote stand upright,   *grew could not*
But to his bed was brought and laid above,°   *upon it*
Like rueful° ghost, unable once to stir or move.   *pitiful*

21

Which, when his mother saw, she in her mind
  Was troubled sore,° ne wist° well what to   *grievously nor knew*
    ween,°   *think*
Ne could by search nor any means out find
The secret cause and nature of his teen°   *hurt*
Whereby she might apply some medicine;
But, weeping, day and night did him attend,
And mourned to see her loss before her eyen,°   *eyes*
Which grieved her more that she it could not mend:
To see an helpless° evil double grief doth lend.   *beyond remedy*†

22

Nought° could she read° the root of his   *In no way discern*
    disease,
  Ne ween° what mister° malady it is   *think kind of**
Whereby to seek some means it to appease.°   *relieve*
Most° did she think (but most she thought amiss)   *Mostly*
That that same former fatal wound of his
Whilere° by Tryphon was not thoroughly healed,   *Formerly*
But closely° rankled° under the orifice: *secretly festered*‡

Least did she think that which he most concealed
That love it was which in his heart lay unrevealed.

23

Therefore to Tryphon she again doth haste,
 And him doth chide as false and fraudulent°   *deceitful*
 That failed the trust which she in him had placed
 To cure her son, as he his faith° had lent,°   *pledge given*
 Who now was fallen into new languishment°   *illness*†
 Of his old hurt which was not thoroughly cured.
 So back he came unto her patient
 Where, searching every part, her well assured
That it was no old sore° which his new pain   *wound*
  procured,°   *caused*

24

But that it was some other malady
 Or grief unknown, which he could not discern:
 So left her he withouten remedy.
 Then 'gan her heart to faint, and quake, and
  earn,°   *grieve greatly*†
 And inly troubled was the truth to learn.
 Unto himself she came, and him besought,
 Now with fair speeches, now with threatenings stern,
 If aught lay hidden in his grieved thought,
It to reveal: who still her answered, there was nought.

25

Natheless° she rested not so satisfied   *Nevertheless*
 But, leaving watery gods as booting° nought,   *availing*
 Unto the shiny heaven in haste she hied,
 And thence Apollo, king of leeches,° brought. *physicians*
 Apollo came – who, soon as he had sought°   *searched**
 Through his disease, did by and by out find°   *find out*
 That he did languish° of some inward thought *was ill*
 The which afflicted his engrieved° mind, *vexed;*† *grieving*†
Which love he read° to be, that leads each living *understood*
  kind.

26

Which, when he had unto his mother told,
　　She 'gan thereto to fret and greatly grieve,
　　And, coming to her son, 'gan first to scold
　　And chide at him that made her misbelieve.°　　*believe wrongly*
　　But afterwards she 'gan him soft° to shrieve°　　*gently question‡*
　　And woo with fair entreaty to disclose
　　Which of the nymphs his heart so sore° did　　　　　*grievously*
　　　　mieve:°　　　　　　　　　　　　　　　　　　*move**
　　For sure she weened it was some one of those
Which he had lately seen that for his love he chose.

27

Now less she feared that same fatal° rede°　　*prophetic counsel*
　　That warned him of women's love beware
　　(Which, being meant of mortal creature's seed,
　　For love of nymphs she thought she need not care),
　　But promised him, whatever wight she were,
　　That she her love to him would shortly gain.
　　So he her told. But soon as she did hear
　　That Florimell it was which wrought° his pain,　　*caused*
She 'gan afresh to chafe and grieve in every vein.

28

Yet since she saw the strait° extremity　　　　　*severe*
　　In which his life unluckily was laid,
　　It was no time to scan the prophecy —
　　Whether old Proteus true or false had said
　　That his decay° should happen by a maid:　　　*downfall**
　　It's late° in death of danger to advise,°　　*too late   consider**
　　Or love forbid him that is life denied;
　　But rather 'gan in troubled mind devise
How she that lady's liberty might enterprise.°　　*undertake to gain*

29

To Proteus self° to sue she thought it vain,　　*himself*
　　Who was the root and worker of her woe;
　　Nor unto any meaner to complain,
　　But unto great King Neptune self did go,
　　And on her knees before him falling low,
　　Made humble suit unto his majesty

To grant to her her son's life, which his foe,
A cruel tyrant, had presumptuously
By wicked doom° condemned a wretched death to die.   *sentence*

30

To whom god Neptune, softly° smiling, thus: *gently*
  'Daughter, me seems of double wrong ye plain:°   *complain*
  'Gainst one that hath been wronged, and us.°   *i.e., Neptune*
  For death to award, I weened,° did appertain   *thought*
  To none but to the seas' sole sovereign.
  Read,° therefore, who it is which this hath wrought,   *Declare*
  And for what cause – the truth discover°   *disclose*
    plain.°   *clearly*†
  For never wight so° evil did or thought   *so much*
But would some rightful cause pretend,° though rightly   *claim*
  nought.

31

To whom she answered: 'Then it is, by name,
  Proteus that hath ordained my son to die,
  For that° a waif,° the which by   *Because ownerless property*
    Fortune came
  Upon your seas, he claimed as property:
  And yet nor° his, nor his in equity,   *neither*
  But yours the waif by high prerogative.
  Therefore I humbly crave your majesty
  It to replevy° and my son reprieve: *recover*†
So shall you by one gift save all us three alive.'

32

He granted it, and straight° his warrant made   *straight away*
  Under the sea-god's seal authentical,°   *authentic*‡
  Commanding Proteus straight to enlarge° the maid   *release*
  Which, wandering on his seas imperial,
  He lately took and sithence° kept as thrall.°   *since then prisoner*
  Which she, receiving with meet° thankfulness,   *fitting*
  Departed straight to Proteus therewithal
  Who, reading it with inward loathfulness,°   *reluctance*†
Was grieved to restore the pledge he did possess.

33

Yet durst he not the warrant to withstand,
  But unto her delivered Florimell –
Whom she, receiving by the lily hand,
Admired her beauty much (as she mote well,°   *well she might*
For she all living creatures did excel),
And was right joyous that she gotten had
So fair a wife for her son Marinell.
So home with her she straight the virgin led,
And showed her to him then being sore°   *grievously*
  bestad.°   *beset*†

34

Who, soon as he beheld that angel's face
  Adorned with all divine perfection,
His cheered heart eftsoons° away 'gan chase   *forthwith*
Sad death, revived with her sweet inspection,°   *sight**†
And feeble spirit inly felt refection:°   *refreshment*
As withered weed through cruel winter's tine°   *affliction*†
That feels the warmth of sunny beams' reflection
Lifts up his head, that did before decline,
And 'gins to spread his leaf before the fair sunshine.

35

Right so himself did Marinell uprear°   *uplift*
  When he in place° his dearest love did spy;   *before him*
And though his limbs could not his body bear,
Ne° former strength return so suddenly,   *Nor*
Yet cheerful signs he showed outwardly.
Ne less was she in secret heart affected,
But that she masked it with modesty,
For fear she should of lightness° be   *wantonness*
  detected:°   *accused*
Which to another place I leave to be perfected.

From The Sixth Book of *The Fairy Queen*, Containing the Legend of Sir Calidore, or, Of Courtesy

[In this core canto to Book 6, Calidore, who has fallen in love with 'the fair Pastorella' (6. 9. 46) and abandoned his knightly quest for the Blatant Beast, catches a glimpse of Colin Clout and Venus's Graces.]

CANTO 10

Calidore sees the Graces dance
    To Colin's melody;
The whiles his Pastorell' is led
    Into captivity.

1

Who now does follow the foul Blatant Beast
   Whiles Calidore does follow that fair maid,°   *i.e., Pastorella*
   Unmindful of his vow and high behest° –   *command*
   Which by the Fairy Queen was on him laid –
   That he should never leave nor be delayed
   From chasing him till he had it achieved?°   *accomplished*
   But now, entrapped of° love, which him betrayed,   *by*
   He mindeth more how he may be relieved
With grace from her whose love his heart hath sore°   *much*
   engrieved,°   *distressed*

2

That° from henceforth he means no more to sue°   *So that pursue*
   His former quest, so full of toil and pain.
   Another quest, another game in view
   He hath: the guerdon° of his love° to gain,   *reward beloved*
   With whom he minds° for ever to remain   *has in mind*
   And set his rest° among the rustic sort°   *dwell folk*
   Rather than hunt still after shadows vain

Of courtly favour, fed with light° report   *untrustworthy*
Of every blast, and sailing always on the° port.   *towards*

3

Ne° certes° mote° he greatly blamed be   *Nor indeed may*
  From so high step to stoop unto so low;
  For who° had tasted once (as oft did he)   *he who*
  The happy peace which there doth overflow,
  And proved° the perfect pleasures which do grow   *experienced*
  Amongst poor hinds° in hills, in woods, in dales,   *country folk*
  Would never more delight in painted show
  Of such false bliss as there° is set for stales°   *i.e., at court lures*
To entrap unwary fools in° their eternal bales.°   *into torment*

4

For what hath all that goodly° glorious gaze°   *supremely sight‡*
  Like to one sight which Calidore did view? –
  The glance whereof their dimmed eyes would daze
  That° never more they should endure the show   *So that*
  Of that sunshine that makes them look askew.°   *sidelong‡*
  Ne° aught in all that world of beauties rare°   *Neither exceeding*
  (Save only Gloriana's heavenly hue,°   *aspect*
  To which what can compare?) can it compare,°   *rival*
The which, as cometh now, by course° I will   *in due course*
    declare.°   *describe*

5

One day, as he did range° the fields abroad   *rove‡*
  Whilst his fair Pastorella was elsewhere,
  He chanced to come far from all people's troad,°   *path‡*
  Unto a place whose
    pleasance° did appear   *agreeableness; pleasure-garden qualities‡*
  To pass° all others on the earth which were.   *surpass*
  For all that ever was by Nature's skill
  Devised to work delight was gathered there,
  And there by her were poured forth at fill°   *overflowingly*
As if this to adorn she all the rest did pill.°   *plunder*

6

It was an hill placed in an open plain
   That round about was bordered with a wood
   Of matchless height that seemed the earth to disdain,
   In which all trees of honour° stately stood   *beauty; nobility*
   And did all winter, as in summer, bud,
   Spreading pavilions° for the birds to   *canopies* *
      bower,°   *inhabit†*
   Which in their lower branches sung aloud;
   And in their tops the soaring hawk did
      tower,°   *mount ready to swoop‡*
Sitting like king of fowls in majesty and power.

7

And at the foot thereof a gentle flood°   *stream*
   His silver waves did softly tumble down,
   Unmarred with ragged moss or filthy mud,
   Ne° mote° wild beasts, ne° mote the ruder   *Neither might nor*
      clown°   *rustic*
   Thereto approach, ne filth mote therein drown;°   *sink*
   But nymphs and fairies by the banks did sit
   In the wood's shade (which did the waters crown,
   Keeping all noisome things away from it)
And to the water's fall tuning their accents°   *voices‡*
      fit.°   *appropriately*

8

And on the top thereof a spacious plain
   Did spread itself to serve to all delight,
   Either to dance (when they to dance would fain),°   *wish*
   Or else to course° about their bases°   *chase‡ prisoners' base*
      light;°   *quickly*
   Ne aught there wanted° which for pleasure might   *lacked*
   Desired be, or thence to banish bale.°   *evil; harm*
   So° pleasantly the hill with equal° height   *thus level*
   Did seem to overlook the lowly vale;
Therefore it rightly cleped° was Mount Acidale.   *called*

9

They say that Venus, when she did dispose°   *incline*
 Herself to pleasance,° used to resort *delight; recreation*
 Unto this place and therein to repose
 And rest herself as in a gladsome port,
 Or with the Graces there to play and sport,
 That° even her own Cytheron (though in it   *So that*
 She used most to keep her royal court,
 And in her sovereign majesty to sit),
She in regard° hereof refused and thought unfit. *comparison*

10

Unto this place whenas° the elfin knight   *when*
 Approached, him seemed that the merry sound
 Of a shrill pipe° he playing heard on height,° *bagpipe   loudly*
 And many feet fast thumping the hollow ground,
 That° through the woods their echo did rebound. *So that*
 He nigher drew to weet° what mote it be: *discover*
 There he a troop of ladies dancing found
 Full merrily, and making gladful° glee,° *joyful* sport**
And in the midst a shepherd piping he did see.

11

He durst° not enter into the open green,   *dared*
 For dread of them unwares° to be descried *unexpectedly*
 For° breaking of their dance if he were seen; *For fear of*
 But in the covert° of the wood did bide, *shelter; thicket*
 Beholding all, yet of them unespied.
 There he did see, that° pleased much his sight *what*
 (That° even he himself his eyes envied), *So that*
 An hundred naked maidens lily white,
All ranged° in a ring and dancing in delight. *ordered; disposed*

12

All they without° were ranged in a ring   *outside*
 And danced round; but, in the midst of them,
 Three other ladies did both dance and sing
 The whilst the rest them round about did hem° *enclose‡*
 And like a garland did in compass° stem.° *a circle   surround†*

And in the middest of those same three was placed
   Another damsel, as a precious gem
   Amidst a ring most richly well enchased,°   *engraved; set*†
That with her goodly presence all the rest much graced.

13

Look how the crown – which Ariadne wore
   Upon her ivory forehead that same day
   That Theseus her unto his bridal° bore   *wedding feast*
   When the bold centaurs made that bloody fray
   With the fierce Lapiths, which did them dismay° –   *vanquish*
   Being now placed in the firmament,
   Through the bright heaven doth her beams display
   And is unto the stars an ornament
Which round about her move in order excellent:

14

Such was the beauty of this goodly band,
   Whose sundry parts were here too long to tell;
   But she that in the midst of them did stand
   Seemed all the rest in beauty to excel,
   Crowned with a rosy° garland that right well   *made of roses*
   Did her beseem.° And ever as the crew°   *suit   company*
   About her danced, sweet flowers that far did smell,
   And fragrant odours,° they upon her threw;   *incense; spices*
But most of all those three did her with gifts endue.°   *endow*

15

Those were the Graces, daughters of delight,
   Handmaids of Venus, which are wont° to   *accustomed*
     haunt°   *resort; dwell*
   Upon this hill and dance there day and night:
   Those three to men all gifts of grace do grant,
   And all that Venus in herself doth vaunt°   *boast*
   Is borrowed of them. But that fair one,
   That in the midst was placed paravaunt,°   *pre-eminent*†
   Was she to whom that shepherd piped alone,
That made him pipe so° merrily as never   *as*
   one.°   *no one had [before]*

16

She was to weet° that jolly° shepherd lass   *indeed beautiful*
  Which piped there unto that merry rout;°   *gathering*
  That jolly° shepherd which there piped   *handsome; amorous*
    was
  Poor Colin Clout (who knows not Colin Clout?):
  He piped apace whilst they him danced about.
  Pipe, jolly shepherd, pipe thou now apace
  Unto thy love that made thee low to lout:°   *bow in submission*
  Thy love is present there with thee in place;°   *in that very spot*
Thy love is there advanced to be another Grace.

17

Much wondered Calidore at this strange sight,
  Whose like before his eye had never seen;
  And, standing long astonished in sprite°   *mind*
  And rapt with pleasance,° wist° not what to   *delight knew*
    ween:°   *think*
  Whether it were the train° of beauty's queen,   *following*
  Or nymphs, or fairies, or enchanted show,
  With which his eyes mote° have deluded been.   *might*
  Therefore resolving what it was to know,
Out of the wood he rose, and toward them did go.

18

But soon as he appeared to their view,
  They vanished all away out of his sight,
  And clean were gone, which way he never knew –
  All save the shepherd, who, for fell°   *fierce*
    despite°   *indignation*
  Of that displeasure,° broke his bagpipe   *offence*
    quite,°   *completely*
  And made great moan for that unhappy turn.°   *occurrence*
  But Calidore, though no less sorry wight°   *a person**
  For that mishap, yet, seeing him to mourn,
Drew near that° he the truth of all by him mote° *so that might*
    learn,

19

And, first him greeting, thus unto him spake:
　'Hail, jolly shepherd, which thy glorious days
　Here leadest in this goodly° merry-make,°　　*fine merry-making*†
　Frequented of° these gentle° nymphs always,　　*by noble*
　Which to thee flock to hear thy lovely lays.°　　*songs of love*
　Tell me, what mote these dainty damsels be
　Which here with thee do make their pleasant°　　*merry*
　　plays?°　　　　　　　　　　　　　　　　*games*
　Right happy thou, that mayest them freely see –
But why, when I them saw, fled they away from me?'

20

'Not I so happy,' answered then that swain,
　'As thou unhappy which them thence did chase,
　Whom by no means thou canst recall again;
　For, being gone, none can them bring in
　　place°　　　　　　　　　　　　　　*to their presence*
　But whom they of themselves list° so to grace.'°　*wish favour*
　'Right sorry, I,' (said then Sir Calidore)
　'That my ill fortune did them hence displace.
　But since things past none may now restore,
Tell me, what were they all whose lack thee grieves so
　　sore?'°　　　　　　　　　　　　　　*extremely*

21

Tho° 'gan the shepherd thus for to dilate:°　*Then explain at length*
　'Then wote° thou, shepherd, whatsoever thou be,　*know*
　That all those ladies which thou sawest late°　*just now*
　Are Venus' damsels, all within her fee,°　　*service*
　But differing in honour and degree.°　　　*rank*
　They all are Graces, which on her depend,
　Besides a thousand more which ready be
　Her to adorn when so she forth doth wend;°　*venture*
But those three in the midst do chief° on her attend.　*chiefly*

22

'They are the daughters of sky-ruling Jove,
　By him begot of fair Eurynome,
　The Ocean's daughter, in this pleasant° grove　*delightful*
　As he this way coming from feastful°　　　*festive*

glee°   *entertainment*
Of Thetis' wedding with Æacide
In summer's shade himself here rested weary.
The first of them hight° mild Euphrosyne;   *is called**†*
Next fair Aglaia; last Thalia merry:
Sweet goddesses all three which me in mirth do cherry.° *cheer†*

23

'These three on men all gracious gifts bestow
    Which deck the body or adorn the mind
    To make them lovely or well-favoured show:
    As comely carriage°; entertainment° kind;   *bearing hospitality*
    Sweet semblant°; friendly offices° that   *favour* attentions*
        bind;°   *form bonds*
    And all the complements° of courtesy.   *accomplishments*
    They teach us how, to each degree° and kind,°   *nature class*
    We should ourselves demean° to low and high: *behave*
To friends, to foes – which skill° men call Civility. *knowledge*

24

'Therefore they always smoothly° seem to smile   *gently*
    That° we likewise should mild and gentle be;   *To tell us that*
    And also naked are that° without guile   *so that*
    Or false dissemblance° all them plain°   *dissimulation† clearly†*
        may see,
    Simple and true from covert° malice° free.   *secret evil*
    And eke° themselves so° in their dance they bore   *also thus*
    That two of them still froward° seemed to be;   *facing away**
    But one still towards showed herself afore,°   *before*
That good should from us go, then come in greater
        store.°   *abundance*

25

'Such were those goddesses which ye did see;
    But that fourth maid which there amidst them
        traced,°   *stepped*
    Who can aread° what creature mote she be –   *declare*
    Whether a creature, or a goddess graced°   *favoured*
    With heavenly gifts from heaven first enraced?°   *implanted‡**
    But whatso sure° she was, she worthy was   *indeed*
    To be the fourth with those three other placed.

Ye was she certes° but a country lass: *certainly*
Yet she all other country lasses far did pass.°   *surpass*

26

'So far as doth the daughter of the
    day°   *i.e., Venus, the morning star*
All other, lesser, lights in light excel,
So far doth she in beautiful array
Above all other lasses bear the bell:°   *is pre-eminent*
Ne° less in virtue that beseems° her well   *Nor befits*
Doth she exceed the rest of all her race;
For which° the Graces that here   *i.e., reason*
    wont° to dwell   *are accustomed*
Have for more honour brought her to this place
And graced° her so much to be° another   *favoured so as to be*
    Grace.

27

'Another Grace she well deserves to be
    In whom so many graces gathered are,
Excelling much the mien° of her degree:°   *bearing class*
Divine resemblance,° beauty sovereign rare,   *appearance*
Firm° chastity, that spite ne° blemish dare;   *Steadfast will not*
All which she with such courtesy doth grace
That all her peers° cannot with her compare,   *companions*
But quite° are dimmed when she is in place.°   *utterly present*
She made me often pipe, and now to pipe apace.

28

'Sun of the world, great glory of the sky,
    That all the earth dost lighten with thy rays:
Great Gloriana, greatest majesty,
Pardon thy shepherd – 'mongst so many lays°   *songs*
As he hath sung of thee in all his days –
To make one minim° of° thy poor handmaid,   *small space‡ for*
And underneath thy feet to place her praise
That,° when thy glory shall be far   *So that*
    displayed°   *spread abroad*
To future age, of her this mention may be made.'

29

When thus that shepherd ended had his speech,
   Said Calidore: 'Now, sure,° it irketh° me   *indeed vexes*
   That to thy bliss I made this luckless° breach   *unfortunate*
   As now the author of thy bale° to be,   *torment*
   Thus to bereave° thy love's dear sight from thee.   *steal*
   But, gentle° shepherd, pardon thou my shame,   *courteous*
   Who rashly sought that which I mote° not see.'   *may*
   Thus did the courteous knight excuse his blame,
And, to recomfort° him, all comely° means   *comfort civil*
   did frame.°   *devise*

30

In such discourses they together spent
   Long time, as fit occasion° forth them led,   *opportunity*
   With which the knight himself did much content
   And with delight his greedy fancy° fed –   *imagination*
   Both of his words (which he with reason read),°   *interpreted*
   And also of the place (whose pleasures rare°   *exceptional*
   With such regard° his senses ravished),   *sight*
   That thence he had no will away to fare,
But wished that with that shepherd he mote dwelling share.

31

But that envenomed sting, the which of yore
   His poisonous point deep fixed in his heart
   Had left, now 'gan afresh to rankle°   *fester*
     sore°   *greatly; painfully*
   And to renew the rigour of his smart° –   *wound*
   Which to recure° no skill of leech's° art   *heal physician's*
   Mote him avail, but to return again
   To his wound's worker° that, with   *i.e., Pastorella*
     lovely° dart,   *of love*
   Dinting° his breast, had bred his restless pain,   *Striking*
Like as the wounded whale to shore flies from the main.°   *sea*

32

So, taking leave of that same gentle swain,
   He back returned to his rustic wone,°   *dwelling**
   Where his fair Pastorella did remain;
   To whom, in sort° as he at first begun,   *the same fashion*

He daily did apply himself to done°   *perform*
All dueful° service void of thoughts   *due; fitting†*
   impair.°   *unfitting†*
Ne° any pains ne° peril did he shun   *Neither nor*
By which he might her to his love allure,
And liking in her yet untamed heart procure.

33
And ever more the shepherd Coridon,
  Whatever thing he did her to aggrate,°   *gratify†*
  Did strive to match with strong contention,
  And all his pains° did closely emulate: *attentions*
  Whether it were to carol as they sat
  Keeping their sheep, or games to exercise,°   *practise*
  Or to present her with their labours late:°   *recent*
  Through which, if any grace° chanced to arise   *favour*
To him, the shepherd straight with jealousy did freeze.

34
One day, as they all three together went
  To the greenwood to gather strawberries,
  There chanced to them a dangerous accident:
  A tiger forth out of the woods did rise
  That, with fell claws full of fierce° gourmandise,°   *cruel greed*
  And greedy mouth wide gaping like hell gate,
  Did run at Pastorell' her to surprise;
  Whom she beholding, now all desolate,
'Gan cry to them aloud to help her, all too late.

35
Which Coridon, first hearing, ran in haste
  To rescue her; but when he saw the fiend,
  Through coward fear he fled away as fast,
  Ne° durst° abide° the danger of the end: *Nor dared await*
  His life he esteemed dearer than his friend.
  But Calidore, soon coming to her aid,
  When he the beast saw ready now to rend
  His love's dear spoil,° in° which his heart   *plunder through*
    was preyed,°   *preyed upon*
He ran at him enraged instead of being afraid.

36

He had no weapon but his shepherd's hook°   *crook*
 To serve the vengeance of his wrathful will,
  With which so sternly° he the monster struck *fiercely*
  That to the ground astonished° he fell, *stunned*
  Whence, ere he could recover, he did him kill,
  And, hewing off his head, it presented
  Before the feet of the fair Pastorell' –
  Who, scarcely yet from former fear exempted,° *removed*‡
A thousand times him thanked that had her death prevented.

37

From that day forth she 'gan him to affect,°   *love*‡
 And daily more her favour to augment,
  But Coridon for cowardice reject,
  Fit to keep sheep, unfit for love's content:
  The gentle heart scorns base
   disparagement.° *dishonour by marrying an unequal*
  Yet Calidore did not despise him quite,° *utterly*
  But used him friendly° for further intent *as a friend*
  That° by his fellowship he colour° might *So that disguise*
Both his estate° and love from skill° of any *status knowledge*
  wight.°   *person**

38

So well he wooed her and so well he wrought° her *worked on*
 With humble service and with daily suit,
  That at the last unto his will he brought her:
  Which he so wisely well did prosecute
  That of his love he reaped the timely fruit,
  And joyed° long in close° felicity, *enjoyed himself secret*
  Till Fortune, fraught° with malice, blind and *filled*
   brute,°   *irrational*‡
  That envies lovers' long prosperity,
Blew up a bitter storm of foul adversity.

39

It fortuned one day, when Calidore
 Was hunting in the woods (as was his trade),° *habit*
  A lawless people, 'Brigands' hight° of yore,° *called**† *anciently*
  That never used° to live by plough nor spade, *were accustomed*

But fed on spoil and booty which they made
Upon their neighbours which did nigh them border –
The dwelling of these shepherds did invade,
And spoiled° their houses and themselves did   *plundered*
  murder,
And drove away their flocks, with other much disorder.

40

Amongst the rest the which they then did prey°   *plunder*
  They spoiled° old Meliboeus of all he had,   *robbed*
  And all his people captive led away,
  'Mongst which this luckless maid away was led –
  Fair Pastorella, sorrowful and sad;
  Most sorrowful, most sad that ever sighed,
  Now made the spoil of thieves and brigands bad
  Which was the conquest of the gentlest° knight   *most courteous*
That ever lived, and the only° glory of his might.   *supreme*

41

With them also was taken Coridon,
  And carried captive by those thieves away,
  Who, in° the covert° of the night (that   *under cover; secrecy*
    none
  Mote° them descry, nor rescue from their   *Might*
    prey)°   *plundering*
  Unto their dwelling did them close° convey.   *secretly*
  Their dwelling in a little island was,
  Covered with shrubby woods in which no way
  Appeared for people in or out to pass,
Nor any footing° find for° overgrown grass.   *track‡ because of*

42

For underneath the ground their way was made
  Through hollow caves that no man mote discover
  For the thick shrubs which did them always shade
  From view of living wight and covered over.
  But darkness dread and daily night did hover
  Through all the inner parts wherein they dwelt,
  Ne° lightened was with window, nor with   *Neither*
    louver,°   *chimney-hole*

But with continual candle light, which dealt
A doubtful sense of things not so well seen as felt.

43

Hither those brigands brought their present prey
  And kept them with continual watch and ward,°   *guard*
  Meaning, so soon as they convenient
    may,°   *i.e., could find it convenient*
  For slaves to sell them (for no small reward)
  To merchants, which them kept° in bondage   *would have kept*
  hard
  Or sold again, Now, when fair Pastorell'
  Into this place was brought and kept with guard
  Of grisly° thieves, she thought herself in hell   *terrifying*
Where with such damned fiends she should in darkness dwell.

44

But for to tell the doleful° dreariment°   *dismal   desolation*†
  And pitiful complaints° which there she made –   *laments*
  Where day and night she nought did but lament
  Her wretched life, shut up in deadly shade
  And waste her goodly beauty, which did fade
  Like to a flower that feels no heat of sun
  Which may her feeble leaves with comfort glade° –   *gladden*
  And what befell her in that thievish wone°   *dwelling*
Will in another canto better be begun.

[In cantos 11 and 12 Calidore rescues Pastorella (who turns out to be
of noble birth) and tames the Blatant Beast – who, however, escapes
and remains at large, maligning those who deserve it as well as those
who do not.]

[Book 7]
TWO CANTOS OF MUTABILITY,
Which, both for form and matter, appear to be
parcel° of some following book of the   *part*
FAIRY QUEEN,
Under the Legend of Constancy.
Never before imprinted.

CANTO 6

> Proud Change (not pleased, in mortal things
>   Beneath the moon, to reign)
> Pretends,° as well of gods as men   *Claims*
>   To be the sovereign.

1

What man that sees the ever-whirling wheel
    Of Change, the which all mortal things doth sway,°   *control*
But that thereby doth find and plainly feel
How Mutability in them doth play
    Her cruel sports, to many men's decay?°   *downfall*
Which, that to all may better yet appear
I will rehearse° that° whilom° I heard say,   *narrate what once**
How she at first herself began to rear°   *raise*
'Gainst all the gods, and the empire sought from them to bear.

2

But first here falleth° fittest to unfold   *it befalls*
    Her antique° race and lineage ancient,   *ancient‡*
As I have found it registered of old
In Fairyland 'mongst records permanent:
    She was, to weet,° a daughter by descent   *indeed*
Of those old Titans that did whilom strive
With Saturn's son for heaven's regiment,°   *government*

Whom, though high Jove of kingdom° did   *i.e., their kingdom*
    deprive,
Yet many of their stem° long after did survive.   *stock*

3

And many of them afterwards obtained
    Great power of° Jove, and high authority;   *from*
    As° Hecate, in whose almighty hand   *Such as*
    He placed all rule and principality°   *sovereignty*
    To be by her disposed diversely°   *variously*
    To gods and men as she them list° divide;°   *wished apportion*[†]
    And dread Bellona, that doth sound on high°   *loudly*
    Wars and alarms unto nations wide°   *far and wide*
That makes both heaven and earth to tremble at her pride.

4

So likewise did this Titaness aspire
    Rule and dominion in herself to gain,
    That° as a goddess men might her admire,   *So that*
    And heavenly honours yield as to them
        twain.°   *those two [Hecate, Bellona]*
    And first on earth she sought it to obtain,
    Where she such proof and sad examples showed
    Of her great power to many ones' great pain,
    That not men only (whom she soon subdued)
But eke° all other creatures her bad doings rued.°   *also grieved at*

5

For she the face of earthly things so changed
    That all which Nature had established first
    In good estate,° and in meet° order   *condition appropriate*
        ranged,
    She did pervert° and all their statutes°   *upset decrees*
        burst;°   *broke*
    And all the world's fair° frame° (which   *beautiful structure*
        none yet durst°   *dared*
    Of gods or men to alter or misguide)
    She altered quite° and made them all accursed   *completely*
    That God had blessed and did at first provide
In that still° happy state for ever to abide.   *permanently*

6

Ne she° the laws of Nature only break,   *She did not*
  But eke of Justice and of Policy,°   *Government*
  And wrong of right and bad of good did make,
  And death for life exchanged foolishly:
  Since which, all living wights° have learned to die   *creatures**
  And all this world is woxen° daily worse.   *grown*
  O piteous work of Mutability! –
  By which we all are subject to that curse,
And death instead of life have sucked from our
     nurse.°   *i.e., Nature*

7

And now, when all the earth she thus had brought
  To her behest° and thralled° to her   *command made captive*
     might,
  She 'gan to cast° in her ambitious thought   *plan*
  To attempt the empire of the heavens' height°   *high*
  And Jove himself to shoulder from his right.
  And first she passed the region of the air
  And of the fire, whose substance thin and slight
  Made no resistance, ne° could her contrair,°   *nor oppose*
But ready passage to her pleasure did prepare.

8

Thence to the circle° of the Moon she clamb,°   *sphere climbed*
  Where Cynthia reigns in everlasting glory,
  To whose bright shining palace straight she came,
  All fairly decked with heavens' goodly story,°   *sculpted history*
  Whose silver gates (by which there sat an
     hoary°   *white; venerable*
  Old aged sire with hour-glass in hand,
  Hight° Time) she entered, were he lief° or   *Called** *glad*
     sorry;
  Ne stayed till she the highest stage° had   *level*
     scanned°   *climbed†*
Where Cynthia did sit that never still did stand.

9

Her sitting on an ivory throne she found,
    Drawn of° two steeds, the one black, the other white,   *by*
    Environed° with ten thousand stars around   *Encircled*
    That duly her attended day and night;
    And by her side there ran her page, that hight
    Vesper, whom we the Evening Star intend,°   *name‡*
    That with his torch, still twinkling like twilight,
    Her° lightened° all the way where she should   *For her lit up*
       wend°   *go*
And joy to weary wandering travellers did lend.°   *bestow*

10

That when the hardy° Titaness beheld –   *bold*
    The goodly building of her palace bright,
    Made of the heavens' substance and upheld
    With thousand crystal pillars of huge height –
    She' gan to burn in her ambitious sprite°   *mind*
    And to envy her that in such glory reigned.
    Eftsoons° she cast° by force and   *Forthwith resolved*
       tortious° might   *illegal*
    Her to displace and to herself to have gained
The kingdom of the Night and waters by her wained.°   *moved**

11

Boldly she bid the goddess down descend
    And let herself into that ivory throne,
    For she herself more worthy thereof weened,°   *believed*
    And better able it to guide alone:
    Whether to men (whose fall she did bemoan),°   *lament*
    Or unto gods (whose state she did malign),°   *begrudge;‡ resent*
    Or to the infernal powers, her need° give loan   *requirement to*
    Of her fair light and bounty° most benign   *kindness; virtue*
Herself of all that rule she deemed° most   *judged*
      condign.°   *worthy**

12

But she that had to her that sovereign seat
    By highest Jove assigned, therein to bear
    Night's burning lamp, regarded not her threat,
    Ne yielded aught for favour or for fear;

But, with stern countenance and disdainful cheer,°   *aspect*
Bending her horned brows, did put her back,
And, boldly blaming her for coming there,
Bade her at once from heaven's coast° to pack°   *border   depart*
Or at her peril bide the wrathful thunder's wrack.°   *destruction*

13

Yet nathemore° the Giantess forbare°   *not at all   desisted*
  But, boldly pressing on, raught° from her hand   *reached*
  To pluck her down perforce° from off her   *by force*
    chair°   *throne*
  And, therewith lifting up her golden wand,
  Threatened to strike her if she did withstand.
  Whereat the stars which round about her blazed,
  And eke the Moon's bright wagon, still did stand,
  All being with so bold attempt amazed,°   *stunned*
And on her uncouth° habit and stern look still gazed.   *unfamiliar*

14

Meanwhile the lower world (which nothing knew
  Of all that chanced here) was darkened quite,°   *utterly*
  And eke the heavens and all the heavenly crew°   *company*
  Of happy wights,° now unpurveyed°   *beings*   unprovided**
    of° light,   *with*
  Were much afraid, and wondered at that sight,
  Fearing lest Chaos broken had his chain
  And brought again on them eternal night:
  But chiefly Mercury, that next doth reign,
Ran forth in haste unto the king of gods to plain.°   *complain*

15

All ran together with a great outcry
  To Jove's fair palace fixed in heaven's height
  And, beating at his gates full earnestly,
  'Gan call to him aloud with all their might
  To know what meant that suden lack of light.
  The father of the gods, when this he heard,
  Was troubled much at their so strange°   *unusual*
    affright,°   *fear†*
  Doubting° lest Typhon were again upreared,°   *Afraid   raised up*
Or other his old foes that once him sorely° feared.   *extremely*

16

Eftsoons° the son of Maia° forth he sent   *Forthwith i.e., Mercury*
  Down to the circle° of the Moon to know   *sphere*
  The cause of this so strange astonishment,°   *cause of wonder*†
  And why she did her wonted course forslow;°   *neglect*
  And, if that any were on earth below
  That did with charms and magic her molest,
  Him to attach° and down to hell to throw: *seize*
  But if from heaven it were, then to arrest
The author, and him bring before his presence prest.°   *quickly**

17

The winged-foot god so fast his plumes did beat
  That soon he came whereas° the Titaness   *to where*
  Was striving with fair Cynthia for her seat;
  At whose strange sight and haughty hardiness°   *daring*
  He wondered much, and feared her no less.
  Yet, laying fear aside to do his charge,°   *duty*
  At last he bade her (with bold steadfastness)
  Cease to molest° the Moon to walk at   *prevent*
    large,°   *walking freely*
Or come before high Jove her doings to discharge.°   *justify*†

18

And therewithal he on her shoulder laid
  His snaky-wreathed mace, whose awful° power   *awe-inspiring*
  Doth make both gods and hellish fiends afraid;
  Whereat the Titaness did sternly° lour,°   *fiercely frown*
  And stoutly° answered that in evil hour   *boldly*
  He from his Jove such message to her brought
  To bid her leave fair Cynthia's silver bower,°   *chamber*
  Sith° she his Jove and him esteemed nought   *Since*
No more than Cynthia's self; but all their kingdoms sought.

19

The heavens' herald stayed not to reply,
  But passed away his doings° to relate   *experiences*
  Unto his lord, who now in the highest sky
  Was placed in his principal° estate°   *sovereign position*
  With all the gods about him congregate.°   *congregated**
  To whom, when Hermes had his message told,

It did them all exceedingly amate°   *astound*
  Save Jove, who, changing nought his countenance bold,
Did unto them at length these speeches wise unfold:

20

'Hearken to me a while, ye heavenly powers:
  Ye may remember since° the Earth's cursed seed   *when*
  Sought to assail the heavens' eternal towers,
  And to us all exceeding fear did breed.
  But how we then defeated all their deed
  Ye all do know, and them destroyed quite;°   *completely*
  Yet not so quite but that there did succeed
  An offspring of their blood which did alight
Upon the fruitful Earth, which doth us yet
  despite.°   *treat contemptuously*

21

'Of that bad seed is this bold woman bred
  That now with bold presumption doth aspire
  To thrust fair Phoebe from her silver bed,
  And eke° ourseves from heaven's high empire,   *also*
  If that her might were match to her desire.
  Wherefore it now behoves us to advise°   *ponder*
  What way is best to drive her to retire:°   *withdraw†*
  Whether by open force or counsel wise,
Aread,° ye sons of god, as best ye can devise.'   *Declare*

22

So having said, he ceased, and with his brow
  (His black eyebrow, whose doomful° dreaded   *fateful†*
    beck°   *sign of command*
  Is wont° to wield° the world unto his   *accustomed direct*
    vow,°   *desire‡*
  And even the highest powers of heaven to check)
  Made sign to them in their degrees° to speak, *ranks; hierarchies*
  Who straight° 'gan cast° their counsel grave *forthwith present*
    and wise.
  Meanwhile the Earth's daughter – though she nought did
    reck°   *care*
  Of° Hermes' message – yet 'gan now advise°   *About consider*

What course were best to take in this hot, bold
    emprise.°   *undertaking*

23

Eftsoons she thus resolved that, whilst the gods
    (After return of Hermes' embassy)°   *ambassadorial mission*†
    Were troubled and amongst themselves at odds,
    Before they could new counsels re-ally°   *reassemble*
    To set upon them in that ecstasy,°   *upheaval; frenzy*
    And take what fortune time and place would lend.
    So forth she rose, and through the clearest sky
    To Jove's high palace straight cast° to ascend   *determined*
To prosecute her plot: good onset° bodes good end.   *beginning*‡

24

She, there arriving, boldly in did pass,
    Where all the gods she found in counsel close,°   *secret*
    All quite unarmed, as then their manner was.
    At sight of her they sudden all arose
    In great amaze,° ne wist° what way to *panic*† *neither knew they*
      choose.
    But Jove, all fearless, forced them to aby,°   *remain**
    And in his sovereign throne 'gan straight dispose
    Himself more full of grace and majesty
That mote° encheer° his friends, and foes mote   *might   cheer*
    terrify.

25

That, when the haughty° Titaness beheld,   *tall;‡ arrogant*
    All° were she fraught° with pride and   *Although filled*†
      impudence,
    Yet with the sight thereof was almost quelled
    And, inly° quaking, seemed as° reft° of   *inwardly as if robbed*
      sense
    And void of speech in that dread audience,°   *judicial hearing*
    Until that Jove himself herself bespake:°   *addressed*†
    'Speak, thou frail woman, speak with confidence:
    Whence art thou, and what dost thou here now
      make?°   *what is your purpose?*
What idle errand hast thou, Earth's mansion° to   *dwelling*
    forsake?'

26

She, half confused with his great command,°   *exercise of authority*‡
   Yet gathering spirit° of° her nature's pride,   *courage   from*
   Him boldly answered thus to his demand:
   'I am a daughter, by the mother's side,
   Of her that is grandmother magnified°   *glorified*
   Of° all the gods – great Earth, great Chaos' child.   *By*
   But by the father's (be it not envied)°   *also: denied*‡
   I greater am in blood (whereon I build)
Than all the gods, though wrongfully from heaven exiled.

27

'For Titan – as ye all acknowledge must –
   Was Saturn's elder brother by birth right:
   Both sons of Uranus. But by unjust
   And guileful means, through Corybantes' sleight,
   The younger thrust the elder from his right;
   Since which thou, Jove, injuriously° hast held   *wrongfully*‡
   The heathens' rule from Titans' sons by might,
   And them to hellish dungeons down hast felled:
Witness, ye heavens, the truth of all that I have telled.'°   *told*

28

Whilst thus she spake the gods, that gave good ear
   To her bold words and marked well her grace
   (Being of stature tall as any there
   Of all the gods, and beautiful of face
   As any of the goddesses in place),°   *present*
   Stood all astonied,° like a sort° of steers   *thunderstruck   herd*
   'Mongst whom some beast of strange and foreign race
   Unwares is chanced,° far straying from his   *has happened*
      peers:°   *companions*
So did their ghastly° gaze bewray° their hidden   *fearful*‡   *reveal*
   fears.

29

Till, having paused a while, Jove thus bespake.°   *spoke*‡
   'Will never mortal thoughts cease to aspire
   In this bold° sort to heaven claim to make,   *manner*
   And touch celestial seats with earthly mire?
   I would have thought that bold Procrustes' hire,°   *punishment*

Or Typhon's fall, or proud Ixion's pain,
  Or great Prometheus' tasting of our ire,
  Would have sufficed the rest for to restrain,
And warned all men by their example to refrain.

30

'But now this offscum° of that cursed fry°   *dross^t* *progeny*
  Dare to renew the like bold enterprise,
  And challenge the heritage° of this our sky –   *inheritance*
  Whom what should hinder° but that we likewise   *stop us*
  Should handle as the rest of her allies,
  And thunder-drive° to hell?' With that he   *drive with thunder^t*
    shook
  His nectar-dewed locks, with which the skies
  And all the world beneath for terror quook,°   *quaked*
And eft° his burning levin-brand° in hand   *after lightning bolt^t*
    he took.

31

But when he looked on her lovely face,
  In which fair beams of beauty did appear
  That could the greatest wrath soon turn to grace°   *favour*
  (Such sway doth beauty even in heaven bear),
  He stayed his hand and, having changed his cheer,°   *aspect*
  He thus again in milder wise° began: *fashion*
  'But ah!, if gods should strive with° flesh   *against*
    yfere,°   *together*
  Then shortly should the progeny of man
Be rooted out if Jove should do still what he can.

32

'But thee, fair Titans' child, I rather ween°   *believe*
  Through some vain error or inducement light°   *trifling*
  To see that° mortal eyes have never seen,   *what*
  Or through example of thy sister's might,
  Bellona, whose great glory thou dost spite°   *begrudge*
  Since thou hast seen her dreadful power below,
  'Mongst wretched men dismayed° with her   *overcome*
    affright,°   *fear^t of her*
  To bandy° crowns, and kingdoms to bestow: *toss around^t*
And sure, thy worth no less than hers doth seem to show.

33

'But wote° thou this, thou hardy° Titaness,   *know   bold*
  That not the worth of any living wight°   *creature**
  May challenge° aught in heaven's interess,°   *claim   legal title*
  Much less the title of old Titans' right;
  For we by conquest of our sovereign might,
  And by eternal doom° of Fate's decree,   *sentence*
  Have won the empire of the heavens bright
  Which to ourselves we hold, and to whom we
Shall worthy deem° partakers of our bliss to be.   *judge*

34

'Then cease thy idle claim, thou foolish girl,
  And seek by grace and goodness to obtain
  That place from which by folly Titan fell;
  Thereto thou mayest, perhaps, if so thou fain,°   *wish*
  Have Jove thy gracious lord and sovereign.'
  So having said, she thus to him replied:
  'Cease, Saturn's son, to seek by proffers vain
  Of idle hopes to allure me to thy side
For° to betray my right before I have it tried.   *In order*

35

'But thee, O Jove, no equal judge I deem
  Of my desert, or of my dueful° right,   *due*
  That in thine own behalf mayest partial seem:
  But to the highest him that is behight°   *called†*
  Father of gods and men by equal might –
  To weet,° the god° of Nature, I appeal.'   *Namely   deity*
  Thereat Jove waxed wrath and in his sprite°   *mind*
  Did inly° grudge,° yet did it well conceal,   *inwardly   grumble*
And bade Dan° Phoebus' scribe her appellation°   *Lord   appeal*
    seal.

36

Eftsoons° the time and place appointed were   *Forthwith*
  Where all – both heavenly powers and earthly wights –
  Before great Nature's presence should appear
  For trial of their titles and best rights:
  That was, to weet, upon the highest heights
  Of Arlo Hill (who knows not Arlo Hill?),

That is the highest head in all men's sights
Of my old father Mole, whom shepherd's quill°   *i.e., pen*
Renowned hath with hymns fit for a rural skill.°   *expertise*

37

And, were it not ill-fitting for this file°   *narrative thread*[†]
 To sing of hills and woods 'mongst wars and knights,
 I would abate the sternness° of my style   *severity*
 'Mongst these stern° stounds° to mingle soft   *fierce conflicts*
  delights,
 And tell how Arlo, through Diana's spites°   *anger*
 (Being of old the best and fairest hill
 That was in all this holy island's heights),
 Was made the most unpleasant and most ill;
Meanwhile, O Clio, lend Calliope thy quill:

38

Whilom,° when Ireland flourished in fame   *Once upon a time*[*]
 Of wealths° and goodness far above the rest *collective property*
 Of all that bear the British Islands' name,
 The gods then used, for pleasure and for rest,
 Oft to resort thereto when seemed them best.
 But none of all therein more pleasure found
 Than Cynthia, that is the sovereign queen
  professed°   *acknowledged*
 Of woods and forests, which therein abound
Sprinkled with wholesome waters more than most on ground.

39

But 'mongst them all, as fittest for her game° –   *recreation*
 Either for chase of beasts with hound or bow,
 Or for to shroud° in shade from Phoebus' flame,   *shelter*
 Or bathe in fountains that do freshly flow
 Or° from high hills or from the dales below –   *Either*
 She chose this Arlo, where she did resort
 With all her nymphs enranged° in a row,   *arranged*[†]
 With whom the woody° gods did oft consort;   *woodland*
For with the nymphs the satyrs love to play and sport.

40

Amongst the which there was a nymph that hight°   *was called*†*
  Molanna, daughter of old father Mole
  And sister unto Mulla, fair and bright,
  Unto whose bed false Bregog whilom° stole,   *formerly**
  That° shepherd Colin dearly° did   *Which much*
    condole,°   *lament†*
  And made her luckless loves well known to be.
  But this Molanna, were she not so shoal,°   *shallow*
  Were no less fair and beautiful than she:
Yet as she is a fairer flood may no man see.

41

For, first, she springs out of two marble rocks,
  On which a grove of oaks high-mounted grows
  That as a garland seems to deck the locks
  Of some fair bride brought forth with pompous
    shows°   *ceremony*
  Out of her bower,° that many flowers strews: *chamber*
  So through the flowery dales she, tumbling down,
  Through many woods and shady coverts° flows   *hiding places*
  (That on each side her silver channel crown)
Till to the plain she come, whose valleys she doth drown.° *cover*

42

In her sweet streams Diana used oft –
  After her sweaty chase and toilsome play –
  To bathe herself; and after, on the soft
  And downy grass, her dainty limbs to lay
  In covert° shade where none behold her may,   *secret; covering*
  For much she hated sight of living eye.
  Foolish god Faunus, though full many a day
  He saw her clad, yet longed foolishly
To see her naked 'mongst her nymphs in privity.°   *secret*

43

No way he found to compass° his desire   *achieve*
  But to corrupt Molanna, this her maid,
  Her to discover° for some secret hire.°   *reveal reward*
  So her with flattering words he first assayed,°   *tested*
  And after, pleasing gifts for her purveyed° –   *supplied*

Queen apples and red cherries from the tree,
With which he her allured and betrayed
To tell what time he might her lady see
When she herself did bathe, that he might secret be.

44

Thereto he promised, if she would him pleasure°   *gratify*‡
   With this small boon, to quite° her with a better: *repay*
   To weet,° that whereas she had out of   *Namely*
      measure°   *excessively*
   Long loved the Fanchin° (who by nought did   *i.e., Funsheon*
      set° her)   *esteem*
   That he would undertake, for this, to get her
   To be his love, and of° him liked well.   *by*
   Besides all which, he vowed to be her debtor
   For many mo'° good turns than he would tell,   *more*
The least of which this little pleasure° should excel. *gratification*

45

The simple° maid did yield to him anon,°   *humble; naive soon*
   And eft° him placed where he close° might view *after secretly*
   That° never any saw, save only one   *What*
   (Who for his hire° so° foolhardy°   *reward such foolhardiness*‡
      due
   Was of° his hounds devoured in hunter's hue).°   *by form*
   Tho,° as her manner° was on sunny day,   *Then custom*
   Diana, with her nymphs about her, drew
   To this sweet spring where, doffing° her   *removing*
      array,°   *attire*
She bathed her lovely limbs, for Jove a likely° prey.   *suitable*

46

There Faunus saw that° pleased much his eye,   *what*
   And made his heart to tickle° in his   *be stirred with pleasure*
      breast,
   That° for great joy of somewhat° he   *So that i.e., the pudenda*
      did spy
   He could him not contain in silent rest
   But, breaking forth in laughter, loud professed°   *declared*
   His foolish thought: a foolish Faun' indeed
   That couldest not hold° thyself so hidden blessed,   *keep*

But wouldest needs thine own conceit°   *thought*
   aread° –   *declare*
Babblers unworthy been of so divine a meed.°   *reward*

47

The goddess, all abashed with that noise,
   In haste forth started from the guilty brook
   And, running straight whereas° she heard   *to the place where*
   his voice,
   Enclosed the bush about and there him took,
   Like dared° lark, not daring up to look   *dazzled*‡
   On her whose sight before so much he sought.
   Thence forth they drew him by the horns and shook
   Nigh° all to pieces that° they left him   *Nearly   so that*
   nought,°   *as nothing*
And then into the open light they forth him brought.

48

Like as an housewife that with busy care
   Thinks of her dairy to make wondrous gain,
   Finding whereas° some wicked beast   *where*
   unware°   *unknown to her;* * unexpectedly*
   That breaks into her dairy house there doth drain
   Her creaming pans and frustrate all her pain,°   *trouble*
   Hath in some snare or gin set close° behind   *secretly*
   Entrapped him and caught into her train,°   *trap*
   Then thinks what punishment were best assigned,
And thousand deaths deviseth in her vengeful mind:

49

So did Diana and her maidens all
   Use silly° Faunus, now within their bail:°   *ignorant   power* *
   They mock him and scorn him, and him foul°   *foully*
   miscall;°   *vilify*
   Some by the nose him plucked, some by the tail,
   And by his goatish beard some did him hale.°   *drag*
   Yet he (poor soul) with patience all did bear,
   For nought against their wills might
   countervail;°   *balance itself*†
   Ne aught he said,° whatever he did hear   *And he said nothing*

But, hanging down his head, did like a Mome°   *Momus: i.e., fool*
   appear.

                              50
At length, when they had flouted° him their fill,   *mocked*‡
   They 'gan to cast° what penance to him give.   *consider*
   Some would have gelt° him (but that same would   *castrated*
      spill°   *destroy*
   The wood-gods breed, which must for ever live);
   Others would through the river him have drive'°   *driven*
   And ducked deep (but that seemed penance light);
   But most agreed, and did this sentence give,
   Him in deerskin to clad and, in that plight,°   *condition*
To hunt him with their hounds, himself save how he might.

                              51
But Cynthia's self, more angry than the rest,
   Thought not enough to punish him in sport
   And of her shame to make a gamesome° jest,   *merry*
   But 'gan examine him in stricter sort°   *fashion*
   Which of her nymphs, or other close°   *secret*
      consort,°   *companion*
   Him thither brought and her to him betrayed?
   He, much afeared, to her confessed short°   *without delay*
   That 'twas Molanna which her so bewrayed.°   *exposed*
Then all at once° their hands upon Molanna laid.   *together*

                              52
But him (according as they had decreed)
   With a deerskin they covered, and then chased
   With all their hounds that after him did speed.
   But he, more speedy, from them fled more fast
   Than any deer: so sore° him dread°   *greatly fear*
      aghast.°   *terrified**
   They after followed all with shrill outcry,
   Shouting as° they the heavens would have   *as if*
      brast,°   *burst asunder*
   That° all the wood and dales where he did fly   *So that*
Did ring again, and loud° re-echo to the sky.   *loudly*

53

So they him followed till they weary were,
  When, back returning to Molann' again,
  They, by commandment of Diana, there
  Her whelmed° with stones. Yet Faunus (for her pain)   *buried‡*
  Of° her beloved Fanchin did obtain   *From*
  That her he would receive unto his bed:
  So now her waves pass through a pleasant° plain   *delightful*
  Till with the Fanchin she herself do wed
And, both combined, themselves in one fair river spread.

54

Natheless° Diana, full of indignation,   *Nevertheless*
  Thenceforth abandoned her delicious brook
  In whose sweet stream, before that bad occasion,
  So much delight to bathe her limbs she took:
  Ne° only her, but also quite° forsook   *And not completely*
  All those fair° forests about Arlo hid,   *beautiful*
  And all that mountain which doth overlook
  The richest champaign° that may else be   *plain*
    rid,°   *ridden over*
And the fair Suir, in which a thousand salmons bred.

55

Them all, and all that she so dear did weigh,
  Thenceforth she left; and, parting° from the place,   *departing*
  Thereon an heavy, hapless° curse did lay,   *unlucky‡*
  To weet,° that wolves, where she was wont to   *Namely*
    space,°   *roam‡*
  Should harboured be, and all those woods deface,
  And thieves should rob and spoil° that coast around.   *plunder*
  Since which, those woods and all that goodly
    chase°   *hunting ground*
  Doth to this day with wolves and thieves abound –
Which too, too true that land's indwellers° since   *inhabitants*
    have found.

CANTO 7

Appealing from Jove to Nature's bar,
   Bold Alteration pleads
Large° evidence: but Nature soon   *Much*
   Her righteous doom° areads.°   *sentence declares*

1

Ah, whither dost thou now, thou greater Muse,
  Me from these woods and pleasing forests bring?
  And my frail spirit – that doth oft refuse
  This too high flight, unfit for her weak wing –
  Lift up aloft to tell of heaven's king
  (Thy sovereign sire) his fortunate success
  And victory in bigger° notes to sing,   *louder*
  Which he obtained against that Titaness
That him of heaven's empire sought to dispossess.

2

Yet sith° I needs must follow thy behest,°   *since bidding*
  Do thou my weaker wit° with skill° *understanding knowledge*
    inspire
  Fit for this turn;° and in my feeble breast   *change of subject*
  Kindle fresh sparks of that immortal fire
  Which learned minds inflameth with desire
  Of heavenly things; for who but thou alone,
  That art yborn of heaven and heavenly sire,
  Can tell things done in heaven so long ygone° – *gone;* ago**
So far past memory of man that may be known.

3

Now, at the time that was before agreed,
  The gods assembled all on Arlo hill:
  As well those that are sprung of heavenly seed
  As those that all the other world° do fill   *i.e., the earth*
  And rule both sea and land unto their will.
  Only the infernal powers might not appear,
  As well for horror of their countenance ill°   *evil*

As for the unruly fiends which they° did   *i.e., the other gods*
  fear;
Yet Pluto and Proserpina were present there.

4

And thither also came all other creatures
  Whatever° life and motion do retain,   *Which*
  According to their sundry kinds of features,
  That° Arlo scarcely could them all contain,   *So that*
  So full they filled every hill and plain.
  And had not Nature's sergeant (that is, Order)
  Them well disposed by his busy pain°   *care*
  And ranged° far abroad in every border,°   *arranged boundary*
They would have caused much confusion and disorder.

5

Then forth issued – great goddess! – great Dame Nature,
  With goodly° port° and gracious majesty,   *fine bearing*
  Being far greater and more tall of stature
  Than any of the gods or powers on high.
  Yet, certes,° by her face and   *indeed*
    physnomy,°   *physiognomy; face*
  Whether she man or woman inly° were,   *inwardly; intimately*
  That could not any creature well descry;°   *perceive*
  For, with a veil that wimpled° everywhere,   *covered*
Her head and face was hid that mote° to none   *so that it might*
  appear.

6

That, some do say, was so by skill° devised   *cunningly*
  To hide the terror of her uncouth°   *strange; unknown*
    hue°   *appearance*
  From mortal eyes that should be sore°   *greatly*
    agrised,°   *terrified**
  For that her face did like a lion show
  That° eye of wight° could not endure to   *So that anybody**
    view.
  But others tell that it so beauteous was,
  And round about such beams of splendour threw,
  That it the sun a thousand times did pass,°   *surpass*
Ne° could be seen but° like an image in a glass.   *Nor except*

7

That well may seemen true; for well I ween°   *believe*
   That this same day, when she on Arlo sat,
     Her garment was so bright and wondrous sheen°   *resplendent*
     That my frail° wit° cannot devise to what   *feeble understanding*
   It to compare, nor find like stuff° to that;   *fabric*
   As those three sacred saints, though else most wise,
   Yet on Mount Tabor quite their wits forgot
   When they their glorious lord in strange disguise
Transfigured saw – his garments so did daze their eyes.

8

In a fair plain upon an equal° hill   *level-topped*
   She placed was in° a pavilion° –   *under canopy*
     Not such as craftsmen by their idle° skill   *empty; vain*
     Are wont for princes' states° to fashion;   *canopied thrones*
   But the Earth herself, of her own motion,
   Out of her fruitful bosom, made to grow
   Most dainty trees that, shooting up anon,°   *forthwith*
   Did seem to bow their blooming heads full low
For homage unto her, and like a throne° did   *i.e., canopied throne*
   show.°   *appear*

9

So hard it is for any living wight°   *creature**
   All her array and vestments to tell
     That old Dan° Geoffrey (in whose gentle°   *Master noble*
     sprite°   *soul; mind*
   The pure well-head° of poesy did dwell)   *source*
   In his *Fowls' Parley* durst° not with it   *dared*
   mell,°   *concern himself*
   But it transferred° to Alan, who, he thought,   *handed over*
   Had in his *Plaint of Kinds* described it well:
   Which who will read set forth so as it ought,
Go seek he out that Alan where he may be sought.

10

And all the Earth far underneath her feet
   Was dight° with flowers that voluntary grew   *adorned*
     Out of the ground and sent forth odours sweet:
     Ten thousand mores° of sundry scent and   *roots; plants*

hue°   colour
That might delight the smell or please the view° –   sight‡
The which the nymphs from all the brooks thereby
Had gathered – which they at her footstool threw,
That richer seemed than any tapestry
That princes' bowers° adorn with painted imagery.   chambers

11

And Mole himself, to honour her the more,
  Did deck himself in freshest° fair° attire,   brightest splendid
  And his high head (that seemeth always hoar°   white
  With hardened frosts of former winters' ire)
  He with an oaken garland now did tire°   dress
  As if the love of some new nymph late° seen   recently
  Had in him kindled youthful fresh desire,
  And made him change his grey attire to green:
Ah, gentle Mole! such joyance° hath thee well   festivity
  beseen.°   suited

12

Was never so great joyance° since the day   rejoicing†
  That all the gods whilom° assembled were   once*
  On Haemus hill in their divine array°   order; hierarchy
  To celebrate the solemn bridal cheer
  'Twixt Peleus and Dame Thetis 'pointed° there;   appointed
  Where Phoebus self,° that god of poets   himself
  hight,°   was called*†
  They say did sing the spousal° hymn full clear   marriage
  That° all the gods were ravished with delight   So that
Of his celestial song and music's wondrous might.

13

This great grandmother of all creatures bred –
  Great Nature, ever young yet full of eld,°   age
  Still° moving, yet unmoved from her stead,°   Ever place
  Unseen of° any, yet of all beheld –   By
  Thus sitting on her throne, as I have telled,
  Before her came Dame Mutability
  And, being low before her presence felled°   fallen
  With meek obeisance and humility,
Thus 'gan her plaintiff plea with words to amplify:°   expatiate‡

14

'To thee, O greatest goddess, only° great,   *uniquely*
   An humble suppliant, lo, I lowly fly
   Seeking for right, which I of thee entreat,
   Who right to all dost deal indifferently,°   *impartially*
   Damning all wrongs and tortious° injury   *illegal*
   Which any of thy creatures do to other,
   Oppressing them with power unequally,
   Sith° of them all thou art the equal mother   *Since*
And knittest each to each, as brother unto brother.

15

'To thee, therefore, of this same Jove I plain,°   *complain*
   And of his fellow gods that feign to be,
   That challenge to° themselves the whole world's   *claim for*
     reign,
   Of which the greatest part is due to me,
   And heaven itself by heritage° in fee:°   *inheritance   absolute*‡
   For heaven and earth I both alike do deem,°   *judge*
   Sith° heaven and earth are both alike to thee,   *Since*
   And gods no more than men thou dost esteem,
For even the gods to thee, as men to gods, do seem.

16

'Then weigh, O sovereign goddess, by what right
   These gods do claim the world's whole sovereignty,
   And that° is only due unto thy might   *that which*
   Arrogate° to themselves ambitiously.   *Assume*‡
   As for the gods' own principality°   *sovereignty*
   Which Jove usurps unjustly: that to be
   My heritage Jove's self° cannot deny,   *Jove himself*
   From my great grandsire Titan unto me
Derived by due descent, as is well known to thee.

17

'Yet, maugre° Jove and all his gods beside,   *in spite of*
   I do possess the world's most regiment°   *management*
   As, if ye please it into parts divide,
   And every part's inholders° to convent,°   *tenants*‡   *convene*‡
   Shall to your eyes appear incontinent.°   *forthwith*

And first the Earth (great mother of us all),
That only° seems unmoved and permanent   *alone*
And unto Mutability not thrall:
Yet is she changed in part° and eke° in general.   *particular also*

18

'For, all that from her springs and is ybred,
However fair it flourish for a time,
Yet see we soon decay and, being dead,
To turn again unto their earthly slime.°   *corruption*‡
Yet out of their decay and mortal crime°   *sin*
We daily see new creatures to arise,
And of their winter spring another prime,°   *spring; infancy*
Unlike in form and changed by strange disguise:
So turn they still about, and change in restless wise.°   *fashion*

19

'As for her tenants – that is, man and beasts –
The beasts we daily see massacred, die
As thralls and vassals unto men's behests;°   *orders*
And men themselves do change continually
From youth to eld,° from wealth to poverty,   *age*
From good to bad, from bad to worst of all.
Ne° do their bodies only flit° and fly,°   *Nor change alter*
But eke their minds (which they immortal call)
Still° change and vary thoughts as new occasions   *Ever*
    fall.°   *befall*

20

'Ne° is the water in more constant case,   *Neither*
Whether those same on high or those below;
For the ocean moveth still from place to place,
And every river still doth ebb and flow;
Ne° any lake that seems most still and slow,   *Neither is there*
Ne° pool so small, that can his smoothness hold   *Nor*
When any wind doth under heaven blow –
With which the clouds are also tossed and rolled,
Now like great hills, and straight° like sluices them   *forthwith*
    unfold.

21

'So likewise are all watery living wights
  Still tossed and turned with continual change,
  Never abiding in their steadfast plights.°   *states*
  The fish, still° floating,° do at random   *ever swimming*‡
    range,°   *rove*‡
  And never rest, but evermore exchange°   *change**
  Their dwelling places as the streams them carry;
  Ne have the watery fowls a certain° grange°   *fixed abode*‡
  Wherein to rest, ne in one stead° do tarry,   *place*
But flitting° still do fly and still their places vary.   *moving*

22

'Next is the air, which who feels not by sense
  (For of all sense it is the middle mean)°   *intermediary*
  To flit° still,° and with subtle influence   *change always*
  Of his thin spirit° all creatures to maintain   *breath*
  In state of life? O weak life, that does lean
  On thing so tickle° as the unsteady° air,   *uncertain inconstant*
  Which every hour is changed and altered clean°   *completely*
  With every blast that bloweth foul or fair –
The fair doth it prolong, the foul doth it impair.°   *weaken*

23

'Therein the changes infinite behold
  Which to her creatures every minute chance:°   *happen*
  Now boiling hot; straight° freezing deadly cold; *immediately*
  Now fair sunshine that makes all skip and dance;
  Straight, bitter storms and baleful°   *malign*
    countenance°   *aspect*
  That makes them all to shiver and to shake.
  Rain, hail, and snow do pay them sad°   *melancholy; heavy*
    penance,
  And dreadful thunder claps that make them quake
With flames and flashing lights that thousand changes make.

24

'Last is the fire, which, though it live for ever,
  Ne can° be quenched quite,° yet every day *Cannot completely*
  We see his parts, so soon as they do sever,

To lose their heat and shortly to decay° –   *deteriorate*
So makes himself his own consuming prey.
Ne any living creatures doth he breed,
But all that are of° others bred, doth slay   *from*
And, with their death, his cruel life doth feed,
Nought leaving but their barren ashes without seed.

                              25
'Thus all these four (the which the groundwork be
   Of all the world and of all living wights)
   To thousand sorts of change we subject see.
   Yet are they changed (by other wondrous sleights)°   *devices*
   Into themselves, and lose their native mights:°   *powers*
   The fire to air, and the air to water sheer,°   *clear*
   And water into earth – yet water fights
   With fire, and air with earth, approaching near;
Yet all are in one body, and as one appear.

                              26
'So in them all reigns Mutability,
   However these, that gods themselves do call,
   Of them do claim the rule and sovereignty –
   As° Vesta, of the fire ethereal;   *Such as*
   Vulcan, of this with us so usual;
   Ops of the earth; and Juno of the air;
   Neptune of seas; and nymphs, of rivers all.
   For all those rivers to me subject are,
And all the rest, which they usurp, be all my share.

                              27
'Which to approven° true, as I have told,   *prove*
   Vouchsafe,° O goddess, to thy presence call   *Grant*
   The rest which do the world in being hold,
   As,° times and seasons of the year that fall;°   *Such as occur*
   Of all the which demand in general,
   Or judge thyself by verdict of thine eye,
   Whether to me they are not subject all.'
   Nature did yield thereto, and by and
      by°   *straight away; in order*
Bade Order call them all before her majesty.

28

So forth issued the seasons of the year:
  First, lusty Spring, all dight° in leaves of flowers   *decked*
  That freshly budded and new blooms did bear,
  In which a thousand birds had built their bowers,°   *nests*
  That sweetly sung to call forth paramours;°   *mates; lovers*
  And in his hand a javelin he did bear,
  And on his head – as fit for warlike stours° –   *encounters*
  A gilt engraven morion° he did wear,   *visorless helmet*‡
That° as some did him love, so others did him fear.   *So that*

29

Then came the jolly° Summer, being   *cheerful; lively*
    dight°   *dressed*
  In a thin silken cassock, coloured green,
  That was unlined all to be more light;
  And on his head a garland well beseen°   *handsome*
  He wore, from which, as° he had chafed°   *as if overheated*
    been,
  The sweat did drop; and in his hand he bore
  A bow and shafts, as° he in forest green   *as if*
  Had hunted late the leopard or the boar,
And now would bathe his limbs, with labour heated
    sore.°   *extremely*

30

Then came the Autumn, all in yellow clad,
  As though he joyed° in his plenteous   *rejoiced*
    store,°   *abundance*
  Laden with fruits, that made him laugh full glad
  That he had banished hunger, which to-fore°   *hitherto*
  Had by the belly oft him pinched° sore.   *tormented*
  Upon his head a wreath, that was enrolled°   *wrapped round*
  With ears of corn, of every sort° he bore,   *type [of plant]*
  And in his hand a sickle he did hold
To reap the ripened fruits the which the earth had yold.° *yielded*

31

Lastly came Winter, clothed all in frieze,°   *coarse woollen cloth*
  Chattering his teeth for cold that did him chill,
  Whilst on his hoary beard his breath did freeze,

And the dull drops that from his purpled bill,°   *nose*
As from a limbeck,° did adown distill.   *alembic*
In his right hand a tipped staff he held,
With which his feeble steps he stayed° still;° *supported   always*
For he was faint with cold and weak with eld,°   *age*
That° scarce his loosed limbs he able was to   *So that*
 wield.°   *control*

32

These, marching softly,° thus in order went,   *slowly‡*
 And after them the months all riding came:
First, sturdy March, with brows full sternly° bent, *fiercely*
 And armed strongly, rode upon a Ram –
 The same which over Hellespontus swam;
 Yet in his hand a spade he also hent,°   *grasped*
 And in a bag all sorts of seeds ysame°   *together**
 Which on the earth he strewed as he went,
And filled her womb with fruitful hope of nourishment.

33

Next came fresh° April, full of lustihead° *young   vigour; lust*
 And wanton° as a kid whose horn new buds: *frisky; lustful*
 Upon a Bull he rode – the same which led
 Europa floating° through the Argolic° *swimming   Greek*
  floods.°   *waters*
 His horns were gilden° all with golden studs,° *gilded   discs‡*
 And garnished° with garlands goodly   *decorated*
  dight°   *adorned*
 Of all the fairest flowers and freshest buds
 Which the earth brings forth: and wet he seemed in
  sight°   *to one's view*
With waves, through which he waded for his love's delight.

34

Then came fair May, the fairest maid on ground,
 Decked all with dainties of her season's pride° *magnificence*
 And throwing flowers out of her lap around.
 Upon two brethren's shoulders she did ride –
 The Twins of Leda – which on either side
 Supported her like to their sovereign queen.
 Lord, how all creatures laughed when her they spied,

And leaped and danced as they had
    ravished° been!   *filled with ecstasy; transported*
And Cupid self° about her fluttered all in green.   *himself*

35

And after her came jolly June, arrayed
    All in green leaves as he a player° were: *actor*
    Yet in his time he wrought° as well as played,   *worked*
    That by his plough-irons mote° right well appear.   *might*
    Upon a Crab he rode, that him did bear
    With crooked, crawling steps (an uncouth° pace)   *strange*
    And backward yode,° as bargemen   *went*
        wont to fare,°   *customarily go*
    Bending their force contrary to their face,
Like that ungracious° crew which feigns demurest   *graceless*
    grace.

36

Then came hot July, boiling like to fire,
    That° all his garments he had cast away.   *So that*
    Upon a Lion, raging yet with ire,
    He boldly rode and made him to obey:
    It was the beast that whilom° did foray°   *once° ravage*
    The Nemean forest, till the Amphytrionide°   *son of Amphitryon*
    Him slew and with his hide did him array.
    Behind his back a scythe, and by his side
Under his belt he bore a sickle circling wide.

37

The sixth was August, being rich arrayed
    In garment all of gold down to the ground.
    Yet rode he not, but led a lovely maid
    Forth by the lily hand – the which was crowned
    With ears of corn; and full her hand was found.
    That was the righteous virgin which of old
    Lived here on earth and plenty made abound;
    But, after Wrong was loved and Justice sold,°   *betrayed*
She left the unrighteous world and was to heaven
    extolled.°   *raised*[1]

38

Next him, September marched, eke° on foot: also
  Yet was he heavy laden with the spoil
    Of harvest riches, which he made his boot°   booty
  And him enriched with bounty° of the soil.   excellence; gift
  In his one hand, as fit for harvest's toil,
  He held a knife-hook; and in the other hand
    A pair of weights,° with which he did   scales [Libra]
      assoil°   resolve
  Both more and less where it in doubt did stand,
And equal gave to each as Justice duly scanned.°   judged‡

39

Then came October, full of merry glee,
  For yet his noll° was totty of° the   head tipsy with
    must°   new wine
  Which he was treading in the wine-vat's sea,
  And of the joyous oil, whose gentle° gust°   noble taste
  Made him so frolic and so full of lust.
  Upon a dreadful° Scorpion he did ride –   terrifying
  The same which by Diana's doom° unjust   sentence
  Slew great Orion. And eke by his side
He had his ploughing share° and coulter°   rear blade front blade
  ready tied.

40

Next was November – he full gross and fat
  As° fed with lard: and that right well might seem,   As if
  For he had been a-fatting hogs of late°   recently
  That° yet his brows with sweat did reek° and   So that smoke
    steam,
  And yet° the season was full° sharp and   Although very
    breme;°   bitter
  In planting eke he took no small delight.
  Whereon he rode not easy was to deem,°   discern*
  For it a dreadful Centaur was in sight° –   to view
The seed of Saturn and fair Nais, Chiron hight.   named*†

41

And after him came next the chill December:
  Yet he, through merry feasting which he made,
  And great bonfires, did not the cold remember –
  His Saviour's birth his mind so much did glad.
  Upon a shaggy-bearded Goat he rode:
  The same wherewith Dan° Jove in tender years,°   *Lord infancy*
  They say, was nourished by the Idaean maid.
  And in his hand a broad, deep bowl he bears,
Of which he freely drinks an health to all his peers.°   *companions*

42

Then came old January, wrapped well
  In many weeds° to keep the cold away: *clothes*
  Yet did he quake and quiver like to quell,°   *as if dying*
  And blow his nails to warm them if he may;°   *might*
  For they were numbed with holding all the day
  An hatchet keen,° with which he felled wood   *sharp*
  And from the trees did lop the needless spray.°   *twigs*
  Upon an huge great earth-pot stean° he stood,   *pitcher*
From whose wide mouth there flowed forth the Roman
    flood.°   *river*

43

And lastly came cold February, sitting
  In an old wagon (for he could not ride)
  Drawn of° two Fishes, for the season°   *by i.e., Lent*
    fitting,°   *appropriate*
  Which through the flood before did softly slide
  And swim away. Yet had he by his side
  His plough and harness fit to till the ground,
  And tools to prune the trees, before the pride°   *abundance*
  Of hasting prime° did make them burgeon round.   *spring*
So passed the twelve months forth, and their due places found.

44

And after these there came the Day and Night,
  Riding together both with equal pace –
  The one on a palfrey black, the other white.
  But Night had covered her uncomely face
  With a black veil, and held in hand a mace

On top whereof the moon and stars were pight,°   placed
And Sleep and Darkness round about did trace.°   step
But Day did bear upon his sceptre's height
The goodly Sun, encompassed° all with beams   surrounded‡
  bright.

45

Then came the Hours, fair daughters of high Jove
  And timely° Night, the which were all indued   belonging to time
  With wondrous beauty fit to kindle love;
  But they were virgins all, and love eschewed
  That might forslack° the charge to them   cause to neglect
    foreshowed°   ordained‡
  By mighty Jove, who did them porters make
  Of heaven's gate (whence all the gods issued),
  Which they did daily watch and nightly wake°   tend
By even° turns, ne° ever did their charge°   equal nor duty
  forsake.

46

And after all came Life and, lastly, Death:
  Death with most grim and grisly° visage seen   terrifying
  (Yet is he nought but parting° of the breath),   departing
  Ne aught to see, but like a shade° to   shadow; ghost
    ween° –   indeed
  Unbodied, unsouled, unheard, unseen.
  But Life was like a fair,° young, lusty boy,   handsome
  Such as they feign° Dan Cupid to have been –   fable
  Full of delightful health and lively joy,
Decked all with flowers, and wings of gold fit to employ.°   use

47

When these were past, thus 'gan the Titaness:
  'Lo, mighty mother, now be judge, and say
  Whether in all thy creatures, more° or less,°   greater lesser
  Change doth not reign and bear the greatest sway;°   control
  For who sees not that Time on all doth prey? –
  But times do change and move continually.
  So nothing here long standeth in one stay.
  Wherefore, this lower world who can deny
But to be subject still° to Mutability?'   always

48

Then thus 'gan Jove: 'Right true it is that these,
  And all things else that under heaven dwell,
  Are changed of° Time, who doth them all   *by*
    disseise°   *dispossess*
  Of being. But who is it – to me tell –
  That Time himself doth move and still° compel   *always*
  To keep his course? Is not that namely° we   *above all*
  Which pour that virtue° from our heavenly   *power*
    cell°   *dwelling*
  That moves them all, and makes them changed be?
So then we gods do rule, and in them also thee.'

49

To whom thus Mutability: 'The things
  Which we see not how they are moved and swayed
  Ye may attribute to yourselves as kings,
  And say they by your secret power are made –
  But what we see not, who shall us persuade?
  But were they so – as ye them feign to be –
  Moved by your might and ordered by your aid:
  Yet what if I can prove that even ye
Yourselves are likewise changed and subject unto me?

50

'And first concerning her that is the first –
  Even you, fair Cynthia, whom so much ye make
  Jove's dearest darling. She was bred and nursed
  On Cynthus hill, whence she her name did take:
  Then is she mortal born, how so ye crake.°   *brag*
  Besides, her face and countenance every day
  We changed see, and sundry forms partake° –   *adopt*†
  Now horned, now round, now bright, now brown° and *dark*
    grey;
So that "as changeful as the moon" men use° to   *are accustomed*
  say.

51

'Next Mercury, who, though he less appear
  To change his hue° and always seem as one,   *aspect*
  Yet he his course doth alter every year,

And is of late far out of order gone.
So Venus eke, that goodly
    paragon,°   *companion; pattern [of beauty]*
Though fair all night yet is she dark all day;
And Phoebus self,° who lightsome° is   *himself   luminous*
    alone,°   *uniquely*
Yet is he oft eclipsed by the way°   *on his course*
And fills the darkened world with terror and dismay.

52

'Now Mars – that valiant man – is changed most;
    For he sometimes so far runs out of square
    That he his way doth seem quite° to have lost,   *completely*
    And clean° without° his usual sphere to fare,   *utterly   outside*
    That° even those star-gazers astonished are   *So that*
    At sight thereof, and damn their lying books.
    So, likewise, grim Saturn oft doth spare°   *relieve*
    His stern aspect and calm his crabbed looks:
So many turning cranks° these have, so many   *twists‡*
    crooks.°   *bends*

53

'But you, Dan Jove, that only° constant are   *alone*
    And king of all the rest, as ye do claim:
    Are you not subject eke to this misfare?°   *going astray**
    Then let me ask you this, withouten blame –
    Where were ye born? Some say in Crete by name,
    Others in Thebes, and others other-where;
    But wheresoever they comment° the same,   *devise**
    They all consent that ye begotten were,
And born, here in this world – ne other
    can° appear.   *nor otherwise can it*

54

'Then are ye mortal born and thrall to me,
    Unless the kingdom of the sky ye make
    Immortal and unchangeable to be.
    Besides, that power and virtue which ye spake,°   *spoke of*
    That ye here work, doth many changes take,°   *operate*
    And your own natures change: for each of you
    That virtue° have or° this or that to make,   *power   either*

Is checked and changed from his nature true
By others' opposition or obliqued° view.°   skewed† aspect

55

'Besides, the sundry motions of your spheres
  So° sundry ways and fashions as clerks°   Such scholars
    feign° –   allege
  Some in short space, and some in longer years –
  What is the same but alteration plain?°   clear
  Only the starry sky doth still remain.
  Yet do the stars and signs therein still move,
  And even itself is moved, as wizards° sayen.°   wise men say
  But all that moveth doth mutation° love –   alteration
Therefore both you and them to me I subject prove.

56

'Then since within this wide, great universe
  Nothing doth firm and permanent appear,
  But all things tossed and turned by transverse:°   crosswise†
  What then should let° but I aloft should rear°   prevent lift
  My trophy, and from all the triumph bear?
  Now judge then (O thou greatest goddess true),
  According as thyself dost see and hear,
  And unto me addoom° that° is my due: adjudge† what
That is, the rule of all, all being ruled by you.'

57

So having ended, silence long ensued;
  Ne Nature to or fro° spoke for a space°   for or against while
  But, with firm eyes affixed, the ground still viewed.
  Meanwhile all creatures, looking in her face,
  Expecting° the end of this so doubtful case,   Awaiting
  Did hang in long suspense what would ensue,
  To whether° side should fall the sovereign place.   which
  At length she, looking up with cheerful view,°   aspect
The silence brake and gave her doom° in   judgement
    speeches° few: phrases†

58

'I well consider all that ye have said,
 And find that all things steadfastness° do hate,   *constancy*
 And changed be. Yet, being rightly weighed,°   *considered*
 They are not changed from their first° estate° *original state*
 But, by their change, their being° do dilate° *nature expand*
 And, turning° to themselves at length again,   *returning*
 Do work their own perfection° so by Fate: *completion*
 Then, over them Change doth not rule and reign,
But they reign over Change and do their states maintain.

59

'Cease therefore, daughter, further to aspire,
 And thee content thus to be ruled by me;
 For thy decay° thou seekest by thy desire.   *downfall*
 But time shall come that all shall changed be,
 And from thenceforth none no more change shall see.'
 So was the Titaness put down and whist,°   *silenced*
 And Jove confirmed in his imperial see.°   *throne*
 Then was that whole assembly quite° dismissed *completely*
And Nature's° self° did vanish – whither no man *Nature herself*
 wist.°   *knew*

The 8th Canto, imperfect

I

When I bethink me on that speech whilere°   *a while back*
 Of Mutability, and well it weigh,°   *ponder*
 Me seems that, though she all unworthy were
 Of the heavens' rule, yet, very sooth° to say, *true indeed*
 In all things else she bears the greatest sway:° *control*
 Which makes me loathe this state of life so tickle,° *unstable*
 And love of things so vain to cast away,
 Whose flowering pride° – so fading and so *splendour*
  fickle° –   *uncertain*
Short° Time shall soon cut down with his consuming *Brief*
 sickle.

2

Then 'gin I think on that which Nature said,
   Of that same time when no more Change shall be,
   But steadfast rest of all things firmly stayed°   *supported*
   Upon the pillars of Eternity
   That is contrary to Mutability.
   For all that moveth doth in Change delight;
   But thenceforth all shall rest eternally
   With Him that is the God of Sabaoth° hight:°   *Hosts   called**†
O that great Sabaoth God, grant me that
      sabaoth's° sight.   *host's; also sabbath's = eternal rest's*

APPENDIX

A Letter of the Author's,
expounding his whole intention in the course of this work,
which, for that it giveth great light to the reader, for the
better understanding is hereunto annexed.

To the Right Honourable and valorous Sir Walter Ralegh,
Knight, Lord Warden of the Stannaries, and her Majesty's
lieutenant of the County of Cornwall.

Sir: knowing how doubtfully all allegories may be construed,
and this book of mine (which I have entitled *The Fairy Queen*),
being a continued allegory or dark conceit, I have thought good,   10
as well for avoiding of jealous opinions and misconstructions,
as also for your better light in reading thereof (being so by you
commanded), to discover unto you the general intention and
meaning, which in the whole course thereof I have fashioned,
without expressing of any particular purposes or bye-accidents   15
therein occasioned. The general end, therefore, of all the book is
to fashion a gentleman or noble person in virtuous and gentle
discipline – which, for that I conceived should be most plausible
and pleasing, being coloured with an historical fiction (the which
the most part of men delight to read rather for variety of matter   20
than for profit of the example), I chose the history of King
Arthur as most fit, for the excellency of his person (being made
famous by many men's former works), and also furthest from
the danger of envy and suspicion of present time. In which I
have followed all the antique poets historical: first, Homer (who   25
in the persons of Agamemnon and Ulysses hath exampled a
good governor and a virtuous man, the one in his *Iliad*, the
other in his *Odyssey*); then Virgil (whose like intention was to
do in the person of Aeneas). After him Ariosto comprised them
both in his *Orlando*; and lately, Tasso dissevered them again,   30
and formed both parts in two persons: namely, that part which

they in philosophy call *ethic* (or virtues of a private man), coloured in his Rinaldo; the other, named *politic*, in his Godfredo. By example of which excellent poets, I labour to portrait in Arthur, before he was king, the image of a brave knight, 35 perfected in the twelve private moral virtues, as Aristotle hath devised – the which is the purpose of these first twelve books; which, if I find to be well accepted, I may be perhaps encouraged to frame the other part – of politic virtues – in his person after that he came to be king.   40

To some, I know, this method will seem displeasant, which had rather have good discipline delivered plainly in way of precepts, or sermoned at large, as they used, than thus cloudily enwrapped in allegorical devices. But such, me seem, should be satisfied with the use of these days, seeing all things accounted 45 by their shows, and nothing esteemed of that is not delightful and pleasing to common sense. For this cause is Xenophon preferred before Plato, for that the one, in the exquisite depth of his judgement, formed a commonwealth such as it should be; but the other, in the person of Cyrus and the Persians, fashioned 50 a government as might best be: so much more profitable and gracious is doctrine by example than by rule. So have I laboured to do in the person of Arthur, whom I conceive, after his long education by Timon (to whom he was by Merlin delivered to be brought up so soon as he was born of the Lady Ygraine), to have 55 seen in a dream or vision the Fairy Queen – with whose excellent beauty ravished, he, awaking, resolved to seek her out and, so being by Merlin armed, and by Timon thoroughly instructed, he went to seek her forth in Fairyland.

In that Fairy Queen, I mean 'glory' in my general intention; 60 but in my particular, I conceive the most excellent and glorious person of our sovereign Queen, and her kingdom in Fairyland. And yet, in some places else I do otherwise shadow her. For, considering she beareth two persons (the one, of a most royal Queen or Empress, the other of a most virtuous and beautiful 65 lady), this latter part in some places I do express in Belphoebe: fashioning her name according to your own excellent conceit of Cynthia – Phoebe and Cynthia being both names of Diana. So, in the person of Prince Arthur, I set forth magnificence in particular, which virtue – for that, according to Aristotle 70 and he rest, it is the perfection of all the rest and containeth in it them all – therefore, in the whole course, I mention the deeds of Arthur applicable to that virtue which I write of in that book.

But of the twelve other virtues I make twelve other knights the patrons, for the more variety of the history, of which these three books contain three: the first, of the knight of the Red Cross, in whom I express Holiness; the second, of Sir Guyon, in whom I set forth Temperance; the third, of Britomartis, a lady knight, in whom I picture Chastity. But because the beginning of the whole work seemeth abrupt and as depending upon other antecedents, it needs that ye know the occasion of these three knights' several adventures. For the method of a poet historical is not such as of an historiographer; for an historiographer discourseth of affairs orderly as they were done, accounting as well the times as the actions; but a poet thrusteth into the midst, even where it most concerneth him, and there recoursing to the things forepast, and divining of things to come, maketh a pleasing analysis of all. The beginning, therefore, of my history – if it were to be told by an historiographer – should be the twelfth book, which is the last, where I devise that the Fairy Queen kept her annual feast twelve days, upon which twelve several days the occasion of the twelve several adventures happened, which, being undertaken by twelve several knights, are in these twelve books severally handled and discoursed.

The first was this. In the beginning of the feast, there presented himself a tall, clownish, young man, who, falling before the Queen of Fairies, desired a boon (as the manner then was) which, during that feast, she might not refuse: which was, that he might have the achievement of any adventure which during that feast should happen. That being granted, he rested him on the floor, unfit through his rusticity for a better place. Soon after entered a fair lady in mourning weeds, riding on a white ass, with a dwarf behind her leading a warlike steed, that bore the arms of a knight, and his spear in the dwarf's hand. She, falling before the Queen of Fairies, complained that her father and mother – an ancient king and queen – had been by an huge dragon many years shut up in a brazen castle, who thence suffered them not to issue; and therefore besought the Fairy Queen to assign her some one of her knights to take on him that exploit. Presently, that clownish person, upstarting, desired that adventure: whereat the Queen much wondering, and the lady much gainsaying, yet he earnestly importuned his desire. In the end the lady told him that, unless that armour which she brought would serve him (that is, the armour of a Christian man specified by St Paul – see Ephesians), that he could not succeed in 115 thatenterprise; which, being forthwith put upon him with due furnitures thereunto, he seemed the goodliest man in all that company, and was well liked of the lady; and eftsoons taking on him knighthood, and mounting on that strange courser, he went forth with her on that adventure. Where beginneth the first 120 book, viz.: 'A gentle knight was pricking on the plain', etc.

The second day there came in a Palmer bearing an infant with bloody hands, whose parents he complained to have been slain by an enchantress called Acrasia; and therefore craved of the Fairy Queen to appoint him some knight to perform that 125 adventure, which, being assigned to Sir Guyon, he presently went forth with that same Palmer – which is the beginning of the second book and the whole subject thereof.

The third day there came in a groom, who complained before the Fairy Queen that a vile enchanter called Busirane had in 130 hand a most fair lady called Amoretta, whom he kept in most grievous torment because she would not yield him the pleasures of her body. Whereupon Sir Scudamour, the lover of that lady, presently took on him that adventure. But, being unable to perform it by reason of the hard enchantments, after long 135 sorrow, in the end met with Britomartis, who succoured him, and rescued his love. But by occasion hereof, many other adventures are intermeddled, but rather as accidents than intendments: as the love of Britomart; the overthrow of Mari-nell; the misery of Florimell; the virtuousness of Belphoebe; the 140 lasciviousness of Hellenore, and many the like. Thus much, Sir, I have briefly overrun to direct your understanding to the well-head of the history, that, from thence gathering the whole intention of the conceit, ye may – as in a handful – grip all the discourse which otherwise may haply seem tedious and con- 145 fused. So, humbly craving the continuance of your honourable favour towards me and the eternal establishment of your happiness, I humbly take leave.

23 January 1589
Yours, most humbly affectionate,
EDMUND SPENSER

NOTES

___

Note: Stanza numbers are printed in bold type; biblical quotations are from the Geneva Bible (1560; I have used a London 1599 edition). In addition to the common abbreviations for biblical books, the following abbreviations have been used:

Agrippa	H. C. Agrippa, *Three Books of Occult Philosophy*, trans. J.F., 1651
Am	Spenser, *Amoretti*
Ansell Robin	P. Ansell Robin, *Animal Lore in English Literature*, 1932
Brooks-Davies 1977	D. Brooks-Davies, *Spenser's 'Faerie Queene': A Critical Commentary on Books 1 and 2*, 1977
Brooks-Davies 1983	——, *The Mercurian Monarch: Magical Politics from Spenser to Pope*, 1983
Brooks-Davies 1995	—— (ed.), *Edmund Spenser: Selected Shorter Poems*, 1995
Colin Clout	Spenser, *Colin Clout's Come Home Again*
Curtius	E. R. Curtius, *European Literature and the Latin Middle Ages*, trans. W. R. Trask, 1967
Eade	J. C. Eade, *The Forgotten Sky: A Guide to Astrology in English Literature*, 1984
Epith	Spenser, *Epithalamion*
Fowler 1964	A. D. S. Fowler, *Spenser and the Numbers of Time*, 1964
Fowler 1970	——, *Triumphal Forms: Structural Patterns in Elizabethan Poetry*, 1970
FQ	Spenser, *The Fairy Queen*
Ger. lib.	T. Tasso, *Gerusalemme liberata*, 1581
Hamilton	A. C. Hamilton (ed.), *Spenser: 'The Faerie Queene'*, 1977
HHB	Spenser, *An Hymn of Heavenly Beauty*
HL	Spenser, *An Hymn in Honour of Love*

Kermode	F. Kermode, *Shakespeare, Spenser, Donne*, 1971
Klibansky	R. Klibansky, E. Panofsky, F. Saxl, *Saturn and Melancholy*, 1964
LA	Spenser, *Letter of the Author's* (appendix to *FQ*)
Lewis	C. S. Lewis, *Spenser's Images of Life*, ed. A. D. S. Fowler, 1967
Lotspeich	H. G. Lotspeich, *Classical Mythology in the Poetry of Edmund Spenser*, 1932
Lynche	R. Lynche, *The Fountain of Ancient Fiction*, 1599. The Renaissance and the Gods, 13.
Met.	Ovid, *Metamorphoses*, Loeb Classical Library edn, trans. F. J. Miller, 2 vols, 1916
Mutab.	Spenser, *Two Cantos of Mutability* (*FQ*, Book 7)
OF	L. Ariosto, *Orlando Furioso*, 1532
Panofsky 1955	E. Panofsky, *Meaning in the Visual Arts*, 1955
Panofsky 1962	——, *Studies in Iconology*, 1962
Ripa	C. Ripa, *Iconologia*, 1603, intr. E. Mandowsky, repr. 1970
Ross	A. Ross, *Mystagogus Poeticus, Or, The Muses' Interpreter*, 1648. The Renaissance and the Gods, 30
SC	Spenser, *The Shepherds' Calendar*
SpE	A. C. Hamilton et al. (eds), *The Spenser Encyclopedia*, 1990
Steadman	J. M. Steadman, *Nature into Myth*, 1979
Strong	R. Strong, *The Cult of Elizabeth*, 1987
Tervarent	G. de Tervarent, *Attributs et Symboles dans l'Art Profane 1450–1600*, 1958
Tooke	A. Tooke, *The Pantheon*, 1713. The Renaissance and the Gods, 35
Tuve	R. Tuve, *Allegorical Imagery*, 1977
Valeriano	G. P. Valeriano, *Hieroglyphica*, 1602. The Renaissance and the Gods, 17
Var.	E. Greenlaw, C. G. Osgood et al. (eds), *The Works of Edmund Spenser: A Variorum Edition*, 11 vols, 1932–57
Whitney	G. Whitney, *A Choice of Emblems, and other Devices*, 1586
Wilson	E. C. Wilson, *England's Eliza*, 1939

| Wind | E. Wind, *Pagan Mysteries in the Renaissance*, rev. edn, 1967 |
| Yates | F. A. Yates, *Astraea: The Imperial Theme in the Sixteenth Century*, 1975 |

BOOK I

PROEM 1 echoes the opening of Renaissance editions of the *Aeneid* (sometimes still printed), telling of Virgil's progress from pastoral poetry to martial epic. Spenser's own first published poem had been the pastoral *SC*. *Trumpets*: emblems of war; *oaten reeds*: shepherds' flutes. *Fierce wars . . . loves*: echoing the opening of *OF*. 2 *Virgin*: the Muse of st. 1, who appears to be a conflation of Clio, Muse of history, and Calliope, Muse of epic verse (cf. *Mutab.*, 6. 37); *Tanaquil*: wife of the Roman king Tarquinius Priscus, she was a type of chastity; *Briton Prince* = Arthur, the overall hero of the poem. 3 invokes celestial Cupid, god of divine love (son of Jupiter and Venus), and the traditional theme, fundamental to *FQ*, of the reconciliation of Mars (god of war) with Venus (goddess of love): see Wind, pp. 85–96. 4 celebrates Queen Elizabeth I as the *mirror* of truth, prudence, and Venus (Tervarent, cols 271–4); as deity of an island, like Venus (associated with the island of Cyprus, etc.); and as a solar monarch (*Phoebus*): the sun is a traditional emblem of monarchical power.

Canto 1

1 Redcross wears 'the whole armour of God' (Ephesians 6:11–17 and *LA*). 2 *bloody cross*: St George's arms (st. 4–5n.) are a red cross on a white ground (see 1. 10. 66n.); *dead as living*: Rev. 1:18; *shield*: 'above all, take the shield of faith' (Ephes. 6:16); *faithful true*: Christ on a white horse and 'called faithful and true' (Rev. 19:11); *solemn sad*: the tendency to melancholy expressed later when he encounters Sansjoy (Joyless) at 1. 4 and 5, and Despair at 1. 9. It is purged at 1. 10 46ff. when he meets the positive melancholy of Contemplation. See also 2 Cor. 7:10 ('worldly sorrow causeth death'). 3 *dragon*: in the St George legend, the knight kills a dragon that has been terrorising a kingdom by demanding child sacrifices, thereby preventing the king's daughter from being offered to him; the dragon in *FQ* is also 'the dragon . . . which is the devil and Satan' of Rev. 20:2. 4–5 Una (named at st. 45) = Oneness; Truth: Queen Elizabeth as the head of the Anglican Church. Her *ass* signifies humility and kingship (Zech. 9:9; Judges 5:10; Matt.

21:5ff.); *white* signifies purity, though *white* and *black* were Elizabeth's personal colours; the *veil* suggests the concealing of truth until mankind is ready for it; the *stole* was an ancient emblem of monarchy; the *lamb* represents innocence; also Christ as the 'lamb of God which taketh away the sin of the world' (John 1:29). The princess of the St George legend was sometimes accompanied by a lamb. Una's parents are Adam and Eve (see 1. 7. 43n.; 1. 12. 26); as the primal sovereigns over the earth (Gen. 1:26), they signify Elizabeth's claim to universal rule (see Yates, Parts 1 and 2). **6** *dwarf*: perhaps symbolising reason or prudence. **7–9** *paths . . . wide*: cf. 1. 4. 2n. Book 1 begins, like that of Dante's *Divine Comedy*, with a dark wood as a symbol of chaos, ignorance and error (Latin *errare* = to wander, or deviate from the path of rectitude). The tree catalogue is a commonplace (e.g., Chaucer, *Parliament of Fowls*, 176ff. and Curtius, pp. 194–5), and Spenser exploits traditional attributes of the trees named. Note the emphasis on *pride* (st. **7, 8**), which hints at the tree of knowledge and the myth of the Fall of Man in Gen. 3. The *elm* supporting the *vine* symbolised fidelity in love (Whitney, p. 62); the *poplar* weeps (*Met.*, 2. 346ff.); for the *laurel* and victory, see *Met.*, 1. 553ff.; the *myrrh* bleeds gum; the *plane tree* with its large circumference was noted for its splendour. **12** Una uses proverbs to convey truth and wisdom. **13–16** *Error*, as a general principle governing the fallen world, and also as specific theological doctrinal error (i.e., adherence to Catholicism and Puritan extremism rather than Elizabethan Protestantism: the *books* of st. **20**), is based on the archetypal cave-dwelling snake woman Echidna, whose offspring were destructive to mankind (Hesiod, *Theogony*, 295ff.). The serpent in depictions of the Fall myth frequently has a woman's face and torso. Error is associated with darkness; Redcross, in contrast, is compared to a *lion* (st. **17**), emblem of the sun as well as of wrath and justice tempered with mercy (Tervarent, cols 242–8; cf. 1. 3. 5–7n.). **19** *Add faith . . . force*: Error has seized the 'shield of faith' (st. **2**n.); *force* = moral strength, fortitude (Tuve, pp. 94–5, 120). **20** *frogs*: unclean spirits like frogs come from the mouth of the dragon at Rev. 16:13; *toads* were believed to be poisonous. **21** for spontaneous generation from the *Nile* mud, see *Met.* 1. 416ff. Egypt is connected with evil because of the Jewish captivity there. **22–3** the comparison of the baby serpents to *gnats* anticipates the *flies* simile of st. **38**: both are symbols of the deceiving power of the imagination and of evil (Beelzebub, Lord of the Flies, is 'prince of devils' (Matt. 12:24)). **29** Archimago (see st. **43**) is depicted as a hermit in accordance with contemporary depictions of Hypocrisy (Argument stanza to 1. 1, and Ripa, pp. 200–1): contrast the true hermit, Contemplation, at 1. 10. 46ff. Archimago is a Catholic (st. 35) and thus the enemy as Antichrist according to Elizabethan Protestant thought. He is also the Arch-magus (magician) because Reformation propaganda frequently wrote of priestly and papal black magic (Kermode, pp. 44–5); and the *arch*etypal *image*-creator, satanically generating false images in the external world in the form of idols and deceptive phantoms in the minds of men. Angelica meets an old hermit-magician at *OF*, 2. 12ff. **30** *Bidding . . . beads: bead* = prayer was obsolete by the mid sixteenth century, after which it primarily signified 'rosary beads'. **33** note Redcross's association with the *sun*, and cf. 1. 5. 2n. and 1. 11. 31ff. **36–7** *Morpheus* is god of sleep and bringer of dreams, and *Pluto* is the king of hell whose *dame* (wife) is Proserpina; *Gorgon* (i.e., Demogorgon) is the primal and traditionally unmentionable grandfather of the gods: cf. 1. 5. 22; *Cocytus* and *Styx* are two of the four infernal rivers. **38** *two*: the number of duplicity, as in Duessa's name (1. 2. 12–19n.). **39** *Tethys*, wife of Oceanus, is goddess of the sea; *Cynthia* is the moon (*Mut.*, 6. 8–10n.). **40** alluding to the *gates* of sleep in Homer's *Odyssey*, 19. 562ff. and Virgil's *Aeneid*, 6. 893ff., which symbolise true dreams and false visions. The *ivory* gate is that of false visions (and see st. **44**). **43** *Hecate* is the goddess of witches and identified with *Proserpina* as queen of hell and night: see also *Mut.*, 6. 3n. **45–50** Redcross's imagination is tempted by a dream of a false Una collaborating with Venus (now the goddess of lust, not love: contrast 1 proem 2) accompanied by her companion three Graces (see 6. 10. 9n.). *Hymen* is the Graeco-Roman god of marriage, and the cry *io Hymen* was common at weddings in antiquity; *Flora*, the Roman goddess of flowers with whom Elizabeth I was sometimes identified, was also known anciently as a harlot. The *false . . . boy* (st. **47**) is Cupid. Redcross's mental faculties are so far under Archimago's power that the false Una survives into his waking world (st. **49**). **51** *blind god*: lust-inducing Cupid (for his blindness, see Panofsky 1962, ch. 4).

Canto 2

1 the *waggoner* is the constellation Boötes, the Ploughman (cf. Redcross at 1. 10. 66 found in a furrow by a ploughman), guiding the *seven* main stars of Ursa major; the *steadfast star* is the Pole Star. *Phoebus* is the sun. **2** *Proserpina*: 1. 1. 36–7n. **3–5** another vision that defines Redcross's sin: he suffers from a predominance of anger and lust, the two extremes of the tripartite soul identified by Plato that should be controlled by *reason*, which in Redcross's case here is inoperative. 6–7 *Hesperus*: the planet Venus in her role as the evening star, though the name was often (as here) used to signify her role as morning star (cf. 1. 7. 30; 1. 12. 21 and n.; Brooks-Davies 1995, p. 297 (*Epith.*, 95n.); *Tithonus* was the husband of *morning* (Aurora); *Titan* was a name for the sun. 10 *Proteus*: the sea god fabled to be capable of infinite metamorphoses (*Met.*, 8. 730–7): he was a symbol of formlessness, deception, and the power of magic. See also 3. 4. 25n. 12–19 Redcross can overcome faithlessness (the pagan Sansfoy) for reasons given in st. 18–19 but, still under Archimago's sway, succumbs to Fidessa (false faith), that is, Duessa (doubleness) in disguise (st. 44). As a parody of faith (we meet true Faith in 1. 10. 12–13), she appears in the form of the Whore of Babylon (Rev. 17:4: 'arrayed in purple and scarlet, and gilded with gold, and . . . pearls'), identified by Protestants as the Catholic Antichrist (her father rules from Rome – 'where Tiberis [the river Tiber] doth pass' – and her lover, Christ, can no longer be seen by her: st. 22–4). Spenser alludes to Elizabethan claims to the Holy Roman Empire and hence to world dominion: see Yates, Parts 1 and 2. Fidessa contrasts with Una at 1. 1. 4–5. Redcross will remain with her until canto 7. 25 *Sans joy*: see 1. 4. 38ff.; *Sans loy* (Lawless): see 1. 3. 33ff. and, for their lineage, 1. 5. 20ff. In early editions of *FQ* the names were separated, as here, on their early appearances, into their component syllables to make their etymology obvious. 28–30 there are *two* trees for doubleness (see 1. 2. 9 and the meaning of Duessa's name), as well as to recall the trees of life and knowledge in the Garden of Eden (Gen. 2:9). Redcross has thus escaped into a false paradise from the heat of the sun (*Phoebus*) which should, rather, have been endured since it signifies Christ's judgement (Malachi 4:2 and Geneva gloss; Panofsky 1955, p. 262). Cf. the shade of 1. 7. 2ff. and, for the motif of the bleeding tree, *Aeneid*, 3. 22ff. 33 *Fradubio* means Brother Doubt; *Boreas* is the north wind, and the north was associated with pestilence (Jeremiah 1:14): note the parallel between Fradubio and Redcross. 37 *Fraelissa* (Italian *fralezza*) signifies frailty (but note that *elissa/elisa* suggests *Eliza*beth), while the *roses* denote beauty and mutability. 40–1 cf. 1. 8. 46–8, the stripping of Duessa. *Origan* and *thyme* supposedly cured skin ailments. 43 the *well* symbolises divine grace (John 4:14; Rev. 22:1).

Canto 3

3–4 the wandering woman motif derives from Song of Solomon 3:1ff. and Rev. 12:1–6, the 'woman clothed with the sun' who flees into the wilderness, interpreted by Reformation propagandists as the Protestant

Church. Una–Truth's escape into the shade is, unlike Redcross's in 1. 2 and 1. 7, without culpability: it signifies that she is unrecognised by humanity, to whom she remains veiled. She lies down like the Fairy Queen herself at 1. 9. 13–15. **5–7** the lion, solar emblem of wrath (1. 1. 13–16n.), and, here, representative of natural law, succumbs to Una since lions traditionally protect virgins and instinctively recognise and revere royalty (New Arden Shakespeare, *1 Henry IV*, 2. 4. 267–8). **10–20** the *wench* is *Abessa* (both abbess and the clerical abuse of absenteeism, from Latin *abesse* = to be absent). Her deafness, etc. (st. 11) indicate that she is closed to God's kingdom (Mark 4:9–12: 'He that hath ears to hear, let him hear'); her *mother* is *Corceca* (st. 18), i.e., blind heart (cf. Ephes. 4:18 on darkness of understanding caused by hardness of heart). Together with *Kirkrapine* (church plunderer; st. 17, 22), they represent abuses which Anglicanism had inherited from Catholicism. The lion's defeat of Kirkrapine suggests wrathful Puritan reform within the English Church. **16** *Aldebaran* is a star in Taurus associated with 'the destruction ... of buildings' (Agrippa, 2. 33, p. 286); *Cassiopeia* was stellified for boasting of her daughter, Andromeda's, beauty. As an Ethiopian she is black. On the astronomy, see Eade, pp. 173–5. **21** the *Greek* is Ulysses, who refused Calypso's offer of immortality in order that he could return to his wife, Penelope (*Odyssey*, 5). **26–30** in a world of multiplying darkness even Truth can, for the purposes of narrative at least, be misled. **31** *Tethys*: 1. 1. 39n. *Orion's hound* is Sirius, the heat-bringing Dog Star (Canis major, located south-east of Orion, bringer of storms); *Nereus* is the Old Man of the Sea (Homer, *Iliad*, 18. 141). **33–9** *Sansloy* embodies absolute lawlessness, symbolically coinciding with, then vanquishing, Archimago who himself originates from chaos. **36** *Lethe* was the infernal river of forgetfulness; the three *Furies* guard hell and perpetually punish guilt. **42–4** the lion's world of natural law yields to the historically prior demon of lawlessness himself. On another level, the episode suggests the dangers of the Church's succumbing to over-zealous (Puritan) reform.

Canto 4

2 *broad highway*: Matt. 7:13 ('it is the ... broad way that leadeth to destruction'), and cf. 1. 1. 7–9n. and contrast 1. 10. 5. **4–5** cf. Alcina's city: *OF*, 6. 59ff. The *dial tells* and *tolls* ominously, since this palace is the house built on sand of Matt. 7:26–7, Reformation emblem of the Catholic Church. The *brick* and *towers* suggest brick-built Babel (Gen. 11:3–4); and *without mortar* confirms its vulnerability to God's wrath

(Ezek. 13:14). Readers would have identified the palace's description as a satiric glance at the splendid houses built by Elizabeth's leading statesmen. 6 *Malvenù* means Ill-come. 7 like Duessa–Fidessa, Lucifera (st. 12) is connected with Persian wealth and paganism (1. 2. 13). 8 Lucifera is a solar *maiden queen* like the Virgin Queen Elizabeth (1 Proem 4) and Una (1. 3. 4; 1. 12. 8, 23); but we recall the virgin daughter of Babylon of Isaiah 47: 1. 9 *Phoebus . . . child*: Phaethon, son of the sun god, stole his father's chariot and nearly destroyed the world (*Met.*, 2. 1ff.). 10 *dragon*: the Whore of Babylon rides on one (Rev. 17:3, and Geneva gloss): cf. Duessa at 1. 7. 16–18. Contrast Arthur's dragon at 1. 7. 31n. *Mirror*: emblem of Venus, Vanity and Lechery (Tervarent, cols 273–4; contrast 1 proem 4n.). 11 cf. 1. 1. 36–7n. 12 *Lucifera* recalls Lucifer (i.e., Satan) and the proud King of Babylon, Nebuchadnezzar (Isaiah 14:12). Lucifer is also the planet Venus as the morning star (here = lust). Politically, as a self-elected tyrant associated with Machiavellian 'policy' (st. 12), Lucifera offers a contrast to Elizabeth's constitutional role. 16 *Aurora*: 1. 2. 6–7n. 17 *Flora*: 1. 1. 45–50n.; *Juno* was the proud queen of heaven, one of whose emblems was the *peacock*, the eyes on whose tail belonged to *Argus*, the watchman of *Met.*, 1. 717–23. 18–36 Lucifera heads the procession of Deadly Sins, ordered according to a scheme deriving from Christ's temptation (e.g., Matt. 4), in which Sloth, Gluttony and Lust were sins of the Flesh; Avarice the Worldly sin; Envy, Wrath and Pride (*Satan*, st. 36) were sins of the Devil. Each of Spenser's sins has its usual iconographical attributes, deriving from classical and biblical sources: Brooks-Davies 1977, pp. 47–51. 38 Redcross now succumbs to the joylessness born of faithlessness, the worldly (not godly) sorrow of 2 Cor. 7:8–11 (see 1. 1. 2n.). 44, 48 *Morpheus, Stygian*: 1. 1. 36–7n.

Canto 5

2 *Phoebus . . . bridegroom*: Psalm 19:4–5 on the sun as bridegroom. 5 parodies Elizabeth as she surveyed her Accession Day tilts (on which see Strong, ch. 5); *laurel garlands*: 1. 1. 7–9n. 8 *griffin*: fabled creature with eagle's head and wings attached to the body of a lion, frequently used as an emblem of Christ. The *dragon* represents Satanic Sansjoy. 10 *Stygian lake*: 1. 4. 48n. 13 Sansjoy is vanquished, not killed, because sins and temptations can always return to taunt the unwary. For the *cloud*, see *Aeneid*, 5. 808ff. 17 *wine and oil*: Luke 10:34. 18 the *crocodile* that supposedly wept for its prey was an emblem of hypocrisy (Ansell Robin, pp. 53–5); the Nile's *seven mouths* were linked with the seven sins: cf. 1. 1. 21 and n. 19 *Jove's . . . house*: the heavens.

20 *Night*: see *Aeneid*, 5. 721ff.; Lotspeich, p. 91. 22 *ancient*: Hesiod, *Theogony*, 116ff.; *Demogorgon*: 1. 1. 36–7n. 23 *Aveugle* means Blind One. 30 Hecate (1. 1. 43n.) is associated with *dogs* and *wolves*; the *owl* is associated with Night and Death (Tervarent, cols 96–7). 31 *Avernus* was the poisonous entrance to hell (*Aeneid*, 6. 237ff.). 33 *Acheron* was the underworld river of grief, *Phlegethon* the river of fire. 34 *Cerberus* was the triple-headed canine guardian of hell-gate. 35–40 traditional list of sufferers in hell with their usual punishments: e.g., *Odyssey*, 11. 582ff.; *Aeneid*, 6. 617ff.; *Met.* 4. 458ff. and 10. 41ff. 35 *Ixion* was bound on a wheel by Jove for attempting to seduce Juno; *Sisyphus* was a thief, punished by having to roll a huge stone perpetually up a hill; *Tantalus* revealed the secrets of the gods and was punished by being placed in a lake from which he could not drink with overhanging fruit trees from which he could not eat; *Tityus* assaulted Latona and was condemned to being stretched out in hell and having his liver devoured by a vulture; *Typhoeus/Typhon* (see *Mut.*, 6. 15n.) has been given Tityus's punishment by Spenser; *Theseus* was punished for attempting to abduct Proserpina (see 4. 10. 27n.); the *sisters* are the Danaids, punished for killing their bridegrooms. 36 *Æsculapius*, god of healing and son of Phoebus (st. 44), is a parody of Christ here, curing body rather than soul. 37–8 *Hippolytus* was killed in his chariot after being (falsely) accused of making love to his stepmother, Phaedra. His *sea-god sire* was Poseidon. For his presumption in reviving him, Aesculapius was thrown into hell by Jupiter: see *Aeneid*, 7.765ff. 47 the *proud king* is Nebuchadnezzar (Daniel 3, 4); *Croesus* was the wealthy last king of Lydia; *Antiochus* persecuted the Jews (1 Maccabees 1). 48 *Nimrod* was reputedly the first tyrant and builder of the tower of Babel (Gen. 10, 11 and Geneva marginal glosses); *Ninus* founded Nineveh; his wife, Semiramis, was reputed to have founded Babylon; the *mighty monarch* is Alexander the Great, supposed son of Jupiter *Ammon*, who died outside Babylon. The Babylon references identify Lucifera's palace as the depraved city of the world and of Antichrist (1. 2. 12–19n.). Roman references follow because the city was, as the centre of Catholicism, the second Babylon in Protestant thought. 49 *Romulus* founded Rome; *proud*: *Tarquinius* Superbus (i.e., The Proud One), the last Roman king; *Lentulus*: the name of a proud patrician family; *Scipio* Africanus conquered the Carthaginian general *Hannibal*; *Sylla* (first name Cornelius) was a vainglorious Roman dictator whose rival was the consul *Marius*; *Caesar* (Julius) defeated *Pompey* at Pharsalia; *Antonius* is Mark Anthony, lover of Cleopatra (st. 50). 50 *Semiramis* (st. 48n.) lusted after, and was killed by, her son; *Sthenoboea*, wife of Proetus,

loved Bellerophon in vain. 53 *laystall*: also a dung-heap (reinforcing the parallel with Duessa's foul rear at 1. 8. 48).

Canto 6

4 *rock of diamond*: see 1. 7. 33n. 7 *lion*: 2 Timothy 4:17 (on deliverance from 'the mouth of the lion'); *fauns* and *satyrs*: both were wood-gods and goat-men, who here represent appetitive human nature, higher on the scale of being than Sansloy and the lion. In terms of religious history, they represent humanity in a pre-Christian state of nature rather than of grace; hence their tendency to idolatry. *Sylvanus* was a wood-god, identified with Faunus (2. 2. 6n.) and Pan, the nature god; according to one tradition he loved the boy Cyparissus (st. 14, 17). 13 the *olive*, virginal Athena's tree, signifies peace and reconciliation: Tervarent, col. 290 and cf. the crowning of Una at 1. 12. 8. 15 *Bacchus* was the god of wine; *Cybele*, the great earth mother, was worshipped drunkenly and noisily; *mirror*: cf. 1 proem 4n.; *Dryope* loved Faunus; *Pholoe* was loved by Pan. 16 recalls Aeneas's reaction to Venus disguised as a nymph of virginal Diana at *Aeneid*, 1. 314ff. (Una combines Venus and Diana, love and virginity, into a mystery of chaste love: see Wind, pp. 75ff. and *SC April*, emblems. Like Belphoebe, another Venus–Diana composite, at 2. 3. 21–31n., she is also Diana as goddess of the wood.) 18 *hamadryads* were tree deities; *naiads* were water nymphs. 19 *ass worship*: draws on a familiar emblem: Steadman, ch. 9. 21 *Satyrane* (st. 28), son of a satyr and of *Thyamis* (from Greek *thymos* = passion) is a wild man whose hunting of beasts symbolises his control of his passions. *Labryde* derives from Greek *labros* = furious; *Therion* from the Greek for wild beast. 35 reintroduces Archimago, disguised as a pilgrim who has been to the Spanish shrine of St James (*Jacobus* in Latin) of Compostela.

Canto 7

2–3 Redcross escapes from the sun's heat into a *locus amoenus* or false paradise: cf. 1. 2. 29 and, for the tradition, Curtius, pp. 195–200. He has removed his Christian armour (1. 1. 1n.). 4–5 the enervating fountain recalls that of Salmacis (*Met.*, 4. 285ff.): contrast 1. 2. 43, 1. 11. 29–30; *Phoebe* is the moon goddess Diana; *disgrace* (st. 5) can also mean 'remove from one's favour' – as such it is a Spenserian first. 8–10 Orgoglio (Italian for pride; st. 14) is, like all the traditionally rebellious giants (or Titans: see *Mutab.* 6. 2n.), the offspring of Earth and Heaven. But his heavenly father is *Æolus*, the wind god; so that Orgoglio is puffed up with pride. Note the parody of Gen. 2:7 (Adam created of earth and made a living soul with the breath of life). If Lucifera represents worldly pride, then Orgoglio is the demonically corrupt root of spiritual pride itself, the most deadly of the sins. His tree parallels that of Sylvanus (1. 6. 14) and is the traditional attribute of the lawless wild man (*Aeneid*, 3. 665ff., the Cyclops). The Pope was sometimes depicted as a wild man Antichrist in Reformation propaganda. 13 *Furies*: 1. 3. 36n. 16 the Whore of Babylon is dressed in scarlet, purple and gold, and is seated on a seven-headed beast interpreted in Geneva glosses as a type of Roman Catholicism (rev. 17:3 and cf. 1. 2. 12–19n.). 17 *Alcides* (Hercules) killed the many-headed Lernean hydra, symbol of sin's multiplicity. 29–36 Arthur arrives, bringing grace and exemplifying the inclusive virtue of magnificence (see *LA*). He is a sun god (st. 29) to dispel the darkness of ignorance. 30 *lady's head*: the Fairy Queen, Gloriana herself. The legendary Arthur's shield bore an image of the Virgin Mary; *Hesperus*: 1. 2. 6–7n. 31 *dragon*: another detail from the Arthurian legend, it was a reminder of his father, Uther Pendragon, whose kingship was prophesied by a dragon-shaped ball of fire. It is also the dragon of Cadwallader, last king of the Britons and ancestor of Henry VII, Elizabeth's grandfather. Cf. also Turnus's helmet at *Aeneid*, 7. 785–6. 32 *almond*: mount *Selinus* was palmy (*Aeneid*, 3. 705); the *almond* represents priesthood via Numbers 17:8, and world-rule (*monde* is French for world). 33 this is the 'shield of faith' (Ephes. 6:16), the archetype of Redcross's at 1. 1. 2n., since the *diamond* signifies good faith (Tervarent, col. 148). Cf. *OF*, 2. 55–6 and *OF*, 22. 81ff. (Atlante's veiled shield of carbuncle) and Minerva's petrifying shield with the Gorgon's head on it. 37 *squire*: Timias (from Greek *timē* = honour). Cf. 3. 1. 18, etc. 43 *Pishon . . . Gihon*: three of the four paradisal rivers (Gen. 2:10–14). 44 *Dragon . . . four years*: Rev. 12:4–6. 46 *order*: parallels the Order of the Garter, headed by the monarch; its patron saints were Saint George and the Virgin Mary: see Strong, ch. 6. *Cleopolis* (cf. 1. 10. 58): the name means city of glory (Greek *kleos* = fame, glory + *polis* = city).

Canto 8

3 *horn*: cf. Astolfo's horn in *OF*. 15. 14–15. 4 cf. Joshua 6 on the fall of the walls of Jericho, and the trumpets of Rev. 8 and 9. The battle is between Christ and Antichrist, Protestantism and Catholicism. 6 *beast*: the beast of the Whore (1. 7. 16n.). 10 parodies Exodus 17:5–6 and 1 Cor. 10:2–4 (water from the rock signifying divine grace). 11 *Cymbria*: the Cimbri lived in north Germany (the evil north again: 1. 2. 33n.). 14 *cup*: the Whore has 'a cup of gold in her hand full of abomination' at

Rev. 17:4, parodying the eucharistic chalice. Cf. Circe's cup filled with the drug of forgetfulness in Homer's *Odyssey*, 10, and contrast Fidelia's chalice at 1. 10. 13. 19 see 1. 7. 33n. **30–4** *Ignaro* is Ignorance (Ephes. 4: 17–18). The *rusty keys* (st. 30) parody the 'key of knowledge' of Luke 11:52. **35–6** the *babes* recall the victims of Herod's Massacre (Matt. 2:16); together with the slaughtered *innocents*, the passage as a whole echoes Rev. 6:9–10 on the souls of the Christian martyrs. There is also a suggestion of the St Bartholomew's Day massacre of French Protestants (August 1572). The *cunning imagery* combines black magic with Catholic iconography (1. 1. 29n.). **46–50** the stripping of Duessa echoes Isaiah 3 (the stripping of the proud daughters of Zion) and Isaiah 47 (the uncovering of Babylon's daughter); and cf. *OF*, 7. 71–3. The *fox* signifies cunning; the *eagle's claw* is from personifications of Deceit (Ripa, pp. 173–5); the *bear's paw* is from Rev. 13:2; the *bear* is also a type of the devil (via interpreters of 1 Sam. 17:36). At Rev. 17:16 we read that the Whore shall one day be made 'naked'.

Canto 9
1 *golden chain*: symbol of the universe held together by concord and hierarchy; derives from *Iliad*, 7. 18–27. **4** *Timon*: Greek *timē* again (1. 7. 37n.). Arthur talks allegorically. *Rauran*: hill in Merioneth, a county with strong Tudor connections. The *Dee* divides (and links) North Wales and England. **13–15** the underlying story of the poem is really that of Arthur's quest for the Fairy Queen, who appears to him here as Diana did to Endymion (an image of union with the divine for neo-Platonists: Wind, p. 154) or, more riddlingly, as the elf queen to Chaucer's Sir Thopas in his parody romance *Sir Thopas*, 778ff. Technically Arthur's dream is what the Renaissance reader would have called a revelation, unlike that of Redcross at 1. 1. 47ff., which is an evil illusion. **19** *diamond*: 1. 7. 33n; *liquor pure*: cf. 1. 11. 29–30. **21** *Pegasus*: the winged horse of Greek mythology. **29** *rope* and *knife*: traditional emblems of Despair, the deadly sin born of an overwhelming sense of guilt and unworthiness, leading one to deny God's mercy and grace (and hence His omnipotence). **33–6** the iconography of the cave is suitably infernal and melancholic, echoing Error's cave (1. 1) and hell's mouth as described in Sackville's Introduction to *A Mirror for Magistrates* (1563). **38–47** Despair's seductive speech parodies and perverts commonplaces of the 'art of dying' (*ars moriendi*) tradition, which drew on ancient and biblical texts to encourage composure and hope (see K. Koller in *Studies in Philology*, 61 (1964), 128–39. **38** cf. Romans 6:23 ('the wages of sin is death') and the trick Faustus plays

on himself in the opening scene of Marlowe's *Dr Faustus*. 39 echoing Cicero, *De senectute*, 19, etc. 41 *De senectute*, 20. 43 answered at st. 52-3. 53 *chosen*: cf. 2 Thessalonians 2:13 ('God hath from the beginning chosen you to salvation'; does not necessarily imply the Calvinistic sense of predestined election).

Canto 10

1 *grace*: e.g., Ephes. 2: 8-9 ('by grace are ye saved through faith ... it is the gift of God'). But Celia's house exemplifies good works as well, thereby defining its Anglican position. 3 *ancient house*: the 'spiritual house' of 1 Peter 2:5, and the Elizabethan Church understood as the Catholic Church restored to its primitive purity. This episode marks Redcross's repentance and his recognition of the goal of the Christian's pilgrimage, the Heavenly City or New Jerusalem (which, described at st. 57-8, undoes Lucifera's Babylon at 1. 4-5, St Augustine's image of the corrupt earthly city). 4 *Celia*: Heavenly One: the origin (and mother) of the three theological virtues, Faith, Hope and Charity (1 Cor. 13:13). 5 *knocked*: Matt. 7:7 ('knock, and it shall be opened unto you'); *Humiltà*: Humility is the virtue which traditionally opposes the sin of Pride (and see Luke 14:11); *strait and narrow*: Matt. 7:14 (the way leading to life): contrast 1. 4. 2n.; cf. st. 10. 12-13 the white robe of purity, together with the eucharistic chalice, are emblems of Christian Faith personified (Ripa, p. 149): contrast 1. 8. 14n. *Crystal*: emblem of faith and purity (original spelling: *Christ*all); the book is the Bible; *dark things*: 2 Peter 3:16; *serpent*: emblem of Christ from John 3:14 (contrast Book 1's evil dragons). 14 *blue*: the heavenly colour; *anchor*: Hebrews 6: 18-19 (hope as an anchor). 16 *Charissa*: see st. 30-1n. 20 alludes respectively to Joshua 10:12-13 (sun standing still), 2 Kings 20: 10-11 (Hezekiah and the dial of Ahaz), Judges 7 (Gideon's victory), Exodus 14: 21-31 (the passage over the Red Sea), Matt. 21:21 and 1 Cor. 13:2 (faith moving mountains). 21-8 Faith produces repentance, the formal stages of which Redcross now undergoes. 28 the *lion* of sin (1 Peter 5:8): a different aspect of the leonine Redcross referred to by Una at 1. 3. 7. 29 *kissed*: the kiss of greeting and charity (Romans 16:16; 1 Peter 5:14). 30-1 Charity (love) is the supreme and last of the theological virtues, without which we are 'nothing' (1 Cor. 13:2). she is traditionally represented with several babies, suckling at least one (Ripa, p. 64). The *yellow* and *doves* are both emblematic of marriage and of Venus. The *tiara* combines Charity's usual crown of flames with the gold crown of virtue (Tervarent, cols 126-8). 34-5 *Mercy*: Luke 6:36. 36 *beadsmen*: contrasting with the seven sins of 1. 4, they exemplify

the seven corporal works of mercy which originate with Matt. 25: 35–6. 40 *he . . . hell*: Christ's three-day descent into, and harrowing of, hell (Matt. 12:40) was narrated in the apocryphal Gospel of Nicodemus, 2. 6. 41 *as the tree does fall*: Ecclesiastes 11:3 42 *bridal bed . . . spouse*: Matt. 25: 2; *workmanship . . . hand*: Gen. 1:26–7. 46 contrast Archimago's hermitage at 1. 1. 34 and Despair's cave at 1. 9. Redcross has now moved for a moment from the active life to the contemplative as he enjoys a vision of the Heavenly City with Contemplation himself on the traditional mountain of meditation and virtue. 47 *eagle*: cf. 1. 11. 34n. It was believed to be able to gaze on the sun (symbolising Christ). 50 *keys*: of heaven (Matt. 16:19): contrast 1. 8. 30–4n. 53 Sinai (Exodus 24), and cf. Rev. 21:10 (the mountain from which John sees the New Jerusalem); *billows*: Exodus 14. 54 *sacred hill*: the Mount of Olives (e.g., Luke 22:39ff.); *pleasant mount*: Parnassus, home of the Muses. The hills signify the progress from the Old Law to the New and thence to a vision of the prophetic and religious power of poetry (on the latter see Klibansky, p. 245). 55 *city*: the New Jerusalem of Rev. 21. 56 *angels*: Genesis 28:12 (Jacob's dream); Hebrews 12:22 (the Heavenly Jerusalem and innumerable angels). 57 *Lamb*: John 1:29. 58 *Cleopolis*: 1. 7. 46n; *Panthea*: (Greek for all the gods), recalling the Roman Pantheon. 66 (cf. st. 61): *Met.*, 15. 553ff. tells of the similar discovery by a ploughman of Tages, who became an instructor of the Etruscans in the art of prophecy. *George* derives from Greek *gēorgos* = ploughman; so that Redcross is, like the biblical Adam, 'of the earth, earthly' (1 Cor. 15:47; cf. st. 52; Adam means *earthly*). For the St George legend, see 1. 1. 3, 4–5nn. George as ploughman and bearer of the red cross (1. 1. 2n.) affirms the essential message of peace and unity underlying Book 1 and *FQ* as a whole. Specifically, it recalls Isaiah 2:4 on turning swords into ploughshares, a text which was, early on, interpreted as a prophecy of world unity (cf. Elizabeth as world emperor at 1. 2. 12–19n.); furthermore, Justin, Irenaeus and others identified the plough with the Christian cross (J. Daniélou, *Primitive Christian Symbols*, trans. D. Attwater (1964), ch. 6).

Canto 11

3 omitted by mistake in 1590 edn. 5 *Muse*: Clio, the Muse of history, daughter of the sun god (*Phoebus*) and Memory (cf. 1 Proem 2). 7 *second*: supporting; *tenor* also means tone, mood. Cf. *SC October*, 50; *HHL*, 13–14; *Epith.*, 9. 8–15 the dragon combines the Leviathan of Job 41, the dragon of Rev. 12:9, the serpent vanquished by Cadmus

(*Met.*, 3. 31ff.), and the dragon of the St George legend and related mummers' plays. He is like a *mountain* – moveable by faith (1. 10. 20) – because of Rev. 8:8 (mountain identified in the Geneva gloss with 'sects of heretics'). 11 *stings*: 1 Cor. 15:55–6 (the sting of death is sin); 2 Cor. 12:17. 26–7 *arms to leave*: cf. 1. 7. 2. Redcross now burns like Hercules (*champion*), a type of Christ, poisoned by Deianira with a coat soaked in the blood of the centaur Nessus (*Met.*, 9. 101ff.). 29 *Well of Life*: cf. Rev. 22:1 and John 4:14: grace, baptism and purification are all suggested. 30 *Silo*: John 9:7; Christ was baptised in the *Jordan* (Matt. 3:13–16); *Bath* had been established as a spa by the Romans; *Spau* (Spa) is near Liège; the *Cephisus* washed sheep white; the *Hebrus*, traditionally pure, saw Orpheus's death and reunion with Eurydice (*Met.*, 11. 1–60). 33 *Titan*: like Phoebus, a name for the sun. 34 another solar *eagle* myth (cf. 1. 10. 47), alluding to the bird's supposed ability to renew itself by flying to the sun and then immersing itself in water. This was allegorised as a myth of regeneration: cf. Psalm 103:5. 39 *Five joints*: the five senses, as at 2. 11. 7–13; and cf. Rev. 17:10 ('five are fallen'). 41 *Cerberus* (cf. 1. 5. 34n.) was defeated by Hercules. 44 *Etna*: cf. 2. 9. 29n. 45 *pestilence*: deliverance from pestilence is promised in Psalm 91:3, but Redcross is still a spiritual backslider (*backward*). The *mire* is from Psalm 69:2. 46–7 the two trees are the tree of life and the tree of knowledge of Genesis 2:9. 48 cf. Rev. 22:2 ('and the leaves of the tree served to heal the nations with'), and contrast Orgoglio at 1. 8. 10. 51 answers 1. 2. 7. 53 the dragon is killed through the mouth to suggest hell's mouth and the destruction of hell (Rev. 20:14 and Geneva gloss: 'hell ... shall be destroyed'). 54 *down ... down*: 'Babylon that great city is fallen, it is fallen' (Rev. 14:8).

Canto 12

6 cf. the crowd's strewing of branches when Christ enters Jerusalem (Matt. 21:18). For the *laurel* of victory, see 1. 1. 7–9n. 7 *Diana*: 1. 6. 16n. 8 with the crowning of Una, cf. 1. 6. 13 and *SC April*, 55–60. 18 Redcross and Una are betrothed; their marriage (on one level representing that of Christ and the true Church) will occur at the end of time: i.e., in the eternal sabbath which succeeds the six ages (*six years*) of the world. Cf. *Mutab.*, 8.2n., and Hebrews 4:3–4. 21 *morning star*: cf. 1. 7. 30 and 1. 2. 6–7n. Christ is the morning star at Rev. 22:16 and the bride-Church of Song of Solomon 6:8 is an 'only daughter' and 'looketh forth as the morning'. The phrase is also used of the Virgin Mary. 22 *white ... spot*: the bride of the Lamb (i.e., the true Church) arrayed for

her marriage at Rev. 19:7–8 ('pure fine linen and shining') and 21:2
('as a bride trimmed for her husband'); also the bride in Song of
Solomon 4:7 (who has 'no spot'). This is an apocalyptic vision of the
victory of English Protestantism over Rome. 23 *sunshiny*: cf. 1. 3.
3–4n. 26 *King of Eden*: cf. 1. 7. 43n. 36 cf. the temporary binding of
Satan at Rev. 20:2–3. 37–8 recalling Roman marriage customs: see
Spenser's own *Epithalamion*. 39 *trinal triplicities*: the nine orders of
angels were divided into three sets of three, following Pseudo-Diony-
sius's *Celestial Hierarchies* (starting with those nearest to God, the
order is: seraphim, cherubim, thrones; dominations, virtues, powers;
principalities, archangels, angels).

BOOK 2

PROEM 2 *Peru*: conquered by the Spaniards in the mid sixteenth
century; *now found true*: i.e., in 1541; *Virginia*: named after the Virgin
Queen, Elizabeth I, after Ralegh's return from North America in 1584.
4 *princess*: Elizabeth I. 5 *Guyon*: named from *gyon*, a wrestler
(S. Snyder, *Renaissance News*, 14 (1961), 249–52); from the paradisal
river *Gihon* (1. 7. 43n.), sometimes interpreted as the virtue of
Temperance (A. D. S. Fowler, *Modern Language Notes*, 75 (1960),
289–92); and with hints of the celebrated romance hero, Guy of
Warwick.

Canto 1
1 *architect*: Archimago. 5 *knight*: Sir Guyon. 6 *Huon*: the favourite of
Oberon in the thirteenth-century mediaeval romance *Huon de Bor-
deaux*. 7 *Palmer*: a pilgrim who has visited the Holy Land and carries
a palm leaf as testament to this. Here he embodies Christian faith and
reason's power to control the passions. Contrast and cf. Archimago's
appearance at 1. 1. 29. 14–15 *lady*: i.e., Duessa (st. 21). 19 *errant
damsel*: Una. 22 cf. 1. 8. 50. 28 *heavenly maid*: the Fairy Queen,
Gloriana, hinting also at the Marian cult of Elizabeth (on which see
R. H. Wells, *Spenser's 'Faerie Queene' and the Cult of Elizabeth*,
1983). 35–55 *Amavia* (named in Argument stanza to 2. 1; Italian
amare + *via* = way of love; Latin *amavi* = I have loved) loves and tries
to redeem Mortdant (death-giver, Argument stanza and st. 49) from his
enslavement to the flesh (concupiscence). The Christian depth of her
love is shown by her disguise as a palmer (st. 52), though since hers is
only a human love, she has not the power finally to redeem him from

his curse. In his death we see the corruption of the old Adam (Colossians 3:9), who bequeathes the fact of his and Amavia's death (so that she is also as Eve), and thereby the ineradicable blood of original sin, upon his baby (see 2. 2. 1–4n.). 51 *Acrasia*, the witch of the Bower of Bliss (2. 12. 42ff.), is the ultimate symbol of intemperance (Greek, *akrasia* = ill-mixture; *akratos* = intemperance). She is based on Circe (*Odyssey*, 10), Alcina in *OF*, 5, 6, 10, and Armida in *Ger. lib.*, 16. 53 *Lucina* is the moon goddess Cynthia–Diana in her role as goddess of childbirth. 55 *Bacchus* is wine; the *nymph* is water (nymphs were traditionally freshwater deities). Mortdant dies from an intemperate clashing of extreme opposites. 58 *squire*: temperance is the middle point between extremes (Aristotle, *Nicomachean Ethics*, 1106B), and the *set-square* is the symbol of virtue derived from right reason symbolised by the rectangle (*Nicomachean Ethics*, 1100B). It is *golden* because gold was believed to contain the elements in perfect (i.e., temperate) balance. 60 *cypress*: associated with death because dark and yet also evergreen, hence symbolising immortality.

Canto 2

Argument: *Golden Mean*: Medina, who controls her castle of warring extremes at st. 12ff. Guyon leaves the baby with her (2. 3. 2.). 1–4 baptism promises rebirth but cannot eradicate original sin (Articles 9 and 27 of the Anglican Thirty-nine Articles). But the point is, presumably, that this is *not* holy water, as the fable that follows indicates. Note the analogy with Ezekiel 16:4–9 ('I saw thee polluted in thine own blood': Geneva gloss: 'before God wash his Church and give life, there is nothing but filthiness and death'). 6 *Dame Nature*: Mutab., 7. 5ff.; *Flora*: 1. 1. 45–50n. 7–10 cf. 1. 7. 5. The tale is Ovidian in style (e.g., *Met.*, 5. 572ff., the story of Arethusa; *Met.*, 1. 548ff., the story of Daphne), but is Spenser's invention (Ovidian metamorphic tales were popular at the time). *Faunus* was a wood deity, half man, half goat, often identified with Pan, and a symbol of lust (cf. 1. 6. 7n. and *Mutab.*, 6. 42n.). 11 the *steed*, Brigadore (named at 5. 3. 34), has been stolen by Braggadocchio (2. 3. 4). Orlando's steed in *OF* is called Brigliadoro, i.e., golden bridle (both elements in the name suggest temperance and restraint).

Canto 3

Argument: *Braggadocchio*: braggart, a *miles gloriosus* (vainglorious soldier) in the tradition of Shakespeare's Ancient Pistol (see *Henry V*); *Belphoebe* means beautiful (Italian *bella* + Phoebe = shining, glittering (a name for the moon goddess): she is a manifestation of the private, chaste and loving, self of Elizabeth I (see *LA*). 2 *Ruddimane*: bloody hand. 10 *Trompart*: the trumpet of vanity (Tervarent, col. 388); also French *tromper* = to deceive. 21–31 Belphoebe temperately combines Diana, virginal goddess of the woods (hunting, bow and arrows, etc.; cf. 1. 6. 16n.) and Venus: she has Venerean *roses* at st. 22, and *Graces* at st. 25 (see 6. 10. 9 and 12–15nn.), as well as possessing hair of Venus's colour, yellow (st. 30; and cf. Ptolemy, *Tetrabiblos*, 2. 9 and *Am.* 73, 81). Hence she is greeted as Aeneas greeted Venus when disguised as a nymph of Diana at *Aeneid*, 1 (see 1. 6. 16n.). The *pillars* (st. 28) are from Song of Solomon, 5:15. 31 *Diana ... Cynthus*: *Aeneid*, 1. 502–3 (Dido was also a name applied to Elizabeth) and cf. *Mutab.*, 6. 8–10n.; *queen ... Troy*: Penthesilea (*Aeneid*, 1. 490ff.); *Pyrrhus*: the son of Achilles; *Priam*: king of Troy. 38 *moon*: Braggadocchio is committed to the moon as the planet of Fortune, mutability and secular honour (although *above the moon* would take him to the realm of immutability: *Mutab.*, headnote). Redcross, in contrast, belongs to the super-solar regions (2. 1. 32).

Canto 7

2 *trumpet*: traditional emblem of Fame (Ripa, p. 143). 3ff.: Guyon's equivalent to the epic hero's descent to the underworld (e.g., Odysseus in *Odyssey*, 11; Aeneas in *Aeneid*, 6) which in his case is a temptation to avarice or, in the words of Christ's Sermon on the Mount, to lay up treasure on earth rather than 'in heaven, where neither the moth nor canker corrupteth' (Matt. 6:19ff.). Mammon (named in **Argument stanza**) signifies riches (the translation of the word in the Geneva version of Matt. 6:24, though the Vulgate, Tindale and other translations read *Mammon*); he was also the demon of covetousness and leader of the devils who tempt and ensnare (Agrippa, 3. 18, p. 399). Avarice is a branch of concupiscence; so that this temptation complements the sexual temptations of Phaedria (canto 6) and Acrasia (canto 12). Mammon is described as a blacksmith (and as a parody alchemist devoted to material rather than spiritual gold) and also as a Saturnian melancholic because Hades (the underworld) means *gloomy, melancholy*. Mammon also represents the world's loss of innocence in terms of its fall from a primal Golden Age to a corrupt Age of Iron: see st. 17n. 5 *Mulciber*: Greek equivalent of Vulcan, blacksmith to the gods (cf. st. 36). 8–10 cf. Satan's temptation to Christ in the wilderness to 'all the kingdoms of the world' (Matt. 4:8). 14 *Caspian, Adrian*: notoriously stormy. 17 cf. Ovid's account of the loss of the Golden

Age, *Met.*, 1. 127ff.). 21-5 the traditional iconography of hell (e.g., *Aeneid*, 6. 262ff.); *broad highway* (st. 21): see 1. 4. 2n.; *Pluto*: see 1. 1. 36-7n.; *Celeno* (st. 23) was the chief harpy, a rapacious bird-woman (*Aeneid*, 3. 245-6). 28 Arachne was changed into a spider for her presumption in challenging Minerva to a weaving contest (*Met.*, 6. 5ff.). 31 *iron door*: cf. Acts 12:10 ('they came unto the iron gate ..., which opened ... by its own accord'), which thus equates Mammon with Herod. 35-6 cf. the Cyclopes' furnaces at *Aeneid*, 8. 416ff.; *Vulcan's rage*: flames. 41 *Titan*: gigantic offspring of Earth: cf. 1. 7. 8-10n. and *Mutab.*, 6. 2n. 44-50 *Philotime* (st. 49, from Greek *philos* (lover) + *timē* (honour)) has affinities with Lucifera (1. 4. 5) as a vainglorious parody Fairy Queen. The pressing crowds suggest those in Dante, *Inferno*, 3 and the souls at *Aeneid*, 6. 305ff. The *chain* in st. 46 parodies the chain of love (1. 9. 1n.). 51-3 *Proserpina* was the queen of hell (1. 1. 36-7n.); the plants are all connected with death, melancholy, or sleep: *cypress* and *ebony* were dedicated to Saturn, god of melancholy, as was *hellebore*; *poppy* was an emblem of Night and Death; *coloquintida* is the deathly gourd of 2 Kings 4:39-40 (Geneva gloss: 'which the apothecaries call coloquintida, and is most dangerous and venomous in purging'); *tetra* is deadly nightshade (*tetrum solanum*); *samnitis* has not been identified; *cicuta* (hemlock) killed Socrates, but Crito (not *Critias*) was his *belamy*. 54 *Atlas' daughters* were the Hesperides, whose western island garden contained golden apples guarded by a dragon; *Hercules*, however, as one of his labours, stole some of them. The *Euboean* was Hippomenes (or Meilanion), who slowed Atalanta down by dropping golden apples which she picked up (*Met.*, 10. 560ff.). 55 *Acontius* tricked Cydippe into marriage with an inscribed apple (Ovid, *Heroides*, 20, 21); *Ate*, goddess of discord, flung the golden apple inscribed 'to the fairest' into the banqueting hall where the marriage of Peleus and Thetis was being celebrated. Juno, Minerva, and Venus quarrelled over which of them it described. Paris judged Venus the Victor; Helen was his reward, and the Trojan war the consequence: cf. 3. 9. 36. 56 *Cocytus*: the infernal river of lamentation. 57-60 *Tantalus*: cf. 1. 5. 36n. 61-2 *Pilate*: John 18:36-8, Matt. 27: 23-4. 65 *three days*: cf. Christ's three-day harrowing of hell, 1. 10. 40n.

Canto 8

Argument: *Acrates' sons*: Cymochles (from Greek *kyma* = wave + *ochleo* = to move) and Pyrochles (Greek *pyr* = fire). They represent concupiscence and anger respectively. Their pedigree is given at 2. 4.

41 and is similar to the infernal pedigree of the Sans brothers (1. 5. 22–3n). For *Acrates*, see also 2. 1. 51n. 1–2: see Matt. 4:11, 'the angels came and ministered unto him' [Christ] after the temptation in the wilderness. 5–6 the angel (representing divine love) is portrayed as a heavenly Cupid (cf. 1 proem 3n.), whose mother, Venus, frequented Mount *Ida*. *Graces*: cf. 2. 3. 21–31n. 16 *raven, kite*: the undignified fate promised by David to Goliath (1 Sam. 17:46). 17 *Lybian steed*: particularly fine horses, and a reminder of North African crusades against the infidel. 20 *sword . . . Merlin*: cf. 1. 7. 36; *meadwort* heals wounds; the name contains hints of the terrible magical power of the witch Medea (2. 12. 44–5n.); *Etna*: 2. 9. 29n.; *Styx*: 1. 1. 36–7n. 21 *Mordure*: from French *mordre* (to bite) + *dur* (hard). 30 *Termagant*: supposed Muslim god. 52 Pyrochles echoes Turnus's last speech to Aeneas (*Aeneid*, 12. 932 – 'enjoy your good fortune').

Canto 9

2–4 *lady's head*: for Guyon's shield, see 2. 1. 28n.; *morning star*: 1. 12. 21n. 6 *Artegall*, the beloved of Book 3's Britomart, is the hero of Book 5; *Sophy* is never mentioned again (Greek *sophia* = wisdom). 12 *enemies*: see canto 11; *seven*, because of the planets and seven ages of man, signifies earthly life and mortality. 16 *gnats*: cf. 1. 1. 23; the reference is to the bogs in central Ireland. Note Spenser's colonialist association of the Irish landscape with rebellion. 18–19 *Alma* in Latin means gracious, nourishing (an adjective often applied to Ceres and the Virgin Mary); in Italian it means soul. She is the rational soul, which includes, and is superior to, the sensitive and vegetative souls (see S. K. Heninger, Jr, *The Cosmographical Glass* (1977), ch. 6). Like Belphoebe (2. 3. 21–31n.), she combines virgin and Venus in the forms of *lily* and *rose* and *yellow hair*. 21 Alma's castle (representing the temperate human body) is made in part of corrupt earth. For Ninus, Nimrod and Babel, see 1. 5. 48n. The tower of Babel was held together by *slime* (Gen. 11:3), *Egyptian* because of the fertile Nile mud (1. 1. 21n.) and because Cairo was sometimes called Babylon. 22 for a full account of the number symbolism, see Fowler 1964, pp. 260–88. Spenser draws on the Pythagorean and Platonic belief, still much alive in the Renaissance, of the symbolic power of numbers. Briefly, he expresses in geometrical and arithmetical terms the mystery of the union of spirit and flesh in the human body. The *circle* represents the shape of the head (and, abstractly, perfection); the *quadrate* represents the trunk (and virtue, the Aristotelian meaning of the square: *Nicomachean Ethics*, 1100B); the *triangle* represents the legs (and imperfection).

These figures were also identified with the rational, sensitive and vegetative souls respectively. *Seven* is mutable and mortal (st. 12n.); *nine* is heavenly because of the nine orders of angels (1. 12. 39n.), and because, in the Ptolemaic system, the sphere of fixed stars was ninth counting from, and including, the earth. The arithmetical logic of the last line is: join (*compact*) seven and nine and you get harmonious eight (the octave or *diapase*), the temperate mean between them. 27ff. the journey is an ascent following the Platonic anatomy of (1) belly (st. 27–32), breast and heart (st. 33–4), and head (st. 45–60): *Timaeus*, 69–73; Agrippa, 2. 6, p. 182. 29 *Mongiball*: Mongibello, another name for volcanic Mount Etna on Sicily; compare the furnace at 2. 7. 35–7. 32 *Port Esquiline*: the Esquiline Gate in Rome was a sewer and dump haunted by carrion birds. 35 the heart's passions are divided here into four concupiscible and five irascible (after Plato's division of the soul into concupiscible, rational and irascible faculties). 37–9 *Praise-Desire* lies at the root of Arthur's quest for the Fairy Queen. *Purple* and *gold* are both royal; and purple, as a mixture of red and blue, symbolises temperance, as does gold (2. 1. 58n.). The *poplar* is an attribute of virtuous and heroic Hercules (Virgil, *Eclogues*, 7. 61). 40–3 *Shamefastness* (st. 43) is Guyon's impelling virtue, described here according to emblematic convention (e.g., Ripa, p. 420). Her *bird* remains unidentified: see Brooks-Davies 1977, p. 167. Aristotle, *Nicomachean Ethics*, 1116A, talks of the balance between fear of shame and desire of praise in courageous men. 44 *ten*: numerologically the number of perfection as they approach the head. 45 *Cadmus* founded *Thebes*, which was destroyed by *Alexander* (see 1. 5. 48n.) in 335 BC; *Hector*'s son Astyanax was flung from *Troy*'s walls by the Greeks (*Met.*, 13. 415–17). 47 *heavenly tower*: the New Jerusalem (1. 10. 55–7). 48ff.: the rooms and their inhabitants signify the three ventricles of the brain, recognised as containing Imagination, Reason (or Judgement), and Memory. Spenser correlates these with the three parts of time (future, present, past). 48 *the wisest*: Socrates (referring to Plato, *Apology of Socrates*, 21A); *Pylian*: wise Nestor, who advised the Greeks during the war against Troy, of which *Priam* was king. 49–52: *Phantastes* (st. 52) embodies Imagination (or Fancy, the image-making faculty): cf. the *flies* of st. 51 and 1. 1. 22–3n. and 1. 1. 38. Phantastes is melancholic because Saturn, god of melancholy, governed visionaries, madmen, etc. 53–4 *goodly reason* modifies Imagination's excesses and works in conjunction with *Memory* (st. 55–8). 56 *Nine*: st. 21n. above, the first person to wage war; *Assaracus* was an early king of Troy and greatgrandfather of Aeneas; *Inachus* was a river god and first king of Argos.

57 *Nestor* (st. 48n.) was reputedly 300 at the time of the Trojan war; for Methuselah see Gen. 5:27.

Canto 11

6–7: the *twelve* troops are divided into *seven* deadly sins attacking body and soul (cf. 1. 4. 18–36), and *five* evils which attack the senses, presented in their traditional order of Sight, Hearing, Smell, Taste, Touch. The animals are the conventional emblematic attributes of the senses to which Spenser attaches them. 19 *Spumador* means Golden Foam (Italian *spuma d'oro*). *Laomedon* was Aeneas's grandfather. 20–3 *Maleger* means Badly Sick (Latin *male* + *aeger*) and Ill Omen (Italian *malaugurio*). He signifies original sin as it corrupts the body. The *tiger* signifies destructive swiftness since the Armenian word for *arrow* was *tigris* (Valeriano, Book 42, p. 445). 45–6 cf. the myth of the giant Antaeus, son of Poseidon and Earth, who received renewed strength from his mother when he was thrown to the ground. He was defeated by Hercules as Arthur defeats Maleger.

Canto 12

2ff.: echoing Odysseus's voyages in *Odyssey*, 12; those of Aeneas (*Aeneid*, 2, 3); and those of Ubaldo and Carlo in *Ger. lib.*, 15. 3–8 *Gulf, Rock*: the Charybdis and Scylla of *Odyssey*, 12. 73ff. and 234ff. 6 *Tartarus*: hell. 11 *Wandering Islands*: cf. the Wandering Rocks (*Odyssey*, 12. 59ff.) and the unstable Isle of Fortune in G. de Lorris and J. de Meun's *Romance of the Rose*, 5921ff. 13 *Latona*: her story is told in *Met.*, 6. 184ff. The *twins* were Apollo and Diana; Jupiter, Juno's husband, was their father. 17 *Phaedria*: as in Book 2, canto 6. 22 *Neptune*: king of the seas. 23 the *hydra* was the many-headed snake of antiquity; when one head was struck off, another grew in its place. 26 *Tethys*: 1. 1. 39n. 31 *Heliconian maids*: the Muses (dwellers on Mount Helicon). 30–2 the *mermaids* are based on the Sirens of *Odyssey*, 12. 39ff. and 166ff. 33 *Zephyrus*: the west wind of spring, associated with lust through his rape of Chloris. 36 all the birds have infernal associations; *harpies*: 2. 7. 21–5n. 39 cf. Circe's island, *Odyssey*, 10 (followed also by Ariosto, Tasso and Trissino). 41 Mercury's *rod* (the caduceus) brings peace and harmony; symbolises reason; gives sleep; and guides the souls of the dead: Brooks-Davies 1983, pp. 38–9. And cf. Ubaldo's magic wand at *Ger. lib.*, 14. 73. *Orcus* is Pluto, the god of hell. 42 note that *art* so improves *nature* here that it causes deception. 43 *enclosed*: echoes and parodies Song of Solomon 4:12, the 'garden enclosed' as the body of the bride-Church and Virgin Mary. 44–5 for the tale of the Argonauts see Apollonius Rhodius, *Argonautica*. The witch *Medea* was *Jason*'s wife. When he abandoned her for *Creusa* she killed her with a poisoned garment. The *boy* is Absyrtus, Medea's brother, killed by her as she and Jason fled with the Golden Fleece from her father, Aeetes. The *ivory* (st. 44) recalls the gate of false dreams (1. 1. 40n.). 47–8 *Genius*: the god of generation, here perverted. His true form appears at 3. 6. 31–3. *Agdistis* (st. 48), the hermaphroditic son of Zeus and Earth (Pausanias, *Description of Greece*, 7. 17. 5), was a nature deity identified by the mythographers with Genius. A *staff* is an emblem of office and authority. 50 *Flora*: 1. 1. 45–50n. 52 *Rhodope* gave birth to a giant sired by Neptune (*Met.*, 6. 87–9); *Phoebus*: Apollo chased after Daphne in *Tempe*, where she was changed into a laurel (*Met.*, 1. 452ff.); *Ida*: see 2. 8. 5–6n.; *Parnassus*: 1. 10. 54n.; *Eden*: Gen. 2, 3. 54 *hyacinth*: ancient name for what was probably the sapphire (dedicated to jovial Jupiter); the *rubine* (ruby) was associated with love; the *emerald* was dedicated to Venus. 60 *midst*: parodies Rev. 22:1–2 (river of water of life flowing through middle of New Jerusalem; cf. Gen. 2: 9). 62 *jasper*: parodies Rev. 21:11. 63–8 derived from Tasso, *Ger. lib.*, 15. 58ff. The *Cyprian* (st. 65) is Venus, particularly worshipped on *Cyprus* and born from the foam of the sea: 3. 5. 8n.; she is also Phosphor, the morning star (1. 2. 6–7n.). 69 *Acrasia*: 2. 1. 51n. 72 *lover*: Verdant (st. 82), whose name means giver of spring (Latin *ver* = spring): he is a parody Adonis (3. 1. 34–8n., 3. 4. 29n.) and the opposite of Mortdant (2. 1. 35–55n.). 74–5 translated from *Ger. lib.*, 16. 14–15; for the *rose*, see 1. 2. 37n. The song is in the 'seize the day' tradition of Catullus, *Carmina*, 5 ('Let us live and love, my Lesbia'). 77 *Arachne*: 2. 7. 28n. 86 *Grill* means pig (Greek *gryllos*). According to Plutarch, 'Whether the Beasts Have the Use of Reason', he had been a companion of Odysseus who, changed into a pig by Circe, had refused to be turned back to human shape again (*Moralia*, 985Dff.). The story was repeated in G. B. Gelli's *Circe* (1549; English trans., 1557.)

BOOK 3

PROEM 1 *Chastity*: fidelity in love and the control of lust, as ideally fulfilled in marriage (and thus, in effect, sexual continence, a branch of temperance). Historically it can also mean celibacy and virginity. Hence the polarity in Book 3 between Venus and Diana summed up in the twins Amoret and Belphoebe (see Canto 6). 2 *Zeuxis*, a celebrated Greek painter, and *Praxiteles*, the celebrated Greek sculptor, lived in the fifth and fourth centuries BC respectively. 3 *sovereign*: Elizabeth I. 4 *servant*: Sir Walter Ralegh, *The Ocean's Love to Cynthia* (i.e., Elizabeth as moon goddess: *Mutab.*, 6. 8–10n.); *LA* is addressed to Ralegh and mentions the 'excellent conceit [image] of Cynthia'.

Canto 1

1 *Prince*: Arthur; *fairy knight*: Guyon; *Alma*: Book 2, cantos 9–11. 2 *Acrasia*: Book 2, canto 12. 4 *lion ... field*: the arms of Britomart's ancestor Brutus, great-grandson of Aeneas and founder of Britain. 7–8 *Britomart*: Britomartis was anciently identified with Artemis–Diana, virginal lunar huntress; the *spear* was an attribute of wise, virginal Minerva (Tervarent, col. 230). The name also suggests *British Mars* while simultaneously recalling heroic Bradamante, whose magic spear is described in *OF*, 23. 15. *Venus ... glass*: for the mirror of Venus, see Tervarent, col. 274 (but this is actually Merlin's magic globe: 3. 2. 17–22). 15–16: i.e., Florimell (3. 5. 8), from Latin *Flora* (a flower goddess: 1. 1. 45–50n.) and Latin *mel* = honey; also suggesting Italian *mela* = apple, emblem of love and Venus. For *beaten gold*, see Psalm 45:9 (the queen in a vesture of gold); *blazing star*: comet (from Greek *komē* = head hair), symbol of rarity and love as well as being ominous. *Yellow locks*: 2. 3. 21–31n. She is modelled on Angelica in *OF*, 1. 33ff. 17 the *forester* was a contemporary symbol of lust and the mysterious chaos represented by the woods. 18 *Timias*: 1. 7. 37n. 20 *six knights*: see st. 45n. 31 *Castle Joyous*: the castle of pleasure familiar in mediaeval and Renaissance romance. Its description parodies that of the New Jerusalem (Rev. 21:18ff.). 34–8 the key myth of Book 3, it reappears explicitly in canto 6 (and see Lewis, ch. 3). For the ancient story, see *Met.*, 10. 519ff. *Rosemary* symbolises remembrance; *violets*, love (they are dedicated to Venus); pansies represent thoughts (French *pensée*), usually of death; Adonis was transformed into an anemone. 40 *Lydian*: the musical mode associated with sensuality. 41 *Persian*: cf. 1. 4. 7n. 45 the six parody the ladder of love: L. J. Friedman, *Romance Philology*, 19 (1965–6), 167–77; A. H. Gilbert, *Modern Language Notes*, 56 (1941), 594–7; A. D. S. Fowler, *Studies in Philology*, 56 (1959), 167–77. 51 *Ceres*: mother goddess of the corn; *Lyaeus* is Bacchus, the wine god (so both together represent the food and wine essential to love's success): cf. Chaucer, *Parliament of Fowls*, 275–6. 57 *Malecasta* (Italian *male* + *casta*) = badly chaste; *moist daughters*: the Hyades, stars in the constellation, Taurus, bringers of rain, called by Renaissance mythographers daughters of the giant *Atlas*. See Eade, p. 180 for the astronomy. 59 *scarlet*: reminiscent of the Whore of

Babylon of Rev. 17:4 (cf. Duessa, 1. 2. 13); *ermine*: emblem of royalty and chastity (it reputedly would do anything to preserve the purity of its white winter coat), it was particularly associated with Minerva and Elizabeth I as the Virgin Queen.

Canto 4

2 the Amazonian queen *Penthesilea* fought with the Trojans and is mentioned by Virgil (not Homer): 2. 3. 31n.; *Deborah*, used as a cult name for Elizabeth I (Wilson, ch. 2): judge and prophet who helped arrange Sisera's death in Judges 4; *Camilla* kills Orsilochus at *Aeneid*, 11. 690ff. 8–10 combine biblical (Psalm 69: 1–15) and Petrarchan (*Canzoniere*, 189) ideas in conventional fashion. 17 *Marinell*: a combination of Narcissus (in his self-preservingness and connection with water) and Adonis (in his role as wounded lover who revives: 3. 1. 34–8n.), he is associated with the sea (Latin/Italian *mare*) and also reluctant to marry (French *mari* = husband + Latin *nolle* = to be unwilling). 18 Britomart rejects the *gold* because Chastity defeats Avarice (Ripa, p. 66). 19 *Cymoent*: named as *Cymodoce* at 4. 11. 50 and 53 (where again she is a Nereid, i.e. daughter of the sea god Nereus); she cares for her son as Thetis cares for Achilles (*Met.*, 13. 162ff.). Greek *kyma* = wave (cf. 2. 8 Arg. stanza). *Dumarin* means of the sea. 25 *Proteus*: tricky shape-changer; old man of the sea; sophist; magician: cf. 1. 2. 10n. 29 *daffadillies*: the flower of Narcissus (st. 17n. and *Met.*, 3. 341ff., especially 509–10); but *daffodils* signify grief because Proserpine was gathering them when she was abducted into the underworld (Ross, p. 307; Shakespeare, *Winter's Tale* (New Arden), 4. 4. 116ff.). The time spent by Proserpine underground represented winter and dormant seed; her six months in the upper world with her mother Ceres, the corn goddess, signified spring and summer: another seasonal myth thus enters the book to complement that of Adonis (see 3. 6. 46–9n.). 30 *continent*: note the pun (temperate) as at st. 10, line 2. 32 *Neptune*: king of the seas. 33 *Triton*: Neptune's son; he had control over sea creatures; *dolphins*: symbols of love and (because of the dolphin's rescue of Arion), salvation (Valeriano, Book 27, pp. 274–7; Ross, p. 31). 41 *Liagore*: a Nereid in Hesiod's catalogue (*Theogony*, 257). Spenser tells of her the story recounted of Oenone in Ovid, *Heroides*, 5. 145ff. *Apollo* discovered the art of healing (he will cure Marinell at 4. 12. 25): *Met.*, 1. 521–2; *Paeon* was the gods' physician (*Iliad*, 5. 401). 43 *Tryphon*: following Boccaccio, *De genealogia deorum*, 7. 36 in the name and in making him Aesculapius' (1. 5. 36–44) brother. 45 *Archimago*'s last appearance in the poem (his first

is in Book 1, canto 1). 51 *Hesperus*: the evening star (1. 2. 6–7n.). 54 cf. 1. 9. 13–15. 55 *Night* is the author of strife, lies, etc. at Hesiod, *Theogony*, 224ff.; cf. 1. 5. 20ff.; *Cocytus*: 2. 7. 56n.; *Herebus*: personification of the underworld. 59 cf. 1. 5. 25.

Canto 5

5–6: cf. 3. 1. 15–16nn. 8 *Florimell* has a seasonal function as Flora (1. 1. 45–50n.), goddess of spring; her relationship with the sea (through Marinell and her adventure in canto 8) suggests an additional role as Venus born from the sea (Venus anadyomene), as in Botticelli's *Birth of Venus* (and see *Met.*, 4. 537–9). 15 *three . . . graceless*: a grotesque triad of anti-Graces in contrast to Belphoebe, Amoret and Florimell, perhaps to suggest the three lusts of 1 John 2:16. 27 *Braggadocchio*; *Belphoebe*: cf. 2. 3 argt stanza. 29 cf. Marinell; Adonis in 3. 6; and Mortdant and Verdant at 2. 1. 41 and 2. 12. 79. 32 *Tobacco*: recently introduced (1584) by Sir Walter Ralegh (3 proem 4n.), and supposedly curative (this is apparently its first mention in English literature); Venus gives *Panacea* (Greek for cure-all) to Aeneas at *Aeneid*, 12. 419; *Polygony* prevents blood flowing and is good for slow-healing wounds and frostbite (*frozen*, st. 31). 40 a true *locus amoenus* in contrast to 1. 2. 28–30n., 1. 7. 2–3 and the Bower of Bliss at 2. 12. *Myrtle* belongs to Venus; *laurel* to virginal Daphne (*Met.*, 1. 548–67). 42 Adonis was gored in the thigh by the boar (3. 1. 34–38n., and 3. 6. 48); the wound has obvious sexual significance. 51 suggests the *rose* of virginity, of Venus, and the Tudor rose, combined with the thornless rose that flourished in *paradise* (st. 40; Gen. 3:18), emblem of the Virgin Mary and Elizabeth (Wilson, p. 219n.; Strong, pp. 68–75).

Canto 6

2 *Jove, Venus, Phoebus*: an astrologically fortunate conjunction (Fowler 1964, p. 83n., noting that neo-Platonists regarded the three planets as equivalent to the three *Graces* (on whom see 6. 10. 9, 12–15 and 22nn.)). 3 *morning dew*: Psalm 110:3, often interpreted as referring to Christ's conception (Sternhold and Hopkins metrical version as in Geneva Bible appendix: 'Thy birth due is the dew that doth/From womb of morning fall'): cf. the mediaeval carol 'I sing of a maiden': 'He came all so still . . . As dew in April.' Like Christ, but also like Mary, she is born free of original sin. 4 *Chrysogone*: from Greek *chrysos + gonē* (race) – i.e., gold-producing (note also Greek *gynē* = woman). The Greeks used the word *chrysogonos* of the Persians, supposedly descendants of Perseus, son of Danaë after she was impreg-

nated by Jove in the form of a shower of gold (Aeschylus, *Persians*, 79–80; cf. 3. 11. 31). An epithet of the Virgin Mary in her Litany is *house of gold*; and the sunbeams piercing Chrysogone's womb (st. 7) recall an image frequently used of Mary's impregnation (Upton in *Var.*, 3. 250). *Amphisa*: double-natured (Greek). 6 *roses, violets*: mean love and chastity respectively, though the violet is also Venerean. 7–9 on spontaneous generation from the *Nile* mud acted on by sunbeams, see 1. 1. 21n. The moon, Phoebus Apollo's *sister*, governs moisture, menstruation and childbirth. The allegorical significance of sun and moon here is supported by the echo of Rev. 12:6, where the 'woman clothed with the sun, and the moon ... under her feet', having given birth, 'fled into the wilderness'. 11–26: cf. Moschus, *Idyll* 4, 'Love the Runaway': the source of *SC, March.* 20 *Cytherea* is Venus (from the island by which she was born from the sea). 24 *Mars*: 1 proem 3n. 27 *withouten pain*: like the Virgin Mary, unlike Eve, upon whom child-birth pain was bestowed as a curse (Gen. 3:16); *Lucina*: 2. 1. 53n. 29 *Paphos* was an important centre of Venus worship; *Cytheron hill*: 6. 10. 9n.; *Gnidus*: site of the Praxitelean (3 proem 2n.) statue of Venus. 29–30 on the plurality of matter in Eden, cf. Gen. 1:24, 2:5. The name *Adonis* was associated with *Eden* (which means pleasure); *Garden of Adonis* (st. 29) was a phrase signifying place of fruitful and fast-growing plants (Plato, *Phaedrus*, 276B); on Venus and Adonis, see 3. 1. 34–8n. 31 the *gates* signify life and death, and suggest the womb (Job 3:10) and double-headed *Janus*, guardian of the gates of the year and identified with Apollo and Diana (Macrobius, *Saturnalia*, 1. 9; cf. 3. 6. 7–9.). *Janus* sounds like (but is not directly related to) the figure *Genius* understood as a priest of nature: contrast the false Agdistis at 2. 12. 47–8. 32–3 cf. Virgil, *Aeneid*, 6. 713ff. 34 *increase and multiply*: Gen. 1:22, 28. 35 *some ... some*: 1 Cor. 15:39: 'All flesh is not the same flesh; but there is one flesh of men, and another flesh of beasts, and another of fishes, and another of birds.' 36 *Chaos*: *Met.*, 1. 5–20 and Gen. 1:1 and cf. *HL*, 57ff. 42 traditionally the seasons (excluding winter, which did not exist) were simultaneous in Eden and in the Golden Age (Gen. 1:12, *Met.*, 1. 107–10). 43 *middest*: 2. 12. 60n.; *myrtle*: 3. 5. 40n. 44 *ivy, eglantine, caprifole*: the first is Bacchic, the others are plants of Venus. *Aeolus*: the wind god. 45 *Hyacinthus*: beloved of *Phoebus* Apollo, who killed him with a discus misdirected by the jealous wind god (*Met.*, 10. 162ff; *Narcissus*: 3. 4. 17 and 29nn.; *amaranthus* (Greek: immortal, unfading) was one of the flowers being gathered by Proserpine's attendants when she was abducted into Hades (Ovid, *Fasti*, 4. 439): cf. 3. 4. 29n. In Thomas Watson's *Amyntas*

(1585), the eponymous lover dies through grief over Phyllis and is changed into an amaranthus. **46–9** *transformed oft* because Adonis is, in the Orphic *Hymn to Adonis* (in *The Orphic Hymns*, trans. A. N. Athanassakis, 1977), described as many-formed. Adonis was commonly interpreted as the sun, the killing boar as time and winter, and Venus as the earth, barren or fruitful according to the time of the year. **50** *Psyche* (Greek for soul) quests for, and is finally married to, *Cupid*. The tale, seen by neo-Platonists as an allegory of the suffering soul's eventual union with the principle of divine love, was originally told in Apuleius, *The Golden Ass*, Book 5. Their child, *Pleasure*, is punningly, the meaning of *Eden* (3. 6. 29–30n.). **53** *Scudamour* means shield of love; he is Amoret's lover and husband.

Canto 7

1ff. cf. Angelica in *OF*, 1. 33ff. **2** alludes to the Platonic image of the unrestrained horse of the passions. **11** *Diana's crew*: 2. 2. 7–10n. **14** *Stygian shores*: 1. 1. 36–7n. **22** *Hyena*: traditionally treacherous and believed to desecrate corpses buried in consecrated ground. Here, it represents Florimell's view of male sexual appetite. **26–7** *Myrrha*: mother of Adonis, she committed incest with her father (*Met.*, 10. 312ff.); *Daphne* was pursued by Apollo (2. 12. 52n.). Florimell turns to the sea, the site of Venus's birth (3. 5. 8n.). Britomartis (3. 1. 7–8n.) was saved by *fishermen* (Diodorus Siculus, *Library*, 5. 76. 3–4); but *fish* and *fishermen* are associated with lust (A. Alciati, *Emblemata* (Lyons, 1551), p. 83). The zodiacal sign Pisces (the Fish marks the exaltation of Venus (cf. 3. 8. 20ff.). **30** *Satyrane*: 1. 6. 21n. **31** *girdle*: contested for in Book 4, canto 5, it is the symbol of 'chaste love' and originally belonged to Venus (4. 5. 3; Homer, *Iliad*, 14. 214ff.). In Latin it is the *cestus*, which suggests *castus* (spotless, chaste). **41** *Olympus*: Spenser, like many, thought the Olympic Games were held there. **47–8** as a *giantess*, *Argante* (a pagan warrior in *Ger. lib.*), is earth-born (see 1. 7. 8–10n.), not sea-born like Venus, and hence 'of the earth, earthly' (1 Cor. 15:47). *Typhoeus* (1. 5. 35n.), giant of storms (typhoons), rebelled against Jupiter (*Mutab.*, 6. 15n.). *Ollyphant* is a mace-bearing giant in Chaucer's fragmentary *Tale of Sir Thopas*. These terrible twins parody Belphoebe and Amoret and, more remotely, Apollo and Diana. **51** *Columbell* means beautiful dove (Italian *colomba* + *bella*), which was Venus's bird, emblem of chaste love. **52** *Palladine*: a paladin was a knight errant, originally associated with Charlemagne. The name also recalls *Pallas*, the Greek virgin goddess of wisdom. **61** *Alcides*: Hercules, and his celebrated twelve labours.

Canto 8

5-9 *Riphoean hills*: perpetually snowy Scythian mountains. The creation of the phantom Florimell recalls Archimago's machinations in Book 1, canto 1 as well as Paracelsian theories of the creation of living creatures. She is described in terms of Petrarchan sonnet convention: *Canzoniere*, 90 and cf. *Am* 37 and 81. Her creation also recalls the story of the two Helens, the real one of whom remained in Egypt while the phantom one, made out of clouds, accompanied Paris to Troy (Plato, *Republic*, 586C and Euripides, *Helen*). **11** *Braggadocchio*: see Book 2, canto 3. **13** *Trompart*: Braggadocchio's companion (also 2. 3). **15** *armed knight*: Sir Ferraugh (named at 4. 2. 4). **21** *Aeolus*: 3. 6. 44n. **24-6** based on OF, 8. 30ff. On *fish*, see 3. 7. 26-7n. **28** *Peridure*: one who endures; traditionally one of the Arthurian knights; *Calidore*: the courteous knight of Book 6 (but Latin *calidus* = fierce, fiery). **30** *Proteus*: see 3. 4. 25n. The flower maiden now succumbs to the tyrannical force of winter (st. 35); she will be released in 4. 12. **37** for the topography, see Virgil, *Georgics*, 4. 418ff.; *Panope* is named as a Nereid at 4. 11. 49, following Hesiod's *Theogony* catalogue (cf. 3. 4. 41n.). **41** cf. Archimago at 1. 2. 10. **45** *Paridell* suggests Trojan *Paris*; his emblem is that of Lechery at 1. 4. 25. **47** *Knights of Maidenhead*: 1. 7. 46n.

Canto 9

3-7 *Malbecco* means evil goat (Italian *male* + *becco*), symbol of lust and of the horned cuckold. Married to Hellenore (Helen-over-again; Helen-whore), he is Menelaus to Paridell's abducting Paris (see st. 34-6 below). A parody of the outbreak of the Trojan war follows. The conjunction of old man and young woman traditionally symbolised disorder. **7** *Argus*: had a hundred eyes and was set by jealous Juno to keep watch over Io, after whom she knew her husband, Jove, lusted (*Met.*, 1. 622ff.). **11-18** following OF, 32. 65ff. **19** *Vulcan*: blacksmith to the gods and Venus's cuckolded husband. **22** *Minerva* (*Bellona* in 1590 text), armed goddess of wisdom (*SC, October*, 114 gloss identifies Bellona with Pallas). The reference is to the battle of the giants against the gods (*Mutab.*, 6. 2n.). The giant *Enceladus* was reputedly killed by Minerva's chariot (Pausanias, *Description of Greece*, 8. 47. 1); but it was Jove who killed Typhoeus on Mount *Haemus*. Minerva bore the *Gorgon*'s head on her shield, symbol of chastity's power over lust; but in Britomart's case there is an additional suggestion of the virtuous Venus armed with a Gorgonian shield (Wind, p. 91n.). Cf. 1. 7. 33. **30** *Bacchus*: 3. 1. 51n. The game, *cottabos*, was played by Helen and Paris (Ovid, *Heroides*, 17. 75ff.). Spenser glances, of course, at the *mystery* of Eucharistic wine. 33–51: completes the historical background of the British myth, begun in Book 2, canto 10 and continued in Book 3, canto 3. Its sources lie, among others, in the *Iliad*; the *Aeneid*; and Geoffrey of Monmouth's twelfth-century *History of the Kings of Britain*. 34–6 *Paris, Helen*: 2. 7. 55n. Paris abandoned his beloved *Oenone*, who lived with him on Mount *Ida*, for Helen. The usual name for their son is Corythus. *Scamander, Xanthus* (st. 35): the same Trojan river. *Priam* (st. 36): king of Troy at the time of its destruction, and Paris's father (cf. 2. 9. 48n.). 41–2 *Latium*: the western land in Italy which Aeneas was directed to colonise in order to repair the ruin of Troy; *Latinus*, king of Latium, permitted Aeneas to marry his daughter, Lavinia, who was already betrothed to the Rutulian leader, Turnus (the *rival*): see *Aeneid*, 7–12. 43 *long Alba*: Alba longa, in Latium; *Romulus* founded *Rome*. 44–5 *Troynovant*: London (the third Troy after the original and Rome). 47 *Mnemon*: Memory (Greek). 49–51 cf. 2. 10. 5–12; and, for *Cleopolis*, 1. 7. 46n. and 1. 10. 58.

Canto 10

1 *fairy knight*: Satyrane. 8 *bransles*: songs accompanying dances; *virelays*: songs with short-line stanzas having only two rhymes. 12 *Helen*: cf. *Aeneid*, 6. 517–19. 15 Malbecco lusts, the victim of cupidity in both its avaricious and sexual senses. Cf. 3. 4. 18n., and Guyon's battle with Mammon (2. 7) and Acrasia (2. 12). 19 parodying the Florimell–Marinell story. 23 *Braggadocchio, Trompart*: 3. 8. 11, 13nn. 31 *doucepeer*: one of Charlemagne's twelve (French *douze*) paladins (3. 7. 52n.). 32 *Sanglamort*: bloody death: 33 the *steed* was *stolen* from Guyon at 2. 3. 4. 43 *bagpipes*: traditionally associated with lust. Cf. Una and the satyrs at Book 1, canto 6. 55–8 Jealousy is depicted as many-eyed (cf. Argus at 3. 9. 7n.), carrying a *thorny* (st. 55) branch symbolising self-laceration: Ripa, pp. 181–2, who includes a cockerel among Jealousy's emblems: hence, in part, the *claws* of st. 57.

Canto 11

1 *Proserpine* was queen of *hell* (2. 7. 51–3n., 3. 4. 29n.), and associated with *serpents* because of her name (Latin *serpere* = to crawl like a serpent): Tervarent, col. 344. The *Furies* were snake-haired; *snakes* were also attributes of Envy (see 1. 4. 31). 3 *Ollyphant, Argante*: 3. 7. 47–8n. 5 *base*: 6. 10. 8n. 7 *winged boy*: Cupid. 10 *Busirane*: Egyptian tyrant associated with blood lust and killed by Hercules (*Met.*, 9. 182–3), identified with the pharaoh of Exodus (Steadman, ch. 13); *seven months*: Florimell, too, is imprisoned for this period (4. 11. 4),

suggesting the duration of winter (Proteus, her gaoler, recalls the Egyptian King Proteus to parallel Egyptian Busiris: Ross, p. 371). **22** *Earth's children*: the giants/Titans (3. 9. 22n.). **25** the barrier of fire is a familiar romance motif (cf. Tasso's *Rinaldo*, 5; *Ger. lib.*, 13. 33ff.); *itself divide*: as the Red Sea parted to allow the Israelites to escape Busiris's bondage in Egypt (Exodus, 14:21ff.). **26** *Mulciber*: i.e., Vulcan (3. 9. 19n.): the fire is that of lust or envy (Tervarent, col. 183). **28–46** cf. Arachne's tapestry of love's lusts at *Met.*, 6. 103–28, and the tapestry in Malecasta's castle at 3. 1. 34–8. **30–1** *Helle*: Ovid. *Fasti*, 3. 852ff.; *Europa*: *Met.*, 2. 847ff.; *Danaë*: Ross, pp. 89–91. **32** *Leda*: *Met.*, 6. 109; Wind, ch. 10. **33** *Semele*: *Met.*, 3. 259ff.; *Alcmena*: Tooke, pp. 332–3. **34** *Asterie*: *Met.*, 6. 108; *Ganymede*: *Met.*, 10. 155–61. **35** *Antiopa*: *Met.*, 6. 110–11; *Mnemosyne*: Ross, pp. 297–8. For the details of Apollo's exploits, see *Met.*, 4. 171ff. (Venus and Mars) and 2. 12. 52n. (*Daphne*) (st. 36); *Met.*, 10. 162ff. (*Hyacinth*) and 2. 542ff. (Coronis) (st. 37); *Met.*, 2. 1ff. (st. 38; *son of Climene* = Phaethon); *Met.*, 6. 124 (Isse) (st. 39). **40–2** cf. *Aeneid*, 1. 145ff. **42** cf. *Met.*, 6. 115–20. **43** *Saturn*: *Met.*, 6. 125–6. **45–6** cf. Petrarch's *Triumph of Love*. **47–9** the *pavone* (peacock) of pride derives its eyes from Argus (3. 10. 55–8n.); *Iris* is the rainbow goddess. This is the Cupid of lust and earthly love in contrast to the celestial Cupid of 2. 8. 5. The *dragon* (st. 48) that traditionally guards virginity is, symbolically, wounded. **54** *Be bold*: the Bluebeard story was known in the Renaissance: this motto appears over the Fox's hall portal (e.g., R. Chambers, *Book of Days* (1869), 1. 291–2).

Canto 12

2 smoke, etc. is symbolic of the manifestation of a deity (Exodus 19:16, 1 Kings 19:11–12). **3** *laurel*: an emblem of victory (Tervarent, col. 233). Spenser's masque of Cupid draws on classical (Ovidian), mediaeval, Petrarchan and theatrical conventions. The procession of paired masquers depicts the effects of love. **7** *Fancy*: on the imagination, see 2. 9. 49–52n.; *imp*: Ganymede (3. 11. 34); *Alcides* (Hercules) loved *Hylas* (Apollonius Rhodius, *Argonautica*, 1. 1207ff.). **10** *Albanese*: alluding to the Scottish fashion of wearing full-sleeved shirts (*Spenser Newsletter*, 16 (1985), 15–16). **13** *Hope*: the secular counterpart of Speranza (1. 10. 14), just as *Fear* (st. 12) is the secular counterpart of Obedience at 1. 10. 7, since obedience there means *fear* of the lord (*timor domini*): Brooks-Davies 1977, p. 95. **16** *Grief ... pincers*: cf. Amendment's pincers at 1. 10. 26. **17** *Fury*: cf. 1. 4. 33–4; 2. 4. 7ff. **18** *honey-lady bee*: Cupid is linked with bees (his arrows are traditionally the stings of love); and note the honey in Florimell's name (3. 1. 15–16n.). **20–1** the arrow-pierced heart is emblematic of love (Tervarent, col. 102): cf. 2. 1. 37; 3. 4. 6. **22–3** Cupid is at the sovereign centre of his triumph (Fowler 1970, p. 52). He rides on a *lion* to signify love's power (cf. *SC*, *December*, 57–8; and Tervarent, col. 247). For his blindness, etc., see Panofsky 1962, ch. 4. **30–1** the iconography suggests Amoret's fear of the male. The *brass* that predominates (st. 29, 30) is Venerean (Agrippa, 1. 28, p. 59); the *pillar* signifies both chastity and virtue in general (Tervarent, cols 107–8). **31** *figuring*: like Merlin at 3. 3. 14. **36** *reverse*: reversing black magic charms restores normality: e.g., Circe at *Met.*, 14. 300–1. **42** cf. Guyon's effect on the Bower of Bliss at 2. 12. 83. [**1590 ending to Book 3**: *dear*: the deer/dear pun was a commonplace because of the hunt of love *topos*: cf. Petrarch, *Canzoniere*, 190 and *Am*, 67. *Hermaphrodite*: the neo-Platonic image of perfect mystical union from Aristophanes' fable in Plato's *Symposium*: Wind, pp. 200–2, 211–14. It also signifies marriage (the 'one flesh' of Gen. 2:24). The *Roman* is unidentified (see Donald Cheney in *Publications of the Modern Language Association of America*, 87 (1972), 192–200), but Roman Ovid tells the story of Hermaphroditus in *Met.*, 4. 285–388. The notion of growing together like tree trunks (*stocks*) comes from *Met.*, 11. 375–7. The *swains* are Amoret and Scudamour.]

BOOK 4

Canto 10

1 *gall ... honey*: proverbial, and used as Thomalin's emblem in *SC*, *March*. **5** *Paphos, Cyprus*: the first was a specific, the second a more general centre of Venus worship: see 3. 6. 29n. **6** *Doric*: one of the three ancient types of column, originally designed to reflect the proportions of the male body, and thus appropriate for the approach to the temple of a hermaphroditic deity (Vitruvius, *Ten Books on Architecture*, 4. 1. 5–6.). **7** *twenty knights*: twenty anciently signified servitude: P. Bongus, *Numerorum mysteria* (1599), 426, 428. **12** on double-faced Janus, god of gates, beginnings, and the year (hence January), see 3. 6. 31n. In general, compare the guardian personifications here with those guarding the castle of the lady's virtue in G. de Lorris and J. de Meun, *The Romance of the Rose*. **17** *Danger* (Coyness): see 3. 12. 11 and *Romance of the Rose*, 2824–3158. **20** lovers should not look backward, as Orpheus discovered when he lost Eurydice (1. 11. 30n.); and cf. 1. 3. 30. For the *hindparts*, cf. the misshapen nether parts of Duessa at 1. 8.

48. 22 Eden, too, contained every kind of tree (Gen. 2:9). *Juniper*,
sweetly scented but with prickly leaves, signifies love and its barriers;
cedar: aromatic and traditionally beautiful. 23 *Elysian fields*: paradisal
abode of the blessed dead in the ancient underworld: e.g., *Aeneid*, 6.
638–59. *To life returned*: in the Virgilian underworld, where the dead
souls have to be made to forget their bliss in order to return to the pains
of the upper world. 27 Lists traditional pairs of male friends: *Hylas* was
Hercules's beloved (3. 12. 7); the story of *David* and *Jonathan* appears
in 1 Samuel 18:3ff.; *Theseus* helped *Pirithous* against the Centaurs and
in his attempt to abduct Proserpina from hell: *Met.*, 12. 210ff. and
Aeneid, 6. 393ff.; *Pylades* and *Orestes* are named as friends in Statius,
Thebaid, 1. 476–7; the story of *Titus* and *Gisippus* is told in Boccaccio,
Decameron, 10. 8 and Sir Thomas Eliot's *The Book named the
Governor*, 2. 12; *Damon* and *Pythias*: Pythagoreans, the former of
whom offered to die for the latter. 30 *temple of Diana*: Acts 19;
celebrated for its statue of the many-breasted Diana. *Seven wonders*: the
other six of the ancient world were: the Egyptian pyramids: the Mau-
soleum at Halicarnassus; the statue of Zeus by Phidias; the Colossus of
Rhodes; the hanging gardens of Babylon; the lighthouse (pharos) at
Alexandria. *King of Jewry*: Solomon, for whose magnificent Temple at
Jerusalem, see 1 Kings 6. 32 another neo-Platonic mystery of reconciled
opposites: Wind, p. 211; Belphoebe at 2. 3; and cf. the hermaphrodite
herself. On the youth yet strength of *Love*, see Plato, *Symposium*,
178A–C and, on his control of hate, *HL*, 83–4. 34–5 *Concord*: for the
personification, see Ripa, p. 81. The binding of the elements (as at *HL*,
57ff.) derives from Plato, *Timaeus*, 32C. 37–8 among other sources,
draws on the Temple of Venus in *Aeneid*, 1. 416–17 (a hundred altars
warm with incense). 39 *in the midst*: the position of sovereignty (3. 12.
22–3n.); the unnamed substance recalls the purity and fidelity signified
by *crystal* (see 1. 10. 12–13n.). For ancient crystal statues, see Lynche,
C1 verso. 40 *Phidias* of *Paphos* (see 4. 10. 5n.) did make statues of
Venus; but Spenser refers to a statue of Venus made by Praxiteles on
Cnidus, with which a youth fell in love (Pliny, *Natural History*, 36. 5.
21). The snake with its head in its mouth (the ouroboros) signifies
eternity: Tervarent, cols 346–7. 41 the *veil* conceals a neo-Platonic
mystery of reconciled opposites (Wind, pp. 211ff.). There was a particularly strong neo-Platonic tradition of hermaphroditic deities, which
included commentaries on Gen. 1:27. Cf. Dame Nature at *Mutab.*, 7.
5–6n. and Agrippa, 3. 8, p. 362: 'out of the divinity of *Orpheus*,
[Apuleius] produceth this verse of [concerning] *Jupiter*: Jove is both
male and female.' 42 for the description, compare Enobarbus's account

of Venerean Cleopatra in Shakespeare's *Antony and Cleopatra*, 2. 2; and on the similarity of Cupids and angels, 2. 8. 5–6n. above. **44–7** the hymn closely echoes the celebrated invocation to the procreative Venus at the beginning of Lucretius' *De rerum natura*, 1. **47** *all the world . . . made*: Venus as the creator of the world derives from Natalis Comes, *Mythologiae*, 4. 13 (Lotspeich, p. 116); *queen of the air*: the air is associated with the sanguinic (youthful and lustful) temperament which was governed by Venus; *laughter*: traditionally Venerean: Hesiod, *Theogony*, 989. **49–51** lists the ideal womanly virtues, culminating in Obedience, the marital virtue demanded by St Paul (Ephes. 5:22: 'wives, submit yourselves unto your husbands'). On Shamefastness, see 2. 9. 40–3; Ben Jonson satirises the ideally silent woman in *Epicoene* (1609). The Virtues are seated in a circle (symbol of perfection); and they total six, the number of harmony and of Venus (Martianus Capella, *Marriage of Philology and Mercury*, 7. 736). **52** *lily white* and *linen* recall the purity of the saints and of the bridal New Jerusalem at Rev. 19. **55** *the pledge . . . hand*: the pledge of faith in marriage (*Book of Common Prayer* (1559), p. 123); *hind*: the deer/dear of love again (see notes to 1590 ending to Book 3, above). **58** in retrospect Scudamour rescues Amoret as Orpheus rescued his wife Eurydice from Hades (the guardian of which was the dog *Cerberus*: 1. 11. 30, 41nn.). She had died during their wedding feast with the marriage unconsummated (*Met.*, 10. 1–85; 11. 1–84). *Styx*: 4. 11. 4n.; the *prince* is Pluto.

From *Canto* 11

1–2 Florimell was imprisoned by Proteus in 3. 8. **4** *Styx*: underworld river, the daughter of Erebus and Night; *seven months*: cf. 3. 11. 10n. **5** *Marinell*: recalling 3. 4. **6** *Tryphon*: 3. 4. 43n. **8** the river marriage was a common Elizabethan poetic subject (e.g., Spenser's own projected *Epithalamium Thamesis*; hints in *SC, July*, 79–84 and *Prothalamion*; John Leland's *Cygnia Cantio* (1545); William Camden's *De connubio Tamae et Isis* in his *Britannia* (1586). The Medway was celebrated for its naval yards, and the Thames as a trading waterway that was also the site of the main royal palaces (Greenwich, Hampton Court, Windsor).

Canto 12

2 *Venus . . . bred*: cf. 3. 5. 8n. **3** *Cymodoce*: see 3. 4. 19n. **5** *stone*: Marinell's heart in st. 7, equating the lover's hard heart with that of the faithless in Ephes. 4:18. **6** Florimell's prison, near to *lowest hell*, recalls Despair's cave at 1. 9. **13** for Cupid riding the lover see Petrarch, *Canzoniere*, 161 and cf. Panofsky 1962, pp. 116–17, figs 90–1, where

Cupid rides the Platonic horse of the libido. **14** *former charge*: 3. 4. 26.
19–20 Marinell now suffers the traditional symptoms of love melancholy (Chaucer, *Knight's Tale*, A. 1361ff.), akin to the effects of
imprisonment on Redcross (1. 8. 41). **22** *Tryphon*: 4. 11. 6n. **25** for
Apollo as physician, see 3. 4. 41n.). **28** refers to Proteus's prophecy at
3. 4. 25–7. **29** *Neptune*: sovereign over all the world's oceans.
Resistance against *tyranny* had become a common sixteenth-century
political concern. **34** *angel's face*: more than mere hyperbole: see *Am*,
61; *withered weed ... sunshine*: confirming Marinell as a vegetation
god, like Adonis and Narcissus: see 3. 4. 17 and 29nn., and 3. 6.
46–9n. **35** *another place*: the pair marry in Book 5, canto 3.

BOOK 6

Canto 10

1–3 the *Beast* represents slander and detraction. Ironically, given the
corruption of the court world, Calidore's withdrawal into the pastoral
world here is described in terms of the traditional lapse into lust that
interrupts the epic hero's quest: Odysseus sojourns with Calypso
(*Odyssey*, 5) and Circe (*Odyssey*, 10); Aeneas with Dido (*Aeneid*, 4);
Ruggiero with Alcina (*OF*, 6–8), etc. **4** *Gloriana* – *FQ*'s persona for
Elizabeth I – is prudently removed from the general censure; but the
painted show (st. 3) of the court is, nevertheless, very close to the world
of Lucifera's palace (1. 4–5); and cf. Spenser's complaint in *Prothalamion*, st. 1. **5** *pleasance*: a true earthly paradise recalling 3. 6 (the
Garden of Adonis) and in contrast to 1. 7. 2–4, 2. 12, etc. It shares the
simultaneity of seasons with Eden (except that, unlike Eden, it does
know winter): 3. 6. 42n. Eden was traditionally located on a mountain
top, and contained a river, as do all subsequent paradisal places,
together with trees and bird song (Curtius, pp. 195–200). **8** *bases*:
game of chase involving two sides. *Acidale*: a surname of Venus, from
Greek *akēdēs* = free from care (cf. Hesiod, *Theogony*, 989). Also,
Greek *akis* = pointed; *dēlos* = visible (i.e., visible mountain). **9** *Graces*:
the three Graces were traditionally the main attendants on Venus:
Wind, chs 2, 3. See also st. 12–15n. below. *Cytheron*: 3. 6. 29 and
Chaucer, *Knight's Tale*, A. 1936–7, 'mount Cytheroun ... [W]here
Venus hath her principal dwelling' (confusing Venus's island of
Cytherea with Mount Cytheron in Boeotia, dedicated to Jupiter). When
at Acidale, Venus, like Calidore, is freed from care. **10** the *pipe*, symbol
of sexual excitement, recalls (but contrasts with) that played at 3. 10.

43 (and cf. 1. 6. 7–14). For the *thumping* feet, cf. Horace, *Odes*, 1. 4. 5–7 (Venus and Graces stamping on the ground as they dance). *Echo* may (but need not) recall Narcissus's beloved, who faded away into a mere echo because he refused to love her: *Met.*, 3. 379–401. 12–15 *Ariadne* (st. 13) helped Theseus escape from the Cretan labyrinth but he then abandoned her, whereupon Bacchus took pity on her, married her, and stellified her wedding crown as the constellation *corona borealis* (*Met.*, 8. 169–82). Spenser conflates this tale with that of the wedding of Pirithous and Hippodamia, at which Theseus battled against the Centaurs who were fighting the Lapiths: *Met.*, 12. 210ff. *Rosy garland* because roses were dedicated to Venus. The *Graces*, Aglaia (Brightness), Euphrosyne (Good Cheer), and Thalia (Joyfulness), symbolised *delight* (st. 15). The convention of the fourth Grace is used in *SC*, *April*, 109–17. 16 the *lass* is Colin's beloved, and as complex as *SC*'s Rosalind. She is simultaneously Elizabeth I (as in *SC*, *April*), Elizabeth Boyle (the subject of *Am*), and any other female ideal Spenser wished to implicate. *Colin Clout* had been Spenser's pseudonym of pastoral humility since *SC* (see D. R. Shore in *SpE*, pp. 172–3). 18 for the breaking of the pipe as a gesture of despair, see *SC*, *January*, 72; *April*, 3, 14–15. The vanishing of the nymphs recalls the disappearance of the dancers at the knight's approach in Chaucer's *Wife of Bath's Tale*, D 990ff., and is more distantly related to Actaeon's culpable spying on Diana and her nymphs while they were bathing: he was punished because he had seen what no mortal should see (*Met.*, 3. 155–252; Ross, p. 7). 22 the *Jove–Eurynome* parentage derives from Hesiod, *Theogony*, 907–11 (contrast 2. 8. 6; the various parentages were listed in Renaissance mythological handbooks), though it is Spenser who makes the Graces' conception coincide with the wedding of Thetis with Peleus (son of Aeacus, hence *Æacide*). 23–4 the symbolism of the Graces in terms of the receiving and bestowing of gifts, etc., is described in Wind, chs 2, 3. On their names, see st. 12–15 above. 24 *froward* and *towards*: the traditional pattern is two facing and one with her back to us (*SC*, *April*, 109 gloss), which Spenser here reverses for a reason which is not clear. 26 *daughter . . . day*: Venus as morning star (1. 2. 6–7n; Una as morning star at 1. 12. 21n.). *Bear the bell*: an appropriate pastoral image (it alludes to the bell-wether, or leading sheep of a flock). 31 the effects of Cupid's poisoned darts – that cause love's sorrows – are described in *HL*, 120–33 (Brooks-Davies 1995, pp. 331–2n.). *wounded whale*: cf. 2 *Henry IV*, 4. 4. 40–1 (New Arden, ed. A. R. Humphreys (1967); also Appendix 1, p. 204). 34 *strawberries*: symbols of love and the pastoral golden age (*Met.* 1. 104).

Tiger: lust (because the animal of drunken Bacchus: *Met.*, 3. 668–9); and see 2. 11. 20–3n. **39** *brigands*: ancient northern Britons, according to Renaissance mythographers. **44** vegetation myth again (cf. 3. 12. 34n.): for Pastorella as Proserpina (3. 4. 29n.), and hence a link with the ancient Eleusinian mystery religion as understood in the Renaissance, see D. Brooks-Davies in *SpE*, pp. 485–7.

[BOOK 7]

TWO CANTOS OF MUTABILITY

First published in the 1609 folio edition of the *FQ*, and clearly by Spenser, we do not know for certain that the title, canto numberings and running head 'the seventh book' are Spenser's. The claim of Mutability – a goddess invented by Spenser – to govern the whole universe is a direct challenge to the structure of the cosmos as it was understood from ancient times through to the end of the sixteenth century. For the accepted view – which depended on the cosmos as interpreted by Ptolemy – was that mutability was limited to the earth and the region between it and the sphere of the immediately adjacent planet, the moon (i.e., the sublunary region). Above the moon, counting outward from it, the spheres of the six other planets (Mercury, Venus, the sun, Mars, Jupiter, Saturn), together with the sphere of the fixed stars, the crystalline sphere, and the *primum mobile*, participated in time but were thought to be immutable. Spenser's Mutability challenges this, but is disproved by Nature, who combines neo-Platonism's recognition of a world of perfect stasis with Christianity's doctrine of a world beyond time and change known as the eternal sabbath. Their debate is, in effect, an expansion of Theseus's concluding speech in Chaucer's *Knight's Tale*, A. 2987ff., which accepts the power of mutability but still gives control to 'Jupiter the king'.

Canto 6

2 the *Titans* (often called merely Giants in the Renaissance), offspring of Uranus (Heaven) and Gaea (Earth), included Saturn, who overthrew his father and was in turn overthrown, and castrated, by his son, Jupiter (Jove), who instituted the rule of the Olympians (Mars, Venus, Juno, etc.). The titans warred against the Olympians but were defeated and buried under the earth in the underworld (Apollodorus, *Library*, 1. 1. 1ff.). Cf. 1. 7. 8–10n. and st. 27n. below. **3** *Hecate*: the powerful underworld aspect of the triple moon goddess, Hecate–Diana–Cynthia (cf. Hecate at 1. 1. 43n.). See Hesiod, *Theogony*, 411–52 and Ross, pp. 151–4. *Bellona*: Roman goddess of war, not normally regarded as a Titan. 6 Spenser laments the effects of change on the cosmos in the proem to Book 5; it was a common Renaissance topos. The *curse* of death is usually regarded as a result of the Fall of Man (Gen. 3:3ff.). 7 *air, fire*: in the Ptolemaic cosmology, the earth was regarded as being surrounded by an envelope of water, then air, then fire; these in turn were enclosed by the sphere of the moon and then the planetary spheres as outlined in the headnote. 8–10 cf. Phaethon's ascent to the palace of the sun (*Met.*, 2. 1ff.). *Cynthia* was a name of the moon goddess, Diana–Phoebe, from the fact that she was born on Mount Cynthus (*Mutab.*, 7. 50n.; *Cynthia* was also a cult name for Queen Elizabeth I (Wilson, ch. 7): just as Phaethon presumed upon the sun, symbol of monarchy, so Mutability presumes upon a persona of the Virgin Queen. *Silver*: dedicated to the moon (Agrippa, 1. 24, p. 54); *Time*: for the iconography, see Panofsky 1962, ch. 3. He is associated with the moon because, as the planet with the swiftest orbit, she was the planet of mutability. 9 *Ivory*: symbol of purity; while the dark and light steeds are traditional attributes, symbolising the moon's dark and light faces (Lynche, p. G4 verso-H). For *Vesper* (i.e., Hesperus), see 3. 4. 51n. 10 *crystal pillars*: Agrippa, 1. 24 (p. 54) allocates crystal to Diana–Cynthia. 12 *horned brows*: the crescent moon; *thunder's wrack*: destruction by Jupiter, whose attribute was the thunderbolt (st. 30n.). 14 *Chaos*: the primal mass of unreconciled elements from which the cosmos was created by being bound into order by Love (*HL*, 57ff.). *Mercury* is *next* in the Ptolemaic order to the moon (see headnote). He is also the messenger of the gods. 15 *Typhon*: one of the giants/Titans buried by Jupiter after his victory in the war in heaven (st. 2n.). 16 *Maia*: the mother of Mercury by Jupiter. 17–18 *winged-foot*: for the iconography of Mercury (which included winged sandals, helmet, and the wand called the caduceus, with its entwined snakes and its power over the souls of the dead (see 2. 12. 41n.)), see Virgil, *Aeneid*, 4. 239ff. 19 *principal estate*: appropriate to Jove (Jupiter) as king of heaven; *Hermes*: Greek name for Mercury; it means *interpreter*. 20 *Earth's . . . seed*: the giants/Titans (see st. 2n.). 21 *Phoebe* (= glittering one, in Greek): the moon goddess in her role as sister of the sun god, Phoebus Apollo. 22 cf. the frown of Zeus (Greek equivalent of Jupiter) in *Iliad*, 1. 528–30. 26 *Earth* – the *child* of *Chaos* because formed from it – is *grandmother of . . . the gods* at Statius, *Thebaid*, 8. 303. 27 the *sleight* of the *Corybantes* – the orgiastic priestesses of the earth goddess, Cybele, who was also Jupiter's mother – was to drown out his infant cries by their noise so that Saturn, unable to hear the infant, was deceived into devouring a stone instead of him (Apollodorus, *Library*, 1. 1. 5–7). Mutability refers to a version of the story found in some Renaissance mythographers which regards Jove as a usurper because Titan allowed Saturn to succeed him only if he devoured all his offspring, thereby allowing the succession to revert to Titan himself. **29** *Procrustes* stretched and hacked at his guests to that they would fit his bed; Theseus punished him in like fashion; *Typhon*: st. 15n.; *Ixion*: 1. 5. 35n.; *Prometheus* was punished for his presumption in stealing fire for mankind by being bound to a rock and having his liver perpetually torn at by a vulture. **30** *levin-brand*: *Met.*, 1. 197 and st. 12n. **31** *gods . . . flesh*: Gen. 6:3. *Bellona*: st. 3n. above. **35** for Mercury as scribe, see J. Seznec, *The Survival of the Pagan Gods*, trans. B. Sessions (1961), pp. 158–60. **36** Mutability's illegitimate claim is to be settled in the Irish countryside, to which the English laid claim by right of conquest. The name *Arlo* derives from the Aherlow valley, in County Tipperary, which is overlooked by Galtymore, the highest in a mountain range near Spenser's Kilcolman Castle in County Cork. For *Mole* (Spenser's name for the whole range), see *Colin Clout*, 56–69, 104–5. **37** recalls 1 proem 1, where the poet announces he has abandoned pastoral for epic. The tale that follows of *Cynthia* (or Diana, the hunting goddess: see 2. 3. 21–31n.) is original with Spenser. *Clio, Calliope*: 1 proem 2n. and 1. 11. 5n. **38** Spenser refers to the mediaeval (sixth–ninth centuries) tradition of learning and Christian art in his *View of the Present State of Ireland* (first published 1633), where he also alludes to Ireland's ancient name, *sacra insula* (i.e., holy island). **39** cf. Acidale as Venus's resort in Book 6, canto 10. **40** *Molanna*: the River Behanagh runs near Kilcolman; Spenser combines its name with that of Mole (st. 36); *Mulla*: Spenser's name for the Awbeg, which again flows near Kilcolman (*Colin Clout*, 92ff., telling the story of the marriage of Mulla and Bregog (and see *Var. Minor Poems*, 1. 454–5)). On Colin Clout, see 6. 10. 16n. **41** *grove of oaks*: St Bridget, patroness of Ireland, built her cell under an oak. **42** *Faunus*: 2. 2. 7–10n. The story that follows is based on Actaeon's punishment for spying on the naked Diana (6. 10. 18n.), with details from Diana's banishment of Callisto (*Met.*, 2. 463–5), and the tale of the conjunction of the River Alpheus and the well Arethusa (*Met.*, 5. 577ff.). In Ovid's *Fasti*, 2. 335ff., Faunus tries to rape Omphale but suffers ridicule. **43** *queen apples, red cherries*: love tokens; the queen apple is referred to commonly in sixteenth-century English poetry; but the exact kind is now unknown. **45** *only one*: Actaeon (st. 42n.) who was turned into a deer by Diana and destroyed by his own hounds; *Jove . . . prey*: see Jove's amours at 3. 11. 30–5. **46** Faunus destroys his vision as Calidore destroys the dance before Colin Clout at 6. 10. **47** *dared lark*: larks were caught in nets after being dazzled by mirrors. **49** *Mome*: Momus was the personification of mockery and censure (Hesiod, *Theogony*, 214). **50** *deerskin . . . hounds*: exactly the punishment of Actaeon. **53** the Bregog is punished in the same way at *Colin Clout*, 148–55. **54** *Suir*: the river flows through the Vale of Aherlow: st. 36n. above. **55** on *wolves* and *thieves* in Ireland, see *Colin Clout*, 318–19, and *Epithalamion*, 69.

Canto 7

1 *greater Muse*: Mutab., 6. 37n. *spirit . . . wing*: the flight metaphor was originally Platonic (*Phaedrus* 246C–247C) and is common in Spenser: e.g., *Am*, 72, *HL*, 176ff.; *sire*: Apollo was father of the Muses, Jupiter (*heaven's king*) their paternal grandfather. **3** *Pluto* (1. 1. 36–7n.) and *Proserpina* (3. 11. 1n., 3. 6. 45n.) are included because they govern the growth of seed under the earth and are hence under Nature's dominion. **5–6** *Nature*: cf. the description in Chaucer's *Parliament of Fowls*, 302ff. Her sexual ambiguity is traceable to neo-Platonic and Hermetic ideas of divine androgyny (4. 10. 41n., commenting also on the *veil*, on which see, in addition, veiled Una at 1. 1. 4 and 1. 3. 4.). *Face . . . lion*: perhaps because lions were emblems of Cybele, the earth mother (Tervarent, col. 246), and because a lion was the Egyptian hieroglyph for the Nile inundation, supreme symbol of Nature's power (Valeriano, Book 1, pp. 7–8; cf. 3. 6. 7–9n.). *Beams . . . glass*: recall divine brightness as at 2 Cor. 3:18 ('we all behold as in a mirror the glory of the Lord') and *HHB*, 183ff. **7** refers to Peter, James and John's vision of the transfigured Jesus on Mount Tabor (Matt. 17:1–8; Mark 9: 2–8 and Geneva gloss); *wits forgot*: the account in Mark 9:6 (Peter 'knew not what he said'). **8–9** follow *Parliament of Fowls*, 302ff. (Spenser claims, incidentally, to have directly inherited Chaucer's *spirit* at 4. 2. 32–4). Chaucer mentions Alanus de Insulis, *De planctu Naturae* (*Of the complaint of Nature*) at *Parliament of Fowls*, 316; though Spenser may well never have seen a copy of the *Complaint*, since it remained unprinted at this time. **10** spontaneous flowering: cf. the spontaneity of nature in the Golden Age (*Met.*, 1. 101–2), and the densely flowered ground in Botticelli's *Primavera*. **11** *Mole*: the mountains near Spenser's home: *Mutab.*, 6. 36n. above. **12** the wedding of *Peleus* and *Thetis* was celebrated for being the scene of the quarrel over the golden apple that led to the Trojan war (3. 9. 34–6n.), though it did not take place on *Haemus*, a Thracian mountain that had once been a mortal who had been transformed as a punishment for claiming divinity (*Met.*, 6. 87–9). 13 *young ... eld*: for precedents, including Claudian's Natura, see Curtius, pp. 101–5; *moving ... unmoved*: cf. Boethius, *Consolation of Philosophy*, trans. Chaucer, Book 3, Metre 9; *unseen ... beheld*: HHB, 120–33; Romans 1:20. 16 *Titan*: *Mutab.*, 6. 2n. 17–25 Mutability lists the elements in their traditional order (*Mutab.*, 6. 7n.). 22 *all sense*: air is only the medium through which we see, hear, and smell: Fowler (1970), 59n corrects her hyperbole. 26 *Vesta* is goddess of celestial and elemental *fire* (*Fasti*, 6. 291–2; Lotspeich, p. 117); *Vulcan* (3. 9. 19n.), god of fire as known on earth; *Ops*: one of the names of the earth goddess (Lynche, p. M2 verso); for *Juno* and air, see Ripa, p. 121; for *Neptune*, see 4. 12. 29n.; for *nymphs*, see 2. 1. 55n. 28–31 Spenser draws on traditional attributes, including the identification of the seasons with the four ages of man. 32–43 the procession of the months, beginning, as was traditional, with March, the first month of the legal year (General Argument, *SC* and ed. Brooks-Davies 1995, p. 10), combines the usual labours associated with the months with their zodiacal attributes (and their mythological origins) together with their expected emblems: e.g., Ripa, pp. 315–26. Note that, as with the woodcuts to *SC*, the sign per month tradition is followed (see E. H. Gombrich, *Symbolic Images*, 1978, pp. 109–18). 32 *Ram ... swam*: Aries; and see 3. 11. 30. 33 *Bull ... Europa*: Taurus (*Fasti*, 5. 603–17) and see 3. 11. 30. 34 *Twins of Leda*: Castor and Pollux, sons resulting from Jove's congress with her as a swan (3. 11. 32); the sign Gemini. *May* is traditionally associated with sexual activity. 35 *green leaves ... player*: June is portrayed as a wild man of the summer forest out of an Elizabethan pageant; *Crab*: Cancer; appropriate, because in June the sun begins to retrograde. 36 *Lion*: the sign Leo, identified as the creature killed by Hercules, son of *Amphitrion*, in Nemea; the lion is traditionally wrathful. 37 *maid*: Astraea, goddess of Justice, who left the earth after it became corrupt with the advent of the Iron Age (*Met.*, 1. 149–50). She was stellified as Virgo and understood as a corn goddess (literalising the concept of the Golden Age which she represented: Yates, pp. 29–87). 38 *weights*: the scales of Libra. 39 *Scorpion*: Scorpio, the creature sent by Diana to slay Orion after he boasted of his mastery over wild beasts (Ovid, *Fasti*, 5. 493). 40 *Centaur ... Chiron*: the sign Sagittarius. Spenser conflates two traditions concerning the centaur Chiron's parentage: that he was the son of Saturn and Philyra; that he was the son of Magnes and Nais. 41 *Saviour*: Christ, whose nativity is celebrated on 25 December; the *Goat* (stellified as Capricorn) nursed Jove when, as an infant, he was tended by Amalthea on Mount Ida (*Fasti*, 5. 111–28). **42** *Janus* (4. 10. 12n.) founded the Janiculum on the banks of the Tiber (*Aeneid*, 8. 356–8): hence the *Roman flood* which pours from the earthenware pot to signify Aquarius, the water-pourer. **43** *two Fishes*: appropriate for the fasting associated with Lent, and representing the sign of Pisces. **44** *Day, Night*: Ripa, pp. 183–4 and 360–1 respectively (also 1. 5. 20n.). **45** *Hours*: traditionally guardians of *heaven's gate*, they were usually regarded as the daughters of *Jove* and Themis, though Spenser has them as the offspring of Day and Night at *Epith*, 98–102. **46** *Cupid*: for the convention of Cupid as an adolescent boy, see Panofsky 1962, ch. 4. **49** Mutability is ignorant of (or ignores) 2 Cor. 4: 18: 'the things which are not seen, are eternal'. **50–3** Mutability lists the planets in their Ptolemaic order counting from earth, except that she reverses Saturn and Jupiter (thus recognising Jupiter's claim of sovereignty). Her point is that the planets (named from Greek *planētēs* = wanderer) are erratic in their orbits. **50** *Cynthus*: on Delos, site of the birth of Diana and Apollo. **53** as Mutability rightly points out, there were various traditions concerning Jove's birthplace. **55** the *starry sky* is the crystalline sphere with its fixed stars (but a new star had been noted in 1572; so it was *not* immutable). **59** *no more change*: 1 Cor. 15:51ff. looking forward to the time when 'this corruptible hath put on incorruption'.

The 8th Canto, imperfect

1 *Time's sickle* is conventional (*Mutab.*, 6. 8–10n. above). Time abbreviates (*shortens*) and is also *short* himself in relation to eternity (cf. 'short time' in *Epith*, last line). **2** *pillars*: emblems of constancy (Tervarent, col. 107). *Sabaoth*: the meaning Lord of Hosts (Romans 9:29, James 5:4) is primary, referring to the multitude of blessed saints at the end of time (and cf. Rev. 19, 20). But the end of time is the eternal rest of the 'perpetual sabbath' envisioned by St Augustine in *The City of God*, 22. 30: 'we shall become that sabbath [i.e., seventh day of rest]; we shall be still . . .'; and this meaning is therefore present as well. Spenser thus says: Great Lord of Hosts, grant me sight of your host of saints and participation in the eternal sabbath.

APPENDIX

Note: the *Letter of the Author's* was appended to the 1590 edition of *The Fairy Queen* (containing Books 1–3 only). It was not published with the six-book text of 1596.

l. 5 *Ralegh*: 1552–1618; had an estate near Spenser's at Kilcolman; stayed with Spenser in 1589, accompanying him to England with the presentation copy of *FQ* for Elizabeth. *Stannaries*: the Devon and Cornwall tin mines. l. 10 *dark conceit*: riddling, shadowy, idea. ll. 17–18 *fashion . . . discipline*: combines the traditionally instructive function of poetry (e.g., Horace, *Ars poetica*, 333ff.) with the contemporary courtesy book (e.g. Sir Thomas Eliot's *Book named the Governor*; 1531). *Gentle*: noble; courteous. l. 19 *coloured*: embellished;* disguised. l. 25 *antique*: ancient.‡ ll. 29–30 *Ariosto . . . Orlando*: *Orlando furioso* (1532). ll. 32–3 *ethic*: moral;‡ treating of morals; *politic*: i.e., political (pertaining to public affairs). Spenser refers to Tasso's *Rinaldo* (1562) and *Ger. lib.*, and Aristotle's *Nicomachean Ethics* and *Politics*. l. 34 *portrait*: portray,‡ represent.‡ l. 37 *devised*: distributed* [them]; ordered [them]. l. 39 *frame*: fashion. Eliot, similarly, had promised a second, political, volume to succeed his published volume of private moral education (*the Governor*). It did not appear: see A. L. DeNeef in *SpE*, pp. 581–4. l. 41 *displeasant*: disagreeable. l. 44 *they used*: was their custom. ll. 47–50 *Xenophon . . . Cyrus*: Plato's *Republic*; Xenophon's (fourth century BC) *Cyropaedia*, a political treatise based on the life of the virtuous, wise and brave founder of the Persian empire, Cyrus the Great. ll. 54–5 *Timon*: 1. 9. 4n.; *Ygraine*: Geoffrey of Monmouth, *History of the Kings of Britain*, 8. 19–20; *dream*: *FQ*, 1. 9. 13–15. l. 60. *glory*: honourable fame; splendour and magnificence; bright light. l. 64 *two persons*: the doctrine of the monarch's two bodies, the private and fallible self and the public self which is divine and shares the immortality of the realm which it governs: E. H. Kantorowicz, *The King's Two Bodies*, 1957. ll. 66–8 *Belphoebe, Cynthia, Diana*: 2. 3. argt stanza n. and 21–31n; 3 proem 1 and 4nn. l. 69 *magnificence*: the undertaking of great deeds for glory and honour: for the tradition drawn on by Spenser, see H. MacLachlan and P. B. Rollinson in *SpE*, p. 448. ll. 83–5 *historiographer . . . midst*: poet and history writer were traditionally opposed: e.g. Philip Sidney, *Apology for Poetry* (1595), ed. G. Shepherd (1977), p. 97. Historians narrate in chronological order; epic poets begin their narrative 'in the middle of things' (Horace, *Ars poetica*, 148–9). l. 91 *annual feast*: presumably based on the annual commemoration of Elizabeth's accession on 17 November (see Strong, chaps 4, 5). l. 96 *clownish*: rustic;‡ uncultivated.‡ l. 114–15 *armour . . . Ephesians*: 1. 1. 1n. l. 149 *1589*: i.e., 1590; England still used the Julian calendar (see *Mutab.*, 7. 32–43n.).

SUGGESTIONS FOR FURTHER READING

Editions

J. C. Smith (ed.), *Spenser's 'Faerie Queene'*, 2 vols, 1909; E. A. Greenlaw, F. M. Padelford, C. G. Osgood et al. (eds), *The Works of Edmund Spenser: A Variorum Edition*, 11 vols, 1932–57; Graham Hough, introd., *Edmund Spenser: 'The Faerie Queene', 1596* (facsimile), 1976; A. C. Hamilton (ed.), *Spenser: 'The Faerie Queene'*, 1977 (rev. edn forthcoming); T. P. Roche and C. P. O'Donnell (eds), *Spenser: 'The Faerie Queene'*, 1978; W. A. Oram et al. (eds), *The Yale Edition of the Shorter Poems of Edmund Spenser*, 1989; D. Brooks-Davies (ed.), *Edmund Spenser: Selected Shorter Poems*, Longman Annotated Texts, 1995.

Background reading

Essential background material will be found in: Plato's *Symposium* (for the essentials of Spenser's theory of love, which he inherited direct from Plato and also through the medium of Renaissance commentators: e.g., Marsilio Ficino's *Commentary on Plato's 'Symposium'*, trans. Sears Jayne; 1944, repr. 1985); Virgil's *Aeneid* and Ariosto's *Orlando Furioso* (for the epic and romance sources); Ovid's *Metamorphoses* (for many of Spenser's mythological tales); the Bible (especially Genesis; the Song of Songs; Isaiah; Revelation); Geoffrey of Monmouth's *History of the Kings of Britain* (source for much of Spenser's view of British history and its myths).

For symbolism and ideological backgrounds the following are especially recommended: D. C. Allen, *Mysteriously Meant: The Rediscovery of Pagan Symbolism and Allegorical Interpretation in the Renaissance*, 1970; Eamon Duffy, *The Stripping of the Altars: Traditional Religion in England 1400–1580*, 1992 (impact of Reformation and strength of residual Catholicism); Erwin Panofsky, *Studies in Iconology*, 1939; Gareth Roberts, *The Mirror of Alchemy*, 1994; Murray Roston, *Renaissance Perspectives in Literature and the Visual*

Arts, 1987; Roy Strong, *The Cult of Elizabeth*, 1977; Edgar Wind, *Pagan Mysteries in the Renaissance*, rev. edn 1967; Jean Wilson (ed.), *Entertainments for Elizabeth I*, 1980 (courtly texts sharing assumptions with *FQ*).

Critical reading on The Fairy Queen

There is an overabundance of material, so the following list is very selective and personal.

(1) GENERAL CRITICISM

The primary resource is now A. C. Hamilton et al. (eds), *The Spenser Encyclopedia*, 1990, which will answer or offer pointers to answers to most enquiries. It also has excellent bibliographies.

General or introductory studies include:

Alpers, P. *The Poetry of 'The Faerie Queene'*, 1967
—— *Edmund Spenser: A Critical Anthology*, 1969
Bayley, P. C. *Edmund Spenser: Prince of Poets*, 1971
—— *Spenser: 'The Faerie Queene': A Casebook*, 1977
Bennett, J. W. *The Evolution of 'The Faerie Queen'*, 1942
Berger, H., Jr *The Allegorical Temper*, 1957 (on Book 2)
—— *Spenser: A Collection of Critical Essays*, 1968
—— *Revisionary Play: Studies in the Spenserian Dynamics*, 1988 (collects some of Berger's idiosyncratic and suggestive essays on *FQ*)
Bieman, E. *Plato Baptized: Towards the Interpretation of Spenser's Mimetic Fictions*, 1989
Brooks-Davies, D. *Spenser's 'Faerie Queene': A Critical Commentary on Books 1 and 2*, 1977 (stanza-by-stanza reading emphasising iconography)
Cullen, P. *Infernal Triad: The Flesh, the World, and the Devil in Spenser and Milton*, 1974
Evans, M. *Spenser's Anatomy of Heroism: A Commentary on 'The Faerie Queene'*, 1970
Fowler, A. D. S. *Edmund Spenser*, 1977
Giamatti, A. B. *Play of Double Senses: Spenser's 'Faerie Queene'*, 1975
Hamilton, A. C. *The Structure of Allegory in 'The Faerie Queene'*, 1961
—— *Essential Articles for the Study of Edmund Spenser*, 1972
Hankins, J. E. *Source and Meaning in Spenser's Allegory: A Study of 'The Faerie Queene'*, 1971

Hough, G. *A Preface to 'The Faerie Queene'*, 1962

Jones, H. S. V. *A Spenser Handbook*, 1930

Krier, T. M. *Gazing on Secret Sights: Spenser, Classical Imitation, and the Decorums of Vision*, 1990.

Lewis, C. S. *Spenser's Images of Life*, ed. A. Fowler, 1967

McCaffrey, I. G. *Spenser's Allegory: The Anatomy of Imagination*, 1976

Nelson, W. *The Poetry of Edmund Spenser*, 1963 (best single introduction)

Nohrnberg, J. *The Analogy of 'The Faerie Queene'*, 1976 (monumental reading of imagery, structure, etc. Best single overall book on *FQ*)

Roche, T. P., Jr *The Kindly Flame: A Study of the Third and Fourth Books of Spenser's 'Faerie Queene'*, 1964

Rose, M. *Spenser's Art: A Companion to Book One of 'The Faerie Queene'*, 1975

Tonkin, H. *The Faerie Queene*, 1989 (good basic introduction)

Waller, G. F. *English Poetry of the Sixteenth Century*, 1986 (contains New Historicist approach to *FQ*)

(2) MORE SPECIALISED STUDIES

Brooks-Davies, D. *The Mercurian Monarch: Magical Politics from Spenser to Pope*, 1983 (first chapter on magic, alchemy, etc. in *FQ*)

Cheney, P. *Spenser's Famous Flight: A Renaissance Idea of a Literary Career*, 1993

Dundas, J. *The Spider and the Bee: The Artistry of Spenser's 'Faerie Queene'*, 1985 (imagery, rhetoric, etc.)

Ellrodt, R. *Neoplatonism in the Poetry of Spenser*, 1960

Fowler, A. D. S. *Spenser and the Numbers of Time*, 1964 (iconography, astrology, numerology in *FQ*)

Goldberg, J. *Endlesse Worke: Spenser and the Structures of Discourse*, 1981 (modernist/postmodernist)

Hume, A. *Edmund Spenser: Protestant Poet*, 1984 (religion)

King, J. N. *Spenser's Poetry and the Reformation Tradition*, 1990 (religion)

Leslie, M. *Spenser's 'Fierce Warres and Faithfull Loves': Martial and Chivalric Symbolism in 'The Faerie Queene'*, 1983 (includes Garter symbolism)

Lotspeich, H. G. *Classical Mythology in the Poetry of Edmund Spenser*, 1932 (alphabetical handbook of references)

Miller, D. L. *The Poem's Two Bodies: The Poetics of the 1590 'Faerie Queene'*, 1989 (postmodernist reading)

Norbrook, D. *Poetry and Politics in the English Renaissance*, 1984 (includes New Historicist reading of Spenser)

Quilligan, M. *Milton's Spenser: The Politics of Reading*, 1983 (rhetoric and reader-response theory)

Rambuss, R. *Spenser's Secret Career*, 1993

Smith, C. G. *Spenser's Proverb Lore*, 1970 (alphabetical list of proverbs)

Suzuki, M. *Metamorphoses of Helen: Authority, Difference, and the Epic*, 1989 (feminist, with a section on *FQ*)

Wells, R. H. *Spenser's 'Faerie Queene' and the Cult of Elizabeth*, 1983 (icons of the queen in *FQ*)

Yates, F. A. *Astraea: The Imperial Theme in the Sixteenth Century*, 1975 (iconography of empire in *FQ* and other texts)

——*The Occult Philosophy in the Elizabethan Age*, 1979 (includes suggestive magical reading of *FQ*)

Note: For those with access to a major library, *Spenser Studies: A Renaissance Poetry Annual* contains excellent articles representing the varying persuasions of current Spenser critics.